SOHO Networking

A Guide to Installing a Small-Office/Home-Office Network

PETE MOULTON

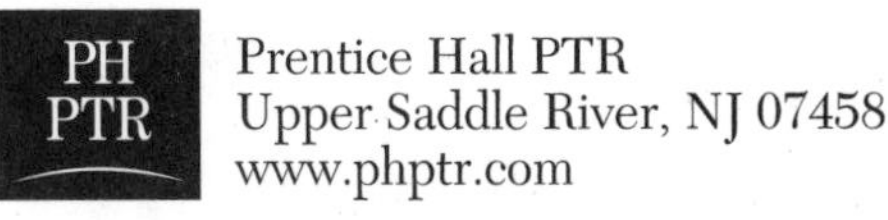

Prentice Hall PTR
Upper Saddle River, NJ 07458
www.phptr.com

A CIP catalog record for this book can be obtained from the Library of Congress.

Editorial/Production Supervision: *Faye Gemmellaro*
Senior Managing Editor: *Mary Franz*
Editorial Assistant: *Noreen Regina*
Marketing Manager: *Dan DePasquale*
Manufacturing Manager: *Alexis R. Heydt-Long*
Manufacturing Buyer: *Maura Zaldivar*
Interior Designer: *Gail Cocker-Bogusz*
Cover Design Director: *Jerry Votta*
Cover Designer: *Nina Scuderi*

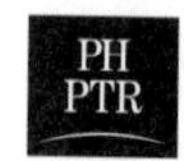

Publishing as Prentice Hall PTR
Upper Saddle River, New Jersey 07458

Prentice Hall books are widely used by corporations and government agencies for training, marketing, and resale.

For information regarding corporate and government bulk discounts, contact:

Corporate and Government Sales (800) 382-3419 or corpsales@pearsontechgroup.com

Printed in the United States of America

10 9 8 7 6 5 4 3 2 1

ISBN 0-13-047331-6

Pearson Education Limited
Pearson Education Australia Pty., Limited
Pearson Education Singapore, Pte. Ltd.
Pearson Education North Asia Ltd.
Pearson Education Canada, Ltd.
Pearson Educación de Mexico, S.A. de C.V.
Pearson Education—Japan
Pearson Education Malaysia, Pte. Ltd.

This book is dedicated to Cate Dolan and my surrogate autistic grandson Paddy Dolan who constantly help me discover more about life, more about myself, and how PCs and technology can positively influence our lives.

CONTENTS

Introduction

SOHO LANs

Chapter Syllabus

- SOHO LANs Defined
- Book Objectives
- Who Needs This Book
- What This Book Covers
- Summary
- Key Technical Terms
- Review Questions

This book describes and examines from a plain language and practical viewpoint the technologies, technical terminology, installation, and operation of small office/home office (SOHO) Local Area Networks (LANs). SOHO LANs started in 1983, with PC Net and Ethernet-like disk and printer sharing networks using PCs and XTs.

SOHO LANs have evolved today into inexpensive home and office networks that support a variety of home and office applications. Home applications include the ubiquitous disk and printer sharing as well as sharing high-speed Internet access. Business applications add Web serving and telephony applications. Newer applications encompass networking home appliances to provide inventory control and centralized management of the home. Business applications are expanding to include all office communications, e-business, research, and telecommunications functions.

Such SOHO LANs are the key communications fabric used by businesses today and into the future. Knowledge and understanding of the technologies, configuration, and operation of them is vital for everyone's personal and professional life.

SOHO LANs Defined

SOHO stands for small office or home office. It describes a working environment and a business culture. Virtual office is sometimes used as a synonym for SOHO. A SOHO LAN is a local area network that supports the SOHO work environment.

At the low end, a SOHO LAN consists of two or more computers (typically, Windows or Macintosh PCs) linked together to share disks and printers. These computers are all labeled "hosts," even though they do not necessarily host anything.

Larger small-office LANs may involve a hundred Windows or Macintosh PCs and a variety of other computer and communications equipment to provide basic LAN disk and printer sharing. Since small-office LANs are larger, they use more sophisticated software. This permits sharing disks and the files on those disks as well as printers. Larger SOHO LANs use more sophisticated software and networking components to support a wider variety of applications and functions. File sharing capabilities on larger SOHO PC LANs provide greater data security than file sharing on simpler home office LANs by providing more features limiting access to sensitive files. In a two-PC SOHO LAN, such added file security features contribute little to overall LAN security.

What makes SOHO LANs more appealing today is that the cost of implementing them is hugely reduced. My original SOHO LAN was Orchid Technology PCnet. It was designed to facilitate sharing resources on PC XT computers. The cost of my network was about $800 per Network Interface Card (NIC), the hardware component installed in each PC to connect it to the network. The software for resource sharing was provided with the boards. My cost for three computers was around $2,500 when the cost of the cabling was included.

This SOHO LAN used coaxial cable equivalent to the coaxial cable used by cable TV, also known as Community Antenna Television (CATV), systems. Any break in the cable meant that the entire LAN became inoperative.

An equivalent SOHO LAN today would cost $15 per NIC, $50 for a hub, and $30 for three cables, for a total cost of around $150. Some SOHO networking kits, including a hub, two NICs, and two cables, cost as little as $50. Windows, Macintosh, and other software supports basic networking, so no added software cost is needed. Each added PC would require around $25 of hardware and cable to add to the network up to the hub's limit of four to eight devices. Not only is a basic SOHO LAN cheaper than my original SOHO LAN, but it is also much more reliable. The hub isolates each cable from every other cable so that in the event one cable fails, only one PC is affected and the remainder of the LAN operates as usual.

My points so far regarding SOHO LANs are that they vary in size and sophistication, and newer SOHO LANs are cheap and reliable. These trends are the underlying forces that catapult SOHO sales forward.

Brain Teaser: LAN Kits

Check a local computer or electronics retail store for LAN kits. What do they include? Compare this with the Linksys EW5PCISK network kit:

www.linksys.com/products/product.asp?prid=90&grid=12

What kind of price can you find online at *www.pricewatch.com* by searching for Linksys EW5PCISK? My prices ranged from $47 to $56.

SOHO LAN Components

A SOHO LAN uses PCs running Windows. Such personal computers are ready to network. Windows software provides basic networking capabilities, which requires the addition of a NIC to each PC to build a simple SOHO network. Many laptops and other newer PCs have the NIC built into the main logic board, such as the Sony Vaio PCG-GR300 laptop that I am using to add this comment.

Any network and any SOHO network are constructed from three basic components. See Figure 0.1. These components include the following:

- Hardware—The tools a network is built from is the hardware. Hardware includes PCs (referred to as hosts), NICs, and all the network hardware components used to construct the network. Hardware is the tools used to build a network.

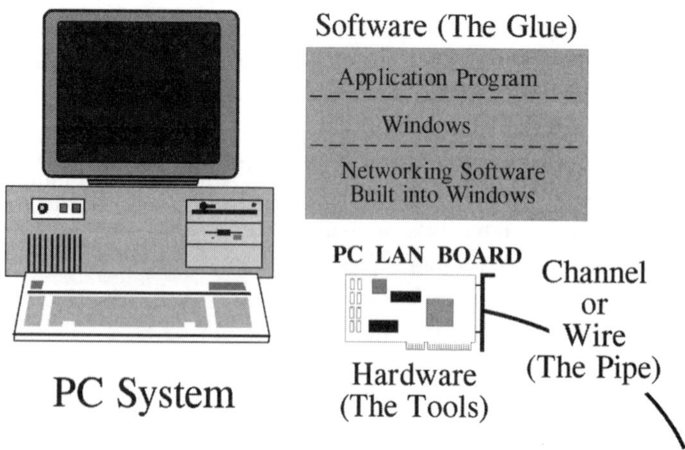

Figure 0.1 Networking components.

- Channel—The pipe used to interconnect network components is the channel or wire. A channel or wire interconnects all components in a SOHO LAN. In some cases the channel is not wire but rather a radio frequency (RF) connection between two hardware components. A channel is the pipe that interconnects all network PCs (or hosts) and components. Channels work just like pipe; you stuff bits into one end and they pour out the other end, similar to the way water poured into one end of a pipe soon flows out the other end. Channels, like pipe, come in different sizes or capacities. We can have large pipes like water mains from the central reservoir that carry millions of gallons. Similarly, smaller pipes distribute the water to the faucet in our homes. In SOHO LANs the channel (or pipe) capacity is measured in bits per second (bps). It can be thousands of bits per second (Kbps), millions of bits per second (Mbps), billions of bits (gigabits) per second (Gbps), or higher. Most SOHO LANs use 100 Mbps channels. Some older SOHO LANs still run at 10 Mbps because the components that implement them are capable of no higher speed.
- Software—The glue that holds the network together as a cohesive whole is the software. Software as presented earlier is generally built into Windows and other operating systems. Since most SOHO LAN hosts are Windows-based PCs, we focus primarily on Windows here. Software provides a variety of functions, such as connecting applications programs to the network, providing security, transferring data from network host to network host, and interfacing to network hardware. The only software that is sometimes not provided by Windows is the software that interfaces the NIC to Windows. Later in this book we examine how the functions performed by Windows software are organized in a logical fashion. Under-

standing this logical organization helps when configuring a Windows SOHO LAN.

When configuring or troubleshooting a SOHO LAN, we focus our efforts in these three areas because they are the highest level at which a SOHO LAN can be readily subdivided. Problems in hardware, software, and channels have unique distinguishing characteristics that help identify their source and resolution.

Small SOHO "Peer-to-Peer" LANs

A small SOHO LAN ranges in size from two to 10 personal computer systems. In two-PC SOHO LANs the PCs can be directly connected to one another, but most often small SOHO LAN hardware components consist of NICs installed in each PC and a wiring hub. See Figure 0.2. The channel is the wire from the PC NIC to the wiring hub. This wire is referred to as Ethernet cable, or as networking cable. Sometimes networking nerds call this Ethernet patch cable, especially when it is used for short runs. The software used is a driver program provided with the NICs to interface them to Windows, and then Windows software to transfer data between the PCs and set up disk and printer sharing. The operation of the Windows software is described as "peer-to-peer," which infers that each PC host participates and shares equally in network responsibilities. Each PC designates which disk drives or folders to share and sets the level of security for those disks and folders.

In our two-PC SOHO LAN, performance is not an issue. The PCs are connected directly to each other using the wire and the hub. The entire communications capacity of the wire is available to transfer data between the PCs,

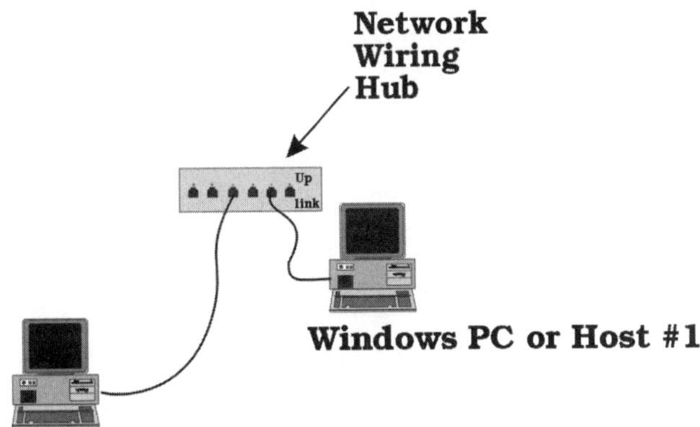

Figure 0.2
Two-PC SOHO LAN.

making exchanges quite fast. Only files that are hundreds of Mbytes in size, like videos and large photos, would make the transfer seem slow to the casual SOHO LAN user. Even if this network were to expand to three, four, or five PCs, performance should not be an issue because file transfers among PCs rarely all happen at exactly the same instant. Network users work with the disks of their PC and occasionally transfer a file to another PC as needed to share data.

One network application is e-mail. When I switched my early SOHO LAN to Novell's NetWare, an e-mail application came with the Novell software. This application, an internal e-mail system, was promptly implemented. Although I (the boss) thought it was very useful for sending directives to all employees, the employees (emulating Dilbert) rarely used the internal e-mail.

In the small SOHO LAN case, it is more effective to use a free Internet mail service like Yahoo! e-mail or a subscription Internet e-mail service like AOL for both internal and external e-mail. In this manner, SOHO LAN users can communicate with vendors, customers, and internal company personnel using one e-mail service. Just select professional-sounding screen names like TMCMktDir or TMCOwner and not ones like Philtrout or DialANerd for a more professional e-mail demeanor. My e-mail address is DialANerd, so I present a somewhat less professional image, which matched with my TV persona and not my business persona.

Larger Small-Office Client/Server LANs

The cutover point between small and larger SOHO LANs is around 10 Windows PCs. Windows peer-to-peer capabilities support up to 10 PCs simultaneously accessing the disk drive of your PC. There could be 20 PCs on the network that are permitted to access your disk drive, but only 10 can access it at any instant in time. There are many reasons for this limitation beyond the obvious need to sell Windows server software and make more money for Microsoft.

Microsoft's server software is implemented in Windows NT Server and Windows 2000 Server software. This software implements a client/server network model where the PC running the server software provides centralized services to the client PCs. Only the centralized server needs to run the server software; the client PCs can run any version of Windows. The central server PC manages all network security and access. See Figure 0.3.

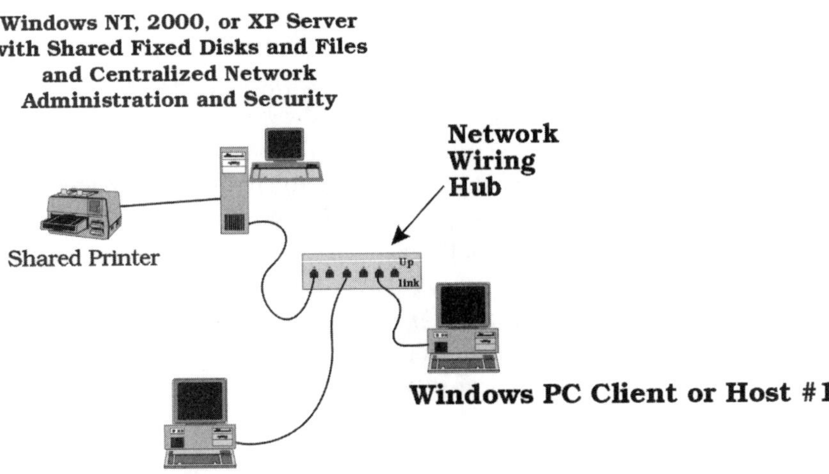

Figure 0.3 Client/server small-office LAN.

The most prominent reasons for moving to client/server networking software are performance and network administration. When a Windows 9x PC has network activities running in the background or actively, it consumes significant CPU cycles or processing power, as well as other PC resources. If there are more than 10 connections into a Windows 9x PC that are actively accessing files and printers on that PC, the performance of that PC can be easily degraded significantly. The PC user just sees the PC seemingly stop dead in its tracks while in reality it is performing the networking tasks requested from it. Once these networking tasks are complete the Windows 9x PC again becomes responsive to its user. There have been instances when my Windows 9x PC would lock waiting for network communications to complete a simple task, while it was really supporting any number of other computing tasks. Such Windows 9x PC network performance is unacceptable in a busy office.

Windows NT, Windows 2000, and Windows XP are all designed to support network operations much more efficiently. The core of their software design more effectively distributes the CPU cycles or processing power across the variety of tasks the Windows NT/2K/XP PC is performing simultaneously. Because these CPU cycles are distributed across all processes more evenly, performance under significant network loads is much better than performance for Windows 9x.

Network administration is another major reason for moving to a client/server network model. In peer-to-peer networks, security is administered at each individual PC. If anything goes wrong with a PC, then the network administrator may need to rebuild the data, security access, and passwords at that PC. This means the network administrator must travel from PC to PC to manage a network. For 10 PCs this is not too bad, but when we reach 20 or more, the administrative work can be very time consuming. In a client/server network all network administration is performed at a single server. Every client gets security permissions from that single server. Network administration is performed using the server and not many individual PC hosts. Such centralized network management reduces the network administrative workload significantly. This is especially true where access to some network resources must be restricted to special groups of users.

In larger small-office LANs, a wider variety of networking equipment is used to provide more services and better performance for network users. Instead of simple hubs, switches are used to increase network transmission speed between PC hosts and PC servers. Gateways support high-speed Internet access. Printers attach directly to the network. Special servers sometimes support internal Web site hosting and e-mail. We examine these components in greater detail later in this book.

SOHO LAN Technologies

In the 1980s several LAN technologies fought for market dominance. These technologies included Xerox-Intel-DEC Ethernet, IBM's Token Ring, and DataPoint's ARCnet. Each LAN technology had several positive and negative points. The early implementation of each LAN technology met the simple networking needs of the 1980s, but those implementations did not provide sufficient performance and reliability to support current and future SOHO LAN uses. Over several years the Xerox-Intel-DEC Ethernet technology evolved more rapidly to meet the needs of modern LANs. ARCnet dropped by the wayside, and IBM's Token Ring fills a niche market need but is expensive compared with today's Ethernet products.

The overriding factor in selecting SOHO LAN technology is cost. Cheaper products are more widely used than more expensive products. The cheapest networking products today are products based upon the original Xerox-Intel-DEC Ethernet technology. This is generally known as 802.3 Ethernet. Ethernet technology is implemented in NICs and other network hardware components. It uses a protocol or language labeled CSMA/CD, which stands for Carrier Sense Multiple Access with Collision Detection. This protocol (communications language) manages access to the communications media or wire. It functions similar to citizens band (CB) radios that permit any user to broadcast a message at any time.

Ethernet of the 1980s carried data at 10 Mbps. As an example, the size of the electronic files that comprise this book—including the diagrams—is about

250 MB. To backup these files at 10 Mbps would take a calculated three minutes, but in reality five to 10 minutes. In the 1990s the Ethernet transmission speed was increased to 100 Mbps. The same 250 MB backup would require a calculated 20 seconds, but in reality one to three minutes. Ethernet operates at these speeds—and up to 1 Gbps—today, and someday 10 Gbps components will be commonly available. Most SOHO LANs use Ethernet components operating at 100 Mbps because these are the most prevalent and cheapest network components. Both the Token Ring and ARCnet technologies lagged behind Ethernet technology in the increases in transmission speed. Further, the Token Ring technology was more expensive than Ethernet to implement. More on the operation and evolution of Ethernet and Token Ring technologies is presented later in this book.

SOHO LAN Applications

As described earlier, the basic applications of SOHO LAN are simple disk, file, and printer sharing. Such sharing turns every SOHO-network-attached PC and printer into resources available to an entire office. Particularly in an office of 10 people or smaller, sharing a printer makes sense because a shared printer is just a few short steps from everyone's desk. In the home where cost is of primary consideration, sharing one printer among all PCs saves money. Similarly, sharing one large-capacity disk drive among all office personnel as a master electronic file cabinet spreads the cost across every PC. Having two big disk drives containing copies of all key data provides instant online backup of that key data. This does not, however, relieve any home office of the need to keep offsite copies of data to provide disaster protection.

A new key application for the SOHO LAN is to provide a mechanism to share high-speed Internet access among all SOHO LAN-attached PCs. This is readily accomplished by either using the Windows connection sharing capability or installing a Digital Subscriber Line (DSL) or cable modem router. This is rapidly becoming an increasingly important application that drives the implementation of home office LANs.

Some newer SOHO LAN applications are beginning to emerge. I've been running a SOHO LAN since 1983 and once made the bold prediction that I would one day attach my SOHO LAN to my refrigerator. Consequently, new applications do not seem cutting edge to me. However, you should be aware of what looms over the horizon.

Home PCs are used for multimedia applications and Internet access. Multimedia applications include playing music encoded in MP3 and other formats, playing DVDs, and processing and managing photographic images. Increasingly, the entertainment and image information that we use in our daily lives is fast becoming digital information stored on our PCs. Consequently, we will soon find that having a PC with a large, reliable disk drive is a necessary part of our homes; this drive will store all our key entertainment and image files. My SOHO LAN has two servers, each with over 300 GB of storage. Each server contains about 100 GB of MP3 music that can be played on any PC attached to my SOHO LAN. These PCs act like the "smart house" systems of the 1980's, providing music in any room of the house. Their attached amplified speakers with subwoofer reproduce music adequately for my untrained ear and can certainly reproduce the music loud enough to deafen any teenager.

One PC is my television. It is attached to a 42-inch diagonal flat panel display, the CATV feed for the house, and my SOHO LAN with a high-speed Internet connection. The Internet connection is used to download weekly program guides. These guides are used to tune in TV programs for viewing off the CATV connection. The PC also plays DVDs and MP3 files. The SOHO LAN permits the MP3s to be stored on my servers, and it supports access to the Guide Plus+ Web site containing the weekly CATV program schedules.

These are the simplest of home entertainment applications. When we get to business applications, the SOHO LAN is central to accessing remote data at our office, permitting us to work at home. Further, the SOHO LAN at a central office can have an internal company Web site reside on a server that publishes key company information like policy and procedures manuals. Such an internal company Web site is usually called an intranet. An intranet brings Internet technologies into a closed corporate LAN or a SOHO LAN. An intranet is basically any SOHO LAN segregated from the Internet, whether it hosts an internal Web site or not. Most intranets host internal Web sites.

Depending upon business and related network activity, company Web site hosting and e-commerce applications may be implemented externally by an Internet service provider, or internally on a small office LAN. To implement Web site hosting and e-commerce applications on a SOHO LAN would require more expensive and higher-speed Internet access than is currently offered by DSL or cable modem connections. While Web hosting and e-commerce is possible using DSL or cable modem connections, it is not prudent because anything other than a very light Web site or e-commerce network transmission load could easily overload a DSL or cable modem link. When e-commerce is intended to be a key part of a business, overloaded Internet links and servers are highly undesirable.

E-mail is the backbone of most business communications. Have you tried to reach someone by telephone lately? It is almost impossible. E-mail and fax communications are more effective. SOHO LANs provide access to external e-mail services like Yahoo!, AOL, and Hotmail, or they can support an internal e-mail post office server. Internal e-mail post office servers act just like a post office; they receive mail destined for company e-mail addresses from external e-mail servers and hold that mail until the e-mail recipient logs onto the e-mail server. The e-mail is then sent to their PC when they request it. Similarly, e-mail sent from internal PCs is relayed by the internal e-mail post office server to external e-mail servers for forwarding to the destination e-mail address.

The next killer application is mixing voice communications or telephony with the SOHO LAN. This general class of application is labeled Voice over Internet Protocol (VoIP). In this case our client PCs can become telephones or we use special VoIP telephones and we have a special server or Private Branch Exchange (PBX) that interfaces those PC telephones to other PC telephones across the Internet and to other ordinary telephone company-connected telephones found in everyone's home. Soon such VoIP applications turn into full video telephony applications. At that time AT&T's 1950s vision of the video telephone will become everyday reality. This is about 10 to a maximum of 20 years away.

The next step will be when the SOHO LAN connects to everything in our homes, including the refrigerator. This permits us to readily monitor everything we consume (permitting easy reordering of our everyday consumables) and the operation of everything in the home (permitting us to control our environment). So you see, my refrigerator LAN connection is not really off the wall. The refrigerator would have a sensor mounted around the door so that anything placed into or removed from the refrigerator would be recorded. Diets will never be the same.

Brain Teaser: SOHO LAN Use

Write down a list of what you plan to do with your SOHO LAN. Arrange it in order from what you think will be the easiest and least costly to implement to most difficult and costly to implement. Please save this list for later comparison.

Book Objectives

This is an essential guide that shows readers how to:

- Install
- Configure
- Operate

a small office/home office network. Non-engineering professionals and other nontechnical home users are shown in easy-to-understand steps how to select, install, and configure networking components for a small or home office to support disk, printer, and Internet connection sharing.

SOHO LAN technologies and terminology are explained using simple and hopefully sometimes humorous analogies to facilitate learning. Network design principles are discussed to permit readers to understand the most effective SOHO LAN configurations to support SOHO LAN applications. Design principles help readers understand LAN performance and reliability issues. Network security and management issues are presented and discussed. Throughout the book Brain Teaser exercises are used to illustrate the practical aspects of the concepts presented.

Who Needs This Book

The target audience of this book is my grandparents, Paul D. and Edna Moulton, rest their souls, because they truly represent nontechnical PC users and non-engineering professionals who need to install and operate a small-office or home-office network. The book includes practical explanations of selecting networking hardware components, configuring Windows software, and operating a network. This is a "how to" book, as well as a book that explains the technical terminology of SOHO LANs.

Most people think that they can escape advancing technology. They believe they do not need to know anything about how PCs and networks work. This thinking is generally correct because all computer products are becoming easier to implement and use. They are also incorrect in that they do not need to be able to understand PC design, but rather they only need to learn how to make a PC and a SOHO LAN do what they would like it to do. There is no escape, or as a Borg in Star Trek would state, "Resistance is futile!" Let me illustrate.

In 1965 Dr. Gordon Moore of Intel Corporation observed that the number of transistors per integrated circuit would double every 18 months. He forecast that this trend would continue for 10 years through 1975. Moore's Law, as his observation came to be called, has continued far longer and is still true as we enter the 21st century. Everyone has seen the implications of Moore's Law. PC and PC component prices have continuously dropped as the capabilities and capacities of PCs have increased.

Low PC prices and increased PC capabilities have made it possible for the PC usability research performed by a wide variety of companies and institutions to be implemented in each new generation of PCs. Unfortunately, there are no ready measurements for ease of use. If there were, I could postulate Pete's Law stating that ease of use increases twofold with each new generation of PCs. Because manufacturers implement new ease of use designs in their latest PC products, much simpler PC and SOHO LAN operation and installation result. Thus the axiom to Pete's Law would be something like, "Automatic and default settings work best."

For example, early PCs used DOS, requiring all users to remember cryptic commands like format, deltree, and fdisk. This made the PCs of the 1980s impossible for my grandparents to use. The PCs evolved to Windows and the graphical user interface (GUI), making them somewhat easier to use. However, the implementation of Web browsers and the Hypertext Markup Language (HTML) providing a point and click interface really made computers accessible to most all users (including my grandparents). This trend toward easier to use computers is a direct result Moore's Law.

The trend toward easier to use computers is spilling over into networking, with networking components becoming easier to install and configure. A simple rule to remember that can fix most networking and PC problems is that "default settings most often work best." Hopefully, this book can guide you to those PC and SOHO Networking components that are easy to install and can prepare you to work with those components that are almost "ready for prime time," but not quite as easy to install and configure as we'd like them to be.

We cannot escape the relentless advance of microelectronic technologies. They will soon invade every aspect of our lives. Once I was being interviewed on TV for a year 2000 show, and I made the comment that at least we didn't have to worry about the computers that run our toilets failing. My co-panelist disagreed because he had a computer-controlled toilet (imported from Japan). There is no escape and resistance is truly futile. So the more we learn about how to make computers and networks do what we want them to do for us, the better off we'll be. There is a finite risk that the only surviving life form from planet Earth may be some future cyber being that we humans created. Regardless of this warning, there is no turning back because we are already too committed to following the slippery slope of technology wherever it may lead us.

What This Book Covers

This book explains the applications of SOHO network hardware, wiring, and software. It presents the information using many pictures, with supporting text making it easy for the reader to understand how to select components and install, configure, and operate a SOHO network. Where helpful, information identifies and explains the technical specifications describing the most effective SOHO LAN technologies used in today's SOHO networking product offerings. These technical specifications are associated with SOHO LAN products that implement them. Such technical specifications are a step in ensuring that products conforming to those specifications interoperate in SOHO networks. They also help explain how SOHO network components work.

Concepts and procedures are illustrated using practical, real-life networking experiences as well as current industry product and service offerings. Practical exercises are included to reinforce the concepts and procedures presented in each chapter.

In Chapter 1 we look at SOHO LAN applications in detail. We expand on the applications described in this Introduction and see how they are implemented.

Chapter 2 details SOHO networking components, their function, their features, and their selection. Then, in Chapter 3, we examine installing and configuring a SOHO LAN. In most cases this is a direct and simple implementation process. However, when there are curves you will be alerted and shown how to avert or resolve problems.

Chapter 4 delves into wireless networking technologies because they promise to make SOHO LAN installation easy for everyone. However, there are some cautions to using wireless LAN technology, the most significant of which is security. Chapter 5 examines high-speed Internet access in detail. Configuring a router is covered step by step.

Telecommuting technologies are covered in Chapter 6. Chapter 7 presents SOHO networking security issues. Security is an increasingly important aspect of SOHO networks because a security breach can impact every network-attached PC and result in the loss of thousands or more dollars.

Chapter 8 looks into VoIP networking, a rapidly emerging application that is now in a key transitional period. As VoIP becomes mainstream, it will represent a real cost savings potential to all businesses. In Chapter 9 we try to bring everything into a practical perspective, wrapping up this book.

Finally, in the Appendix we look at multimedia entertainment PCs and discuss in detail how to build a multimedia entertainment PC. What executive office can be without a TV today, so why not turn executive PC hosts into televisions?

Summary

In this chapter we started by describing in high-level terms what a small and a large SOHO LAN is. We examined both peer-to-peer and client/server LAN configuration and operation. These basic descriptions are expanded upon later in the book as we examine SOHO LAN applications, components, installation, security, and more. SOHO LAN technologies and applications were introduced and described. The chapter concluded with the objectives of this book, a description of who needs this book, and what the book covers.

Key Technical Terms

Cable Modem—This is a technology used by cable television companies to provide high-speed Internet access over CATV cabling.

CATV—Community Antenna Television.

Client/Server—A type of network operation with a central server PC sharing resources and managing network resource access and security.

CSMA/CD—Carrier Sense Multiple Access with Collision Detection is a protocol (communications language) used by Ethernet to manage access to the communications media or wire.

DSL—Digital Subscriber Line is a telephone company technology that provides high-speed Internet access using telephone cabling.

Ethernet—A LAN technology developed by Xerox, Intel, and DEC; used in most SOHO LANs.

Gbps—(Giga) Billions of bits per second; a measure of transmission speed.

GUI—A graphical user interface, such as that used in Macintosh and Windows systems, provides a user interface with mouse controlled pointer and icons.

Host—Any PC that is attached to a SOHO LAN or the Internet.

HTML—Hypertext Markup Language is a page-description technology that implements point and click capabilities in Web browsing software.

Kbps—Thousands of bits per second; a measure of transmission speed.

LAN—Local Area Network is a network that serves a confined geographic area like a home or a small office.

Mbps—Millions of bits per second; a measure of transmission speed.

NIC—Network Interface Card.

PC—Personal computer that usually runs some version of the Microsoft Windows operating system.

Peer-to-Peer—A type of network operation in which all PCs participate as equals.

SOHO LAN—Small office/home office Local Area Network.

Virtual Office—This is another term for a SOHO.

VoIP—Voice over Internet Protocol is a set of technologies and products that implements voice telephony across SOHO LANs.

Review Questions

1. What three components comprise all SOHO LANs?

   Answer: Hardware, channel, and software.

2. A two-PC SOHO LAN has what physical components?

   Answer: Two PCs, two patch cables, and a wiring hub.

3. What makes a small-office LAN different from a home-office LAN?

   Answer: Small-office LAN is generally a client/server LAN and a home-office LAN is a peer-to-peer LAN.

4. Why are computers easier to use today than they were a decade ago?

   Answer: Because PC processing power and capacities have increased as predicted by Moore's Law, we can build PCs that are easier to use. These PCs implement HTML and point-and-click Web browsing.

5. What are the two most common SOHO applications?

   Answer: Disk/file sharing and printer sharing.

6. What application is driving home-office LAN sales?

   Answer: Sharing high-speed Internet access.

Chapter 1

SOHO Network Uses/ Applications

Chapter Syllabus

- Basic Network Applications
- Internet Access
- Web Serving
- Voice over Internet Protocol (VoIP) Telephony
- Telecommuting
- General Networking Approaches
- Summary
- Key Technical Terms
- Review Questions

This chapter examines in more detail the basic SOHO applications. These applications as identified in the introduction are disk/file sharing and printer sharing. Sharing high-speed connections to the Internet are a new application that is driving installation of many home office LANs.

Small office/home office network applications include the traditional disk, file, and printer sharing. These form the base for other small-office LAN applications. Intranet Web serving and e-mail applications rely on accessing key files on a server computer.

Sharing high-speed Internet access is quite different from sharing disk and printer resources. This relies on connection-sharing software or a router to merge Web page and other network information requests into a composite data stream to the Internet and in turn separate the replies and forward them to the requesting SOHO host PCs. Voice over Internet Protocol (VoIP) telephony is a demanding SOHO application. It requires a low-latency (minimum transmission delay) network and specialized telephony servers connected to the Internet and/or the Public Switched Telephone Network (PSTN).

Telecommuting applications require secure access to centralized organization LANs and data. Each application presents special challenges. This chapter examines how these applications benefit organizations and generally how they may be implemented. Finally, the basic networking approaches identified in the Introduction are expanded upon to provide greater insight into SOHO networking technologies.

Basic Networking Applications

The primary SOHO network applications are disk, file, and printer sharing. PC fixed disk drives hold files that are either data or software. The disk drive and its files may be shared across a SOHO LAN. Similarly, data may be printed on any printer attached to a SOHO LAN. Let's examine this in more detail.

Disk Sharing

PC disk drives under Windows store both data and programs in a file hierarchy. There is a root directory for each drive and under that subdirectories or folders containing either more subdirectories or files. In both home office peer-to-peer and small office client/server networks, all attached PC hosts can share their disk drives. This disk drive sharing is a two-step process. The first step is installing the disk and file sharing networking software provided with Windows and the second step is actually sharing the disk drives. When the drives are shared, access to them is specified for all users using passwords, or for specific users as determined by the central network security provider. To make this clear we look at disk sharing in our two-PC host, peer-to-peer home office LAN first, and then we look at disk sharing in a centrally administered small-office client/server LAN.

Disk sharing between two PC hosts on a simple SOHO LAN is shown in Figure 1.1. Each disk drive has its own file structure that can be viewed using

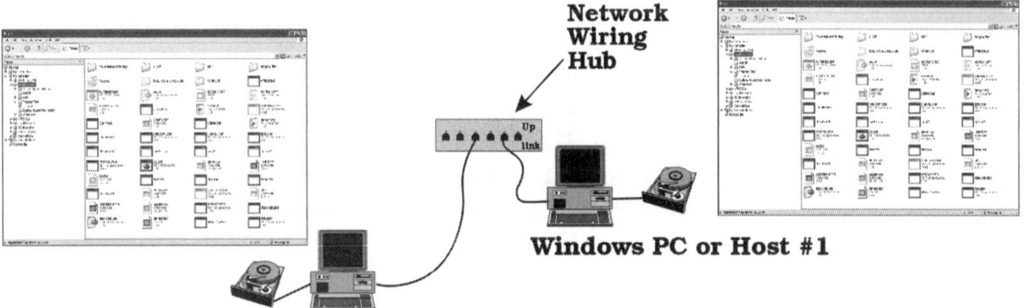

Figure 1.1 Two-PC host disk sharing.

the Windows Explorer. This structure is somewhat standardized by Windows on drive C: Documents and other files are contained in the folder My Documents under Windows 9x and in the folder Documents and Settings under Windows XP/2000. Programs are installed in the Program Files folder and Windows itself resides in the Windows or WinNT folder. In each folder there are either files or more folders. When a PC host shares its disk drive in a simple peer-to-peer network, there are two steps. Windows file and print sharing software must be installed, and then the disk drive or folder itself must be shared. Without performing both steps, the host PC is like a car with an engine (Windows file and print sharing software) but no transmission (sharing the disk drives with a designated security assignment).

We can tell that the disk drives are shared in the figure because the disk drive has a sharing icon associated with it. See Figure 1.2.

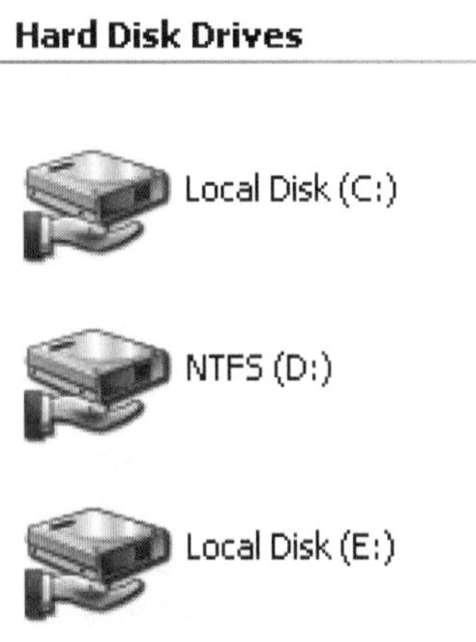

Figure 1.2
Windows XP Disk Sharing icon.

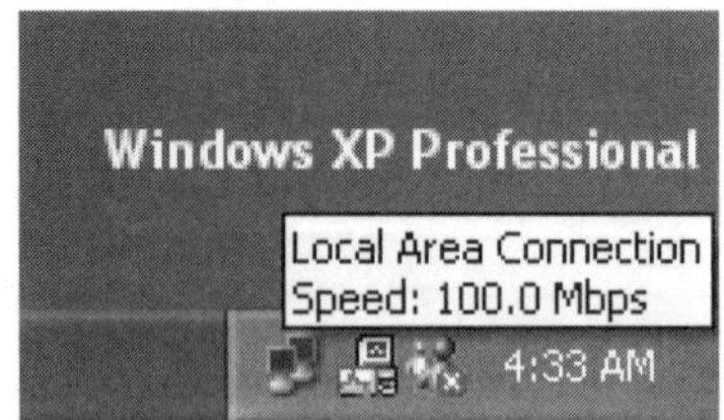

Figure 1.3
SYSTRAY Network icon.

The general procedure to check out disk drive sharing on any PC host attached to a LAN is similar for Windows 9x and Windows XP/2000/NT except that some of the labels vary. Windows XP provides network access through a network icon appearing in the SYSTRAY. The SYSTRAY is a Windows feature that displays icons for some programs and services running in the background under Windows. It provides a convenient mechanism for opening those programs and services like opening the network service running when the PC host is connected to a SOHO LAN. See Figure 1.3.

In Windows 9X we most commonly use Network Neighborhood to examine disk sharing setup. In Windows ME and Windows 2000 the same icon is labeled My Network Places. To look at disk drives we use the My Computer icon. In this case let me illustrate disk sharing using a Windows XP PC. The examples show screen captures from Windows XP. All versions of Windows follow similar disk sharing set up screens, but some Windows ME and Windows XP/2000/NT screens have different labels.

Brain Teaser: SOHO LAN Disk Sharing

Open the My Computer icon on your Windows desktop and see if any of the disk drives are shared. Shared drives have the Sharing icon, a hand supporting the disk drive. If there are no hands supporting your disk drives, they are not shared.

The easiest way to determine whether disk drives are shared on a SOHO LAN is to use the Windows Explorer and open My Network Places, as shown in Figure 1.4.

When the Entire Network icon is expanded, the Microsoft Windows network is expanded, and the domain "TMChqtrs" is expanded, we see the PC hosts in the domain listed. Clicking on one of these PC hosts, in this case NTServer, lists the shared resources, including the disk drives. When disks are not shared, we see no shared drives listed.

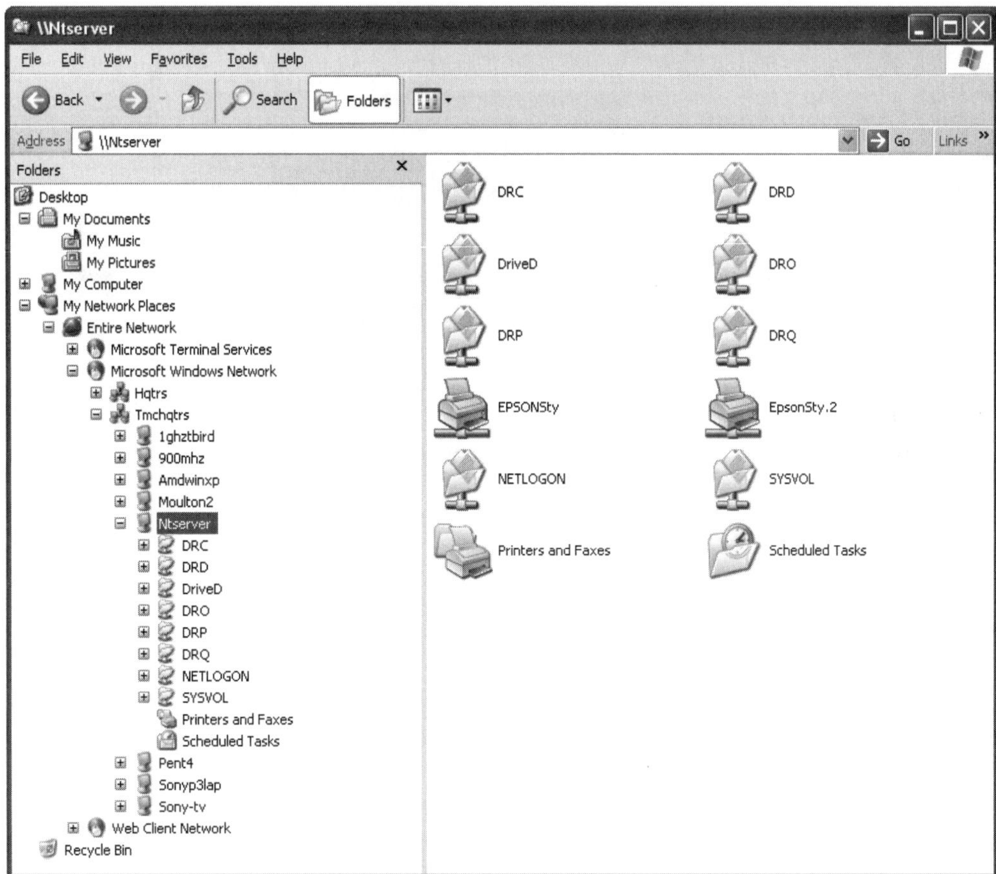

Figure 1.4 NTServer shared network drives.

File Level Access Control or File Sharing

Sharing individual files by a Windows PC host or server on a SOHO LAN is not performed with the older File Allocation Table (FAT) disk file system. Sharing folders is supported by both the FAT and Windows XP's NTFS (NT File System) on Windows PC hosts. File level access control or file sharing is supported on Windows XP Professional and Windows servers using NTFS. File-level access control or file sharing is performed using the inherited rights and the added security tab for files provided by NTFS. To determine if a file, folder, or disk is shared on a FAT or an NTFS partition, click on the file, folder, or disk icon to highlight the file, folder, or disk, and then right click to select Properties. The Windows XP File Properties screen pops up. See Figure 1.5.

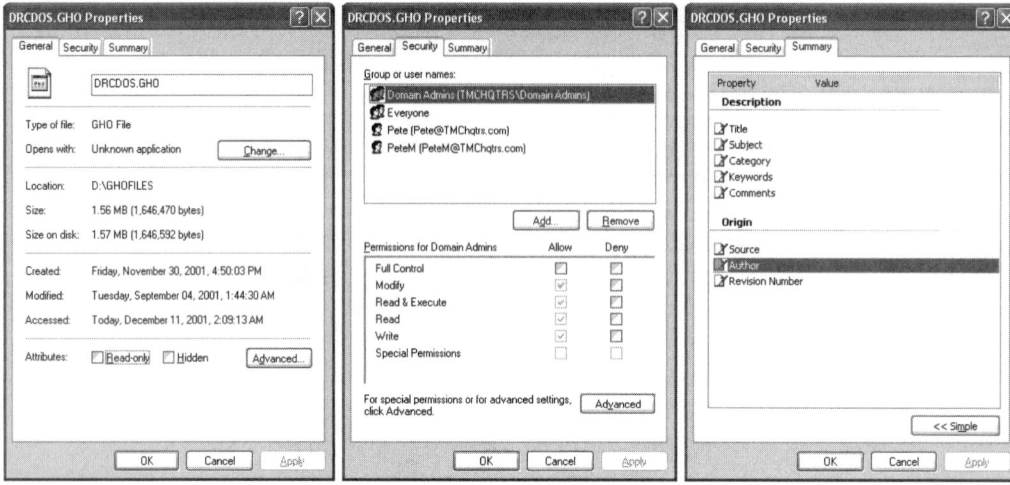

Figure 1.5 Windows XP File Properties.

The three tabs describe the shared file. The General tab provides overall information on the file. The Security tab regulates file-level access control or file sharing. The file-level access control or file-sharing rights are inherited under NTFS when the disk drive is shared. However, the file-level access control or file-sharing security tab permits us to further restrict access to the shared file for network users and groups based upon inherited security rights. The Summary tab provides added information on the file.

File-level access control or file sharing is an additional inherited security parameter for folder sharing and disk sharing. Sharing files is typically set up using inherited rights from a shared disk drive or a shared folder. See Figure 1.6.

Disk sharing rights lay the foundation for Folder sharing. Folder sharing generally places more restrictions on drive contents than does disk sharing. Finally,

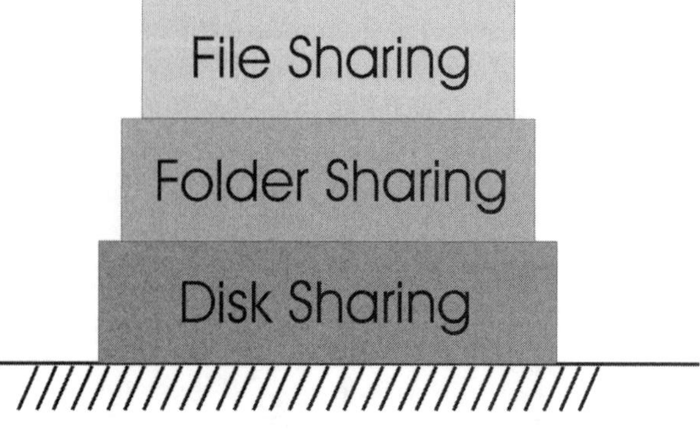

Figure 1.6
Windows disk, folder, and file-level access control or file sharing.

file sharing protects individual files more than disk or folder sharing. A strategy is to give open access to the disk drive and then protect critical areas on the drive from access by using increased folder and file level access control or file sharing restrictions. Windows supports other strategies as well.

For home office LANs, the typical installation strategy is to install the LAN with relaxed security restrictions, then tighten the restrictions when the LAN operates as they expect. For larger small-office LANs only specific folders and files are shared as needed. This protects critical PC host configuration information from being accessible to ordinary users. Administrative personnel generally set up a network so that they can get at critical configuration information to facilitate centralized network administration.

Printer Sharing

Printers attached directly to a PC host or other network printers may be shared. When sharing a network printer, the PC host connects to it using a TCP/IP port that acts like a local parallel or serial port. Once shared, the printer, similar to a disk drive, has an associated Sharing icon.

To determine in Windows XP if a printer is shared, use the Control Panel to open the printer's icon and view the printers. Network printers have an associated Network icon and local shared printers have the associated Sharing icon. See Figure 1.7.

In the figure the Tektronix printer is shared and the HP LaserJet printers are all network printers attached to other network PC hosts. This concludes the traditional SOHO LAN applications. These applications have been supported by SOHO LANs since the mid-1980s. Newer applications are based upon enhanced LAN technologies and high-speed communications.

Brain Teaser: SOHO LAN Printer Sharing

Using the Start button in Windows, go to Settings, and open the Printers icon to see if a printer attached to your PC is shared. Shared printers, similar to shared drives, have the Sharing icon—a hand supporting the printer. If there are no hands supporting your locally attached printer, it is not shared.

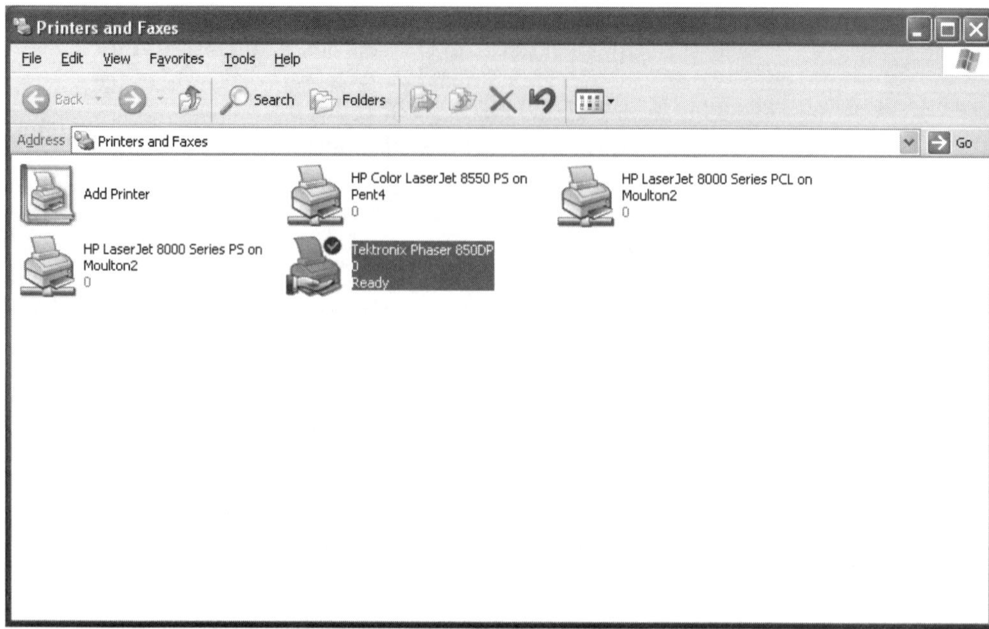

Figure 1.7 Windows XP network and shared printers.

Internet Access

Sharing high-speed connections to the Internet is a hot application area for SOHO LANs. In homes and offices today, cable modems or Digital Subscriber Line (DSL) modems provide 10-Mbps Ethernet connections into the SOHO LAN. These cable modems and DSL connections do not operate at the full Ethernet 10-Mbps speed, but rather they typically provide an uplink from the SOHO LAN to the Internet at a speed of 128 to 384 Kbps and a downlink from the Internet to the SOHO LAN of 400 Kbps to 1.544 Mbps for a $49 to $99 monthly fee. The cable modem or DSL modem provides the buffering needed to match the 10-Mbps Ethernet speed to the slower speeds of the uplink and downlink to the Internet.

Internet connection sharing is accomplished in two ways (see Figure 1.8):

1. The cable modem link is attached to a SOHO network component called a router.
2. A Windows XP PC host is configured to support Internet connection sharing with all Internet traffic then routed through a single Windows XP host PC.

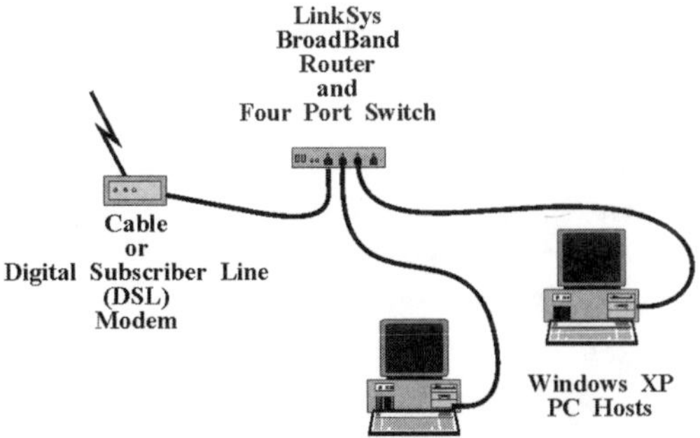

Router Configuration

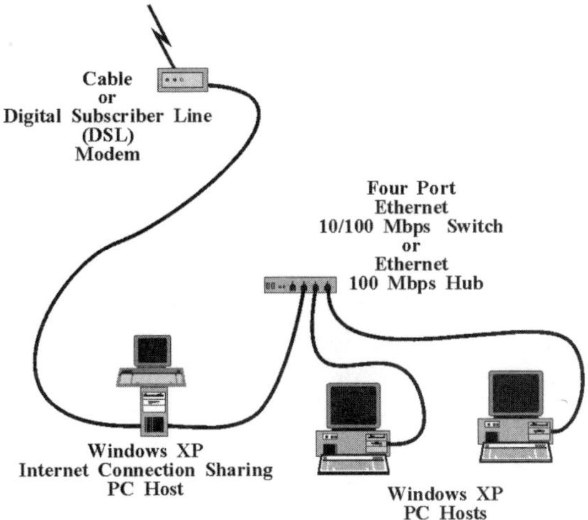

XP Internet Connection Sharing Configuration

Figure 1.8 Router and Internet connection sharing configurations.

At the top of the figure there are two Windows XP PC hosts connected via a switch/router to the cable or DSL modem. We examine the functions of these SOHO network components in greater detail in Chapter 5. In the bottom of the figure a Windows XP PC host has been configured to share the high-speed cable or DSL modem Internet connection. This is a configuration of the software components built into Windows XP that we shall also examine later in the book.

Cable Modems

Cable modems use the CATV coaxial cable to connect to central facilities at the CATV provider's head end facility. There the data stream from the cable modem is routed to a LAN that in turn is connected to the Internet. The LAN has local server computers, Internet caching servers, mail servers, and more. Typically the CATV provider also acts as an Internet service provider. It provides caching of frequently accessed Web pages on the local Internet caching servers, e-mail services, news group services, Web page storage, and sometimes more.

The cable modems are just a high-speed modem capable of 40-Mbps transmission speed, but centrally configured by the CATV provider to operate at 128 Kbps on the uplink and 400 to 800 Kbps on the downlink. The uplink and downlink speeds can vary depending upon network traffic. During high traffic periods the speeds are often lower. Unfortunately, the uplink speed of 128 Kbps never gets higher during low traffic periods. The downlink speed may exceed 800 Kbps.

Cable modems conform to a Data Over Cable Service Interface Specification (DOCSIS). These cable modems can be controlled from a central CATV head-end network facility. A central controller can vary the speed at which they send and receive data. Most CATV providers sell multiple addresses that can be assigned to each cable modem. My cable modem provider sells up to four addresses that can be assigned to a single cable modem.

The basic cable modem cost is about $40 per month, with added addresses costing about $10 per month. However, added addresses do not translate into added cable modem transmission capacity. All addresses for the cable modem share the cable modem's assigned transmission capacity. Such capacity sharing is also required for the router and Internet connection-sharing configurations. For small networks of two to 20 PC hosts, sharing is typically not a problem. There is no apparent performance degradation owing to multiple users. For larger networks multiple cable modems or higher-speed DSL modems could be deployed. Groups of PC hosts can be assigned to a specific cable modem, spreading a heavy load over multiple $40 per month cable modem connections.

For larger networks a T-1 connection may be needed to provide the requisite performance. A T-1 connection is a channel leased from the telephone company; it operates at 1.544 Mbps. Costs for such a leased channel vary from $600 to $1,000 per month plus a significant installation fee.

Cable modems can be purchased at retail computer outlets (what I refer to as computer grocery stores) like Best Buy and CompUSA. They come in a kit that SOHO LAN operators can readily install. Comcast runs a funny advertisement showing that a klutz who cannot fix anything at home can easily install a cable modem. Installation is not quite as easy as they imply in the advertisement, but most SOHO LAN operators can accomplish it.

Digital Subscriber Line (DSL)

A Digital subscriber line is a pair of modems that convert an ordinary telephone line into a high-speed Internet connection. DSL modems provide equivalent uplink and downlink speeds to a cable modem. The connection to the SOHO LAN is a 10-Mbps Ethernet connection. We discuss Ethernet in more detail in Chapter 2. For a SOHO LAN both DSL and cable modems provide basically equivalent high-speed Internet access.

Similar to cable modems, there is central control of DSL modems. SOHO LAN operators in some cases can install DSL modems. If not, telephone company service personnel can assist with the installation.

One limiting factor for DSL modems is that they must meet specific criteria to be able to function on the existing telephone wire. There are distance limitations from the telephone company central office that when exceeded prohibit the use of DSL modems. When the distance exceeds 18,000 feet the DSL modem typically does not operate. In my case, my facility is 27,000 feet from a telephone company central office, so I cannot get a DSL modem.

Cable modems do not have distance limitations like DSL modems. If you have CATV service and the CATV service supports cable modems, then you can get a cable modem.

Some DSL modems require that you logon to the DSL provider's network to use the DSL. When a PC host does not logon, the high-speed DSL Internet link is not available. This can be irksome. However, routers provide the capability to automatically logon to a DSL provider network whenever there is SOHO LAN activity requesting high-speed Internet access.

Web Serving

Web serving brings Internet-style Web site hosting capabilities into the SOHO LAN. Here we're interested in publishing Web sites over the company's internal network—its *intranet*. These sites are not available to anyone outside the network. In this case a PC host acts as a Web site server that is accessible using any Web browser. A special Internet Information Services (IIS) Windows XP software component is added to Windows PC hosts that permit them to act as a Web site server. While it is possible to set up an internal Web-style site by sharing a folder containing an index.HTM file, the IIS, and other Web server software make the reference to this intranet Web site more general and easier to use. Linux hosts with Apache and Samba Web serving software and other network components like the Sun Cobalt Cube and RaQ server appliances support Web site hosting and other functions. The Linux operating system can be obtained for free, but a PC host is required to run it. The Sun Cobalt Qube costs around $1,100 and the Sun RaQ can run as high as $2,200.

Windows computers can install personal Web server software to provide similar functions. Web pages are created using Web page creation software like FrontPage and then stored on the PC host running the IIS software. Web browser software like Internet Explorer can now display the Web pages stored internally on the intranet.

This application permits businesses to publish frequently changed information electronically. Because of its electronic form and universal availability to every PC host that is SOHO LAN attached, the information can be easily maintained and disseminated to SOHO LAN users. Take for instance an internal telephone directory. Such a document changes often and needs to be referred to by everyone. Publishing it as a Web page on an intranet saves significant time and money for any business.

There are a couple of cautions when publishing Web pages. First, links require continual testing to ensure that they always work. Second, Linux (and UNIX) servers use links that are case sensitive, while Windows does not.

When mixed case is used in a Web site name and a Web site link (a uniform resource locator—URL), Windows servers ignore the mixed case and Linux servers do not. This can cause problems unless the site is targeted at Linux servers by using only lowercase site names and URLs.

Web serving is an application that is used more by larger enterprises and much less frequently used by home office LANs. In a home office there is little need to publish internal Web documents. However, they can be published with pictures, so this may be the way to keep family photos in the future. Web publishing in a business can be much more useful. Instruction manuals, policy and procedure manuals, sales documents, memos to groups of employees, and other information that changes periodically and needs wide internal distribution are all candidates for intranet Web serving.

Internet Information Services

The IIS software is required to establish an internal Web server on a SOHO network. The IIS software is automatically installed with the Windows 2000 server software and can be manually installed in Windows XP or Windows 2000 Professional. Windows 9x versions use different software to perform the same Web page publishing functions.

When installed, the Windows XP Control Panel provides access to the administrative tools, which in turn has the shortcut to the IIS manager. See Figure 1.9.

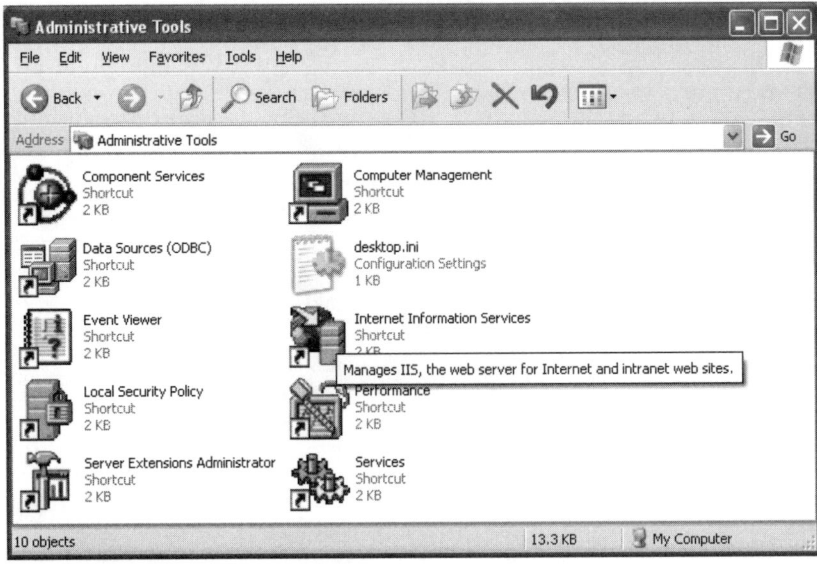

Figure 1.9 Administrative tools.

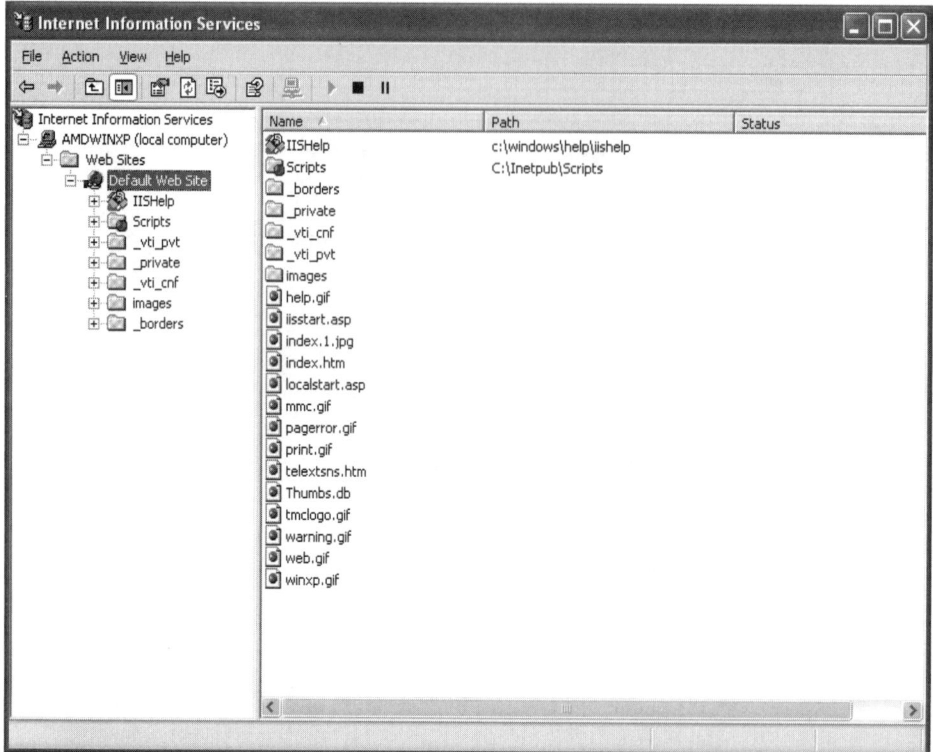

Figure 1.10 IIS default Web site display.

Once the administrative tools are opened, they show the contents of the default Web page. See Figure 1.10.

This figure shows the Windows XP intranet Web site server and the Web pages and files contained in the default Web site. For my intranet, two Web pages were created, INDEX.HTM and TELEXTSNS.HTM. These pages were created using FrontPage, and then published to the intranet default Web site.

FrontPage

Microsoft's FrontPage software creates Web pages. In our case we opened FrontPage to create a new Web page. Then we created the INDEX.HTM page and linked it to the TELEXTSNS.HTM page. On the index page, a graphic logo TMCLOGO.GIF was used. See Figure 1.11.

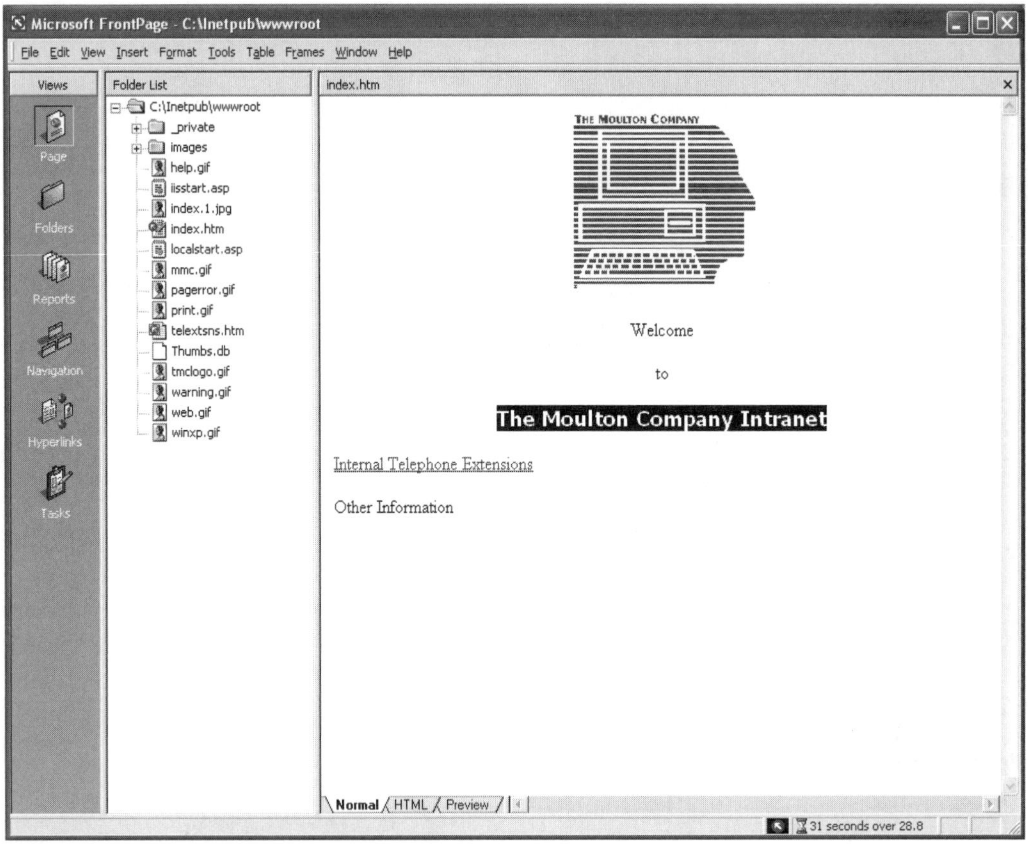

Figure 1.11 FrontPage creating index page.

FrontPage software comes with full versions of Microsoft Office software. FrontPage provides a variety of Web page publishing and formatting capabilities. Its major drawback is that the raw HTML code it creates is cumbersome and difficult to understand. However, for simple SOHO intranet publishing it functions adequately.

Intranet and Internet Publishing

Once FrontPage creates a Web site, the site is published to the intranet using the default Web site. The published Web page can be viewed by all SOHO LAN-attached PC hosts by using the URL http://*server_name*. See Figure 1.12.

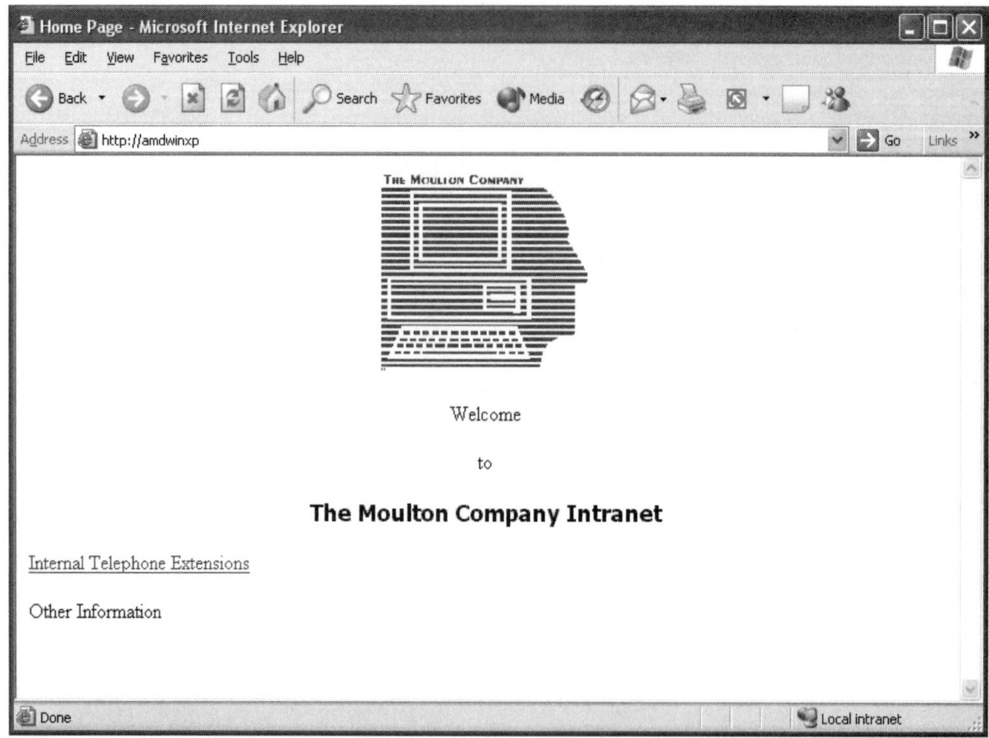

Figure 1.12 IE intranet Web page display.

An intranet Web site can be used for internal testing of Internet Web site content or just to provide information to enterprise employees. In the intranet site shown in Figure 1.13 there is a link to a Web page that lists all the telephone extensions throughout my home office. See Figure 1.13.

In my intranet the URL *http://amdwinxp* accesses the intranet Web page. The "*amdwinxp*" designates the Windows XP Professional PC host acting as an intranet Web server. When *http://amdwinxp* is entered into the IE browser, the intranet Web page pops up.

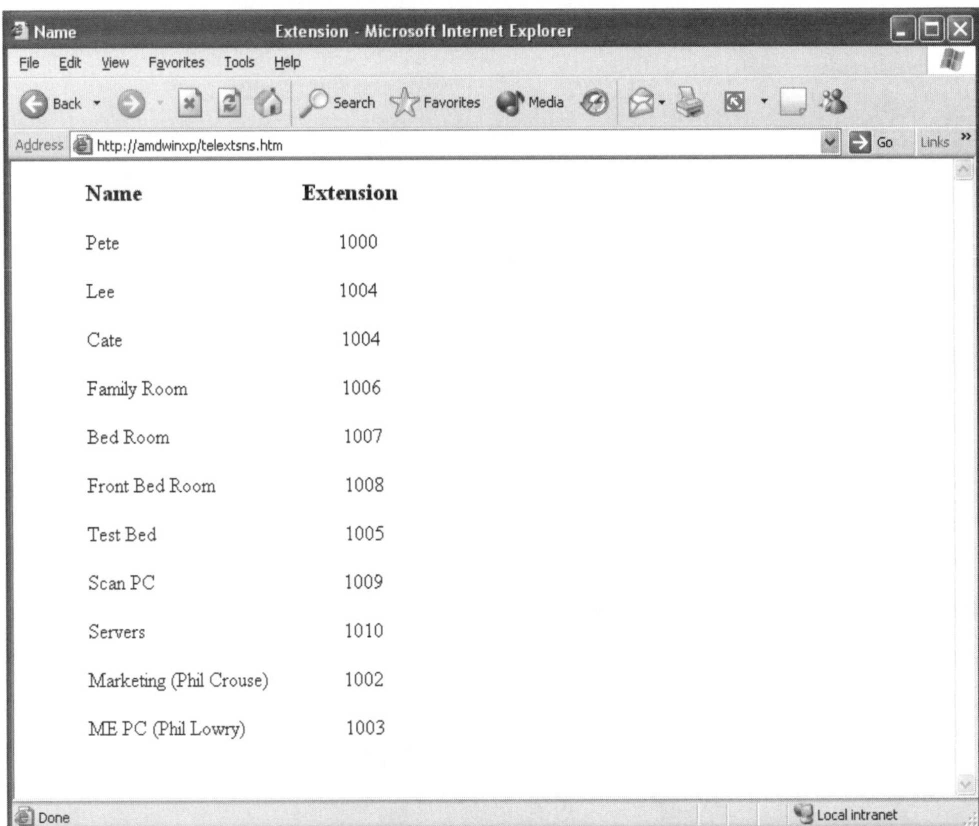

Name	Extension
Pete	1000
Lee	1004
Cate	1004
Family Room	1006
Bed Room	1007
Front Bed Room	1008
Test Bed	1005
Scan PC	1009
Servers	1010
Marketing (Phil Crouse)	1002
ME PC (Phil Lowry)	1003

Figure 1.13 Telephone extensions intranet Web page.

Voice over Internet Protocol (VoIP) Telephony

Voice over Internet Protocol (VoIP) telephony marries an enterprise's telephone system to its SOHO LAN. Marrying a Private Branch Exchange (PBX) to a SOHO LAN is not really a home office application because how many homes besides mine have their own PBX? However, there are low-end VoIP components for the home-office LAN that can be used to reduce long distance costs by providing free PC-to-PC VoIP connections and home-office LAN to Public Switched Telephone Network (PSTN) connections. Typically, a special telephony server or gate keeper is needed to provide the translation

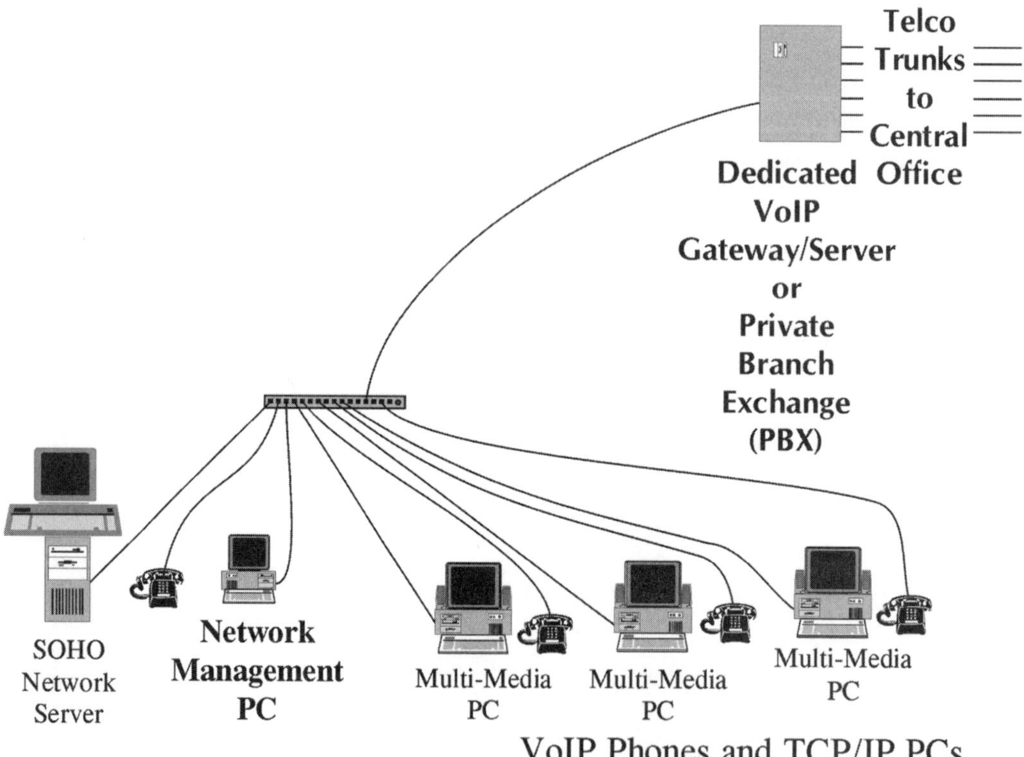

Figure 1.14 VoIP LAN configuration.

from the internal SOHO IP network to the dialup operation of the PSTN. See Figure 1.14.

In Figure 1.14 both PC hosts and telephones connect by the same wiring to the hub. The PC host traffic flows into the SOHO network server, while the VoIP traffic is routed to the dedicated VoIP gateway/server or PBX. Such VoIP applications depend upon the SOHO network using TCP/IP as its protocol.

TCP/IP

Transmission Control Protocol/Internet Protocol (TCP/IP) is the Internet protocol used by most LANs. Virtually all Windows operating systems support TCP/IP protocol, even Windows 3.1. TCP/IP performs routing and message delivery functionality. It operates efficiently.

TCP/IP is the basic communication language of the Internet. It is also frequently used as a communication protocol in SOHO networks. When a Windows PC host has a direct connection to the Internet, that PC host generally uses Windows' TCP/IP software components to send and receive messages and other data from Internet-connected host computers. Those computers also run TCP/IP software components.

TCP/IP provides two functions that are layered upon one another. The two parts of TCP/IP identify these functions. The higher layer is TCP and the lower layer is IP.

The higher-layer function, TCP, breaks apart messages or files into smaller packets that are transmitted over the TCP/IP network. At the destination host computer the TCP layer in turn receives these smaller packets and reassembles the packets into the original message.

The lower-layer function, IP, provides packet addressing so that the packets get to their destination. In a SOHO network Windows computers typically use the Active Directory Domain Name Service (DNS) or Windows Internet Name Service (WINS) to track IP addresses for each PC host and server. WINS is used for internal address resolution and DNS is used for both internal and external (Internet) address resolution. Each PC host uses the DNS or WINS information to send data and messages to the correct destination PC host address. In the Internet routers and gateway computers check the IP address to see where to forward data and messages. Sometimes packets from the same message get routed differently through a network than others. Regardless of such diverse routing, all packets are reassembled at the destination host computer.

TCP/IP uses client/server communication operation in which a network host client requests and is provided a service such as transmitting a Web page by network host server. TCP/IP communication is point-to-point, with each communication traveling from one host computer in the network to another point or network host computer. The IP layer is a connectionless service because packets follow no fixed path through the TCP/IP network. The TCP layer is connection-oriented because each message's packets must be received and reassembled to complete the message.

Some higher-level applications that use TCP/IP may also be considered connectionless because each client request is considered a new request unrelated to any previous one. Data requests come in wads and chunks. The wads and chunks arrive irregularly with no guaranteed arrival rate or transmission speed. Because IP is connectionless—sending IP packets only when there is information to send—it frees network paths so that they can be used as needed. In an IP network there are no paths dedicated to a single connection. All communications links or paths are shared by the information being sent across the communications links or paths.

This is different from phone conversations that are circuit switched and require a dedicated 64-Kbps constant bit speed connection for the duration of

a call. In a telephone network, a 64-Kbps link is used for a single call whether there is voice traveling across that link or not.

This highlights the basic conflict between TCP/IP data applications that have no guaranteed connectivity and delivery and telephony applications that require a fixed connection with guaranteed data delivery. Consequently, TCP/IP networks provide delivery guarantees for specific data types so that telephony applications requiring delivery guarantees to provide acceptable voice quality can operate on a TCP/IP network. These delivery guarantees are referred to as quality of service (QoS).

On SOHO LANs a single server using Dynamic Host Configuration Protocol (DHCP) TCP/IP dispenses addresses automatically. This facilitates central management of the network and saves administrative personnel from running between PC hosts when IP addressing problems arise. DHCP IP address assignment is used for Internet connections for SOHO LANs and in SOHO client/server LANs. The DHCP capability is provided by Windows 2000/NT Server software. For SOHO Windows clients using DHCP, the TCP/IP setting is used to obtain an IP address automatically. See Figure 1.15. Clicking on the Windows Network icon in the SYSTRAY and selecting Properties enters this client setup.

SOHO peer-to-peer LANs can use fixed or dynamic IP addresses for the TCP/IP protocol. This is easy enough to manage for two to 10 PC hosts. To set

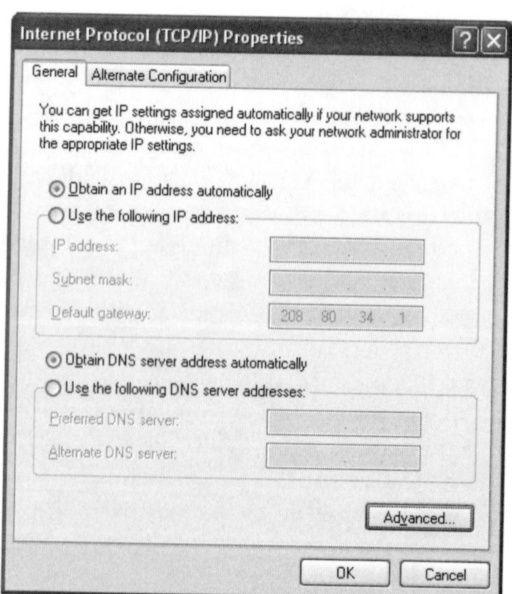

Figure 1.15
TCP/IP DHCP client setup.

a fixed IP address, select "Use the following IP address" and then enter an IP address. IP addresses consist of four numbers that range from 0 to 255.

Some IP addresses to use are 10.10.10.10 to 10.10.10.100 or 172.16.10.10 to 172.16.10.100. The Internet Assigned Numbers Authority (IANA) reserved three blocks of IP address space for private intranets:

10.0.0.0	to	10.255.255.255
172.16.0.0	to	172.31.255.255
192.168.0.0	to	192.168.255.255

Any enterprise using IP addresses in the address space above can do so without any coordination with IANA or an Internet registry.

Each fixed IP address should have the same numbers for the first three settings. The varying number is the last or right-most number, as in 10.10.10.nnn. Because many networks tend to use the addresses near nnn.nnn.nnn.255 and nnn.nnn.nnn.10 for SOHO LAN servers and routers, it is better to use a number greater than 10 or a number not near 255. Other IP addresses can potentially interfere with some TCP/IP network functions. Other TCP/IP network functions use specific IP addresses like the loopback address of 127.0.0.1, the 0.0.0.0 default route address, or the 224.nnn.nnn.nnn to 248.nnn.nnn.nnn addresses used by Internet routers or reserved for future use, so such numbers are good to avoid as well.

Brain Teaser: IP Address Assignment

Using your Windows Start button, go to Control Panel and open the Network and Dialup Connections icon, highlight the LAN connection icon, right click, and select Properties. This should reveal a panel with Internet Protocol (TCP/IP) as a selection. Highlight it and select the Properties button below to see if the PC uses a fixed IP address. Most likely you will find that "Obtain an IP address automatically" has been selected.

Higher-layer application protocols ride on top of TCP/IP to provide PC hosts with special Internet services like Web browsing and e-mail. Such higher-layer protocols include the World Wide Web's Hypertext Transfer Protocol (HTTP); the File Transfer Protocol (FTP); Telnet (TELNET) for logging on remote UNIX/Linux computers as a terminal; and the Simple Mail Transfer Protocol (SMTP), the Post Office Protocol 3 (POP3), and the Internet Message Access Protocol (IMAP) used in combination to manage and deliver e-mail. These protocols are packaged together with Windows TCP/IP

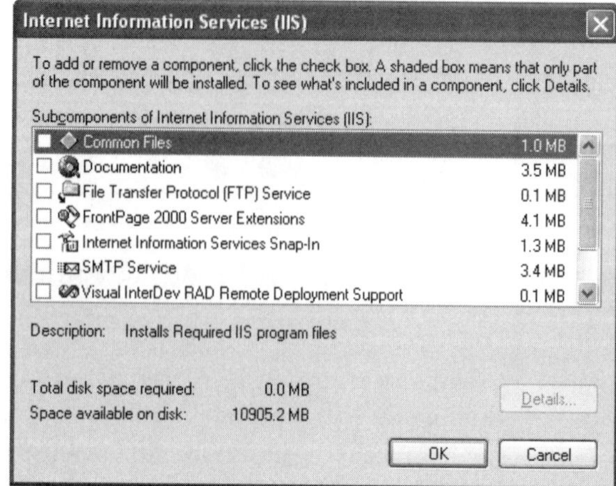

Figure 1.16
IIS-supported functions and protocols.

protocol. The IIS implements FTP, SMTP, and HTTP protocols to provide intranet services. Internet Explorer uses HTTP to retrieve Web pages from intranet and Internet Web sites. See Figure 1.16.

Dialup connections to the Internet use the Serial Line Internet Protocol (SLIP) or the Point-to-Point Protocol (PPP). These protocols operate at a lower level than the IP protocol. They encapsulate the IP packets and send them over dialup phone connections to an Internet service provider.

VoIP

Voice over Internet Protocol uses TCP/IP to transport voice as packetized data across a LAN. In the telephone network each phone line is translated into a continuous 64-Kbps digital stream. In the TCP/IP LAN world, the telephone network 64-Kbps data streams or analog telephone network channels must be translated by a gateway/server into the TCP/IP packets that travel across the TCP/IP LAN. They typically are encoded at a lower speed than in the PSTN. The concern here is that once telephone conversations are translated to TCP/IP packets, the connectionless nature of TCP/IP can cause the voice quality to degrade. If some voice conversation packets were to arrive late, this could cause the voice output to warble or sound unclear. With a VoIP TCP/IP network, performance and guarantees of timely packet delivery is very important.

VoIP benefits include all voice and LAN data traffic running across the same wiring. There is no need to maintain two separate sets of wiring. It is also becoming increasingly possible to route long-distance voice calls across the

Internet or other private IP networks. This can greatly reduce the cost of long distance and overseas voice telephone calls.

Telecommuting

A combined home office and enterprise application is telecommuting. In this case a home office LAN at the telecommuter's residence is linked to the enterprise network, permitting the home office worker to function electronically as though he or she were present in the enterprise's normal office facilities. This electronic link works for many types of office and professional jobs. When telephone calls are routed to a telecommuter's home, the caller can in no way tell that the telecommuter is working from home and not from some central office facility. The only time a telecommuter cannot report to work is when the electronic links between the home and the enterprise office facility are broken or out of service. When telecommuters are spread across a metropolitan area, it would be very difficult to have every telecommuter unable to connect to the central enterprise office facility.

Telecommuters can depend upon Windows Virtual Private Network (VPN) and Remote Access Server (RAS) software to link their home office LAN to the central enterprise network. Windows VPN capability is built into most Windows versions. It permits the remote Windows system to securely connect to a central office Windows system over a virtual connection that travels across a private TCP/IP network or the Internet. A central office Windows or other VPN server routes the data from the remote Windows PC host to the enterprise network servers. A Windows or other RAS server permits remote PC hosts to dial into the central facility network using the Public Switched Telephone Network (PSTN). In other cases remote PC hosts may connect directly as terminals to enterprise network mainframe computers to access and update specific databases. See Figure 1.17.

The Windows Server routing and Remote Access software has several configurations that support SOHO telecommuter configurations and other small office network configurations, as described in Figure 1.17.

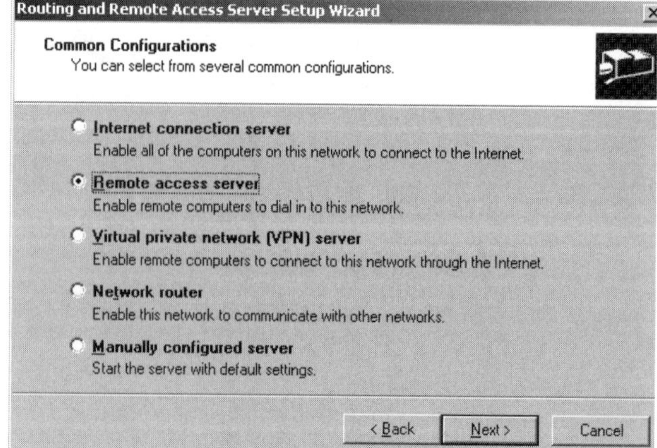

Figure 1.17
Windows 2000 Server Remote Access software.

Virtual Private Networks (VPN)

Virtual Private Networking has been used by enterprises for quite some time. It creates logical software-defined virtual circuit connections between host computers on a TCP/IP network. Both the remote PC host and the central PC server ensure that all communications between them remain private by encrypting data flowing between them. Further, the remote users are connected to the central office network as though they were sitting at a PC host in the office. This means that they must logon to the central office network with their user name (USERID) and password to authenticate them and assign them their requisite network security authorizations. See Figure 1.18.

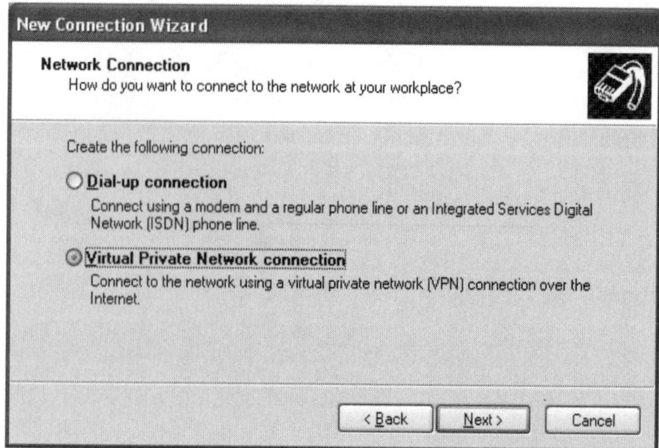

Figure 1.18
Windows XP VPN network connections.

The Windows VPN software is easily configured to connect to a central office companion VPN server. The Windows VPN server permits connections via the Internet. VPN connections run across high-speed cable modems or DSL links into the Internet.

Remote Access Server (RAS)

A Remote Access Server is a server with the Routing and Remote Access Service specially configured to provide remote networking for telecommuters, mobile workers, and network administrators. The Windows routing and remote access service permits telecommuter PCs to dial into the RAS and access the central facility network. RAS permits remote access to file and printer sharing, e-mail, scheduling, and database access.

Windows remote access servers set up secure connections through the PSTN. In this case the telecommuters need to be in a local calling area to avoid expensive toll charges.

Host Network Access

Windows XP PC hosts can use the HyperTerminal program to directly access mainframe computers as though they were terminals attached to the host computer system. The HyperTerminal emulates a variety of dialup terminal types. See Figure 1.19.

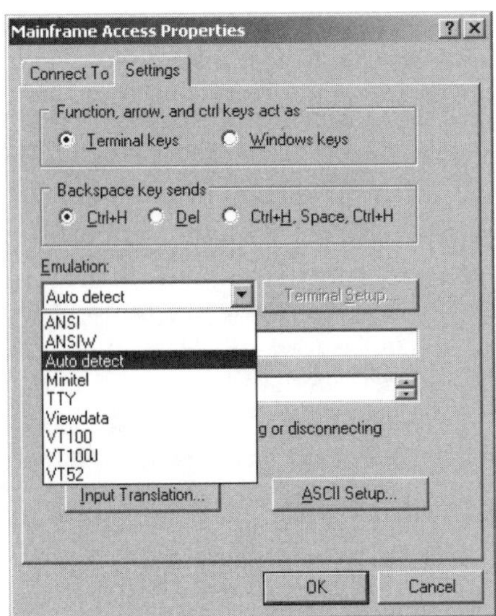

Figure 1.19
HyperTerminal dialup terminal emulation.

The HyperTerminal is configured to use a specific COM port, and its attached modem will call a mainframe computer supporting dialup connectivity. Windows XP dial-up networking configuration is not needed for HyperTerminal. HyperTerminal may be used to directly connect to computer and communications equipment that uses a command line interface such as telecommunications PBX switches, the Linksys 24-port gigabit switch (EF24G2), and Small Computer System Interface (SCSI) Redundant Array of Independent Disks (RAID) controllers. For telecommuters the ability to dialup mainframe computers is the key feature.

Brain Teaser: Finding HyperTerminal

Using the Windows Start button, go to Programs, select Accessories, Communications, and open HyperTerminal. If the Location Information Wizard pops up, enter your area code and any number needed to access an outside line (usually 8, 9, or no number). Click OK and click OK again to set the "My Location" dialing rules. HyperTerminal will then open. Enter any name like "Eat at Joe's" and select OK to connect using COM1. Note the port settings and select OK. Then exit by disconnecting and not saving the "Eat at Joe's" session.

General Networking Approaches

After examining the SOHO LAN applications, we turn our examination to the general approaches to SOHO networking. These approaches deal with the communications channel or wiring and the networking protocols used. An approach is embodied in the Network Interface Card (NIC).

Most often the wire and the networking protocol are married together for life because they are implemented in a NIC. However, it is possible to see a wider variety of networking approaches today. There is nothing that mandates that Ethernet run at 100 Mbps over unshielded twisted pair wire. With that said, I must stress that the more esoteric combinations of wiring and protocol are most often some manufacturer's response to a niche market, and are not anywhere near the market mainstream.

Home Wiring

All SOHO LAN operators would like to use the electrical wiring in the home to act as the communications medium for the SOHO LAN. Linksys at one time provided SOHO LAN products that worked with the electrical wiring in the home. These products seem to be falling victim to emerging 802.11 wireless networking products. Home electrical wiring communications technology does not deliver the transmission speeds (capacity or bandwidth) or the reliability that are realized by special SOHO home wiring tailored to Ethernet and video transmission or to that provided by wireless LAN products.

There are manufacturers that produce special wire tailored to home office networking. They include SEIMON, and OnQ. At one time both IBM and Lucent were developing and selling home wiring products, but they appear to have dropped those product lines.

Most home wiring systems have a central hub. All room outlets are star wired to the central hub. The central hub is used to cross connect the various cables to provide the video and SOHO network connections for a home. Home wiring systems are easy and cost effective to install in a new home, but they are somewhat more costly and difficult to install in an existing home.

Universal Serial Bus (USB) Networking

All PC hosts today have Universal Serial Bus (USB) ports. These ports can be interconnected to network PC hosts. USB operates at 1.5 Mbps or 12 Mbps, with the speed of an individual bus determined by the slowest device on the bus. For a very small network, USB networking would be OK. However, more than two or three devices on a USB network would not work as well as using 100 Mbps Ethernet. USB requires special cables that have special connectors. USB acts like any NIC in that it fulfills the wiring and communications protocol requirements for a network. It falls short when it comes to transmission speed as compared with Ethernet. Higher transmission speeds should be available soon in USB networking components. However, they will still lag behind Ethernet.

Another networking approach similar to USB networking is to use IEEE 1394 FireWire. Sony computers come with this interface. I have networked two Sony laptops using their FireWire ports and Windows built-in software networking protocols. They implemented a peer-to-peer network using FireWire in place of Ethernet NICs.

Both USB and FireWire lack the plethora of networking components found for Ethernet. Further, they both operate at speeds of 12 Mbps, or 480

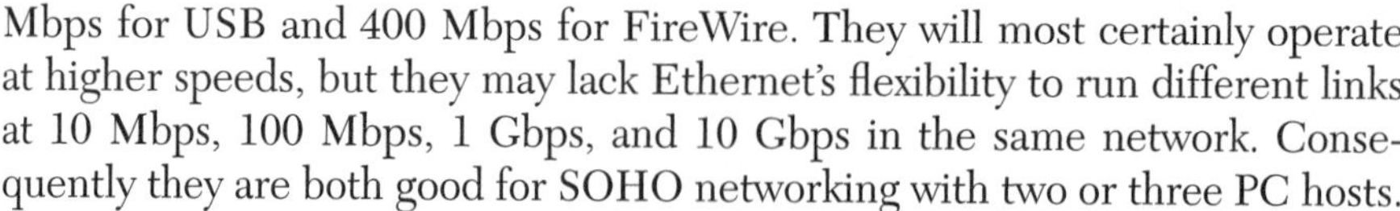

Mbps for USB and 400 Mbps for FireWire. They will most certainly operate at higher speeds, but they may lack Ethernet's flexibility to run different links at 10 Mbps, 100 Mbps, 1 Gbps, and 10 Gbps in the same network. Consequently they are both good for SOHO networking with two or three PC hosts.

Brain Teaser: Finding USB Connections

Look at the rear of your computer for the connections and their symbols. Do you find any rectangular connections? What is the symbol next to them? Does the symbol look like a growing plant? If it does, then these are USB connections. Verify by going to a computer or electronics store and looking for USB cables. The same USB symbol should appear on the USB cable box.

Ethernet

Ethernet is the primary SOHO and LAN networking technology. It operates at speeds of 10 Mbps, 100 Mbps, 1 Gbps, and 10 Gbps. It is easy to migrate a slower SOHO Ethernet LAN from a slower operating speed to a faster operating speed because Ethernet networking hubs, switches, and routers provide built-in speed buffering. Ethernet NICs and other components are cheap. They interconnect directly with cable and DSL modems, and they support TCP/IP. Ethernet networking components can be centrally monitored and managed, and they provide the high speed and QoS network management needed for VoIP networking. This makes Ethernet the primary SOHO LAN technology candidate.

Wireless Networking

Wireless networking technology provides some competition for Ethernet. It too comes from the development and standardization work of the IEEE 802 committee. The major attractiveness of wireless LANs is the lack of fixed wiring. This means that in a home few physical wires need to be run. Some Ethernet wiring at the central network hub point is needed, but this can be confined to a single room. Then a Wireless Access Point (WAP) connects into the existing Ethernet and provides the wireless connections to the PC hosts. These RF links can connect through walls and floors. However, there are limits there. Regardless of these connectivity limits, the higher cost of wireless

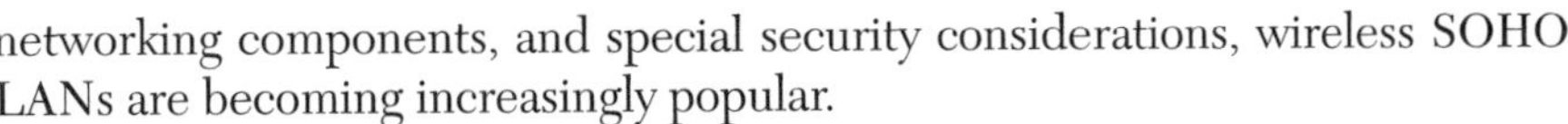

networking components, and special security considerations, wireless SOHO LANs are becoming increasingly popular.

Our Networking Focus

In this book we will focus on market mainstream SOHO LAN networking approaches. This means largely Ethernet and wireless networking. These will be examined in more detail in subsequent chapters. We have also discussed USB and FireWire networking for small SOHO networks because they are inexpensive to implement (one only needs a cable for two PC hosts) and in some cases readily available.

Summary

This chapter has examined basic SOHO LAN applications. It illustrated how to determine if a PC LAN was set up for disk sharing, folder sharing, file sharing, and printer sharing. We then looked at the popular application of sharing high-speed Internet connections. These applications comprise the most common applications for home office LANs.

The chapter then moved to more common small-office LAN applications that included Web serving supporting enterprise intranets, Voice over IP (VoIP) telephony that combines both the small-office LAN and telephony so all communications run across a single wiring plant, and telecommuting applications where Virtual Private Networking (VPN) and Remote Access Service (RAS) software connect telecommuters seamlessly to enterprise networks.

The chapter concluded with a quick tour of the general approaches to SOHO networking. Ethernet and wireless networking (sometimes referred to as WiFi) command the market mainstream. USB and FireWire networking can be used to quickly network two computers. These networking approaches are embodied in the Network Interface Card (NIC). They are combinations of wiring and hardware protocols built into NICs. Our networking focus in this book will be to examine the market mainstream networking approaches.

Key Technical Terms

CATV—Community Antenna Television is the cable network connection that many people rely upon for receiving television channels and programming. CATV networks are also providing high-speed Internet access and are supporting voice telephony.

DHCP—Dynamic Host Configuration Protocol is a software service provided by designated LAN servers that lease IP addresses to PC hosts as requested by the PC hosts. The leased addresses are allocated from a pool of addresses managed by the DHCP server. DHCP clients "Obtain an IP address automatically." DHCP facilitates more centralized TCP/IP LAN management.

DOCSIS—Data Over Cable Service Interface Specification standardizes the design of all cable modems. DOCSIS modems are centrally controlled by the CATV head-end facility. Speed is regulated to 128 Kbps up and 400 to 800 Kbps down to the SOHO LAN connected to the cable modem.

FAT—File Allocation Table is a disk drive format or file layout scheme that was developed for fixed disks under DOS. FAT-32 or a 32-bit FAT is the current incarnation. The alternative disk drive file layout scheme is NTFS or NT File System.

FireWire or IEEE 1394—FireWire or IEEE 1394 is a serial bus technology developed to interface multimedia peripherals such as camcorders and VCRs to PC hosts. It runs at 400 Mbps.

FTP—File Transfer Protocol is a protocol that rides on TCP/IP and supports transferring files of data across the Internet. Whenever we use Windows Update to download software updates to our Windows PC host, we are using FTP.

HTTP—Hypertext Transfer Protocol is the top-layer protocol used to transfer Web page content across the Internet or any other IP network to Web browsing software (e.g., Microsoft's Internet Explorer) for display on a PC host.

IMAP—Internet Message Access Protocol is used to access e-mail or bulletin board messages stored on an e-mail server.

IP—Internet Protocol is the lower-layer protocol part of TCP/IP that uses numeric addresses to route data from source to destination in the Internet or any other IP network. A typical IP address is 208.80.34.183. IP is a connectionless protocol.

NTFS—NT File System is a disk drive format or file layout scheme that was developed for fixed disks under Windows NT. It provides more folder and file control capabilities than does the FAT disk format or file layout scheme. NTFS was designed to be a more secure disk file system to support client/server networking. The alternative disk drive file layout scheme is FAT or File Allocation Table.

PBX—Private Branch Exchange is a voice telephone switch privately owned by an enterprise. It switches internal voice telephone calls, provides voice mail, and more.

POP3—Post Office Protocol 3 is a client/server protocol in which e-mail is received and held by an Internet server. Periodically, an e-mail client checks a mail-box on the e-mail server and downloads any mail.

PPP—Point-to-Point Protocol is a dialup protocol used to connect TCP/IP protocol computers to the Internet or other IP networks.

PSTN—Public Switched Telephone Network is the telephone network that has existed since the late 1800s and that carries in our voice communications traffic. Today it operates as a backbone voice communications network to cellular communications networks and the Internet.

QoS—Quality of Service is the capability to guarantee a specified performance level for a connection across a TCP/IP LAN or other network. QoS is critical on SOHO LANs that mix both voice and data traffic on the same network.

RAID—Redundant Array of Independent Disks is a hardware or software mechanism for distributing data across several disk drives primarily to provide redundancy in the event of a single disk failure. RAID software is built into Windows 2000/NT Server. The Windows RAID software works only on NTFS disk drives.

SCSI—Small Computer System Interface is a disk interface bus used in PCs. SCSI disks are most often found in servers. Several disks can be connected to a single SCSI bus.

SLIP—Serial Line Internet Protocol is a dialup protocol used to connect TCP/IP protocol computers to the Internet or other IP networks.

SMTP—Simple Mail Transfer Protocol runs on top of TCP/IP to exchange e-mail messages between Internet post office computers and e-mail client computers. It works in combination with POP3 and IMAP.

RAS—Remote Access Service is Windows software that permits remote computers to use the PSTN to dial into a central facility network.

T-1—T-1 is a telephone network with a 1.544 Mbps high-speed digital channel that carries voice or data to customer facilities and between telephone network facilities. A T-1 channel is what every nerd lusts for to connect his home into the Internet. T-1 channels run 24 hours a day and 7 days a week.

TCP—Transmission Control Protocol is the upper-layer function of TCP/IP. It is responsible for delivery of messages sent across the Internet and any

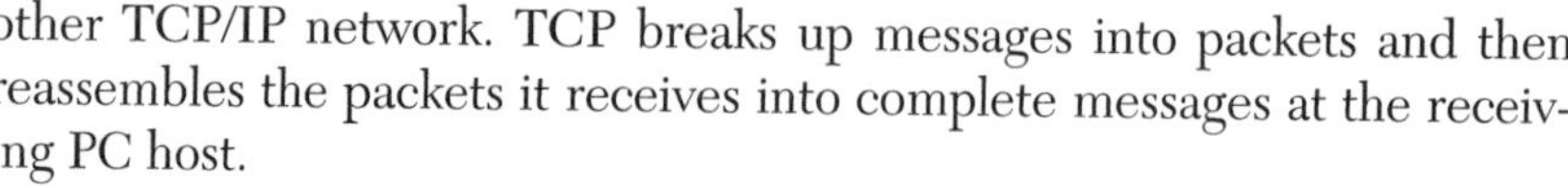

other TCP/IP network. TCP breaks up messages into packets and then reassembles the packets it receives into complete messages at the receiving PC host.

TCP/IP—Transmission Control Protocol/Internet Protocol is the suite or set of protocols that carries data packets across the Internet and many other private networks. IP provides a best-effort, connectionless (no fixed path) packet delivery service. Packets can contain data, voice, image, or video information.

URL—Uniform Resource Locator is the Web page reference used to link to other Web page information or Web sites.

USB—Universal Serial Bus is a high-speed serial bus for connecting various peripheral components to PC hosts. It currently operates at 1.5 Mbps and 12 Mbps. Higher speeds are expected in the future.

VPN—Virtual Private Network is point-to-point virtual connection across the Internet or a packet-switched network implemented and controlled by software. The virtual connection remains private and secure because data is encrypted by the sending PC host and decrypted by the receiving PC host.

WAP—Wireless Access Point is the central radio frequency hub connecting the remote PC hosts using wireless LAN NICs to an Ethernet.

WiFi—Another name for the IEEE 802.11 wireless LAN specification products.

Windows XP—The latest version of Windows. XP is not an acronym for anything special, so create your own meaning for it. Windows NT, or Windows New Technology, was the grandparent of Windows XP. Windows XP, Windows 2000, and Windows NT share many common features.

World Wide Web—The World Wide Web or WWW is a collection of servers that contain Web pages accessed by Web browsing software and HTTP. It is a subset of the Internet host computers because some Internet host computers do not serve HTTP Web pages.

Review Questions

1. What are the common SOHO LAN applications?

   Answer: Disk, folder, file, and printer sharing.

2. What is a newer SOHO LAN application?

   Answer: High-speed Internet connection sharing.

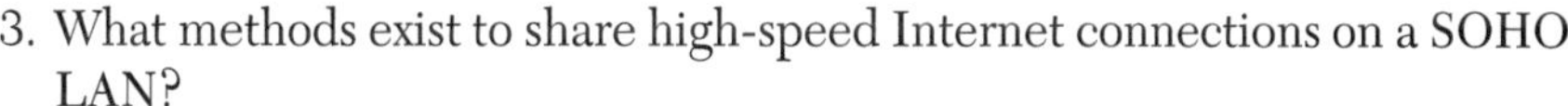

3. What methods exist to share high-speed Internet connections on a SOHO LAN?

   Answer: A small office LAN can share the connections using Internet connection sharing software or can connect to a hardware router.

4. What applications are more aimed at small office networks?

   Answer: Intranet Web serving, VoIP telephone, and telecommuting provide more benefits for enterprises using small office LANs.

5. What are the two most common SOHO networking approaches?

   Answer: Ethernet and wireless LANs.

6. What networking approaches may also be used for two-PC host LANs?

   Answer: USB and FireWire networking.

Chapter 2

NETWORKING COMPONENTS

Chapter Syllabus

- Windows Networking Model
- Networking Hardware
- Cabling
- Software
- Summary
- Key Technical Terms
- Review Questions

This chapter presents the hardware, cabling, and software components needed to implement a SOHO LAN. It covers the differences between Ethernet and Fast Ethernet, CAT-3 and CAT-5 cabling, and relevant Windows software. These components and their role in the Windows networking model are described. The operation and role of other networking hardware is presented with the goal of helping the reader select the components best suited to his or her networking needs.

Windows Networking Model

We begin this chapter by looking at the Windows networking model. This model reflects the SOHO LAN hardware and the Windows XP software installed to build a LAN. Using Windows XP or any other Windows software, you can easily see the Windows networking model. In Windows XP we open the Start menu and select Control Panel. See Figure 2.1.

The Control Panel contains a Network Connections icon. When opened, this icon reveals the network connections panel. When a SOHO LAN is installed, it appears as a LAN or High-Speed Internet connection. See Figure 2.2.

This icon identifies the physical hardware over which the LAN connection communicates. Right clicking reveals a menu with Properties. Opening Properties reveals the Windows XP Local Area Network Connection Properties General tab. See Figure 2.3.

Figure 2.1
Windows XP Start menu.

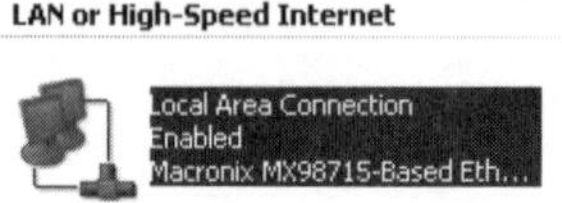

Figure 2.2
Windows XP network connection LAN icon.

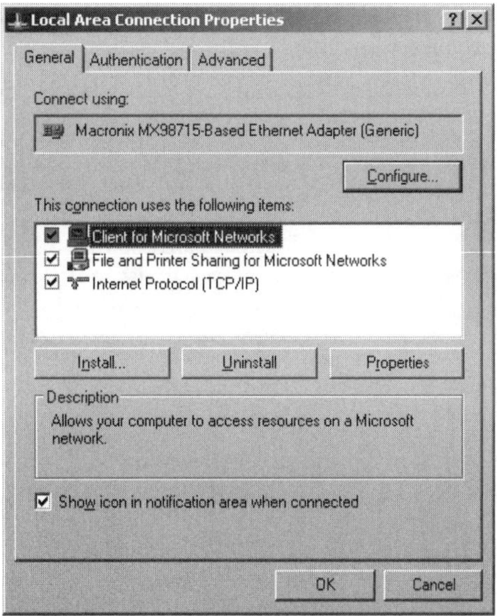

Figure 2.3
Windows XP Local Area Network Connection Properties.

These LAN properties describe the Windows networking model. The Windows networking model is broken into three general layers:

1. A **hardware layer** shown in the "Connect Using" panel that describes the networking adapter and wiring.
2. A **protocol layer** shown at the bottom of the "This connection uses the following items:" panel.
3. A **services layer** shown at the top of the "This connection uses the following items:" panel. Both Client for Microsoft Networks and File and Printer Sharing for Microsoft Networks services are shown in the Figure.

These layers can be further subdivided into more detailed functions. One such division is the ISO seven-layer networking model. This model is discussed in other telecommunications books like *The Telecommunications Survival Book*, but is not discussed in depth here because our focus is on understanding and building SOHO LANs. As we look as SOHO networking under Windows using Windows XP examples, we in truth examine most of the ISO seven layers.

The Windows Networking Model parallels our Introduction Chapter LAN hardware (the tools), channel (the pipe), and software (the glue) networking description. In Figure 2.3 we see both the NIC hardware and the wire configured in the "Connect using" pane. In the bottom pane the Windows network protocol and the services software is listed. This is a further division of the software identified in the Introduction.

The bottom layer of the Windows Networking Model is the Network Interface Card (NIC). A NIC is installed in a Windows XP PC host, and the driver program software for that NIC is installed automatically. NICs are automatically configured by Windows to work with the wire connected to the NIC.

The middle layer of the Windows networking model is the protocol. We focus on the Internet protocol (TCP/IP) because it is fast becoming the only protocol used in networks. Network Basic Input/output System Extended User Interface (NETBEUI) is another popular protocol for simple Windows Networking.

The upper or top-most layers are the services and client software. Services would be file and printer sharing. Client software would be client software for different servers like the Windows Server, Novell NetWare Server, or various UNIX servers.

Networking Hardware

SOHO LAN hardware is more than just a NIC. Other behind-the-scenes SOHO LAN components include the following:

1. Hubs
2. Switches
3. Cable/DSL modem routers
4. Servers
5. RAID servers

Each LAN component performs a different function or role in building a SOHO LAN. Small LANs need fewer components, while bigger LANs have more hardware components to perform a greater variety of services and functions.

Another LAN component is Network Attached Storage (NAS). NAS is a disk server attached directly to the network. NAS devices are not explored here because those devices seem to have either limited capacity or they are very expensive. This is typically beyond the budget for a home office and even a small office user. A more cost-effective approach is to use a cheap server. NAS devices fit a niche market.

Network Interface Cards

All NICs are at the bottom layer of the Windows networking model. Windows supports multiple network adapters. Newer Windows versions have a larger selection of supported NICs than earlier Windows versions. When Windows is installed and the PC hardware is set up, the NIC is chosen. Windows XP uses its plug-and-play capability to install all NICs. NICs are installed when driver programs interface them to the other networking software in Windows. The linkages between networking software are called bindings.

In other Windows versions additional adapters can be added through the Network item in the Control Panel. See Figure 2.4.

Windows NT does not support plug-and-play but Windows 95/98/2000/Me and XP do. This means that installing Windows NT requires knowledge of NIC setup parameters, including the Interrupt Request (IRQ), I/O Port Address, DMA channel, and shared memory addresses. Most NIC problems come from selecting incorrect setup parameters. With Windows XP, incorrect NIC setup is a rare problem because Windows XP's plug-and-play function is very well defined and standardized.

The most popular LAN NICs are Ethernet NICs. Xerox originally designed Ethernet, Intel developed the first Ethernet chip sets, and Digital Equipment Corporation sold the early Ethernet products. Ethernet uses Carrier Sense Multiple Access with Collision Detection (CSMA/CD) protocol. This is not the same as the Windows networking model protocol selection because this protocol is built into the NIC hardware. CSMA/CD is referred to in other networking models as the Media Access Control (MAC) protocol.

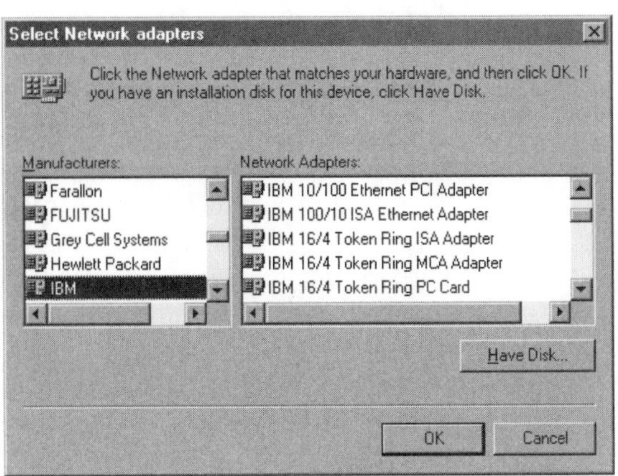

Figure 2.4
Windows 98 IBM NIC selections.

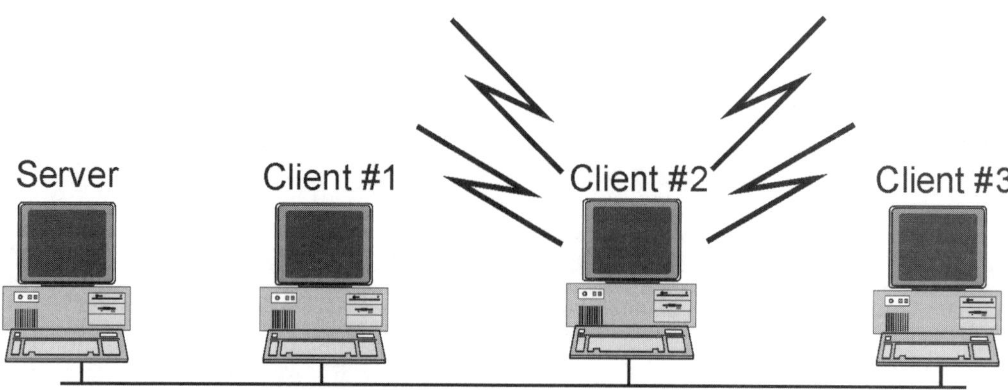

Figure 2.5 Ethernet protocol.

Although CSMA/CD sounds complicated, it is really quite simple to understand because it operates like Citizens Band (CB) radios or like people talking in a room. Considering Figure 2.5 as people talking in a room, each person has a carrier sense capability. What is the carrier they can sense? Sound or voice is correct. All persons have free and equal access (i.e., multiple access) to the communications medium. The communications medium (or Ether) is the air in the room. Any person can speak at any time. When people have something to say, they first listen to hear if the channel is occupied. If they hear nothing, they blast away with their message, "Breaker, breaker one nine, Rubber Ducky are you there?" While they broadcast they listen to the channel. If what they heard was not corrupted, then they assume that their message was transmitted OK.

However, we do not live in a perfect world and sometimes collisions happen. When a collision occurs the transmitting party hears their message garbled. They back off and retry a short time later. To determine how long they wait, they flip a coin. Now both stations having the collision must flip coins to determine how long to wait. One gets heads while the other gets tails. This means the one with heads multiplies the time they wait by one to get one time unit and we (the station with the tails) must multiply our wait time by two to get two time units. So we wait until our time expires and listen again for anyone talking on the channel. We hear the first station blabbing away because its wait time was less than ours. Soon they stop and it looks like we have our chance to transmit. Away we go only to have another collision with a third station. So the third station and we are forced to flip the coins again. This time we get heads and they get tails. Looks good for us, but wait—our time is determined by the "automobile theory of insurance." You know the "automobile insurance theory" don't you? When you have a fender bender, the insurance company ups your rates or yanks your policy so you cannot get out on the road again immediately. In our CSMA/CD case we must multiply our wait time by one and then by three. We end up waiting three time units and the other guy only needs to wait two time units. Is this unfair or what? Doesn't it seem like we could remain the bridesmaid and never become the bride?

CSMA/CD operation may seem backward but it isn't. If every device were, upon detecting a collision, to immediately retry transmitting, the result would be collision after collision and no one would get through. Consider people exiting a room. If they all rushed the door, one or two might get through but the remainder would collide. If those who collided lunged for the door again and again, there would be even more collisions and no one would get out of the room. By forcing those people having one collision to start more or less halfway back across the room and by forcing those people having a second collision to start more or less on the opposite side of the room, all the people would soon exit the room.

The Ethernet collision detection algorithm is technically called a binary exponential back-off algorithm. It makes Ethernet particularly good at handling bursts in network activity but not as good at constant heavy loads. This description of Ethernet's CSMA/CD protocol illustrates one-way-at-one-time or half-duplex operation. Most Ethernet protocol implementations use full-duplex physical channels, so they have basically no collisions.

The key things to understand about Ethernet NICs are the speed at which they operate, whether they support half-duplex or full-duplex data transfers, and the PC bus type the card supports. Basic Ethernet communicates half duplex at 10 Mbps. Fast Ethernet, the most popular SOHO networking NIC, communicates full duplex (or half duplex) at 100 Mbps. Both basic and Fast Ethernet use CAT-5 unshielded twisted pair (UTP) wire.

Most Ethernet NICs are Peripheral Component Interconnect (PCI) bus cards. These cards are plug-and-play cards that can share IRQs with other PCI bus cards. An Industry Standard Architecture (ISA) bus Ethernet card and a PCI bus Ethernet Card are shown in Figure 2.6. The ISA bus Ethernet NIC supports only 10 Mbps half-duplex data transfer operations over UTP wiring. This would not be the best Ethernet NIC for new multimedia LAN applications.

A PCI bus Fast Ethernet NIC works with UTP wiring and is capable of 10 or 100 Mbps transmission with full-duplex data transfer capabilities. Ethernet cards are labeled 10 base T for 10 Mbps half-duplex operation and 100 base TX for 100 Mbps full-duplex operation. Figure 2.7 illustrates 100 Base TX operation. This PCI bus NIC is capable of supporting new telecommunications applications over the Ethernet LAN depending upon the LAN configuration.

Figure 2.6 Ethernet Industry Standard Architecture (ISA) Bus (right) and Peripheral Component Interconnect (PCI) Bus (left) NICs.

Figure 2.7
PCI Ethernet NIC RJ-45 or Mod-8 connector and light-emitting diode 100 Mbps and FDX indicators.

Wireless LAN NICs use protocols that are somewhat similar to CSMA/CD but more specifically tailored to wireless communications. Most wireless LAN NICs use the PC card bus. Card bus NICs work with Windows plug-and-play software. Wireless NICs used the card bus interface because they were originally targeted at laptop and other mobile PCs. Wireless NICs require a special bus adapter to connect them into the PCI bus of a desktop PC host. Wireless NICs are discussed in more detail in Chapter 4.

Brain Teaser: LAN Boards

What type of LAN board connections does your PC have? Check the rear of the PC. Can you find a RJ-45 connector with wire connected to it? Refer to Figure 2.7. This is likely an Ethernet connection. Does your PC have any USB ports? Is anything attached to them?

Hubs

The lowest-layer LAN network component is a hub. Hubs are the central connecting points for all SOHO LAN wiring. Most all hubs are active hubs. See Figure 2.8. Active hubs perform a repeater or signal regenerator function.

Hubs work at the Windows networking model NIC or hardware layer. They work electronically with specific NICs. Some hubs work only with basic Ethernet, such as the hub in Figure 2.8, while other hubs work with Fast Ethernet.

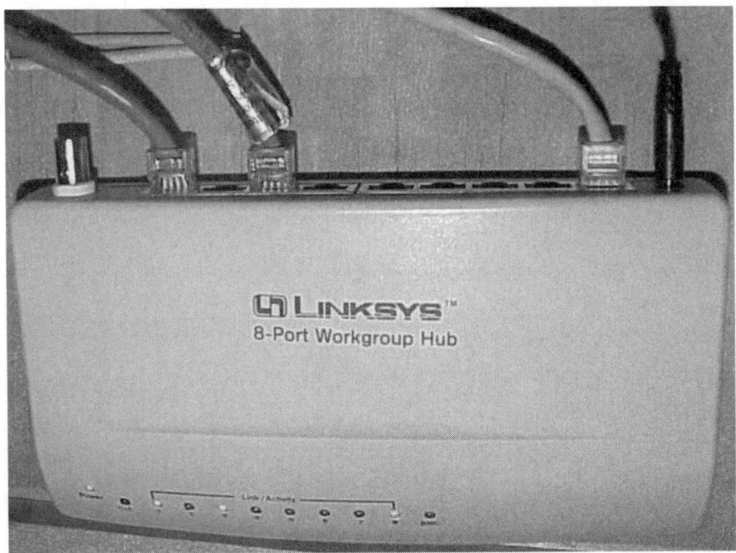

Figure 2.8 Ethernet active 10-Mbps UTP hub with coax connection.

The Repeater Function

To understand the repeater function and SOHO LAN wiring rules, we must understand digital transmission. Refer to Figure 2.9.

Digital transmission can be simply conceived as square waves or pulses. These digital signals are either present or absent, "0" or "1." Digital square waves are soaked up (attenuated) by wire. When they are soaked up they may not exceed the minimum height or voltage level needed for the receiving device to detect them. In this case they must be sent through a digital repeater or signal regenerator that samples the old signal's midpoint and then creates an exact duplicate of the original digital pulse and passes it on to the receiver. Well, this is *almost* an exact duplicate. It is identical in every respect to the original signal except that it is delayed one-half pulse width. While this half pulse width delay does not seem like much, it can cause problems when a SOHO LAN is improperly wired.

To understand how electrical signals work in a SOHO LAN, we need to go way back to when we were children. Think of the summertime when life was simple. No school, hot sunny day, nothing to do, and you had a rope in your hand! So you whip it up then down and see a pulse (digital transmission) travel down the rope. Cool! Now you try a different rope to see that the pulse doesn't travel as far. Then you try several other ropes to see that some are really good while others are not so good at having the pulse travel down them. Next you try whipping a rope really hard. The way up and way down hard whip makes the pulse travel farther down the rope as compared with the distance produced by a wimpy wrist flick. Next you go for high-speed transmission by rapidly whipping the rope up and down. This shortens the distances

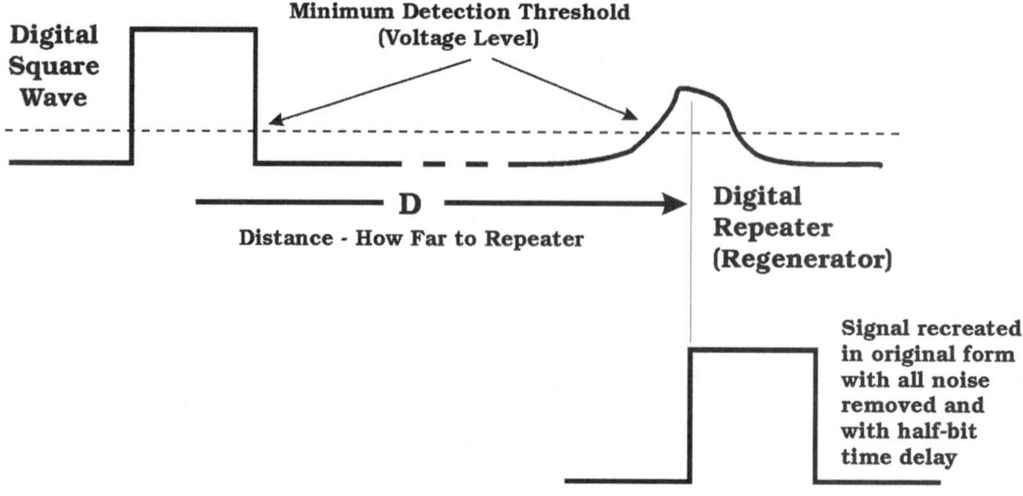

Figure 2.9 Digital transmission.

pulses can travel. Didn't you do this as a child? I sure did. It must have been early training for my present job.

Our simple rope analogy tells us all we need to know about digital transmission across wires. Some wire is better than other wire in carrying digital signals. Category-5 (or CAT-5) wire is better than Category-3 (or CAT-3) wire. We discuss CAT-5 and CAT-3 wires later in this chapter. The stronger the electrical signal, the farther the pulse travels. Different NICs have different electrical properties and hence transmit digital pulses longer or shorter distances. And finally, the higher the transmission speed, the shorter the distance the signal travels. High-speed digital transmission can run over any wire for a short distance before the receiving device has difficulty detecting it.

Digital transmission can be summarized by the following characteristics:

1. Digital transmission occurs in discrete pulses.
2. Digital repeaters or signal regenerators remove transmission noise and retransmit pulses at their original strength.

Hubs perform the digital signal regeneration function. As a result, hubs extend the physical distance a LAN covers and electrically isolate parts of the LAN, thus increasing overall network reliability. Some hubs are more intelligent than others, so that they can support simultaneously a mix of 10-Mbps and 100-Mbps half- and full-duplex Ethernet connections. So the auto-sensing speed translation hubs buffer Ethernet CSMA/CD packets to match speeds among different parts of the network.

Hubs only care about the Windows networking model hardware layer. They work electronically with specific NICs. There are very specific wiring rules for NICs and hubs that depend upon the NIC and hub electronics.

Hubs do not care about what Windows protocol software is used. The protocol software could be TCP/IP or NETBEUI.

Passive, Active, and Managed Hubs

The types of wiring hubs are as follows:

1. Passive hubs—Passive hubs just connect wires. They contain no active electronics and perform no signal regeneration. These are the oldest type of hubs. Passive hubs provide a shared bus to all individual connections.
2. Active hubs—Active hubs perform signal regeneration functions. Similar to passive hubs, active hubs provide a shared bus to all individual connections. However, active hubs isolate individual device connections electrically from one another. Active hubs also perform traffic monitoring, media diagnosis, and transmission speed translation. They translate between 10 Mbps and 100 Mbps half- and full-duplex transmission.

3. Managed hubs—These are intelligent hubs that participate in a centralized network management system. They use the Simple Network Management Protocol (SNMP) to report operating and load status back to a central network management system. See Figure 2.10. Managed hubs monitor themselves and their functioning in the network. Standards-based, open systems are very flexible since they can often control devices based on the same standards. SNMP has been a primary focus in the rise of standards-based management systems. Integrated management systems help users manage networks by establishing a single location to control network operations, regardless of the type and source of devices on the network. Managed LAN hubs have an SNMP agent that monitors network activity and alerts a central management system to cable outages. The central system and the hub exchange messages using TCP/IP and SNMP. Hubs that are more sophisticated permit active testing of the cabling and disabling of cable segments from the central management system. Such hubs are used in larger small-office LANs.

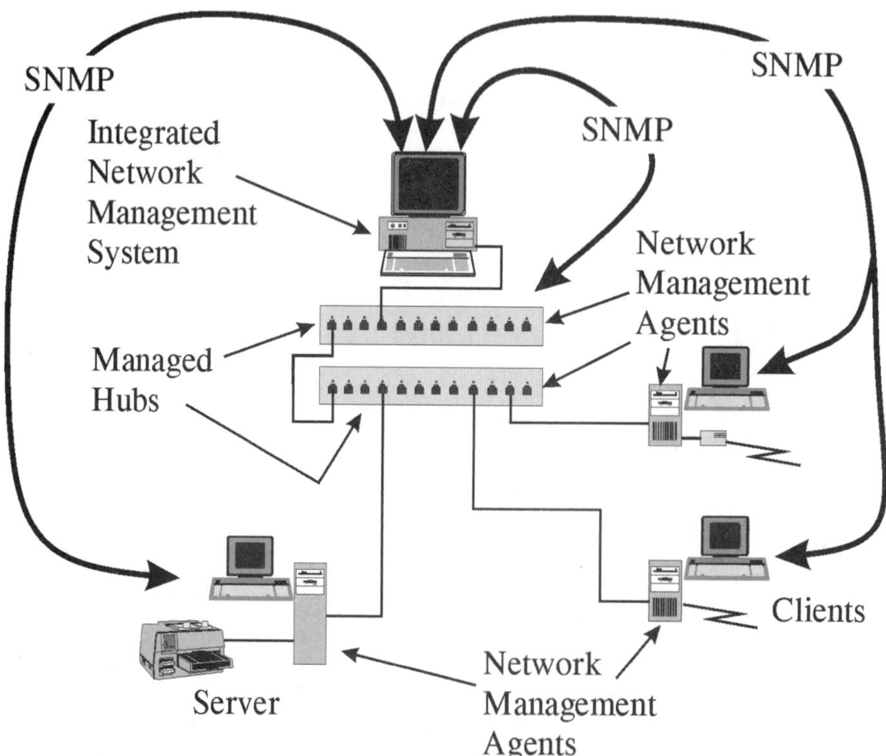

Figure 2.10 LAN management with SNMP.

Wiring Rules Explained

Every LAN technology has specific wiring rules. These rules are based upon signal attenuation in the wire and the signal propagation delays in the network. Digital signal attenuation or soak up was discussed above. Propagation delays have a different impact on wiring rules. Let me illustrate with a simple example.

In half-duplex Ethernet the sending device detects collisions only while it is actually sending data. Once it stops transmitting, it stops detecting collisions as well. In a bus-style, half-duplex Ethernet it would take some time as determined by the signal propagation delay for a station's signal to reach the most remote end of the network. If a station at the remote end transmitted—causing a collision without the original station knowing it—then the Ethernet would not function properly.

Think of it this way: you and I are at opposite ends of a 1,000-foot long room. We use sound as our carrier to send data amongst the stations in the room. When I am speaking, I am also looking to make sure there are no collisions. If I began transmitting a message, how long would I need to transmit to ensure that I never missed a collision? Since sound travels at 1,090 (one thousand feet is close enough for government work) feet per second, it would take one second for my signal to propagate across the room to you. However, if I stopped transmitting at one second, I could miss detecting a collision. Because you might start transmitting a message just an instant before my signal propagated to you, a collision would occur. However, it would take a second for that collision to propagate across the room for me to detect it. Consequently I must transmit two full seconds or enough time for the signal to reach you at the most distant end of the network and return to me so I can detect the collision. The problem would be impacted if my signal had to run through a repeater because each repeater adds a half-bit time of propagation delay to the transmission.

Early half-duplex Ethernets used a "5-4-3" rule to account for repeaters and used propagation delays to ensure all collisions were detected. The "5-4-3" rule worked something like this:

1. An Ethernet could have five segments.
2. The segments could be connected using four repeaters.
3. Three segments could be active (have attached PCs or servers) and two segments would only be segments that extended the physical distance that the LAN covered.
4. A client was separated from its server by no more than two repeaters.

See Figure 2.11.

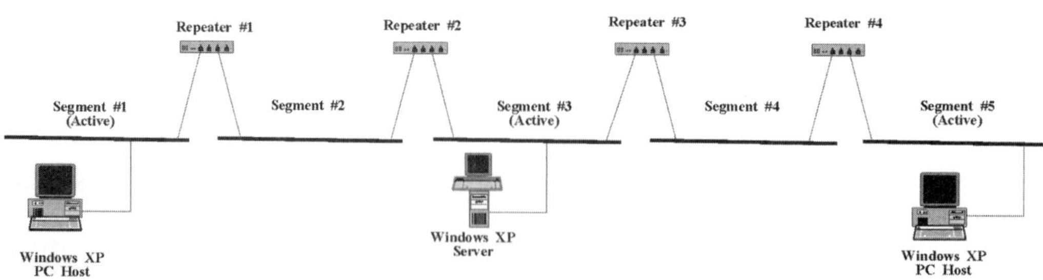

Figure 2.11 5-4-3 repeater rule.

This is changed now with Ethernet switching. However, there is now new wiring that must be followed with switches based upon signal propagation delays and signal attenuation.

In small home-office LANs wiring rules are rarely violated. When they are, the home-office LAN fails to work, and wire is shortened, rectifying the problem. When a LAN behaves erratically, the source of the problem is most likely poor wiring. Hubs have lights that help troubleshoot such problems.

Small-office LANs can have much more extensive wiring; it is important to follow the wiring rules of the LAN component manufacturer to the letter to avoid problems. When the wiring rules are not followed precisely, bad things happen. Such problems caused by poor wiring are very difficult to pinpoint. They can have you, as Jenna, my granddaughter, said, want to kick the living "bad word" out of your LAN.

Switches

Switches are the high-performance LAN components. Many small-office LANs use switches in place of hubs to provide improved network performance because there is only a small difference in the cost of a hub versus the cost of a switch. Switches operate in the Windows networking model NIC layer. Switches provide the intelligence of managed hubs and more. Each RJ-45 (MOD-8) port has its own individual path for data. Any port can be connected to any other port at full transmission speed. To the PC hosts this looks like they have a direct, unshared connection to one another. They appear to be on their own isolated point-to-point LAN. Ports can operate at 10 Mbps or 100 Mbps in half-duplex mode or full-duplex mode. See Figure 2.12.

Switches performing Ethernet switching functions make several separate Ethernet segments look like a single 10 Mbps or 100 Mbps LAN. Switches connect clients on several separate Ethernet segments to servers on several other separate segments. When a client talks with a specific server, the switch

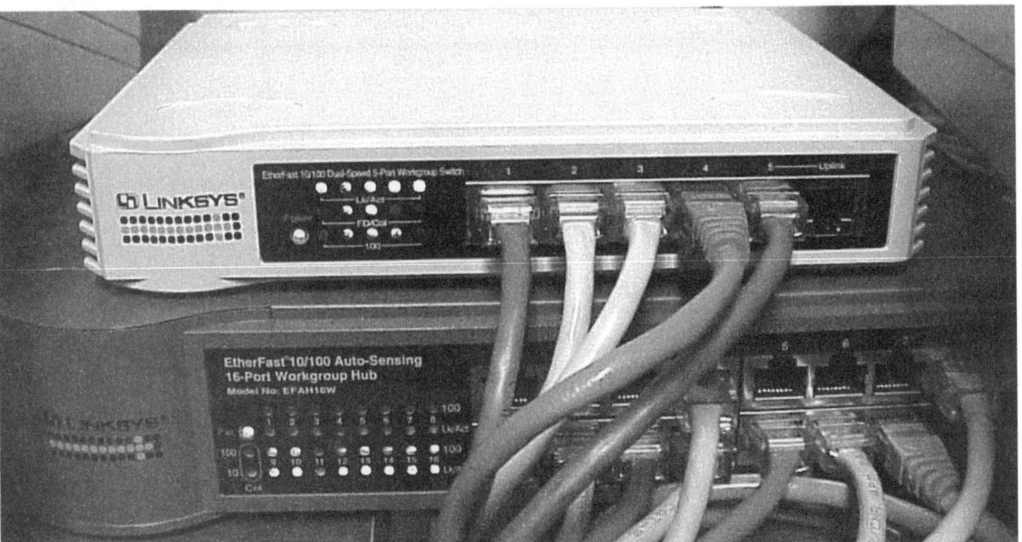

Figure 2.12 Ethernet five-port 10/100 Mbps switch and auto-sensing sixteen-port 10/100 active hub.

connects the client and the server segments together. For that brief instant there is a single 10 Mbps or 100 Mbps connection between that client and that server. Switching significantly improves Ethernet performance.

Switches speed-buffer, that is, translate from one speed to another. They must receive an entire packet at one speed before it can be transmitted out at the other speed. This store and forward switch operation is more commonly used in networks today. This is especially true when migrating from a slower 10 Mbps LAN to a faster 100 Mbps or 1 Gbps LAN.

Switches isolate LAN traffic and implement full-duplex data transmission between LAN servers and clients that have NICs providing full-duplex transmission capabilities. This greatly increases Ethernet performance, virtually eliminating the performance load saturation of the half-duplex CSMA/CD MAC protocol. See Figure 2.13.

Switches change LAN wiring rules because their operation is different from the operation of hubs. The ideal LAN configuration using switching would be to have a single large switch. All clients and servers would be connected to the large switch. This is great in theory, but only practical for small LANs. Larger small-office LANs split between floors requiring wiring runs of hundreds of feet make subdividing the network among several switches more practical. Building a high-performance combined voice and data small-office network can require thoughtful configuration of network switches to isolate the voice traffic and data traffic.

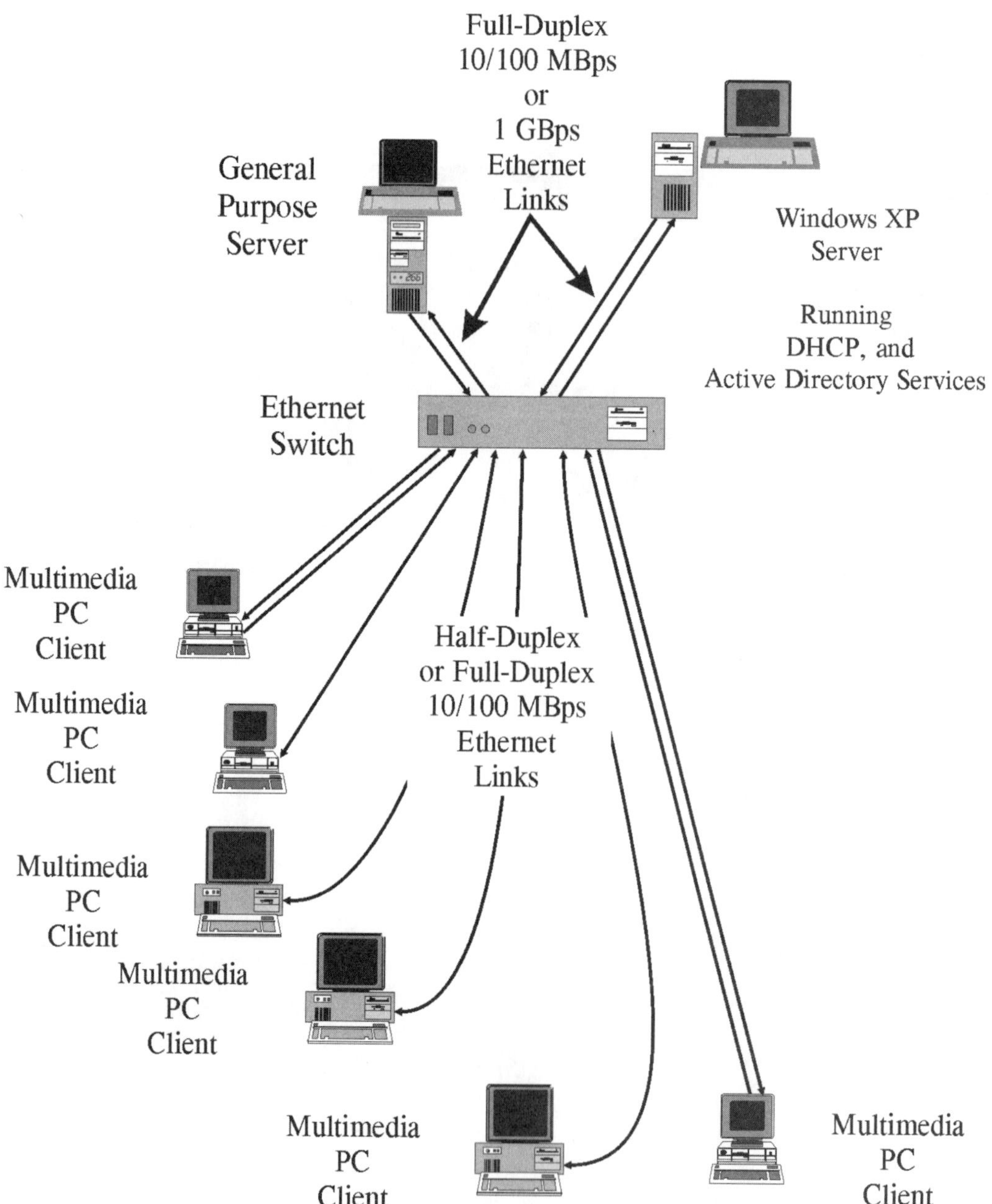

Figure 2.13 Switch operation.

Cable/DSL Modem Routers

Routers work in the protocol and hardware layers of the Windows networking model. Routers connect two or more networks. A router would link a LAN to the Internet in a home-office LAN or to other LANs in a small office LAN. Routers decide which way to send packets based on the routers' current knowledge of the status of the LANs or networks to which they connect. In connecting LANs to the Internet a router is a network component or software in a PC that determines the next network point to which a packet (TCP/IP packet) is forwarded so that the packet can reach its final destination.

Routers create or copy a table of available routes through a network and maintain data on their status. Some routers use this information—combined according to routing algorithms with distance and cost data—to calculate the best route for a packet to follow to reach its final destination. Other routers use simpler hop counts to determine routes. Cable modem and DSL routers use simple routing algorithms to perform routing between a SOHO LAN and the Internet. Typically, packets travel through several routers to reach their final destination on the Internet.

Routers must know something about TCP/IP to work properly. An Internet gateway is a router. Some new routers are a combination of switch and router, as illustrated by the LinkSys cable modem/DSL four-port switch router in Figure 2.14.

Figure 2.14
DSL/cable modem router and four-port ethernet switch.

Routers provide increased network capacity by reducing excess network traffic. They send data from source to destination based upon network routing information contained in the packets. DSL and cable modem routers route only packets that are targeted to Internet sites (PC hosts) out over the DSL and cable modem link to the Internet. Newer DSL and cable modem routers perform some limited firewall functions.

DSL and cable modem router firewalls route and filter packets. The DSL and cable modem firewalls protect a SOHO LAN from unauthorized access and sometimes limit network users in how they can access the Internet. A SOHO LAN with PC hosts accessing the Internet installs a DSL and cable modem router with firewall functions to prevent unauthorized outsiders from accessing private data on the SOHO LAN and for controlling the specific Internet resources (e.g., no Playboy or sex sites permitted) its PC hosts can access.

DSL and cable modem router firewalls examine each packet and its routing information to route data and to filter all network packets. The filtering function determines whether to forward them to their desired destination. DSL and cable modem routers with firewall functions represent a network as a single IP address to the Internet. Packet filtering includes screening packets to ensure they come from previously identified domain names and IP addresses. Packet headers and contents can also be scanned for key words and phrases. These can be used to discard unauthorized packets. DSL and cable modem router firewalls allow laptop users to access a LAN through secure logon procedures and authentication certificates.

DSL and cable modem router firewall features include logging and reporting, automatic alarms at given thresholds of attack, and a Web browser user interface for managing and configuring the firewall.

Because Internet traffic and attacks change so often, it is hard to make DSL and cable modem router firewalls totally impervious to external attacks. Firewall functions require constant maintenance to keep filtering effective. Sometimes firewalls filter too well and block LAN access from sites that are authorized to connect to a LAN.

While firewall functions can prevent unauthorized LAN access from the Internet, they typically cannot effectively filter viruses from packets passing through the firewall. LAN users must use virus scanning programs, must not blindly open files with Visual Basic Script (VBS) macros, and must delete mail from unknown users to keep their chance of getting a virus infection low.

Further, DSL and cable modem router firewalls do not effectively protect against Trojan horse software that gathers passwords and user account information. HAPPY99 was one such program that captured password information and sent them to an Internet account in China. At one time, Microsoft in its update and registration process was capturing Ethernet NIC MAC addresses and storing them.

When surfing authorized Web sites, cookies are exchanged between the surfing PC and the Web site. These cookies and other information are used to track Internet usage. DSL and cable modem router firewalls do not effectively protect against this information-gathering activity on the Internet.

Servers

Servers are the central small-office LAN component. Without them resource sharing and more importantly small office LAN-centric applications could not be implemented. Once users begin to rely on a small-office LAN and its servers to perform their daily work functions, the network and the servers must be highly reliable. If the network or a server is unavailable, then users at PC client hosts cannot work. If a server loses a user's data, months of effort can be lost and may have to be recreated by the irate user. Since most users rely on the LAN and prayer-based backup (what we label PBB) to preserve their critical work, implementing reliable and robust servers is not a luxury, it is a necessity for most small-office LANs. Servers must be extremely reliable and robust to implement VoIP and other specialized telecommunications applications. Understanding what makes a reliable and powerful LAN server is important.

Reliable servers require several key features and technologies, including:

1. Redundant CPUs
2. Error detecting and correcting memory
3. Hot-swappable components
4. Redundant array of independent disks (RAID) data storage

This section examines these special server features.

Redundant CPUs

High-end servers can use as many as eight CPUs. Small-office servers might have two CPUs. Multiple CPUs permit Windows or UNIX software to spread the processing load evenly across all CPUs. In Windows this is called symmetric multiprocessing (SMP). When one CPU fails, the server slows but keeps on running. Multiple CPUs must be matched with each other for the software to run properly. This is described as matching the stepping level of the Intel CPU chip. See Figure 2.15. Multiple CPU configurations improve performance and reliability with Windows XP, Windows 2000, Windows NT, and UNIX servers.

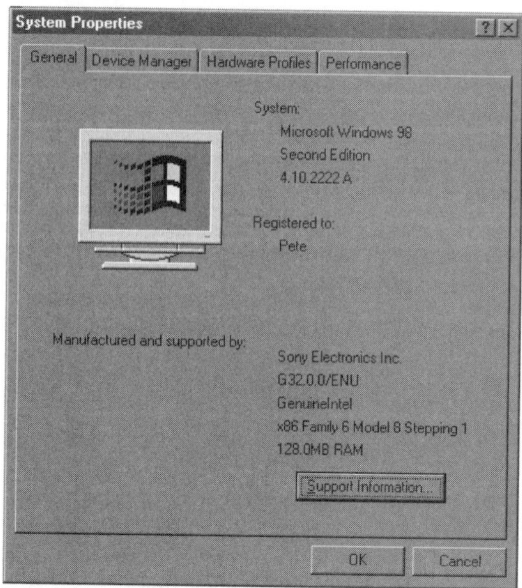

Figure 2.15
Intel CPU stepping.

Some Intel CPUs are designed specifically for servers. However, other Intel Pentium and Celeron chips are used as server CPUs. My servers run with 1.2 GHz Celeron CPU chips. Pentium III and Celeron chips are aimed at the largest PC market, consumer PCs, and consequently they are the cheapest CPU chips. The Celeron chip is equivalent to the Pentium II chip with MultiMedia eXtension (MMX) technology. Single instruction, multiple data (SIMD) technology is in the Pentium III chips. MMX technology enhances multimedia performance and SIMD technology enhances Internet performance for sites that take advantage of it. These technologies are more aimed at PC hosts browsing the Web with a Web browser and are much less important for a server that performs mostly input/output operations.

Factors to consider in selecting a server CPU chip include:

1. Price—Small LAN needs a cheap CPU
2. Clock speed—The higher the better
3. RAM speed—Double Data Rate (DDR) is better than synchronous dynamic random access memory (SDRAM, see below)
4. Chip architecture—Itanium is better than Pentium III Xeon, and Pentium III Xeon is better than Celeron
5. Multiprocessor configuration support

CPU chips differ in their structure and capabilities, making it impossible to predict just on specifications alone the performance of any LAN server using those chips. Only when tests are performed with each chip side by side with precisely the same hardware and LAN software can their performance be compared. A 20 percent or lower increase in performance is not noticeable to human beings. However, this can be significant for LAN servers.

The server design, the CPU chip used, and the LAN software running on the server determine whether multiple CPUs can be used in a server. Windows 2000 Server and Windows NT Server software can run on up to four CPUs out of the box. Special configurations permit Windows to work with up to eight CPUs. Pentium III, Celeron, and Xeon CPUs can be installed in multiple-CPU systems. Some AMD chips should work in multiple-CPU configurations.

RAM and Error Correcting Circuitry (ECC) RAM

Dynamic RAM has been used for PC main memory for years. All memory is some form of dynamic RAM, requiring dynamic or constant refreshing to maintain its contents. When power is lost, the contents of RAM are also lost.

The RAM types used in servers may be:

1. Fast page mode (FPM)—obsolete
2. Extended data out (EDO)—obsolete
3. Burst extended data out (BEDO)—obsolete
4. Synchronous DRAM (SDRAM)
5. Double data rate (DDR) DRAM
6. Rambus DRAM (RDRAM)

Rambus memory, or RDRAM, operates differently from all previous versions of RAM. RDRAM is a general-purpose, high-performance, packet-oriented, dynamic random-access memory. The memory modules use Rambus Signaling Level (RSL) technology to achieve 356 MHz or 400 MHz clock speeds using differential clocks. This type of memory is good for LAN servers.

Double data rate RAM, or DDR RAM, was first used on high-performance video cards. It is more common today in PC systems and provides similar but not equivalent performance to RDRAM at lower cost.

Error correcting codes are used to correct single- and multiple-bit errors in server disk and memory operations. Error correcting codes use multiple bits to detect and correct errors. For server RAM to use error correction circuitry (ECC), each byte of data must be stored in RAM with nine bits. This is specified by RAM dual inline memory modules (DIMMs) being nine by 36 bits or

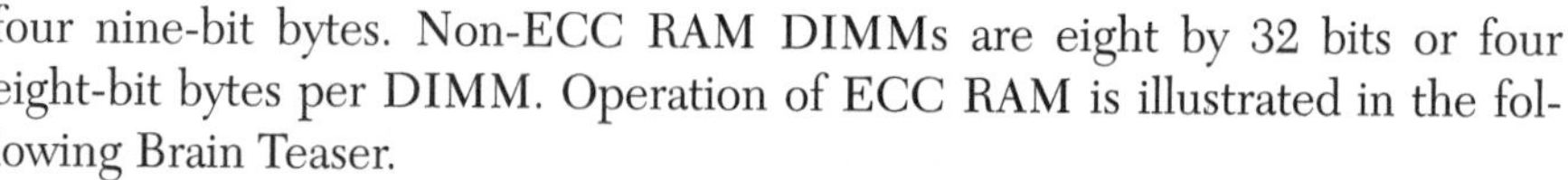

four nine-bit bytes. Non-ECC RAM DIMMs are eight by 32 bits or four eight-bit bytes per DIMM. Operation of ECC RAM is illustrated in the following Brain Teaser.

Brain Teaser: ECC RAM Concepts

To illustrate the operation of error correcting codes we use a simple example. Using three extra bits we can detect and correct single-bit errors in four bits. Use Figure 2.16 to write down any four bits in positions one through four. Next, write these bits down in the circle areas numbered one through four. Then, using even parity ensures an even number of bits are encompassed by circle 5, circle 6, and circle 7. Write these bit values in positions 5, 6, and 7. Now alter a bit position. Any bit position works fine. Using the altered bit value, recalculate bits 5, 6, and 7.

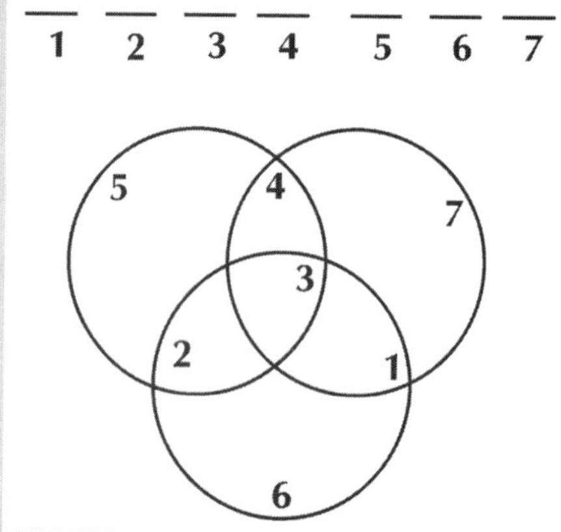

Figure 2.16 ECC exercise.

1. Which bits do not match the originally created bits? The circle area unique to only those mismatched bits is the bit that is in error.
2. Which bits do not match when the center bit is changed? This should be *all* bits; 5, 6, and 7.
3. Which bits do not match when a parity bit 5, 6, or 7 is changed? This should be only the changed parity bit.

This is the simplest illustration of the operation of error correcting codes. Real ECC operation uses three bits to detect and correct single-bit errors in 16 bits or four bits to detect and correct single-bit errors in 32 bits. The goal here is to understand the basics of how bit error detection and correction work.

Hot-Swappable Components

Some small-office LAN servers use hot-swappable components. Redundant hot-swappable power supplies to ensure reliability in the event one fails were the first hot-swappable server component. This has been expanded to include other server components that may fail, such as cooling fans, fixed disk drives (the RAID drives), and PCI bus cards. See Figure 2.17.

Some small-office LAN servers have active monitoring capabilities built into hardware and software. Servers constantly monitor heat and fan operation to help prevent internal component failures. When a failure is detected, it is displayed on the server's control panel. Software may send error notification to a central management system as well.

When the failed component is a power supply or fan, a service person just pops out the old dead unit and replaces it with a new or refurbished unit. During this process the server continues to operate normally. Disk drives and some PCI bus components can be hot swapped in a similar fashion.

Smaller LANs use servers with few if any hot-swappable components. Such smaller LANs can tolerate a server outage for several hours or a day, while larger LANs cannot.

PC hardware today rarely fails. The only hardware failures in my 20 or so PC hosts in the last year have been a main logic board and a power supply. Both were repairable within a day. My servers and many PC hosts run 24 hours a day, 7 days a week.

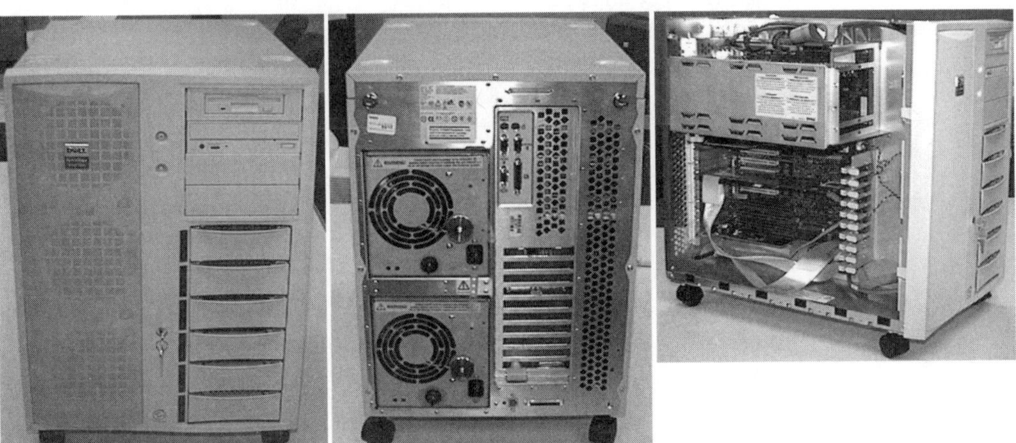

Figure 2.17 Server with hot-swappable, redundant power supplies.

Application Servers

Small-office LAN servers are so inexpensive and reliable that they can be dedicated to a single application on a small LAN. Specialized servers are fax servers that act as a facsimile transmission and storage point, e-mail post office servers, Web servers, remote access servers, proxy servers, VoIP servers, and more.

1. Fax servers support PCs sending faxes. Any PC sending a fax would pass that fax to a facsimile server. The server would transmit the fax to its destination at a time that would save the most money. Incoming faxes would be stored there until retrieved by the client PCs. When a fax is received, the facsimile server may send an e-mail message to the fax recipient to notify him or her that a fax is waiting. Alternatively, network users could check their fax mailboxes periodically for fax messages received for them.
2. Remote Access Server (RAS) permits PCs with Wide Area Network (WAN) access at remote locations to connect to the enterprise LAN and work using it as though they were directly attached to the LAN. The remote PC hosts dialin to the RAS server to connect with the LAN. A VPN server would support private connections from across high-speed links to the Internet. The VPN server permits remote PC hosts to connect to the LAN across DSL or cable modem communication links.
3. A Web server like Windows Internet Information Server (IIS) sets up an intranet for publishing internal information in an electronic browseable HTML format. It establishes a Web site accessible to all PC hosts on the LAN.
4. A database server like a Structured Query Language (SQL) server would implement key enterprise applications such as order entry, inventory management, billing, and other centralized financial functions. SQL servers provide data storage and manipulation functions.
5. The Windows Active Directory server or Primary Domain Controller is the security manager for the LAN. It manages user accounts and provides authorizations for each user to access specific network resources. Generally, resources are managed using group designations; for example, accounting, marketing, and engineering groups have access to different resources.
6. MS Exchange Server is used to implement Microsoft e-mail. Microsoft e-mail is best known for passing those nasty VBS e-mail worm programs that proclaim to love you to hapless Outlook (A.K.A. Lookout) users on the network.
7. An Internet router (proxy server or firewall) provides high-speed access to the Internet for all LAN-attached PCs. This is critical for e-commerce,

business research, communications with customers, downloading audio (like MP3) and video (like DIVX and MOV) files, and other business and non-business activities.

8. A Voice over IP gateway server would interface the internal VoIP network to the public switched telephone network. It must convert digital packetized voice calls into analog connections or 64-Kbps digital streams with associated signaling that can be processed and transmitted through the Public Switched Telephone Network.

This is a brief list of some specialized function servers that can be found on a small-office LAN.

Redundant Array of Independent Disks (RAID) Servers

Small-office LANs may use Redundant Array of Independent (or Inexpensive) Disks (RAID) servers because RAID technology increases storage capacity and makes storage more reliable. IDE disk drives provide a maximum of around 160 GB storage capacity. To have a disk drive that stores several hundred GB (mine store 400 GB), servers use a RAID array of disks that combines the capacity of multiple disks into a single large capacity logical disk drive. Since multiple drives are used, RAID error detecting and correcting technology can prevent data loss when one disk in a RAID array fails.

RAID is implemented in more expensive servers using SCSI bus-attached disk drives or storage arrays. The Small Computer System Interface (SCSI) is an industry standard interface allowing servers to communicate with peripheral hardware. Thirty disk drives may be connected to a dual-port SCSI controller. SCSI is also used to connect to tape drives, CD-ROM drives, printers, and scanners. SCSI is more flexible than earlier parallel data transfer interfaces and operates at higher data rates. The Ultra-2 SCSI for a 16-bit bus can transfer data at up to 80 megabytes per second (Mbps). SCSI allows either 7 or 15 devices to connect to a single SCSI port in daisy-chain fashion. RAID drives are implemented using SCSI interfaces to connect multiple drives to a single server.

In less expensive SOHO LAN servers RAID may also be implemented using IDE drives. A PC host can support two IDE controllers besides the IDE controller built into the main logic board. These controllers can connect up to four IDE disk drives for a total of eight drives plus the four drives that connect to the main logic board IDE controllers. This is more disk drives than can be mounted in a PC. With two extra IDE controllers, I have mounted six 80-GB IDE drives in a PC server to provide about 400 GB of usable RAID storage. RAID was implemented with Windows 2000/NT software. This was not very fast RAID but it was cheap. The upgrade to this configuration can use a hardware RAID ATA controller that supports up to six disk drives. With six ATA 160-GB drives and this controller, a server could have 800 MB of usable RAID storage.

The original RAID configuration required in my server used four-GB SCSI drives and cost about $7,500 per PC server. The IDE RAID cost $2,000 per server and provided 20 times the storage capacity of the SCSI RAID configuration. The new ATA hardware RAID configuration can cost about $1,350 for double the current server's storage capacity.

Numbers identify RAID configurations. The two most common RAID configurations providing data redundancy are RAID 1 and RAID 5. Regardless of how hardware RAID drives are configured, they appear to be a single fixed disk to the software. The different RAID configurations are described below. Refer to Figure 2.18 when reading the RAID descriptions.

RAID-0

RAID-0 stripes data across multiple disk drives. This makes all disks appear to the server as one large disk. RAID-0 can improve performance. RAID-0 commonly uses from two to eight SCSI bus-attached drives. RAID level 0 provides **NO** protection against disk failure. Sometimes RAID-0 is called JBOD (just a bunch of drives or disks). JBOD means lots of drives look like a single disk drive. In Figure 2.18 you see data "d a t a g o e s h e r e" spread across all drives in the RAID array.

RAID-1

RAID-1 is mirroring data by two disk drives. The data on one drive is duplicated on the other drive. Mirroring requires minimally two drives. Data is protected in the event that one drive fails. RAID-1 is quite expensive because each drive storing data needs a twin to store the backup data. Write performance is slower than with RAID-0 because data must be written to both drives before writing is complete. Read performance can be good because data can be read from either drive by using multiple controllers (sometimes called duplexing) and different SCSI buses. In Figure 2.18 you see data "d a t a g o e s h e r e" mirrored on each mirrored set of eight drives in the RAID array.

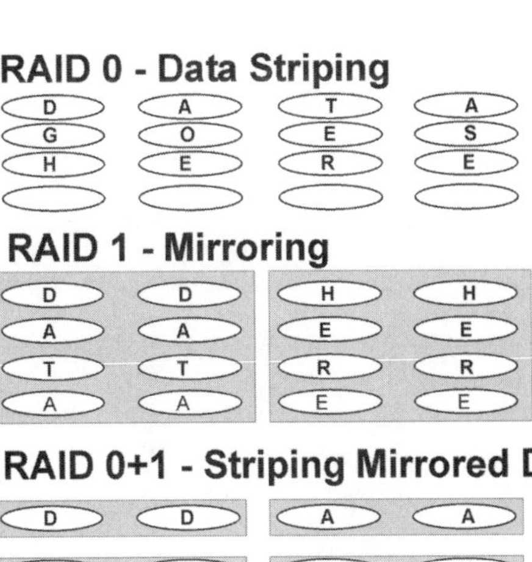

Figure 2.18 RAID types.

RAID-0+1

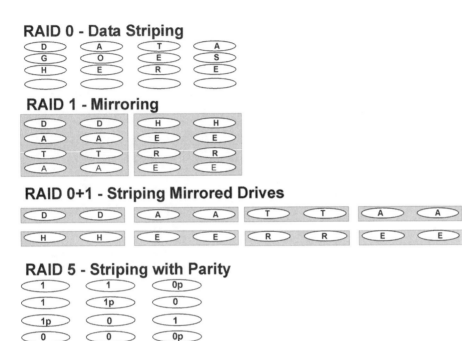

RAID-0+1 is striping mirrored drives. Drives are mirrored on pairs of drives. The mirrored pairs are then added to a RAID-0 stripe set. From four to eight drives can be used. This is striping mirror sets because you mirror first then stripe. It provides excellent reliability but at a high cost. Since twin drives are required for each mirror set, RAID-0+1 is expensive to implement. However, in this configuration multiple drives can fail and your data could be OK. If both drives in a single mirror set fail, then all data is lost. The ultimate in data integrity is mirroring three drives in a mirror set then striping the mirror sets. Now you have one chance in three of losing all three drives and the data in the stripe set. Write performance is not the best, but read performance is excellent. In Figure 2.18 you see data "d a t a g o e s h e r e" mirrored on pairs of drives and then each pair of mirrored drives is striped to store all the data.

RAID-5

RAID-5 is striping both data and parity on multiple disk drives. RAID-5 uses from three to eight SCSI drives. The capacity of one drive is consumed with the parity information. Hence, three four-GB drives in a RAID-5 set yield eight GB of usable data storage. If more than one RAID-5 drive fails at the same time, all data is lost. The position of the drive in the RAID set can be important for some servers. For example, if drive 2 failed and drive 4 was moved into its position, then the RAID recovery could try to rebuild drive 2 using what data it could find on drive 4. This process would destroy any data on drive 2.

Brain Teaser: How RAID-5 Works

Use the RAID-5 illustration to understand how RAID-5 works. RAID-5 is based upon exclusive or (XOR) logic. The truth table for XOR is shown in Figure 2.19.

XOR is the logic used when you are confronted with that age-old dilemma of choosing between two doors, one leading to instant and hellacious death in the volcano and the other to the prince or princess and a kingdom of riches. Two huge guards guard the doors. One guard never lies and the other guard always lies. You get to ask one question of either guard. What is the question? The answer contains a query of whether the guard asked the question is telling a lie and is this correct door to choose?

In the diagram block out any one column of RAID-5 drives and use the bits on the remaining drives and the XOR logic table to create the bits on the missing column of drives.

1. Did the missing data get created correctly?
2. Use a different column. Does the XOR logic recover it as well?

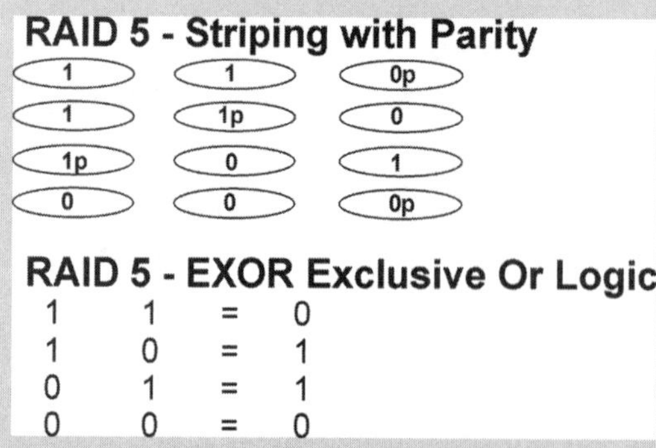

Figure 2.19 RAID-5 striping and exclusive or logic.

This illustrates RAID-5 operation. RAID-5 operation uses from three to eight drives. The goal here is to understand the basics of RAID-5.

Cabling

SOHO LAN clients and servers are wired to hubs or switches using unshielded twisted pair (UTP) wire. In this case, if one cable broke, only that link to the hub or switch is impacted. Demand for higher LAN transmission speeds required reduced signal crosstalk (signal crossover interference from one pair of wires to another, sometimes referred to as near end cross talk—NEXT) within the cable. A cable grading scheme or category level was developed.

SOHO LANs for the large part use CAT-5, CAT-5+, CAT-5e, or CAT-6 unshielded twisted pair wire. This wire is used for telephone wiring as well. These categories of wire support basic 10-Mbps Ethernet and Fast 100-Mbps Ethernet. They are capable of higher speeds for short distances or in special configurations. CAT-5 wire can support 1 Gbps Ethernet by splitting the transmission into four separate 250-Mbps data streams.

General Cabling Schemes

Most home-office LANs use manufactured patch cables connecting to a hub or switch. In that case a wiring scheme is not needed. Consequently, if you are installing a home-office LAN, you can skip this section. Small-office LANs may require significant wiring, necessitating that the wire be installed with an industry standard wiring scheme. This section is more important for small-office LANs that have more than 20 PC hosts.

The Electronic Industries Association/Telecommunications Industry Association (TIA/EIA) has published the TIA/EIA-568 Commercial Building Telecommunications Wiring Standard. This standard specifies minimum requirements for telecommunications wiring within a building. The standard covers cabling systems with a recommended topology and recommended distances, wire, and associated parameters that determine transmission speeds and connectors with pin assignments to ensure devices can be interconnected.

Figure 2.20 illustrates the difference between T-568a and T-568b: Pair 2 and Pair 3 reverse positions. This means that whenever a facility is wired with the T-568a or T-568b wiring specification, additional wiring must follow the original wiring specification or the LAN transmit and receive paths get crossed in the network, causing problems.

Cabling systems include the wire and other components such as punch-down blocks and connectors. The categories are related to the data transmission speeds that the cabling systems can support. The specifications cover

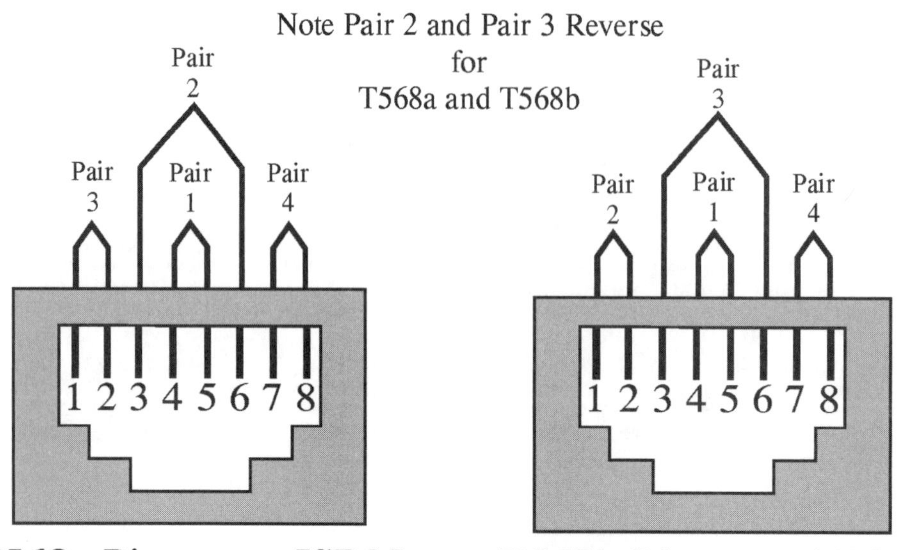

Figure 2.20 T-568a and T-568b Mod 8 connector pair pin assignments.

wire, connectors, and punch-down blocks to be used in order to meet the requirements of a specific category.

Wiring Categories

SOHO LAN wiring is classified according to categories, with the most common being CAT-3, CAT-5, CAT-5+, CAT-5e, and soon CAT-6. Table 2.1 lists different wiring categories and the supported transmission speeds or the common applications of that wiring category.

In addition to wiring categories, SOHO wiring can be plenum or non-plenum wire. Plenum wire has special Teflon exterior insulation to prevent it from easily producing noxious fumes in a fire. Non-plenum wire has only a polyvinyl chloride (PVC) exterior insulation that gives off poisonous fumes during a fire. It must be installed in special wiring trays or metal wiring pipes/ducts to ensure that the PVC fumes do not reach people in the event of a building fire.

Table 2.1 Wiring Categories/Levels vs. Transmission Speed or Application.

Cabling System Classification	Transmission Speed Supported or Common Application
CAT-1	Analog Voice
CAT-2	Digital Voice
CAT-3	16 Mbps
CAT-4	20 Mbps
CAT-5	100 Mbps
CAT-5+ CAT-5e (Data Grade High-End)	155 Mbps
CAT 6	1 Gbps

The most widely used cabling today is UTP CAT-5, with data grade CAT-5 (CAT-5+ or CAT-5e) rated to support transmission at speeds up to about 155 Mbps. This CAT-5 cable is used extensively in both telephony and LAN wiring.

CAT-3 Cabling

Category 3 twisted pair cable was the original telephone-style cable. Category 3 twisted pair cable came with two to four pairs in each cable. It worked for LAN transmission speeds of 10 Mbps. Higher categories have special cable designs that carefully match pairs of wire with more twists in each pair. Figure 2.21 shows CAT-3 UTP three-pair cable used for standard telephones. The

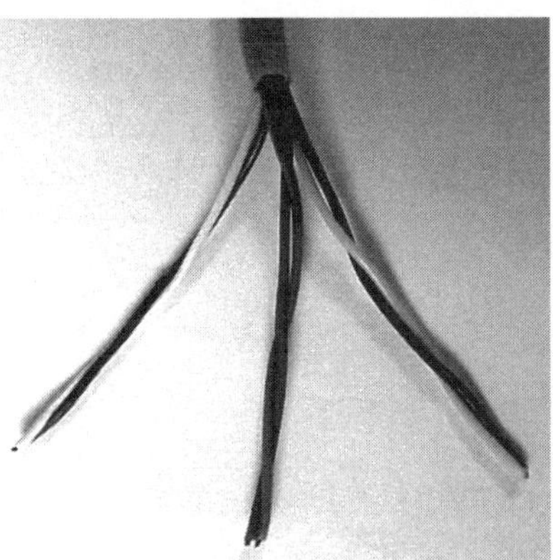

Figure 2.21
CAT-3 telephone wire.

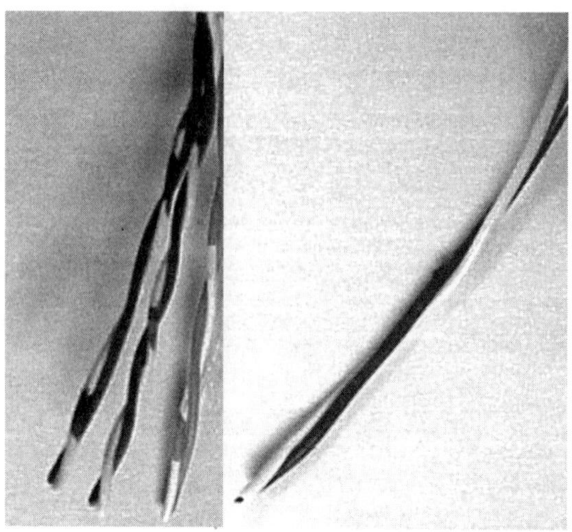

Figure 2.22
CAT-3 vs. CAT-5 pair comparison.

cable has red-green, yellow-black, and blue-white pairs. The red-green pair is for the primary telephone line. The yellow-black pair is for a second telephone line. The blue-white pair on the left in Figure 2.21 carried electrical power for lights on the telephone, like the lighted dial of the Princess phone.

The difference in pair twisting between CAT-3 and CAT-5 UTP wire is illustrated in Figure 2.22.

In Figure 2.22, CAT-5 wire pairs are on the left. Only three of the four pairs are visible. On the right is the CAT-3 UTP wire. The sizes are relatively accurate in the composite photograph, illustrating that CAT-5 is twisted about four times more than CAT-3 wire.

CAT-5 Cabling

While CAT-3 and CAT-5 cables may look identical, CAT-3 is tested at lower transmission speeds. If CAT-3 wire is run at higher speeds, it can cause network transmission errors. CAT-3 cabling is near end cross talk (NEXT) certified for only 16-MHz signals, while CAT-5 cable must pass a 100-MHz signal test, permitting it to carry data at 100 Mbps. Figure 2.23 shows two round CAT-5 cables.

There are more differences between CAT-5 and CAT-3 cable beyond CAT-5 twisted-pair cable having more twists per foot than CAT-3 cable. I cannot quote you chapter and verse on the differences between CAT-3 and CAT-5 cabling, but I can give you an idea of how detailed the differences are between cable types.

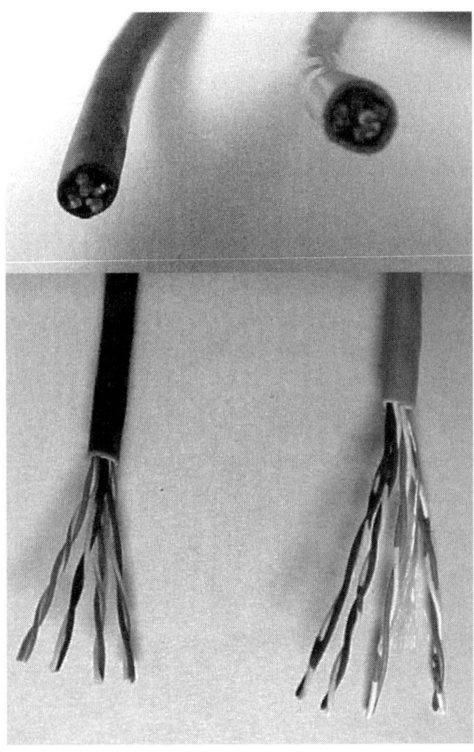

Figure 2.23
CAT-5 round cable.

First, guess how many Eskimo words there are for snow. I do not know the exact number myself but there are a lot of Eskimo words for snow because snow is much more important to Eskimos than it is to us. OK, now how many ways can wiring engineers describe wire? They can describe wire in as many ways as Eskimos can describe snow. There are simple parameters like the gauge (thickness) of the wire, the twists per foot, the copper purity, the capacitance per foot, the resistance per foot, the thickness and type of insulation, the metallic content of the paint coloring the wire pairs, the wire pair coloring—green-green/white, blue-blue/white, orange-orange/white, brown-brown/white, and many more parameters. Now do you have a feeling for the differences between wiring types?

When wiring a LAN or a facility most vendors specify CAT-5 or CAT-5 data grade wiring. They wire according to the TIA/EIA-568a or TIA/EIA-568b wiring scheme. The most likely scheme is T-568b. These schemes determine how the pairs are laid out in the RJ-45 or Mod-8 connectors. Refer back to Figure 2.20 for a refresher on pin assignments.

The pairs in both cables use the standard green-green/white, blue-blue/white, orange-orange/white, and brown-brown/white coloring scheme.

There are different styles of CAT-5 wire. The styles illustrated so far have been round wire, but data grade CAT-5 wire (CAT-5+ or CAT-5e) has a flatter design that places specific pairs next to one another, thus reducing crosstalk of electrical signals between pairs. Figure 2.24 shows CAT-5+ or CAT-5 data grade wire.

In the figure the top four images are of one cable and the bottom two images are another cable. The top cable has like most all LAN cabling the cabling system specifications that it meets printed on the outside of the cable. On the top right there is a close-up of the category 5 designation printed on the cable. Figure 2.25 shows a TIA/EIA-568a CAT-5 cable label.

Although both top and bottom cables in Figure 2.24 are specified as CAT-5 data grade cables (CAT-5+), they are not the same design and quality. The top cable has two separate sheaths, each carrying two of the four twisted pairs found in the cable. While this separates the pairs just fine, it is possible for pairs to bunch up in one or both sheaths. This could alter the data transmission speed characteristics of the cable.

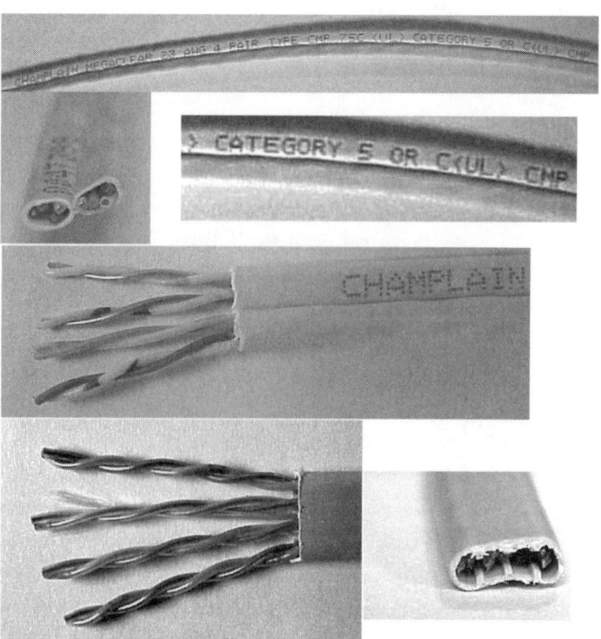

Figure 2.24
CAT-5+ cable.

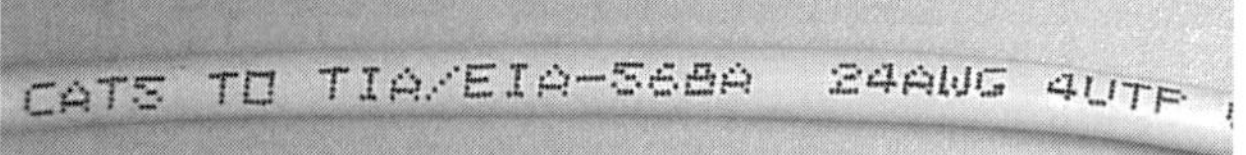

Figure 2.25
CAT-5 cable labeling.

The bottom cable has each individual pair isolated in a specific position in the cable. This prevents bunching of the pairs and would result in more consistent data transmission speed characteristics for the cable. High-speed networks should use the best cable available. The cable should be certified for the transmission speed used in the network and other transmission criteria including signal-to-noise ratio (SNR), pair signal propagation delay skew, and signal attenuation characteristics.

High-speed LAN cabling standards generally meet SNR and maximum noise thresholds standards. But pair signal propagation delay skew and overall signal propagation delay characteristics are important for LANs transmitting data above 100 MHz. Pair signal propagation delay skew applies to components using more than one twisted pair to send data. In this case, transmission is divided between pairs requiring the receiving component to reassemble the data. If data sent on each separate pair arrives at different times because of pair signal propagation delay skew, transmission errors result.

Overall propagation delay, the time it takes for the signal to travel to the receiver, may also determine LAN performance and area of coverage. Overall propagation delay is expressed as the electrical signal speed relative to the theoretical speed of electricity (light). This is sometimes called the velocity of propagation. The LAN speed is measured in megabits per second, not in signal propagation speeds. Overall propagation delays cause delays in conversational handshaking (like talking on a satellite link), but once a transmission is being received it arrives at the designated LAN speed.

Some network component manufacturers resolve electrical loss across cable distances by incorporating signal equalizers into their receivers. The signal equalizers attempt to amplify the received signal based on an anticipated attenuation or electrical signal loss from transmission across the cable. The received signal must be distinguishable from electrical noise picked up during its transmission. Some noise is always present in any cable and is re-amplified along with the data signals. An incorrect interpretation of the original data results in a bit error. Bit errors are detected by LAN components and are corrected by retransmission of the data in error.

In the case of 155-Mbps transmission on CAT-5 cable, signaling errors can occur above the CAT-5 maximum signal frequency of over 100 MHz and as high as 200 MHz. These signaling errors when processed by the equalizer can be amplified as if they were part of the signal. This may cause an unacceptably high bit error rate.

Gigabit Ethernet could use CAT-5 for short distance wiring to the desktop. This would save costs by preserving the CAT-5 twisted-pair wiring most organizations already have in place. Longer runs of Gigabit Ethernet use optical fiber.

Beyond CAT-5 Cabling

Higher-speed transmission is becoming a necessity for the new multimedia LAN applications being used to meet new creative and competitive business challenges. These applications are continuing to consume more and more LAN bandwidth. The Gigabit Ethernet Alliance concluded that high-speed gigabit technology significantly impacts LAN cabling. Gigabit Ethernet pushes cabling speed capabilities to its limits. Regardless of product and installation quality, gigabit Ethernet leaves no room for error when implemented on CAT-5 cabling systems.

New specifications and guidelines for electrical bandwidth in excess of 100 MHz are now required. The Level 5 specification from 1992 was modified to cover the performance requirements for existing CAT-5 cables. More stringent requirements for data grade, High-End CAT-5, or CAT-5+ cables are referred to as Level 6. See Table 2.1. New generation products that support twice the CAT-5 bandwidth requirement are referred to as Level 7. Level 5 is different from the standard CAT-5 because it must meet more stringent requirements included in the international standard ISO 11801. This ISO 11801 standard for cable performance creates a super set of the original Category 5 requirements. Cable that meets Level 7 standards attains performance that has over twice the actual usable electrical bandwidth of the current Category 5 cable. Level 7 compliant cable extends the data bandwidth to 1.2 Gbps, permitting it to be used in gigabit Ethernet networks.

Cabling standards continue to evolve to support higher transmission speeds. As small-office LANs move to combined voice (VoIP) and data networking, network cabling that supports higher transmission speeds becomes increasingly important for them. For home-office LANs with light loads, fast 100 Mbps Ethernet continues to be the favorite network cabling.

Software

Software provides the protocol and services layers of the Windows networking model. When talking about software we focus on the services layer more than the software layer. Client PC hosts can be configured with peer-to-peer networking and client server services. Server software implements the services side of client/server software.

Windows software dominates SOHO LANs because basic networking functions are built in. Windows and other LAN servers perform general and specific network functions as determined by the capabilities of the software installed on them. Some Windows servers can be assigned database operation, others network management functions, while still others can act as fax and e-mail servers. Each special server requires basic Windows server software and then additional network application software for the specific function performed. For example, a Structured Query Language (SQL) Server would need the basic Microsoft Windows XP or Windows 2000 Server Software and then the Microsoft SQL Server software as well. Similarly, an e-mail server would need the Microsoft Windows 2000 Server Software and the Microsoft Exchange Server software. Not all server packages require Windows Server. For example, Microsoft SQL Server can run from Windows 2000 Professional just fine for some small SOHO offices because Windows 2000 Professional supports only 10 simultaneously active connections under peer-to-peer networking.

Basic Windows XP software supports peer-to-peer networking, while special Windows server software is needed to implement client/server networking.

Peer-to-Peer

Virtually all Windows software supports peer-to-peer networking services. This covers Windows 3.1 (Windows for Workgroups), Windows 9x, Windows NT, Windows 2000, and Windows XP. Home-office LANs rely on peer-to-peer networking services, while small-office LANs may use both peer-to-peer networking and client/server networking services.

Windows XP network security hides a Windows PC host on a TCP/IP network. The `PING`, `TRACERT`, and `PATHPING` (Windows 2000/XP) commands cannot find a Windows XP PC host when the firewall function is enabled on that Windows XP PC host.

Windows XP/2000

Windows XP/2000 are significant 21st-century networking products because networking components are neatly integrated into the operating system. Additionally, Windows comes with a broad set of client software for most of the popular network operating systems. This allows Windows to operate as a client for other servers on your network. Windows can also work in a peer-to-peer networking system. Windows provides interoperability to the following networks:

1. Microsoft networks
2. Novell NetWare
3. TCP/IP hosts, including UNIX hosts
4. AppleTalk

Windows supplies this flexibility though modularization of the network components. This means that network components can be added, removed, or updated in some cases without disturbing the other network components. A reboot may be required to activate the component before its change takes effect. The downside here is that Microsoft software products are very much "a la carte." You must buy Windows server software and then add modular Windows application software to support other key small-office network applications. Once added, Microsoft application software intertwines with Windows and cannot be easily removed.

Windows 9x

Similar to Windows XP/2000, Windows 9x software has both peer-to-peer services and client/server client services built in. Windows 9x does not act as a centralized server in client/server networks because it is not as reliable and robust as is Windows XP/2000. With Windows 9x, one server running peer-to-peer services can be designated as a network server, but it is limited to 10 simultaneously active client connections.

Client/Server

Windows 2000 and Windows NT have special server software that implements client/server computing. This server software permits the central network user and TCP/IP management needed in larger small-office LANs.

Windows 2000 Server

Windows 2000 is Microsoft's latest client/server network operating system. It comes in several flavors, with the most powerful being the Windows 2000 Advanced Server software. Windows 2000 in a single integrated network operating system (NOS) provides a Web applications platform, Internet performance and scalability, and security based on the latest standards and technologies to extend enterprise operations using the Internet.

Windows 2000 Server can:

1. Connect employees, customers, and suppliers using the Web, spanning geographic or corporate network boundaries
2. Build internal line-of-business applications
3. Share select enterprise information in an extranet without compromising confidential data

4. Allow mobile users to connect securely to corporate resources from anywhere in the world
5. Increase performance as application load increases
6. Integrate Web and application services

Windows implements Active Server Pages (ASP), allowing the Web to become dynamic and highly personalized. Windows supports Extensible Markup Language (XML). XML integrates data from multiple sources, reduces network traffic, and supports more useful searches. Windows supports streaming media. This allows development and distribution of real-time presentations and rich multimedia content to both internal and external audiences. Streaming media can send full-screen video to PC clients on demand and provide CD-quality audio.

Windows 2000, like Windows NT, is designed to increase performance through symmetric multi-processing (SMP) support. SMP means that Windows takes equal advantage of multiple microprocessors on the same machine. Although microprocessors get faster and faster, real scalability is achieved by adding more processors to a single server. Windows allows demanding high-end applications to access and use more memory. Windows 2000 Server supports four CPUs and Windows 2000 Advanced Server supports eight.

A second approach to increasing performance is combining several servers into a cluster. Microsoft refers to this approach as scaling out. Scaling out distributes a computing workload among multiple servers by clustering or load balancing.

A Windows 2000 Network Load Balancing (NLB) service is part of Advanced Server. With NLB an Internet site can grow by adding more Windows servers. NLB directs traffic on the site, spreading the traffic across multiple servers without requiring new applications development or reengineering.

Enterprise LANs support intranets, Internet sites, and extranets requiring increased system security. Confidential information may be stored on mobile computing devices that can be stolen or lost. Windows has end-to-end security that integrates systems both inside and outside an enterprise into the enterprise LAN while controlling LAN access and protecting data. Security includes identifying who is accessing systems, including digital "keys" to access selected data. A single ID permits users to access their own computer and other shared resources on the enterprise LAN, the Internet, or on an extranet. Windows 2000 Server has comprehensive, standards-based security services, including flexible authentication, data encryption, flexible and secure network access, and protection of virtual private networks (VPNs). Windows 2000 uses core Internet standards such as IP Security (IPSec) and secure transaction processing.

NetWare

For almost a decade Novell claimed the lion's share of the network operating system market. For nearly as long they enjoyed little competition. They provided an easy-to-implement client/server solution for connecting PCs, together. NetWare ran on many network types, including Ethernet and the Token Ring. Originally, NetWare used a flat bindery database approach to user management, providing easy-to-use, menu-driven tools for DOS-based PCs. This was the most successful network operating system package for SOHO DOS-based PC LANs for many years.

NetWare's primary competitor is the Microsoft Windows operating system. Novell redesigned NetWare to work as part of larger and heterogeneous networks, including the Internet. NetWare adopted domain management and a hierarchical network management database structure to support enterprise-wide LANs. This was called NetWare Directory Services (NDS). This jump from simple DOS menu-driven network management to hierarchical network management was very difficult for most NetWare users because the network management paradigm was so different. At that time it was easier to use the Windows network management paradigm to manage enterprise-wide LANs with Windows PC clients.

Windows 2000 now provides a hierarchical network management database structure to support enterprise-wide LANs called Active Directory. The Active Directory in Windows 2000 is easier to transition to than was NetWare's NDS.

Today, Novell offers its NetWare 6 products. NetWare 6 is designed to work with the Internet as a major enabler of Novell's oneNet concept of non-stop access to network services through any device, at any time, and from any location. NetWare 6 is a Web-based network operating system using TCP/IP. NetWare 5.1 originally integrated NDS with the industry standard Domain Name System (DNS) and the Dynamic Host Configuration Protocol (DHCP). NetWare 6 now embraces standards such as HTTP, Java, and XML that comprise the universal conventions of the Internet. NetWare 6 has a multiprocessing kernel. Additional NetWare 6 features include a next generation file system supporting Storage Area Networks (SANs), printing services, and advanced security that has public-key cryptography and Secure Authentication Services—SAS.

NetWare servers and file system are managed through a Web browser from any location in a network. Some tasks performed through the Web browser connecting with a NetWare server include mounting and dismounting volumes, monitoring system resources, browsing the NDS tree, and many other routine management tasks.

NetWare supports all open Internet standards, including Lightweight Directory Access Protocol (LDAP) v3. LDAP accesses directory information from many different directories.

Novell software is predominately client/server LAN software aimed at small-office and enterprise LANs. Novell's NetWare provides the server software and the client software. The server software is licensed for a specific number of active client stations. Novell's NetWare is high-performance disk and print serving LAN server software. NetWare has always been robust server software. Today, Windows and UNIX are more dominant in the small-office LAN market.

UNIX

UNIX is an operating system developed at Bell Labs in 1969 as an interactive time-sharing system. It has evolved as a large freeware product with different extensions and new ideas provided in its many versions. Businesses, universities, and individuals developed these UNIX versions. Because UNIX was not a proprietary operating system owned by a single computer company and because UNIX is written in the standardized C programming language, UNIX became the first standard open operating system. As an open operating system UNIX could be improved or enhanced by anyone.

IEEE standardized the C language and UNIX user command interfaces as the Portable Operating System Interface (POSIX). POSIX interfaces specified in the X/Open Programming Guide 4.2 became known as UNIX 95 or the Single UNIX Specification. Version 2 of the Single UNIX Specification is labeled UNIX 98. The Open Group, an industry standards organization, which certifies and brands UNIX implementations, owns the "official" trademarked UNIX.

UNIX operating systems are used in workstations produced by Sun Microsystems, Silicon Graphics, and IBM. UNIX and its client/server program model played a key role in Internet development and in reshaping computing to center it in networks of computers rather than in individual computers. Linux is a UNIX derivative. Linux has both free software and commercial versions. Linux is increasing in popularity as an alternative to proprietary operating systems.

UNIX software is used heavily in Internet servers. It is server software but has been adapted to perform client operations as well. Client UNIX requires an easy-to-use graphical user interface to front-end the cryptic command-level interface. Availability of hardware driver programs for UNIX software may also be an issue. The best things about UNIX software are as follows:

1. The operating system is free. The Linux version of UNIX can be downloaded off the Internet.

2. UNIX is very efficient. UNIX running on an old, tired 486 CPU can handle communications loads that would stress Windows XP running on a GHz CPU.
3. UNIX has very good security features if you know how to implement them effectively.
4. UNIX supports TCP/IP, SPX/IPX, and NETBEUI.
5. UNIX software is very Internet centric. Many high-performance Internet applications run on UNIX servers.

Linux is free and available for download over the Internet. However, the easiest way to install Linux is to use CD-ROMs because installation from CD-ROM is automatic. Internet installations are done manually. CD-ROM collections known as distributions are purchased for a small fee. A standard distribution typically includes more than just the necessary Linux OS software. A distribution includes programming languages, editors, hardware drivers, window managers, and other CD-ROMs of software that may contain well over 1,000 individual programs.

The primary benefits of UNIX (Linux) as an operating system are the cost—Windows and NetWare licenses cost into the hundreds of thousands of dollars for a large enterprise, and then its robust performance. The main difficulty with Linux and UNIX is that the command line interface is very cryptic. This means that most Linux/UNIX servers install a Windows-like graphical user interface (GUI) shell to make UNIX more usable by less technical humans. Administering a Unix (Linux) server requires different administrative and computer skills and knowledge than administering a Windows server. UNIX and Linux servers are used in small-office LANs as well as in the world's largest server operations.

Summary

In this chapter we examined the Windows networking model with its hardware, protocol, and services layers. We then discussed networking hardware, including NICs, hubs, switches, routers, and servers with RAID technology. The Ethernet CSMA/CD half-duplex protocol operation was presented. The repeater function was explained. RAID technology operation was also presented. SOHO LAN cabling categories were described with emphasis on CAT-5 cabling, which is the most common SOHO LAN cabling. Windows client/server and peer-to-peer networking software was examined along with NetWare and Unix (Linux) software.

Key Technical Terms

10 Base T—10 Mbps baseband (digital) half-duplex transmission over unshielded twisted pair wire.

100 Base TX—100 Mbps baseband (digital) full-duplex transmission over unshielded twisted pair wire.

CAT-3—A common type of unshielded twisted pair wire used for analog telephones and early LANs that ran at 10 Mbps.

CAT-5—The most common type of unshielded twisted pair wire used for LANs that run at 10 Mbps and 100 Mbps.

Celeron—A cheap Intel CPU chip that is equivalent to the Pentium II.

DDR—Double data rate DRAM is a new type of RAM that is twice as fast as SDRAM.

DIMM—Dual inline memory modules; the mounting package for SDRAM.

ECC—Error-correcting circuitry corrects RAM memory and other memory errors.

Firewall—A network component that secures a network from the public Internet. Firewalls filter incoming and outgoing traffic to detect intrusions, stop access to unauthorized Web sites, and hide the network from hackers.

Hub—A networking component connecting PC hosts together. This component typically performs the repeater function.

IDE—Integrated drive electronics is the most common fixed disk drive interface. IDE drives are the least expensive disk drives.

ISO seven-layer networking model—An international standard that divides networking functions among seven layers. These layers are Layer 1—physical, Layer 2—data link, Layer 3—network, Layer 4—transport, Layer 5—session, Layer 6—presentation, and Layer 7—application.

MOD-8—The designation for a modular 8-pin connector more commonly called an RJ-45 connector.

NETBEUI—Network Basic Input/output System Extended User Interface is a Windows protocol layer that is used in simple peer-to-peer LANs.

NetWare—Novell's server software that implements client/server networks.

NOS—Network Operating System is what Novell calls NetWare.

Pentium—An Intel CPU chip that implements the i386 or 32-bit CPU architecture.

PING—Packet Internet (Inter-Network) Groper is a command that tests for active IP addresses.

RAM—Random access memory is the volatile working memory of a PC host.

RDRAM—Rambus DRAM is the RAM type used with Pentium 4 CPU chips.

Router—A networking component connecting one network to another. This component typically represents one LAN to another LAN as a single IP address.

SAN—Storage Area Network is a network that connects storage systems and represents them to a server as a single disk drive. They are used in large networks.

SDRAM—Synchronous Dynamic RAM is a common memory chip.

Servers—A networking component providing disk sharing, print sharing, and application processing services to PC hosts. They are the server side of a client/server network.

SIMD—Single Instruction Multiple Data is a special instruction set extension in Intel Pentium III chips.

SPX/IPX—Sequenced Packet Exchange/Internet Packet Exchange is Novell's protocol layer software equivalent to TCP/IP.

SQL—Structured Query Language is software used to develop database applications.

Switch—A networking component connecting PC hosts together. This component improves LAN performance by connecting PC hosts directly to one another as though they were on a separate network.

TIA/EIA—Telecommunications Industry Association/Electronic Industries Association.

UNIX—An open source code operating system originally developed by Bell Labs. Linux is a variation of UNIX that runs on PC hosts. UNIX is used on many Internet servers.

UTP—Unshielded twisted pair wire has solid copper wire twisted into several individual pairs.

Xeon—An Intel CPU chip used in servers because of large internal cache memory.

Review Questions

1. What is the most popular type of LAN wiring?

   Answer: CAT-5 but higher grade CAT-5+, CAT-5e, and CAT-6 wiring are now being used in its place.

2. How many layers are there in the Windows networking model?

   Answer: Three—the hardware, protocol, and services layers.

3. In what layer do we find NICs?

   Answer: Layer 1—hardware.

4. What functions does TCP/IP perform?

   Answer: IP performs routing and TCP verifies message integrity, among other functions.

5. What type of SOHO LAN does Windows 9.x software implement?

   Answer: Peer-to-peer LANs.

6. What RAID types can Windows server software implement?

   Answer: RAID-0 striping, RAID-1 mirroring, and RAID-5 parity striping or a rotating parity array.

Chapter 3

INSTALLING AND CONFIGURING A BASIC LAN

Chapter Syllabus

- Installing LAN Cabling
- Installing Network Interface Cards
- Configuring Windows Software
- Summary
- Key Technical Terms
- Review Questions

This chapter describes the procedure for installing a basic LAN. It begins with installing the wiring and hubs, continues with installing the PC network interface cards and driver programs, and concludes with configuring Windows software for peer-to-peer network operation using NETBIOS and TCP/IP. Throughout, the Windows networking model is used to illustrate key installation steps.

The first steps in installing a SOHO LAN involve the LAN wiring and LAN wiring hubs and switches. Unless these connections are in place, nothing works with the SOHO LAN. Once the wiring is installed, hardware installation follows. Finally, Windows software configuration completes the process. Windows provides most of the software needed for peer-to-peer networking. So configuring the Windows software is usually the last step in setting up a SOHO LAN.

Some SOHO network configurations and costs are summarized as we discuss their installation. The estimated costs were compared using information obtained from Web sites on the Internet. These costs should give a rough approximation of actual installation costs. Since electronic component prices continue to decline, it should be possible to install a SOHO LAN for less than the estimated costs.

The very first step is installing wiring, wiring hubs, and switches. Determining the manufacturer's wiring rules and following them to the letter is very important for trouble-free SOHO LAN operation. Recall in Chapter 2 the repeater function that regenerates digital signals was described. This is the basis for every manufacturer's wiring rules. Wiring rules for Ethernet are generally defined by industry line standards. Consequently, manufacturers generally described these industry wide standards as their wiring rules, or they will reference them in their documentation as the wiring rules to follow with their equipment.

Installing LAN Cabling

This section discusses the general steps performed in installing SOHO LAN cabling. It then examines the differences between home-office LAN cabling configurations and installation and small-office configurations and installations. Installing wiring hub and switching components is explored along with an in-depth discussion of LAN cables.

General Cabling Tasks

The tasks to perform in installing LAN cabling are the following:

1. Planning
    a. Selecting cable, tools, etc.
    b. Designating cable runs
    c. Determining the central hub and the hub hierarchy
2. Test the cable before installation
3. Install the cable
4. Test the cable after installation
5. Document the installation and label the cables

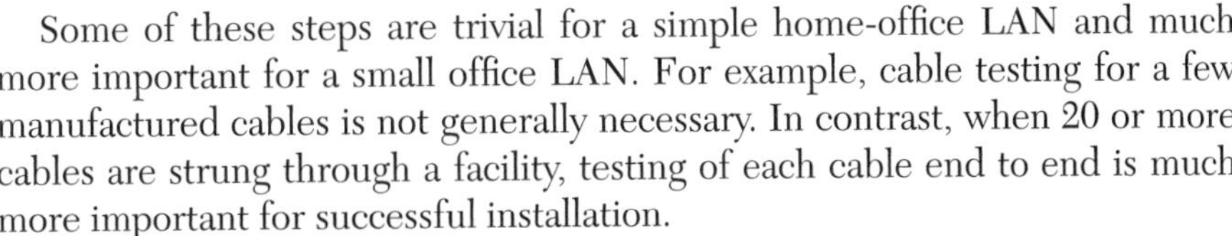

Some of these steps are trivial for a simple home-office LAN and much more important for a small office LAN. For example, cable testing for a few manufactured cables is not generally necessary. In contrast, when 20 or more cables are strung through a facility, testing of each cable end to end is much more important for successful installation.

Brain Teaser: LAN Installation Plan

Draw a layout of the rooms in your facility and check the rooms where PC hosts are installed. Identify precisely the wall they are installed against.

Is there a good spot to locate a central hub? What is the distance between the central hub and the rooms where the PC hosts are located?

Identifying the central hub and determining the distance from it to the remote PC hosts is a first step in planning the SOHO LAN cable installation.

Planning

Planning a LAN installation begins with selecting the cable and wiring terminations, including outlet boxes, snap-in CAT-5e RJ-45 jacks, RJ-45 8-conductor modular plugs, punch down tools, and patch panels. The most readily available cable is CAT-5 or CAT-5e. This cable is available at Radio Shack.

LAN Wiring Components. Radio Shack sells other LAN wiring components and tools but not every component is available at their stores. Some components are only available online at

www.radioshack.com

SOHO LAN cabling and other components are found under computer and then networking; under wire, cable hardware and tools; or telephones and communications. There are some pictures and tutorials at the site under

www.radioshack.com/ProdSupport/ProductSupport.asp#

and selecting online tutorials. In the online tutorials, the networking tutorial is under

www.attenza.com/radioshack/cl/1,,5+30,00.html

Central Hub or Head End. Every LAN should have a central hub or head end. This is the location or room from which all wiring emanates. The wiring is run from the remote SOHO LAN components to the central hub. The central hub usually contains the SOHO network servers and other network equipment. There may be other hubs in the LAN depending upon its size. These other hubs would form a second tier or level in the LAN. In some LANs a third tier may be required to connect all remote PC hosts to the central hub servers. A large LAN is wired in a hierarchical structure from the single central hub. At the hubs, active network hubs or switches are installed. Most LANs use switches at the hubs because they provide the best performance and their cost is little more than the cost of a network hub. The central hub should be where the main LAN servers are installed. Other servers may also have been installed at the remote hubs. These servers will service the local PC hosts connected into the switch at that remote hub.

Test the Cable before Installation

Testing the cable prior to installation ensures that no bad cable is installed. This is especially important for long or difficult cable runs. A simple pre-installation test is to use a voltmeter to check the continuity of the wire while it is still on the reel. A simple resistance test of each wire should show that there are no breaks in the cable. Little or no resistance means that a wire is not broken. High or infinite resistance means that the wire is broken.

In home-office LANs, testing the wire prior to installation is not really necessary. This is especially true when patch cables are used to connect each PC host to the central network switch. However, cables can be quickly tested using the PC hosts closest to the central hub switch. With the switch and the PC both powered up, the network cables are plugged one at a time into both the PC host and the switch. The switch's LEDs are used to test each cable.

More extensive testing is performed once the cable is installed. Such extensive testing would employ special cable test equipment.

Install the Cable

Cable installation requires running the cables from the central point to the remote PC hosts. This may require fishing the cable from ceilings to drop boxes near each remote PC host. In larger small-office LANs cabling may be run across drop ceilings. When there are drop ceilings it is best to install the cabling in a cabling tray. In smaller installations this is often not done. When running cable across drop ceilings, it is best to give fluorescent lights installed in the ceiling a wide berth. Fluorescent lights give off high radio frequency (RF) emissions. Such RF emissions can be readily picked up by unshielded twisted pair (UTP) wire, causing interference with the network electrical signals traveling across the wire. Such interference can easily corrupt data traveling across the network cabling. Network cabling should be separated from fluorescent lights by a distance of two feet or more.

Test the Cable after Installation

More extensive testing is performed once the cable is installed. Such extensive testing would employ special cable test equipment. Special cable test equipment checks cable continuity and measures the electrical signal interference between cable pairs over a wide range of frequencies. Such electrical signal interference can cause problems in larger networks that have long cable runs and that employ punch-down blocks and patch panels.

In a large network every cable should be tested end-to-end with such test equipment. Cable runs that do not pass the test should be identified and fixed. Problems with LAN wiring are very difficult to pinpoint once the network is in full operation. This is especially true when LAN wiring problems result in high error rates and consequently low data transfer speeds. Some remote PC hosts operating at great speed while other remote PC hosts run very slowly—as if they were stuck in tar—is a common manifestation of such problems.

Brain Teaser: Cable Testing

Locate a hub in your network. Examine it and determine what lights are on the hub.

Can the hub be used to test the transmission speed? Does it have a LED that indicates 10 or 100 Mbps operation? Is there a LED that shows half-duplex or full-duplex operation? What operating LEDs are on the NIC in your PC host?

This determines the testing capabilities of hubs and NICs in your network.

Document the Cable Installation

Once the cabling is installed, it should be documented. If the cable is not documented during installation, I promise you it will be documented at some point. Even a small LAN needs to have its cable layout documented because it is virtually impossible to make any cabling configuration changes without having some network documentation.

The documentation on each end of the cable should identify precisely the location of that end of the cable as well as the exact location of the other end of the cable. For example, the label attached to a cable installed at the remote end should identify precisely the room and drop point in that room where the cable is installed as well as the switch and the port on the switch into which the cable is connected. Similarly, the end of the cable at the central hub should identify precisely the switch and port on the switch into which the cable is connected as well as the room and drop point of the remote end of the cable. Such a label may say Floor 3—Room 2 and Switch 1—Port 5. In this manner the cable end in room 2 on floor 3 is identified along with the switch 1 port 5 into which it is inserted. The same label should be attached to both the start and finish ends of the cable.

There should also be prepared a network cabling document that describes each cable run and includes the test results for the after installation test of that specific cable run.

Home-Office LAN Cabling

In a home-office LAN one PC host should be at the central hub. This is illustrated in Figure 3.1. Sometimes this is referred to as a head-end. The PC host located at the central hub or head-end point should be the host sharing its disk drives with all other PC hosts.

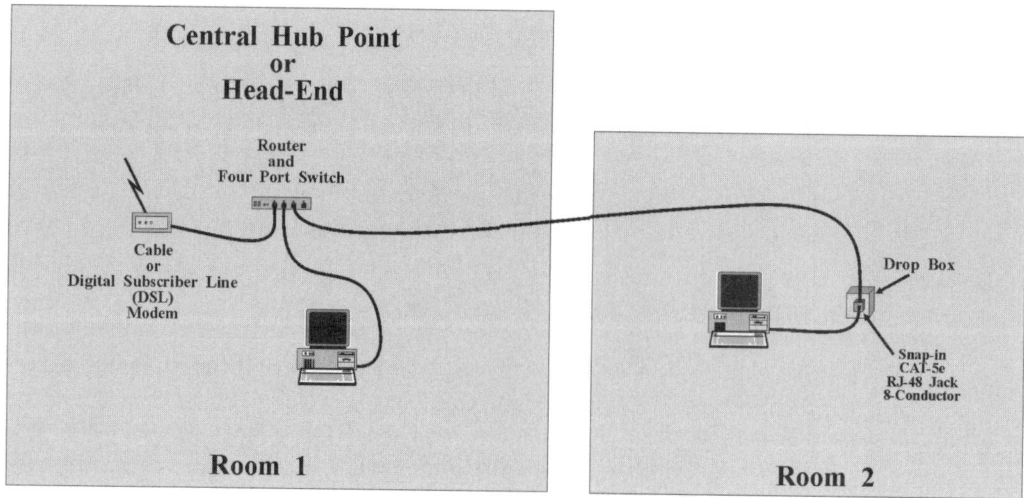

Figure 3.1 Home-office wiring and hub.

A home-office LAN requires simple wiring. In most cases a manufactured patch cable of 10 to 50 feet in length from the central hub to a PC host or two is all that is needed. When a home-office LAN involves two desktop PC hosts and a laptop PC host or two, then more elaborate wiring may be required. In this case the more remote PC hosts may be wired using wall plates. CAT-5 cable is run from the central hub to a drop-down box and a CAT-5 rated snap-in RJ-45 connector. A short patch cable is run from the snap-in RJ-45 connector to the remote PC host. This cabling configuration necessitates constructing the cable from the remote RJ-45 snap-in connector to the central hub.

The cost of wiring this simple configuration is as follows:

Hub—Linksys 20-port hub	$120
CAT-5e—50-foot cable	$27
CAT-5e—25-foot cable	$17
Snap-in CAT-5 jack	$6
Surface mount wall jack	$5
Total Estimated Cost	$175

These estimated costs are based upon prices at the Radio Shack Web site. They are conservative. It is possible to find a hub or switch for less than $120. Some eight-port 10/100 switches are advertised for as little as $35 plus shipping at

www.pricewatch.com

Cables could be shorter and cost less as well. Further, in a home-office configuration the wall jack is not necessarily needed. I have found that with wall-to-wall carpeting there is a space between the baseboard and the carpet that readily hides wires that are pushed into it. See Figure 3.2. This makes it easy to run cable around the walls of a room to any location. This space can accommodate about two cables and maybe more. The cables can be run by using a flat-bladed screwdriver to push the cable into the space between the baseboard and the carpet. It is an effective means to wire a home-office LAN without using drop-down boxes.

The cables used should follow the standard Ethernet patch cable configuration. This wiring configuration is discussed in more detail later in this chapter.

Home office wiring cables are tested effectively using lights on hubs or switches. When hub LEDs do not light, then the wire is bad. For hub lights to light, both the remote PC host and the hub must be powered and operating.

Figure 3.2 Baseboard wire installation.

Figure 3.3 illustrates how the LEDs are used to test the wiring. In the figure, the yellow cable connects to an uplink port, and the gray cable is connected to a standard port. The yellow cable connects to another active switch, as shown by the green light on the switch. The gray cable is not functioning or not connected because the LED associated with its port is not lit. Power is applied to the switch because the power LED is lit in red. The collision light on the switch can also be an effective diagnostic tool. If the collision LED remains continuously and brightly lit, then there is most likely a problem with the cabling causing excess of collisions. Consequently, a continuously and brightly lit collision LED indicates a potential cabling problem.

Often other LEDs on the switch or hub indicate 10 Mbps or 100 Mbps and full duplex operation. When the LEDs on the switch or hub do not indicate a match with the PC host NIC capabilities, then there is likely a configuration problem.

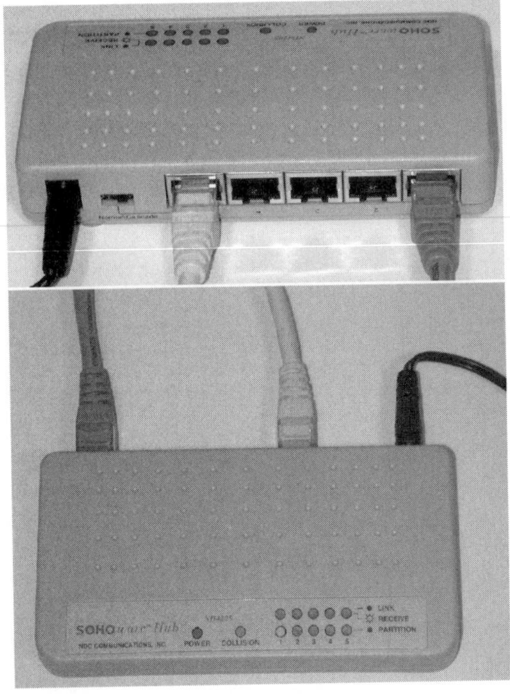

Figure 3.3
SOHO switch LEDs.

Small-Office LAN Cabling

In a small-office LAN the server PCs should all be located at the central hub. For best LAN performance the servers should be connected to switches. The central hub switches are then connected to remote switches or hubs. The remote switches/hubs are connected to the central hub using uplink ports or crossover cables. A crossover cable or an uplink port on a hub crosses the transmit pairs and the receive pairs. Crossover cable configurations are discussed later in this chapter.

Refer to Figure 3.4. In the figure the central hub has a 16-port switch connecting to two servers and a router to a high-speed Internet connection. In this manner the network load can be split between the two servers and the Internet router and distributed among the LAN switches. The remote PC hosts could be connected to the central switch using hubs or switches. Hubs would be used when there is no local switching required at the remote hub. If a server was installed at the remote hub, then a switch could increase network performance by keeping traffic to that server within the remote switch. Only traffic for the central servers would travel across the wiring links to the central switch.

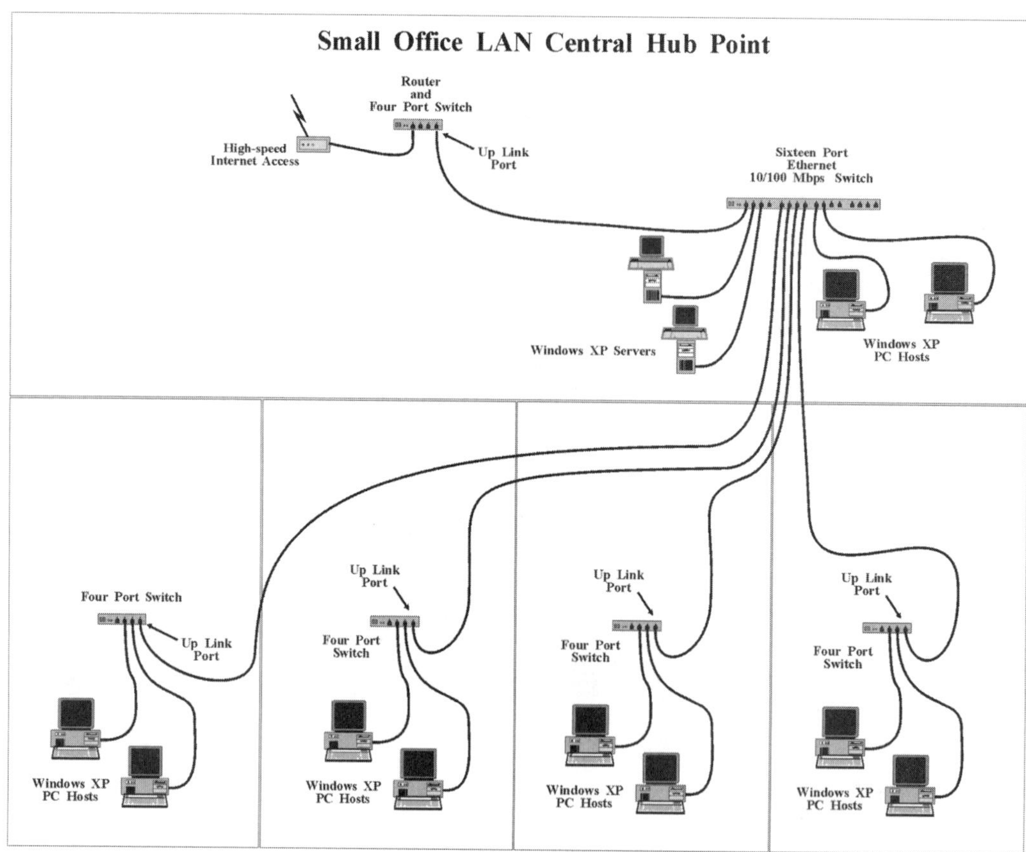

Figure 3.4 Small-office wiring and hubs.

Sometimes extensive wiring is required with punch down-blocks and other wiring hardware. When using punch-down blocks and other wiring hardware, make sure that it is rated the same as the wire being installed. A punch-down block is sometimes referred to as a Type 66 or Type 110 punch-down block. CAT-5 wiring should be connected with punch-down blocks that are rated the same as CAT-5 wire, and CAT-3 wiring should be connected with punch-down blocks that are rated the same as CAT-3 wire.

Brain Teaser: LAN Hubs

Locate the LAN hub or switch connected to your PC host. Find a hub by tracing the cables from your PC host to the nearest wiring closet.

Is your PC host connected to a hub? Or is your PC host connected to a switch? At what speeds can the switch or hub operate? Does the switch or hub support full-duplex transmission?

Labels on the hub or switch typically reveal the maximum transmission speed and whether the hub or switch can support full-duplex operation. If the hub or switch labels do not list the maximum transmission speed or the half- or full-duplex transmission capability, sometimes the LED labels will identify these attributes.

In Figure 3.5 the use of a punch-down block is illustrated. The punch-down block is an easy way to run CAT-5 cable without connectors on each end to a remote outlet. The punch-down block terminates and cross connects the connectorless CAT-5 cable ends. At the remote end the connectorless CAT-5 cable end is terminated in a drop box. A standard patch cable is then used to connect the drop box to the PC host. At the central hub an RJ-45 connector is installed on the cable end that is inserted into a switch port.

Similarly, a patch panel may be substituted for the punch-down block. In this case a patch panel terminates the connectorless end of the CAT-5 cable running to the remote PC host. The remote connectorless end of the CAT-5 cable terminates in a drop box. Again a simple patch cable runs from the wall outlet to the remote PC host. The benefit of the patch panel over the punch-down block is that the central hub switch is connected to the patch panel using manufactured patch cables. The manufactured patch cables have RJ-45 connectors at each end. One RJ-45 connector plugs into the central hub switch; any other plugs into the central hub patch panel. The patch panel also provides a convenient termination point for the connectorless cable ends of the CAT-5 cables running from the central hub to the remote PC hosts. These cables can be simply terminated in the patch panel and do not require installation of an RJ-45 plug on the cable. A patch panel configuration is illustrated in Figure 3.6.

Wiring configurations using punch-down blocks and patch panels are more sophisticated than those used in a simple home-office LAN. This greater sophistication provides an opportunity to better organize the wiring at the central hub. Organized wiring is needed for larger small-office LANs. Documented and organized wiring is needed to properly install and maintain larger SOHO LANs.

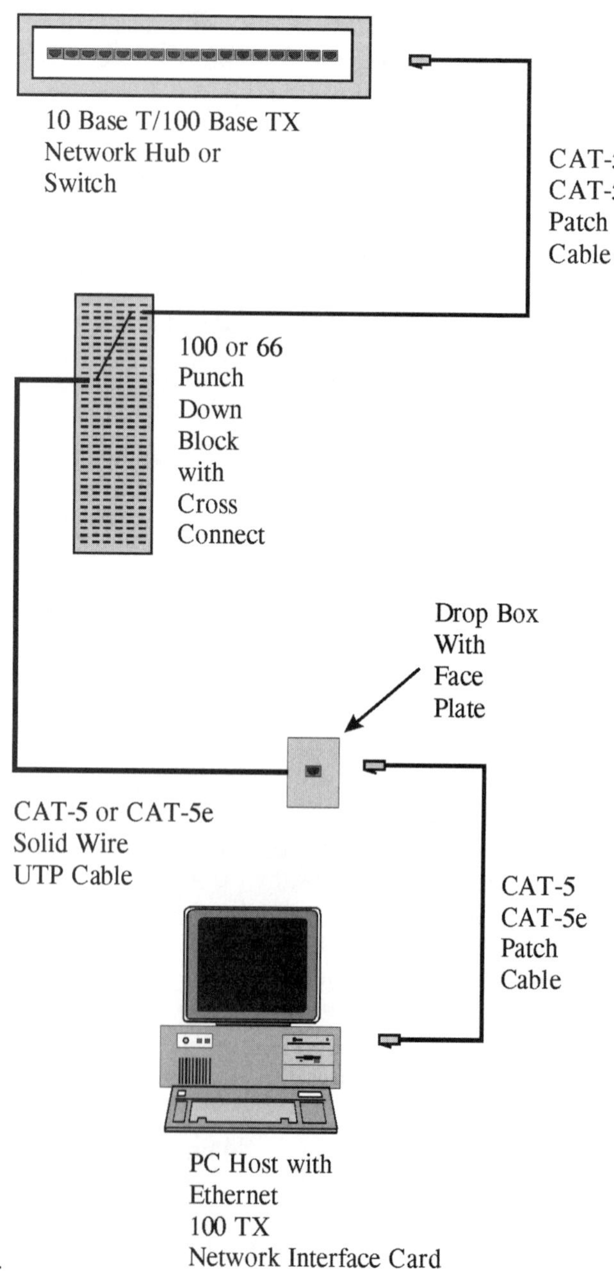

Figure 3.5
Punch-down block wiring configuration.

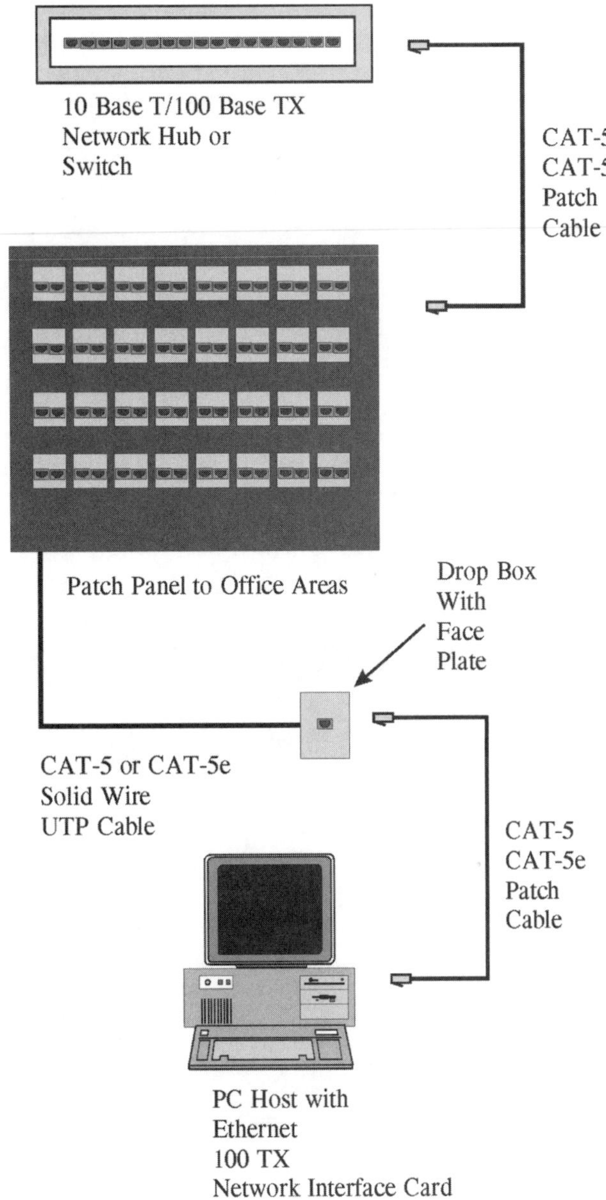

Figure 3.6
Patch panel wiring configuration.

The estimated cost of wiring a more complex configuration is:

Central Switch—Linksys 16-port 10/100 switch	$329
Remote Hubs—(4) Linksys 20-port 10/100 hubs	$480
CAT-5e—(20) 100-foot cables, or 2,000 feet	$650
RJ-45 connectors and misc. hardware	$50
CAT-5e—(16) 25-foot patch cables	$272
Snap-in CAT-5 jack (16)	$96
Surface mount wall jack (16)	$80
Total Estimated Cost	$1,957

This estimated cost is for wiring up a 16-PC host SOHO LAN. This results in an approximate cost of $125 to wire each PC host into the SOHO LAN.

Brain Teaser: Patch Panels or Punch-Down Blocks

Follow the SOHO LAN cable from your PC host to the nearest wiring closet. Examine the wiring closet for punch-down blocks or patch panels.

Can you find patch panels in the wiring closet? Are punch-down blocks used in place of patch panels? If there are no punch-down blocks or patch panels in the closest wiring closet to your PC host, go to the central hub for your facility. Are patch panels or punch-down blocks used there?

Small-office networks typically use patch panels or punch-down blocks in the network cabling configuration. If they are used, has cable testing been performed that tests not only the cable but also tests the punch-down block or patch-panel connections?

Installing a Hub

Installing a hub is a relatively easy process. Hubs require power, so the first step is to plug the hub's transformer into a nearby wall outlet. Next, the transformer is connected to the hub. Now the hub should be powered on. This can be verified by observing the power LED on the hub. Once the hub is powered on, the network cables can be plugged into it. As each cable is plugged into the hub, verify that the cable is operating properly by observing the LEDs for the cable connection. The LEDs should indicate the NIC cable connection is active, operating at 10 or 100 Mbps, and functioning in half- or full-duplex mode. The LEDs will only light when the PC host at the opposite end of the cable is powered on and the cable is installed into its NIC. The hub installation is complete when all the cables are plugged into the hub. When a SOHO LAN is operating normally, all the lights on the hub are blinking as data travels across the LAN wiring. The collision LED lights frequently when there is heavy traffic on the LAN.

Installing a Switch

Switch installation is similar to hub installation. Unmanaged switches are self-configuring so there is virtually no software setup. Managed switches like HP's Procurve require setup depending upon how it is used in the SOHO LAN. Switches require power just as hubs require power. Consequently, the first step is to plug the switch's power transformer into a wall outlet. The switch's power LED should now be lit, verifying that the switch has electrical power. Next, key LAN cables are plugged into the switch ports. As each cable is plugged in, the port LEDs should light up, verifying cable integrity and the transmission speed, in half- or full-duplex operation. The switch port LEDs only light when the PC host at the opposite and of the cable is powered on and the cable is plugged into its NIC.

Additional verification of the cable link operation should be performed using Windows XP. The LAN icon in the SYSTRAY should display the expected LAN operating speed, as illustrated in Figure 3.7.

Basic switch installation is complete when all the cables are plugged into the switch. With a switch, however, some additional configuration is needed. A switch can only improve LAN performance when the servers are connected to it using high-speed links. Consequently, the server connections should be made using the highest possible LAN speed. This speed is either 100 Mbps or 1 Gbps. The higher speed provides increased performance for the remote PC hosts connecting through the switch to the servers.

For large small-office LANs, stackable switches at the central hub are required. The stackable switches have special connections between each

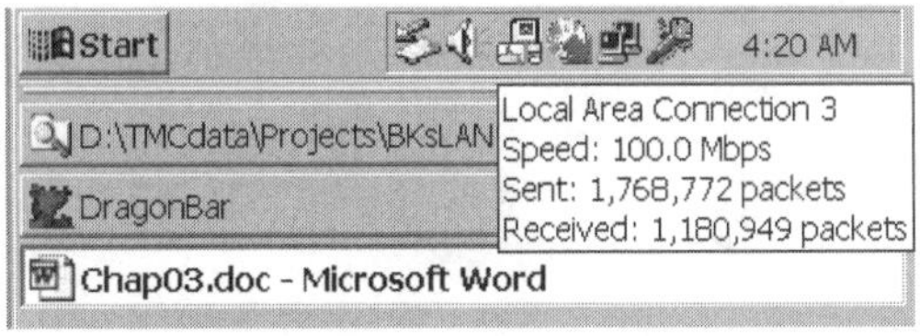

Figure 3.7
SYSTRAY LAN icon operating speed display.

switch that transform all the stackable switches into the equivalent of one very large switch. These special connections connect the internal circuitry of each switch directly to the internal circuitry of the next switch, providing increased performance for the switch stack.

Linking Hubs and Switches

In large small-office networks, remote hubs and switches are connected to the central hub switches. These connections are made using uplink ports. The uplink ports should be operated at the highest transmission speed and in full-duplex mode to provide the best overall LAN performance. If an uplink port is not available to connect a hub or a switch into a central hub switch, then a crossover cable may be used. A crossover cable is connected into an ordinary hub or switch port and then into an equivalent switch port on the central hub switches. It is best to use a single tier, or level, of remote hubs. If necessary two tiers, or levels, may be used, but having more than two tiers, or levels, is not recommended because it can result in reduced transmission speeds, packet corruption, or other network problems.

As each remote hub is connected into the network, it should be tested. The simplest test is performed using a PC host. The PC host is plugged into a remote hub port, and then it is used to access a central server. When the remote PC host communicates with a central server, the hub and the link between the hub and the central hub switches are functioning properly.

Hub and Switching Hierarchy

In combined Voice over Internet Protocol (VoIP) and data networks, more sophisticated hub and switching hierarchies may be employed. Figure 3.8 illustrates one possible network configuration for a combined VoIP and data network. In this switching hierarchy there are two separate destinations for traffic on the network. One destination is for the VoIP traffic and the other destination is for the servers for the data traffic. The VoIP traffic is switched to a VoIP gateway or VoIP-enabled private branch exchange (PBX) that in turn routes voice traffic over the public switched telephone network (PSTN). The network switches data traffic to central hub servers. Each remote switch has a connection for the VoIP traffic going to the central hub PBX and a separate connection for the data traffic going to the central hub servers. The remote switch would use an uplink port for one connection and a crossover cable for the second connection. In this manner VoIP traffic flows only through the remote switch, where it would be switched to a section of the network dedicated exclusively to VoIP traffic. Similarly the data traffic is switched by the

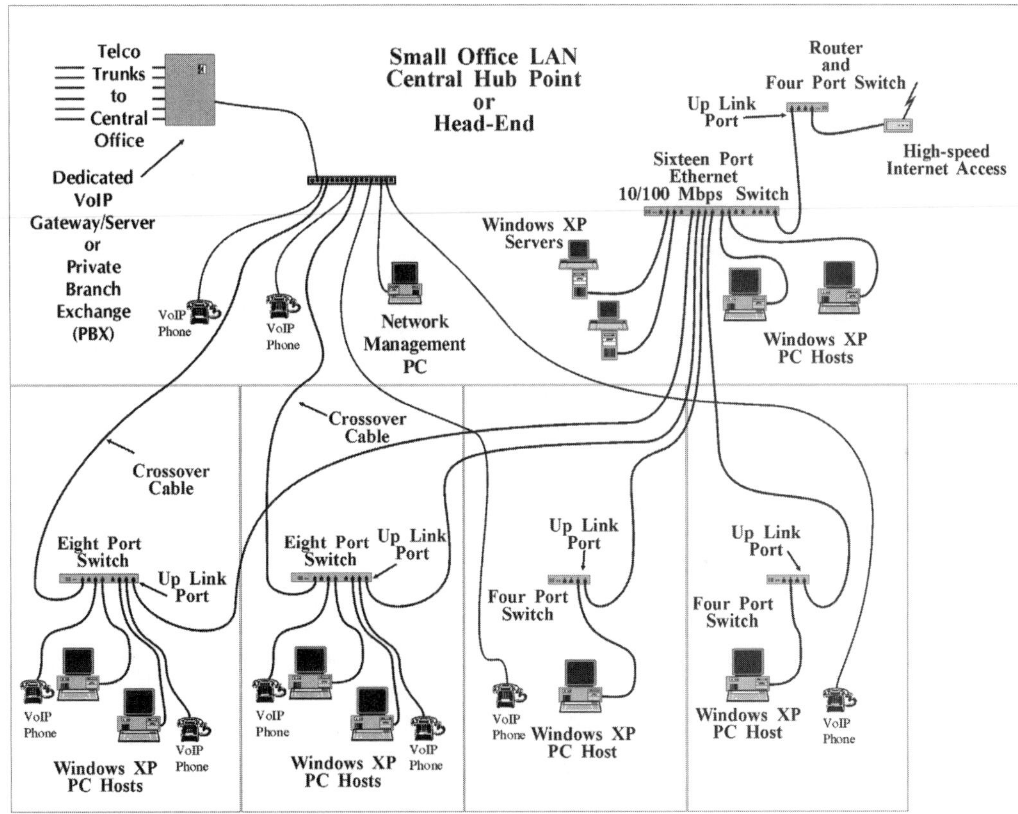

Figure 3.8 Sophisticated switching hierarchy.

remote switch to a section of the network dedicated exclusively to data traffic. The only part of the network shared by both VoIP and data traffic would be the remote switch.

In Figure 3.8, some remote VoIP telephones connect directly to the central VoIP switch. Other VoIP telephones connect to the remote switches and then their voice traffic is switched to the central hub VoIP switch. These connections would depend upon the distance from the central hub VoIP switch to the remote VoIP telephones.

Notice in the figure this is a two-tier or two-level network hierarchy. The remote switches form the bottom level or tier. The top level, or tier, is composed of the central hub switches.

Brain Teaser: Connecting Hubs and Switches

Follow the cable from your local PC host to the closest hub. Examine the hub to see if it connects to other hubs or switches.

Is the connection between the hub and another hub made using an uplink port or a crossover cable?

Draw a diagram of the connections between the hubs and switches in your SOHO LAN. How many tiers or levels are there? If there are more than three tiers or levels, do the PC hosts connecting to the third or greater tier or level hubs seem to work erratically? Do they have more performance problems can PC hosts connected to hubs and switches in the first, second, or third tier?

Ethernet Cable Configuration

Wiring connections for CAT-5 cable are shown in Figure 3.9. The standard Ethernet wiring is as follows:

Pin 1—Orange/White
Pin 2—Orange
Pin 3—Green/White
Pin 4—Blue
Pin 5—Blue/White
Pin 6—Green
Pin 7—Brown/White
Pin 8—Brown

This wiring works with patch cables and direct connections into wiring hubs and switches. These wiring connections use all eight wires or all four pairs in the cable. Four-pair cables are best because all cable pairs will be used as Ethernet transmission speeds increase above 100 Mbps.

It is possible to run Ethernet over cables that have only two pairs or four wires. Such cables do not provide the increased transmission speed capability that is provided by four pairs or eight wire cables.

A crossover cable configuration is illustrated in Figure 3.10. In this cable the transmit and receive pairs are switched. Transmit at one end of the cable connects into receive at the other end of the cable and vice versa. This is accomplished by connecting the orange/white Pin-1 and orange Pin-2 wires on one end into Pin 3 and Pin 6 respectively on the other end, and by connect-

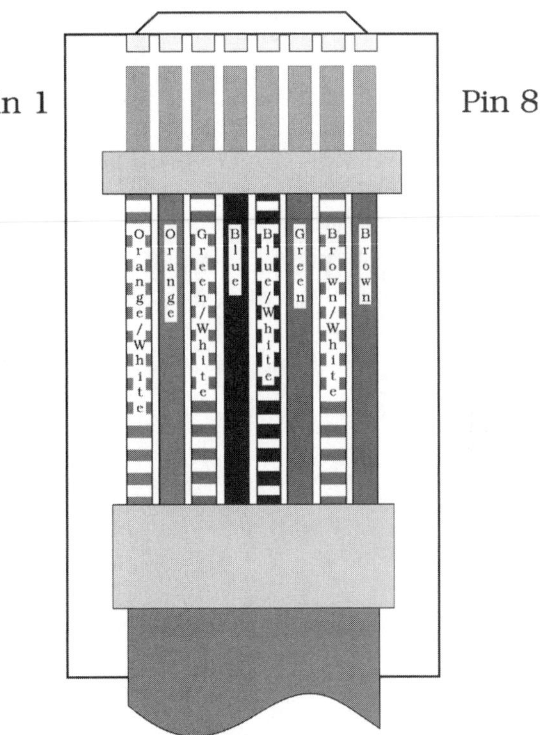

Figure 3.9
RJ-45 connector wiring configuration.

Bottom View of The Connector

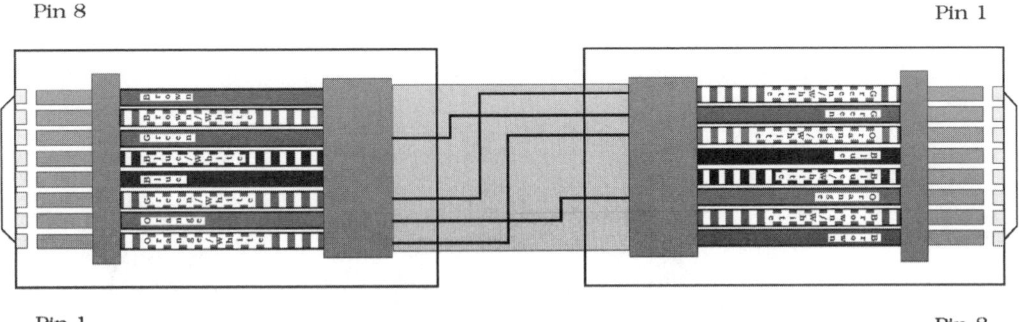

Bottom View of The Connectors

Figure 3.10 Crossover cable configuration.

ing the green/white Pin-3 and the green Pin-6 into Pin 1 and Pin 2, respectively. Such crossing of transmit and receive pairs is performed by crossover ports on switches and hubs.

Crossover cables are used to connect hubs to hubs, hubs to switches, switches to switches, and PC hosts directly to one another without using a hub or a switch.

Brain Teaser: Crossover Cables

Find a crossover cable used in your network or at a store. Place the RJ-45 connectors at each end of the cable next to each other with the tabs facing down. Compare the wiring color codes with the wiring color codes in Figure 3.9.

Do the color codes match? Can you see transmit and receive pairs crossed over?

Building and Testing a Cable

Network cables are relatively easy to build. The key to building a good cable is to make sure the connections between the jack's electrical connectors and the solid copper conductors in the cable are properly mated. Good mating depends upon inserting the wires completely into the jack and applying uniform crimping pressure when mating the jack's electrical connectors to the copper conductors in the cable.

Another consideration in making CAT-5 cables is that the twists in the wire should be maintained as far into the RJ-45 connector as possible. Further, the external PVC cable shield should go into the RJ-45 connector so that the stress relief bar holds it after the connector is crimped. When the stress relief bar holds the external PVC cable shield, it prevents the twisted cable pairs from becoming untwisted.

In Figure 3.11 the connector on the left and center with the blue wire is properly mated while the connector on the right with the gray wire is not well mated. The left-most connector in Figure 3.11 has the cable inserted fully into the RJ-45 jack so that the tips of the cable wires extend fully to the tip of the jack. This ensures that when the jack is crimped the cable wires are properly mated with the jack. Further, the outside insulation is inserted beyond the stress relief bar, ensuring that the wire twists extend into the RJ-45 connector. In the right-most connector in the figure, the outside cable insulation does not extend into the stress relief bar. This means that the cable becomes untwisted outside the RJ-45 connector.

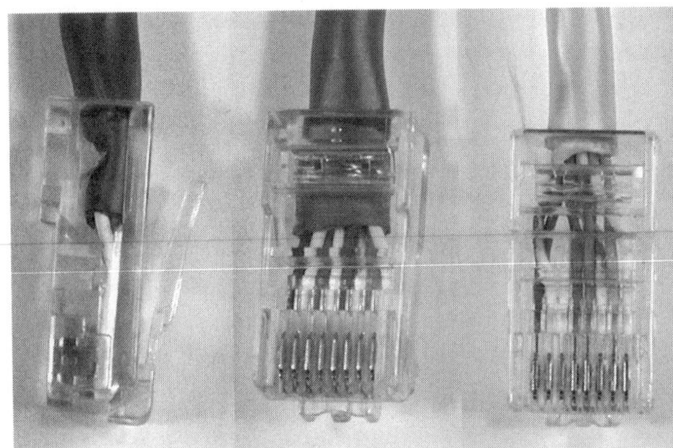

Figure 3.11
RJ-45 jack cable mating.

In manufactured cables this mating process is performed by machines, which ensures consistent and good connections. When making cables it is wisest to use the very best crimping tools to get a consistent mating of the cable wire and the electrical connectors in the RJ-45 jack. Figure 3.12 shows a cable stripper on the left, a modular jack in the center, and a crimping tool on the right.

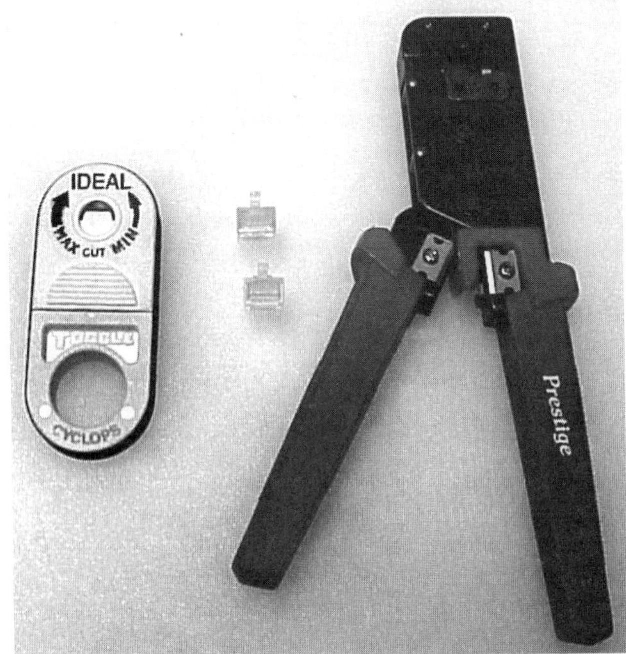

Figure 3.12
Cable stripper, modular jack, and crimping tool.

When making a CAT-5 cable, RJ-45 jacks that are rated CAT-5 must be used for the cable to operate at high speeds. When RJ-45 jacks are not rated CAT-5, the cable is most likely to work improperly and inconsistently. If such a cable is installed in a hub or a switch, the hub or switch lights typically indicate a proper connection, but during data transfer operations there may be excessive collisions indicated. Such excessive collision indications result from data errors caused by the bad cable.

There are two basic types of cable tests. The most fundamental test is a continuity test, which ensures that all pairs are properly connected and that there are no breaks in any wire in the cable. A continuity test can be performed using a voltmeter set to measure resistance. The probes are placed on each individual wire in the RJ-45 connector at each end of the cable to verify electrical continuity. Plugging the cable into a hub and a PC effectively performs a continuity test. When the cable pairs are properly configured and there are no breaks in any wire, the hub light comes on. There are other simple and inexpensive cable testers that perform continuity tests.

Simple continuity tests work for home-office LANs. Larger LANs require more sophisticated cable testing. Figure 3.13 shows special cable test equipment. This equipment has one unit that attaches to one end of the cable being tested and a second unit that attaches to the other or remote end of the cable being tested. The central unit then runs high-frequency signals across each pair of wires that the remote unit returns to the central unit on a different pair of wires. The central unit compares the signal it sent with the signal it received from the remote end to determine the amount of interference between the signals. This interference is referred to as near end cross talk (NEXT). The

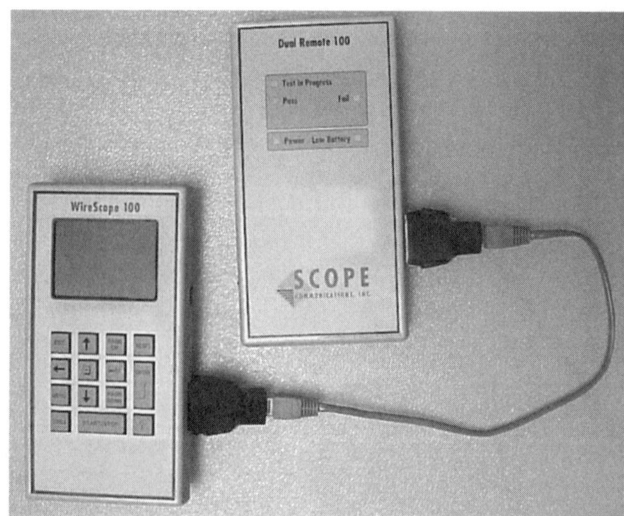

Figure 3.13
Cable test equipment.

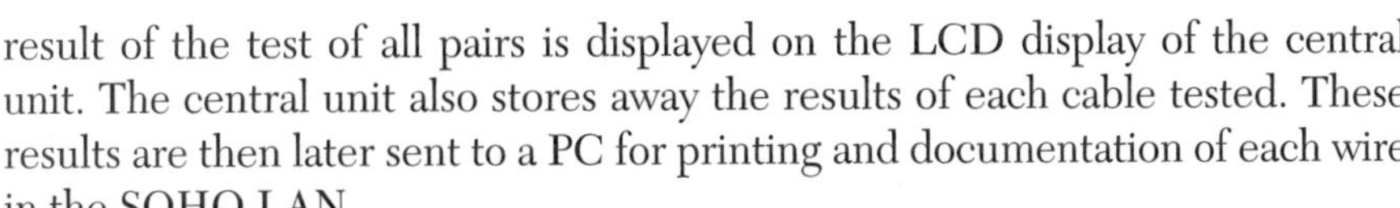

result of the test of all pairs is displayed on the LCD display of the central unit. The central unit also stores away the results of each cable tested. These results are then later sent to a PC for printing and documentation of each wire in the SOHO LAN.

As network transmission speeds increase, the potential for problems from electrical signal interference also increases. This makes sophisticated cable testing very important in larger small-office LANs.

Manufactured Patch Cables

Not all manufactured patch cables are alike. Patch cables are generally CAT-5 cables. Some patch cables are CAT-5e and others are CAT-3. Beyond this, patch cables have other features.

Features

The most obvious patch cable feature is color. Typical colors are gray, blue, red, and green. Crossover cables are generally colored yellow. Manufactured crossover cables are labeled as crossover cables in addition to being colored yellow. See Figure 3.14. It is possible however to find yellow patch cables as well.

An important feature is snagless RJ-45 connectors. This feature prevents the retaining tab on the top of the RJ-45 connector from catching other patch cables as the patch cable is being pulled out of a group of patch cables. When the retaining tab catches another cable it easily breaks off, requiring replacement of the RJ-45 connector. This is illustrated in Figure 3.15. The cable on the left in the figure has its retaining tab almost broken off, and the cable on the right has the retaining tab completely broken off. Breaking the retaining tabs happens often when adjusting cable configurations.

Figure 3.16 shows two types of snagless connectors on the left and a basic RJ-45 connector on the right. The center RJ-45 snagless connector provides the best protection for the retaining tab.

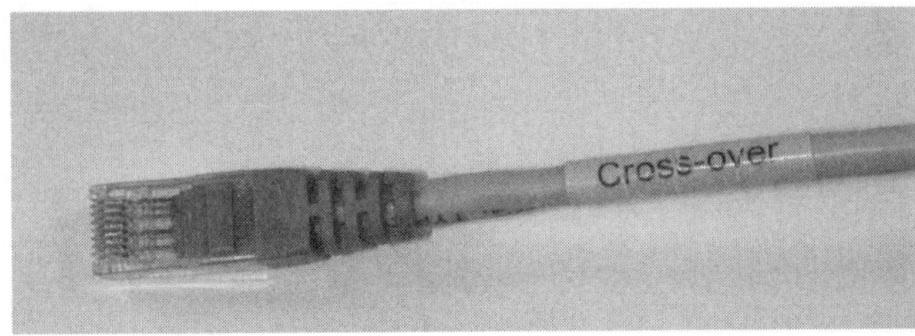

Figure 3.14
Crossover cable.

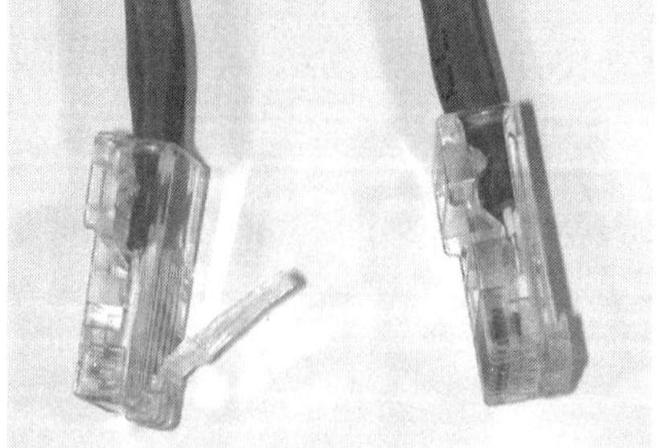

Figure 3.15
RJ-45 connector with damaged retaining tab and broken retaining tab.

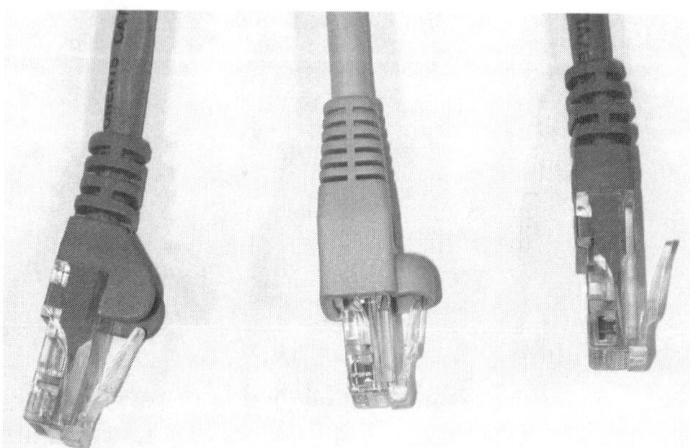

Figure 3.16
Snagless and basic RJ-45 connectors.

Other than category, color, and the snagless RJ-45 connector feature, most patch cables provide equivalent performance and functionality.

Brain Teaser: SOHO LAN Cables

Examine the LAN cable attached to your PC host. Is the cable a manufactured cable? Is the cable a snagless cable?

If the cable is not a manufactured cable, how well is the wire mated to the RJ-45 jack? Does the outside insulation extend into the RJ-45 jack? Is the outside insulation crimped under the stress relief bar of the RJ-45 jack?

Lengths

Patch cables come in many different lengths. Some cables are as short as half a foot while others are 100 feet or longer. Typical patch cable lengths are:

1. Three feet or one meter
2. Six feet or two meters
3. Twelve feet or four meters
4. Twenty-five feet or eight meters
5. Fifty feet or 16 meters

These standard lengths fit most network cabling configurations.

Installing Network Interface Cards

Once the network cabling is installed, we can then install the Network Interface Cards (NICs) in all PC hosts. Many PC hosts already come with built-in NICs. Sometimes the NICs are installed before the cabling is installed. A common practice is to install one NIC in a PC host to test the cabling as the cabling is being installed.

NIC installation is straightforward. A NIC can only be installed one way in a PC host because it does not fit mechanically any other way. The physical NIC installation requires opening the PC, finding an empty slot that matches the NIC bus type, unbolting the rear connector plate, inserting the NIC, and bolting it into the PC host. This process requires five or 10 minutes. For two or three PC hosts the total time to install NICs is not long. In a small-office network with 20 to 100 PC hosts the total time is significant, particularly when the PC hosts are spread throughout a facility.

This first NIC installation step is shown in Figure 3.17. In the figure the side panel has been removed using the screwdriver on the left in the figure. The plate covering the mounting slot has been removed. The mounting slot plate and its bolt are next to the screwdriver on the chassis panel. We have the NIC also lying on the panel ready to install.

The next step is insertion of the NIC into the PC host. Figure 3.18 illustrates this step. To insert the NIC select a compatible bus connector slot. ISA bus connectors are black, while PCI bus connectors are white. The Advanced Graphics Port bus connector used to install the video display card is colored brown. In Figure 3.18 the LAN card is being inserted into a white PCI bus slot. The NIC's bracket slides into a retaining slot at the rear of the PC chassis and the NIC is held in place by a bolt installed at the top of the NIC's metal bracket. The metal bracket is visible in Figure 3.17 on the left-hand side of the NIC.

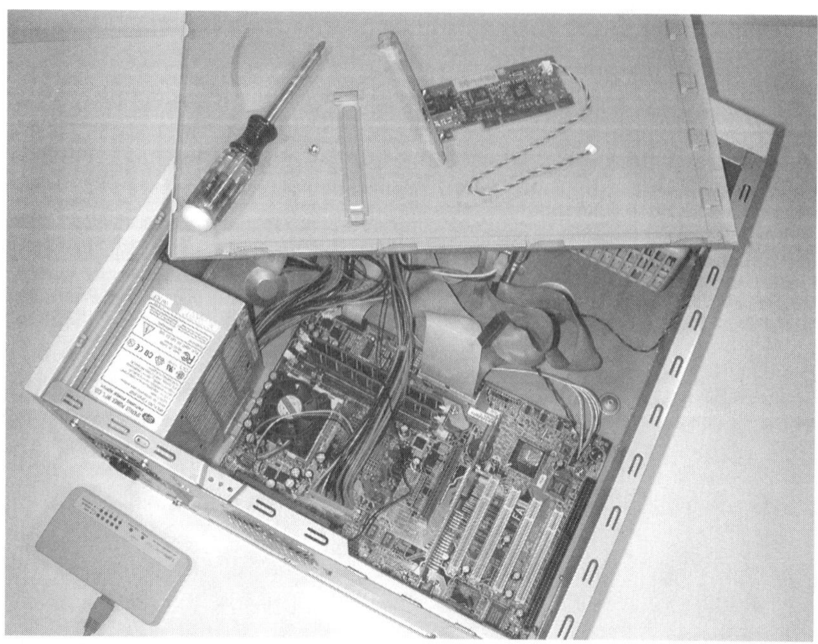

Figure 3.17 PC host with case open.

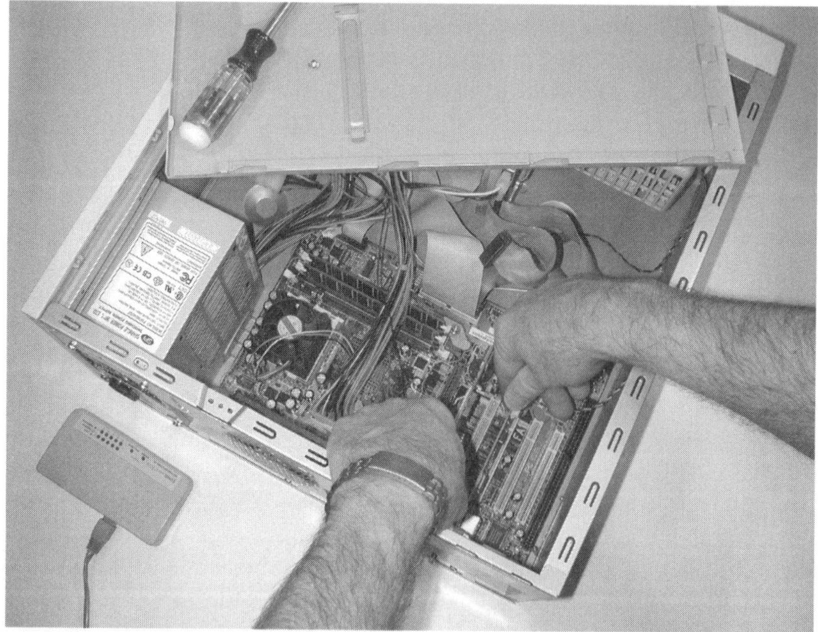

Figure 3.18 PC NIC insertion.

The next step is to connect the wake on LAN (WOL) wire from the NIC to the PC's main logic board (MLB). Most NICs support the WOL feature. WOL is a technology that wakes a PC host from power saving mode to full operating mode when data is sent across the LAN to the PC host. The NIC and the PC host's MLB must both support the WOL feature. The WOL feature was implemented by connecting a physical wire between the NIC and the PC host's MLB. This wire connection permitted the NIC to signal the PC host's MLB whenever it received data for the PC host. In Figure 3.17 our NIC with a WOL connection is shown on the right. The WOL cable runs off the right side of the NIC. Installing the WOL connection is shown in Figure 3.19. To attach the WOL cable, first locate the WOL connector on the MLB. The easiest way to do this is to look in the documentation for its location on the MLB. Otherwise you need to search for a small white connector that has a WOL label painted next to it. Connecting the WOL cable into the wrong connector can possibly damage the MLB or the LAN board, so it is important to locate the correct connector and to plug the WOL cable in properly (Pin 1 connects to Pin 1). The WOL cable connector is keyed to assist with plugging the cable in properly. Once connected, we have installed the NIC into the PC host.

After the WOL LAN cable is attached and the NIC is bolted into place, then the PC host can be closed up and the Ethernet cable attached to its external RJ-45 port. See Figure 3.20. The patch cable RJ-45 connector can

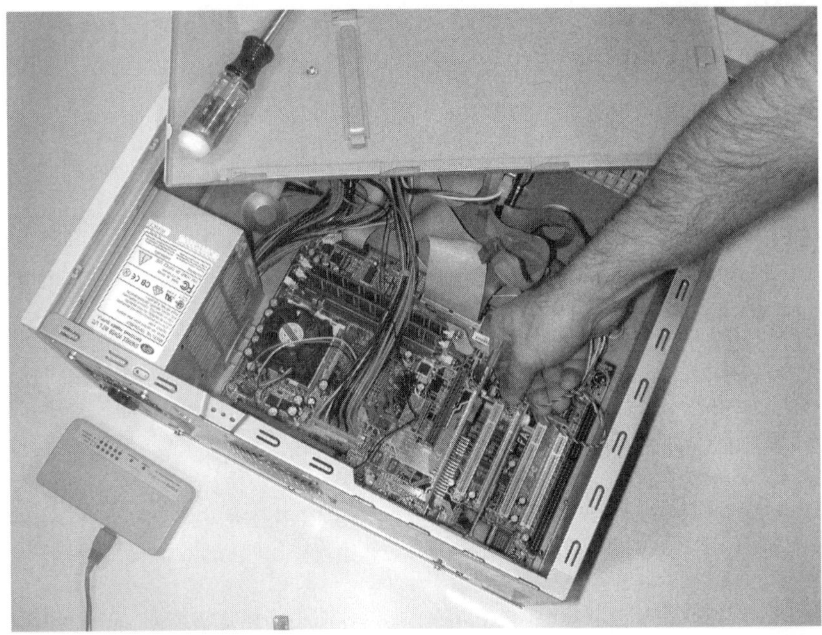

Figure 3.19 Attaching WOL cable to MLB.

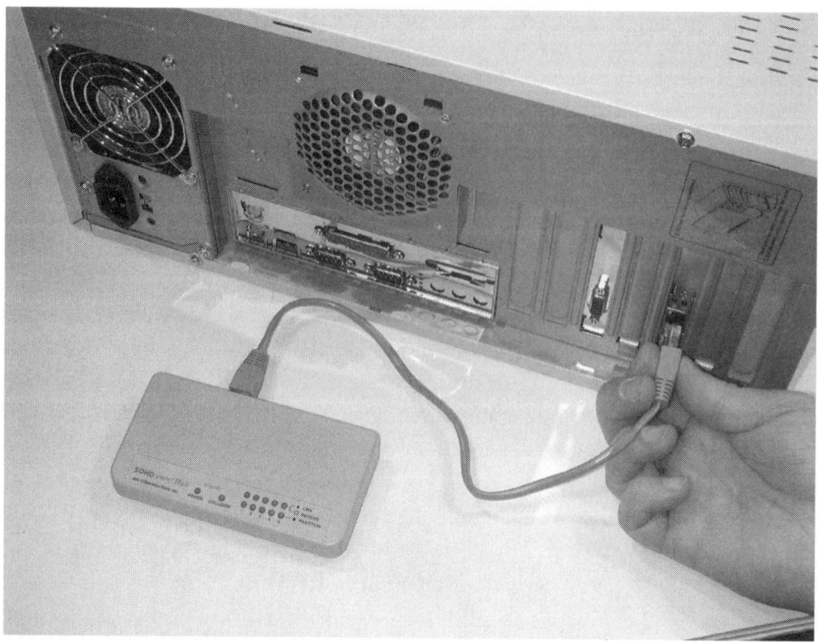

Figure 3.20 Connecting a patch cable to the NIC.

only insert into the RJ-45 jack one way (the correct way) because of the mechanical layout of the connector.

After this final connection is made and the hub and the PC host are powered up, the NIC lights and the hub lights should indicate that the cable and the NIC are functioning properly. Making it a practice to always check the NIC and hub lights can save you a lot of aggravation when there is a bad cable, malfunctioning hub port, or bad NIC.

The final check is to see if the PC host drew blood. It seems that real nerds always cut themselves on the sharp pointy metal soldered pins on PC cards or on some other metal edge in the PC chassis. You cannot be considered a real nerd until you bleed.

Network Interface Card Types

There are several different types of NICs. The PC bus type, the maximum transmission speed, half- or full-duplex operation, and the network protocol used differentiate the types.

NICs use the Peripheral Component Interconnect (PCI) bus, the Industry Standard Architecture (ISA) bus, the PC card bus, or the Universal Serial Bus

(USB) to interface to the PC host. Desktop PC hosts use the PCI or ISA bus NICs. The most popular NIC bus for desktop PC hosts is the PCI bus NIC. Most PCI bus NICs are 32-bit NICs. It is possible to find some 64-bit NICs. The 64-bit NICs are used with 1 Gbps and faster Ethernet. See Figure 3.21.

Both NICs in Figure 3.21 are Fast Ethernet NICs that can operate at 100 Mbps. As I recall they both support full-duplex transmission as well. Newer NICs automatically sense the optimal transmission configuration. They automatically configure the link between themselves and the switch or hub as 10 or 100 Mbps and half- or full-duplex operation. Older NICs sometimes require manual configuration to operate at their full potential over the communication link. If you are not sure what speed and transmission operation is supported, set the NIC for 10 Mbps and half-duplex operation. This should enable it to function with any hub or switch. Configuring the communications link is performed using the NIC driver software in the Windows PC.

Figure 3.21 Ethernet Industry Standard Architecture (ISA) bus (bottom) and Peripheral Component Interconnect (PCI) bus (top) NICs.

A USB NIC is shown in Figure 3.22. The USB NIC is an external PC component. On one end it plugs into the RJ-45 Ethernet cable and the other it plugs into a Type-B USB connector. The Type-A USB connector on the other end of the cable is plugged into the PC hosts USB root hub port. The Type-B USB connector is on the right of the USB cable in the center of Figure 3.22 and the Type-A USB connector is on the left of the cable in the center of the figure. Because USB adjusts itself to the operating speed of the slowest USB device attached to the USB bus, it is best to have only the USB NIC on a single USB root hub port so that it operates at maximum speed (12 Mbps). With a USB NIC it is possible to attach a PC to a LAN without opening the PC.

PC card bus and USB NICs are used for laptop PCs and for wireless connections. PC card bus NICs or Personal Computer Memory Card International Association (PCMCIA) bus NICs may connect directly into the network cabling or may have a pigtail connector that attaches the PC card bus NIC to the network cabling. See Figure 3.23. The card in Figure 3.23 is both a LAN NIC and a WAN modem combined.

Wireless LANs use PC card bus NICs or USB NICs. Desktop PCs require a special adapter that plugs into the PCI bus to use wireless PC card bus NICs. Wireless USB NICs plug directly into desktop PC USB connections. See Figure 3.24.

NICs support a variety of transmission speeds. These speeds vary from 10 Mbps to 10 Gbps. The first Ethernet NICs operated at 10 Mbps. Fast Ethernet NICs operate at 100 Mbps. Fast Ethernet is the most popular SOHO LAN NIC. Some Gbps Ethernet NICs are used to connect servers to the central switching hubs.

NICs can support half- or full-duplex transmission. The 10 Mbps Ethernet NICs operate typically at half duplex. Half-duplex operation is one-way-at-a-time transmission. The NIC is either transmitting data or receiving data. Fast Ethernet 100 Mbps NICs operate in full duplex. In Figure 3.25 the top-left LED indicates full-duplex operation and the bottom-right LED indicates 10/100 Mbps transmission speed. With full-duplex operation the NIC can

Figure 3.22 USB NIC.

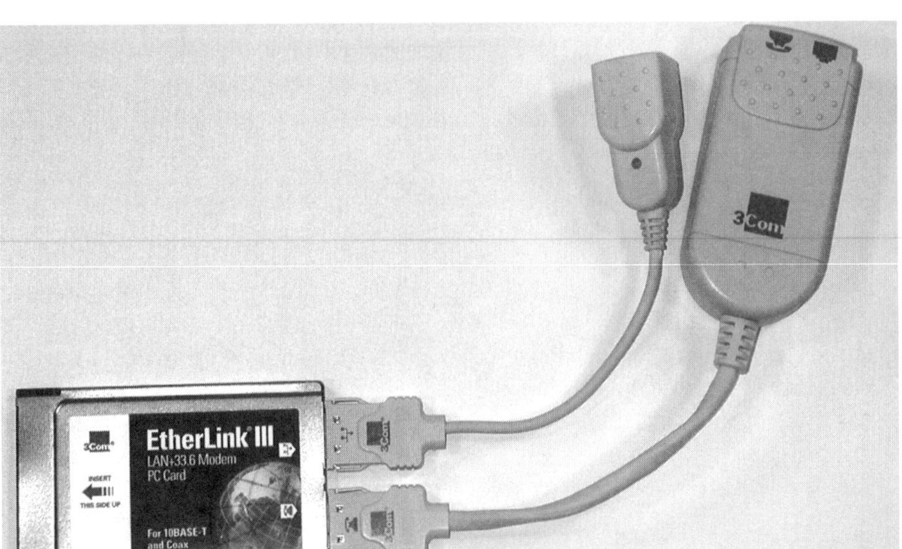

Figure 3.23 PC card bus or PCMCIA bus NIC with pigtail connectors.

Figure 3.24
Wireless NIC.

Figure 3.25
NIC full duplex (top) and 10/100 (bottom) indicator LEDs.

simultaneously send and receive data to a network switch. Depending upon how they connect to the Ethernet switch, Gbps NICs may operate half duplex or full duplex. Although wireless NICs use different frequencies for transmitting and receiving data, their operation is more like half-duplex operation than full-duplex operation.

NICs use different network protocols. Ethernet NICs dominate the marketplace. They use the Carrier Sense Multiple Access with Collision Detection, or CSMA/CD, protocol. This protocol was designed for a bus-type network that supported half-duplex transmission. When two PC hosts transmitted simultaneously, a collision resulted. When CSMA/CD protocol operates in full-duplex channels, collisions are minimized. Because switches provide shared access to transmit pathways into servers, and because their packet buffering capability has limits, collisions can still occur. When several remote PC hosts are transmitting data to a server over a single full-duplex transmit pathway and a switch's data buffering capacity is exceeded, collisions may occur.

Wireless NICs use Carrier Sense Multiple Access with Collision Avoidance, or CSMA/CA, protocol. This protocol is similar to CSMA/CD protocol. With CSMA/CA a transmitting PC host first sends a jam signal, and then it waits a sufficient time for all stations to receive the jam signal before transmitting a data frame. If during data frame transmission the PC host detects a jam signal from another PC host, it ceases transmission and waits a random amount of time before trying to transmit again.

Token Ring NICs use a token passing ring protocol. These NICs may still be found in some small-office LANs. A new protocol, asynchronous transfer mode (ATM), may be found in some small-office LANs. See Figure 3.26. The ATM card shown in the figure operates at 622 Mbps over fiber optic cables.

However, the dominant NIC protocol is Ethernet's CSMA/CD protocol because the Ethernet NICs are so inexpensive.

Figure 3.26 Asynchronous transfer mode (ATM) NIC.

Home-office LANs sometimes employ specially designed NICs that utilize existing telephone or electrical wiring to carry data between PC hosts. While such NICs offer the convenience of plugging into telephone or electrical outlets, they typically operate at lower speeds than Ethernet NICs. NICs using telephone wiring permit the same wiring to be used simultaneously for telephone voice communications and LAN data transfers. This is possible because telephone voice communications are transmitted at lower frequencies than are the LAN data transfers. Similarly, a new transmission technology called Orthogonal Frequency Division Multiplexing (OFDM) and supporting electronic chipsets make it possible to send and receive data reliably using the power outlets in a home. Both of these NICs make wiring a home-office LAN simple at the expense of reduced transmission speed.

Brain Teaser: NICs

Open your PC host to reveal the NIC installed in it. Disconnect the patch cable from the NIC, unbolt the NIC, and remove them from the PC host.

Is the NIC a PCI bus or an ISA bus NIC? Does the NIC support WOL? What LEDs does the NIC have?

Now reinstall the NIC back into your PC host.

NIC Driver Program

A NIC driver program is needed to interface the NIC to the Windows networking software. The driver program works directly with the NIC hardware. It understands the NIC completely. The driver program knows the NIC's I/O port address, its interrupt request (IRQ) level (or number—1 through 15), and the memory address hardware buffers installed on the NIC. Figure 3.27 details the I/O port range, memory buffer address range, and IRQ for a Macronix Ethernet adapter installed in this Windows XP PC host.

Windows XP driver programs know all these details and perform hardware configuration in Windows using the Windows Plug-and-Play standard.

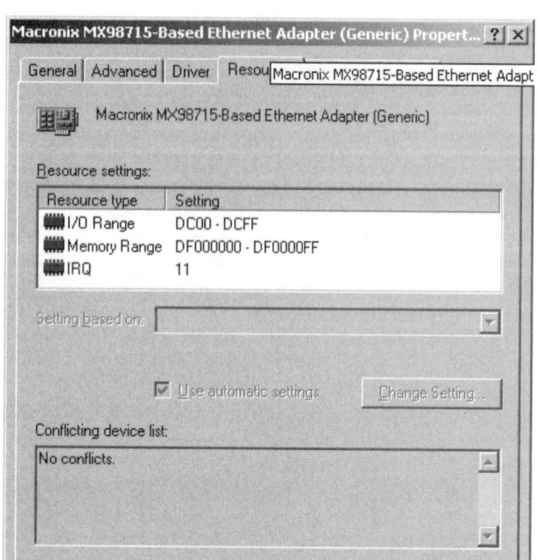

Figure 3.27
NIC control panel properties.

Installing Drivers

Once the PC host is powered up with the new NIC installed, Windows XP displays a New Hardware Found panel. This panel leads to the Wizard that guides you through installing the NIC driver programs. The Wizard steps you along and finally asks where it can find the driver programs for the newly installed NIC. At this point the driver program diskette or CD provided by the NIC manufacturer is inserted into diskette drive A: or the CD-ROM drive, respectively. Windows XP searches the diskette or CD, automatically finds the requisite driver program, and installs it. Sometimes a SETUP.EXE program must be run to install the drivers.

Driver program diskettes or CDs from manufacturers contain Windows XP drivers as well as Windows 9x, Windows 2000, UNIX, and NetWare drivers. Client PC hosts use a wide variety of inexpensive NICs. NIC hardware and software drivers are constantly being changed and upgraded by manufacturers, making it unlikely that Windows XP has the driver software in its installation files for the specific SOHO LAN NIC being installed. Consequently, the driver diskette or CD from the NIC manufacturer is essential to complete driver installation. Once the driver is installed, Windows XP installs the remainder of the network hardware. Opening the Network Connections icon in the Control Panel shows this, as illustrated in Figure 3.28.

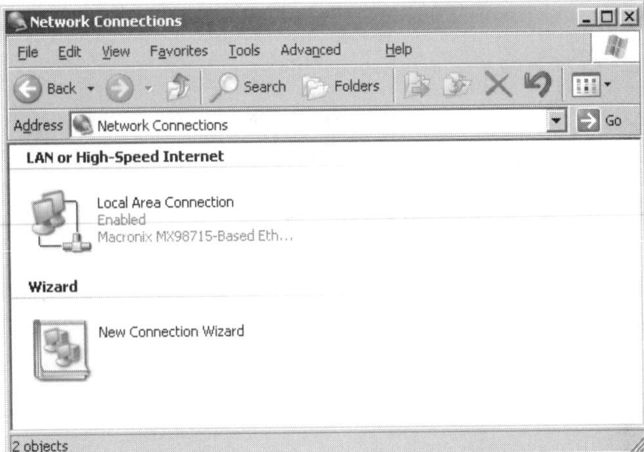

Figure 3.28
Windows XP Network Connections.

In Figure 3.28 the local area network connection is shown as enabled. To finish the NIC installation the Windows XP network software must be configured. This is discussed at the conclusion of this chapter.

Upgrading Drivers

Sometimes the NIC drivers are out of date or they perform poorly, causing Windows errors. In this case the most current upgraded drivers for the NIC should be installed. Sometimes installing new drivers requires that the MLB BIOS be upgraded as well. To upgrade drivers or the MLB BIOS the latest driver programs must be downloaded from the manufacturer's Web site on the Internet. A search engine like iWon.com or the DriversHQ.com Web site can be used to locate the manufacturer Web site for NICs and MLBs. At these sites, look for a technical support menu selection or find the section of the Web site with sales information on the exact NIC with which you are working. This should lead you to where the latest drivers for your NIC can be downloaded.

Making a folder on your C: drive labeled Install and then subfolders under Install for each installed hardware component driver program makes it easy for you to direct Windows XP to any hardware drivers it needs in the event of software reinstallation, driver program corruption, or other Windows XP software reconfiguration problems. The upgraded drivers from the manufacturer's Web site can be directly downloaded into the subfolder for the NIC.

Once downloaded the drivers are expanded by executing the .EXE file they are packaged into or by using the WinZip compressed file expansion program. The expanded files contain an .INF and a .SYS file. The .INF file contains instructions to Windows XP on how to load the driver, and the .SYS file is the driver program itself.

The new driver program can be installed by using the Control Panel, selecting System—Hardware—Device Manager, and then opening Network Adapters. See Figure 3.29.

When Network Adapters is opened Windows XP displays the network hardware installed in the PC host on which you are working. Clicking the left mouse button highlights the network adapter entry, then clicking the right mouse button drops down a menu, permitting selection of Properties. In Windows XP the Properties menu selection is displayed using bold type. Open it by clicking the left mouse button. Windows XP now displays the Properties panel as shown in Figure 3.30.

The driver tab in the middle of the tabs at the top of the panel shown in Figure 3.30 directly installs driver program upgrades for the NIC. There is an Update Driver button that permits pointing to the folder containing the new drivers. The Update Driver button is shown in Figure 3.31.

When Windows XP is pointed to the folder, it finds the .INF file and uses it to upgrade the driver programs. Once upgraded, Windows XP should display new dates for the driver programs.

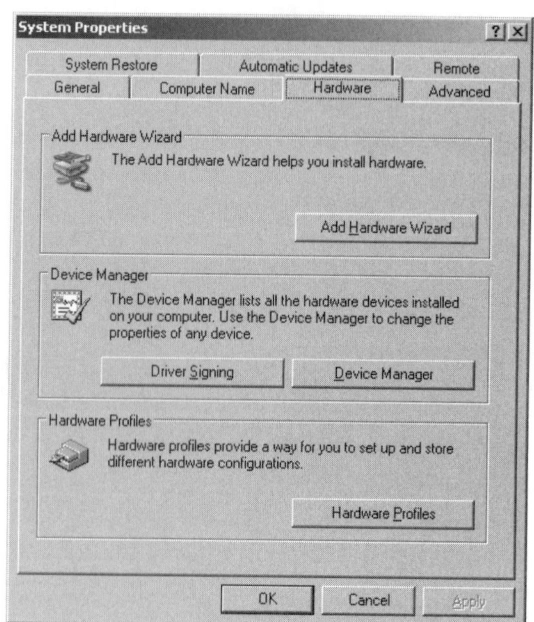

Figure 3.29
System Device Manager selection.

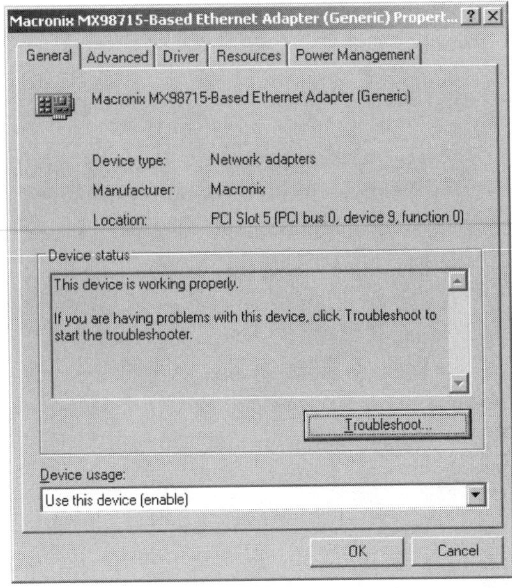

Figure 3.30
NIC properties.

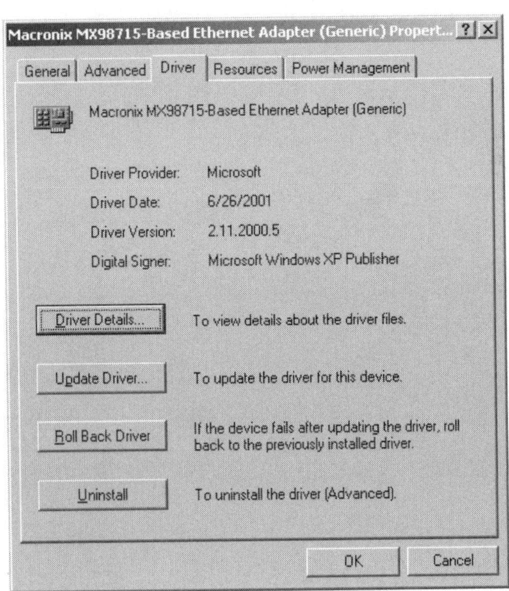

Figure 3.31
NIC panel Driver tab.

Brain Teaser: NIC Controls

On your PC host click on the Start button, select Settings, and open the Control Panel. In the Control Panel, open the System icon, then the Hardware tab, and the Device Manager button. In the list of hardware components shown by the Device Manager, expand the network adapters and select the NIC in your PC host. Double-click to open up the NIC properties panel. Select the Power Management tab.

Is the "Allow this device to bring the computer out of standby" box checked? Is the "Allow the computer to turn off this device to save power" box checked? If these boxes are checked, other PC hosts may have trouble accessing your PC host's disk drives when you have not worked at your computer for a long period of time.

The Advanced tab provides detailed control of the NIC. In this NIC it specifies how the network interface is to operate. See Figure 3.32.

For this particular NIC, the connection types that can be selected using the Advanced tab are shown in Figure 3.32. The Auto Negotiate selection is the default and generally works in most configurations. If the specific LAN link configuration is known and the NIC seems to be misbehaving, setting the NIC operation to that configuration may fix the problems. This was required to make the network operate when I first did the video for the original *A+ Certification Interactive Video Course* for Prentice Hall PTR.

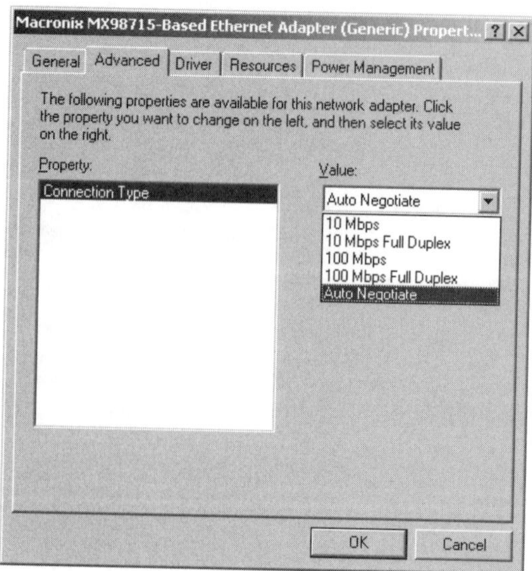

Figure 3.32
NIC panel Advanced tab.

Configuring Windows Software

After the NIC drivers are installed the Windows networking software must be configured for the network to function as expected. This configuration differs for simple two- or three-PC host home-office LANs and for small-office LANs using servers. Some configuration selections are the same for both simple home-office LANs and larger small-office LANs. For example, both would use the ubiquitous TCP/IP protocol, but the configuration for a simple peer-to-peer LAN would use fixed IP addresses while the larger small-office LAN with servers would use DHCP to assign IP addresses automatically to each PC host. As we look at configuring Windows XP network software we contrast the differences between the peer-to-peer software configuration used by home-office LANs and the client/server software configuration used by small-office LANs.

Selecting and Configuring a Protocol

In the Windows networking model we examined in Chapter 2, the lowest layer was the network hardware and cabling. This included the NIC. The next layer was the protocol layer. With Windows generally there are three choices of protocol: TCP/IP, NetBEUI, and Novell's SPX/IPX. Most networks today regardless of size use TCP/IP for the protocol layer. NetBEUI is an old protocol originally used on IBM PC networks. NetBEUI is a simple protocol aimed at small two- to five-station local area networks. NetBEUI is a non-routable protocol so it does not effectively work on LANs that use routers between different network segments. SPX/IPX protocol is used in networks that have Novell servers. SPX/IPX is not restricted to Novell client/server networks. It can be used in peer-to-peer network configurations as well.

TCP/IP is a protocol preferred for most SOHO LANs because it is used in the Internet as well as on most other LANs. TCP/IP is more efficient than Novell's SPX/IPX. The major difficulty with TCP/IP is choosing between using fixed IP addresses or using Dynamic Host Configuration Protocol (DHCP) assigned IP addresses. Home-office peer-to-peer LANs use fixed IP addresses. Fixed IP addresses can be effectively managed in small LANs of two to 10 PC hosts. Managing fixed IP addresses on a large LAN consumes lots of time. Consequently, larger LANs use DHCP to automatically assign PC hosts an IP address for a specific time period from a central pool (scope) of IP addresses. The Windows software configuration discussed here focuses on TCP/IP.

There are several ways to reach the software configuration panels in Windows XP. The approach we use in this book is to open the Control Panel and select the Network Connections icon, as shown in Figure 3.33.

Double clicking on the Network Connections icon opens the Network Connections panel that shows all active network connections and the new connection Wizard. If the NIC is installed properly, is working, and the driver programs were installed, then we'll see an active local area network connection in the Network Connections panel. The local area connection shown in Figure 3.34 is the active network connection. The Network Connections panel and the active local area connection are used to enter the Windows XP network software configuration panels, as we illustrate here. In Figure 3.34 the active network connection has been selected by clicking the left mouse button and then the Properties menu has been displayed by clicking the right mouse button. The Properties menu entry opens up the Windows XP Network Configuration panel.

The Windows Local Area Connection Properties panel is shown in Figure 3.35. At the top of the Local Area Connection Properties panel the LAN NIC is identified. The Configure button jumps us to the NIC Hardware Configuration panel that we examined in the preceding section.

Windows XP software configuration for the Microsoft Networks Client and for the File and Printer Sharing for Microsoft Networks is performed automatically. Consequently, the principal functions performed here are configuring TCP/IP and installing additional protocols or services. For SOHO LANs, we principally configure the TCP/IP protocol. Configuring TCP/IP requires clicking the left mouse button when pointing at TCP/IP and then selecting Properties.

Figure 3.33 Control Panel Network Connections icon.

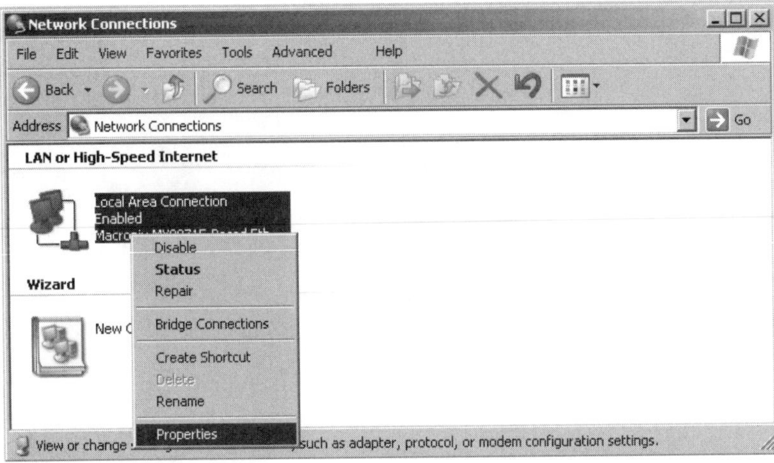

Figure 3.34 Active network connection.

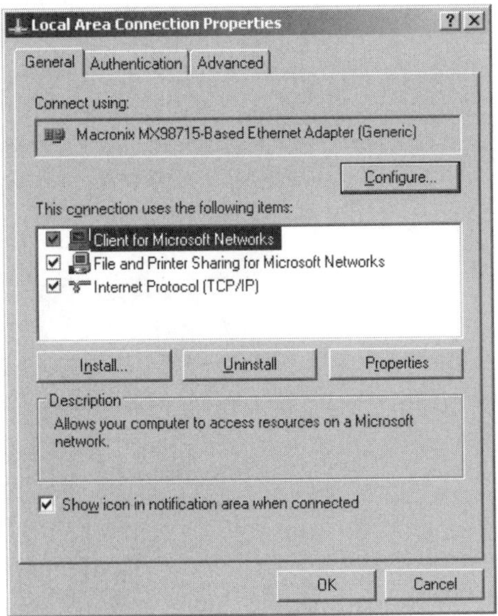

Figure 3.35
Local Area Connection Properties.

This opens the Internet Protocol (TCP/IP) Properties panel that allows us to configure TCP/IP for peer-to-peer or for client/server network operation.

Brain Teaser: Network Connections

Find a Windows 2000 or a Windows XP PC host. Using the Control Panel open the Network Connections icon. Select a local area connection and click on the right mouse button to reveal the local area connection properties.

What services are installed? Is "Client for Microsoft networks" installed? Are file and printer sharing installed? What protocol is being used?

If the protocol used as TCP/IP, select it and click on Properties. How is the IP address set? Is it obtained automatically or is a fixed IP address used? Are DNS servers specified?

Configuring TCP/IP

The Internet Protocol (TCP/IP) Properties panel opens with a General tab as illustrated by Figure 3.36. This panel has a default installation setting of "Obtain an IP addresses automatically." This setting works for Windows client/server networks. In Windows client/server networks that have a DHCP server, this setting is all that is required for most PC hosts. For a peer-to-peer Windows network the setting must be changed to "Use the following IP address." Once this is selected an IP address must be entered into the IP address box. A typical peer-to-peer TCP/IP protocol setup is shown in Figure 3.36.

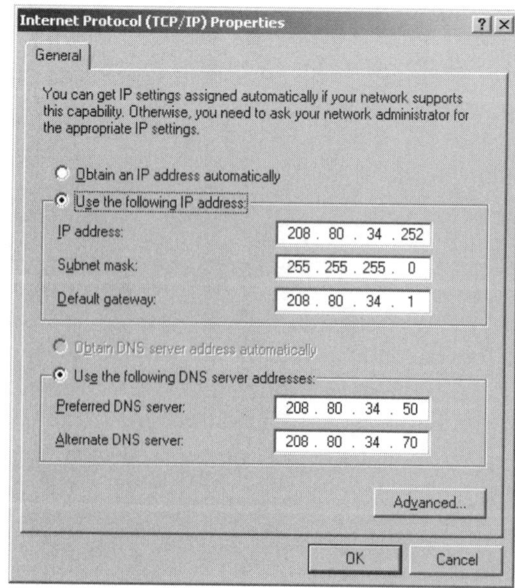

Figure 3.36
Internet Protocol (TCP/IP) Properties.

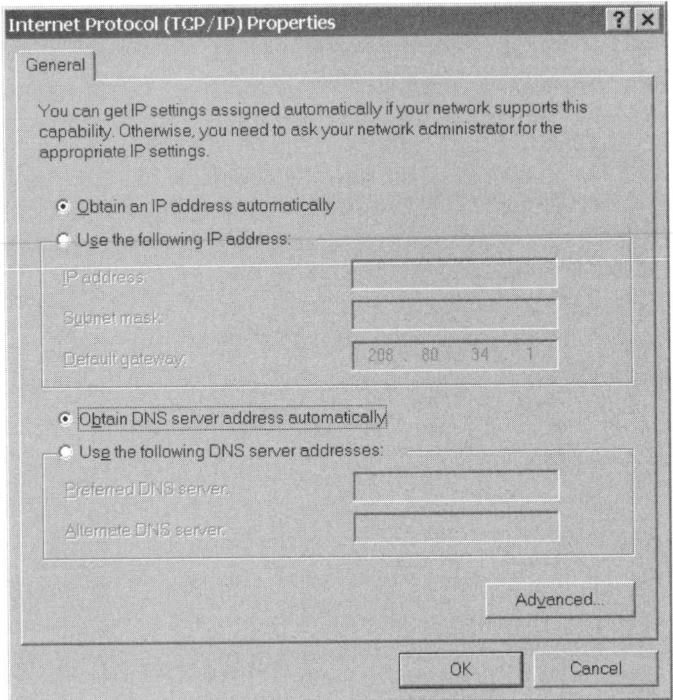

Figure 3.37 Automatic IP address assignment.

In a client/server network IP addresses would be obtained automatically. Figure 3.37 shows the configuration that would be used in client/server networks. When DHCP is used, the IP address is automatically assigned and other network configuration information is sent to the PC host as well. Such information includes the designation of a Domain Name Server (DNS) and a Windows Internet Name Server (WINS).

IP address assignment is critical for proper operation of the TCP/IP protocol. Duplicate IP addresses cause LAN errors. IP addresses that are not in the same network neighborhood or subnet can make it difficult for PC hosts to find one another. A brief explanation of IP addresses helps us understand this.

IP Addresses. An IP address consists of four numbers—each ranging from 0 to 255. Some IP addresses have special functions and cannot be used as fixed IP addresses. For example, some fixed IP addresses to avoid are:

127.0.0.1	The local PC host loopback address
0.0.0.0	An address reserved for the Internet
255.255.255.255	An address reserved for the Internet
nnn.nnn.nnn.0	Designates all local IP networks

There are other IP addresses that are used for special Internet functions such as multicasting, which are not good choices for SOHO LAN IP addresses. Some good address choices are the following:

10.10.10.10
172.16.10.10
192.168.0.10

A three-station, peer-to-peer LAN might use addresses

10.10.10.10
10.10.10.11
10.10.10.12

or addresses

192.168.0.50
192.168.0.51
192.168.0.52

IP addresses are something like postal addresses. A postal address in IP form would look something like this:

Country.State.City.Street
USA.MD.Columbia.7146 Rivers Edge Road

Notice that these postal addresses moved from the largest geographic area on the left to the smallest geographic area on the right, which is the street where my PC host is located. In a peer-to-peer home-office LAN the PC hosts on streets in a city can communicate with other PC hosts on streets in the same city. PC hosts in one city are limited by the subnet mask to communicating only with hosts in that city. The subnet mask 255.255.255.0 imposes that limitation. If the subnet mask were 255.255.0.0, then PC hosts in the same state would be able to communicate with one another. A subnet mask of 255.0.0.0 would permit PC hosts throughout the United States to communicate with each other regardless of the state, city, or street where they were located.

When a network has a high-speed connection to the Internet that uses a gateway, the gateway's address is usually the lowest excluding the "0" address or highest available IP addresses. In Figure 3.36, the gateway address is 208.80.34.1.

For a simple peer-to-peer home-office LAN, assigning a fixed IP address and a subnet mask is all that is required for the TCP/IP protocol to function

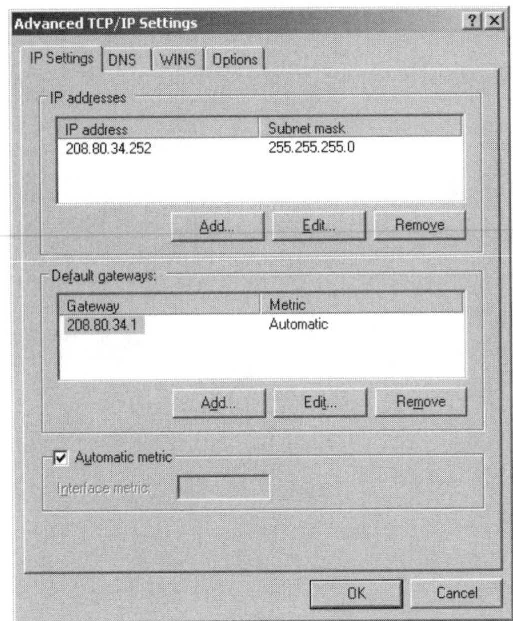

Figure 3.38
Advanced TCP/IP Settings.

properly. Client/server small-office LANs have special servers that perform specific TCP/IP network functions. The DHCP configuration provides information on the special servers to the PC host. When we know the IP address of the special servers we can enter that into the TCP/IP protocol configuration by using the Advanced button. Figure 3.38 shows the first tab displayed when the Advanced button is selected.

This panel displays the configuration settings we have already entered for the TCP/IP protocol.

Domain Name Service (DNS). DNS servers match PC host names to IP addresses. In the Internet, DNS servers match the Internet domain names (e.g., www.phptr.com) and more to their assigned IP addresses. DNS servers are used by the Windows XP Active Directory to translate PC host names into IP addresses on a SOHO LAN.

Clicking on the DNS tab opens the DNS configuration panel shown in Figure 3.39. When we know the network's DNS server IP addresses, we can add them here by clicking on the Add button under "DNS server addresses, and in order of use."

In Figure 3.39 the DNS servers in our network have addresses 208.80.34.50 and 208.80.34.70, with the primary DNS server being 208.80.34.50. It is listed at the top so that our PC host will check it first when trying to match PC host names to IP addresses.

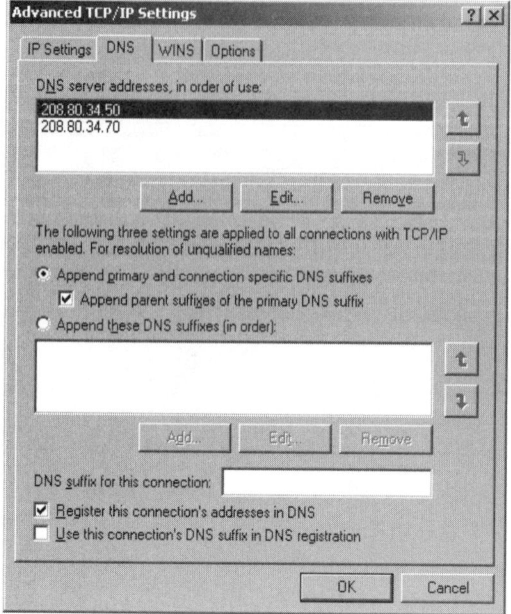

Figure 3.39
TCP/IP DNS setup.

Windows Internet Name Service (WINS). The Windows Internet Name Service (WINS) is a Windows-specific TCP/IP network service that translates NetBIOS names into IP addresses. The WINS service automatically observes the network and builds a database of information to perform this translation process. To use the WINS service a Windows server must have the WINS software installed and activated. To configure our PC host to use WINS, we designate the WINS server IP address using the WINS Setup panel, as shown in Figure 3.40.

WINS's server addresses are added to the TCP/IP configuration by clicking on the Add button in the "WINS addresses, in order of use:" box. Similar to the DNS server designation, our primary WINS server is 208.80.34.50. Because it is listed first in the box, our PC host uses it first to find the IP addresses of other PC hosts in our SOHO LAN.

In our network example the DNS and the WINS server are the same PC host. Because we're using Windows 2000 server, PC host name to IP address translation could be performed by either DNS or WINS. SOHO LANs using Windows NT typically use WINS for PC host name to IP address translation.

LAN Manager Hosts (LMHOSTS). The LMHOSTS is a text file identifying known servers on the SOHO LAN. This is a holdover from the early Windows TCP/IP networking configurations. LM is short for LAN Manager, the name of the early Windows networking software. In most SOHO

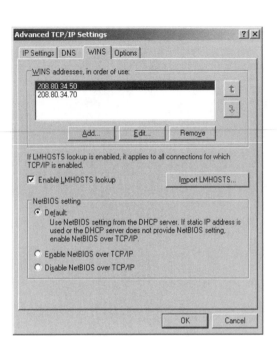

Figure 3.40
TCP/IP WINS Setup.

LANs LMHOSTS lookup is like your appendix, a vestigial organ. It exists but is not used.

Dynamic Host Configuration Protocol (DHCP). Dynamic Host Configuration Protocol (DHCP) is a service that runs on Windows XP/2000/ NT servers. DHCP is used in client/server networks to automatically assign IP addresses to PC hosts. DHCP leases the IP addresses from a pool of IP addresses (referred to as a scope of IP addresses) to a PC host for a specific period of time. The duration of the lease is specified when the DHCP server is set up. DHCP can be used in home-office peer-to-peer LANs. Figure 3.41 shows the setup of a DHCP server in a small-office LAN. The scope identifies the basic network 208.80.34.0. On that basic network an address pool of 10 IP addresses has been set up for dynamic allocation to the PC hosts in the network. This address pool uses the addresses ranging from 208.80.34.230 to 208.80.34.239 because address 208.80.34.240 has been excluded from use.

The red arrow on the server signifies that the scope is not active and leasing addresses are requested by PC hosts on the network. A SOHO LAN only needs one active DHCP server. Multiple DHCP servers can be configured but only one server can be active. A second DHCP server can act as a standby or backup server in the event the primary DHCP server is inoperative. Setting up a backup DHCP server is only required for very large small-office LANs.

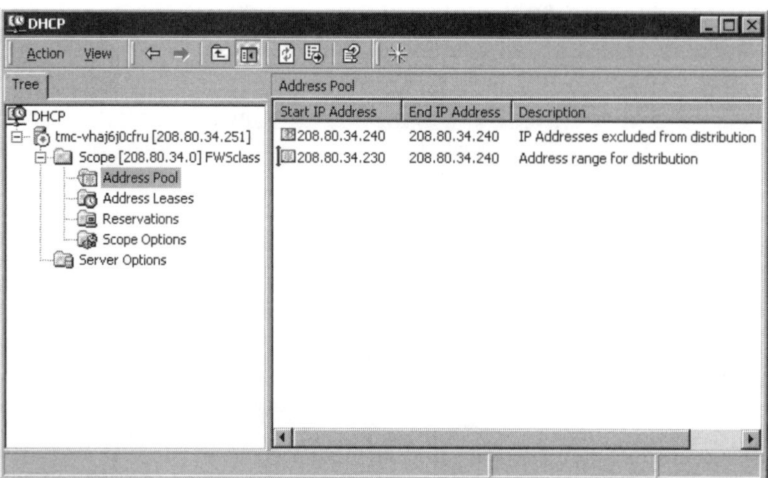

Figure 3.41 DHCP management.

Other TCP/IP Settings. Other TCP/IP settings are used to enhance network security over and above that provided by Windows XP basic user ID and password security. Windows XP supports filtering different TCP/IP packet types, increasing the difficulty of discovering and communicating clandestinely with PC hosts on a SOHO LAN. Figure 3.42 illustrates the other TCP/IP packet filtering settings.

Most SOHO LANs would not use these packet-filtering functions because they can easily be configured incorrectly and consequently create more problems than they solve.

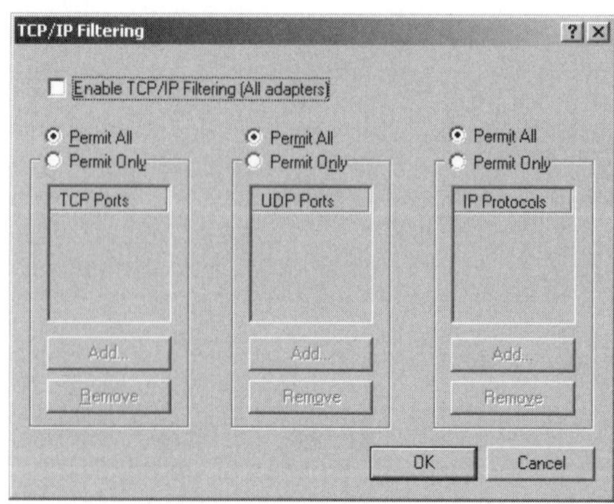

Figure 3.42
Windows XP TCP/IP packet filtering.

Brain Teaser: Configuring TCP/IP

Open a command prompt window on a Windows 2000 or Windows XP PC host by going to the Start button, Programs, Accessories, and then Command Prompt. Enter IPCONFIG /ALL and hit Return. What DNS servers are identified? What DHCP server is identified? What is the default gateway? Are WINS servers identified?

On a Windows 9x host, go to the Start button and select Run. Enter WINIPCFG and select OK. In the panel that appears, click on the arrow to the right of the box containing PPP Adapter to reveal the NIC in this PC host. Select it and click on the More Info button. What DNS servers are identified? What DHCP server is identified? What is the default gateway? Are WINS servers identified?

Configuring NetBEUI

The NetBEUI protocol requires virtually no configuration because it is such a simple protocol, aimed at peer-to-peer home-office LANs. Once NetBEUI is installed it causes the PC host to search the network for other PC hosts. When a PC host is found, the PC hosts negotiate to determine which PC host becomes the browse master. The browse master PC host keeps track of the names of the other PC hosts on the SOHO LAN. When a PC host becomes active on the SOHO LAN, it seeks using NetBEUI protocol the browse master PC host to find other PC hosts active on the SOHO LAN. In this manner NetBEUI protocol configuration is quite automatic and does not deal with the addressing issues that are required to configure TCP/IP. The drawback of this simple configuration is that NetBEUI protocol is not routable and is, consequently, most useful in very simple home-office LAN configurations.

Configuring the PC Host's Network Identification

Once the protocols are configured within the PC, the host's identification on the SOHO LAN needs to be checked. When a PC host is not properly identified on a SOHO LAN, it cannot easily find the other computers on the SOHO LAN. Reviewing and changing the PC host's network identification is performed using the Network Identification menu selection as shown in Figure 3.43.

Selecting Network Identification brings up the System Properties panel shown in Figure 3.44. The Windows XP PC host identified in the System

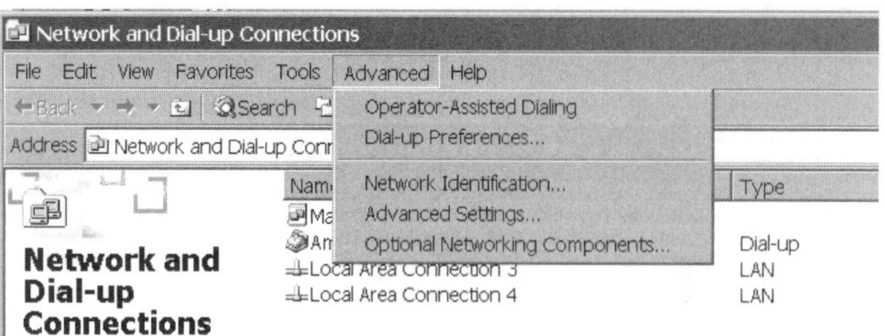

Figure 3.43 Network Identification menu selection.

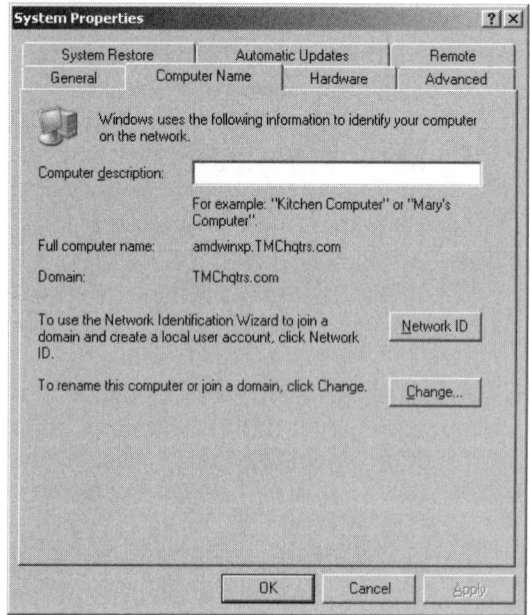

Figure 3.44 System Properties panel.

Properties panel is part of an active directory domain called TMChqtrs.com. The name of the PC host is "amdwinxp." This PC host is configured properly to operate in the domain. When a networking configuration is initially made, the Windows XP default settings are often used. The SOHO LAN can operate with the default settings particularly if it is a very small LAN. Larger small-office LANs can develop conflicts when default Windows XP network identification settings are used. In this case it is best to change the settings to a more logical and descriptive network identification for the PC host. In my case the domain exists at The Moulton Company headquarters. Hence, the name TMChqtrs.com was used to identify the domain. The PC host description was a combination of the CPU chip used in the PC host and the operating system it was running. In a SOHO business LAN a better description may use the operating department and work function to which the PC host is assigned.

Clicking on the Change button opens the Identification Changes panel shown in Figure 3.45. Entering a new computer name in the computer name box changes the PC host name when the PC system is restarted. Client/server networks would have the PC host be a member of a domain. For a home-office LAN the PC host would be a member of a workgroup. The Windows XP default setting for domain name is "domain" and for workgroup name is "workgroup." For small networks these can work just fine. In larger networks these defaults should be changed to avoid conflicts between other PC hosts and network servers.

Changes to the domain and workgroup names require that the PC host be restarted before the changes take effect. After the PC host identification is properly set, the final step in establishing our network is to enable resource sharing. This is illustrated using disk sharing in the next section. Similar procedures are followed to share a PC host's attached printer(s).

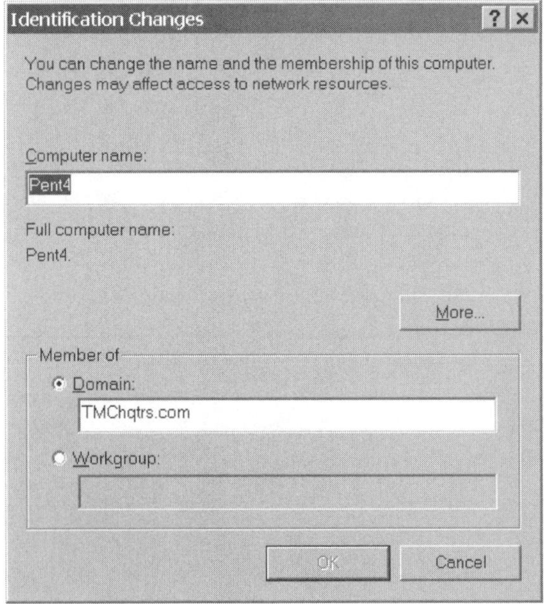

Figure 3.45
Identification Changes panel.

Disk Sharing Configuration

Disk sharing is permitted based upon a user logon with a defined user ID and password. This means that the first step in configuring disk sharing is to define users who are permitted to share the disk drives. For a Windows XP peer-to-peer network the users are defined as local users of the Windows XP PC host. Thus, in a peer-to-peer network a user must be defined on each PC host in the network for him or her to be able to access the PC host's shared resources. This means that if a single user required access to disk drives on five separate PC hosts in a Windows XP peer-to-peer network, that user would need to be defined as a user on each of the five separate PC hosts.

In a client/server Windows XP network the users are defined as network users in the active directory on a Windows XP server. In the client/server network one user definition works on all computers attached to the network.

To define a local PC user on a Windows XP PC host we select My Computer then click the right mouse button and select Manage from the drop-down menu as illustrated in Figure 3.46.

This brings up the Computer Management panel shown in Figure 3.47. For PC hosts in both peer-to-peer and client/server networks, local users and groups can be defined. In Windows XP client/server networks the servers do not support local users and groups. Expanding the Local Users and Groups icon in the Computer Management panel reveals a Users folder and a Groups folder. Clicking on the Users folder we find predefined accounts for administrator and guest. To add users we click on Action in the top menu and then User in the drop-down menu that appears. This permits us to add local users to this PC host. For SOHO LANs the predefined groups need no additions or modifications. For larger networks creating special groups of users with common information interests can be helpful in making a LAN more productive. For home-office and small-office LANs, creating special groups has little benefit.

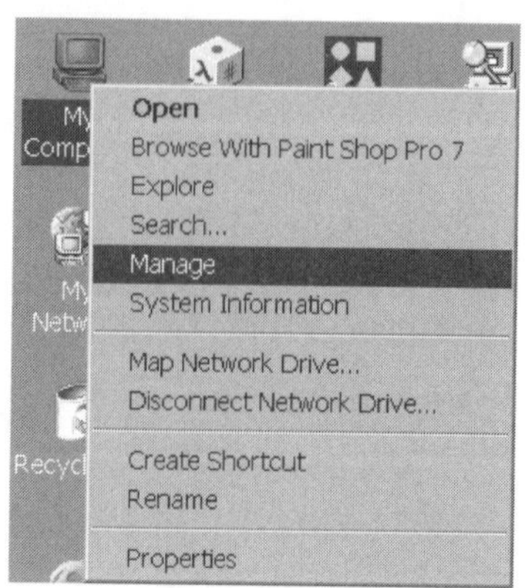

Figure 3.46
Managing users.

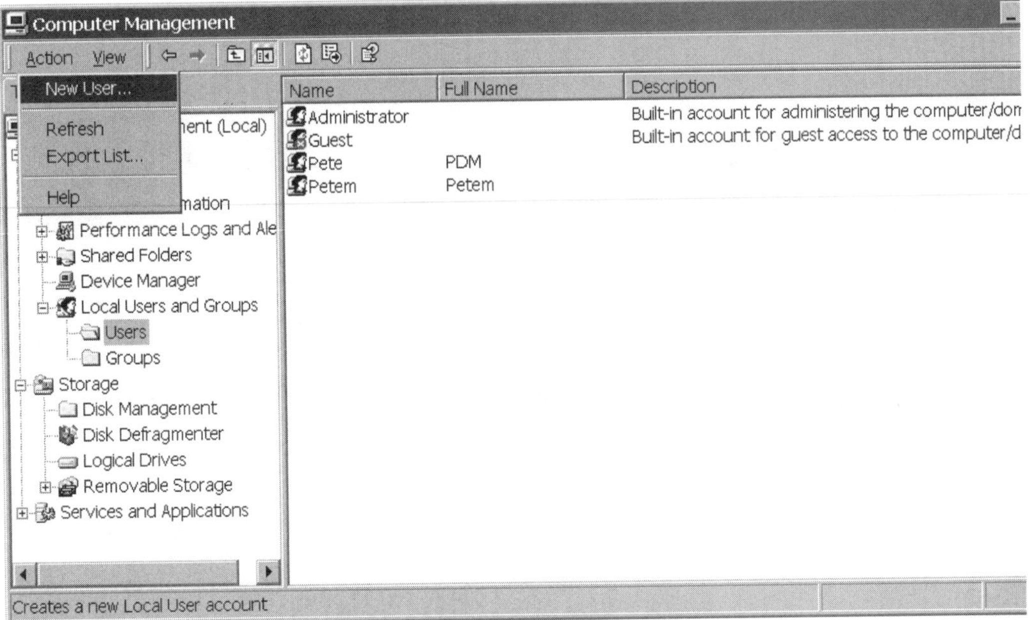

Figure 3.47 Computer Management panel.

After we have defined new users, we would assign them passwords. This is done by selecting each new user with a click of the left mouse button and then clicking the right mouse button to bring up the Set Password and User Properties menu. Once all the users are defined and passwords assigned to each new user, we can then share the PC host's disk drives on the SOHO LAN.

We have now reached the final step in setting up a peer-to-peer SOHO LAN. We now open the My Computer panel, select Disk Drive by clicking on the left mouse button, and click on the right mouse button to reveal the Sharing menu selection. This process is illustrated in Figure 3.48.

This causes the Local Disk Properties menu to pop up with the Sharing tab selected. The default share for the disk drive is displayed. To share the drive a new share must be created. Clicking on New Share allows us to name a new disk share and permit local users and groups as well as network users and groups to access the disk drive. In Figure 3.49 the PC host has shared its drive C: with the share name of DRC. The maximum number of users is permitted to access the drive. For peer-to-peer networks this maximum number is 10 simultaneous users. This is a Windows-imposed limitation as well as a practical performance limitation. If 10 simultaneous users were transferring files from the PC host's shared drive, the PC host would be annoyingly slow. Actually, it would be abysmally slow.

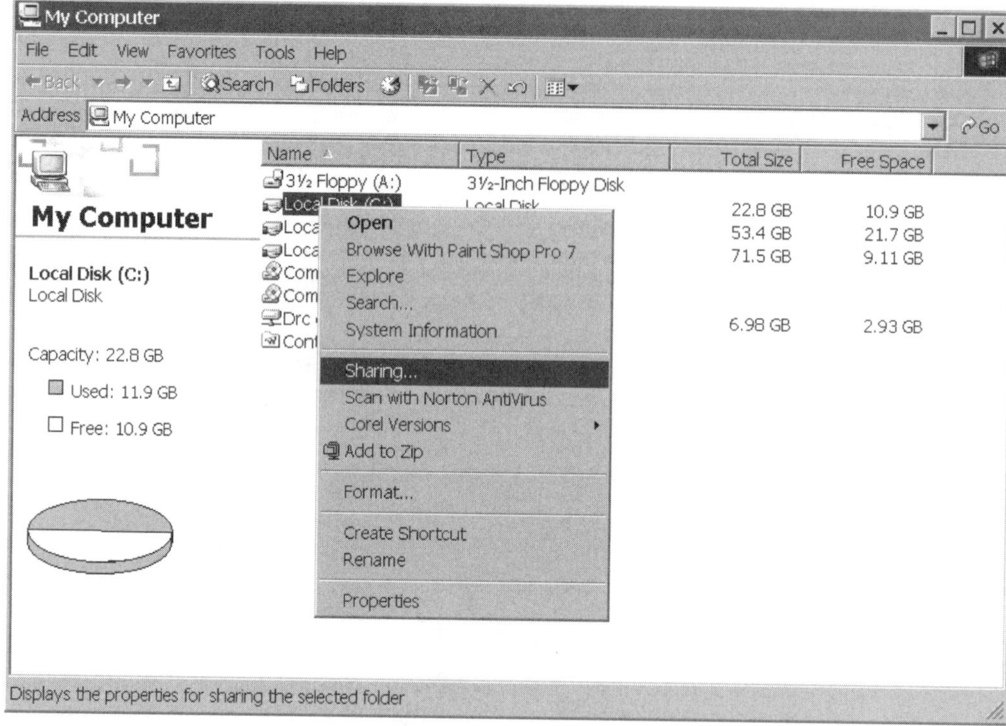

Figure 3.48 My Computer disk sharing.

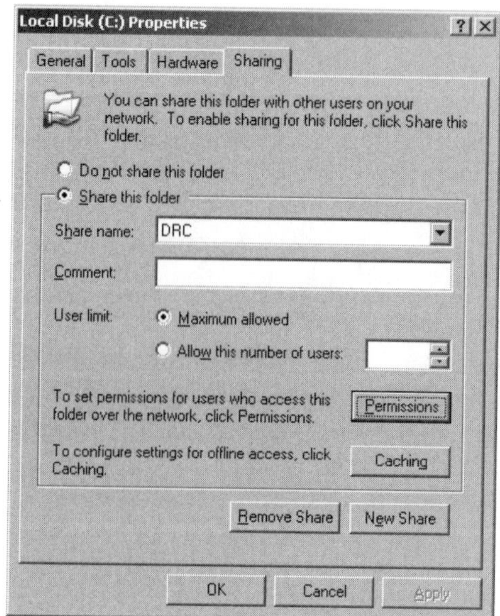

Figure 3.49
DRC share.

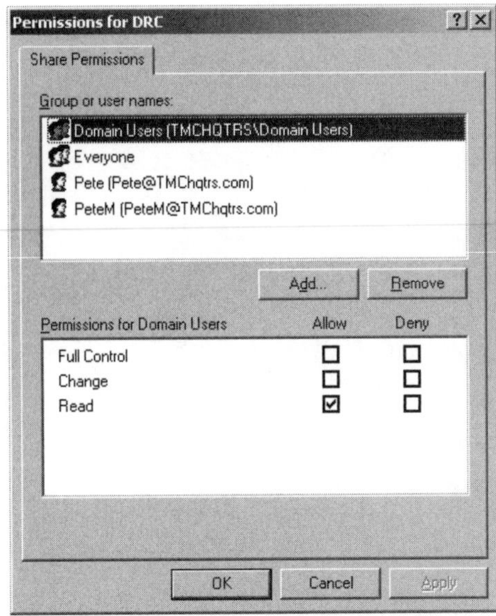

Figure 3.50
Permissions panel.

Clicking on the Permissions button allows us to give users permission to access the drive and designate how they may use the drive. Drive usage may be limited to read only, change, or full control. Read only and full control are self-explanatory permissions. The change permission allows a user to change access to a folder on the disk drive from read only to full control, for example. In Figure 3.50 the top box list the users and groups that have permission to access the shared disk drive on this Windows XP PC host. Highlighting each user or group reveals the permissions they are assigned. When setting permissions, it is best not to deny a particular permission. Permissions denied can easily block users from effectively using the shared disk drive. It is much more effective to just not grant them a particular permission. In our case domain users are only granted the permission to read from the shared disk drive.

The basic disk sharing procedure for any PC host is the same for both peer-to-peer and client/server networks.

Peer-to-Peer Network Disk Sharing

In a peer-to-peer network the disk sharing is permitted for locally defined users and groups. As described earlier, each user must be defined on each peer-to-peer network host PC. In Figure 3.51 the "Look in:" box identifies the local PC host. In the box below appear the users and groups defined on that local PC host.

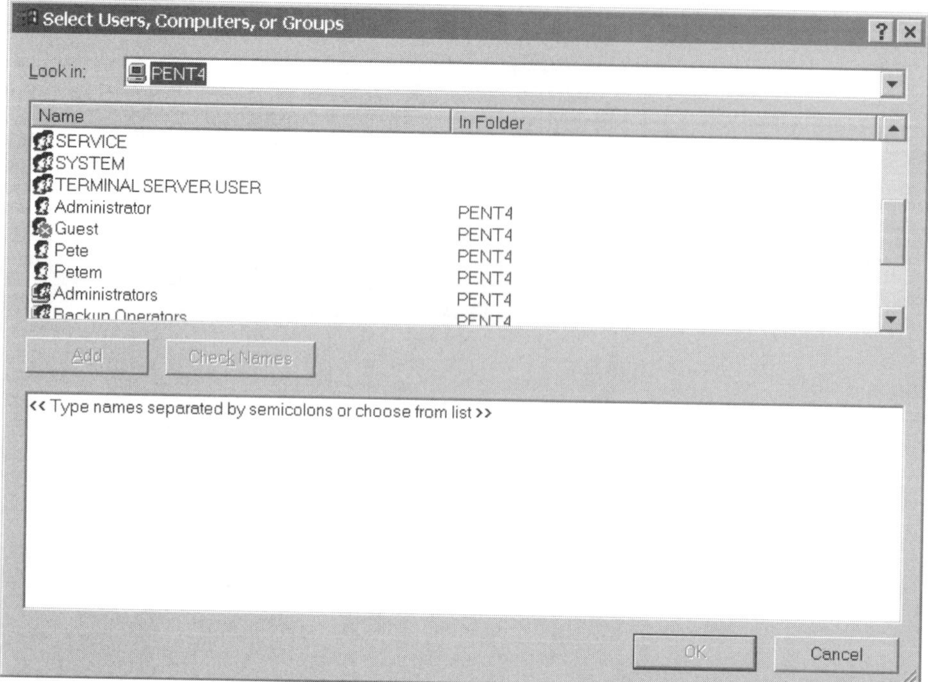

Figure 3.51 Selecting local users.

Selecting from this list of local PC users and groups sets up Windows XP peer-to-peer network disk sharing.

Once users and groups are selected they appear in the bottom box in the Select Users, Computers, or Groups panel.

Client/Server Disk Sharing

Disk sharing in a client/server network is almost the same as disk sharing in a peer-to-peer network. The difference is that when users or groups are selected for sharing a disk drive, they are selected from the active directory maintained by the Windows XP network servers. In Figure 3.52 the domain users are identified as belonging to the TMChqtrs.com domain.

When selecting these users we are setting up a peer-to-peer network using the centralized user management of a Windows XP active directory network. In a client/server network defining user access to share disks on the server is performed similarly. The major difference is that an administrator working at the server sets up the sharing process.

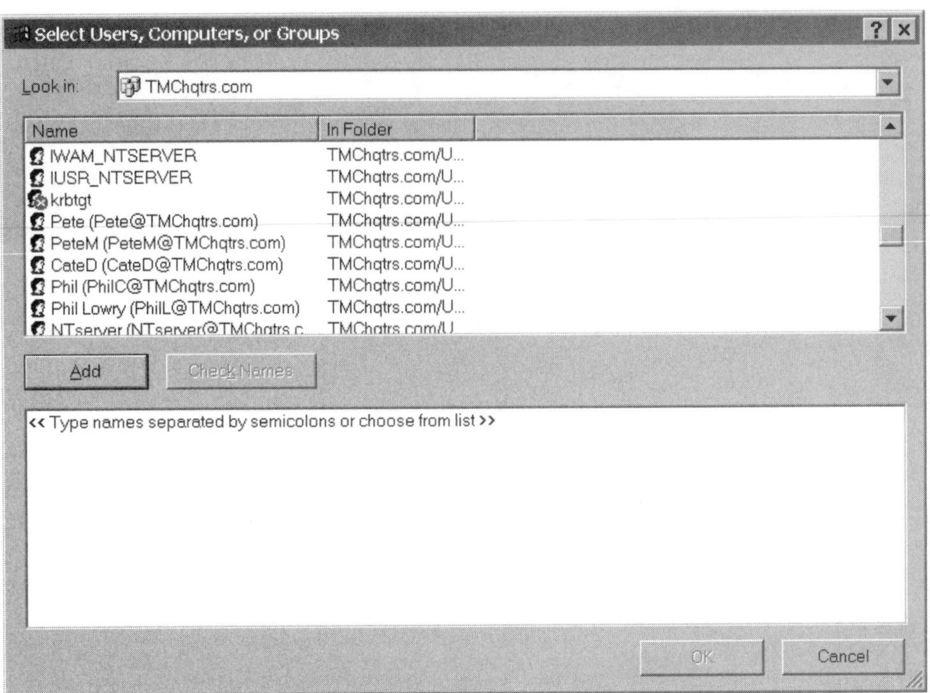

Figure 3.52 Selecting client/server users.

Once we have completed the disk sharing setup, we can verify that resources are shared on our SOHO LAN by using the Windows XP Explorer. Opening the Explorer reveals a My Computer selection and a My Network Places selection in the left panel. Expanding the My Computer selection lists the disk drives that are shared. An icon of the disk drive supported by an open hand designates the shared drives. This hails back to the early days of SOHO LANs and Apple Computer's designating shared resources as a waiter's tray with a hand underneath it holding it up. Figure 3.53 illustrates this. The figure also shows other network computers with shared disk drives. By expanding My Network Places, expanding Microsoft Windows Network, and further expanding the workgroup, domain, and PC host designations, we view the disk drives and printers shared on the network. When a PC host has no shared resources, clicking on it lists nothing. Only PC hosts with shared resources display disk drive icons and printer icons.

We have now completed the setup for peer-to-peer resource sharing among PC hosts attached to simple home-office LANs or attached to more sophisticated small-office client/server LANs. This setup procedure focused on networks with Windows XP/2000. Sharing resources in Windows 9x networks is based upon defining share level or user level access control.

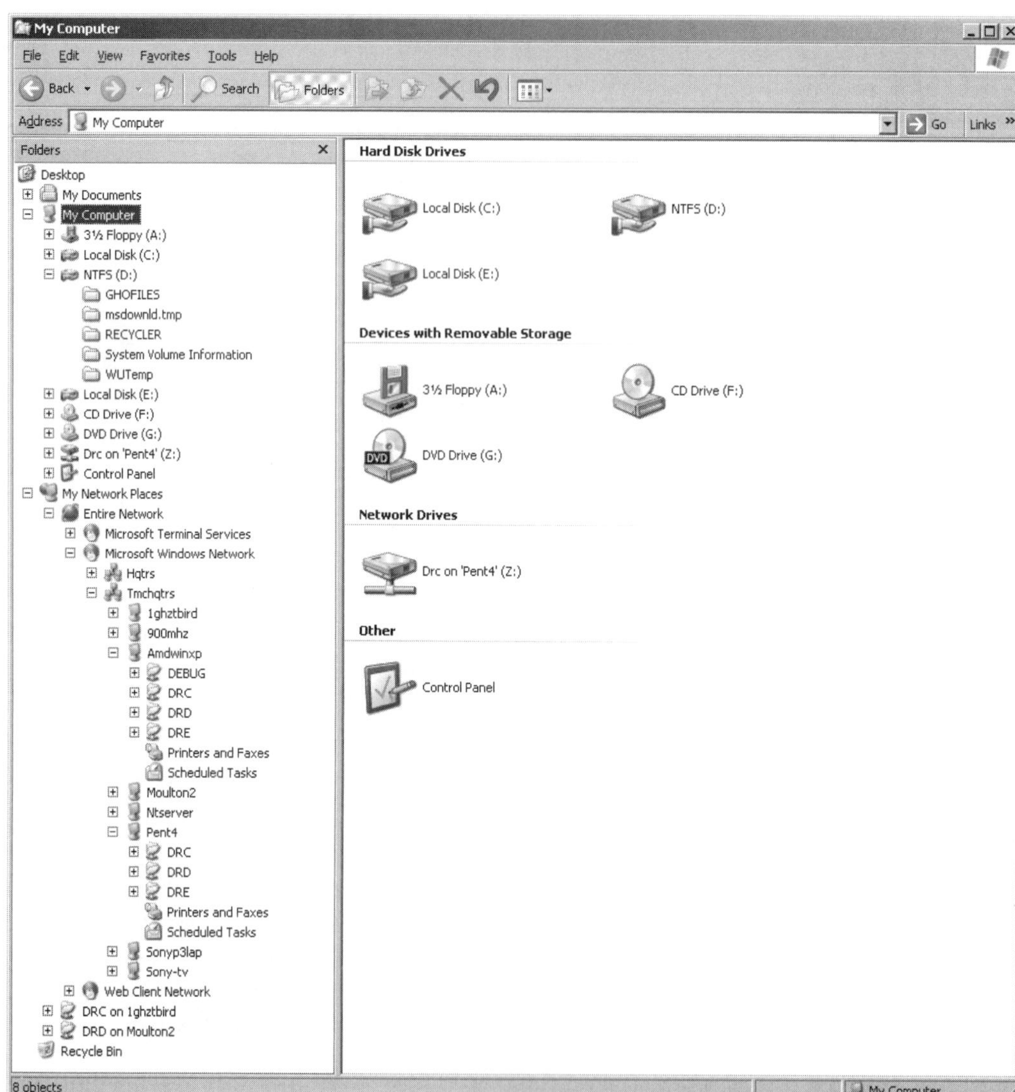

Figure 3.53 Windows XP Explorer's My Computer display.

Windows 9x Share versus User Access Control

Disk sharing security for Windows 9x networks is similar to disk sharing security for Windows XP networks. Disk sharing access control can be defined for each individual PC supporting peer-to-peer disk sharing or it can be defined using client/server domain security authorizations. In Windows 9x networks setting up security on each individual PC host is known as share level access control. When domain server defines security, this is known as user level access control.

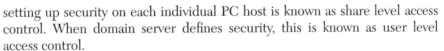

The difference between Windows 9x networks and Windows XP networks is that each PC host in a Windows 9x network defines share level access control by assigning passwords that enable shared disk access to any network user entering those passwords. In a Windows XP network each PC host must have users created for that PC host before those users can be authorized to access the shared resources. Only the users defined for a specific PC host in a Windows XP network can access the shared resources—provided they also enter the correct password authorizing access to those shared resources.

Windows 9x and Windows XP networks are also similar in setting up shared resources in client/server networks. Both Windows 9x and Windows XP networks can specify a domain as the principal security control mechanism. Both support specifying users and groups belonging to the domain with different user level access to the shared PC host resources.

Figure 3.54 shows a Windows 9x shared resource security alternative.

Both share level access control and user level access control set up peer-to-peer networking among PC hosts on a SOHO LAN. The only difference is

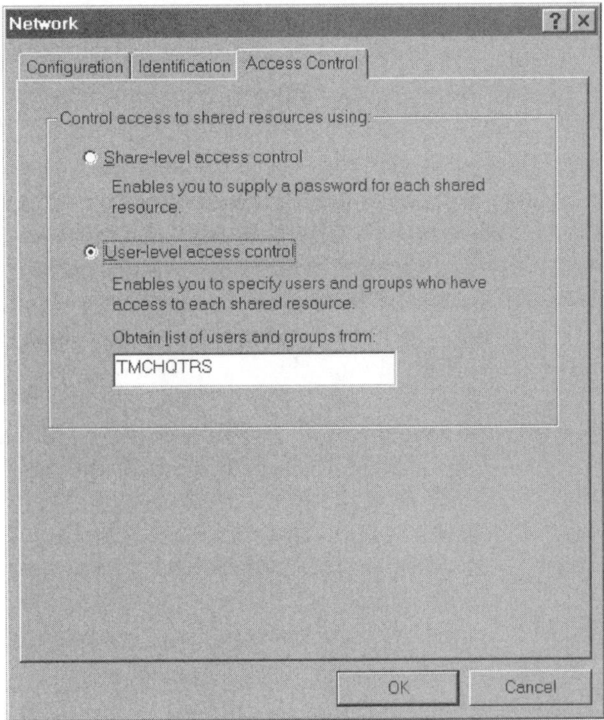

Figure 3.54
Network Access Control.

that user level access control relies on a domain security database to authorize users to access shared resources on remote PC hosts. As with Windows XP, Windows 9x access to shared client/server resources is set up by creating domain users with passwords and defining their level of access authorization to the shared server resources.

Brain Teaser: Disk Sharing

Open the My Computer icon on a Windows 2000 or a Windows XP PC host. Do the disk drive icons indicate that the drives are shared?

Click on a disk drive icon to select it. Click the right mouse button and select Sharing from the drop-down menu. Click on the arrow on the right-hand side of the Shared Name box. Are other shares beyond the default share revealed? The default share has a "$" as the last character.

Click on the New Share button and enter DRC in the box that appears. Click on the Permissions button. What permissions does the group "everyone" have? Add a permission by clicking on the Add button. What does the PC host look in to select the users to which to grant permissions? Is it a domain or is it the local PC host?

Windows 2000

SOHO LAN peer-to-peer network and setup for Windows 2000 networks is nearly identical to the setup for Windows XP networks. The differences between Windows 2000 and Windows XP are largely cosmetic. The underlying protocol setup panels are virtually identical for both Windows 2000 and Windows XP.

Windows XP uses a cleaner desktop that does Windows 2000. The Windows XP Start button reveals a different startup menu that has basically the same elements as Windows 2000, but they are laid out differently. The secret to moving easily between Windows XP and Windows 2000 is to use the Control Panel to access Network Configuration and Security Setup panels.

Client/Server Configuration

To this point we have discussed setting up peer-to-peer networking and networks that operate exclusively as peer-to-peer networks or that function as peer-to-peer networks within the context of a larger client/server network. In the process we have covered and illustrated the setup of a PC host client in a client/server network. This section reviews some of that setup and provides more detail into the server setup in a client/server network.

Windows Server

Windows client/server software is targeted at small-office LANs of 20 or more PC hosts. The Windows Server software uses many of the same software components that the Windows 2000 Professional software uses. The server software has added components that facilitate centralized network management using the Windows Active Directory. The SOHO LAN networking paradigm established by Windows 9x and Windows NT server software is extended and enhanced in the Windows server software. This makes it easy for a Windows NT server administrator to upgrade his or her servers to Windows Server software and administer it with little additional training.

Windows XP/2000 Client Software. PC hosts acting as clients in a Windows XP/2000 client/server network can run Windows 9x, Windows 2000, and Windows XP software. This chapter has already described how to install Windows client software for a Windows XP/2000 client/server network. As our installation process illustrated, the Windows 9x and Windows XP/2000 client software installation is the same for a client/server network as it is for a peer-to-peer network, with some small but important variations.

Server Software. The Windows 2000 Server installation steps are almost the same as the installation steps performed on a Windows XP/2000 network client. The major difference between Windows Server and Windows XP Professional is that the Windows Server performs central network management and user administration. Windows XP Professional has some similar tools for administering local users. These local users are for the specific Windows XP Professional PC host. Windows Server users in contrast are network users who can log on to any PC host attached to the network that is within the domain administered by the Windows server.

Server installation steps are as follows:

1. Install the NIC—This is identical to Windows XP client installation.
2. Load the NIC driver—This also remains the same as the Windows XP client installation.
3. Define users—This differs from Windows XP client installation because now users are defined using domain administration tools.
4. Share disk drives—The sharing of disk drives is the same but they are now shared for network users, not local users. The shared drives should use

the NTFS format, which enables the greatest flexibility in defining user access control (security) to the information stored on the drive.

Once a Windows server is installed in the network, then the bigger job of network administration begins. Network administration not only involves creating users and groups but it also includes setting up special network features such as a DHCP server.

Server Administration. The Windows 2000 server administration is accomplished by using the Windows 2000 administrative tools. These tools or programs are used to perform and manage server administration functions, including the following:

1. Setting up and configuring a DHCP server
2. Initiating and managing a WINS server
3. Administering the active directory
4. Configuring and managing a DNS server
5. Creating, configuring, and managing a distributed file system

Figure 3.55 shows the administrative tools that permit a Windows 2000 server administrator to perform these administrative functions.

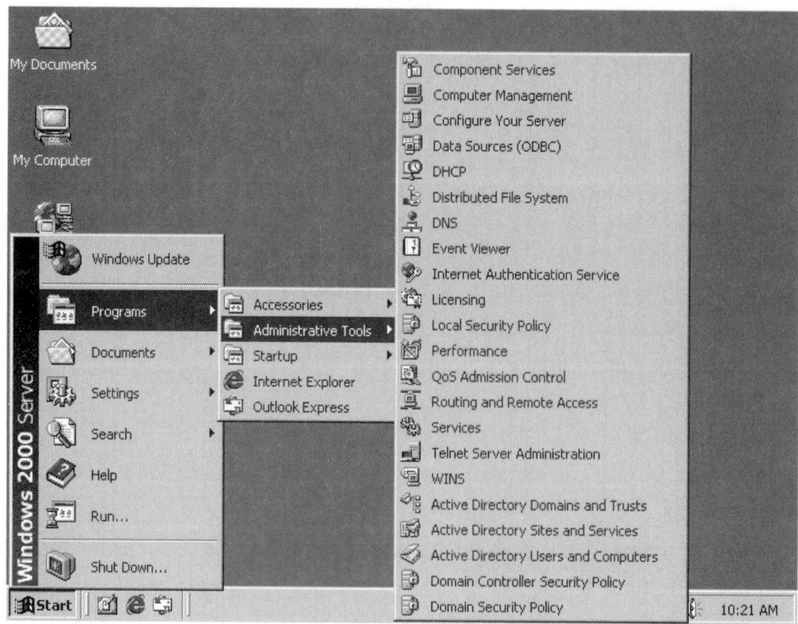

Figure 3.55 Windows 2000 Server administration.

These are not the only server administration functions for a Windows 2000 server. Depending upon the sophistication and size of the SOHO LAN there may be other security-related and application-related administrative functions that must be performed. Other applications supported by a Windows 2000 server are the Remote Access Service (RAS) and the Internet Information Server (IIS).

The RAS service permits remote network users to dial into the RAS server and access network resources as though their PC host was directly connected to the SOHO LAN. Administering the RAS service requires installing the RAS software and defining which network users can dial into the RAS server.

The IIS service sets up an internal intranet. It permits Web pages to be published on the Windows 2000 server. Installing the Windows 2000 Server IIS software is required to set up the IIS service. Microsoft FrontPage can then be used to create and publish Web pages on the Windows 2000/XP IIS server.

NetWare

Novell's NetWare is server software for a client/server SOHO LAN. NetWare originally used SPX/IPX as the network protocol. Now NetWare uses TCP/IP as well as SPX/IPX for the network protocol. In a SOHO LAN NetWare servers work with client PC hosts that run Windows. Both Novell and Microsoft provide Windows client software.

Configuring a Windows PC host client for operation in a NetWare client/server network requires that the Microsoft client for NetWare service be installed as well as the SPX/IPX protocol software.

Because NetWare is client/server software it is used in small-office LANs but not in home-office LANs. Novell's current NetWare focus is to integrate NetWare client/server networks more completely into TCP/IP networks and the Internet. Figure 3.56 shows the Windows XP NWLink SPX IPX/NetBIOS compatible transport protocol installation.

Novell's NetWare client software and Microsoft's client for NetWare integrate into Windows so that Windows client PCs can use the Windows Explorer to manipulate data on Novell NetWare servers. Despite having the dominant market share for networking software throughout most of the 1990s, and perhaps having better performing server software, NetWare continues to lose market share to Windows server software.

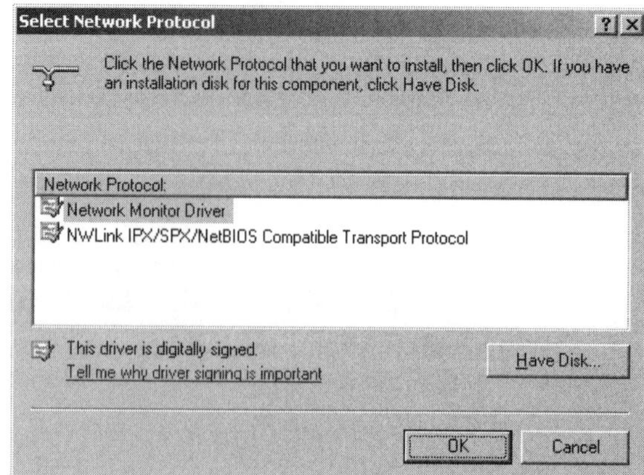

Figure 3.56
SPX/IPX Protocol installation.

Linux

Linux is an operating system that is a variation of the UNIX operating system that runs on Intel-based PC hosts. Both Linux and UNIX are efficient operating systems. They can outperform a Windows server running on a 2 GHz Pentium 4 chip when running an older 200 MHz Pentium chip PC host. Linux and some UNIX versions are open source code software. This means that they are much less costly to license than Microsoft Windows server software. They represent a huge cost savings potential for small-office LANs with more than 50 users. The downside is that Linux or UNIX servers require specially trained administrators as opposed to more readily available administrators for Windows server software.

Similar to NetWare, Linux servers work with Windows clients to form a client/server network. Samba provides full Windows Server Message Block (SMB) support for disk sharing, without any additional software required on the Windows side. As far as the Windows clients are concerned, Linux servers appear to be another Windows server. This completely bypasses the need for NFS software. Samba is readily available for Linux and is included in virtually every Linux distribution.

SOHO LAN PC hosts using Web browsing software can access Linux servers running special Web serving software. Disk sharing is facilitated using Windows File Transfer Protocol (FTP) software. The downside here is that this software does not integrate with the Windows graphical user interface (GUI). The Windows FTP software requires the user to transfer data to and from a Linux server using DOS-like commands.

In some Linux/UNIX installations special software was added to a Windows PC host to fully integrate disk sharing with a Linux/UNIX server into the Win-

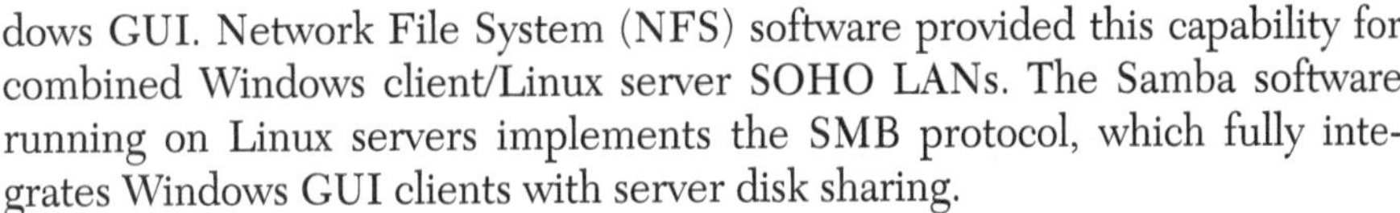

dows GUI. Network File System (NFS) software provided this capability for combined Windows client/Linux server SOHO LANs. The Samba software running on Linux servers implements the SMB protocol, which fully integrates Windows GUI clients with server disk sharing.

Summary

This chapter described installing and configuring SOHO LAN cabling, network interface cards (NICs), and Windows software. The first step was installing LAN cabling, which involved planning the cable installation, installing the cable, testing the cable before and after installation, and documenting the cable installation. The second step was installing the NIC. This was a relatively simple process that involves opening the PC hosts, selecting a PCI bus slot, inserting and bolting down the NIC, closing the PC host, and attaching the NIC to hub and patch cable. The final step that completes the NIC installation is installing the driver programs in Windows XP. To complete our SOHO LAN installation, reconfigure the Windows XP software by selecting and configuring a protocol, verifying an active network connection, naming the PC host on the network, creating local PC host or network users, and finally sharing the PC host's disk drives and printers. Upon completion of these tasks we have an operating home-office or small-office LAN.

Key Technical Terms

ATM—Asynchronous transfer mode. This is a new networking technology that can be used in wide area networks as well as local area networks.

BIOS—Basic input output system. The BIOS is a software code that controls all data transferred to and from the PC host's central processing unit (CPU) or microprocessor chip.

CAT-5e—This designates enhanced CAT-5 cable that can operate at speeds up to 1 Gbps.

Crossover cable—This is a patch cable with transmit and receive pairs switched. Transmit at one end of the cable connects into receive at the other into the cable and vice versa. Crossover cables are used to connect hubs to switches or switches to switches. A crossover cable can also be used to connect one PC host to another PC host bypassing a hub altogether.

CSMA/CA—Carrier Sense Multiple Access/Collision Avoidance. This is the Ethernet-like protocol used in wireless networking.

DHCP—Dynamic Host Configuration Protocol. DHCP assigns IP addresses automatically to each PC host attached to the network when each is first powered on.

DNS—Domain Name Service. DNS servers match PC host names to IP addresses.

Drivers—This refers to driver programs that act as the interface among hardware components in a PC host and the operating system. A driver program retrieves data from a PC component and hands it to the operating system for processing, or vice versa.

FTP—File Transfer Protocol. FTP software transfers data to and from UNIX and Windows servers.

GUI—Graphical user interface. GUI describes the Windows interface that uses icons, a mouse, and other graphical objects on a desktop.

IIS—Internet Information Service. This is Windows XP/2000 software that publishes Web pages on an intranet. The IIS software comes with Windows XP/2000 Professional as well as Windows XP/2000 Server.

I/O—Input/output. This is a designation for receiving external data or sending data to an external source from any computer system.

IP address—This is a TCP/IP address assigned to an individual PC host on a LAN. The address consists of numbers ranging from 0 to 255.

IRQ—Interrupt request. This is the interrupt number or level used by input/output devices in a PC host to gain the attention of the operating system so that data they are transferring can be processed.

ISA—Industry Standard Architecture. The ISA bus is the original PC bus for interfacing expansion cards to the PC MLB.

LCD—Liquid crystal display.

LED—Light-emitting diode. This is a low-power semiconductor lamp that works on direct current (DC) and never burns out.

Linux—This is a popular open source code derivative of the UNIX operating system.

LMHOSTS—LAN Manager HOSTS. LMHOSTS is a text file identifying known servers on a LAN. DHCP performs the functions previously performed by the LMHOSTS file.

MLB—Main logic board. This is the system board, planar board, or motherboard of a PC host. The CPU, the RAM, and all other PC cards connect into the MLB.

NetBEUI—Network BIOS Extended User Interface. This is the original IBM LAN protocol that was used by Microsoft Windows in its early networking software.

NETBIOS—Network Basic Input Output System. This was the DOS interface to the networking software installed in a PC host.

NetWare—This is the general term describing Novell's client/server networking software.

NEXT—Near-end cross talk. This is the electrical interference that causes data errors on LAN cables.

NFS—Network File System. NFS software is added to TCP/IP servers to integrate Windows-based PC host file sharing into the Windows GUI.

OFDM—Orthogonal Frequency Division Multiplexing. This is a special modem encoding technique that permits LAN communications across home electrical wiring.

Patch panel—A wire-terminating LAN hardware component that typically connects cables from remote locations to a panel of fixed RJ-45 connectors that form cross-connections or interconnections using patch cables.

PCI—Peripheral Component Interface. This is the most commonly found bus in PCs for connecting expansion cards to the MLB.

PCMCIA—Personal Computer Memory Card International Association. This is the original designation of the bus used in laptops to connect PC cards into the laptop. This bus is also referred to as the PC CardBus. Of course it's more memorable as the PCMCIA bus.

Punch-down block—A wire-terminating component that secures wire by placing it in a special terminal groove and then pushing it down with a tool designed to shove it into the groove. The process of seating the wire causes the wire insulation to be displaced, making an electrical connection.

PVC—Polyvinyl chloride. PVC is a common compound used in the insulation covering of electrical wire. PVC gives off harmful chemical fumes when it burns.

RJ-45—Recommended jack 45. This connector is used on each end of a patch cable. This is sometimes referred to as a MOD-8 connector. MOD-8 designates an eight-pin modular connector.

SMB—Server Message Block protocol is used by Windows clients and servers to perform disk sharing.

SPX/IPX—Sequenced Packet Exchange/Internet Packet Exchange. SPX/IPX is a protocol used by Novell NetWare. It is generally equivalent to TCP/IP.

SYSTRAY—A Windows feature in the taskbar that displays icons for programs running in the background.

Windows 9x—Windows 9x represents Windows 95, Windows 98, and Windows Me.

WINS—Windows Internet Name Service. WINS is a Windows-specific TCP/IP network service that translates NetBIOS names into IP addresses.

WOL—Wake on LAN. WOL is a NIC feature that wakes a PC host from power saving mode to full operating mode when data is received from the LAN for the PC host.

Review Questions

1. What general steps are required to install a SOHO LAN?

   Answer: A SOHO LAN is installed by cabling the facility, installing NICs in each PC host, installing driver programs, configuring the Windows protocol software, defining users, and sharing PC host resources.

2. A DNS server does what?

   Answer: Domain Name Service (DNS) translates PC host names into IP addresses.

3. What Windows service is similar to DNS?

   Answer: The Windows Internet Name Service (WINS) translates NetBIOS names into IP addresses on a Windows LAN.

4. What SOHO LAN installation task is most often overlooked or left incomplete?

   Answer: Documentation is the task that no one wants to do. However, a SOHO LAN that is not documented will be documented the first time a cabling problem occurs or the network cabling is expanded.

5. What software dominates peer-to-peer LANs?

   Answer: Windows software dominates peer-to-peer LANs. Windows XP will soon replace Windows 9x as the software used on most home-office LANs.

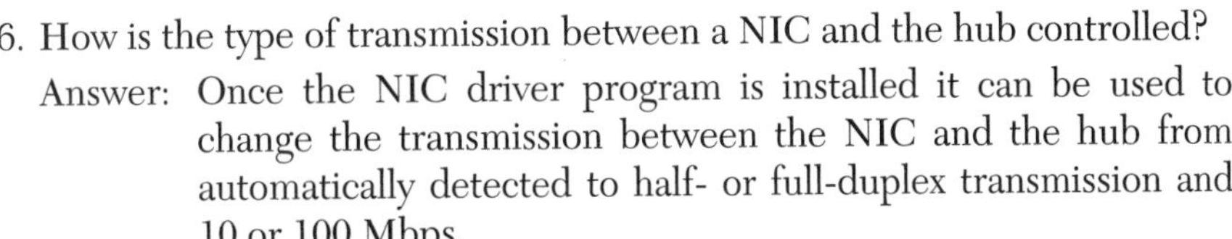

6. How is the type of transmission between a NIC and the hub controlled?

   Answer: Once the NIC driver program is installed it can be used to change the transmission between the NIC and the hub from automatically detected to half- or full-duplex transmission and 10 or 100 Mbps.

Chapter 4

WIRELESS NETWORKING

Chapter Syllabus

- Wireless LAN Technologies and Standards
- Wireless Networking Components
- Installing a Wireless LAN
- Wireless LAN Operation
- Summary
- Key Technical Terms
- Review Questions

This chapter covers installing wireless LAN components. It describes general wireless networking technologies and standards, wireless networking components, configuring a wireless LAN, and integrating a wireless and wired LAN.

SOHO networks use wireless LAN technology because it gets around the problem of wiring a home for the LAN. Wireless LAN technology works in SOHO LAN situations because the current wireless LAN technology can connect PC hosts to wireless LAN access points even when floors and walls separate them. Transmitting through floors and walls reduces the wireless LAN coverage from several hundred feet to less than 100 feet.

Wireless LAN Technologies and Standards

Wireless LAN products conforming to the Institute of Electrical and Electronics Engineers (IEEE) 802.11 standard wireless LAN protocol are sold as PCMCIA (Personal Computer Memory Card International Association) cards or CardBus cards for network laptop computers throughout a facility. The same wireless LAN PCMCIA cards with special PCI to PCMCIA bus adapters are also used to network desktop PC hosts. USB and PCI wireless LAN adapters are also available.

Wireless LAN products conform to IEEE 802.11b or 802.11a specifications. Such wireless LAN products operate at speeds of up to 11 Mbps (802.11b) or up to 54 Mbps (802.11a) and provide network security using data encryption. They work quite well even when signal quality is poor. A new wireless LAN specification is IEEE 802.11g, supporting up to 54 Mbps transmission over short distances. The IEEE 802.11g specification is backward compatible with the IEEE 802.11b specification, allowing 802.11b-equipped computers to operate on an 802.11g network at reduced speed.

Wireless LAN remote clients access a normal LAN through a Wireless LAN Access Point (WAP), as illustrated in Figure 4.1.

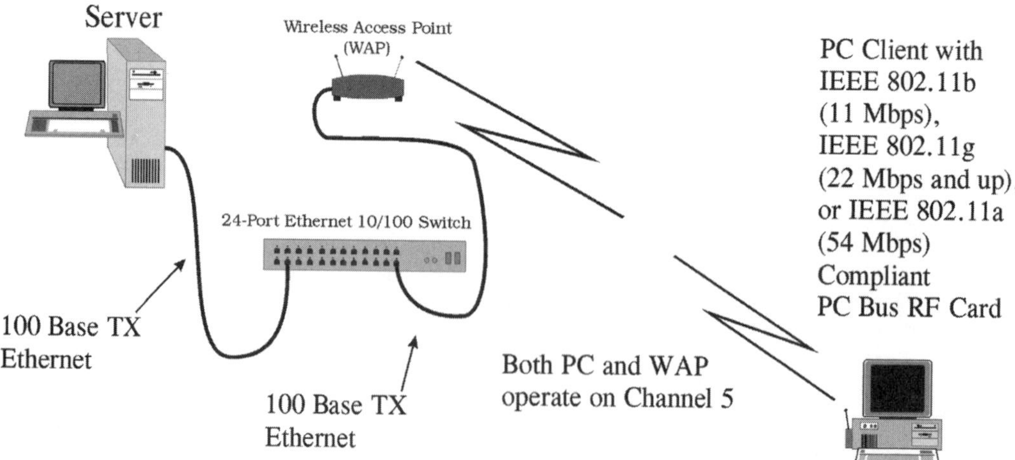

Figure 4.1 Typical wireless LAN configuration.

IEEE Wireless Specifications

Specifications for Wireless Local Area Networks (WLANs) developed by the IEEE are designated as 802.11. There are currently four specifications: 802.11, 802.11a, 802.11b, and 802.11g. All these specifications use the CSMA/CA (Carrier Sense Multiple Access with Collision Avoidance) variation of the Ethernet protocol for radio frequency (RF) media sharing.

802.11b

The 802.11b standard is often referred to as Wi-Fi. It is backward compatible with 802.11. The difference between the 802.11 and 802.11b is in the modulation. In 802.11 phase-shift keying (PSK) was the RF signal modulation technique used. The modulation method selected for 802.11b is known as complementary code keying (CCK). CCK allows higher data speeds and is less susceptible to multi-path propagation interference. There are many inexpensive 802.11b products on the market.

802.11g

The 802.11g standard supports wireless transmission over relatively short distances at up to 54 Mbps. This is faster than the 11 Mbps of the 802.11b standard. Similar to 802.11b, the 802.11g components can operate in the 2.4 GHz RF band and are thus compatible with 802.11b components.

IEEE 802.11g extends the IEEE 802.11 standards with data rates of at least 20 Mbps while remaining compliant with all mandatory portions 802.11b 2.4 GHz band physical layer standard. This is accomplished by using CCK with OFDM (orthogonal frequency division multiplexing) or by using TI's PBCC (packet binary convolutional coding) technologies. Expect to see 802.11g products on the market soon.

802.11a

The 802.11a specification applies to wireless asynchronous transfer mode (ATM) systems and is used in access hubs. The 802.11a-compliant components operate at a RF between 5 GHz and 6 GHz. The modulation technique is orthogonal frequency-division multiplexing (OFDM). OFDM is a sophisticated modulation technique that makes possible data speeds as high as 54 Mbps. Some 802.11a networking equipment supports up to 72 Mbps connections using proprietary compression algorithms packaged with standard

802.11a networking components. A common configuration is eight 54 Mbps channels and two 72 Mbps channels.

Commonly, 802.11a communications operate at 6 Mbps, 12 Mbps, or 24 Mbps speeds. Some 802.11a products are available. More are being offered every year. The main benefit with 802.11a products is that they use the Unlicensed National Information Infrastructure (U-NII) 5 GHz (5.15 to 5.35 GHz) carrier frequencies that don't interfere with many consumer devices. The IEEE 802.11b devices share the 2.4 GHz ISM band with cordless phones, Bluetooth wireless devices, and microwave ovens. These devices can interfere with wireless communications.

Brain Teaser: Wireless LAN Products

Check the Internet to see what wireless LAN products are available. Use the *pricewatch.com* and the *mySimon.com* Web sites to search for IEEE 802.11b, IEEE 802.11a, and IEEE 802.11g products.

What did you find? There should have been lots of IEEE 802.11b products, and some IEEE 802.11a products available. Were you able to find any IEEE 802.11g products?

Spectrum Used

All radio communications share one immutable resource, the electromagnetic spectrum. Two basic pieces of knowledge are needed to put RF communications in perspective. One has to do with the physics of radio communications and the other with the regulation of radio communications. RF telecommunications are governed by the following:

1. The properties of radio frequency transmission
2. Government and international regulation

First let us examine the properties of radio frequency communications. When I was in college and first married, every appliance was a big expenditure. My first wife and I purchased a TV but we lacked the money to buy a TV antenna. Some TVs came with rabbit ears at the time but ours did not. So I proceeded to make an antenna. I went to my general physics textbook and looked up the radio frequency spectrum. Then, I selected the frequency right in the middle of the VHF TV band and divided it out to arrive at the wavelength. It calculated out to be six feet. To make a half wave antenna, I cut three feet of 300-ohm cable (the wide TV cable that is difficult to find anymore), twisted the ends together to get a reasonably precise three-foot length, and soldered them. Next the cable was nailed to a board and in the exact center another 300-ohm cable was tapped into one side to form a "T." This was the antenna. It worked, but not very well.

Good TV antennas, you see, have many elements (the spikes) that run perpendicular to its length. Each spike or element is a very precise length. The length matches the wavelength of a single broadcast TV channel. In that manner the antenna filters the signal received and maximizes it for the broadcast TV channel frequencies. The antenna elements range from about four inches to about three feet in length.

This illustrates that each RF frequency has a wavelength that can be physically measured. There are very long waves (miles in length) that can penetrate the earth and the ocean. They are used to communicate with submarines. As the broadcast radio frequency gets higher and higher, the physical wavelengths get shorter and shorter until they reach the size of a raindrop. At this point, when they travel through the air and it is raining, three things can happen:

1. The radio wave hits the raindrop head on and gets soaked up—it heats the raindrop slightly—being soaked up is bad for us.
2. The radio wave hits the raindrop obliquely and bounces and goes someplace that we do not want it to go—this is also bad for us.
3. The radio wave misses all raindrops and is received correctly by the radio receiver. This is good for us because our message got through.

You can see that rain and water are the enemy of radio communications. Of course, radio waves that are three feet long do not need to worry much about raindrops.

As broadcast radio frequency increases, getting higher and higher, the physical wavelengths get shorter and shorter until they reach the size of a molecule of water in the air. Water molecules are always in the air (it is called humidity) but are mostly invisible to us. Similar to the raindrop example, higher frequency waves are affected by humidity in the air.

What is illustrated here is that the higher the broadcast frequencies the more susceptible to attenuation (absorption) are the radio waves. To overcome this absorption, transmitters and receivers must be closer to one another at the higher frequencies or much more power must be used to burn through the atmosphere. The strength of a radio signal drops quickly as the distance from the broadcast antenna increases. So, high-frequency radio waves need more power or shorter distances between transmitting and receiving devices to get through.

Transmission Frequencies and Characteristics. Microwave communications systems are particularly useful in communicating across difficult natural terrain, in urban areas with signal obstructions (e.g., buildings or bridges), and as a means of continued communications during natural disasters.

A significant advantage is provided by microwave signals' carrying capacity. A single radio channel can carry six thousand voice channels in a bandwidth of 30 MHz. This capability is increasingly important as needs for voice, data, and video communications increase.

Microwave systems typically employ Frequency Modulated Single-Sideband Suppressed Carrier (FM-SSBSC) signal processing. Operation involves generation of an RF signal that is then modulated, amplified, and passed to a transmitting antenna system. The resultant signal travels through free air to a receiving antenna where it is sampled, amplified, and demodulated. In general microwave transmission, characteristics are similar to low frequency radio transmission characteristics except that microwave is considerably more efficient. For example, the wavelength for VHF channel two is about 20 feet. This means that a maximum signal-efficiency receiving antenna would need to be approximately 10 feet long. In contrast, a four-GHz microwave signal has a three-inch wavelength that reduces antenna size and cost.

Line-of-Sight Transmission a Must. Microwave systems must operate over line-of-sight paths. For a signal to pass from transmitter to receiver each antenna system must see the other. This appears restrictive but higher frequency microwave transmissions exhibit similar qualities to light waves; for example, they can be focused. This means for short hauls signal orientation can be manipulated to maintain line of sight by using intermediate antennas or passive reflectors. Over long distances secondary transmission/receiving systems or repeaters maintain the necessary signal levels.

In line-of-sight transmission the path between transmitter and receiver must be clear and unobstructed (e.g., no buildings or hills). This is true of microwave, infrared, and open-air laser transmission. Even when there is a clear, direct transmission path free of obstructions, transmission problems can be caused by rainy weather.

Wireless Frequencies. Wireless communications products operate in the microwave transmission frequency range. These frequencies range from millions of cycles per second (MHz) to billions of cycles per second (GHz). The microwave portion of the electromagnetic spectrum is above about 760 MHz.

To see why dedicated frequency bands are required for wireless data networks, we need to examine the shared transmission bands. Debate on which available frequency band provides optimum transmission for RF networking continues.

Early devices were designed for the extremely crowded 902 to 928 MHz unlicensed Industrial, Scientific, and Medical (ISM) band. Now products have moved up into the other two high-range ISM bands, the 2.4000 to 2.4835 GHz

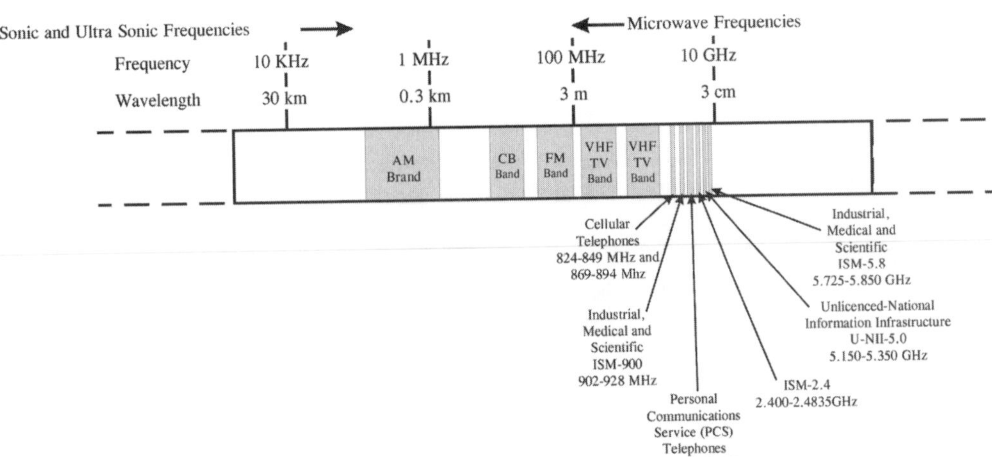

Figure 4.2 RF spectrum assignments.

and the 5.725 to 5.850 GHz bands. Other products use the U-NII 5.15 to 5.35 GHz band. See Figure 4.2.

The ISM bands were originally designated in 1985 for use by factory radio devices. These ISM bands are now used to test cruise missiles, for baby monitors, for cordless phones, for car tracking devices (LoJack), and for wireless networking. That's right, start up your wireless LAN and a cruise missile can now home in on your SOHO LAN.

The ISM bands are the sewer of the radio spectrum because over a period of time, the bands have simply become too crowded. Sharing airwaves in a frequency band wreaks havoc on transmission. To overcome transmission conflicts expensive redundancy and error correction is needed to ensure data integrity in a crowded band. The two higher microwave ISM bands, which are less crowded than the lower 902 MHz band, offer networks less interference. The higher bands have other drawbacks. Higher frequency components cost more. Making components to operate in the 2.4 GHz band it seems is a current upper limit to costs that the market is willing to bear.

Cordless Phones

Cordless phones initially operated in the 900 MHz band as analog devices. Now products are offered in the 2.4 GHz band. A typical product is the Siemens Gigaset and the Panasonic Multi-Handset Cordless Phone System (KX-TG4000B). These are both digital cordless phone systems that operate using frequency hopping digital spread spectrum (FHSS) in the 2.4 GHz ISM band. Cordless FHSS handsets use up to 94 channels for frequency hopping.

These systems typically use a base master unit communicating full duplex with cordless handsets over 2.4GHz FHSS digital RF links for secure, ultra clear conversations. Up to eight cordless handsets can be used to offer full PBX functions without wiring. These phones are installed by hooking up analog phone lines to the base unit and plugging in the AC power for each station. They generally provide a digital voice mail system with mailboxes for each handset so multiple users can retrieve/record messages at the same time. This voice mail with 100-minute capacity and auto attendant is accessed remotely from any cordless handset. These systems often provide call-waiting, Caller ID with a 100-phone number Caller ID memory/dialer, and a 50-phone number directory. Digital full-duplex speakerphone with volume control reduces echo and dropout, providing a more natural-sounding voice. The systems may also provide two-way intercom/paging and three-way conferencing.

The primary difficulty here is that there can be RF interference between these systems and a wireless LAN because they both operate in the same 2.4 GHz ISM frequency band.

Cell Phones

Cell phones operate in several different RF bands. Early North American cell phones operated in the 800 MHz band (824 to 849 MHz uplink and 869 to 894 MHz downlink). Newer PCS digital cell phones operate in a 1.8 GHz (1,710 to 1,785 MHz uplink and 1,805 to 1,880 MHz downlink) and 1.9 GHz (1,850 to 1,910 MHz uplink and 1,930 to 1,990 MHz downlink) frequency bands.

Cell phones can be used to transmit and receive data from personal digital assistants (PDAs) and laptop PCs. However, the cell phone data transmission speeds range from 9,600 to 19,200 Kbps. As a result they are significantly slower than wireless LAN speeds, which range up to 11 and 54 Mbps. Realistically, effective wireless LAN speeds of 6 and 27 Mbps are achieved. This is still much higher than cell phone data transmission speeds.

The important point here is that cellular telephony does not interfere with wireless LANs because they operate in different frequency bands.

Brain Teaser: Wireless and Cellular Phones

Find a cordless phone and a cell phone. If you have neither, go to a local electronics store that sells them. In what frequency ranges do the cordless phone and the cell phone operate?

The operating frequencies should be listed on the box that the cordless phone comes in or on a label attached to the cordless phone base unit. The operating frequency range should be in the unlicensed 900 MHz band for North America.

Cell phone operating frequencies may be more difficult to discover. To determine them precisely you may need to ask your cellular service provider or find specifications for your model of cell phone on the Internet.

Wireless LANs

IEEE 802.11b and IEEE 802.11g operate in the 2.4000 to 2.4835 GHz ISM frequency band. The newer IEEE 802.11a wireless LANs use a higher 5.15 to 5.35 GHz U-NII frequency band that has less potential interference from other wireless devices. RF crowding in the 2.4 GHz ISM band may cause wireless LAN devices to function improperly because of signal interference with other 2.4 GHz devices. The data encoding methodologies employed by wireless LAN products are different from those used by other products, so there is little danger of data being misinterpreted by wireless LAN products.

Bluetooth

Bluetooth is the latest wireless technology. Bluetooth technology enables consumer electronics devices to communicate with each other automatically. The RF transmissions are over very short distances using 2.4 GHz ISM band RF signals. Early devices on the market allow mobile headsets to communicate with phones, permitting hands-free and untethered operation while a caller does other tasks. Soon Bluetooth technology will turn up in business and personal communications devices ranging from desktop and laptop PCs to pagers and PDAs. Automobile manufacturers could install hands-free car kits that work with any Bluetooth-compliant mobile telephone. Because Bluetooth automatically and cordlessly connects a PC and a mobile telephone, the mobile phone could communicate with a PC in a briefcase. Users would be notified of incoming e-mail via the telephone, and they then could read the titles of e-mails on the telephone screen. Eventually Bluetooth devices will be built into cars, refrigerators, and an array of electronic components and home appliances.

Information exchange and synchronization is the initial Bluetooth-enabled product's application. Updating information in personal information manager (PIM) software or business card exchange from a PDA to a PDA, to a cellular phone, or to a business/home PC is very important to many PC users. Money is saved when less time is spent transferring files. This means that a user can spend more time on another project. Eliminating time to interconnect devices makes life more convenient as well as increases time that can be used for other work.

Bluetooth is designed to create personal area networks (PANs) that are always operating and exchanging data in a way that simplifies our lives. Potential applications include cell phones that automatically check schedules on PDAs or laptops to automatically switch into vibrate mode during meetings. Other future applications are cars that recognize your cell phone so they adjust the seats and radio to your personal preferences as you walk toward the car.

Bluetooth communicates via a 2.4 GHz ISM band RF signal for about 10 meters or 30 feet, but distances can increase to 100 meters or 300 feet. The transmission speed is 720,000 bps, or about 72,000 characters per second. This speed is more than adequate for simple text transfers between devices. It may also handle voice and graphics. Slow motion video transmission is also possible. Frequency Hopping Spread Spectrum (FHSS) technology makes the RF signal robust to minimize data loss and encryption provides communications security.

Bluetooth technology is based upon a microchip containing a radio module capable of communicating point to point or from one point to several. Equipped with this chip, a laptop PC could talk to several other handheld devices. Bluetooth developers eventually envision places in commercial establishments where Bluetooth-enabled devices receive signals carrying dining menus, store sale information, games, and the Internet automatically.

Bluetooth was originally pioneered by Ericsson in 1994 and named for a 10th century Danish king who unified Denmark and Norway. Since then many leading communications equipment makers, including Lucent, IBM, Compaq, Motorola, Ericsson, Nokia, and Toshiba are preparing to offer Bluetooth products.

One problem looming on the horizon is that as Bluetooth proliferates, competing radio signals within the various devices are causing signal interference. Because Bluetooth devices are designed to hop through frequencies at a faster rate than 802.11 devices, it is likely that Bluetooth devices will jam wireless LANs as opposed to wireless LANs jamming Bluetooth. Since Bluetooth devices hop through frequencies 600 times faster than 802.11 wireless LAN devices, a Bluetooth device could interfere with a 802.11 transmission many times before the 802.11 device would hop to the next frequency. Such a torrent of RF signals from Bluetooth devices could seriously degrade the performance of an 802.11 wireless LAN.

Regulations and Licensing

Because microwave communications channels broadcast RF signals at high power levels, the Federal Communications Commission (FCC) must license them.

Brain Teaser: Bluetooth

Go to the *hellodirect.com* Web site and check for Bluetooth devices. The easiest way to locate them is to search for Bluetooth.

Did you find any products offered?

Go to the *pricewatch.com* Web site and search for Bluetooth devices. Could you find any? It looks like there are several Bluetooth PC cards, Bluetooth-equipped laptops, and Bluetooth printers currently available.

In the United States, the FCC regulates radio frequencies. The FCC divides up the frequencies into bands and specifies how the frequency bands must be used. The AM (amplitude modulation) and FM (frequency modulation) bands are used to broadcast music, news, and public information. Use of the radio frequencies is regulated through licensing. Originally licensing was to ensure no broadcasting conflicts between stations. A license gives the owner the right to use the frequencies as specified under license guidelines.

Other bands are left open or unlicensed. In this case the federal government does not sell a license for the band, but rather specifies how equipment must operate. This specification covers the frequencies used, the transmit power, and so on. Manufacturers then build RF communications equipment that anyone may purchase to use in these unlicensed bands.

Citizens Band radio is an example of an unlicensed frequency band. There is also an Industrial, Scientific, and Medical (ISM) band that is unlicensed and used for many different commercial applications including wireless LANs and Bluetooth devices, as we just discussed. The unlicensed ISM bands are 900 MHz (902–928 MHz), 2.4 GHz (2,400–2,483.5 MHz), and 5.8 GHz (5,725–5,850 MHz) frequency ranges. The Unlicensed National Information Infrastructure 5.0 GHz (5,150–5,350 MHz) band is also used for IEEE 802.11a wireless LANs. The FCC dictates the use of either FHSS or DSSS technology in the unlicensed 2.4 GHz ISM band. Other more efficient technologies including CCK, OFDM, and PBCC are being deployed in different wireless LAN products.

Coverage and Penetration

The area of coverage for wireless LAN products depends upon whether they are installed within a facility or outside a facility. Within a facility or in an office environment IEEE 802.11b products can communicate from 100 to 300 feet. The 11 Mbps speed operation covers a 100-foot area from the wireless access point. At a lower 1 Mbps speed the office environment coverage can increase to 300 feet. Outside a facility in a more open environment the area of coverage varies from 400 to 1,500 feet. Similar to the closed environment, the 400-foot coverage area is for the higher 11 Mbps speed and the 1,500-foot coverage area is for the lower 1 Mbps speed outside a facility.

Coverage would also vary depending upon antenna placement. The WAP antenna should be mounted as high as possible within the facility. In this manner transmission from a high point to multiple low points would provide better coverage. In my case the WAP antenna is mounted in the basement. It works with devices throughout the house, but these are all less than 100 feet from the WAP.

When a wireless LAN must penetrate walls, floors, and ceilings, its coverage is also a diminished. Multiple wireless LAN access points can be installed to provide seamless roaming throughout a facility and around a campus area with multiple buildings. The access points would be connected to an Ethernet-wired backbone. For multiple WAPs to function properly they must be specifically designed to function in a multiple wireless access point environment. Not every wireless LAN access point is designed this way. Some of Intel's wireless LAN products support multiple wireless access point environments.

Wireless Networking Components

Wireless networking components consist of WAP and wireless network interface cards. Network interface cards come with PC CardBus, USB, or PCI bus interfaces. They connect directly into a PC to support wireless communications between the PC and the WAP or from PC to PC directly.

Wireless Access Point

WAPs are the hubs of a wireless LAN. They are connected into a wired LAN and communicate with the wireless PC hosts. Some WAPs are also configured to bridge between wired LAN segments. WAPs convert the wireless RF data at 11 Mbps from wireless PC hosts into Ethernet packets for transmission at 10 or 100 Mbps.

WAPs use dual antennas and special signal equalization processing to overcome multipath signal propagation. In multipath signal propagation, transmitted signals can combine with signals reflected off walls, ceilings, furniture, and other surfaces to corrupt signals detected by the WAP.

WAPs offer a range of coverage of over 1,000 feet. They also support seamless roaming throughout a wireless LAN infrastructure. The seamless roaming feature is built into the IEEE 802.11b specification. They hand off wireless PC hosts that move throughout a facility from one WAP to another WAP similar to the manner cell phones are handed off between cell sites. This means that several WAPs can be installed in a facility to provide connectivity throughout the facility.

Infrastructure mode also supports roaming capabilities for mobile users. More than one Basic Service Set (BSS) can be configured as an extended service set (ESS). This continuous network allows users to roam freely within an ESS. Wireless PC NICs within one ESS must have the same ESS ID and must use the same radio channel to facilitate roaming. Before setting up an ESS with roaming capability, choose the clearest possible radio channel and the optimum WAP location for maximum signal reception. Locating the WAP as high as possible combined with a clear radio channel signal greatly enhances wireless network performance.

WAPs offer advanced user authentication features to ensure network security. They use either the 64-bit or 128-bit shared key algorithm described in the IEEE 802.11 standard to provide Wired Equivalent Privacy (WEP). This provides a minimal level of security for WiFi RF transmissions. The WEP protocol is an algorithm designed to protect wireless LANs from casual eavesdropping and unauthorized access. WEP uses a secret key that is shared between a mobile station and an access point. The secret key is used to encrypt data packets before they are transmitted and decrypt them when they are received. Further, an integrity check is performed to ensure that packets are not modified in transit. For more secure wireless links, virtual private network (VPN) packet encryption should also be employed.

WAPs are easy to install physically. They plug into electrical power and a wired Ethernet LAN and they are operating. Windows-based configuration and diagnostic software complete the configuration and security setup.

The Linksys WAP shown in Figure 4.3 has dual antennas. USB and Ethernet connections on the rear of the WAP support configuration using the USB connection and LAN data transfer over the Ethernet connection.

The USB port (USB Type B or slave connector) that connects to a USB-ready PC is used exclusively to configure the access point's settings. To work with USB ports, the PC must be running Windows 98, Windows 2000, Win-

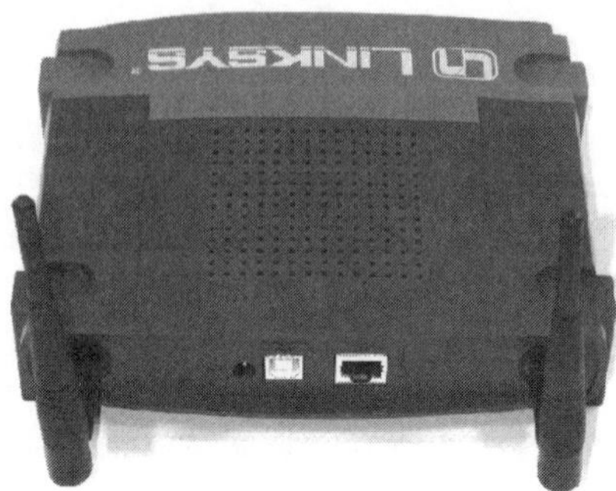

Figure 4.3 Wireless access point.

dows Me, or Windows XP. The USB port does not connect the Linksys Wireless Access Point to a PC host or an Ethernet switch for network data transfers. The USB port's only function is to permit configuration of the WAP's settings. After the access point is initially configured using the USB configuration port, the USB cable connecting the access point to a PC host may be removed.

The WAP can also be configured using Simple Network Management Protocol (SNMP) or a Web browser through the Ethernet connection from any PC host connected to the wired portion of the LAN. Figure 4.4 shows the WAP SNMP Configuration Utility Status tab. This screen appears after the SNMP utility is started with the correct IP address and password for the access point. It shows the regulatory domain preset by the manufacturer for the country in which the WAP was purchased, firmware version, the Ethernet MAC address of the WAP, the WAP operating mode, extended service set identifier (ESSID), the RF channel being used, and the Wired Equivalent Privacy (WEP) key being used. This screen is the same as the configuration screens used by the USB configuration port utility. The only difference is that the SNMP configuration software must have a correct IP address and password to connect to the WAP.

The Basic Setting tab permits entering an ESSID other than the default ID, selecting a different RF channel, and changing the WAP name. The ESSID is a unique network name for the wireless network. The ESSID is shared among all WAPs and wireless PC hosts in a network. It must be identical for every WAP and PC host NIC in the wireless network. The ESSID is case sensitive and has a limit of 30 characters. In North America the channel may be set from 1 to 11. All devices in a wireless LAN must be set to the same

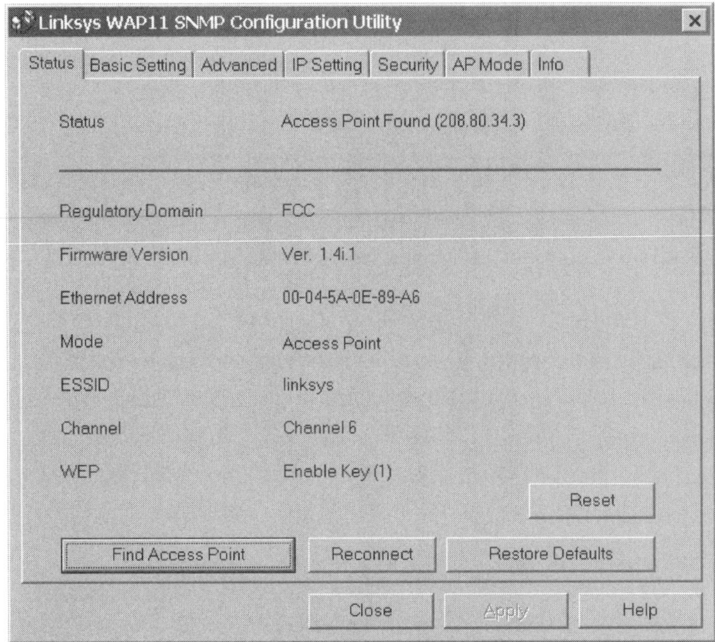

Figure 4.4 SNMP Configuration Utility.

channel to communicate properly. The exception here is a network with wireless bridges and WAPs. The wireless bridges could operate on one channel and the WAPs and the remote PCs could operate on another channel. This would likely reduce the interference between the wireless bridges and the WAPs. A descriptive name may be assigned to a WAP. Unique, descriptive, and memorable names are helpful in understanding your LAN architecture, especially when multiple WAPs are used in the same network. For example, Bridge 1 and Bridge 2 could be used to identify two WAPs that formed a bridge as opposed to a WAP that was used exclusively as an access point.

Brain Teaser: WAP Test

Locate a wireless network access point in your facility. Use a laptop PC with a wireless NIC to measure the received signal strength from the WAP. Next move to a floor above the WAP and test the signal strength again. Move to a floor below the WAP and test the signal strength there.

Where was the signal strength the highest? Was it higher on the floor above the WAP or on the floor below the WAP?

Wireless NICs

Wireless NICs are PC Bus cards, PC Bus cards with PCI Adapters, or USB NICs. Each provides the wireless freedom to work from anywhere, taking full advantage of the mobility of laptop PCs. Laptop PCs with wireless NICs have access to all network resources as they move throughout a facility. High-powered built-in diversity antennas permit RF links to operate at distances of up to 457 meters, or about 1,300 feet. Typical wireless NIC features include:

1. Data transfer at speeds up to 11 Mbps—effective rates are much lower
2. Interoperable with IEEE 802.11b (DSSS) 2.4GHz-compliant equipment
3. Plug-and-play operation with all Windows versions permits easy setup
4. Advanced power management to conserve laptop PC battery power
5. DSSS-compatible to prevent lost connections
6. Integrated antenna
7. Provides 64-bit or 128-bit WEP encryption

NIC installation requires 16-bit PCMCIA Type II or Type III slot with PCMCIA revision 2.10-compliant card and socket services on a Windows 95, Windows 98, Windows Me, Windows NT, Windows 2000, or Windows XP PC host. The configuration utility and NIC driver installation use about 500 Kbytes of disk space.

Installing a Wireless LAN

Installing a wireless LAN can be very simple when you have a few PCs and a single WAP. More thought and configuration testing is required for complex configurations involving roaming and bridging. Installing a wireless LAN uses either an ad-hoc operating mode or an infrastructure operating mode. Bridging WAPs operate in a point-to-point mode. These are the three basic wireless LAN configurations that would be used in SOHO LANs.

Ad-Hoc Mode

When a wireless network is small and resource sharing is only with other computers on the wireless network, then the ad-hoc operating mode is used. Ad-hoc mode allows computers equipped with wireless NICs to communicate directly with each other. This obviates the need for a WAP. The most significant drawback of ad-hoc mode operation is that wireless PC hosts cannot communicate with computers on a wired Ethernet network. Further communication between wireless PC hosts is limited by the distance and interference directly between the wireless PC hosts. Consequently, ad-hoc operating mode is used for wireless PC to wireless PC simple peer-to-peer network configurations. It could also be used to connect several PCs to a single server, but because of distance and interference limitations network traffic is more restricted than if WAPs and infrastructure mode were used.

Figure 4.5 illustrates a simple wireless PC to wireless PC peer-to-peer network. In the configuration shown, all wireless NICs would be configured to operate on the same channel. Any of the PCs could be a server, or they could all support peer-to-peer networking.

In contrast to ad-hoc operating mode, there is infrastructure operating mode, which employs WAPs.

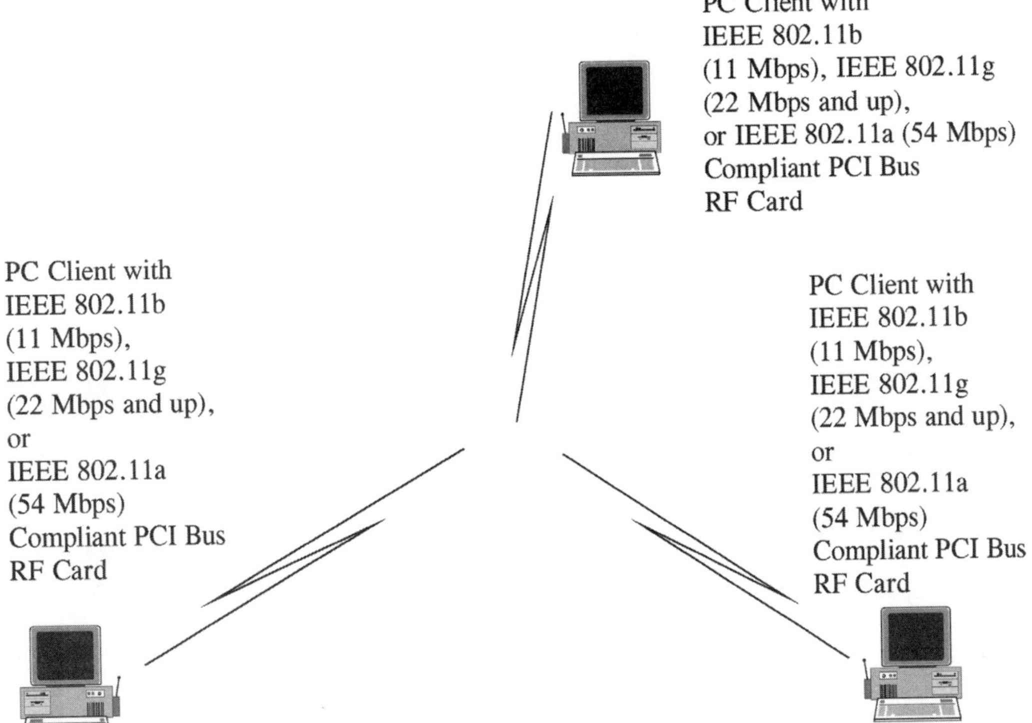

Figure 4.5 Wireless LAN ad-hoc operating mode.

Infrastructure Mode

When PC hosts on the wireless network need access to servers and other resources on a wired Ethernet network or resources such as printers must be shared with the wired network PC hosts, the wireless network is operated in infrastructure mode. Infrastructure mode operation focuses on access points that serve as the main point of communications between the wireless network and the wired network. WAPs transmit data to PCs with wireless NICs, permitting them to roam within several hundred to a little over 1,000 feet of the WAP. Multiple access points can be arranged to permit seamless roaming throughout a facility. In Figure 4.6, both the PC wireless NICs and the WAP use the same RF channel.

In infrastructure mode the WAP to PC host is a one point to many operation. Some small-office wireless LAN configurations use point-to-point communications between WAPs to extend small-office network coverage without wires.

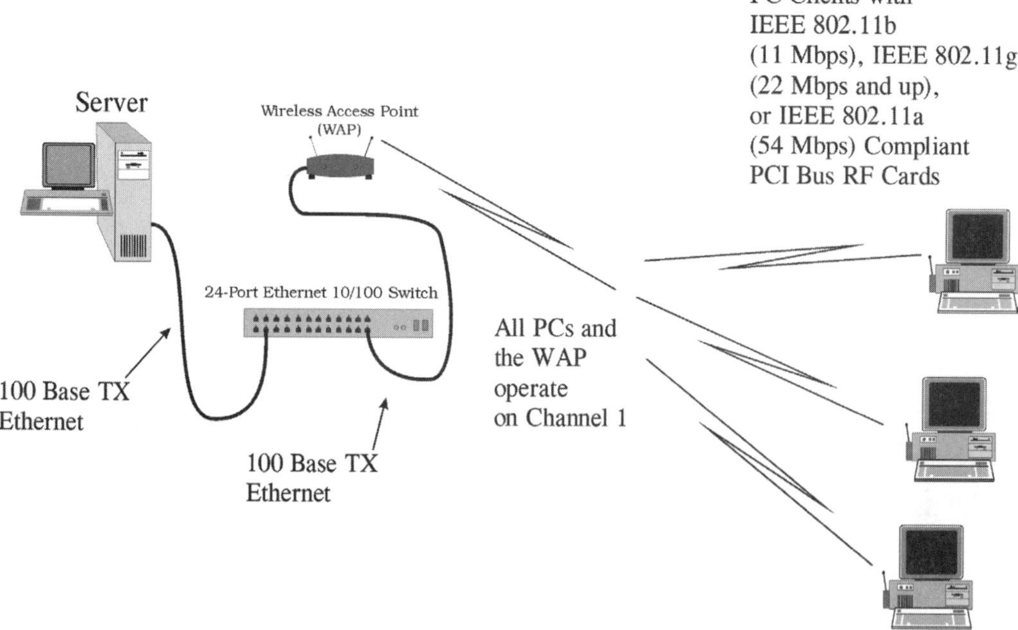

Figure 4.6 Infrastructure mode configuration.

Point-to-Point Mode

In point-to-point mode, as illustrated in Figure 4.7, the WAPs are set up as a wireless bridge between wired SOHO LAN segments. Both WAPs use the same channel and both are configured for point-to-point operation. This configuration would extend the connectivity of a wired SOHO LAN using the RF link between the WAPs. The only drawback in this configuration is that 802.11b links operate at a maximum speed of 11 Mbps and the wired LAN segments run at 100 Mbps. The traffic traveling across the bridge should not overload the 11-Mbps RF link and the significant traffic should stay within each wired LAN on each side of the WAP-to-WAP bridge.

Other configurations are possible as well, as illustrated by the point-to-point configuration between wireless LAN segments shown in Figure 4.8. In this configuration two wireless LANs are bridged by a point-to-point wireless link between WAPs. Wired LAN segments connect the infrastructure mode WAPs servicing the wireless PC hosts to servers and the point-to-point wireless link bridging the wired LAN segments.

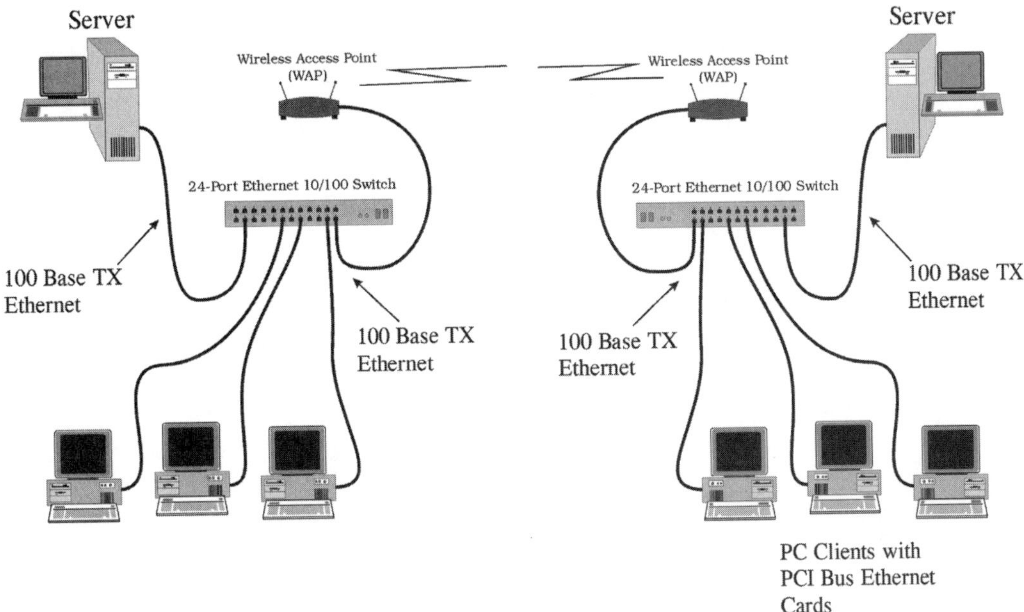

Figure 4.7 WAP point-to-point configuration.

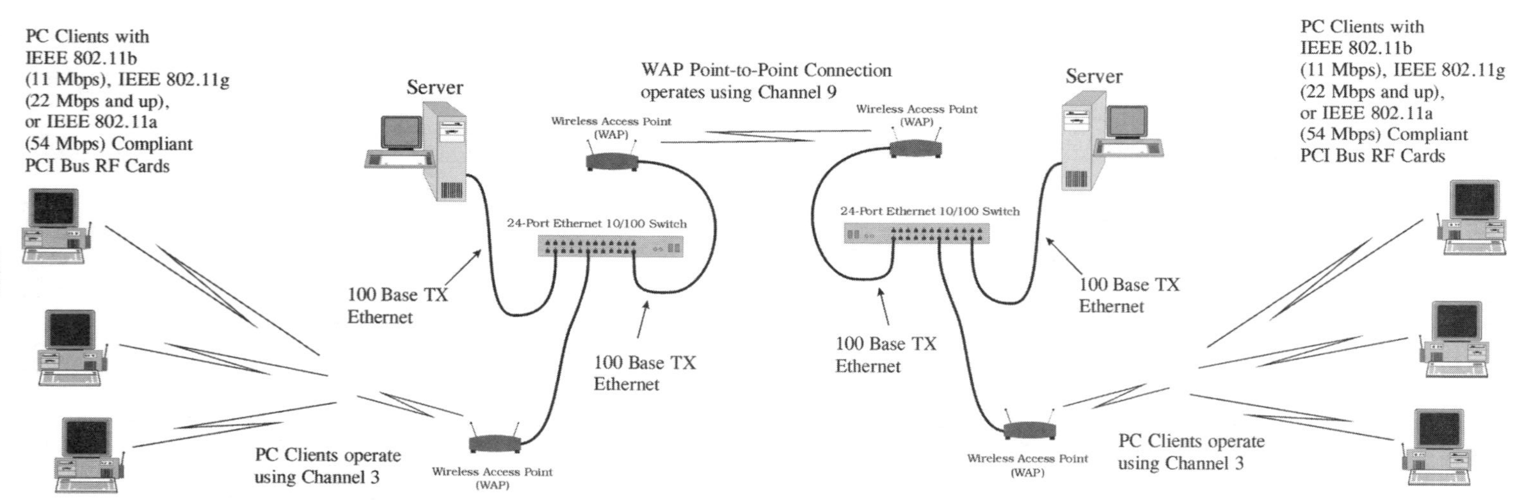

Figure 4.8 Point-to-point wireless LAN segment connections.

These configurations represent a few of the other possible wireless LAN configurations that might be used to solve small-office networking problems. Simpler home-office LANs most often use the ad-hoc, or simple, infrastructure operating modes as compared with more sophisticated wireless LAN configurations.

Point-to-Multipoint Mode

A point-to-multipoint configuration is the last configuration we illustrate here. In this configuration two remote LAN segments are linked to a central LAN segment, as illustrated in Figure 4.9.

In this case the WAPs must be specially configured to implement the point-to-multipoint configuration. This special configuration has the central segment WAP set to multipoint mode operation. Each remote segment WAP is set to point-to-point operation and given the MAC address of the WAP set to multipoint operation. In this manner the central segment WAP can communicate with both remote segment WAPs and the remote segment WAPs communicate only with the central segment WAP. I love this. It is way cool stuff, and it really works.

Brain Teaser: Wireless NIC Test

Find a laptop or a desktop PC that uses a wireless NIC. Click on the LAN icon in the SYSTRAY to open the configuration software.

What operating mode is used for the NIC? Does the NIC use an infrastructure operating mode or an ad-hoc operating mode? If an ad-hoc operating mode is used, can you find a wireless access point in your facility?

Wireless Access Point Installation

WAP installation is very straightforward. WAPs are configured using a USB configuration port or a SNMP connection across a wired Ethernet network. The USB configuration port performs the initial configuration and most importantly assigns a password for subsequent USB or SNMP access. Since SNMP access is from any wired PC host running the SNMP configuration utility software, a password is mandatory for accessing the WAP. Once the configuration utility runs, the setup options and configuration screens are the same for either USB or SNMP access.

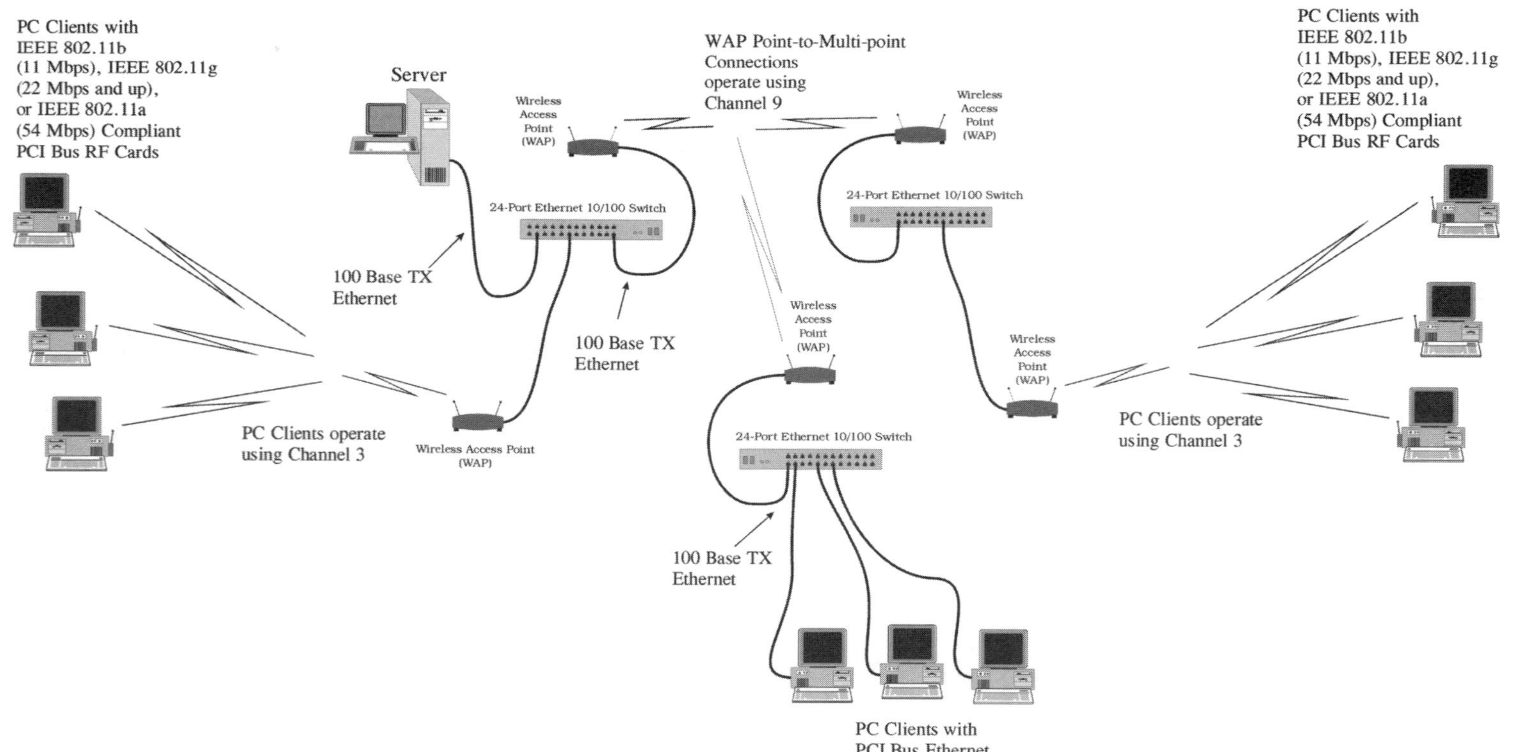

Figure 4.9 Point-to-multipoint wireless LAN configuration.

SNMP (Simple Network Management Protocol)

Simple Network Management Protocol (SNMP) is a protocol that runs on top of the Internet Protocol (IP) and is used to configure and manage network devices. Management agents (programs in firmware) control the network components and use SNMP to communicate with a central management PC. In the case of a WAP, SNMP is used to communicate with any PC running the SNMP configuration utility that has provided the correct login password.

Web Browser

Some WAPs can be configured using a Web browser rather than SNMP protocol. This requires no special PC host configuration software other than IE or Netscape. The user configuring the WAP must enter a login password to activate the Web browser configuration menus.

Configuring a WAP

Once the configuration utility is running the WAP is configured using its menus. The initial screen describing the basic status of the WAP was illustrated back in Figure 4.4. Across the top of the WAP SNMP Configuration Utility window are the tabs for Basic Settings, Advanced Settings, IP Address Settings, Security Settings, Access Point Operating Mode, and General Information.

The basic settings are shown in Figure 4.10. The basic settings include the extended service set identifier (ESSID), which is a 30-character or less text string uniquely identifying the wireless LAN from any other wireless LAN. All WAPs and wireless NICs on a LAN must have the exact same ESSID. This network is using the default setting, making it less secure. Site scanning by some NIC configuration utilities can reveal the ESSIDs in use at the site, rendering this useless for providing security.

A channel is selected from those listed to correspond with the channel settings of all wireless network components. In North America channel settings are between 1 and 11. All WAPs and wireless NICs must use the same channel in order to communicate. Many wireless NICs scan all channels to locate a WAP, so setting a special channel does not increase wireless LAN security.

Access point names may be assigned to help identify and describe where the WAP is located. Creative names like “Outhouse AP” help identify where the access point is in wireless networks employing multiple access points.

The advanced configuration settings are shown in Figure 4.11. In this case the default settings are perhaps the best settings. Only minor modifications

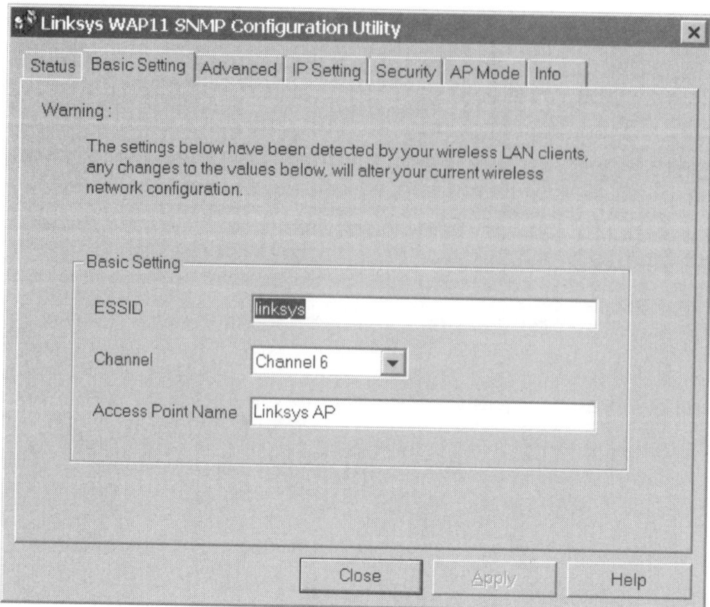

Figure 4.10 WAP Configuration Utility basic settings.

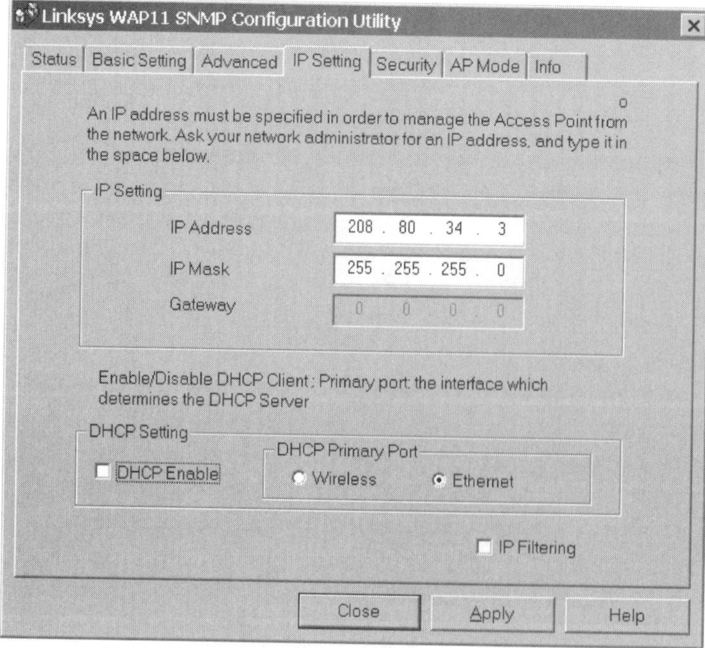

Figure 4.11 Advanced WAP settings.

should be made to the fragmentation threshold and RTS threshold settings. **Do not** try setting them at 1,100 or 3,400 in an attempt to improve wireless LAN performance. Such settings are more likely to cause problems rather than improve performance.

The authentication type defines configuration options for wireless networks to verify the identity and the access privileges of roaming network cards. The choice is among Open System, Shared Key, and Both. The Open System setting has the sender and recipient not sharing a secret key. Both sender and receiver generate a key-pair and ask the receiver or sender respectively to accept the randomly generated key. Once accepted, the key is used for only a short time to encrypt transmissions. When the time expires a new key is generated and agreed upon. Shared Key has both the sender and receiver sharing a secret key. When Both is selected, a WAP accepts either form of authentication.

The preamble type specifies the CRC block length for communication between the WAP and roaming NICs. Long preambles result in lower data errors at the expense of network performance. In high traffic and clear signal situations the short preamble can be used to improve network performance.

The rate setting determines the speed of the wireless network. Enabling all rates and the Auto Rate Fallback setting permits the wireless LAN to fall back to slower speeds when there is signal interference.

Disabling the SSID broadcast somewhat increases network security and makes it less vulnerable to intrusion.

The IP address settings are shown in Figure 4.12.

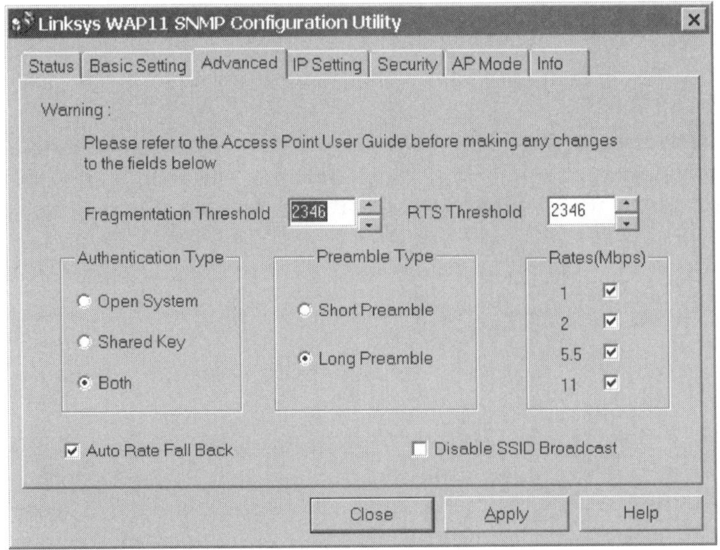

Figure 4.12 WAP IP settings.

The WAP needs a fixed IP address to be accessed using SNMP over an Ethernet. When the WAP is configured using the USB configuration port this IP address setting is not needed.

The IP address assigned must be unique to the SOHO network. The default IP address of 192.168.1.250 may also be used. The WAP address only needs to match the SOHO network addresses when a PC host on the network is going to use SNMP to manage the WAP. Similarly, the IP mask or subnet mask must also match the subnet mask on wired Ethernet network for PC hosts on the wired network to use SNMP to manage the WAP. If the USB software is used to configure the WAP, then IP address assignment is not needed.

Data traffic on the wired Ethernet is accepted by the WAP and rebroadcast over the wireless RF links regardless of its IP address. Similarly, data from the RF links is rebroadcast on the wired Ethernet regardless of its IP address. The WAP is merely a physical layer bridge that converts wired transmissions into wireless transmissions.

The Gateway setting appears only when the DHCP client is enabled. The Gateway setting only indicates that an active gateway was found using DHCP. The WAP does not control the Gateway settings so the Gateway setting cannot be changed.

The DHCP Enable setting allows the WAP to get a dynamic IP address from a DHCP server on the wired network. The WAP may dynamically obtain an IP address from either the wireless network or the wired Ethernet. DHCP changes do not take effect until the WAP has been turned off and turned on again. A static IP address assignment should be no problem because the WAP, gateways, servers, and printers are most of the devices on a network that need a permanent IP address assignment.

IP filtering increases security by filtering packets and allowing only IP packets through the WAP.

The IP Security tab settings are shown in Figure 4.13. These settings implement the security for the network. The algorithms may be unique to the network vendor and may not interoperate with wireless LAN components from other vendors.

The passphrase is the password-like code used when a wireless NIC logs onto the WAP. It is a 32-character text string. WEP key settings are based upon the unique passphrase used here. The same passphrase or WEP key settings must be used for all wireless NICs for the wireless network to communicate properly.

The WEP key setting is the configuration key used in accessing the wireless network via WEP encryption. Entering a 10-digit hexadecimal number in each key field may manually configure these keys. To automatically generate an encryption key, the exact case-sensitive passphrase is typed into the Passphrase field; it is used on all other wireless NICs in the network. Clicking the Done

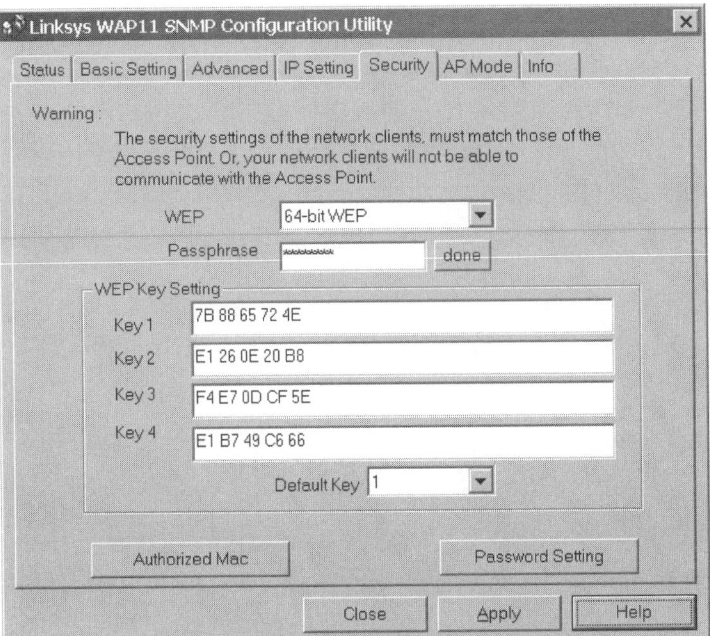

Figure 4.13 WAP IP Security settings.

button creates the encryption keys. A passphrase generates four unique keys. Set the Default key to the same Default key for each wireless network NIC.

Authorized MAC authorizes access to the WAP using MAC address filtering. Only MAC addresses in the authorization table are allowed to communicate with the WAP. This is an additional security measure that can be employed using some WAP products. My original Linksys WAP model WAP11 had this feature while my current Linksys model BEFW11S4 combined WAP, switch, and cable modem router product does not support such settings.

The Password setting allows choosing read/write and/or read only passwords for accessing the WAP. Setting both passwords provides the best security. Set the password by typing in a password and confirming it.

The access point operating mode settings are shown in Figure 4.14.

These settings are used to set up different configurations of WAPs acting as point-to-point and point-to-multipoint bridges.

The default WAP operating mode setting is access point, which connects wireless PCs to a wired network. In most networks the default setting works fine and no change is necessary.

The access point client mode allows a WAP to act as a client of a main WAP access point. A wired LAN attached to a WAP client is wirelessly bridged to the

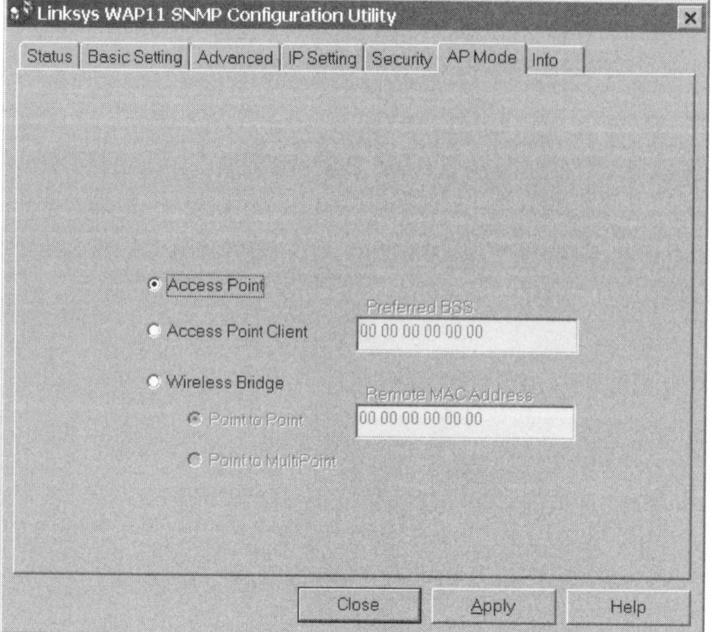

Figure 4.14 WAP AP Mode settings.

central WAP access point. Access Point Client mode requires a MAC address, the same RF channel as the central WAP, but a different SSID is used.

Wireless Bridge is used to make a wireless connection between two wired networks. To connect to another wireless bridge, select Point-to-Point and enter the remote WAP's MAC address. If the main wireless LAN WAP is connecting to multiple client access points, select Point-to-MultiPoint. In these cases, be sure the wireless bridges are configured to use the same SSID and the same RF channel.

In Wireless Bridge mode, the WAP only communicates to other wireless bridges. In order for other wireless devices to access the WAP, it must be reset to access point mode. The wireless bridge and the access point mode are mutually exclusive.

Although we used a specific product here to demonstrate WAP installation, all WAPs are configured similarly.

Wireless NICs

After the WAP is set up, the wireless NICs in the network are configured. Configuring the wireless NICs is very straightforward. They need the same

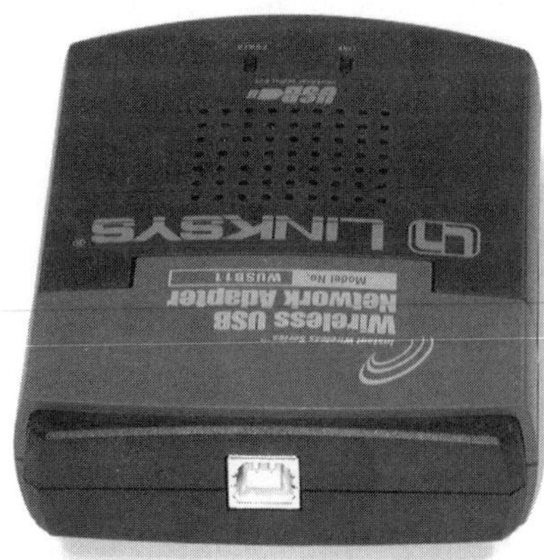

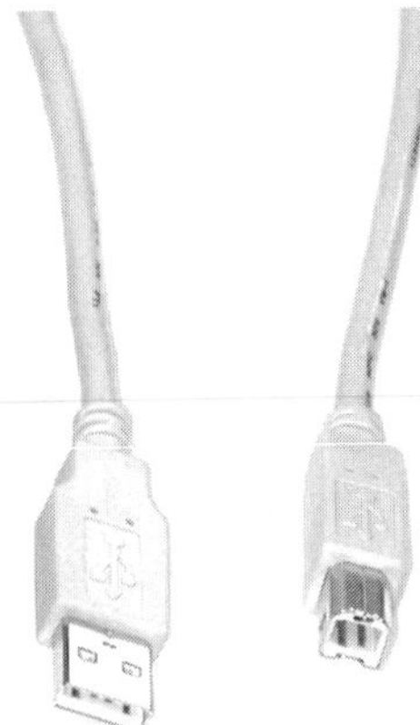

Figure 4.15 USB NIC rear view.

ESSID or SSID as the WAPs and the same encryption keys to communicate with the WAP and the other wireless NICs. Let's first examine the NIC hardware configuration and then look at the software configuration.

USB NICs

USB NICs are the easiest to install. They plug directly into the USB connections on the rear of a PC host. The USB NIC in Figure 4.15 has only a Type B, or slave, connector. It requires no external power connection, only a USB bus connection.

Once connected the drivers load automatically. The configuration software and drivers also readily install from the installation CD.

PCMCIA NICs

PCMCIA NICs are similar to USB NICs. Once plugged in to a PC's CardBus or PCMCIA slot they automatically attempt to load the NIC driver programs. Pointing at the drivers completes the process as well as installing from the installation CD. Running the SETUP program from the installation CD installs the CardBus or PCMCIA NICs as well.

PCI Adapters

Two sets of drivers may be required to install the wireless NIC as a PCI bus adapter. The PCMCIA NIC is inserted into a special PCI bus adapter to connect into a desktop PC host. This necessitates installing the special adapter drivers as well as the PCMCIA bus card adapter drivers. However, the process is generally not difficult. Setup programs can perform the work or the drivers can be located in a drivers directory on the setup CDs or setup diskettes.

Software Configuration

Once the NIC hardware is installed, the software is configured to operate with the WAP or with other wireless NICs. In Windows double clicking on the LAN icon in the SYSTRAY opens the wireless NIC configuration utility. The first tab is the Link Information display, as shown in Figure 4.16. The information display panel shows that the NIC is connected to a WAP that is using channel 5, operating at 11 Mbps transmission speed, the link transmission quality is excellent, and the RF signal strength is also good at 50%. The NIC automatically scans all channels to find an active WAP, so changing channels at the WAP is detected automatically at the NIC.

The Configuration panel determines how the NIC is identified and how it operates in the wireless LAN. This is shown in Figure 4.17. The wireless mode can be ad-hoc or infrastructure. The SSID locks out other wireless NICs using the same RF channels.

The auto rate selection permits the rate to vary depending upon signal interference. The selection permits several fixed rates to be set as opposed to

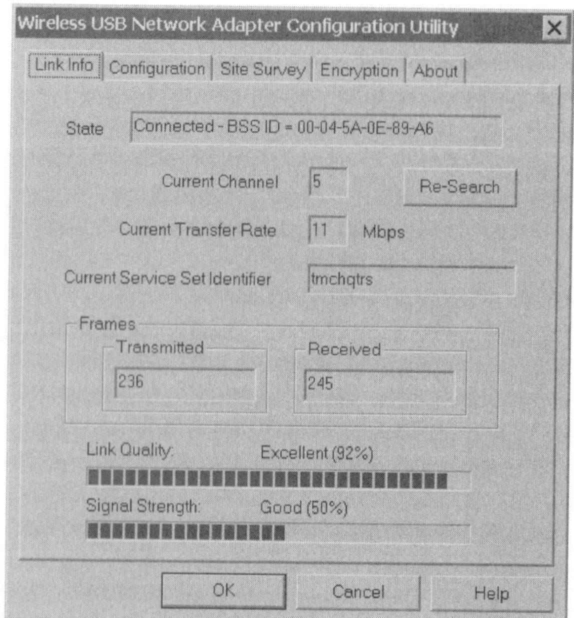

Figure 4.16
Wireless NIC Link Information display.

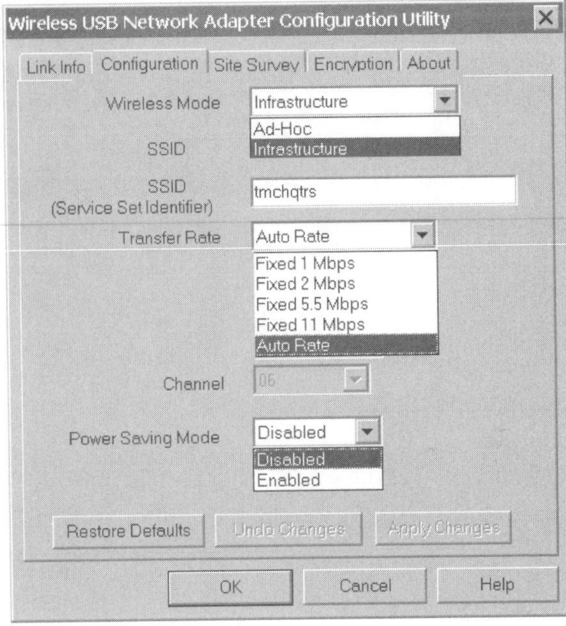

Figure 4.17
Wireless NIC Configuration display.

permitting the rate to vary to accommodate changing signal strength and signal interference.

Power saving mode is important for laptop PCs running on battery power. It can be enabled or disabled. If you pick enabled and the wireless LAN does not work properly, then the only other selection should have it working just fine.

The operating channel is not specified at the NIC. The WAP sets the RF channel selection. The NIC scans all channels and then operates on the wireless channel on which it detects a WAP operating.

The Site Survey tab lists the WAPs found when the NIC scans the channels. As shown in Figure 4.18, this wireless NIC has located a WAP in the default *"tmchqtrs"* Service Set Identifier (SSID) that has the Binary SSID (BSSID) of 00-04-5A-0E-89-A6. The signal strength is 27% using channel 5, and WEP is active. Searching for a new site lists any active WAP. Clicking on the Connect button connects the PC host with the wireless NIC to the selected WAP.

Encryption is the next tab. In Figure 4.19 the encryption screen is open. We can set the encryption at none, 64-bit, or 128-bit levels. A privacy key generation code may be entered to generate all keys or each key may be entered manually. Each key is a 10-digit hexadecimal number.

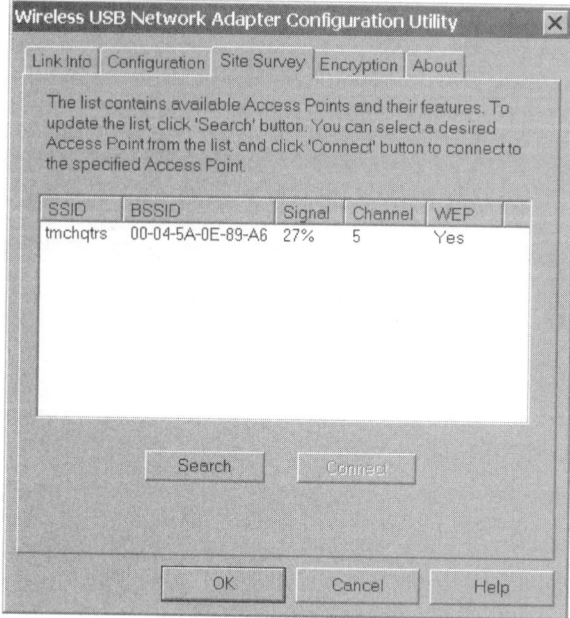

Figure 4.18
Wireless NIC Site Survey.

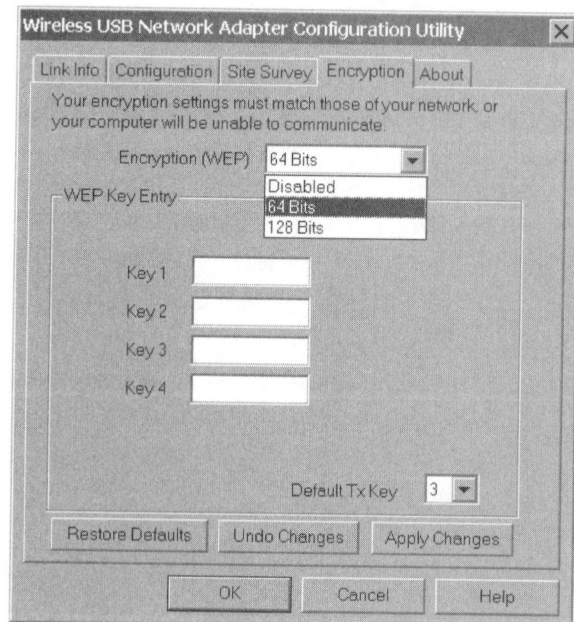

Figure 4.19
Wireless NIC Encryption display.

Picking the default transmit key synchronizes the PC NIC and the WAP. When the WAP and the PC are not using the same default key, communication is blocked.

Brain Teaser: ESSID

Find a laptop or a desktop PC with the wireless NIC. Click on the LAN icon in the SYSTRAY to open-end the configuration software. Go to the Configuration menu and change the SSID or ESSID.

What happens? Change the SSID back to its original setting. What happens? Go to the Security Settings menu. Change the Default Transmit key. What happens?

sIn the first case you should have been disconnected from the LAN. In the second case there may have been a brief disconnection but you should have been able to reconnect to the wireless LAN.

Security

Wireless SOHO LANs need security. However, a simple installation strategy is to first use default settings and minimum security levels. Once you have the wireless network operating and the PCs are communicating with one another, change the configuration from the defaults to other settings and implement WEP security. This makes your wireless network more secure from wiretapping and other intrusions.

One of my consultant trainers, Matt, living in Melbourne, Florida, did a simple test. He loaded his laptop with its wireless LAN NIC into his car and drove around Melbourne. Within 15 minutes to half an hour he had found four wireless LANs operating that he could access. Breaking into a wireless LAN that is unprotected is relatively easy. Setting the wireless LAN NIC on default settings and detecting IP address automatically gets you on any unprotected LAN with the WINS, DNS, and Gateway IP address settings. This at a minimum would permit you to surf the Web using any high-speed link into the Internet from the Gateway address you detected. Running protocol analyzer software in the laptop permits capturing and decoding packets that can yield network user IDs and passwords. This is not rocket science or the FBI sniffing out drug smugglers or terrorists, but it is a matter of employing readily available networking tools to tap into a wireless LAN.

An article at Yahoo! news revealed that wireless home cameras can be easily compromised to reveal what they are taking pictures of in a home. The unscrambled video signals from these cameras are intercepted by a wireless receiver sold with the cameras that is modified with a more sensitive antenna and an amplifier to boost the received signal. When connected to a monitor, the picture on the camera in a home is displayed. There is no rocket science here.

Recently at a network training session run by the U.S. Fish and Wildlife Service we ran both a Cisco and my Linksys WAP in the same room. The Cisco WAP had a default SSID of tsunami and mine was set to its default Linksys. I could survey the site and find both WAPs and connect to either WAP by changing my SSID.

Gaining access to private wireless LANs is relatively easy. Wiretapping and other electronic equipment needed to intercept and interpret wireless LAN communications is relatively cheap. The technical expertise is provided by electronics hobbyist organizations and Internet publications. There are few if any cost effective, commercially available products to detect electronic eavesdropping.

Wiretapping includes all types of communications media. All communications technologies—including satellite, microwave, infrared, and even fiber optics—can be intercepted. Encryption is the primary means to prevent wireless LAN communications from being intercepted and tapped into. The 64-bit or 128-bit WEP encryption is the primary means of securing wireless LANs from unauthorized access. Adding VPN encryption and other security measures to a wireless LAN may be needed to provide sufficient wireless LAN security.

Wireless LAN Operation

Now comes the fun part—operating your SOHO wireless LAN.

The only drawback of a SOHO wireless LAN is that it operates at lower speed than a wired SOHO LAN. However, this is more than adequate for surfing the Web and other casual use and there are no wires tying you down.

The remaining Windows software configuration is the same for a wireless network as it is for a wired network. Once complete, the wireless PC either works in a simple peer-to-peer network or a client/server network.

Figure 4.20 shows the three types of icons. A green wireless communications icon in the PC's SYSTRAY indicates the signal strength is good. A yellow colored icon indicates poor signal strength.

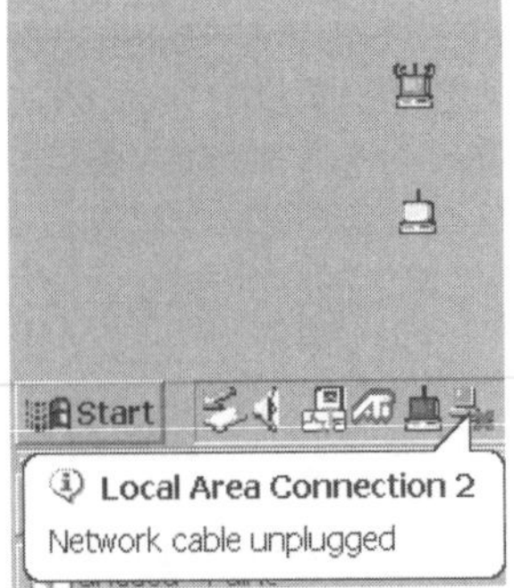

Figure 4.20
Wireless LAN operating icons.

When communication is blocked over the wireless link, a red colored icon is displayed or an icon indicating that there is no operating link appears. This icon is shown in the bottom of the figure. The broken link icon is the same as the broken cable icon shown for wired LAN operation. In addition, a red wireless icon is displayed.

Brain Teaser: Wireless LAN Security

Use a laptop PC with a wireless NIC to locate wireless LANs in your community. Power up the laptop and have a friend drive you around your neighborhood.

Did you locate any wireless LANs? Was encryption enabled on the wireless LANs that you found? Could you surf the Web from your vehicle using someone else's wireless LAN?

Please remember to always use information presented here for good purposes and never for evil purposes. Thank you.

Spread Spectrum Radio Technology

Wireless LANs use spread spectrum radio technology. We examine these technologies here because they are associated with and sometimes used to describe wireless LAN products. Spread spectrum is a form of wireless communications in which the frequency of the transmitted signal is deliberately varied. This produces a much greater bandwidth than the signal would have if its frequency were not varied. This technology was originally conceived and patented in the 1940s by Hedy Lamarr, the actress.

Two common problems with conventional wireless communications are:

1. A signal whose frequency is constant is subject to catastrophic interference. This occurs when another signal is transmitted on, or very near, the frequency of the desired signal. Catastrophic interference can be accidental (as in amateur-radio communications) or it can be deliberate (as in wartime).
2. A constant-frequency signal is easy to intercept, and it is therefore not well suited to applications in which information must be kept confidential between the source (transmitting party) and destination (receiving party).

FHSS is one of two basic modulation techniques used in spread spectrum signal transmission. It is the repeated switching of frequencies during radio transmission to minimize unauthorized interception or jamming of a telecommunications signal. FHSS is known as Frequency-Hopping Code Division Multiple Access (FH-CDMA).

Frequency Hopping Spread Spectrum

In an FHSS system the transmitter hops between available frequencies according to a specified algorithm. The transmitter operates in synchronization with a receiver. Both transmitter and receiver remain tuned to the same center frequency. A short burst of data is transmitted on a narrowband. Then, the transmitter tunes to another frequency and transmits again. The receiver thus is capable of hopping its frequency over a given bandwidth several times a second, transmitting on one frequency for a certain period of time, and then hopping to another frequency and transmitting again. Frequency hopping requires a much wider bandwidth than is needed to transmit the same information using only one carrier frequency.

Direct Sequence Spread Spectrum

Alternatively, DSSS, also known as Direct Sequence—Code Division Multiple Access (DS-CDMA), is the second approach to spread spectrum modulation for digital signal transmission over wireless communications channels. The function of DSSS is to translate digital data into a radio signal suitable for reliable transmission. In DSSS a stream of data to be transmitted is divided into small pieces, each of which is transmitted using a frequency channel within the spectrum. A data signal at the point of transmission is combined with a higher data-rate bit sequence known as a chipping code that divides the data according to a spreading ratio. The redundant chipping code helps the signal resist interference and also enables the original data to be recovered if data bits are damaged during transmission.

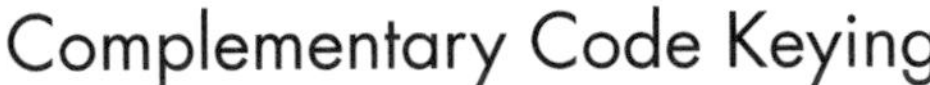

Complementary Code Keying

Complementary Code Keying (CCK) is a modulation technique used in wireless LANs to improve the capability of a radio frequency signal to deliver data in spite of all multipath distortion and interference from other radio signals. CCK is a DSSS technology that combines the data signal with a higher data rate bit sequence (chipping sequence) and modulates that into the RF signal. CCK is used in the IEEE 802.11b standard to achieve the higher 5.5 and 11 Mbps transmission speeds.

Orthogonal Frequency Division Multiplexing

Orthogonal Frequency Division Multiplexing (OFDM) is a modulation technique that sends data across multiple low speed sub-channels simultaneously. The sub-channels are transmitted on different frequencies. They in effect establish parallel transmission paths between the sending and receiving device. OFDM is used in the IEEE 802.11a standard to achieve speeds up to 54 Mbps.

Packet Binary Convolutional Coding

Packet Binary Convolutional Coding (PBCC) is a modulation technology promoted by Texas Instruments. It competes with OFDM for high-speed wireless LAN transmission. PBCC is implemented in the TI ACX100 chip. This chip is fully compatible with the current wireless LAN products, yet using PBCC modulation it provides a high-performance option to the 802.11b standard. The TI ACX100 chip permits products to cover 70% more area or double the 802.11b data rate to 22 Mbps in the 2.4 GHz band.

Brain Teaser: Hedy Lamarr

Use the Google search site to look up Hedy Lamarr. Did you find anything out about her invention?

Summary

In this chapter we first examined wireless LAN technologies and standards. These standards were the IEEE 802.11 standards. The most widely implemented IEEE 802.11 standard is the IEEE 802.11b specification using the 2.4 GHz ISM band to operate at speeds of 11 Mbps. The IEEE 802.11a specification uses a higher frequency band and operates at speeds up to 54 Mbps. Several manufacturers are delivering products conforming to the IEEE 802.11a specification. The newest IEEE specification is the IEEE 802.11g specification that uses a 2.4 GHz ISM band but operates at higher speeds than the IEEE 802.11b specification.

Radio frequency transmission was discussed along with the RF bands used by wireless LANs. These were compared with the frequencies used by cordless and cellular telephones.

The issue surrounding Bluetooth technology was examined along with a discussion of the operation of Bluetooth devices. The potential for interference between wireless LAN and Bluetooth devices was presented.

Several wireless LAN configurations were discussed, illustrating how they could be configured for a small-office environment. This discussion examined ad-hoc mode, infrastructure mode, point-to-point mode, and point-to-multipoint mode configurations.

Installing and configuring wireless LAN access points and network interface cards were examined. The installation menus for a specific vendor's products were used to illustrate IEEE 802.11b-compliant wireless LAN installation and configuration. Wireless LAN security issues and wireless LAN operation were discussed as well in this chapter.

The chapter concluded with a discussion of the operation of various spread spectrum radio technologies. This included explaining Frequency Hopping Spread Spectrum and Direct Sequence Spread Spectrum technologies.

Key Technical Terms

Ad-hoc operating mode—A wireless LAN operating mode supporting simple peer-to-peer communications.

Bluetooth—Bluetooth is a single-chip wireless technology that enables consumer electronics devices to communicate automatically with one another. Bluetooth devices operate in the 2.4 GHz ISM band.

CCK—Complementary code keying is a Direct Sequence Spread Spectrum technology that combines the data signal with a higher data rate bit chipping code and modulates that into an RF signal.

DSSS—Direct Sequence Spread Spectrum is radio transmission that continuously changes frequencies or signal patterns. DSSS, used in Code Division Multiple Access (CDMA) communications, multiplies data bits by a pseudo-random code spreading the data into an encoded bit stream using the full channel bandwidth. The receiving station uses the same pseudo-random code to derive the original data from the encoded bit stream.

ESSID—Extended Service Set ID means that there is more than one SSID. See SSID.

FHSS—Frequency Hopping Spread Spectrum continually changes a conventional carrier frequency several times per second using a pseudo-random set of channels. Because a fixed frequency is not used, unauthorized monitoring of spread spectrum communications is difficult.

IEEE—The Institute of Electrical and Electronics Engineers develops local area network communications standards.

IEEE 802.11a—A specification for wireless LANs operating in the Universal National Information Infrastructure (UNII) 5 GHz RF band and carrying data at speeds up to 54 Mbps.

IEEE 802.11b—A specification for wireless LANs operating in the Industrial, Medical, and Scientific (ISM) 2.4 GHz RF band and carrying data at speeds up to 11 Mbps.

IEEE 802.11g—A specification for wireless LANs operating in the ISM 2.4 GHz RF band and carrying data at speeds of 22 Mbps and higher.

Infrastructure operating mode—A wireless LAN operating mode using access points for wireless PC hosts to connect with a wired LAN.

ISM bands—Industrial, Scientific, and Medical bands are unlicensed RF bands use for wireless LAN and other types of communications.

OFDM—Orthogonal Frequency Division Multiplexing is a modulation technique that sends data across multiple low-speed sub-channels simultaneously.

PBCC—Packet Binary Convolutional Coding (PBCC) is a modulation technology promoted by Texas Instruments that competes with OFDM.

RF—Radio frequency.

SNMP—Simple Network Management Protocol is a protocol running across IP networks that carries network management information between network components.

SSID—Service set identifier is a code word used by a wireless LAN to signal to all wireless LAN components that they are part of the same wireless LAN. Wireless LAN components with a different SSID would be part of a different wireless LAN and unable to communicate with components and other wireless LANs.

UNII—Universal National Information Infrastructure (UNII) is an unlicensed RF band ranging from 5.15 to 5.35 GHz.

WAP—A wireless access point is a hub point in a wireless LAN that connects wireless PC hosts to a wired LAN.

WEP—Wired Equivalent Privacy is the encryption mechanism used in wireless LANs to ensure that communications are private within a single wireless LAN and cannot be monitored by unauthorized PC hosts.

WiFi or Wi-Fi—Wireless Fidelity is a term showing IEEE 802.11-compliant wireless networking components.

Review Questions

1. What IEEE specification supports the highest speed wireless LAN operation?

   Answer: The IEEE 802.11a specification supports wireless LAN communication at speeds up to 54 Mbps.

2. The IEEE 802.11b wireless LANs operate in what frequency band?

   Answer: The IEEE 802.11b wireless LANs use the 2.4 GHz unlicensed ISM band.

3. Can Bluetooth devices and wireless LANs coexist?

   Answer: There are potential problems with wireless LANs that operate in the 2.4 GHz unlicensed ISM band. Wireless LANs operating in higher frequency bands should not interfere with Bluetooth devices.

4. For a large wireless LAN, what would be the preferred operating mode?

   Answer: The preferred operating mode for a large wireless LAN would be infrastructure mode, employing WAPs to connect wireless PC hosts to a wired LAN. The access points would also support PC hosts roaming seamlessly throughout a single facility.

5. What levels of encryption are available for wireless LANs?

   Answer: Wireless LANs can use either 64-, 128-, or 256-bit encryption.

6. What types of wireless LAN NICs are available?

   Answer: There are USB NICs, PC CardBus NICs, and PCI bus adapters that permit using PC CardBus NICs in desktop PCs.

Chapter 5

Internet Access

Chapter Syllabus

- Connecting to the Internet
- Internet Connection Sharing
- Installing and Configuring a Cable Modem/DSL Router
- Summary
- Key Technical Terms
- Review Questions

A key SOHO LAN use is to share high-speed Internet access among all network PCs or hosts. High-speed Internet access is provided through cable modems, digital subscriber line (DSL) modems, and other connections. A SOHO network connected to a router permits all connected PCs to share high-speed Internet access. This chapter shows how to implement such high-speed connection sharing.

The key issues with high-speed Internet access are the following:

1. Availability of service
2. Cost of service
3. Connection speed versus application
4. High-speed connection sharing

The most important consideration is availability of high-speed Internet access. In my case, I used Verizon's Web site to check availability of DSL service by typing in my phone number. I found that I cannot use USL to get to the Internet, since there is no DSL availability for me.

The second consideration is the cost of the high-speed Internet access. For home-office LANs most people would pay around $40 to $60 for high-speed Internet access. A small-office LAN may pay more depending upon the use of the high-speed link.

The third consideration is how the high-speed link is used versus the connection speed. Most high-speed Internet links operate at a slower speed transmitting up to the Internet and a much higher speed delivering data down from the Internet. The asymmetric transmission speeds are generally 128 Kbps up and 400 to 800 Kbps down from the Internet. These speeds are very adequate for surfing the Web, but other applications such as Voice over IP (VoIP) telephony may need higher uplink speeds to function properly.

The final consideration is whether the connection needs to be shared with other computers on the SOHO LAN. Sharing is facilitated by routing data from several PC hosts to a single Internet IP address, then performing the reverse function when data comes from the Internet in response to a request from one SOHO LAN PC host.

Let's examine the SOHO LAN high-speed Internet access alternatives.

Brain Teaser: DSL Availability

Use the Internet to check if DSL is available for your facility. Find the local telco's Web site, click on the DSL link, and follow the directions to enter your phone number and check on availability. What did you find? Was the DSL service available? At what speeds could you get DSL service? What did the highest speed service cost and what did the lowest speed service cost?

Connecting to the Internet

High-speed Internet access alternatives include the most popular cable modem and DSL modem alternatives, the universally available ISDN alternative, and other higher speed and more costly alternatives.

Cable Modems

A cable modem connects a PC to a local cable television or Community Antenna Television (CATV) system's coaxial cable. Cable modems use cable television systems to send and receive high-speed data to and from the Internet.

Cable modems are separate from the cable television set-top box connecting TVs to the cable television network. The set top box distributes television signals to televisions.

Cable modems have two connections: one to the cable television coaxial cable and the other a 10 Mbps Ethernet connection to a PC. Figure 5.1 shows the front and rear view of a cable modem, illustrating the cable and Ethernet connections.

Cable modems modulate digital signals in specific analog frequency ranges. These frequencies coexist on the same coaxial cable as the television signals sent to TV sets. The TV and cable modem signals use different frequency ranges, as shown in Figure 5.2.

Cable modems attach to a cable television company coaxial cable and communicate with a Cable Modem Termination System (CMTS) at the local cable television company head-end office. All cable modems receive from and send signals to the head-end CMTS. They do not communicate directly point-to-point with other cable modems on the same coaxial cable. All communications

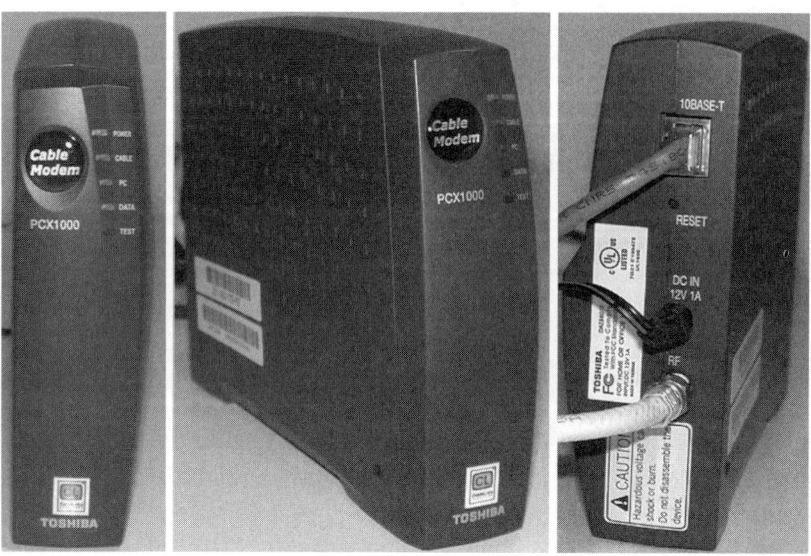

Figure 5.1 Cable modem.

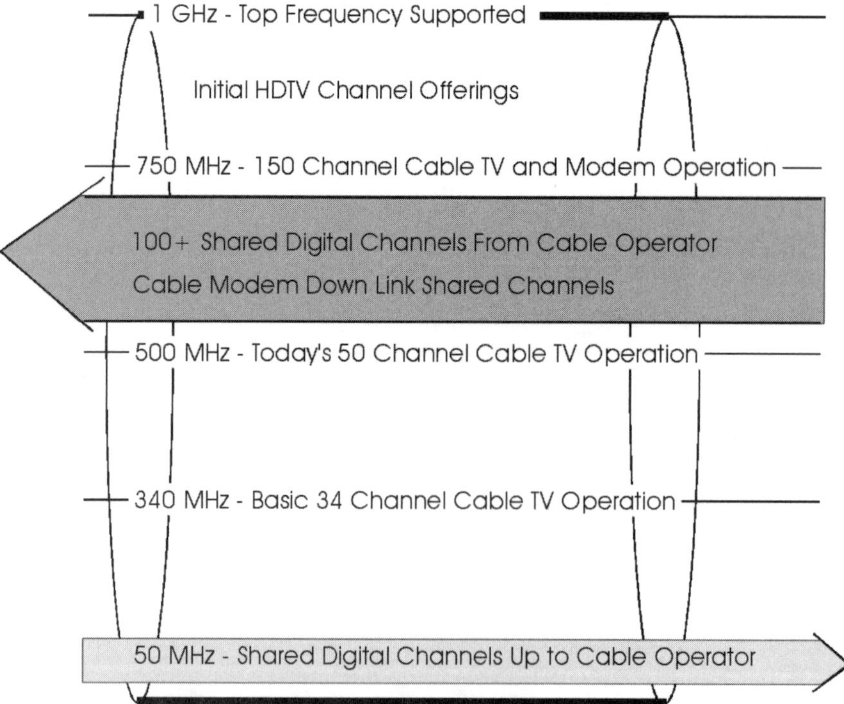

Figure 5.2 Cable television and cable modem frequencies.

pass through a cable television company's head end. Figure 5.3 shows a typical cable modem configuration.

Some cable modem services send upstream signals by telephone rather than the coaxial cable. This is called a telco-return cable modem. The downstream signals travel across the cable television coaxial cable plant to the customer's cable modem.

Cable modems can receive data from the Internet over the cable television cable at speeds up to 30 Mbps and can transmit data at speeds up to 2.5 Mbps. Cable modems are set up to restrict speeds to 128 Kbps up to the Internet and from 400 to 800 Kbps down from the Internet. These speed restrictions vary from cable television system to cable television system.

Comcast's business Internet service restricts uplink speeds to 128 Kbps from a customer's site. This prevents a customer from Web hosting with an onsite server. Comcast provides an offsite managed server facility for Web

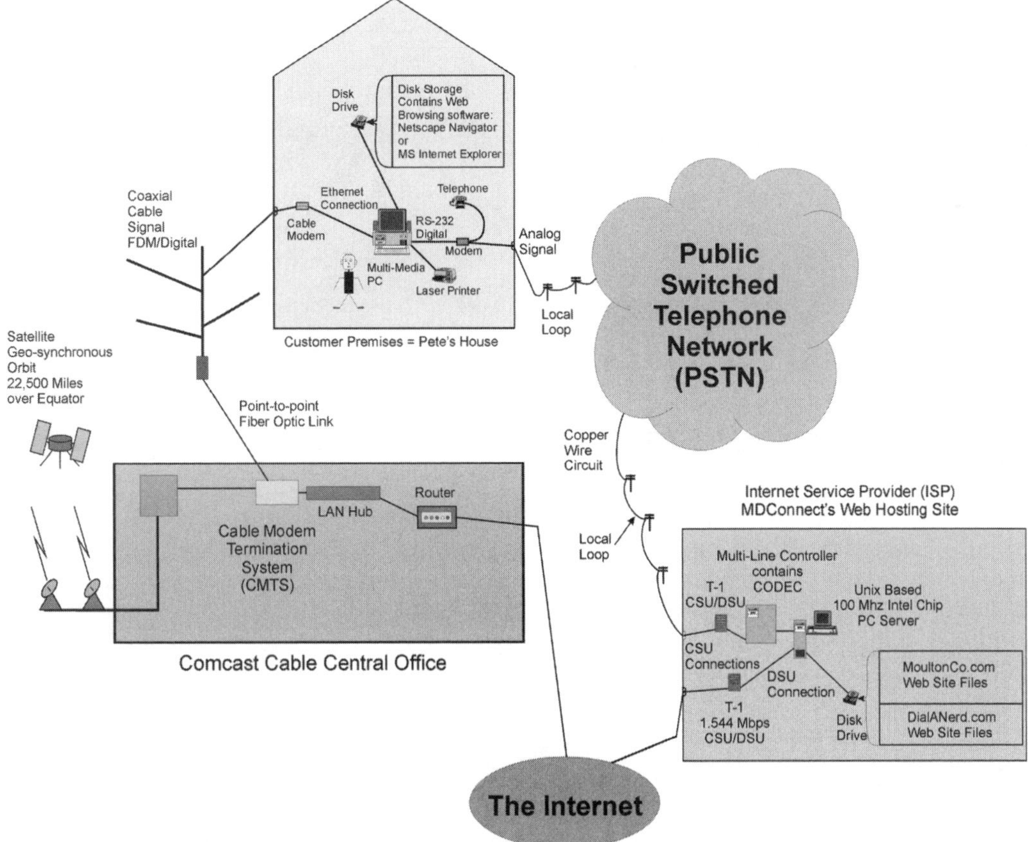

Figure 5.3 Cable modem network components.

hosting, but the 128 Kbps uplink restriction from a customer's facility makes uploading files to such a managed Web server impractical. Further, the cost of Comcast's business services is very high when compared with a more practical approach using a standard cable modem and an off-the-shelf Internet router and firewall and hosting a site at any other managed Web server facility.

In addition to the faster data rates, the advantage of cable modems over telephone Internet access is that cable modems provide continuous high-speed Internet connectivity with either a variable—using DHCP—or fixed IP address 24 hours a day, 7 days a week. There is no phone line sharing with the computer required.

Cable modems have enjoyed an early lead in providing residential users with high-speed Internet access.

Cable modems are purchased at a computer grocery store like Best Buy or CompUSA as a self-installation kit. The kit contains the cable modem and installation software to connect to the cable television provider's network. Windows software has the necessary TCP/IP software built in to operate the cable modem connection. This obviates the need for special installation software.

Brain Teaser: Cable Modems

Go to a local computer store and check for cable modem self -installation kits. Are self-installation kits available? What is their cost? What is the monthly cost of the cable modem service? Does the cable company need to upgrade the cable running into your facility to permit the cable modem to run?

Digital Subscriber Lines

DSL technology brings high-speed Internet access to residences and small businesses using existing copper wire telephone lines. Because DSL is a generic acronym for a family of dedicated services, there are several versions of DSL technology described in Table 5.1.

Table 5.1 DSL Technologies.

Acronym	Type of DSL Technology	Uplink Speed in Mbps	Downlink Speed in Mbps	Comments
ADSL	Asymmetric Digital Subscriber Line	128 to 384 Kbps	384 Kbps to 1.5 Mbps	Original DSL
HDSL	High-Bit-Rate Digital Subscriber Line	1.5 Mbps	1.5 Mbps	4-wire circuit
IDSL	ISDN Digital Subscriber Line	128 Kbps	128 Kbps	An ISDN substitute—who needs it?
RADSL	Rate Adaptive Digital Subscriber Line	128 Kbps	384 Kbps	Too slow for me, but better than nothing!
SDSL	Single-Line Digital Subscriber Line	1.5 Mbps	1.5 Mbps	2-wire circuit
UDSL	Universal Digital Subscriber Line	128 to 384 Kbps	384 Kbps to 1.0 Mbps	Splitter-less DSL or DSL lite
VDSL	Very High Rate Digital Subscriber Line	1.5 to 2.3 Mbps	13 to 52 Mbps	A nerd's dream

A home or small business must be within 18,000 feet of a telephone company central office for DSL service to work. In my case, my facility is 27,000 feet from the nearest telephone company central office, so DSL is not a high-speed Internet access option for me.

DSL connections are capable of very high speeds the closer they are to the telephone company central office. However, DSL connections commonly operate at 1.544 Mbps to 512 Kbps downstream from the Internet and 128 Kbps upstream to the Internet. The basic DSL speeds are similar to the basic cable modem speeds.

A DSL line carries data and at the same time provides a regular voice telephone connection. The data connection is continuous 24 hours a day, 7 days a week. This is shown in Figure 5.4. Similar to cable modems, DSL connections are carried back to a LAN that then connects to the Internet. In the diagram the Internet-connected LAN is shown to reside in the central office facility. This may not be the case. At each central office there could be a high-speed (1.544 Mbps or higher) digital connection that connects the DSL LAN to a LAN at an ISP and thus to the Internet.

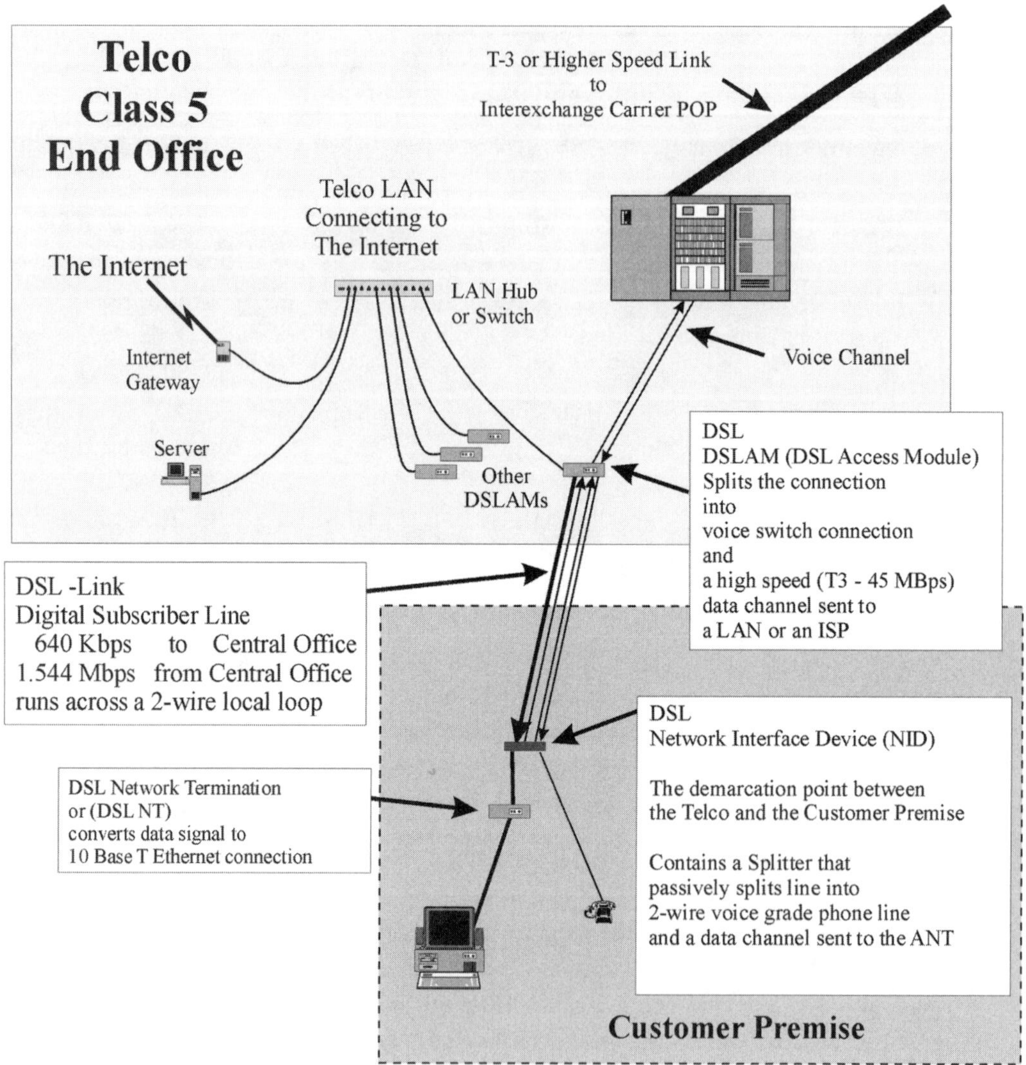

Figure 5.4 DSL network configuration.

DSL competes with cable modems in bringing voice, multimedia video, and 3-D imaging to residential customers and small businesses. Similar to cable modems, DSL installation is also performed with self-install kits. However, DSL kit installation can be more technically challenging to set up than cable modems, sometimes necessitating a technical support installation visit.

DSL speeds and pricing vary. Verizon offers several packages, with the slowest speed costing $49.95 per month after the first three months. This package uploads to the Internet at 128 Kbps and downloads data from the Internet at speeds up to 768 Kbps. The Verizon DSL options and prices are described in Table 5.2.

Table 5.2 DSL Costs and Speeds.

Package Number	Uplink Speed (Kbps)	Downlink Speed (Kbps)	Monthly Fee
1	128	768	$59.95
2	128	1,500	$69.95
3	384	384	$79.95
4	384	1,500	$89.95
5	768	768	$129.95
6	768	7,100	$204.95

The significant feature of theses packages is that the uplink speed can exceed 128 Kbps and the downlink speed can range up to 7.1 Mbps. Where DSL is possible and higher-capacity Internet connectivity is needed to work with a Web site, DSL is the better choice over cable modems.

ISDN

The Integrated Services Digital Network (ISDN) is a telecommunications networking architecture using digital transmission for integrated voice, data, video, and image services over standard twisted-pair telephone wire. ISDN is defined by CCITT/ITU standards specifying digital transmission over ordinary telephone copper wire and other media.

As a digital phone connection, ISDN has been widely available throughout the United States for over a decade. However, in some areas ISDN remains quite expensive. ISDN is a service supporting low-end video conferencing, branch-office LAN-to-LAN interconnection, and Internet access. ISDN meets international standards that define interfaces between telecommunications equipment and intelligent telephone networks.

ISDN provides special telephone services using digital transmission over ordinary telephone lines. Home and business users install ISDN to speed up Internet access to 128 Kbps. Unlike cable modems and DSL, ISDN operates at the same 128 Kbps maximum speed for transmission, both up to and down from the Internet.

Unlike DSL and cable modems, ISDN is generally available from the local exchange carrier in most areas of the United States. Full-period ISDN service varies in cost from relatively inexpensive to very expensive. Full-period ISDN service can cost from $171.45 to $271.45 per month.

The major drawback of ISDN service is that Internet access is initiated with a phone call. ISDN connections use the telephone company central office switch facilities when connecting to the Internet. ISDN connections are not like leased line, cable modem, or DSL connections that provide Internet connectivity 24 hours per day, 7 days per week.

ISDN uses a separate data channel for supervisory signaling. ISDN sends information about a call along with the call. ISDN network configurations are shown in Figure 5.5.

In the figure, LANs connect with ISDN routers and PC hosts with ISDN modems (CSU/DSU) connect to the PSTN. They are thus able to dialup an ISP and connect into the Internet.

ISDN installation is more complex than both cable modem and DSL installation. It requires configuring the ISDN CSU/DSU (ISDN modem) with a Service Profile Identifier (SPID) that specifically tailors the telephone network to work with the ISDN equipment.

An ISDN channel carries voice, data, image, or facsimile information over bearer (B) channels at 64 Kbps. The B channels allow voice or data to be transmitted digitally around the planet. A 64-Kbps B channel is the equivalent of a single phone line. These B channels are clear channels, with the full 64 Kbps being available to handle voice, image, or data transmission.

While ISDN carries voice and data over 64-Kbps B channels, sometimes central office switches limit B channels to a capacity of 56 Kbps. The minimum B channels provided are two and the maximum are 24 for basic ISDN services.

The B channels are combined with a separate channel for signaling transmission. This is the data or delta (D) channel. The D channel carries signaling at 16 to 64 Kbps using HDLC (High Level Data Link Control Protocol)—Link Access Protocol Data (LAPD). The D channel may also carry other packet-switched data to and from an intelligent telephone network.

The two basic types of ISDN service are Basic Rate Interface (BRI) and Primary Rate Interface (PRI).

BRI consists of two 64 Kbps B channels and one 16 Kbps D channel for a total of 144 Kbps usable bandwidth. This basic service is intended for residential users. A BRI is sometimes referred to as 2B+D.

The B channels carry circuit switched voice and other digital transmissions. Control signaling for call establishment, call monitoring, call termination, and

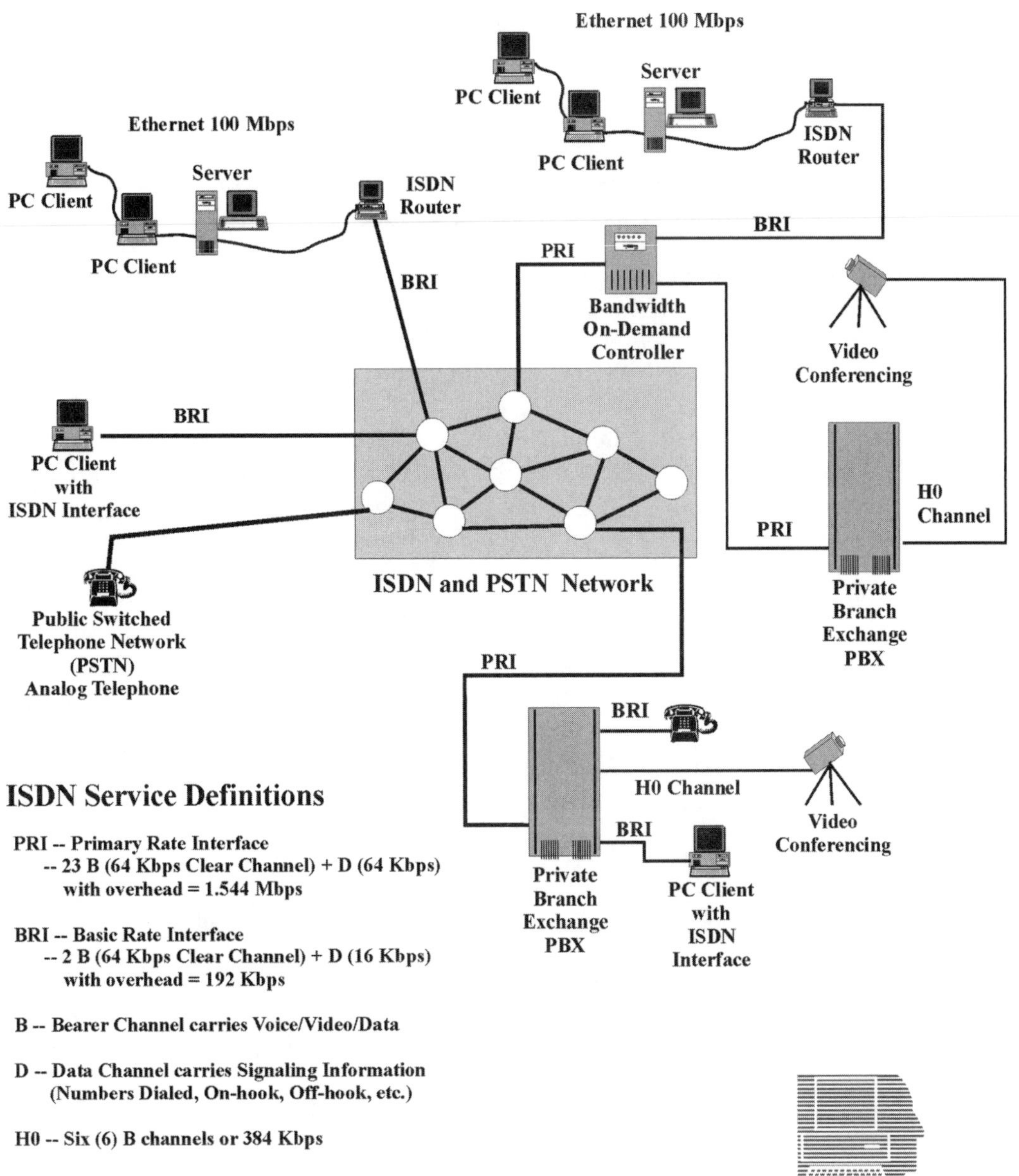

Figure 5.5 ISDN networking architecture.

enhanced telephone features use common channel signaling on the D (data) channel. The D channel speed of 16 Kbps is more than adequate to handle the signaling information for the two B channels in a BRI.

To get BRI service a customer must be within 18,000 feet (about 3.4 miles or 5.5 km) of the telephone company central office. Beyond that distance, repeaters are required, or ISDN service may not be available at all. Customers also need special equipment to communicate with the phone company switch and with other ISDN devices, such as ISDN terminal adapters (TAs), which are sometimes called ISDN modems.

The PRI has 23 B channels and a full 64-Kbps D channel for an aggregate transmission capacity available to the user of 1.536 Mbps. The PRI is provided over a T-1 specification communication link of 1.544 Mbps, with 8 Kbps used for transmission overhead. In Europe PRIs consist of 31 B channels plus one 64 Kbps D channel for a combined speed of 2,048 Kbps. PRIs interconnect medium and large PBXs, ISDN multiplexers, and mainframes to each other or to a telephone company central office.

PRI is targeted at business users with greater capacity requirements. It is possible to cover multiple PRIs with one 64 Kbps D channel using non-facility associated signaling (NFAS). Telephone companies like PRI customers to have at least two PRIs with D channels before they provide a PRI with no D channel. In this manner the customer has a D channel backup in the event of a network outage.

ISDN PRI call-by-call service allows PRI channels to support different mixes of services as needed, such as toll-free telephone numbers. Customer PBXs perform service reconfigurations automatically using the D channel ISDN interface to negotiate the changes with the ISDN network.

H channels aggregate B channels. They are defined as the following:

H0 = 384 Kbps (6 B channels)
H10 = 1,472 Kbps (23 B channels)
H11 = 1,536 Kbps (24 B channels)
H12 = 1,920 Kbps (30 B channels)—international (E1) only

The H channels carry high-speed circuit switched traffic like video teleconferencing calls.

Connection and installation fees vary widely depending on the city where ISDN is installed. See Table 5.3.

Table 5.3 ISDN Costs in Selected U.S. Cities.

City	Installation	Added Costs	Monthly	Per Minute
Memphis Nashville Knoxville (BellSouth)	$41.50 to $59.50	Taxes Extra jacks Inside wiring	$29.50 to $40.50	None
Baltimore Richmond Charlestown, WV (Verizon)	$125 + $48.00	Inside wiring	$30.35	$0.02/minute peak $0.01/minute off peak
Hartford (SNET)	$265	$15 per additional number extra jacks	$50 + $7.50 per additional number	$0.035/minute peak $0.015/minute off peak
St. Louis (SBC)	$400	Inside wiring	$92	None
Dallas and Houston (SBC)	$78.60 to $328.60	Taxes Extra jacks Inside wiring	$58	None
San Francisco San Jose Los Angeles (SBC)	$125	New line $34.75	$29.50	$0.03 first minute, $0.01/ minute thereafter

Without lower ISDN flat rate pricing, ISDN use for high-speed Internet access is only practical when no other high-speed service is available. The costs for a BRI for a business are higher than the cost of an ISDN BRI for a residence. Both the installation cost and monthly fees are greater for business BRIs.

Brain Teaser: ISDN Modems

Check the local computer store (Best Buy, CompUSA, Fry's, etc.) to see if it sells ISDN modems. You do not really have to drop this book and run to the store right now, unless you prefer to do so. Just check next time you are shopping. Are ISDN modems available? How does the kit explain how to order ISDN service? In most cases you may find no ISDN modems sold in these stores because cable modems and DSL services are so much cheaper and better.

Other

The cable modem, DSL, and ISDN BRI connections are mainly used by home-office LANs and some modest size small-office LANs. Other connections like Frame Relay or T-carrier connections are used by larger small-office LANs for high-speed Internet access. Both Frame Relay and T-carrier connections are 24 by 7 connections with capacity varying up to 1.544 Mbps. Typical high-speed Internet connectivity services for small-office LANs—with pricing—are shown for my ISP, MDConnect, in Figure 5.6.

The primary alternatives to cable modems, DSL, and ISDN connectivity for small-office LANs are Frame Relay and T-carrier services. We examine these services in more detail here.

Frame Relay

Frame Relay service offers businesses scaleable, high-speed Internet access. Frame Relay service is a high-speed fast packet network offering connection speeds at committed information rates (CIR) ranging from 128 Kbps to full T-1 1.544 Mbps. This service supports businesses that have moderate to heavy Internet traffic. It can support data, voice, and video applications. Frame Relay service can start with a 128 Kbps connection and then increase the speed up as Internet traffic increases. No additional equipment is needed to speed up the service. Faster service is simply ordered and it is implemented by software commands from the Frame Relay network vendor.

Another advantage of Frame Relay is that it can accommodate bursts of data up to twice the speed of the CIR.

Frame Relay service is designed for cost-efficient data transmission between LANs and the Internet. Frame Relay puts data in a variable-size frame. Error correction is provided by data retransmission. Frame Relay end points determine whether error correction is required, which speeds up data transmission through the Frame Relay network. Frame Relay provides a permanent virtual circuit (PVC), giving the customer 24 by 7 continuous connection. An enterprise can select a quality of service prioritizing specific frames and making other frames less important. Frame Relay provides symmetric transmission speeds to and from the Internet up to 1.544 Mbps. This exceeds the uplink speeds of cable modems and DSL channels for businesses.

Figure 5.7 shows a general Frame Relay network configuration. A LAN at one site is connected to a LAN at a second site or to an ISP for Internet access through a Frame Relay network. The first site has a local access channel con-

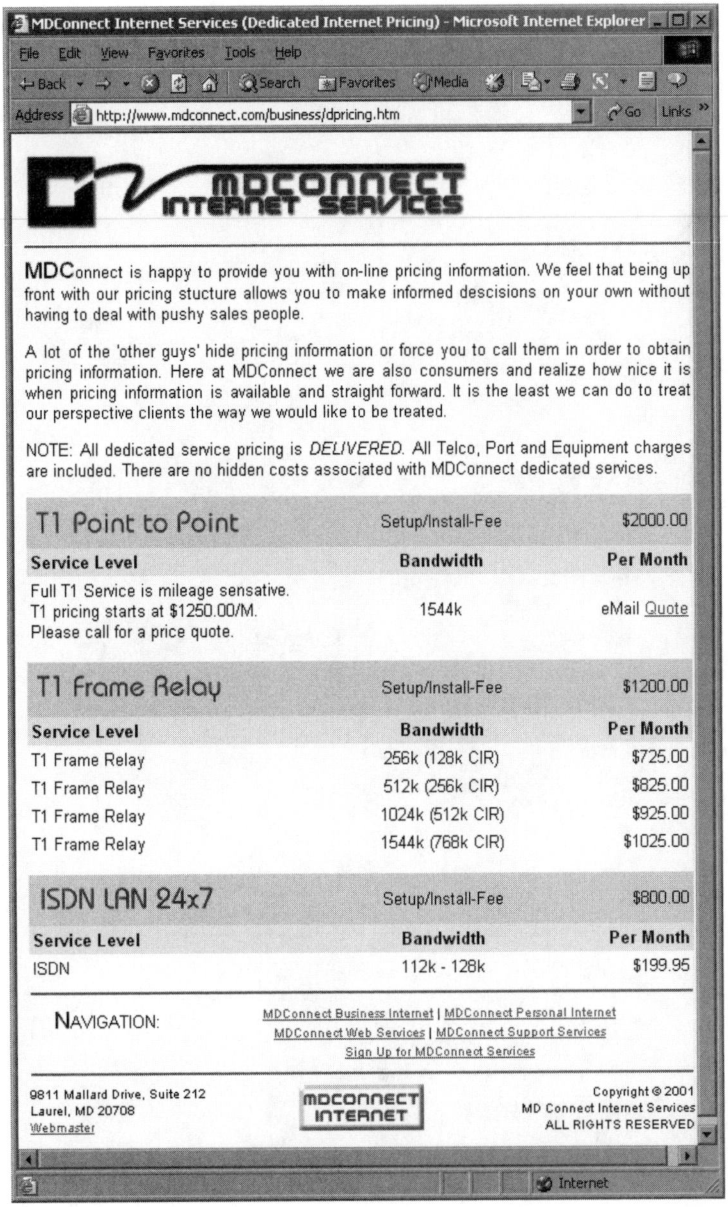

MDConnect Internet Services (Dedicated Internet Pricing) - Microsoft Internet Explorer

File Edit View Favorites Tools Help

Address http://www.mdconnect.com/business/dpricing.htm

MDCONNECT INTERNET SERVICES

MDConnect is happy to provide you with on-line pricing information. We feel that being up front with our pricing stucture allows you to make informed descisions on your own without having to deal with pushy sales people.

A lot of the 'other guys' hide pricing information or force you to call them in order to obtain pricing information. Here at MDConnect we are also consumers and realize how nice it is when pricing information is available and straight forward. It is the least we can do to treat our perspective clients the way we would like to be treated.

NOTE: All dedicated service pricing is *DELIVERED.* All Telco, Port and Equipment charges are included. There are no hidden costs associated with MDConnect dedicated services.

T1 Point to Point	Setup/Install-Fee	$2000.00
Service Level	**Bandwidth**	**Per Month**
Full T1 Service is mileage sensative. T1 pricing starts at $1250.00/M. Please call for a price quote.	1544k	eMail Quote

T1 Frame Relay	Setup/Install-Fee	$1200.00
Service Level	**Bandwidth**	**Per Month**
T1 Frame Relay	256k (128k CIR)	$725.00
T1 Frame Relay	512k (256k CIR)	$825.00
T1 Frame Relay	1024k (512k CIR)	$925.00
T1 Frame Relay	1544k (768k CIR)	$1025.00

ISDN LAN 24x7	Setup/Install-Fee	$800.00
Service Level	**Bandwidth**	**Per Month**
ISDN	112k - 128k	$199.95

NAVIGATION: MDConnect Business Internet | MDConnect Personal Internet
MDConnect Web Services | MDConnect Support Services
Sign Up for MDConnect Services

9811 Mallard Drive, Suite 212
Laurel, MD 20708
Webmaster

MDCONNECT INTERNET

Copyright © 2001
MD Connect Internet Services
ALL RIGHTS RESERVED

Internet

Figure 5.6 High-speed Internet connectivity pricing. Image courtesy MDConnect, ©2002.

necting to a Frame Relay network point of presence (POP). This is a digital channel operating at one of several transmission speeds, up to T-1 channel speeds of 1.544 Mbps. The local access channel speeds are dependent upon

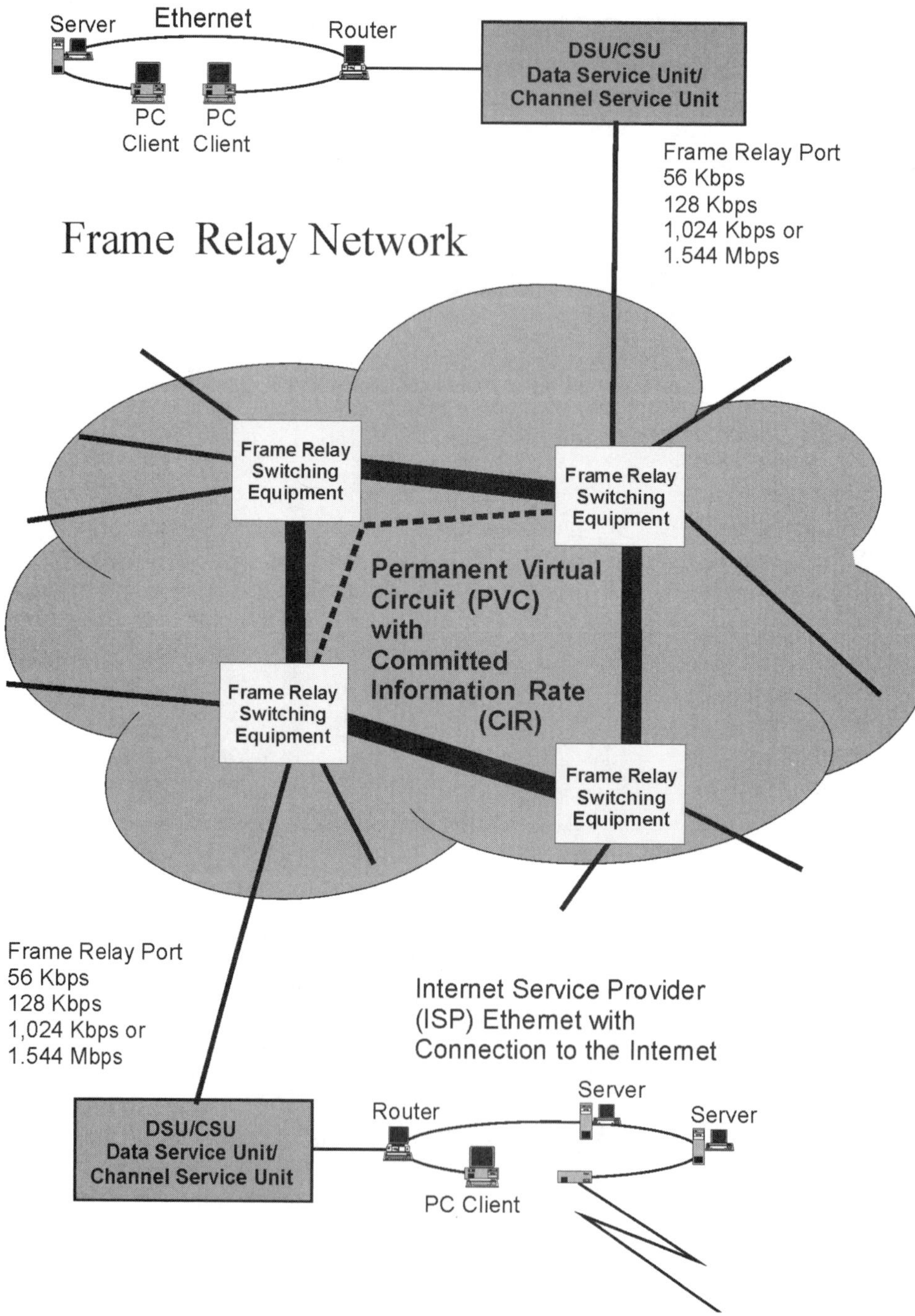

Figure 5.7 Basic Frame Relay network configuration.

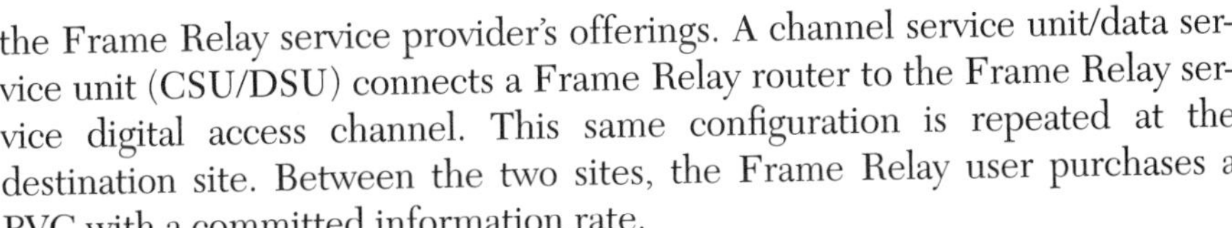

the Frame Relay service provider's offerings. A channel service unit/data service unit (CSU/DSU) connects a Frame Relay router to the Frame Relay service digital access channel. This same configuration is repeated at the destination site. Between the two sites, the Frame Relay user purchases a PVC with a committed information rate.

PVCs are software-defined logical connections between two end points in a Frame Relay network. PVCs permit users to define logical connections and required transmission speeds (bandwidths) between Frame Relay network end points. The Frame Relay network determines how the physical network is used to make the PVC connections and how the PVC traffic is managed. The end points and a stated bandwidth called a committed information rate (CIR) constitute PVCs.

A PVC is similar to a leased line channel between two sites because it guarantees a specific transmission speed between those sites. However, since the PVC runs across shared facilities, it costs the Frame Relay subscriber substantially less than an equivalent leased channel facility would cost. Once a site connects to a Frame Relay POP, it can then connect to many other sites with PVCs.

The CIR is the transmission speed expressed in bits per second assigned to PVCs. In Frame Relay networks different logical connections share the same physical path. Some logical connections are assigned higher transmission speeds or more bandwidth than others. A PVC carrying video would require a 384 Kbps CIR while a LAN-to-LAN connection may only need a 256 Kbps CIR. Both logical connections could run across a Frame Relay network backbone link operating at, say, 1.544 Mbps. A CIR is defined in software permitting a Frame Relay network's mix of traffic bandwidths to be quickly and easily redefined as requirements change. However, it makes no sense to define a 128 Kbps CIR for a site that has a physical connection speed of 64 Kbps.

The CIR is implemented with software buffers. These buffers are like glasses of water. They are one second wide and for a 256 Kbps CIR, 256,000 bits deep. Figure 5.8 illustrates generally how the CIR works. The glass that is the CIR can hold one second's data or, in our example, 256,000 bits. When data arrives at a faster rate than 256 Kbps the CIR buffer overflows into an equivalent glass that is also one second wide and 256,000 bits deep.

In each frame header there is a discard eligibility (DE) bit. The frames below CIR (those that fit in the CIR glass) are not eligible for discard (DE = 0).

The bits falling into the CIR overflow buffer are marked as discard eligible by the Frame Relay router. The DE bit in those frames is set to one (DE-1) and the frame is eligible for discard. In the event of network congestion they can be discarded (spilled on the floor, never to return). Most Frame Relay vendors say that discarded frames in their networks are much less than one

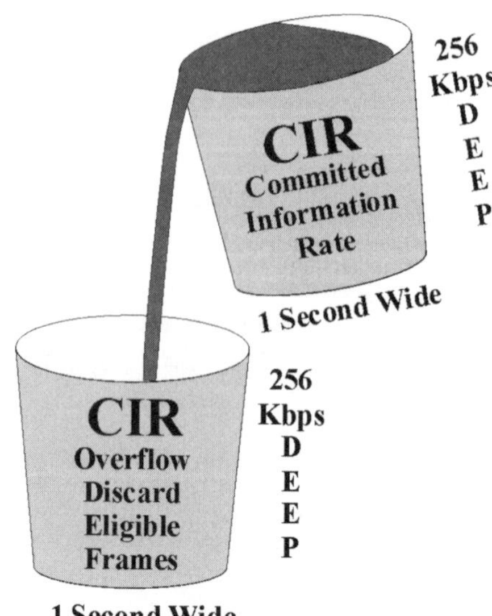

Figure 5.8
Committed Information Rate (CIR) operation.

percent. This is true if you measure them as a percentage of the total data sent through the network, but what really counts is that during periods of data congestion what percent of the active frames are discarded. This would be more a true measure of Frame Relay network performance.

In Frame Relay networks the information field size is negotiated among users and networks and among networks. The maximum size can be as small as 262 characters and as large as several thousand characters. LAN-to-LAN connections generally use a frame size around 1,600 characters. Some Frame Relay services support sizes of 4,096 characters or more. Frame Relay frames have low frame overhead.

T-Carrier Channels and Services

The T-carrier system originally supported digitized voice transmission. AT&T first used it in the 1960s. The basic T-carrier line is a T-1 digital channel with a transmission speed of 1.544 Mbps. T-1 channels are commonly used today for voice transmission and to connect to Internet service providers (ISPs) and the Internet.

The T-carrier system is digital using pulse code modulation and time division multiplexing. The T-carrier channels have full-duplex capability, using four-wire service with two wires for receiving and two for transmitting. T-carrier channels are symmetric with a speed of 1.544 Mbps carrying digital information to and from a facility. The T-1 digital stream consists of 24 DS-0

64-Kbps channels that are time division multiplexed. T-1 channels were originally delivered using two pair twisted-pair copper wires. Coaxial cable, optical fiber, digital microwave, and other media may also deliver T-1 channels.

A typical T-1 site-to-site connection is shown in Figure 5.9. The T-1 channel between the two sites connects to Channel Service Units/Data Service Units that implement Bi-Polar Eight Bit Zero Substitution (B8ZS) and Extended Super Frame (ESF) transmission on the T-carrier channel. T-1 multiplexers attach to the CSU/DSU and split the T-1 channel into DS-0 channels with some routed to the voice PBX and others routed to the data network. The T-1 multiplexer permits the DS-0 channels assigned to voice and data to be varied such that during the daytime most of the DS-0 channels handle voice communications between the two sites. At night the bulk of the DS-0 channels are moved over to the data side to facilitate computer-to-computer data file backups and other file transfers between the sites.

T-1 channels are not cost saving services unless there is sufficient call and data transfer volumes between the two sites. In this case the cost of the T-1 full period leased channel would reduce the long-distance telephone charges between the sites and provide for data transfers. Alternatively, Frame Relay service with voice channels having priority or meeting a specific quality of service (QoS) delay could be less costly than a T-1 channel.

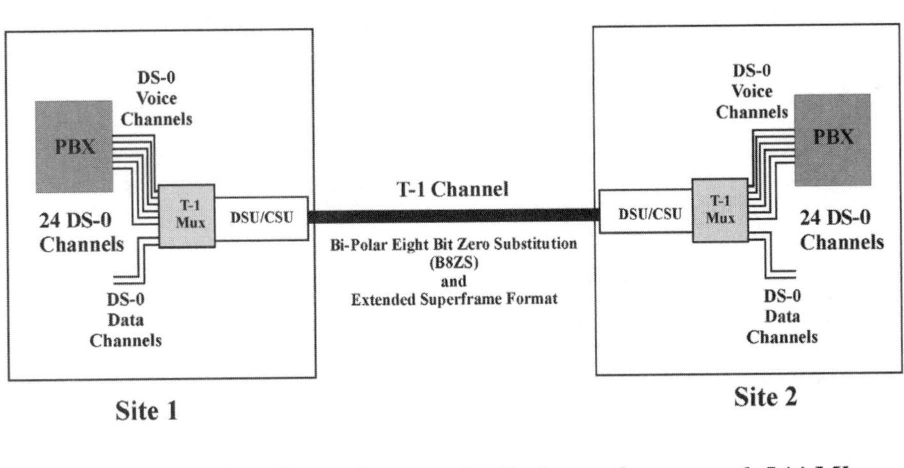

DS-1	*24 voice channels*	*1 T1 channel*	*1.544 Mbps*
DS-1C	*48 voice channels*	*2 T1 channels*	*3.152 Mbps*
DS-2	*96 voice channels*	*4 T1 channels*	*6.312 Mbps*
DS-3	*672 voice channels*	*28 T1 channels*	*44.736 Mbps*

DSU/CSU = Data Service Unit/Channel Service Unit

Figure 5.9 T-1 channel configuration.

T-1 channels are time division multiplexed. This means when DS-0 channels are assigned to voice traffic and there are few calls to carry, the capacity of those channels is wasted.

For sites with significant load and the need for voice and data connectivity, T-carrier facilities present a solution for high-speed Internet access.

A typical quote for a T-1 channel for both voice and data connectivity is shown in Figure 5.10.

INTERNET AND VOICE ACCESS

Qty	Equipment description	Unit cost
1	Cisco 1720 Modular Router	$995
1	IP / Firewall Feature Pack	$830
1	1 port Serial WAN interface card	$335
1	Cable Set	$88
1	Adtran TA 750 *(Provided)*	
1	NX 56/64K V.35 Module	
1	Quad FXS Voice Module	
	Installation	$1,000
	Total one-time costs	$3,248 *

Qty	Internet Access	
1	1024K dedicated Internet access port	$900 **
1	Local T1.5 access channel	$250

Qty	Voice Access	
8	Business line with dail tone and touch tone service	$162
3000	Minutes of long distance traffic at .048 cents	$144

* 24 month service included. Lease option estimated at $250.00 per month.
** 24 month service. 12 month is $1000, 36 month is $800.

Billing of all services by Single Source, Inc. Single Invoice.

Services arranged by East Coast Communications, Inc
804-330-7373 Voice 804-330-4152 Fax

Figure 5.10 T-1 carrier quote.

This quote was for a T-1 channel split between voice services and data services. Eight DS-0 channels would be split off into voice and a local PBX, and the remaining 16 DS-0 channels would service the small-office LAN, providing high-speed access to the Internet. This means that 1,024 Kbps would be dedicated to high-speed Internet access. The installed configuration would use copper wire to deliver the T-1 connection through a V.35 interface to a Cisco router. The router would split the DS-0 channels into voice and data channels, with the data channels being combined into a single 1,024 Kbps Internet access port and the voice channels routed to a PBX. The voice channels would also have 3,000 minutes of long-distance voice service at 48 cents per minute, for a total monthly cost of $144. This configuration has a one-time installation fee of $3,248.

Such a configuration would be ideal for a small business with significant voice and data traffic. Eight shared voice lines can easily service a 20-person office using a PBX. The 1,024 Kbps Internet access is faster than a cable modem or a DSL connection provides, particularly since it is the same speed connection up to the Internet and down from the Internet.

Brain Teaser: Dedicated High-speed Connection

Check the high-speed dedicated connection installation process described at *home.verio.com/products/access/dedicated/moreinfo/install.cfm.*

How much time is estimated to complete the ordering and installation process for a dedicated high-speed link?

Internet Connection Sharing

After determining which type of high-speed Internet connection is best for a SOHO LAN, the next decision is how to share the connection among all the PC hosts in a facility. There are several approaches, all of which involve routing data to and from the PC hosts attached to the SOHO LAN. Routing represents a SOHO network of PC hosts as a single IP address to the next-level ISP. They in turn also represent their network as a single IP address to the next-higher-level ISP. This process continues until the highest-level ISP connects into the top-level Internet backbone.

There are two general approaches to connection sharing: a hardware approach requiring the installation of a hardware router, and a software approach requiring that routing software be installed on a PC host that connects to both the LAN and to the high-speed Internet channel. Windows XP comes with Internet connection sharing software built in, but other connection sharing packages are available.

Windows Internet Connection Sharing (WICS)

Windows Internet Connection Sharing (WICS) connects PC hosts in a SOHO LAN to the Internet using a single connection. A WICS hosting computer needs two network connections. The first is a private LAN connection automatically created by installing a network adapter. The private LAN connection connects to other PC host computers on the SOHO LAN. The second connection, using a modem, an ISDN CSU/DSU, a DSL modem, or a cable modem, connects the home- or small-office network to the Internet. WICS must be enabled on the connection to the Internet connection. By doing this, the shared connection can be used by PC hosts on a SOHO LAN to connect to the Internet. Users outside the SOHO network do not receive IP addresses from the SOHO network that conflict with their ISP-assigned addresses. Duplicate and conflicting ISP addresses cause PC hosts not to work on the Internet.

When choosing a computer to host WICS in a SOHO LAN you should consider the following:

1. The WICS hosting computer should be running Windows XP.
2. The WICS hosting PC should be a fast PC with lots of RAM. A PC with a GHz or higher CPU and with 512 MB of RAM would be better than a 500-MHz machine with 64 MB of RAM.
3. This WICS hosting computer generally operates 24 hours a day and 7 days a week; otherwise, the shared connection to the Internet is not available.
4. The WICS hosting computer should use the highest-speed Internet connection possible, such as a DSL or cable modem.
5. Only one computer can act as a WICS hosting computer. If WICS is running on another computer, turn off WICS on that computer before starting it on another Windows XP host PC.
6. Shared printers should be installed on the WICS hosting PC because it is always running on the SOHO LAN to provide Internet access. Since it is always running, any printers attached to that machine would always be available for printing as well.

When setting WICS on a SOHO network, the Network Setup Wizard in Windows XP Professional can be used to enable Internet connection sharing. The Network Setup Wizard is the easiest way to install WICS because it automatically provides the network settings needed to share an Internet connection with all other PC hosts.

Alternatively, to enable Internet connection sharing on any network connection, click the right mouse button on My Network Places, then select Properties from the drop down menu. Click the right mouse button on the network connection that you are going to share. Select Properties from the drop down menu, and then select the Advanced tab. If the network connection is not sharable, sharing does not appear as an option. This same menu is found when under Network Tasks, the Change Settings Menu option is selected when pointing at a specific network connection and then the Advanced tab is selected. See Figure 5.11.

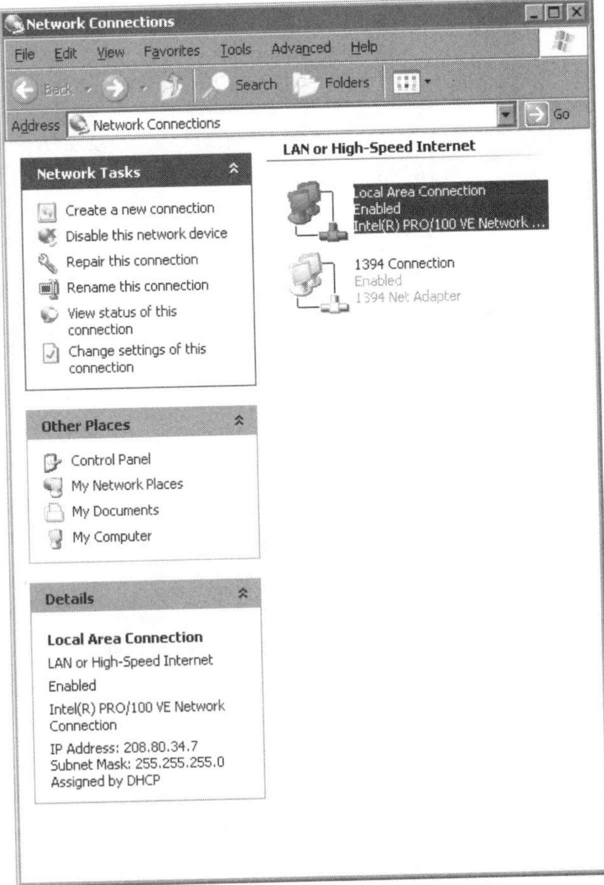

Figure 5.11
Network settings.

One computer connects to the Internet by using a high-speed DSL connection with WICS enabled, then the other computers on the network connect to the Internet through this high-speed connection.

When a network connection is sharable the Internet Connections sharing box appears under the Advanced Settings tab, as shown in Figure 5.12.

Checking off "Allow other network users to connect through this computer's Internet connection" enables WICS. Clicking on the Settings button sets up the specific services that users can access through the shared Internet connection. Typical connections would include every service except perhaps remote desktop and Telnet server. Custom services can be added by clicking on the Add button.

Once WICS is set up and running, make sure that all SOHO network PC hosts communicate with each other and that all PC hosts can access the Internet. Test the Internet connection using Internet Explorer or Netscape to browse the Web.

WICS is used in networks where a single computer hosting WICS controls and directs communication between SOHO PC hosts and the Internet. WICS assumes that in a SOHO LAN, only the computer hosting WICS is connected to the Internet. Other computers on the SOHO LAN can use modems to access the Internet, but their primary Internet connection is through the PC hosting WICS.

WICS may need to be configured so that outside Internet users can access specific PC hosts. When a SOHO LAN hosts a Web server and external Inter-

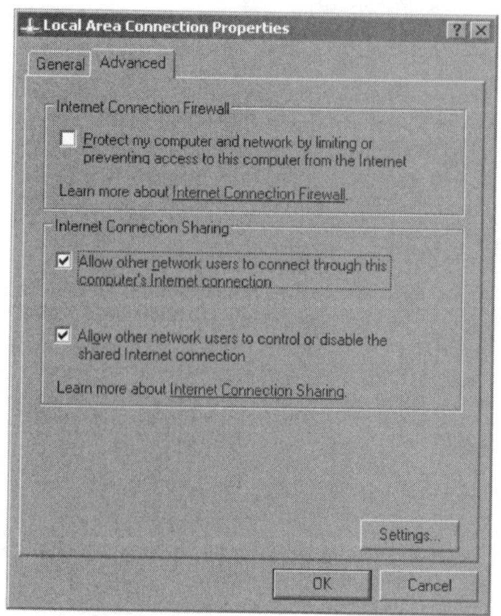

Figure 5.12
Internet Connection Sharing box.

net users need to connect to the Web server, access to the Web server service must be configured on the computer hosting WICS.

WICS is configured on the public connection of the SOHO LAN. When more than one network adapter is installed on a PC hosting WICS, one local area connection—the private network connection—communicates with the other PC hosts on your home- or small-office network. The other network connection—the public network connection—is the shared network connection. When there are three connections in a PC host, two connections are private network connections and the other connection is the public shared network connection. However, in the case of three network adapters the two private network adapters must be bridged. When a network bridge is created that does not include all of the SOHO LAN connections, the bridged connections can be selected as the private connections. The remaining connection is then the shared or public network connection. However, if a network bridge is created that includes all LAN connections into the PC host, the bridge is automatically selected when WICS is enabled because WICS assumes that the shared public connection is included in the bridged connections.

The WICS feature must be specially configured in existing networks with domain controllers, DNS servers, gateways, DHCP servers, or systems configured with static IP addresses. When WICS is enabled, LAN connections to a SOHO network are given a new static IP address. Consequently, TCP/IP connections established between any SOHO PC hosts and the WICS hosting computer are at that time lost and would need to be reestablished. Also, there can be no conflicts between the IP address assigned to the WICS hosting computer and the other PC hosts that have fixed addresses. Also, the proper subnet mask and IP address range must be selected to ensure that all SOHO PC hosts have access to the WICS hosting PC and the shared public Internet connection.

To complete WICS setup, you must be logged in with administrative privileges. When a PC host is connected to a network, network policy settings may also prevent WICS setup.

When a Virtual Private Network (VPN) connection is created on a WICS hosting computer, and WICS uses this connection, then all traffic is routed to the network at the other end of the VPN connection. All PC hosts in the SOHO LAN can access the corporate network and through it the Internet. When WICS is disabled on the VPN connection, other SOHO PC hosts cannot access the corporate network even if the VPN connection is active on the WICS hosting computer.

WICS, Internet Connection Firewall, Discovery and Control, and Network Bridge are not available on Windows XP 64-bit edition; they are only provided with the 32-bit Windows XP software. This is not a big deal because the Windows XP 64-bit edition only runs on 64-bit architecture Itanium CPU chips and not on the more commonly available 32-bit architecture Pentium CPU chips.

Routers

Routers connect two or more networks. A router would link a LAN to the Internet or to other LANs. Routers decide which way to send packets based on the router's current knowledge of the status of the LANs or networks to which it connects. In connecting LANs to the Internet a router is a network component or software in a PC that determines the next network point to which a packet (TCP/IP packet) is forwarded so that the packet can reach its final destination.

Routers create or copy a table of available routes through a network and maintain data on their status. Routers use this information combined according to routing algorithms with distance and cost data to calculate the best route for a packet to follow to reach its final destination. Typically, packets travel through several routers to reach their final destination.

Routers work in the Windows Networking Model Adapter and Protocol Layers. Routers must understand IP routing to function properly. An Internet gateway is a router. Some new routers are a combination of switch and router, as illustrated by the Linksys cable modem/DSL four-port switch router in Figure 5.13.

Figure 5.13
DSL/cable modem router and four-port Ethernet switch.

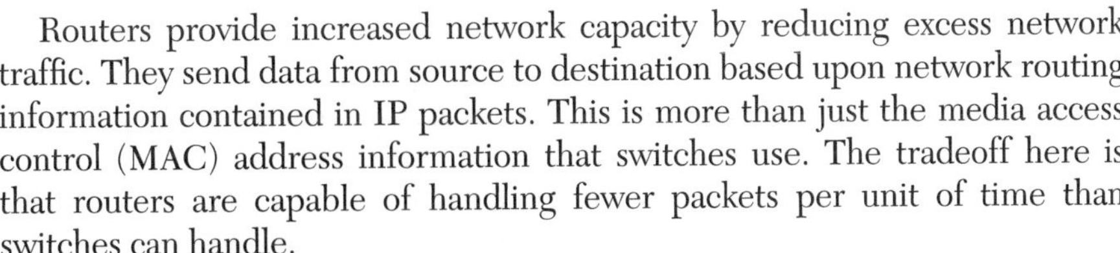

Routers provide increased network capacity by reducing excess network traffic. They send data from source to destination based upon network routing information contained in IP packets. This is more than just the media access control (MAC) address information that switches use. The tradeoff here is that routers are capable of handling fewer packets per unit of time than switches can handle.

Firewalls

A firewall is a security system that provides a protective boundary between the SOHO LAN and the public Internet. A firewall performs routing and packet filtering functions. Firewalls work closely with routing programs. The firewall examines each network packet and determines whether to forward it toward its destination or to discard it.

By protecting the resources of a private network from unauthorized users and sometimes limiting network users in how they can access the public Internet, firewalls provide more functionality than routers alone. An enterprise with employees accessing the public Internet installs a firewall to prevent unauthorized outsiders from accessing its private data and for controlling the specific Internet resources (e.g., no gambling or sex sites permitted) its users can access.

Firewalls represent a network as a single IP address to the Internet. Sometimes a firewall is a specially designated computer separate from the rest of the network or it may be software installed in each PC host. Windows XP provides such firewall software but this is not as effective as firewall software products offered by other software developers.

A firewall may use a separate router and only perform the packet filtering functions. The firewall may physically separate the Internet from a LAN so no packets can directly access the LAN without going through the firewall first.

Firewall packet filtering includes screening packets to ensure they come from previously identified domain names and IP addresses. Firewalls can also scan packet headers and contents for key words and phrases. These can be used to discard unauthorized packets.

Firewalls allow laptop users LAN access through secure logon procedures and authentication certificates.

Firewall features include logging and reporting, automatic alarms at given thresholds of attack, and a Windows user interface for managing and configuring the firewall.

Because Internet traffic and attacks change so often, it is hard to make a firewall totally impervious to external attacks. Firewalls require constant maintenance to keep filtering effective. Sometimes firewalls filter too well and block LAN access from sites that are authorized to connect to a LAN.

While firewalls can prevent unauthorized LAN access from the Internet, they typically cannot effectively filter viruses from packets passing through the firewall. LAN users must use virus scanning programs, must not blindly open files with Visual Basic Script (VBS) macros, and must delete mail from unknown users to keep their chance of getting a virus infection low.

Firewalls must be designed specially to protect against Trojan horse software that gathers passwords and user account information. HAPPY99 was one such program that captured password information and sent them to an Internet account in China. At one time Microsoft in its update and registration process was capturing Ethernet NIC MAC addresses and storing them.

When surfing authorized Web sites, cookies are exchanged between the surfing PC and the Web site. These cookies and other information are used to track Internet usage. Firewalls do not effectively protect against this information gathering activity on the Internet.

Brain Teaser: Firewall Products

Check out the firewall products listed at *ipw.internet.com/protection/firewalls/*.

Did you find both hardware and software firewalls? Use a search engine and see what other firewall products you can find. Can you find firewall products at the *www.pricewatch.com* shopping site? Check Networking Products and then Other to find them.

Windows Internet Connection Firewall (WICF)

Windows XP's Internet Connection Firewall (WICF) is firewall software that sets restrictions on what information is communicated from a PC host to and from the Internet.

When a SOHO LAN uses WICS to monitor Internet access for multiple PC hosts, WICF is enabled on the PC host supporting the WICS Internet connection. WICS and WICF can be used separately.

WICF also protects individual PC hosts connected to the Internet. When a single PC host is connected to the Internet with a cable modem, a DSL modem, or a dialup modem, WICF protects the Internet connection. WICF should be enabled on the Internet connection for all computers that are connected directly to the Internet.

Note that WICF interferes with the operation of file sharing and other VPN functions; consequently, WICF should not be run on VPN connections.

WICF monitors all communications that cross its path and inspects the source and destination address of each message that it handles. To prevent unsolicited traffic from the public Internet connection from entering the private network connection, WICF uses a table listing all communications that have originated from the WICF computer. In a PC host, WICF tracks traffic originated from the PC host. If WICF is used with WICS, WICF tracks all traffic originated from the WICF/WICS computer and all traffic originated from private network PC hosts. Inbound traffic from the Internet is compared against the entries in the table and only allowed to reach PC hosts in a SOHO LAN when an entry matches the table showing a communication exchange initiated from within the PC host or the private SOHO LAN.

Communications originating from Internet sources outside the WICF computer are dropped by the WICF. Special entries may be placed in the table to permit specifically expected traffic to enter the private SOHO LAN. WICF silently discards unsolicited communications, stopping port scanning and other simple network hacking. Instead of notifications WICF creates a security log of activity tracked by the firewall. This log can be viewed to determine if hacking has been attempted.

WICF setup panels are shown in Figure 5.14.

WICF can be configured to permit unsolicited traffic from the Internet to be forwarded by the WICF to the private network. An HTTP Web server would require unsolicited Internet traffic to function. By enabling the HTTP service on the WICF, unsolicited HTTP traffic is forwarded by the WICF to the HTTP server. Operational information, known as a service definition, is required by WICF to allow the unsolicited Internet traffic to be forwarded to a Web server on a private SOHO LAN.

Proxy Servers

Proxy servers act as an intermediary between a PC client and the Internet. Proxy servers perform some security, administrative control, and data caching functions. A proxy server receives a request for an Internet Web page from a client PC. The proxy server filters the request similar to a firewall. If the Web page request is OK to service, the proxy server searches for the Web page in a local cache of previously downloaded Web pages. When the proxy server finds the page, it returns it to the client PC without needing to retrieve the Web page from the Internet. If the requested Web page is not in the cache, the proxy server acts as a surrogate for the client PC and requests the Web page from the server on the Internet. When the requested Web page is returned, the proxy server matches it to the original request and forwards it on to the client PC. It then stores that page in its local cache.

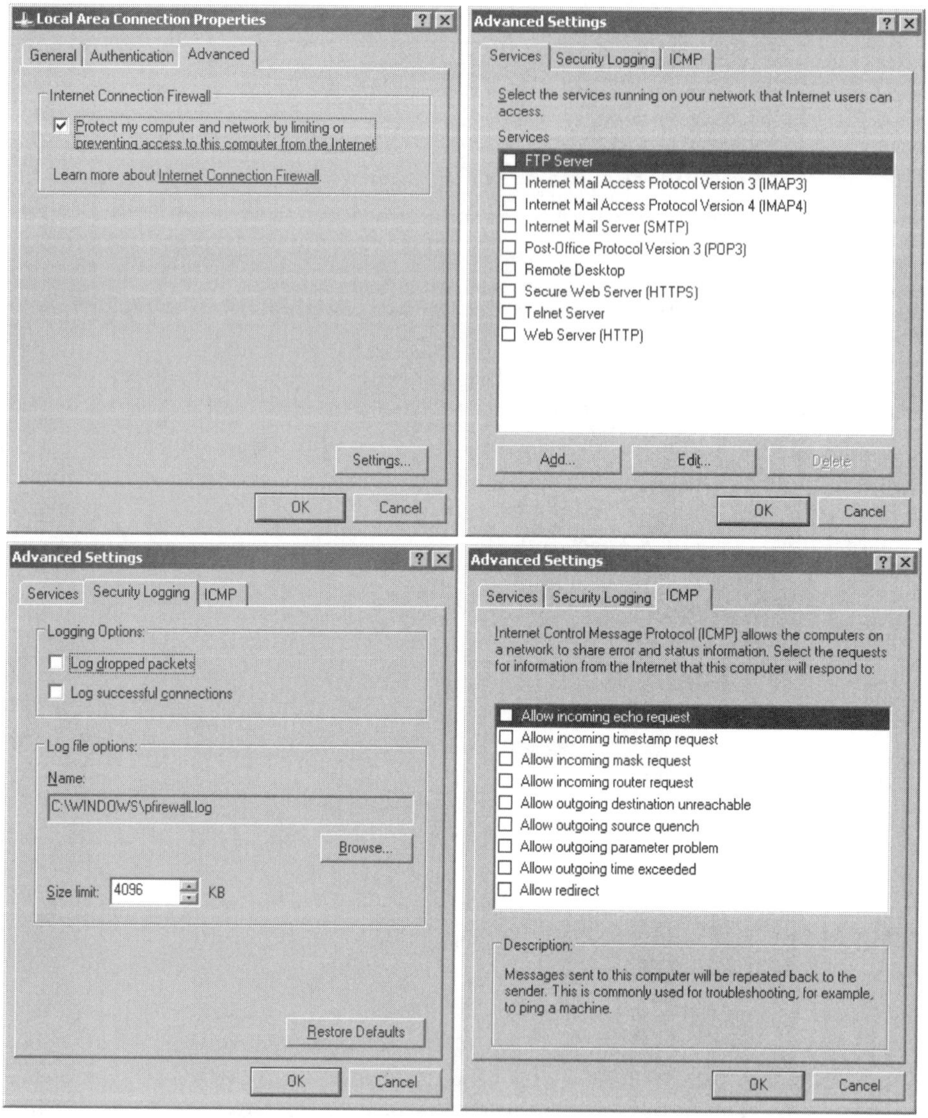

Figure 5.14 WICF setup panels.

Proxy servers are transparent to client PCs. Internet requests and responses appear to be services of the Internet Web page server. The proxy server is not totally invisible to PC clients because its IP address has to be specified as a configuration option for the PC networking software. Further, Web browsers and other programs need to know the specific proxy server ports they use to access the Internet. See Figure 5.15.

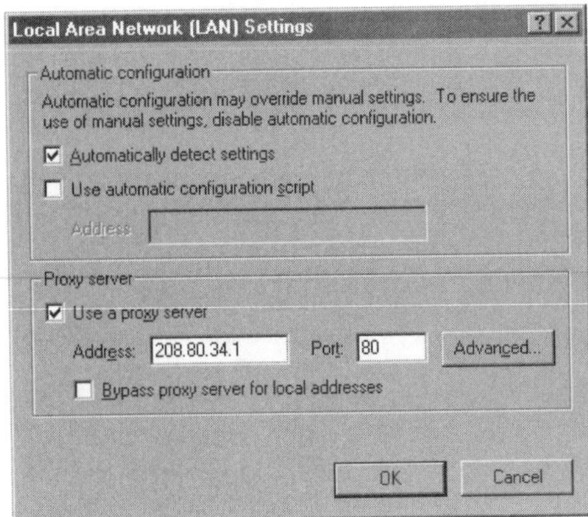

Figure 5.15
Proxy server settings.

A proxy server's cache serves all LAN PC clients. If an Internet site's Web pages are frequently requested, these are likely to be stored in the proxy server's cache and retrieved from there rather than the Internet Web site. This can greatly improve Internet response time. Proxy servers can log Internet request and response activity.

Proxy servers can be associated with a gateway server separating a LAN from the Internet and with a firewall server protecting a LAN from Internet intrusion. The functions of proxy server and firewall can be in separate server programs or combined in a single package. Firewall and proxy server programs can run in different computers. For example, proxy server software may run in the same machine with firewall software or it may run in a separate server and forward requests through a firewall server.

Network Address Translation

Network Address Translation (NAT) is mapping of an Internet Protocol address (IP address) used in one network to a different IP address in another network. NAT designates one network as the inside network and the other network as the outside network. An internal LAN can use NAT to map its local inside network addresses to one or more global outside IP addresses.

Packets are sent from an IP address inside a LAN to the Internet using the global Internet IP address. Packets returned to the global Internet IP address are then translated back into the local LAN IP addresses.

The mapping process helps ensure security since each outgoing or incoming request goes through the mapping process. The mapping provides the ability to qualify or authenticate requests by matching them to previous requests. NAT reduces the number of global Internet IP addresses needed by representing a LAN to the Internet using a single Internet IP address.

NAT is part of a router and is often part of a firewall. LAN administrators create NAT tables that map global-to-local and local-to-global IP addresses. NAT can be static, using few addresses, or it can be dynamic, translating from and to a pool of IP addresses. NAT can support mapping the following:

1. A local IP address to one global IP address
2. A local IP address to any global IP addresses in a rotating pool of global IP addresses
3. A local IP address plus a specific TCP port to a single or pooled global IP address
4. A global IP address to a pool of local IP addresses

NAT reduces the need for publicly known IP addresses by mapping publicly known to privately known IP addresses. Classless interdomain routing (CIDR) aggregates publicly known IP addresses into blocks—as opposed to the previous hierarchical class IP address structure—so that fewer IP addresses are wasted. The goal is to extend the use of the existing IP version 4 (IP V4) IP addresses for several more years before the new IP version 6 (IP V6) addressing is widely supported on the Internet. IP V4 addresses are 32-bit addresses while IP V6 addresses are 128-bit addresses.

The function of all these devices is to permit a SOHO LAN to connect to the Internet over a high-speed link and represent all the PC hosts on the LAN as a single IP address to the ISP, which provides the high-speed link.

Installing and Configuring a Cable Modem/DSL Router

This chapter concludes with an examination of the installation and configuration of a cable modem/DSL router. The installation covers the hardware installation steps. Configuration involves setting up the router for operation with the Wide Area Network (WAN) high-speed Internet connection and the SOHO LAN private network connection.

Installing a Router

Router hardware installation is quite simple. It involves connecting the router with a 10-Mbps Ethernet connection to the cable modem or DSL connection, connecting the power, and connecting to the SOHO LAN private network. The physical connectors on a router are clearly labeled, as shown in Figure 5.16.

The WAN connector on the left is a 10 Mbps Ethernet connection for either a cable modem or a DSL modem. The power connector is on the right and the 10/100 Mbps Ethernet switched connections in the middle are labeled 1, 2, 3, and 4. The uplink connection is a crossover connection that permits the router to be connected into other switches or Ethernet hubs. When it is used the number 4 connection is disabled. Making the physical connections is very easy. Next comes the software configuration.

Configuring the Router Software

This section uses the Linksys routers to illustrate router setup. These routers were chosen for our example because they are inexpensive, they are easy to configure and operate, and they seem to work well. They also provide many of the typical configuration settings found in other cable modem and DSL routers.

To configure the router, a PC with a Web browser is used. The router has a default fixed IP address of 192.168.1.1, as shown in Figure 5.17. This requires assigning a fixed IP address temporarily to the PC host configuring the router so that it can connect to the router using the Web browser. In my case I chose the address 192.168.1.2.

Figure 5.16 Router connections.

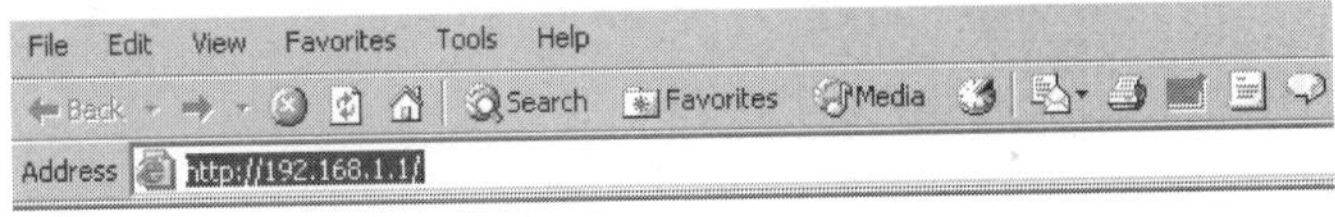

Figure 5.17 Router default IP address.

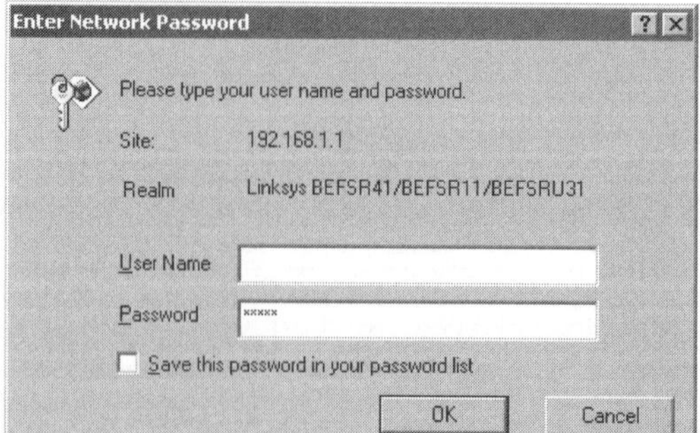

Figure 5.18
Router login.

Once the address is entered the router comes up with its login screen, as shown in Figure 5.18.

A default password is entered to connect to the router configuration menus. All router software configurations are performed using Web browser software directly connected to the router. The first configuration steps are to assign a new router password and to change the router's IP address to an IP address valid on the SOHO LAN. Changing the password first using the password tab causes the router to request a second login with the new password. Once the password change is complete, the router's IP address can be changed. After it is changed the router is no longer accessible from our PC host because its IP address is set up to operate with the router's default IP address. Changing the PC host's IP address to get the IP address automatically returns its IP address to the range of IP addresses used in our SOHO LAN—provided we are using a DHCP server. We can then use the newly assigned router IP address and password to reestablish the connection with the router.

Router WAN Configuration

The router default configuration menu appears. See Figure 5.19.

The Basic Setup screen is the first screen you see when you access the router by typing its IP address into your Web browser location window. You may configure the device and get it working properly using only the settings on this screen.

For most users, all you need to do is give the device a name and select the Obtain an IP Address Automatically option. Some ISPs require that you enter the DNS information. These settings can be obtained from your ISP if they are required.

The key steps to establishing basic router operation are to assign a host name and a domain name. The LAN IP address has been previously set in our first configuration steps. We do not need to set that again.

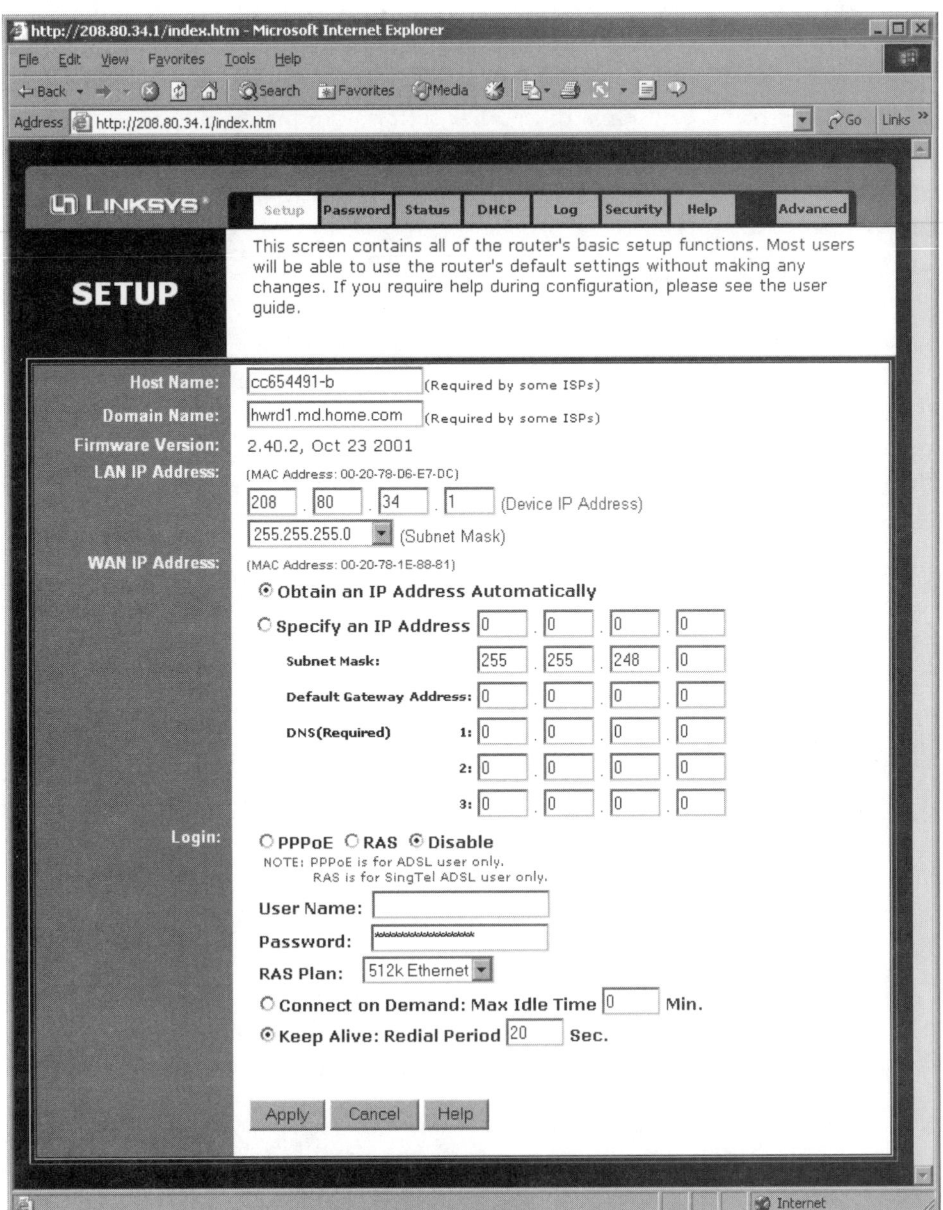

Figure 5.19 Router default configuration menu.

Cable modem and DSL ISPs assign their IP addresses automatically. This means that the next setting to check is the "Obtain an IP address automatically." When fixed IP addresses are used, then specifying the IP address, the subnet mask, the default gateway, and the DNS servers is required. Dynamic IP address assignment is much simpler.

DSL connections can require login parameters including the type of login, the user name, and password. Other settings permit keeping the link active when idle periods occur.

Applying these basic LAN settings should bring the router online and permit SOHO LAN PC hosts to access the Internet. Routers are typically capable of more sophisticated functions that we need to discuss here.

The setup parameters on the basic setup screen are as follows:

1. Host name—This is the name given the router. Some ISPs authenticate connections using the host name. When an ISP requires a host name, enter the name in the host name field. Host names are often assigned by the ISP, but you can make up a name if none has been assigned.
2. Domain name—This name is also assigned by the ISP. Some ISPs authenticate connections and set up DNS using the domain name. If an ISP requires a domain name, enter the name in the domain name field. Domain names, like host names, are often assigned by the ISP. You can make up a name if none has been assigned.
3. Firmware version—This tells the software release used in the router. Newer software releases can change the features of the router to keep pace with how ISPs run their networks. Such software is obtained from the router manufacturer and specially uploaded into the router's non-volatile RAM (NVRAM).
4. LAN IP address—This shows the MAC address and the assigned IP address for the router on the private SOHO LAN. The SOHO LAN hosts would specify this IP address as a gateway address. The default value for the Linksys LAN IP address is 192.168.1.1 and 255.255.255.0 for subnet mask. These values are the initial values needed to begin the router setup process.
5. WAN IP address—The first address listed is the MAC address (00-20-78-1E-88-81). The second address listed is the IP address used on the high-speed cable modem or DSL public link to the Internet. The MAC address operates at the Windows networking modem adapter layer and the IP address is in the Windows networking model protocol layer.

   ISP authentication can be based upon MAC address: When an ISP requires a MAC address to authenticate for Internet access, the router's MAC address, as listed after the WAN IP Address caption on the Setup page, should be provided by the ISP. In some cases MAC addresses are now being used by ISP routers as a means of identifying the physical devices to which data is routed. This MAC address is now included in my cable modem ISP's router's routing tables.

These addresses represent the entire SOHO LAN to external Internet users. The WAN label is used because at some point there is a WAN connection to the public Internet.

When an ISP runs a Dynamic Host Configuration Protocol (DHCP) server, as almost all of them do, select the "Obtain an IP Address Automatically" option. The ISP then leases an IP address to the router. When a static (or fixed) IP address, subnet mask, and gateway setting are used, check the "Specify an IP address" option and enter the settings assigned by the ISP. The critical address is the assigned Domain Name Server (DNS) address. The DNS is absolutely required to navigate the Internet.

6. Login—This is more often used for DSL connections. There are several parameters to set. The parameters include:

   Point-to-Point Protocol over Ethernet (PPPoE)—This protocol connects multiple PC hosts on (you guessed it) an Ethernet LAN to the Internet through a common cable modem, DSL, or wireless connection. PPPoE combines the Point-to-Point Protocol (PPP) used in dialup connections with the Ethernet protocol. The PPP protocol information is encapsulated within Ethernet frames.

   PPPoE requires that neither the telephone company nor the ISP provide special support. Cable modem and DSL connections, unlike dialup connections, are always available. Because many users can share the same physical connection to the Internet, a tracking system is needed to match remote traffic to each user and to identify which users should be billed for the traffic.

   For each session, PPPoE provides a mechanism for an initial discovery exchange to learn each other's network address. After the session is established between a PC host on a SOHO LAN and an Internet site, the session can be monitored for billing purposes if desired. This permits apartment houses, hotels, and the like to bill users for shared Internet access over DSL connections.

   Check with the ISP to determine whether PPPoE must be enabled. If PPPoE is used, the User Name and Password fields need to be completed with information provided by your ISP. The Connect on Demand option can be used to connect/disconnect the PPPoE link automatically. After selecting the Connect on Demand feature, the PPPoE connection is disconnected if it has been idle for a period more than the Max Idle Time setting. When the Keep Alive option is selected, the router tries continually to keep the line connected.

Remote Access Service (RAS)—The RAS settings are for ISPs that use the Alcatel Remote Access Service (RAS). The Alcatel RAS is an access technology to authenticate with ADSL servers. This method uses TCP port 5555. The configuration steps are as follows:

a. Select RAS as the login method.
b. Enter the assigned username. A 512k Ethernet user should use a format like "username" or "username@INT512."
c. Enter the assigned password.
d. Select a RAS plan. A 512k user would choose 512k Ethernet.
e. Click the Apply button. The RAS status can be viewed using the router's Status menu.

7. Double check the settings entered and click the Apply button to save the data to the router. Next test the settings by connecting to the Internet and clicking in the Status tab. Cable or DSL modems should be reset before testing the status of the router.

In most situations, default values should work satisfactorily. This router works in most network scenarios without changing any settings. Some ISPs require additional information in order to connect to the Internet.

Password access to the router is assigned using the password tab. The password tab panel is shown in Figure 5.20. The default password is "admin." The very first step we did in configuring our router was to change the password. This is necessary to provide the minimal level of security needed for the SOHO LAN. After a password is set, anyone accessing the router is prompted to enter the password. The password can be up to 64 characters long. It cannot contain any spaces or asterisk characters. Simple alphanumeric passwords like "zyxsex123tree" should work best here. The password is repeated to verify to the router that it is entered correctly.

SNMP Community—Simple Network Management Protocol (SNMP) community is the name used by SNMP management systems to control access to Management Information Base (MIB) variables. This router supports four community names, SNMP access, and management. The SNMP access for each community can be set to "Read-Only" or "Read-Write." This enables the SNMP management system to use community names to read or write the MIB. SNMP community names must be less than 31 characters.

Restoring the factory defaults sets the router back to its original factory configuration. This necessitates restarting the setup process using the default IP address and password.

Figure 5.21 shows the current router configuration and the DHCP address leased from the ISP's DHCP server.

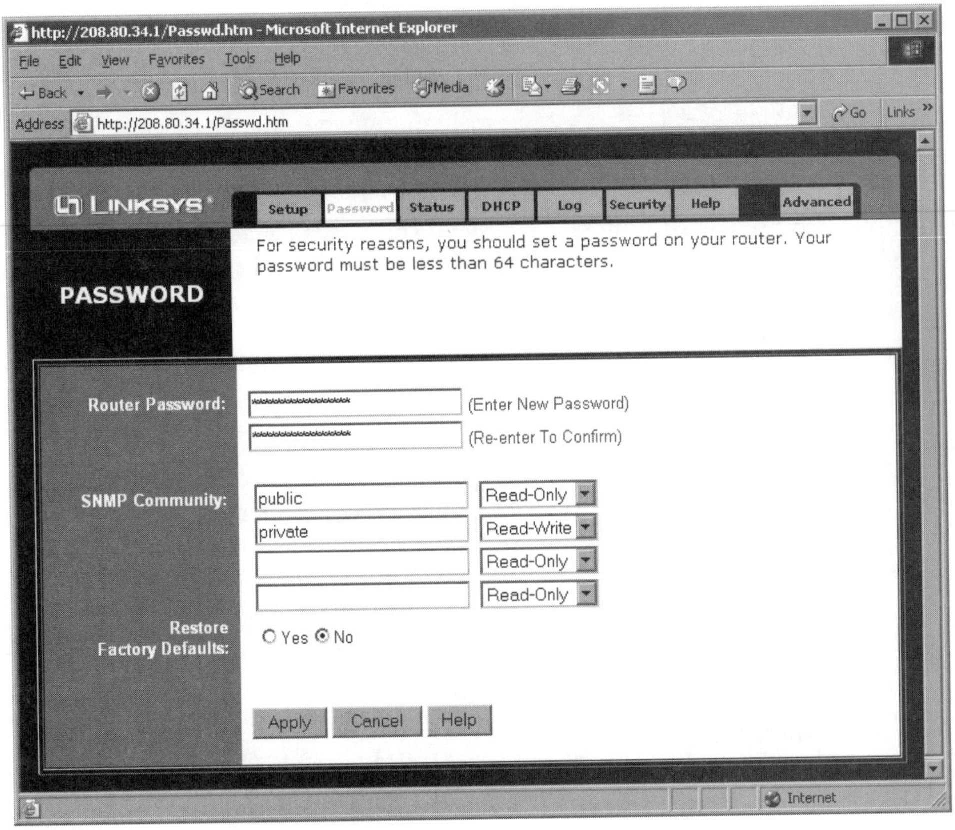

Figure 5.20 Password assignment.

The status screen displays the following parameters for a cable modem ISP setup:

1. Host Name—This is the name assigned to this device as entered in the initial setup. It could be assigned by the ISP.
2. Firmware Version—This identifies the software version used in the router.
3. Login—This displays the WAN login status. When PPPoE or RAS is used as the login method, pressing the Connect button logs the router into the ISP's network. Pressing the Disconnect button disconnects the router from the ISP's network. The router does not connect again until the Connect button is again pressed.
4. LAN—This field shows the IP address and subnet mask of this router on the internal SOHO LAN. This address is the gateway address every PC

host should have in its configuration to facilitate high-speed access to the Internet.

5. DHCP Server—This displays the status of the router's DHCP server function. The DHCP server function is either enabled or disabled. When enabled the router provides dynamic IP addresses to the private network PC hosts as specified by the DHCP settings tab. This is discussed soon.
6. WAN—The IP address, network mask, and default gateway of the router as seen by external users on the Internet are displayed here. When values appear here it means that the router is accepted by the ISP and is able to access the Internet.
7. DNS—This identifies the ISP's domain name servers' IP addresses. These addresses are assigned by the ISP. When addresses appear here it means that communications from the router are able to be routed to the Internet.
8. DHCP—This field shows the time remaining on the DHCP-leased IP address. The address leased to this router is good for a little over 136 years. Right, like the router, my network and I will be around that long. Nonetheless it is nice to know that they trust my network that much.
9. DHCP Release and DHCP Renew—These buttons cause the router to give up all its WAN DHCP settings and to request from the DHCP server new settings.
10. DHCP Clients Table—This button displays the DHCP IP address leases made by the router on the private SOHO LAN to PC hosts. These addresses would be assigned only when the DHCP server is enabled.

Login error messages may be displayed. These messages would show PPPoE error messages such as the following:

a. "Cannot connect to PPPoE server" or "No PPPoE response from ISP."
b. "PPPoE LCP negotiation failed" or "Can't finish PPP Link Control Protocol (LCP) negotiation."
c. "PPPoE authentication failed" or "Wrong username or password."
d. "Cannot get an IP address from PPPoE server" or "Can't finish PPP Internet Protocol Control Protocol (IPCP) negotiation."

RAS error messages such as the following:

a. "Cannot connect to RAS server" or "No RAS response from ISP."
b. "RAS negotiation fails" or "Can't finish RAS control negotiation."
c. "RAS authentication fails" or "Wrong username or password."
d. "Many sessions active! Try again later!" or "Abnormal disconnect. Wait a moment and dial up again."

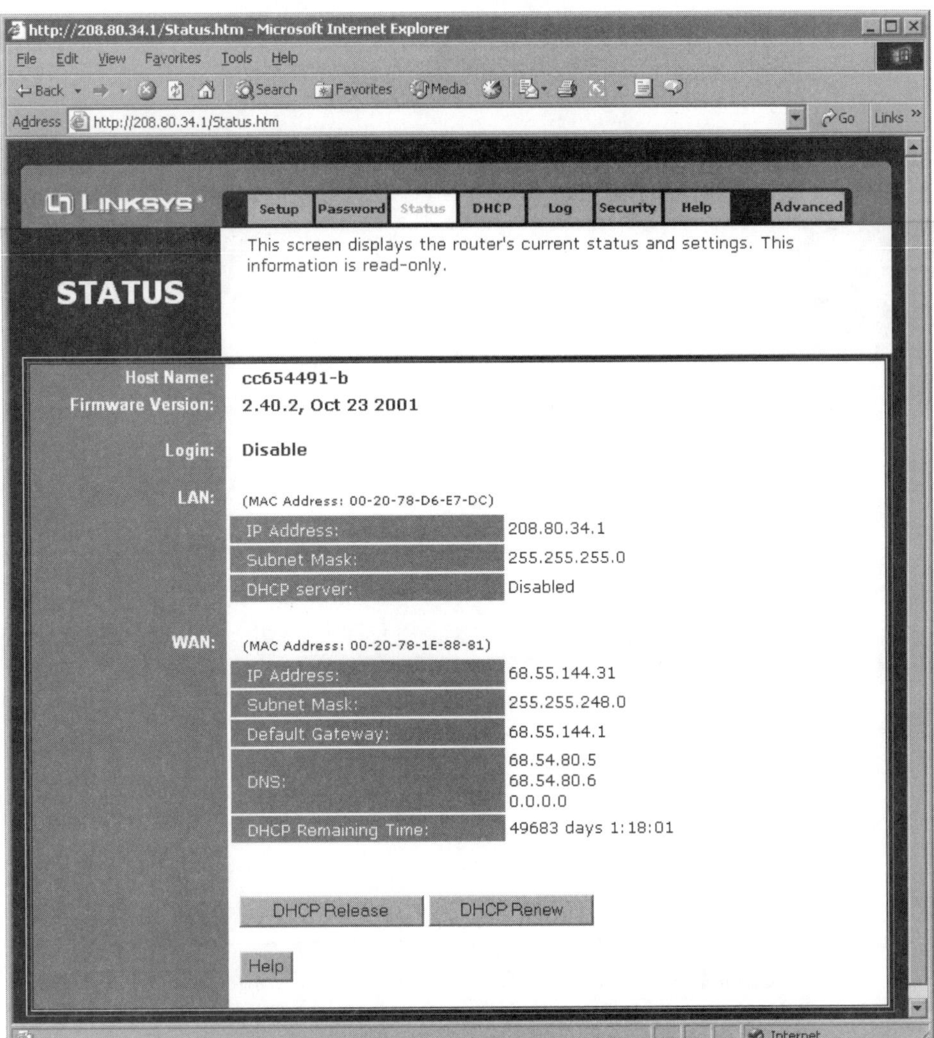

Figure 5.21 Router status panel.

When these error messages appear, check the high-speed connection to the DSL modem or call the ISP for help.

The status panel displays current router status. The information displayed is read-only.

Routers can be set up to be DHCP servers on a SOHO LAN. DHCP servers lease IP addresses to SOHO LAN PC hosts automatically as they request them. When the DHCP server option is enabled, the PCs on the SOHO LAN

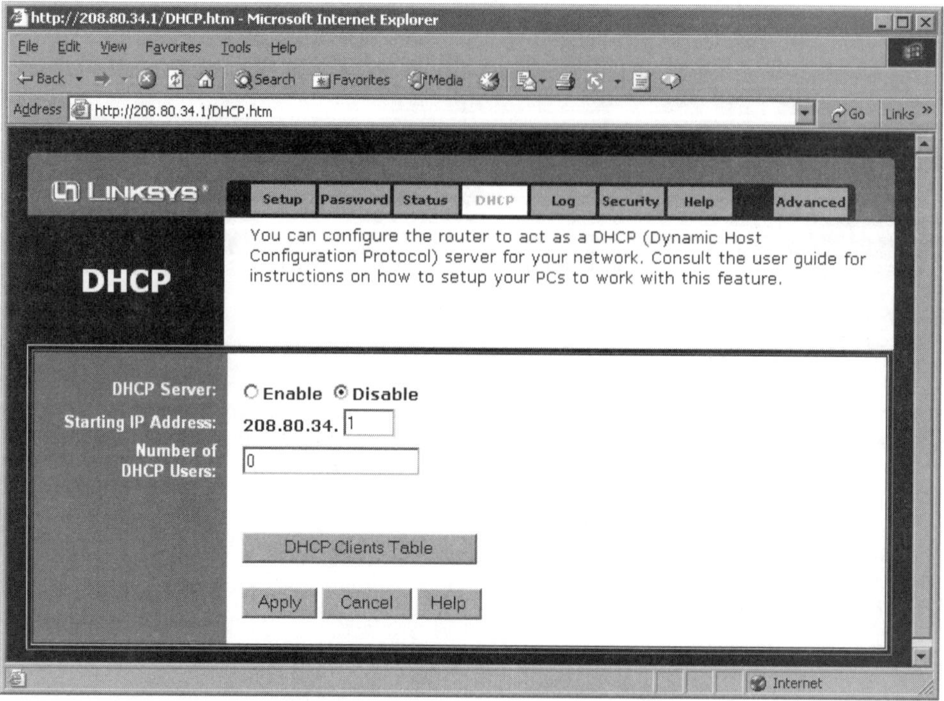

Figure 5.22 Router DHCP configuration.

must be configured to use a DHCP server. The DHCP server configuration panel is shown in Figure 5.22.

This router is capable of assigning DHCP addresses to a single network of no more than 256 PC hosts because the router IP address assignments can only vary from 0 to 255. Practically, several addresses on a SOHO LAN would be assigned as fixed IP addresses. These addresses would be assigned to the router, to servers, and to network attached printers. Thus, the DHCP assignments would realistically serve about 200 PC hosts maximum. A good starting address is 50 with about 100 to 150 DHCP users. This permits the first 50 IP addresses to be assigned to the network (this is always the 0 address) and other PC hosts requiring fixed IP addresses.

A network with a Windows 2000 server could have the Windows server perform the DHCP function. In this case the router's DHCP would be disabled. When there is no DHCP function on your network, all IP addresses, subnet masks, and DNS settings must be manually configured for every PC host on the network. Duplicate IP addresses cause network errors that are readily identified and corrected.

Routers can also log incoming and outgoing transmissions. This is a form of security monitoring but not quite the same as a true firewall. The access log settings are quite simple: The log is either enabled or disabled. When enabled, the router records incoming and outgoing transmissions. The "send log to IP address" option permits the log to be sent to a private network host address. Figure 5.23 shows the access log setup panel.

Copies of the incoming and outgoing access logs are shown in Figure 5.24.

Routers record the access for both LAN hosts and WAN hosts. The router sends the log messages to a PC host on the SOHO LAN but special Linksys-provided Logviewer software is needed to record and display the log messages. Logs are checked using the log page or by using the Logviewer Windows application that can be downloaded from Linksys.com.

The access log function is activated by selecting Enable. Clicking on the Incoming Access Log button displays WAN PC hosts accessing the SOHO LAN. The log display includes WAN host IP address and the port number accessed. Port 80 is used for Web browser access. Clicking on the Outgoing Access Log button displays the SOHO LAN host's access log. This log displays

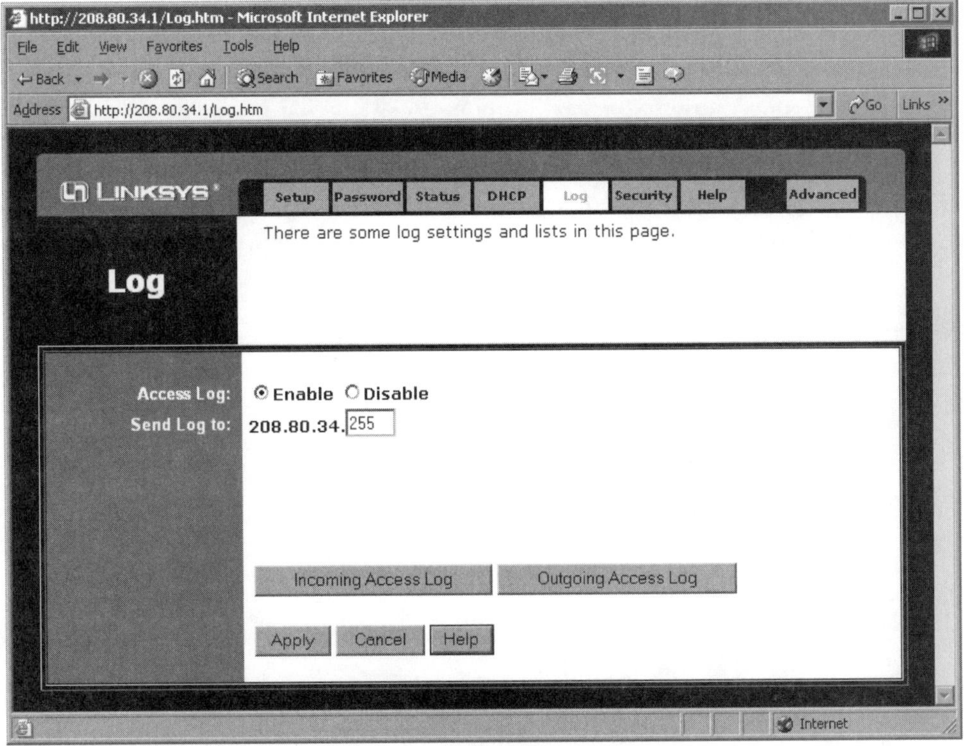

Figure 5.23 Router access log.

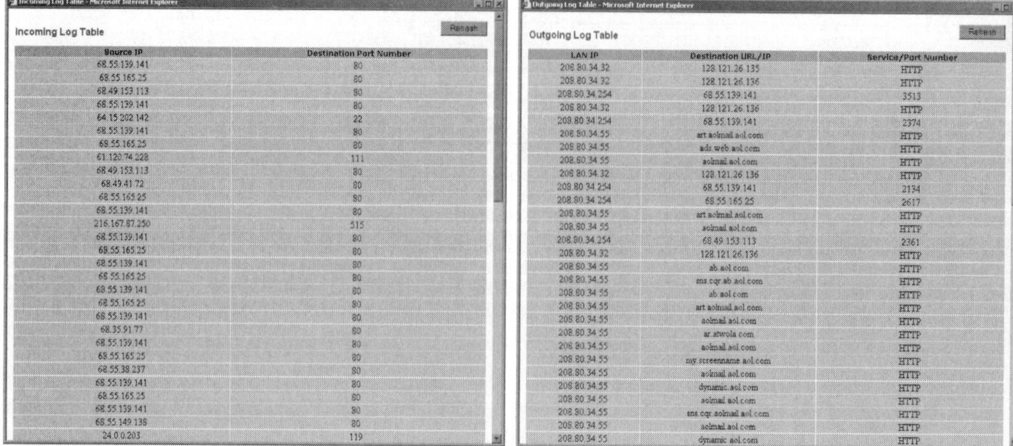

Incoming Log Table

Source IP	Destination Port Number
68.55.139.141	80
68.55.165.25	80
68.49.153.113	80
68.55.139.141	80
64.15.202.142	22
68.55.139.141	80
68.55.165.25	80
61.120.74.228	111
68.49.153.113	80
68.49.41.72	80
68.55.165.25	80
68.55.139.141	80
216.167.87.250	515
68.55.139.141	80
68.55.165.25	80
68.55.139.141	80
68.55.165.25	80
68.55.139.141	80
68.55.165.25	80
68.55.139.141	80
68.35.91.77	80
68.55.139.141	80
68.55.165.25	80
68.55.38.237	80
68.55.139.141	80
68.55.165.25	80
68.55.139.141	80
68.55.149.138	80
24.0.0.203	119

Outgoing Log Table

LAN IP	Destination URL/IP	Service/Port Number
208.80.34.32	128.121.26.135	HTTP
208.80.34.32	128.121.26.136	HTTP
208.80.34.254	68.55.139.141	3513
208.80.34.32	128.121.26.136	HTTP
208.80.34.254	68.55.139.141	2374
208.80.34.55	art.aolmail.aol.com	HTTP
208.80.34.55	ads.web.aol.com	HTTP
208.80.34.55	aolmail.aol.com	HTTP
208.80.34.32	128.121.26.136	HTTP
208.80.34.254	68.55.139.141	2134
208.80.34.254	68.55.165.25	2617
208.80.34.55	art.aolmail.aol.com	HTTP
208.80.34.55	aolmail.aol.com	HTTP
208.80.34.254	68.49.153.113	2361
208.80.34.32	128.121.26.136	HTTP
208.80.34.55	ab.aol.com	HTTP
208.80.34.55	sns.cqr.ab.aol.com	HTTP
208.80.34.55	ab.aol.com	HTTP
208.80.34.55	art.aolmail.aol.com	HTTP
208.80.34.55	aolmail.aol.com	HTTP
208.80.34.55	ar.atwola.com	HTTP
208.80.34.55	aolmail.aol.com	HTTP
208.80.34.55	my.screenname.aol.com	HTTP
208.80.34.55	aolmail.aol.com	HTTP
208.80.34.55	dynamic.aol.com	HTTP
208.80.34.55	aolmail.aol.com	HTTP
208.80.34.55	sns.cqr.aolmail.aol.com	HTTP
208.80.34.55	aolmail.aol.com	HTTP
208.80.34.55	dynamic.aol.com	HTTP

Figure 5.24 Access logs.

LAN PC host IP address, the destination URL or IP address, and the service or port number.

Routers can provide an additional security capability when combined with special software programs. This router works with the ZoneAlarm Pro firewall software and the PC-cillin virus detection software, as shown in Figure 5.25. This router's security capability requires installation of the firewall software and the virus detection software on each PC in the SOHO LAN.

All PC host requests for Internet access are blocked and an error code is displayed on a PC host's browsers if the request has not been cleared by ZoneAlarm or PC-cillin. PC host requests validated by ZoneAlarm Pro or PC-cillin are passed to the Internet for service. Trojan horse or spyware programs can easily open a PC host up to external access. Installing ZoneAlarm and PC-cillin software on a PC host before connecting it through the router to the Internet greatly reduces the risk of successful Trojan horse or spyware attacks. The Exempt Computers setting permits some IP addresses to be specified as exceptions from ZoneAlarm security and PC-cillin antivirus enforcement.

The Help tab connects the router to the manufacturer's online help resources. See Figure 5.26.

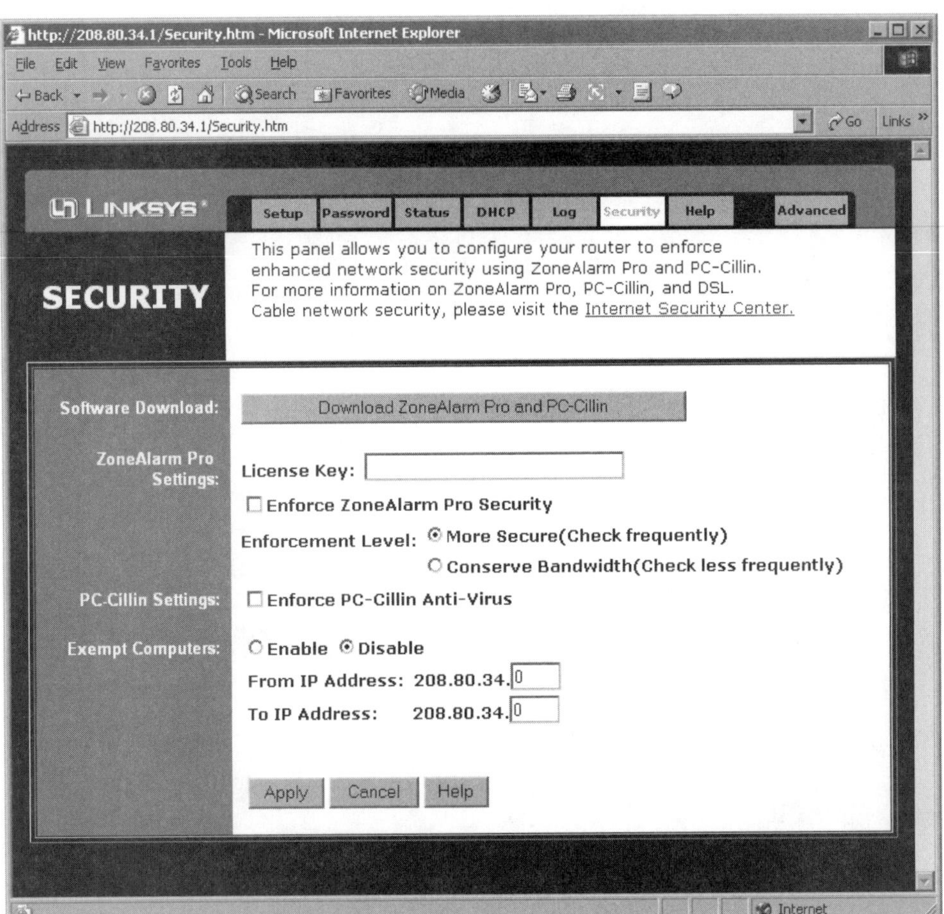

Figure 5.25 Router security.

The key resource here is the ability to upgrade the router firmware. The firmware upgrade program used the Ethernet connection to send the upgrade file to the router. The firmware upgrade is downloaded from the router manufacturer and placed on a PC host disk drive. The router upgrade program is run to perform the upgrade, as shown in Figure 5.27.

The router provides a filtering capability to limit access to the Internet. This filtering is in addition to the security settings. The filtering panel is shown in Figure 5.28.

Filters block specific SOHO LAN PC hosts from accessing the Internet. Different filters are set up for different SOHO LAN PC hosts based on IP addresses or a network port number.

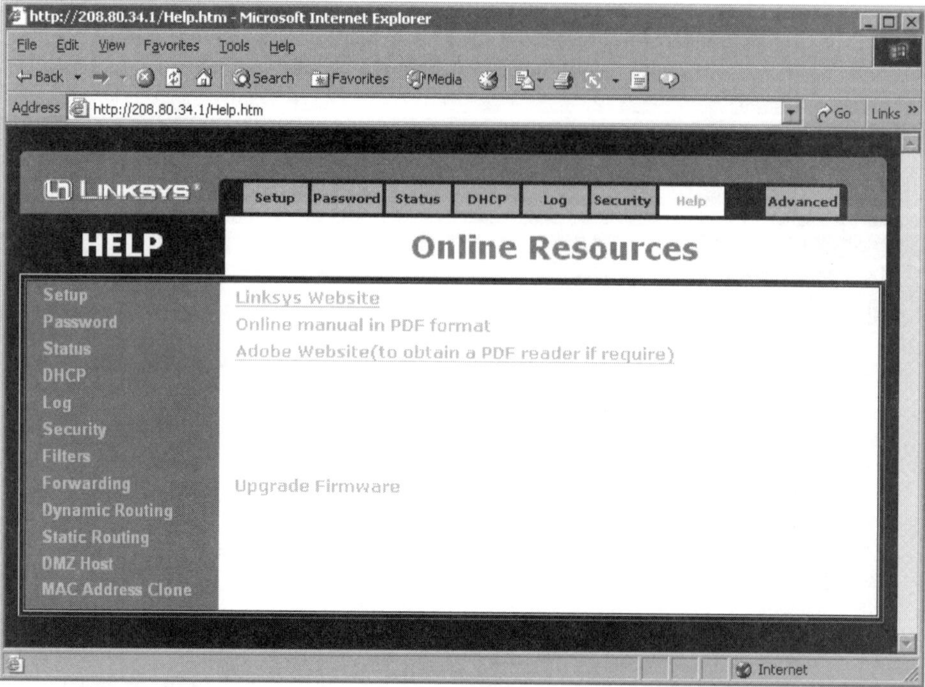

Figure 5.26 Router firmware upgrade program.

http://208.80.34.1/Upgrade.htm - Microsoft Internet Explorer

File Edit View Favorites Tools Help

Back Search Favorites Media

Address http://208.80.34.1/Upgrade.htm

Go Links

Upgrade Firmware

Password:

File Path: Browse

Upgrade

NOTICE !!

- Currently, this Firmware Upgrade utility support only IE 5.0 and above.
- If the file dialog does not appear after pressing 'Browse' button, you should try to set lower security level in the 'Tools/Internet Options/Security/Internet&Local intranet/Custom Level/Java Custom Settings' of your browser.

Done Internet

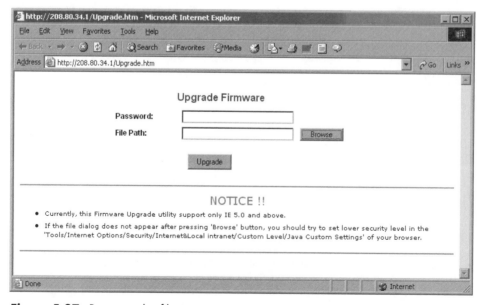

Figure 5.27 Router packet filtering.

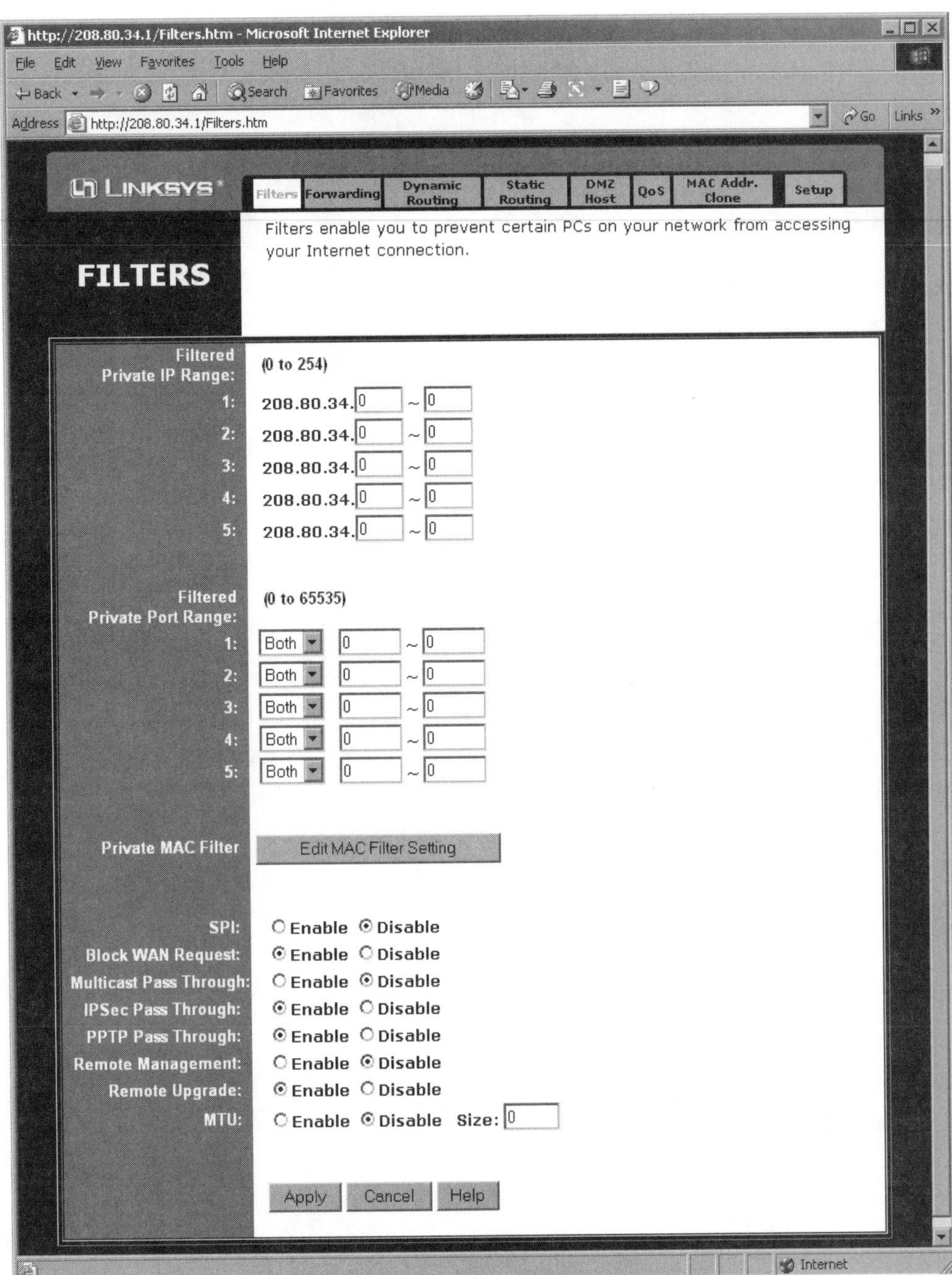

Figure 5.28 Router packet filtering.

Filter settings are made by selecting the range of IP addresses to filter and entering them into the IP address range fields. The SOHO PC hosts using these IP addresses are then blocked from accessing the Internet. SOHO PC hosts can also be filtered using network port numbers. Select the protocols and enter the range of port numbers to block into the port number range fields. SOHO LAN PC hosts using these ports are then not able to access the Internet. SOHO PC hosts can also be blocked by using their MAC address. Select Edit MAC Filter Setting and enter the MAC addresses to filter into the MAC address fields. The PC hosts with those MAC addresses then cannot access the Internet.

The Block WAN Request capability is designed to prevent attacks from the Internet. When Block WAN Request is enabled, the router drops unaccepted TCP requests and ICMP packets from WAN sites. ICMP packets are used by the `PING` and `TRACERT` commands. Hackers cannot find the router by pinging WAN IP addresses.

Stateful Packet Inspection (SPI) operates like the Windows Internet Connectivity Firewall (WICF). SPI checks packets to verify that the destination IP address matches the source IP of the original request. To use the SPI firewall, check Enable. The Disable setting uses the NAT firewall.

The router supports passing through Multicast, IPSec, and PPTP packets. These options can be either enabled or disabled. Point-to-Point Tunneling Protocol (PPTP) is used to enable Virtual Private Networking (VPN) connections. This pass-through must be enabled for VPN to work. IPsec is used for secure IP connections to different Web sites like shopping sites.

The Remote Management selection permits managing the router through the WAN connection. Selecting Enable and using port 8080 on an Internet PC host allows remote management of the router. To upgrade the firmware of the router through the WAN, enabling the remote upgrade option is required.

The Maximum Transmission Unit (MTU) can improve or worsen the routers' performance. To set the MTU size select Enable and enter an MTU size. The recommended packet sizes are in the 1,200 to 1,500 range. Most DSL users benefit from using 1,492. The default is 1,500. When the MTU setting is disabled, the 1,500 default size is used.

Port forwarding is used to set up public services on a SOHO LAN. When Internet PC hosts request specific services on a SOHO LAN, the router forwards those requests to designated PC hosts configured to service the requests. See Figure 5.29.

Forwarding requests from port number 80—the HTTP port—to IP address 192.168.1.2 sends all HTTP requests from Internet PC hosts to 192.168.1.2. To ensure that the requests are sent to the correct PC host, the PC host must have a fixed IP address and cannot be using DHCP. Port forwarding is used to specify a PC host to act as a Web or FTP server via the router.

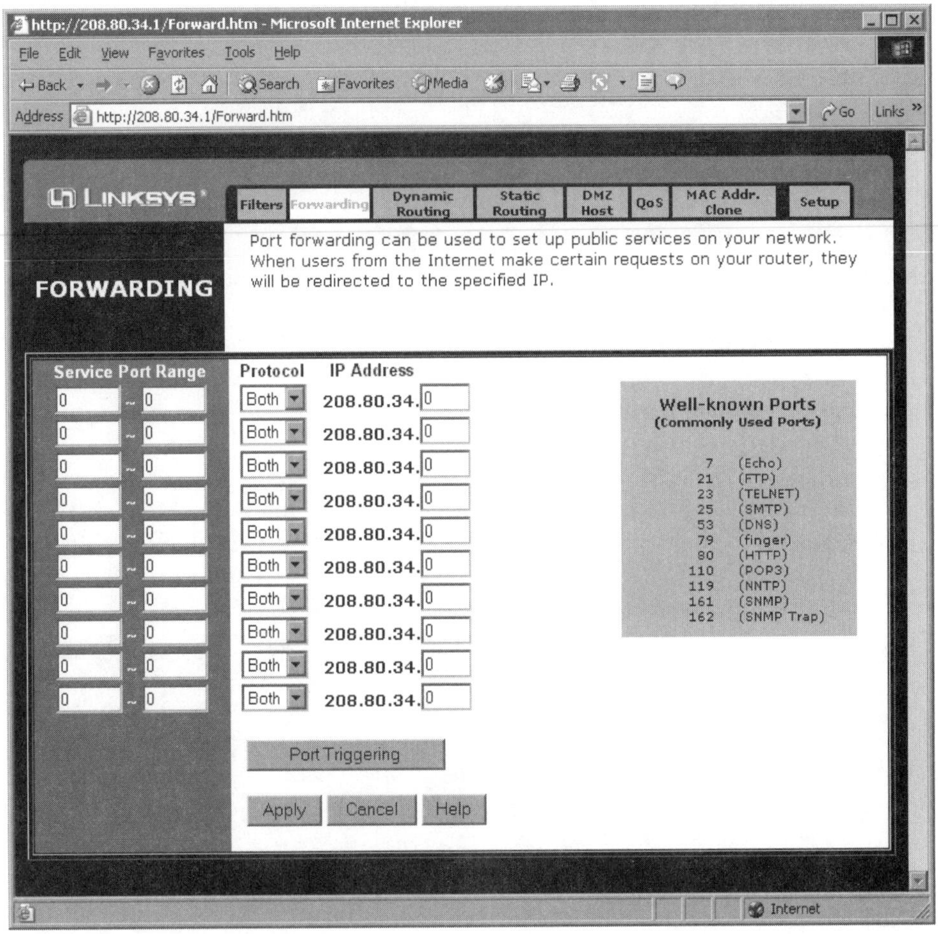

Figure 5.29 Service port forwarding.

Internet users can communicate with the server, but they are not directly connected to the server. Packets from the Internet are forwarded through the router to the designated server.

To configure forwarding, enter the port number range and select either Transmission Control Protocol (TCP), User Datagram Protocol (UDP), or both protocols used by the server. Next enter the IP address of the server that the Internet users need to access, and filtering is configured. To remove a server entry just delete the port range number and IP address from the fields.

Port triggering is needed by some important Internet applications like games. They communicate between server and LAN host using alternate ports. When you want to use those applications, find out the ports used by

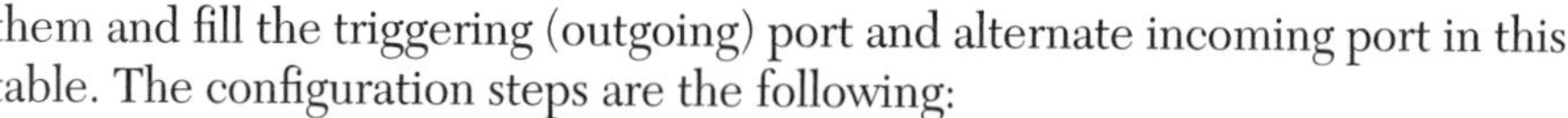

them and fill the triggering (outgoing) port and alternate incoming port in this table. The configuration steps are the following:

1. Enter the application name of the trigger.
2. Enter the port range used by the application.
3. Enter the incoming port range used by the application.
4. Click the Apply button to continue.

Port triggering allows the router to watch outgoing data for specific port numbers and forward the incoming packets to the LAN host.

The IP address of the PC host sending the matching data is remembered by the router, so that when the requested data returns through the firewall, the data is pulled back to the proper PC host using the remembered IP address and port mapping rules.

Dynamic routing uses routing protocols to keep routing tables dynamically updated. Routing protocols run on each Internet router or host. The goal of routing protocols is to notify all other routers of the networks that a router knows and to alert all other routers to any changes to a network, such as a link failure necessitating reaching a remote network via a different route.

Dynamic routing can use distance vector algorithms that determine the best route based on distance metrics. Routers running the distance-vector algorithm send all or a portion of their routing tables in routing-update messages to their neighbors. Or they can use link-state algorithms that send link-state advertisements (LSAs) to all other routers within the same hierarchical area. Information on attached interfaces, metrics used, and other variables are included in LSAs. Link-state routers accumulate link-state information, which they then use in a shortest path first (SPF) algorithm to calculate the shortest path to each node.

Our sample router supports dynamic routing, as shown in Figure 5.30. In the figure the routing protocol selections are shown in the lower right. The transmit (TX) selections are RIP-1, RIP-1 Compatible, RIP-2, or disabled. Similarly the receive (RX) routing protocol choices are RIP-1, RIP-2, or disabled. The best choice for both transmit and receive protocols is RIP-2, the newest of the routing information protocols. These protocols use distance vector algorithms to determine the route.

RIP sends the routing table to other routers so they know how to route IP packets to PC hosts in the SOHO LAN.

Dynamic routing allows the router to automatically adjust to physical changes in a network's layout. The dynamic Routing Information Protocol (RIP) determines the route that packets take based on the fewest number of hops between the source and the destination. RIP regularly broadcasts routing information to other routers on the network. RIP is adequate for routing

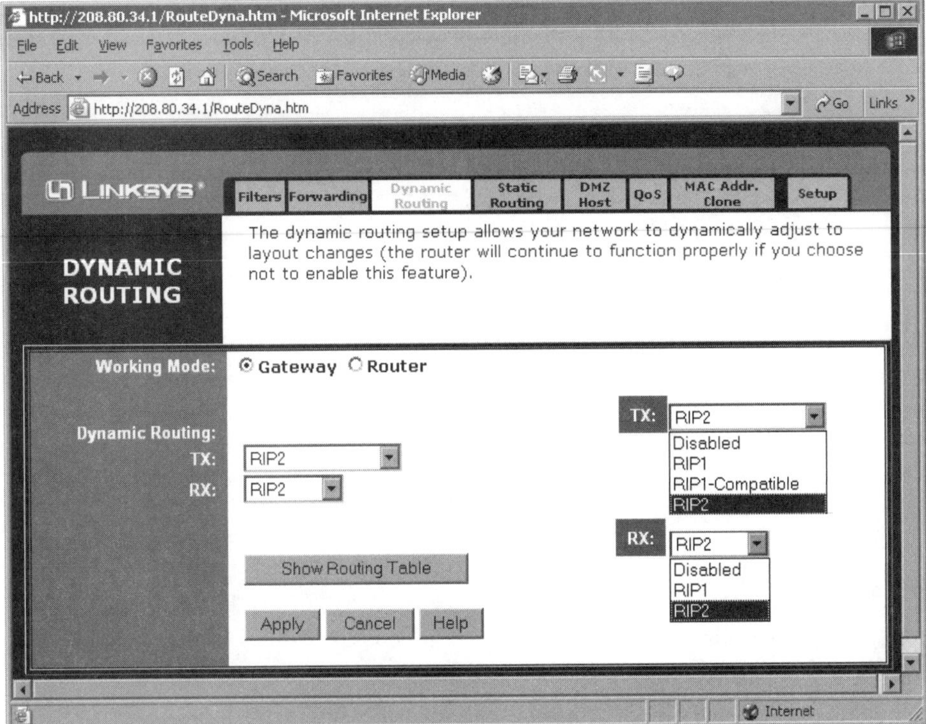

Figure 5.30 Dynamic routing.

data in smaller SOHO LANs. More sophisticated routing protocols are used in the backbone Internet to route data efficiently among large numbers of devices. To view the routing tables use the Show Routing Table button. When selected, routing tables like those in Figure 5.31 are displayed. These routing tables display the valid dynamic route entries. For small networks there are very few entries.

Dynamic routing has two operating modes: gateway and router mode. The gateway mode is used when the router is the SOHO LAN's connection to the Internet. Router mode is used when the router is on a network with other routers, including a separate network gateway providing the Internet connection.

The final setup choices are for the routing protocol the router uses to transmit data on the Internet and the routing protocol the router uses to receive data from the Internet. These choices are variations of RIP.

If there are multiple routers installed on a SOHO LAN, static routing is used instead of dynamic routing. Static routing determines the path that data follows over a SOHO LAN before and after it passes through the router. Static routing is configured using the Static Routing panel, shown in Figure 5.32.

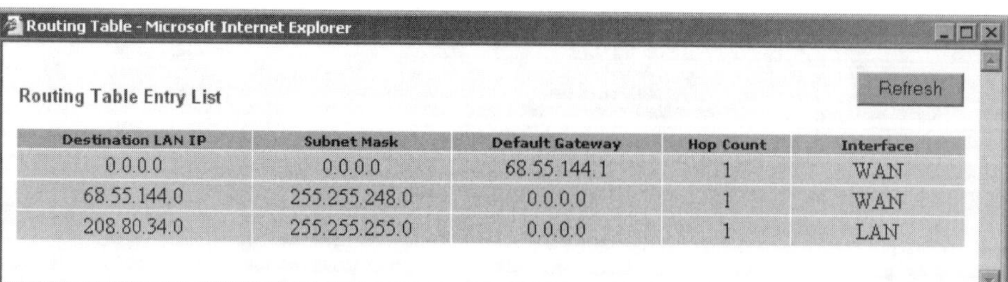
Routing Table - Microsoft Internet Explorer

Routing Table Entry List

Refresh

Destination LAN IP	Subnet Mask	Default Gateway	Hop Count	Interface
0.0.0.0	0.0.0.0	68.55.144.1	1	WAN
68.55.144.0	255.255.248.0	0.0.0.0	1	WAN
208.80.34.0	255.255.255.0	0.0.0.0	1	LAN

Figure 5.31 Routing tables.

http://208.80.34.1/RouteStatic.htm - Microsoft Internet Explorer

File Edit View Favorites Tools Help

Address http://208.80.34.1/RouteStatic.htm

LINKSYS

Filters | Forwarding | Dynamic Routing | Static Routing | DMZ Host | QoS | MAC Addr. Clone | Setup

STATIC ROUTING

This feature sets a fixed path for data to follow on the network. The router will continue to function properly if you choose not to enable this feature.

Static Routing: 1— (Select Route entry)

Delete this entry

Destination LAN IP: 0 . 0 . 0 . 0

Subnet Mask: 0 . 0 . 0 . 0

Default Gateway: 0 . 0 . 0 . 0

Hop Count (Metric, max. is 15): 0

interface: LAN

Show Routing Table

Apply Cancel Help

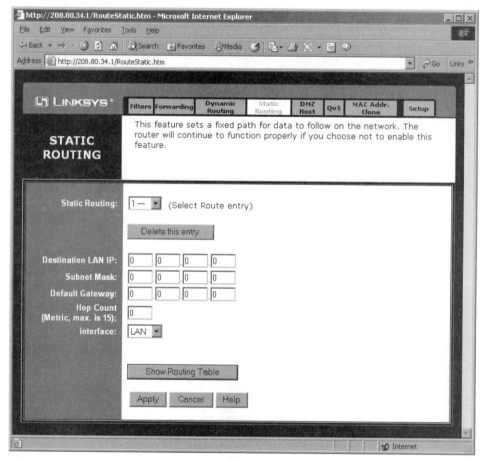

Figure 5.32 Static routing configuration menus.

Static routing requires manual configuration. Usually, an experienced network administrator seeks to avoid manual configurations. For exterior routing, static routing offers some advantages when routing between Internet sites. These advantages are the following:

1. Complete flexibility over subnet advertisement and their next hop routers.
2. No routing protocol traffic travels over the link connecting the Internet sites.
3. Because no routing protocol runs over the inter-Internet link, a faulty router in one part of the Internet cannot affect routers in another part of the Internet.

Obviously, static routes do not bypass link failures, and manual configuration is a heavy maintenance task. Despite this, static routing is a popular choice for connecting Internets that don't "trust" each other.

Static routing can be used to allow different IP domain users to access the Internet through the router. Static routing requires that the router's DHCP settings be disabled.

Static routing is set up by adding routing entries in the router's table that tell the router where to send incoming packets. All of the network's routers should direct the default route entry to the static router. The current routing table is viewed by using the Show Routing Table button. This displays the valid static route entries being used.

Adding a static routing entry is done by selecting a Static Route Entry number from the drop-down list. The router can support up to 20 static route entries.

Enter the following data for each of the 20 possible static routes:

1. Destination LAN IP—Enter the IP address of the remote LAN. Class C IP address domains of 256 host addresses use the first three fields of the destination LAN IP address. The right-most and last field is set to 0.
2. Subnet mask—Enter the subnet mask used on the remote LAN. Class C IP address domains always use a subnet mask of 255.255.255.0.
3. Default gateway—When the router connects the SOHO LAN to the Internet, then the gateway IP address is the IP address of the router. When another router is used to connect the SOHO LAN to the Internet, enter the IP address of the router connecting the SOHO LAN to the Internet as the default gateway.

Deleting a static route is easy. Select a static route entry from the Static Routing drop-down list and click on the Delete this Entry button underneath the drop-down list to delete the entry.

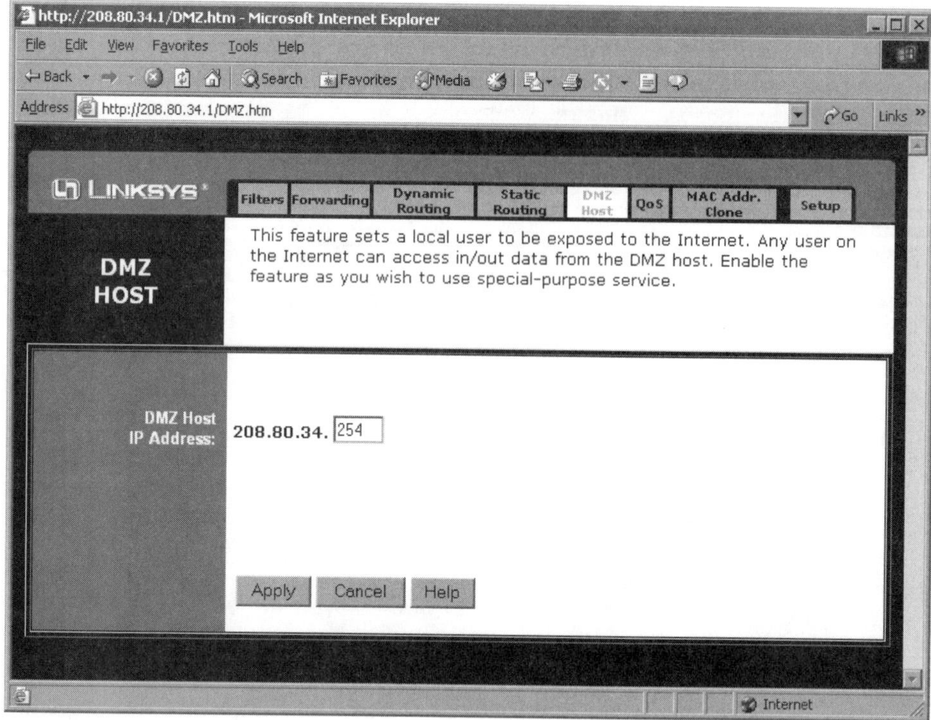

Figure 5.33 DMZ host.

The "demilitarized zone" (DMZ) host setting shown in Figure 5.33 connects a SOHO LAN PC host directly to the Internet.

Some special-purpose services, Internet games, or videoconferencing may require a direct Internet connection. To expose a PC host with a fixed IP address to the Internet, fill in the IP address and select the Apply button. The 0 address is inactive. When this setting is used, firewall protection for the DMZ PC host is disabled.

Quality of Service (QoS) measures transmission rates, error rates, and other characteristics so that the router can improve them and in some manner guarantee them in advance. QoS helps with continuous transmission of high-bandwidth voice, video, and multimedia information. However, the concept applies to other Internet data as well. Transmitting voice and video information dependably on the public Internet using standard best-effort protocols is difficult.

This router supports QoS by giving higher priority to some types of traffic over other types of traffic. This is illustrated in Figure 5.34.

QoS is enabled or disabled. Then the applications needing high QoS are selected from the standard applications accessing the Internet. The applica-

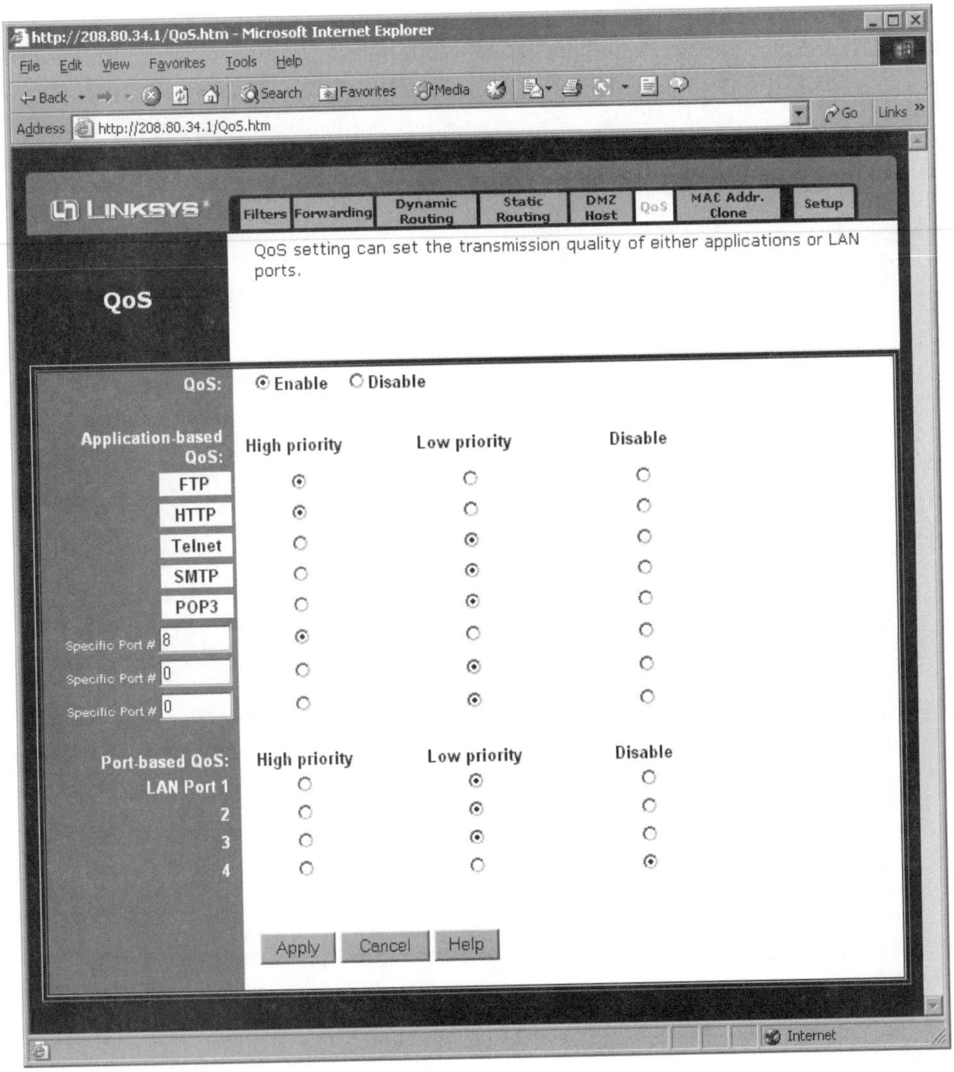

Figure 5.34 Router QoS configuration.

tion-based QoS settings determine the priority for five default services. The services can be set to high priority, low priority, or disable. Three user-defined services can be similarly set. The port-based QoS setting sets QoS for the four physical router ports (Port 1 to Port 4).

These are relatively unsophisticated QoS settings, but they do give some priority to different SOHO LAN applications and the router's Ethernet ports. In the case of this router there is more FTP and Web surfing activity than mail activity, so those applications are given higher priority or a higher QoS.

ISPs are now setting up their routers to use a PC host's NIC hardware or MAC address to set their routing tables. This means that two PCs cannot easily share the same high-speed Internet connection without it requiring half an hour to be reset to the new MAC address. In some cases the ISP will not troubleshoot a router configuration. They require diagnostics to run on one PC host that is directly connected to the cable modem or the DSL modem.

The router provides a means of cloning an internal SOHO LAN MAC address and using it on the high-speed WAN connection. The MAC Address Clone tab sets this up, as shown in Figure 5.35. By changing the router's MAC address to the MAC address of a DMZ PC host that is directly exposed to the high-speed Internet connection, the ISP can be fooled into thinking that it is communicating directly to the SOHO LAN PC host.

Setting the MAC address of the router can also help when an application or an ISP authenticates with a specific MAC address.

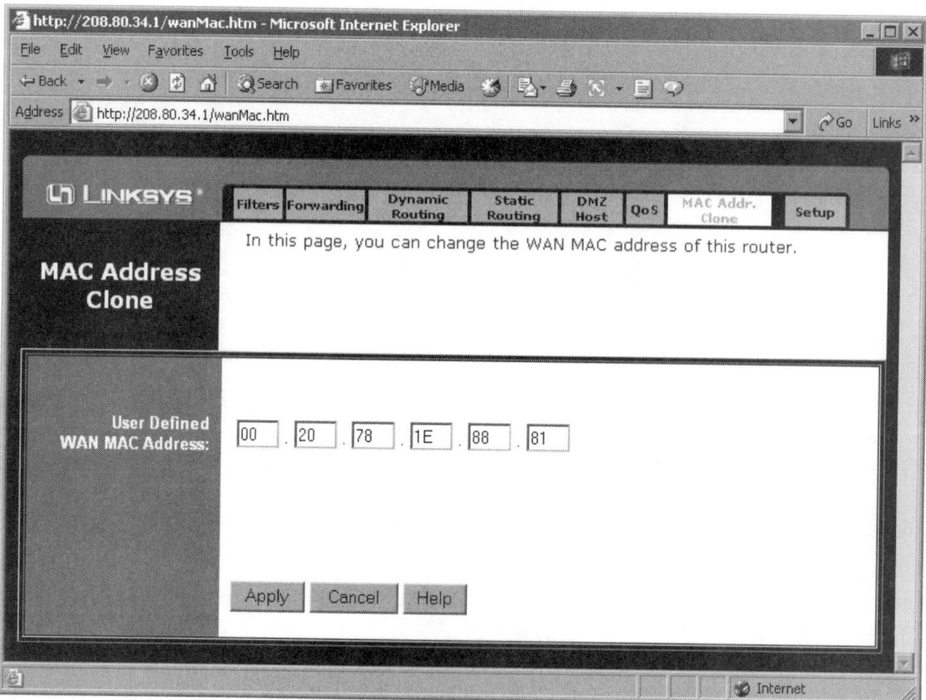

Figure 5.35 MAC Address Clone tab.

Brain Teaser: Internet Gateways

Download the manual for the D-Link DI-704 Ethernet Cable/DSL Internet gateway. Go to the D-Link Web site *www.dlink.com,* select Tech Support, select Products, select the broadband product entry for the DI-704, and click on the Manual button. Save the PDF document to your local disk drive. Compare the features with the features of the Linksys router used as an example in this book.

Do the features of the D-Link router generally match the features of the Linksys router we examined? What does DMZ stand for according to D-Link? Does it conform to the technical terms definition presented here?

Summary

This chapter has examined connecting SOHO LANs to the Internet using high-speed links. These links for home-office LANs connect using cable modems, DSL modems, or ISDN, depending upon availability. Cable modems and DSL are very competitive, but DSL offers higher connection speeds (at appropriately but not excessively higher cost). ISDN is only used where no other high-speed service is available.

Small-office LAN connections could also employ Frame Relay connections or T-carrier connections depending upon the data load and voice networking requirements. These alternatives are considerably more expensive than cable modems and DSL.

Next the chapter explored sharing high-speed Internet connections. It first discussed Windows XP's Internet Connection Sharing software. Then firewalls and routers were covered.

The chapter concluded with the details of installing and configuring a router for high-speed Internet connection sharing. Router setup parameters for this specific router were examined and explained. Setup parameters for other routers are similar to the setup parameters for this router.

Key Technical Terms

24×7—24 hours-a-day 7 days-a-week operation.

B-Channel—The B channel is a 64 Kbps ISDN bearer channel carrying digital voice or data.

BRI—Basic Rate Interface is the smallest capacity ISDN channel. It consists of two B channels operating at 64 Kbps and one D channel operating at 16 Kbps.

CATV—Community Antenna Television is the local cable television network.

CCITT—Consultative Committee on International Telephone and Telegraph is an old standards body now merged into the International Telecommunications Union (ITU).

CIDR—Classless Inter-Domain Routing is an Internet specification for aggregating public (Internet) IP addresses into blocks, as opposed to the previous A, B, and C hierarchical IP address classification structure so that few IP addresses are wasted. CIDR makes routing on the Internet more efficient.

CIR—Committed information rate is the guaranteed Frame Relay transmission speed.

CMTS—Cable Modem Termination System describes the electronic components at the central cable television provider's facility into which all cable modems terminate.

CSU—Channel Service Unit is the part of an ISDN or T-carrier termination that faces the telephone company. The CSU permits the telephone company to test the digital channel by sending digital test packets that are looped back to the telephone company. Comparing such packets determines the error rate of the digital channel.

D-Channel—The D channel is a 16 Kbps or a 64 Kbps ISDN data channel carrying signaling and data packets.

DHCP—Dynamic Host Configuration Protocol is a protocol used by a server to dynamically assign IP addresses to SOHO LAN PC hosts as they are needed.

DMZ—Demilitarized zone specifies an IP host exposed directly to the Internet that is without the protection of a firewall. The DMZ is a computer host inserted between an enterprise's private network and the public Internet, exposing it directly to the Internet. Public Internet users can access a DMZ host. In this way the DMZ host can have an enterprise's Web site so these are served to the public Internet. However, the DMZ blocks to other company data. In the event that an outside user penetrates the DMZ host's security, the Web site might be corrupted but no other enterprise information would be exposed.

DNS—Domain Name Service is an Internet and IP network service that translates domain names into IP addresses.

DSL—Digital Subscriber Line is a set of modems that provide high-speed digital transmission and voice communications on the same pair of copper wires.

DSU—Data Service Unit is the part of an ISDN or T-carrier channel that provides the interface to the customer's equipment. For ISDN this may be on a board that is plugged into a PC or it may be a V.35 copper wire interface to a router.

Frame Relay Network—A high-speed fast packet network service designed to carry data. It can also carry voice and video communications.

FTP—File Transfer Protocol supports file transfers across a TCP/IP network and the Internet.

HTTP—Hypertext Transfer Protocol supports Web browsing over TCP/IP networks and the Internet.

ICMP—Internet Control Message Protocol is a control and error-reporting protocol sent between PC hosts and other Internet components. ICMP is encapsulated in Internet Protocol (IP) datagrams. The ICMP messages are processed directly by IP software. ICMP messages implement `PING` and `TRACERT` commands.

IPsec—Internet Protocol Security is a standard for security at the network or packet processing layer of a network. Traditional security was implemented by the application. IPsec is especially useful in virtual private networks. The advantage of IPsec is that security is provided without changing PC hosts. IPsec supports Authentication Header (AH) that authenticates the data sender and Encapsulating Security Payload (ESP) that authenticates the sender and encrypts the data.

IP V4—Internet Protocol version 4 using 32-bit IP addresses.

IP V6—Internet Protocol version 6 using 128-bit IP addresses.

ISDN—Integrated Services Digital Network is a digital telephone service based upon ITU standards that runs over telephone copper wire. ISDN is a dialup service used by homes and businesses to access the Internet at 64 Kbps or 128 Kbps. ISDN is generally available from a local phone company in most urban areas.

ISP—Internet service provider is a company providing Internet access. This is typically the phone company or a cable television company.

ITU—International Telecommunications Union is an international standards body that sets telecommunications standards, including the standards that specify ISDN.

LSA—Link-state algorithm is a routing mechanism that sends link-state advertising messages between routers. The link-state advertising messages contain information on attached interfaces, metrics used, and other variables. LAS are used by more sophisticated Internet backbone routers.

MAC address—The media access control (MAC) address is the hardware address found on the NIC. It is a six hexadecimal character (48-bit) address unique to the physical hardware. The MAC address is in the Windows Networking Model Adapter Layer.

MIB—Management Information Base is the database residing in network components that dictates their functioning in the network.

MTU—Maximum Transmission Unit is the largest size packet or frame that can be sent in a TCP/IP or other packet network. Transmission Control Protocol (TCP) uses the MTU to determine the size of each packet in any transmission. When the MTU size is too large it can require two packets at the Ethernet level to send the data (Ethernet frames are 1,514 characters maximum size). An MTU of 1,515 requires two Ethernet frames to send—one chalked to the rafters with data and the other carrying a single character. This causes lots of network overhead. If the MTU size is very small the transmission requires more frames to send the data than is necessary. In this case more overhead characters and more acknowledgements have to be processed during message transmission but not twice the amount that would be sent if the MTU were too large.

Window 95 operating systems set a default MTU value of 1,500 characters, which was suitable for most communications. This is the Ethernet standard MTU (remember Ethernet frames are 1,514 characters maximum size). The Internet standard MTU is 576. ISPs often suggest using 1,500. Often, Web site access that passes through routers using 576-character MTUs breaks up 1,500 character MTUs into two smaller 576-character and one 348-character packet (about 0.6 of a 576 character MTU). This results in a slight increase in transmission overhead. Newer Windows operating systems are able to automatically sense whether a connection should use a 1,500-character or a 576-character MTU and automatically set the MTU size accordingly.

NVRAM—Non-Volatile RAM is a technology that saves programs in a random access memory that does not lose its contents when a PC host is powered off. With special software NVRAM can be reprogrammed to update the operating software and BIOS of PC hosts and other network equipment.

PBX—Private Branch Exchange is a voice telephone switch installed on a customer's premise.

PPPoE—Point-to-Point Protocol over Ethernet combines the dialup Point-to-Point Protocol (PPP) with the Ethernet CSMA/CD protocol. PPP protocol data is encapsulated within Ethernet frames for transmission over a DSL communications link.

PPTP—Point-to-Point Tunneling Protocol is a protocol that extends a network through private secure tunnels through the public Internet. Security and privacy are maintained by encrypting and decrypting data at both ends of the PPTP link. Using PPTP a wide-area network can be combined with several private SOHO LANs to form a single virtual private network. Leased lines are not needed for wide-area communication between SOHO LANs because they are replaced by secure PPTP links through the public Internet.

PRI—Primary Rate Interface is a larger capacity ISDN channel. It consists of 23 B channels operating at 64 Kbps and one D channel operating at 64 Kbps.

PVC—Permanent Virtual Circuit is a point-to-point logical connection through a Frame Relay network that operates at a specific guaranteed CIR. Many PVCs share a Frame Relay network's physical transmission facilities.

QoS—Quality of Service is an attempt to measure and adjust IP-based transmission services to provide better performance to specific applications that need performance guarantees.

RAS—Remote Access Service is a service used to authenticate users remotely accessing a network.

RIP—Routing Information Protocol is a protocol that broadcasts routing information between routers on a TCP/IP network. RIP uses distance vectors or metrics to determine the route for data through a network. These distance vectors are typically simple hop counts between the router and the destination Internet host.

SNMP Community—Simple Network Management Protocol Community is the name used by SNMP management systems to access the control data base in networking components.

SPF—Shortest path first is an algorithm used to select routes through IP networks. The SPF algorithm uses link-state information to determine the shortest path through a TCP/IP network or the Internet.

SPI—Stateful Packet Inspection is a firewall security mechanism that matches IP addresses on packets to make sure that all traffic from the public Internet matches a request from the private IP network.

Spyware—Software that is secretly sent to and then accidentally loaded into PC host computers on a private network. The spyware then sends passwords and other access information to destinations outside the private network.

T-1—A high-speed digital channel that operates at 1.544 Mbps. It is divided into 24 DS-0 64-Kbps voice channels or 56-Kbps data channels.

T-3—An even higher-speed channel than a T-1 channel. It is not just three times the capacity of a T-1 channel; it operates at over 44 Mbps.

V.35—This is a T-carrier channel high-speed copper wire interface to a router.

WAN—Wide Area Network that in our case represents the public Internet.

WICF—Windows Internet Connection Firewall Sharing is the software built into Windows XP to protect SOHO LANs from security threats when using a high-speed connection into the Internet.

WICS—Windows Internet Connection Sharing is the software built into Windows XP to permit sharing a high-speed connection from one PC into the Internet.

Review Questions

1. What are the most popular ways to connect a home-office LAN to the Internet at speeds above 56 Kbps?

   Answer: Cable modems and DSL are the two most popular ways to connect home-office LANs to the Internet at speeds of 128 Kbps up to the Internet and 400 Kbps to 800 Kbps down from the Internet.

2. How can a high-speed Internet connection be shared on a SOHO LAN?

   Answer: Software sharing can be implemented using Windows Internet Connection Sharing (WICS) and Windows Internet Connection Firewall (WICF) or by using a hardware cable modem or DSL router.

3. Which high-speed connection services would be used to connect small-office LANs with a heavy load to the Internet?

   Answer: Frame Relay and T-carrier services are the best candidates for providing high-speed Internet connectivity to a small-office LAN.

4. What is a MAC address?

   Answer: It is the 48-bit or 6-hexadecimal digit hardware address found on network interface cards. It is used today to configure ISP routers supporting high-speed Internet connections.

5. What device or feature protects a SOHO LAN from unauthorized access from the Internet?

   Answer: A firewall checks that packets coming in from the Internet match requests for data from the Internet to ensure that unauthorized accesses from the Internet are blocked.

6. What router setting makes sure that packets coming from the Internet are matched with requests for those packets?

   Answer: Stateful Packet Filtering (SPF) should be enabled.

Chapter 6

NETWORKING FOR TELECOMMUTING

Chapter Syllabus

- Telecommuting System Configuration
- Video Teleconferencing
- Telecommuting Administration
- Summary
- Key Technical Terms
- Review Questions

Telecommuting has become part of working life. This chapter describes how to use new telecommunications networking technologies, products, and services, and it illustrates how they might be used to reduce communications costs.

Today's technology seems like it can turn any room with a phone, anywhere in the world, into a satellite office. This is somewhat true. However, to effectively work offsite requires more technology than just a phone line.

Telecommuting is either a dream come true or a company's worst nightmare. On the one hand, telecommuting sounds like a great idea and the ultimate in employee empowerment. There are many potential benefits to an enterprise, including the following:

- Increased productivity and flexibility—no long commutes to work means that employees are never late for the job and they always arrive fresh.
- More direct contact with customers—sales people can work on the road while at customer sites as opposed to impersonal contacts from the office.
- Decreased downtime—bad weather and disasters cannot disable all home workers.

Telecommuting seems like a great way to avoid investing in money-draining bricks and mortar when bricks and mortar can be replaced by assigning employees a laptop PC and a voice mail box.

On the other hand, there are many pitfalls to telecommuting, both legal and practical. Are work-at-home employees injured on the job entitled to workman's comp? How can managers and supervisors monitor employees' workloads and results? How are the following policies and procedures to be ensured?

As a result of developing a seminar on managing telecommuting, I enabled two employees to telecommute. The results were not entirely satisfactory. While they saved money by not coming into the office every day, it was not clear what they accomplished while working at home. If the results had been more measurable, then the telecommuting would have worked better. My work on this book is somewhat like telecommuting for Prentice Hall. The results are decidedly measurable; the chapters are posted in electronic form on the Web within a certain schedule. If the schedule is not met, Prentice Hall is informed of why.

The other key to telecommuting success was the technology employed. In my case telecommuters had PCs at home provided by the company. They had cell phones and high-speed Internet access. However, the details of connecting into the office network were not resolved, so that their access and use of data at the office was seamless. This was particularly true of one remote telecommuter site. The problem appeared to me to be caused by an ID10T error at the remote telecommuter office.

As a consequence of 9/11 and the general economic recession of 2001, the training business, like many other businesses, experienced a dramatic decline in sales. The personnel who were telecommuters have since left their positions. However, in the last few months of their tenure it seemed like their telecommuting was more a way to not work on company business and to work unobserved on personal business. The end result was the suspension of the telecommuting and requiring the employees to be in the office every day. Soon we discovered that they were sick about a week's worth of time each month.

In a different work situation with more measurable results, I believe that telecommuting would have been more successful. However, on days when commuting is difficult and hazardous the ability to work at home is very useful to a business.

From a technical viewpoint, telecommuting needs PC and communications tools that link telecommuters to the office to a greater or lesser degree. These PC and communications tools are tailored to the work performed and the volume of data exchanged.

Using as an example again my work on this book for Prentice Hall, I am working as a telecommuter because I do not go to work at Prentice Hall in New Jersey each day and write. I walk down the hall from my bedroom to the office filled with PCs (I use three in the office and a network of 10 more PCs in the house to write and test how products operate) where I write. The problem arises when I need to send the written material to Prentice Hall. The text data is small in size, ranging from 50 KB to 2 MB. Sending this to Prentice Hall presents no problem because it can be attached to an e-mail message. However, considerable difficulty arises with the figures and diagrams because they are much larger in size. The compressed figure files range from 600 KB to 50 MB for any given chapter. A 50 MB file cannot be sent via AOL e-mail. So the procedure is to post the files on the Web for Prentice Hall to download. This works fine, but uploading 50 MB over my cable modem link at 128 Kbps requires about an hour under ideal circumstances. Since New Jersey is several hours' drive from here, uploading the figures makes perfect sense. However, if the upload was over a telephone line, it could easily require several hours because of the lower speed and less reliable transmission path.

A telecommuter with a different job like entering sales orders could easily operate with a phone line because a sales order is a few thousand characters at most. The data volume and need for access to central data files dictates the PC and telecommunication technology required for each telecommuter.

Besides the administrative and management setup required in establishing a telecommuter, the technical setup requires a careful assessment of the data used and communicated to the organization. When I am on the road teaching it is nice to know that if I need a file from the office, I can connect to my SOHO LAN and download the file to my laptop.

Despite my lukewarm support of telecommuting, when the economy gets hot again, the pressure for organizations to support telecommuters will return. In the long run there will be more telecommuting workers than workers commuting to the office. This means that every business has to managerially and technically address the problems of telecommuting.

Telecommuting System Configuration

Telecommuting and SOHO LANs requires both central site and remote site network configurations. Two access methods to the central site network support telecommuters and other mobile workers. These methods are Remote Access Service (RAS) and Virtual Private Networking (VPN). Both methods connect remote offices to the central site LAN, but the type of connection supported by each service differs. RAS is used to support dialup connections and VPN supports connections made through the Internet.

RAS uses the Public Switched Telephone Network to call a RAS server attached to the central site LAN. This RAS validates the users and permits them to access the central site network as though they were sitting in a central site office directly connected to the LAN. Security with RAS is not the same as with VPN because the connection to the central site network is a direct point-to-point dialup telephone link not shared by other users.

VPN in contrast runs across the Internet with lots of other traffic. To provide security and privacy, VPN connections use encryption/decryption at each end of the communications link. Data is encrypted before transmission and decrypted after reception. In this manner VPN constructs a private and secure connection from the remote facility to the central facility. This connection is not absolutely secure (nothing is absolutely secure), but to break the Windows VPN encryption security is not a trivial task and requires some decided commitment and intent. The VPN server must be directly exposed to the Internet. This means that hiding it behind a firewall prevents establishing VPN connections unless the firewall routes the VPN packets directly to and from the VPN server. While having packets routed directly to a VPN server by a firewall is possible, it is far easier to connect a VPN server directly to the Internet.

One of my reviewers, Charles Prael, pointed out that there are a large number of people attempting to exploit Windows 2000 servers. This means that an externally exposed Windows 2000 server running an IIS server, an Exchange server with outside connectivity, as a VPN server, or as a RAS server are often subject to attacks. To provide SOHO network security Windows vulnerabilities should be continually fixed by keeping Windows critical security updates current. Externally exposed servers that do not have current critical updates installed can very quickly become a security breach.

These differences suggest several differing central site configurations to support RAS and VPN access.

Brain Teaser: Telecommuters

Check to see if your organization has telecommuters.

Did you find that telecommuting was an option for some jobs in your enterprise? Which jobs? Does your job qualify as a telecommuting job?

Central Site Configuration

Central site communications hardware supporting remote telecommuters is usually centered on a local area network (LAN) and perhaps a Private Branch Exchange (PBX). A PBX is a telephone switch owned and maintained by a private company. Figure 6.1 identifies the potential Windows servers at a central site that could be employed in varying degrees to permit telecommuters to work from remote locations. In Figure 6.1 the VPN server has a direct connection through a cable modem to the Internet. A second Internet connection for the central site LAN is made through a separate cable modem.

Cable modems can support multiple addresses. For example my cable modem has a **cc...b-b** address, but at one time it supported a **cc...b-a** address as well. The cable modem network Domain Name Servers (DNS) translated these addresses into Internet IP addresses. The single cable modem provided access to the Internet through my Linksys router/switch and at the same time connected the second address to the VPN server, exposing it directly to the Internet. While this serves both uses with a single cable modem at an additional charge of about $10.00 per month or about $50.00 total cost, it also shares the total transmission capacity of the single cable modem between both the VPN server and the Linksys router/switch. Whatever data is being transmitted from the central site LAN to the Internet from both the VPN server and the Linksys router/switch shares the 128-Kbps uplink transmission capacity from the cable modem to the Internet. Two separate cable modems would double this capacity to 256 Kbps, with 128 Kbps dedicated to the VPN server and 128 Kbps dedicated to the Linksys router/switch. This would incur a total monthly cost of about $80.00 or an increased cost of $30.00.

The RAS server in the upper right of Figure 6.1 is directly connected to dialup telephone lines. This permits remote telecommuters to call the RAS server and connect to the central site network. Once called, the RAS server verifies the users network ID and connects them into the central site LAN as though they were directly connected.

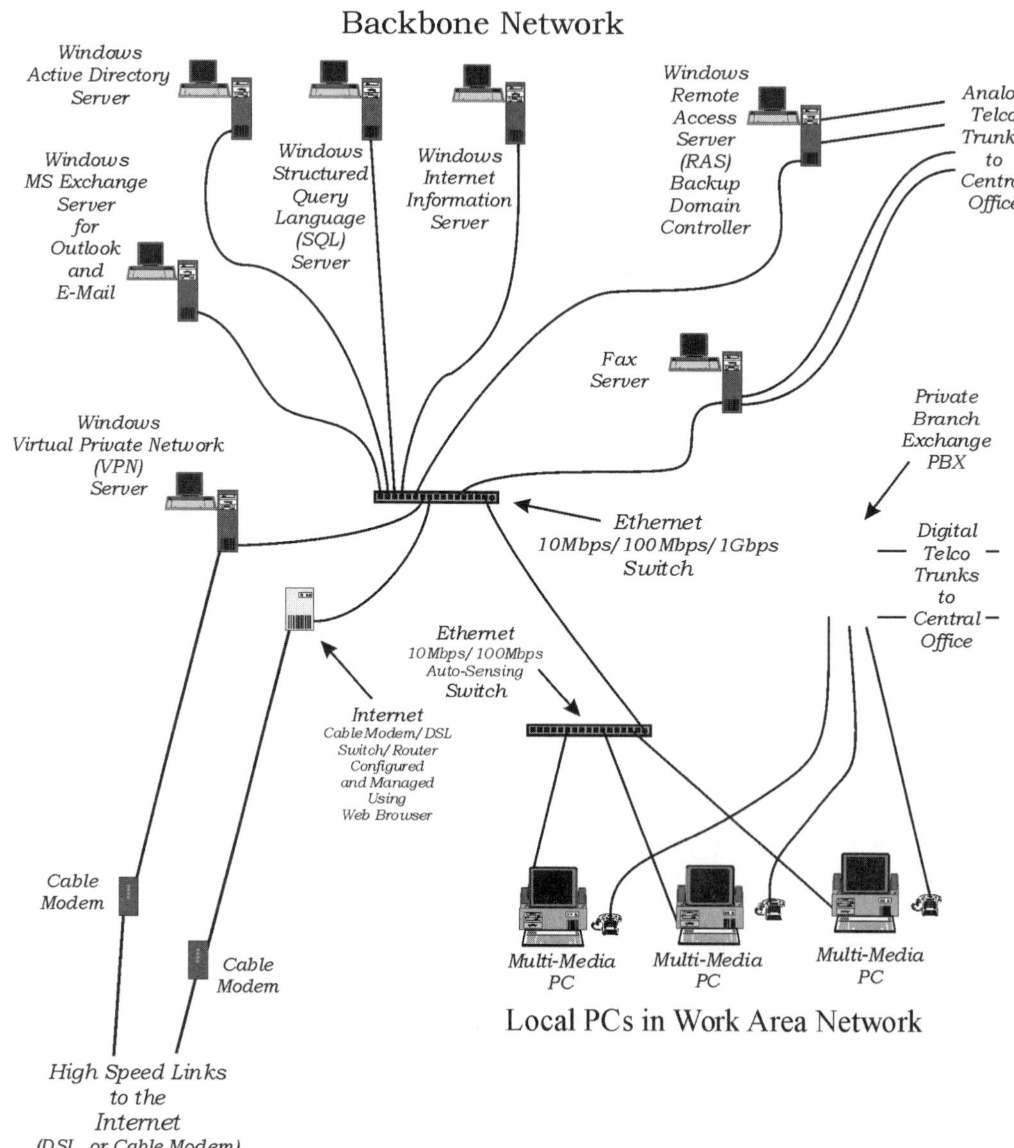

Figure 6.1 Telecommuter central site configuration.

A fax server is similarly connected to dialup telephone lines. It sends and receives faxes with an internal fax modem across the analog telephone lines. Some fax servers connect directly to the Internet and send faxes as digital images that are later translated and sent across analog telephone lines to receiving fax machines or PCs. Any PC with a modem can send and receive faxes today because virtually all modems have a fax send/receive capability. So, an enterprise can send and receive faxes from any PC host equipped with a modem or from a fax server. The benefit of receiving faxes with a fax server is that they are received using a single fax phone number in electronic form. With optical character recognition (OCR) the electronic fax can be converted into text for use in desktop publishing and other Windows applications.

Other servers perform different telecommuter and central site support functions. The Windows Active Directory Server is the network security monitor validating all users and passwords. A database or SQL server implements database and information processing applications. Sales order entry, accounting, inventory control, and other business applications are implemented using a database server. A Web server or a Windows Internet Information server publishes Web pages for an internal intranet or hosts a Web site accessible from the Internet. An e-mail server or a Windows Exchange server provides a post office function for e-mail. It also supports other Microsoft Outlook calendar and contact management functions.

The central site must provide the means for remote telecommuters to receive faxes, connect to the main server databases, send/receive organization wide e-mail, electronically text conference (e.g., Lotus Notes), send/receive voice mail, setup/conduct teleconferences, and other communications functions.

This means that a central site PBX telephone switch must have features that support voice mail and remote teleconferencing.

Smaller small-office LANs can support telecommuting as well. Figure 6.2 shows a remote telecommuter connecting to a small-office LAN through the public switched telephone network (PSTN).

A typical small-office LAN is likely to be Windows Server-based, with a RAS server to permit several simultaneous remote connections to the LAN. The remote telecommuters could connect using an ISDN dialup link into a central RAS server connected via ISDN to the dialup telephone network. This would provide a full-duplex (two-way simultaneous), 128-Kbps, all-digital communications link into the small-office LAN. Such a link would support most telecommuter communications needs with the central office including video conferencing using a Web camera and Microsoft NetMeeting software.

An alternate small-office LAN configuration supporting remote telecommuters is shown in Figure 6.3. In this configuration a cable modem connects a VPN server to the Internet. The telecommuter has a similar cable modem connection to the Internet. The cable modem connections are 24/7 connections that require no telephone dialing. However, the remote PC host must know the IP address or the host name of the VPN server to connect to it. The VPN server must be directly connected to the Internet so that its name is listed in Internet Domain Name Server (DNS) routing tables.

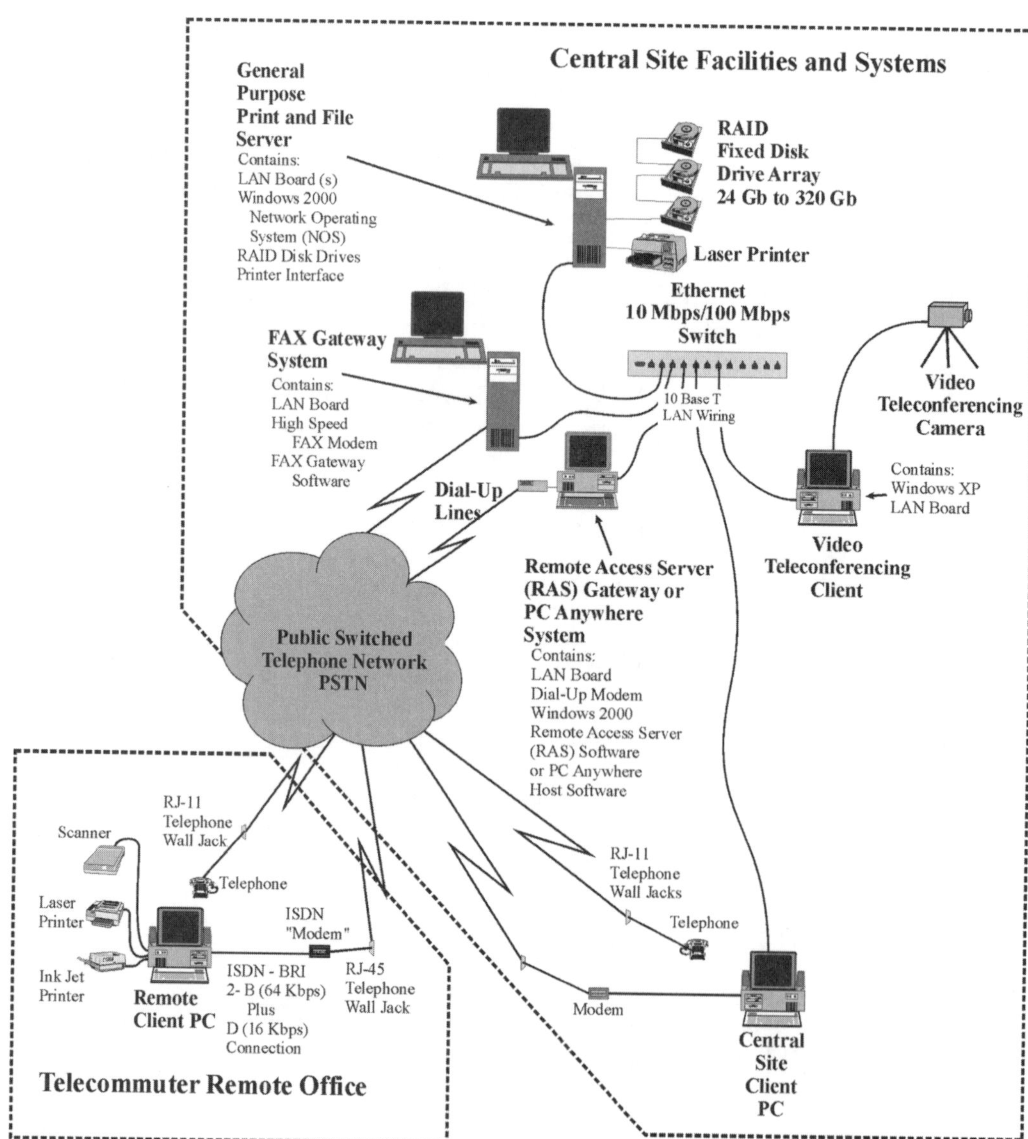

Figure 6.2 Small-office telecommuter RAS connectivity.

In this case the communications out of the central site small-office LAN is at 128 Kbps because cable modems are set up to provide asymmetrical Internet access (128 Kbps uplink and 400 to 800 Kbps downlink). This configuration is good for a few remote telecommuters, but many active telecommuters could easily saturate the 128 Kbps uplink connection from the small-office LAN into the Internet.

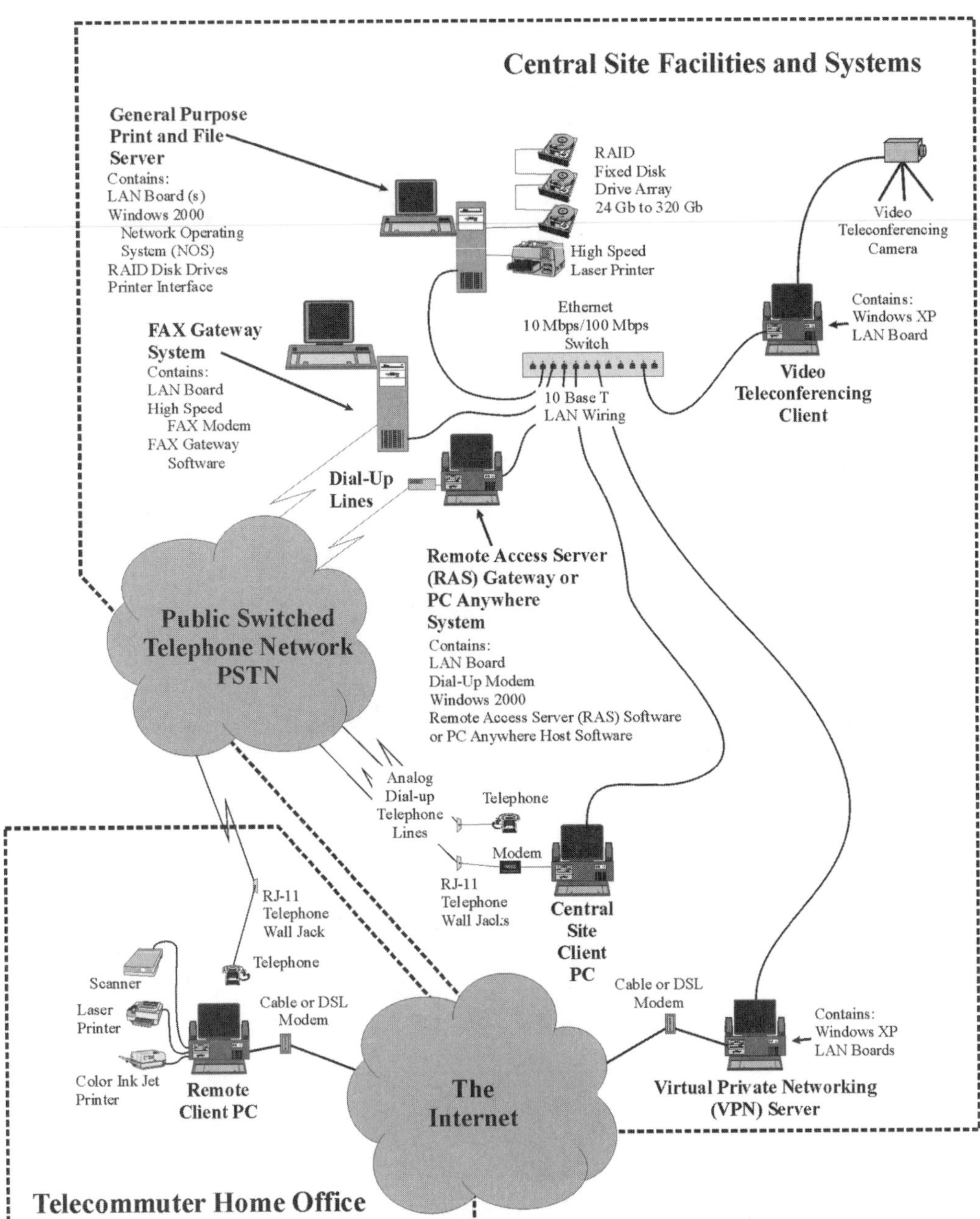

Figure 6.3 Small-office telecommuter VPN connectivity.

PC hosts at the central site and at the remote telecommuter site equipped with modems could simultaneously send faxes using the dialup telephone network and communicate with the central small-office LAN over the cable modem. The central-office communication would appear to the remote telecommuter as though they were sitting at a PC host directly attached to the central site small-office LAN. The file they were faxing over the dialup fax modem could reside on the central site Windows server. It could be simultaneously be downloaded to the PC and then faxed over the dialup network fax connection. This capability is not illustrated in Figure 6.3.

The telecommuter and the central site offices would also be equipped with a telephone for voice communications to contact other employees and customers.

As important as the central-office configurations are, the remote telecommuter-office configurations are equally important. These configurations should be matched to the work that the telecommuter performs while at the remote office. In some cases the telecommuter only requires an inexpensive laptop PC while in others a cheap or expensive desktop model would be used.

Brain Teaser: RAS-VPN Servers

Check to see if your central facility has a RAS server or a VPN server.

How many remote users can the central site RAS server or VPN server support? How many remote telecommuting users are there?

SOHO Configurations

Remote site data communications hardware focuses around the Personal Computer. The PC can be configured for a variety of office, educational, and home entertainment functions. A basic PC system today should have the following features:

1. Pentium CPU that operates at 1 GHz or better
2. Installed RAM of 256 or more
3. Fixed disk drive of 40 GB or larger
4. Data/fax modem that operates at 56 Kbps and 14.4 Kbps respectively, or alternatively a cable modem providing high-speed Internet access
5. Sound board
6. CD-RW with 32X/10X/40X or greater speed

7. Backup power for short outages and excellent surge suppression
8. Monitor, 17 to 21 inches or larger and capable of 1,600 by 1,200 resolution
9. AGP bus video board with 32 MB or more of VRAM able to display 32-bit color

The printer supporting the PC should be either a laser printer capable of 600 dpi printing or a high-resolution color inkjet printer. High-speed, high-volume printing demands the higher-speed laser printer.

These features are available in many laptop PCs for prices ranging from $1,500 to $2,000. A similarly equipped desktop PC may run around $1,000 less than the equivalent laptop. When a telecommuter is a mobile worker, the best match is the laptop PC.

Having a built-in Ethernet connection in the laptop can be a great benefit, particularly when the central site supports VPN. This means that at any customer facility with direct Internet connectivity, the laptop PC can use its Ethernet connection to access the Internet and potentially VPN into the central facility LAN. I have been at Digital Equipment Corporation's and government facilities with my laptops. With their Ethernet connections I was able to access the Internet, share files with other computers, and more.

Let us quickly examine a low-cost, medium-cost, and high-cost remote telecommuter PC host system. When we price these systems out there is perhaps a few hundred dollars at best difference in cost between each system. When buying a single system it might seem like a waste of time to differentiate, but when you are buying several systems, the overall savings can mount quickly. Figure 6.4 shows a PC host with basic components including a modem and a printer. The least expensive PC hosts use Intel Celeron or AMD Duron CPUs. The Celeron CPU is equivalent to the Pentium II CPU. The Celeron and Duron CPUs are not as well designed to support multimedia-intensive applications so they would operate somewhat slower when working with video, video-intensive Web pages, and image-intensive documents. However, despite measurable differences in data manipulation speed between these CPU chips, most people would not notice a difference. What we humans perceive is much different from what most performance tests measure.

A small 40-GB disk drive and a 17-inch display are probably fine for many office administrative tasks. When a larger display costs only $50 to $100 more, then getting it is probably cost effective. A CD-RW drive that writes 700-MB CDs may make transporting data (700 MB or less) between the remote telecommuter PC and the central office easier. CD-ROM drives cost about the same as CD-RW drives. A very fast CD-RW drive can drive the PC host system cost up by $100 or more. Inkjet printers are very inexpensive to purchase, but the true cost to operate them over a year is found when replacing the color ink cartridges. A color ink cartridge can easily cost as much as one-third of the price

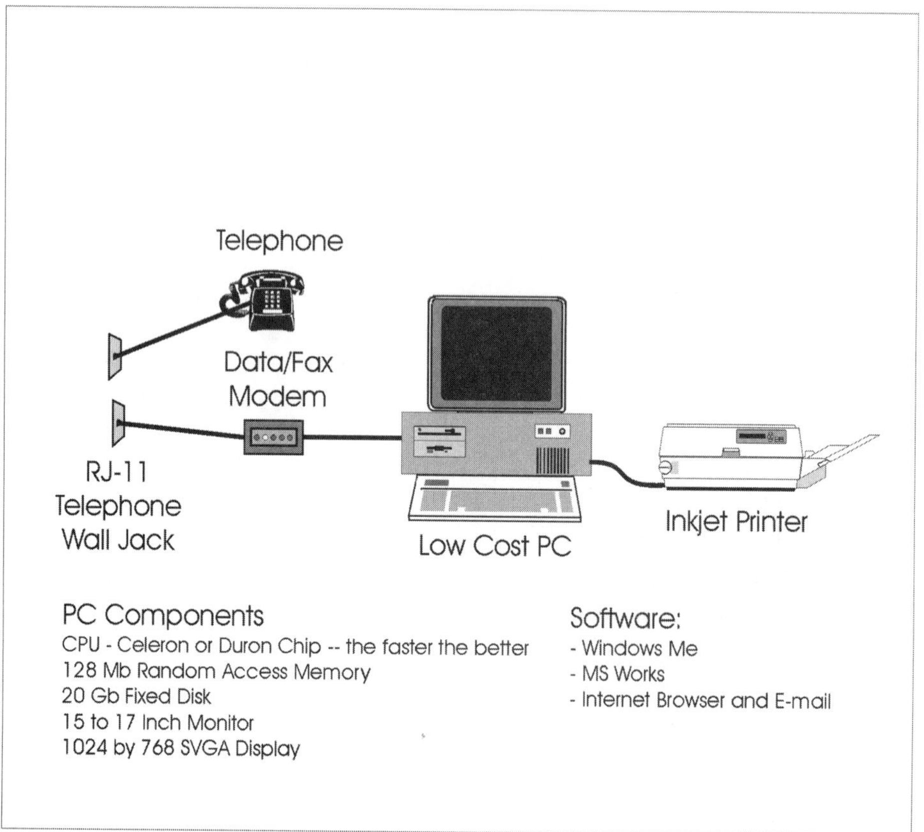

Figure 6.4 Low-cost remote-office system.

of the printer. What is saved in capital expenditures can quickly be lost in buying ink cartridges (red, blue, green, and black) for the printer. This would depend upon the amount of printing performed at the remote telecommuter office.

With a RAS or VPN connection, volume printing could easily be performed by a central site LAN-attached printer. This could save both time and money. Because central site network-attached printers look like all other network-attached printers, high-volume printing could be routed to them. This would work especially well where the central site printer has some specific administrative support for telecommuter printing and where many pages of the same small document need to be printed.

This low-cost configuration would operate with dialup telephone connectivity into the central site RAS server. The remote telecommuter telephone connection would be used to send faxes as well, but not at the same time as the telecommuter's home PC host is connected into the central-office LAN.

Although Windows Me is not well liked, it could be used as the operating system for the low-cost telecommuter PC host system, but Microsoft's Windows XP Home Edition would be a better operating system choice.

In Figure 6.5 the PC host capabilities are increased. A Pentium CPU in this case would be a Pentium III. Pentium IIIs operate at speeds over 1 GHz and are better at processing more complex multimedia, video, and image files. This system may have the addition of a scanner, Web camera, or other image input devices. The larger disk drive and larger monitor make the moderately priced PC host more capable of desktop publishing and other more resource-intensive functions than the low cost system. Windows XP Professional or Windows XP Home Edition would be a good operating system for the moderate-cost remote-office PC host system.

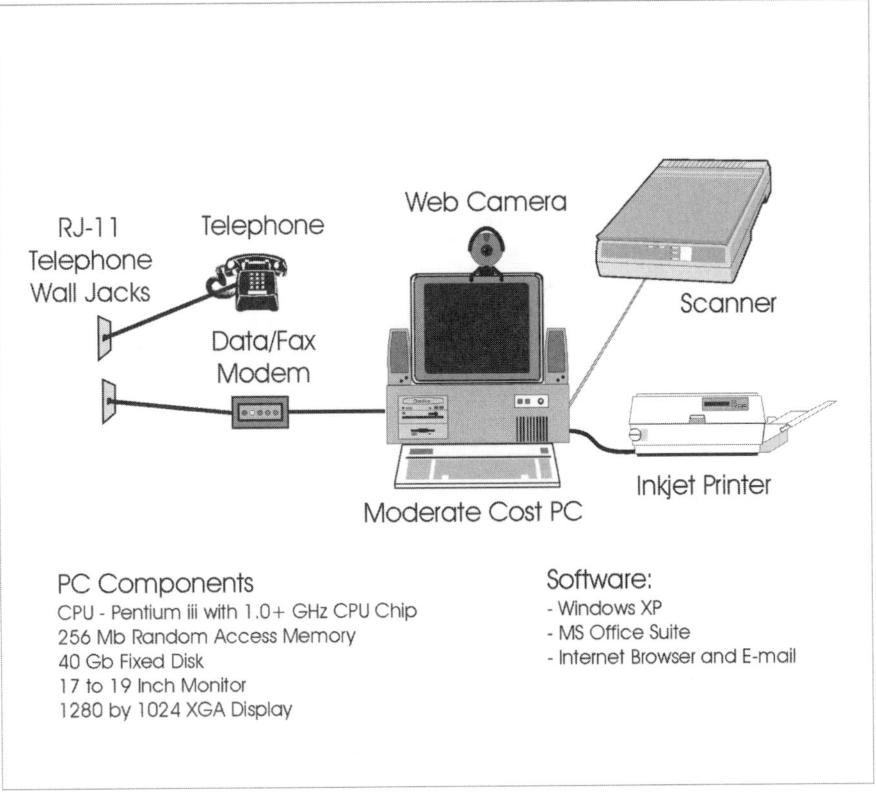

Figure 6.5 Moderate-cost remote-office system.

For a high-cost remote-office system, the PC host would use a Pentuim 4 CPU operating at speeds at 2.0 GHz or higher. This system may have a second monitor for two monitors total. The second monitor makes the PC host better equipped for more complex desktop publishing jobs. Windows XP Professional and Microsoft Office XP Pro along with voice input would likely be the operating system and office suite software used on the high-cost remote-office PC host system (see Figure 6.6).

Most important to us from a data communications viewpoint is the modem and the phone line. To most effectively use the World Wide Web's capabilities, a high-speed cable modem or DSL connectivity is required.

Most home phone lines use analog transmission. Once the signal reaches the telephone company central office, it is converted to a digital signal by the channel bank. Sometimes the PC may operate using ISDN. In this case the

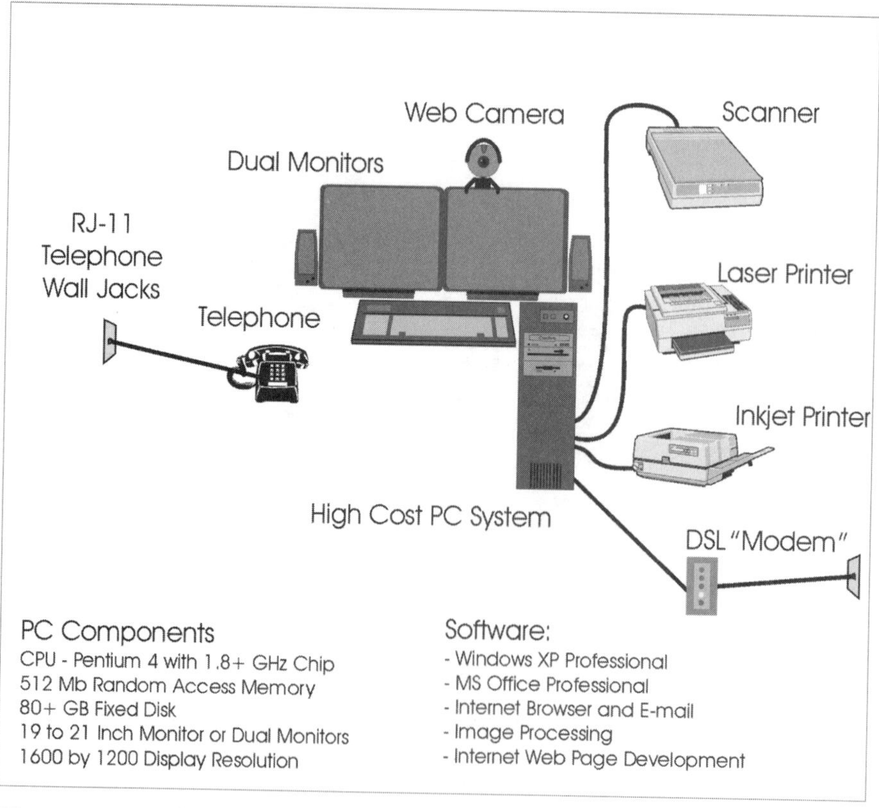

Figure 6.6 High-cost remote-office system.

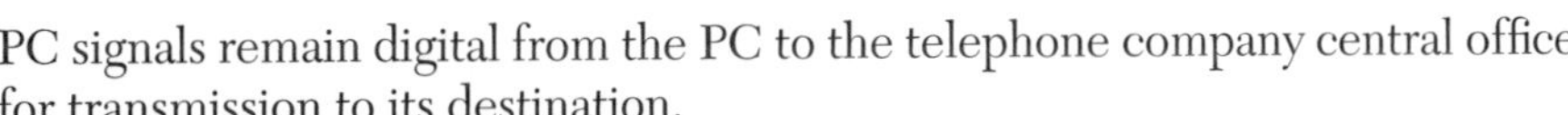

PC signals remain digital from the PC to the telephone company central office for transmission to its destination.

Modems have a variety of capabilities and features. Today virtually all modems can send both data and facsimile transmissions. Some modems with the proper software can also act as voice mail answering machines. Others, although called modems, operate with ISDN and are not really modems at all because they do not modulate or demodulate digital data.

Today, modems typically interface with a RJ-11 jack to a two-wire telephone channel. ISDN modems interface with an eight-wire RJ-45 connector on a special ISDN channel.

Remote site communications hardware consists of a PC, a data/fax modem, and the telephone line from the local exchange carrier.

Some devices that are not shown are LAN connections, connections to video input, color scanners, voice dictation systems, and infrared or RF links to pocket organizers.

Brain Teaser: Home PC Assessment

Make an assessment of your home PC. Determine what CPU, fixed disk, RAM, and other capabilities it has.

How well does your home PC stack up to our low, medium, and high-cost telecommuter remote client PC hosts?

Configuring SOHO Telecommuting Software

SOHO telecommuting software is both client and server software. The same software modules support both RAS and VPN. The configuration of the software varies depending upon whether you are configuring for RAS or for VPN. The initial configuration screens for both the server software and the client software are the same. As the configuration proceeds you come to a point where the software configures either the RAS software or the VPN software. Let's examine this in more detail, starting with first the server software and then the client software. We follow this same process for first the RAS software and then the VPN software.

The initial steps in configuring the server software for remote access are to open Programs, then Administrative Tools, and finally Routing and Remote Access, as shown in Figure 6.7.

This menu selection launches the routing and remote access software.

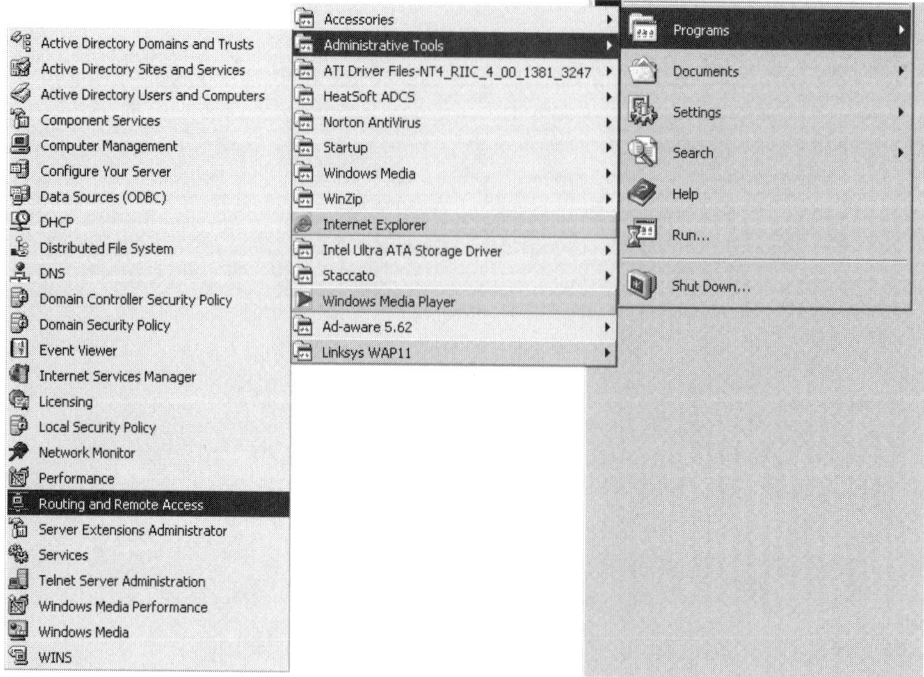

Figure 6.7 Starting routing and remote access software configuration.

RAS Server Configuration

Once the routing and remote access software is launched it starts the remote access server configuration software. The next step is to add a remote access server to handle incoming telephone calls. The initial menu guides us by requesting that we add a server. This is the initial configuration step as shown in Figure 6.8.

Clicking on the Add Server menu entry causes the Add Server panel shown in Figure 6.9 to pop up. The default selection is to make this computer the RAS server. When initially setting up RAS or VPN, the best strategy is to initially go with the default settings that Windows presents. After the server is running using the default settings, then set-up parameters can be varied one at a time to tailor the configuration to the small-office LAN needs. Clicking on OK sets this computer as the RAS server.

After the computer is set as the RAS server it must be configured. Figure 6.10 shows the menu selection for starting the RAS configuration wizard.

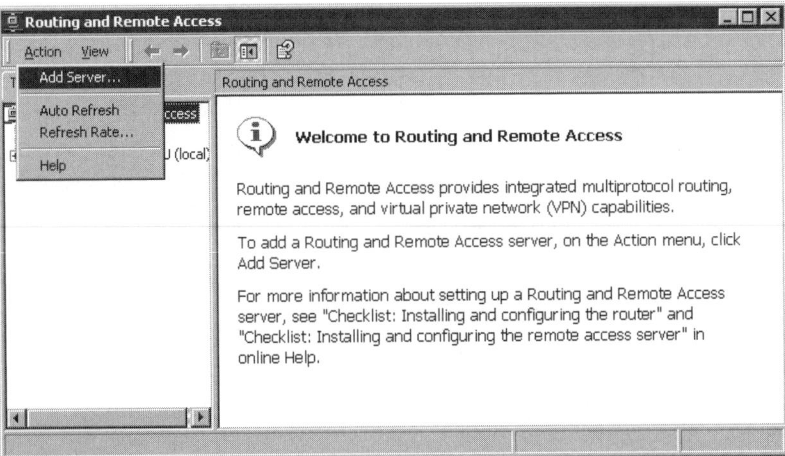

Figure 6.8 Adding remote access server.

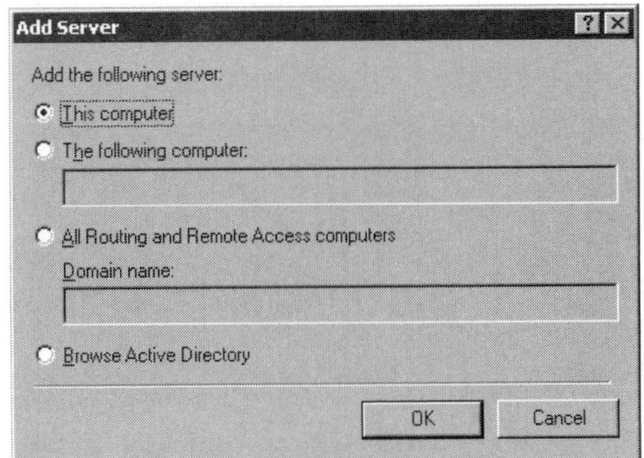

Figure 6.9
Add server panel.

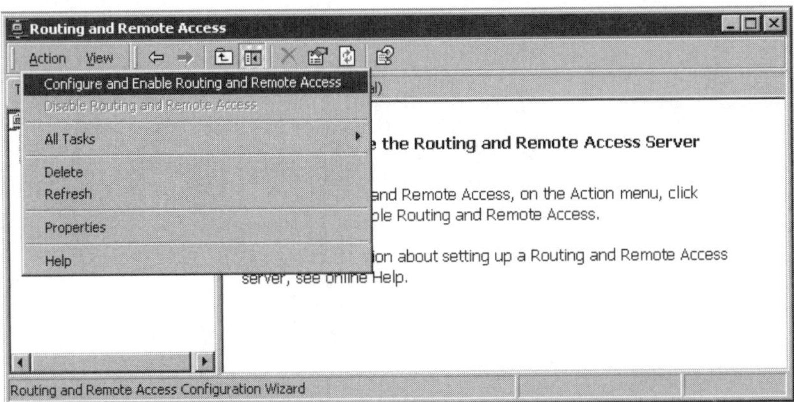

Figure 6.10 Configure and enable routing and remote access.

The routing and remote access server setup wizard leads us step-by-step through the final steps in configuring the RAS server. This wizard sets up both RAS and VPN servers as well as other Windows routing functions. In this case the remote access server selection is picked, as shown in Figure 6.11.

Clicking the Next button moves us to the next step in the configuration process, assigning IP addresses to PC hosts calling the RAS server. Figure 6.12 shows that the IP addresses can be assigned automatically or from a narrow range of IP addresses.

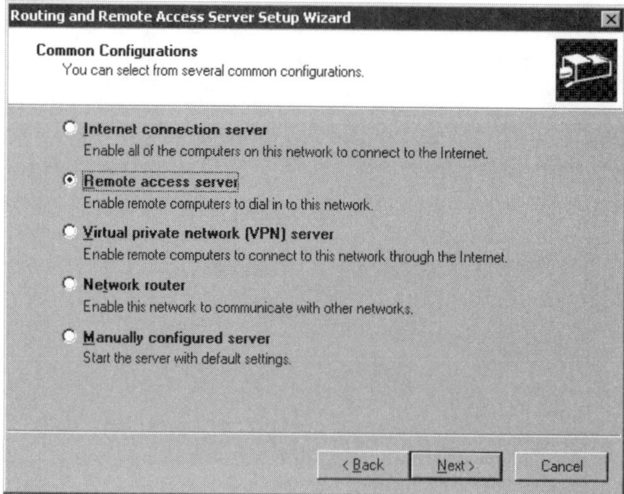

Figure 6.11 Setup Wizard remote access server selection.

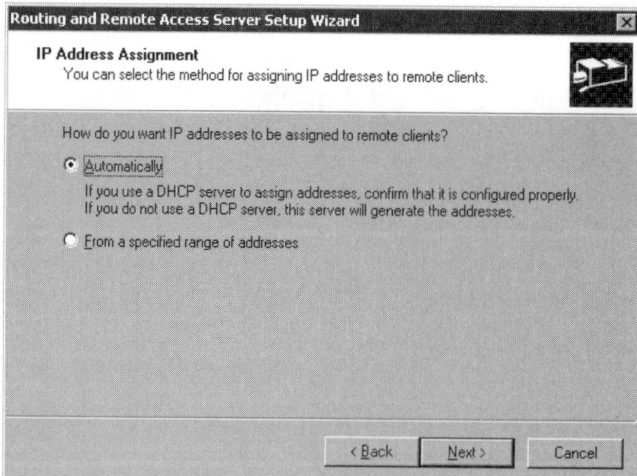

Figure 6.12 IP address assignment options.

In our case we go with the default setting, which is to automatically assign IP addresses. Next the wizard presents us with the option of managing multiple remote access servers. This is called the RADIUS service. Selecting the RADIUS service is shown in Figure 6.13.

In simple small-office LANs the RADIUS service is not really required so we opt to not use this server as a RADIUS server. Clicking on the Next button moves us to the final wizard configuration panel shown in Figure 6.14.

Clicking on Finish completes the configuration process for the RAS server. The next step would be to set up the telecommuter's client PC to access the RAS server.

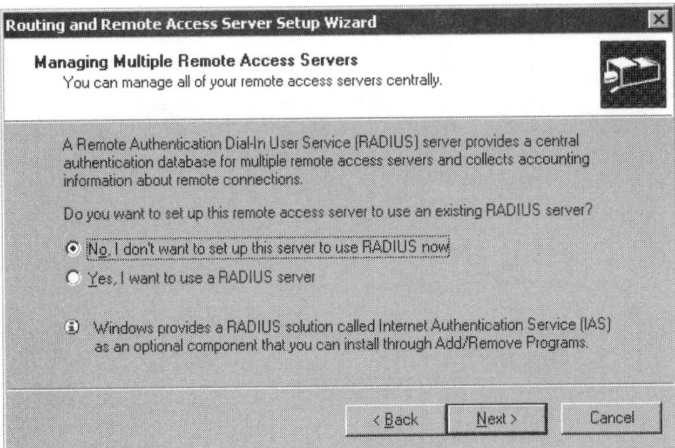

Figure 6.13 Selecting RADIUS service.

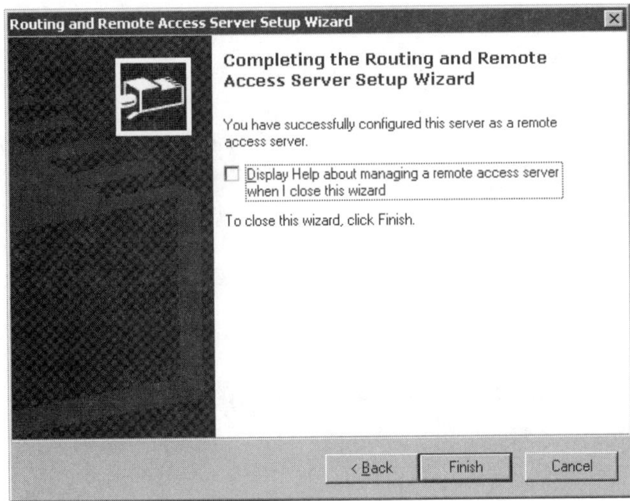

Figure 6.14 Closing the Wizard.

RAS Client Configuration

To set up a client PC for dialup remote access we go to the Control Panel and select the Network Connections icon as shown in Figure 6.15. This same process is used to set up all network connections including LAN connections, VPN connections, dialup connections, and RAS server connections.

The wizard leads you step by step through the software configuration process for the RAS dialup connection software. The initial selection is to "Connect to a private network ...," which in turn permits selecting "Connect to the network at my workplace." At this point we begin the specific configuration steps for the RAS server dialup connection software. The "dialup connection" selection is picked as shown in Figure 6.16.

Figure 6.15 Control Panel Network Connections.

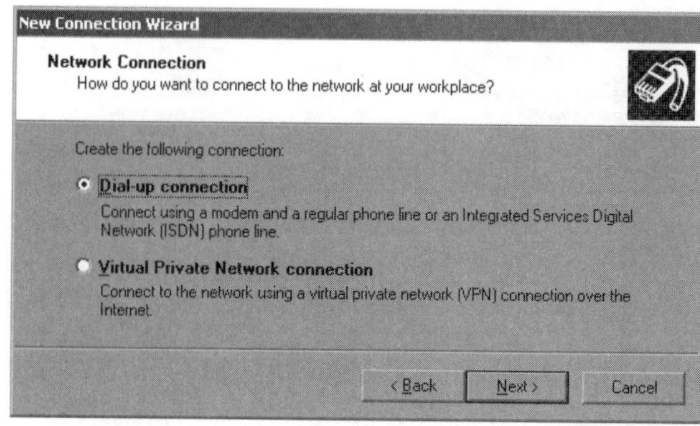

Figure 6.16
New Connection wizard dialup connection.

Clicking Next has the wizard request us to type a name for this connection in the box that is presented. Above the box appears "Company Name," which is somewhat confusing to me. My guess is that the Microsoft thinking there is that you might be calling multiple companies, so the name for the connection should be a company name. Generally, everyone works for one company at a time. However, as telecommuters we may want to access small-office LANs at several different facilities. I'd say "Facility Name" would probably be a more accurate label for the box, but in any event, the name entered here only appears as the label for the remote connection and can be usually edited later. Consequently, any unique name will do the job.

The next step is to enter the phone number that the RAS server answers. The final step is to select a security option for this connection. The security option selections are either for the exclusive use of the person making this configuration or for anyone using this computer. It's probably best to select the most secure option setting, since this connection is for the exclusive use of the person making the configuration. Clicking on Finish in the final wizard panel completes the initial phase of the client setup. The final steps in the client set up are performed when making the first connection to the RAS server.

Clicking on My Network Places then clicking the right mouse button to bring up the menus permits us to select the Properties option. Clicking on Properties brings up the Network Connections panel, as shown in Figure 6.17.

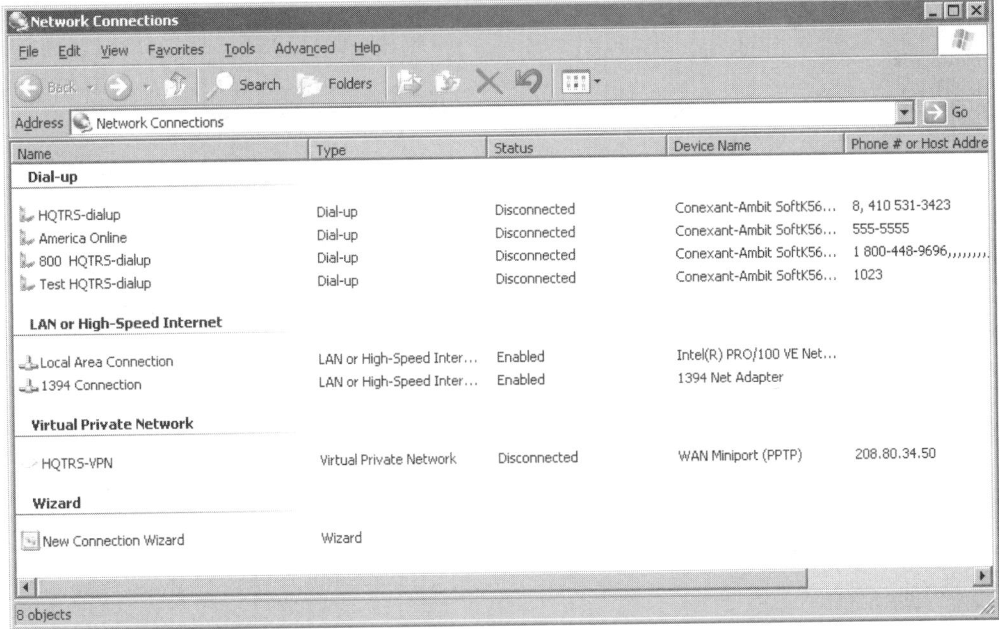

Figure 6.17 Network Connections panel.

Our RAS server connection should be listed under the dialup connections. Opening the connection reveals the Connect panel as shown in Figure 6.18. To sign into the RAS server we enter our user ID for the central-office LAN and our password. For security purposes is best to save this username and password for the exclusive use of the person making the connection. The phone number to call should appear in the Dial panel. The complete phone number with any special dialing digits can be entered here. Windows XP can also be set up for special dialing rules to be followed when calling from specific remote locations. The dialing rules can be configured by selecting the Properties button.

The final step in establishing remote access is to change the user's account on the small-office LAN to permit access from remote locations. Figure 6.19 shows enabling dial-in access for me as remote user. This panel would be accessed by the system administrator for the central-office LAN.

Once the small-office LAN system administrator enables dial-in access for the specific user, the RAS server permits him or her to connect to the central-office LAN. This completes the RAS server client setup. Next we examine a virtual private network connection setup.

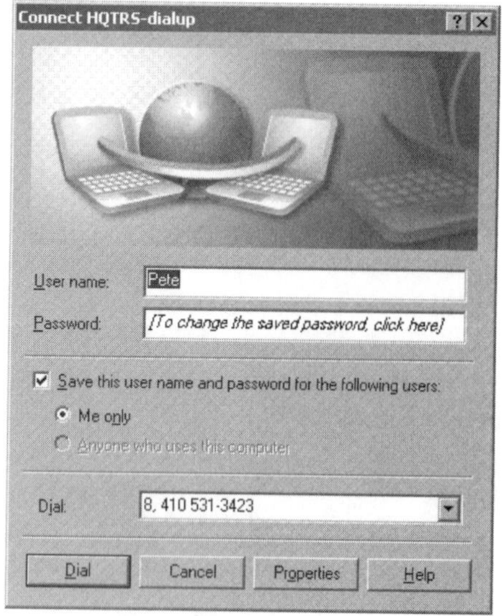

Figure 6.18
Dialup Connect panel.

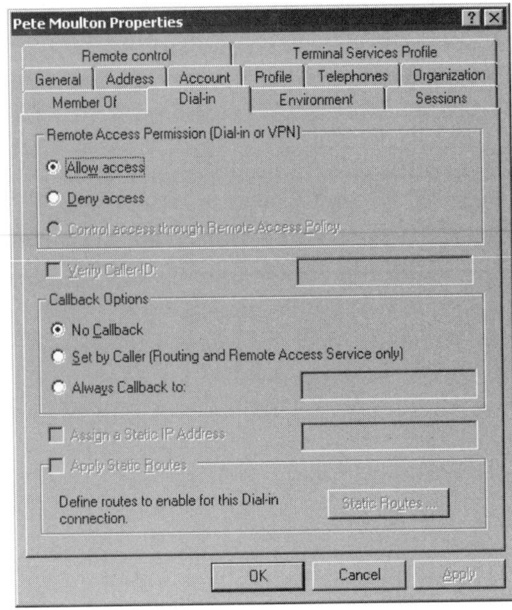

Figure 6.19
User Properties.

VPN Server Configuration

The VPN server configuration is performed using the routing and remote access server wizard, just as is the RAS configuration. The only difference is that when the common configurations panel is displayed the VPN server selection is picked, as shown by Figure 6.20.

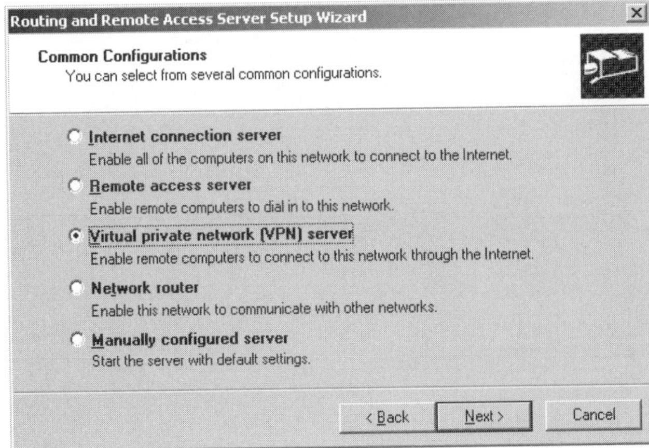

Figure 6.20 VPN Wizard Selection.

Similar to the RAS setup, the IP address of the client contacting the VPN server can be assigned automatically. Otherwise the panel for verifying the remote client protocols is presented. Of these protocols TCP/IP is the protocol that must be present to establish a VPN connection across the Internet. The next wizard panel is used to identify which LAN NIC directly connects the VPN server to the Internet. VPN servers require two NICs, one connecting to the SOHO LAN and the other connecting to the Internet. The VPN connection data transmission is routed from one NIC to the other NIC. In this manner data travels to and from the remote telecommuter PC host through the VPN server to the SOHO LAN.

Similar to the RAS server setup, the VPN software queries as whether to set up the IP address automatically or to work from a specific range of IP addresses. When the SOHO LAN uses DHCP and has a DHCP server, the DHCP server can automatically assign IP addresses to the PC hosts using the VPN connection. When DHCP is used to assign IP addresses to remote clients, the remote clients sometimes need to send DHCP messages to the DHCP server in the SOHO LAN. This requires that the VPN server relay the DHCP messages from the remote VPN client to the DHCP server and the SOHO LAN. To do this the VPN server must have the DHCP relay agent configured with the IP address of the SOHO LAN DHCP server.

Otherwise the VPN server can assign IP addresses itself to remote PC hosts. Having the VPN server assign IP addresses is shown in Figure 6.21. In this figure six addresses have been set aside within the address range 208.80.34.190 to 208.80.34.195 for use by remote VPN PC hosts. As each remote VPN PC host connects to the VPN server, it would be assigned an IP address from this group of six IP addresses.

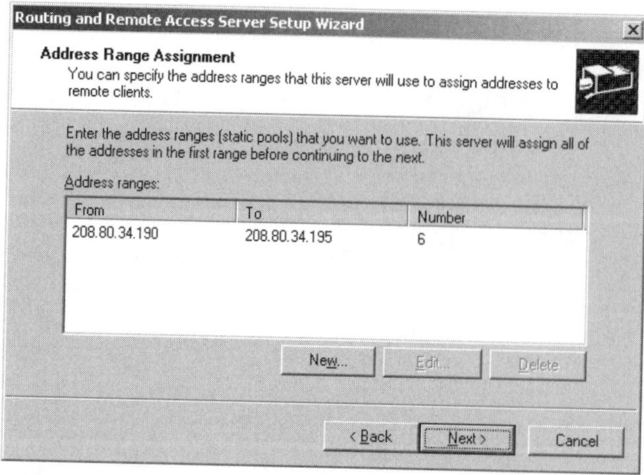

Figure 6.21 Address Range Assignment.

After specifying how the IP addresses are assigned to the remote PC hosts, the VPN setup wizard queries as to whether this VPN server is to be a RADIUS server. A RADIUS server acts as a central authentication authority for multiple RAS and VPN servers. RADIUS servers collect information about remote connections for accounting and logging purposes. When initially setting up a VPN server, a good strategy is to not make it a RADIUS server. Once the VPN connections are working, then the RADIUS server function could be enabled.

In the final phase of VPN server setup a remote access policy is established. Managing remote access security using policies is a new security paradigm. In Figure 6.22 the security policy or set of access rules is given a name.

Once the policy is named, then the conditions that must be met by the policy are created from a standard set of conditions. The standard conditions are shown in Figure 6.23.

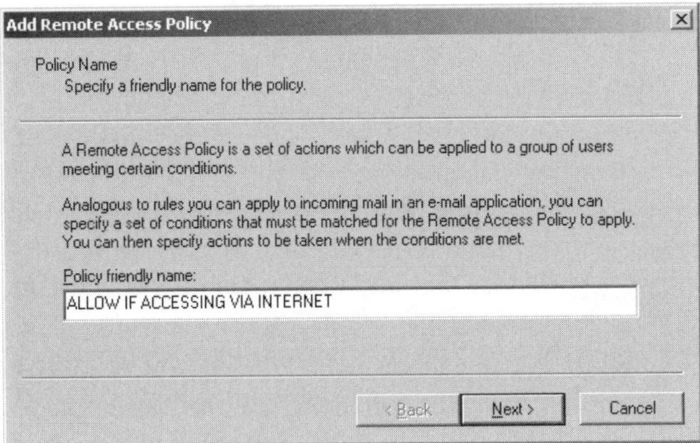

Figure 6.22 Remote Access Policy.

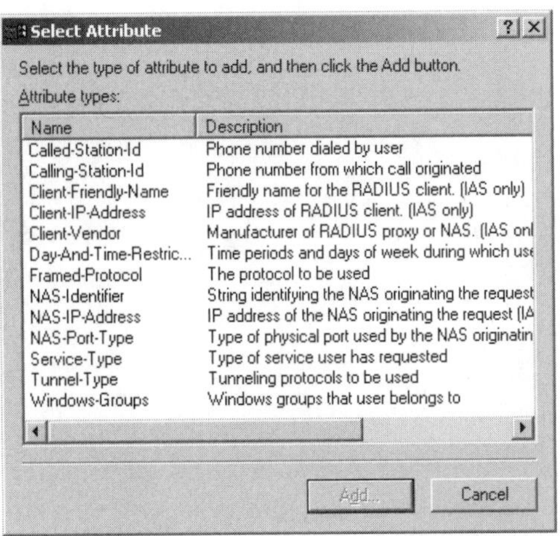

Figure 6.23
Remote access policy attributes.

For our remote access policy we selected the Windows-Groups attribute that restricts access based upon the group to which the remote user belongs. We then had to specify the group to that access would be granted. We specified the group Domain Admins. The VPN setup wizard opened a panel that required us to specifically grant remote access permission to the users fitting the attributes of this security policy. This finished setting up the VPN server.

VPN Client Configuration

Similar to RAS client PC configuration, VPN client configuration is accessed from the Control Panel and the Network Connections icon. This opens the Network Connections panel. We use the new connection wizard to set up our VPN client just as we use it to set up our RAS client. In the opening wizard panel we select "Connect to a private network..." and then in the next panel we select "Connect to the network at my workplace." These steps are basically the same for configuring both RAS and VPN clients.

The next panel directs us to the steps that specifically set up the VPN client. Picking the virtual private network connection configures the VPN client. The VPN connection is first given a name, similar to the step that gave the RAS client a name. The next choice presented is whether we need to first dial a connection to the Internet or whether we have a permanent Internet connection such as a cable modem or DSL connection. This is shown in Figure 6.24. The final wizard configuration step is to set the connection so that it may be used exclusively by one user or by any user logged onto the remote PC host. This completes the wizard panels and the initial VPN client setup.

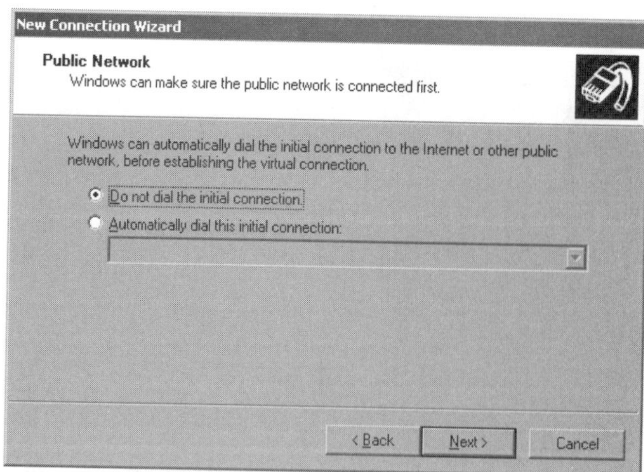

Figure 6.24 Public Network connection.

Opening the VPN connection we have just created requires us to enter a username and password. The username and password can be saved for our exclusive use or for anyone who is logged onto this computer. See Figure 6.25.

Once this information is entered, we click on the Properties button to set the final VPN client properties. The most important property to set—and the one property required for that VPN client to connect to the VPN server—is to identify the VPN server under the General Properties tab. The VPN server can be identified using its Internet IP address or a name that can be resolved by an Internet Domain Name Server (DNS). The identification step is shown in Figure 6.26.

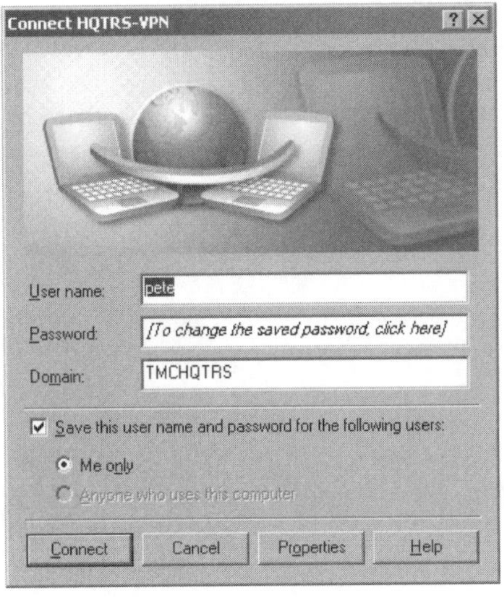

Figure 6.25
VPN Connect.

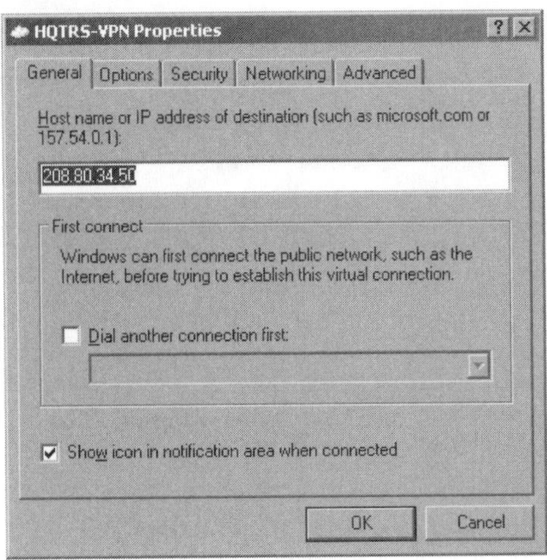

Figure 6.26
Identifying VPN server.

Clicking the OK button completes the VPN client setup. We should now be able to connect to our VPN server and to our SOHO LAN.

When setting up both RAS and VPN connections into a SOHO LAN, the best strategy to follow is to use the default configuration settings to the greatest extent possible. We've tried to illustrate here the minimum settings required to set up both RAS and VPN connections. Whenever I have selected something other than the defaults in an attempt to make a better configuration, I have inevitably caused myself problems. In many cases whatever I was attempting to configure usually did not work. As a result, I have found that staying with the defaults for any initial networking configuration is always the best strategy. Keep in mind Pete's configuration rule No. 1: Defaults always work best.

Brain Teaser: RAS Client

Try setting up a RAS client connection on your PC host. You may use any phone number you choose for the RAS connection or if you know of a RAS server then use its phone number.

Was it easy to set up the RAS server client?

Video Teleconferencing

Telecommuters can use a SOHO LAN to perform collaborative work and video teleconferencing. This is not the same video teleconferencing that would be delivered by a special video teleconferencing facility. It is video teleconferencing and remote collaboration using PC hosts, the SOHO LAN, and RAS and VPN connections.

PC Components

Simple videoconferencing over a SOHO LAN requires a Web camera and Microsoft's NetMeeting software. The Web camera provides both the video and audio input for NetMeeting. NetMeeting establishes connections with other PCs running NetMeeting software, provides video teleconferencing capabilities, and supports collaboration among NetMeeting users.

Web Camera

Web cameras do not provide the same high-quality video as a high-quality video teleconferencing facility provides. The frame rate and the resolution are much lower for Web cameras than they are for video teleconferencing facilities. While a Web camera can produce motion video, even with the best connections the frames per second display speed is less than the 30 frames per second needed for full-motion video. Some Web cams advertise 30 frames per second as their video rate. However, I have yet to see one that delivered true full-motion video. Nonetheless, the video produced by Web cams is adequate for telecommuter video teleconferencing. Once a Web cam is installed, NetMeeting finds it and uses its video input to send images to other NetMeeting software.

NetMeeting Software

NetMeeting software provides both video teleconferencing and remote collaboration functions. NetMeeting supports transferring files between PC hosts, sharing data in programs running on a PC host between other PC hosts in a NetMeeting conference, chatting with users on other NetMeeting PC hosts, and sending whiteboard drawings to other NetMeeting PC hosts. These functions are shown in Figure 6.27. In the figure the NetMeeting function panels are opened. The file transfer panel is in the upper right-hand corner of the figure. Immediately below it appears the program sharing panel. At the bottom right is the chat panel. To the left of that is the whiteboard. The whiteboard function is implemented using the Windows Paint applet. In this case the connection exists between my computer, called Pete M, and the television controlling computer, called Sony TV. The videoconferencing image I see appears in the center panel of the figure. Since no one is sitting in front of the television PC, there's no one with whom to really videoconference. In the panel on the left is my picture that is being sent to the Sony TV PC host.

NetMeeting software establishes connections in two ways. It can connect the PC hosts to one another using a common server. This server acts like a telephone switch connecting active users to one another. In the event a specific user is called but cannot be located as an active user, an indication that he or she was called but was unavailable is left for him or her.

Figure 6.27 NetMeeting features.

Server Connections

The other approach that NetMeeting supports is directly calling another NetMeeting PC host. The target host must be running NetMeeting and be set up to automatically accept incoming phone calls. This works after a fashion. In the case of my Sony television PC host, the television program does not run while NetMeeting is waiting to receive a telephone call. This means that if I'm going to be using NetMeeting for video teleconferencing between PC hosts, the PC hosts must be dedicated to that NetMeeting video teleconference. I am unable to watch television on my home entertainment PC host while waiting for a NetMeeting video conference call.

Setting up NetMeeting to make connections through a common server is performed when NetMeeting is first started by the NetMeeting setup wizard. The information provided to NetMeeting by the setup wizard is used to identify you on the server. See Figure 6.28.

The NetMeeting setup wizard also points NetMeeting at a directory server. The directory server lists your name and permits other people logged onto the directory server to call you using NetMeeting. The directory server identification panel and the NetMeeting setup wizard are shown in Figure 6.29.

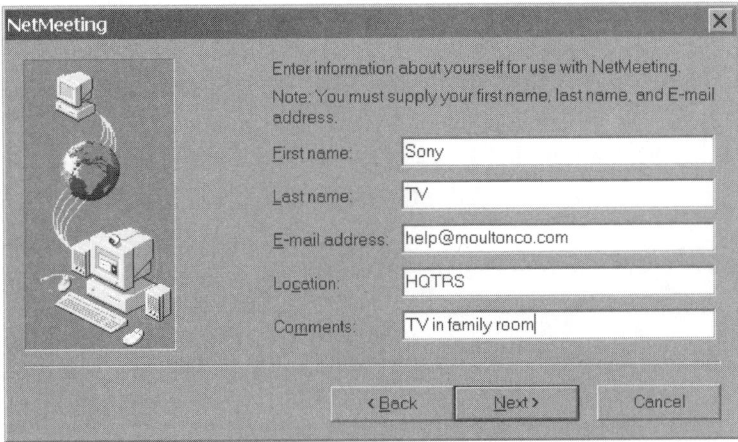

Figure 6.28 NetMeeting user identification.

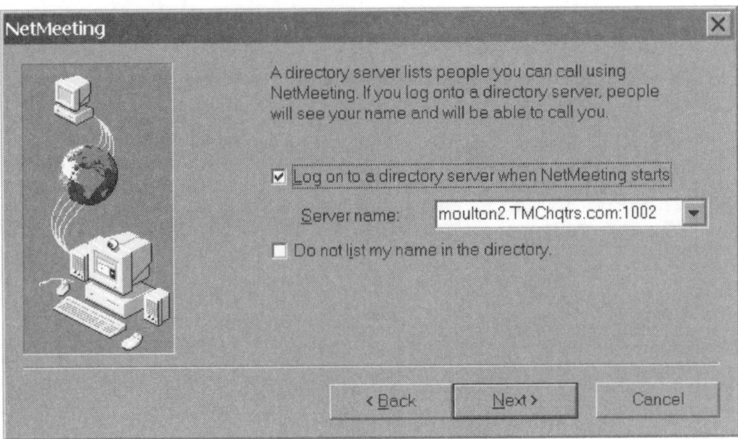

Figure 6.29 NetMeeting directory server setup.

Once the directory server is identified then the communications link speed is specified to NetMeeting. This speed varies from a dialup connection at 28,800 bps to a LAN connection. Despite configuring NetMeeting for a LAN connection, the transmission video was not 30 frames per second full-motion video. So the video quality did not really depend or vary based upon the speed of the communications link between the two NetMeeting PC hosts.

PC to PC Connections

NetMeeting PC to PC connections are easy to set up. They can be set up to accept calls automatically or the NetMeeting users can manually answer incoming calls. Configuring NetMeeting to accept calls automatically is performed using the call menu option. In Figure 6.30 the "automatically accept calls" option is checked. With this option checked, whenever an incoming call is detected by this NetMeeting PC host it is automatically answered.

The PC host placing the call can use the call menu and select new call or can click on the phone icon on the NetMeeting control panel. This causes the Place a Call panel to appear. Entering the IP address of the target station or its name causes a call to be placed. This is shown in Figure 6.31.

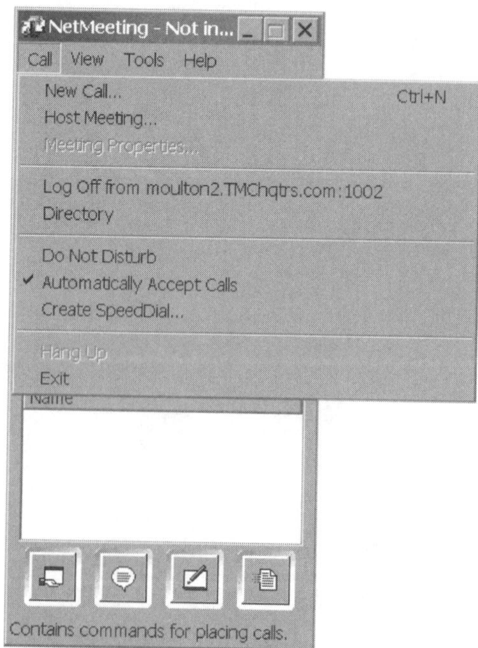

Figure 6.30
NetMeeting automatic call answering.

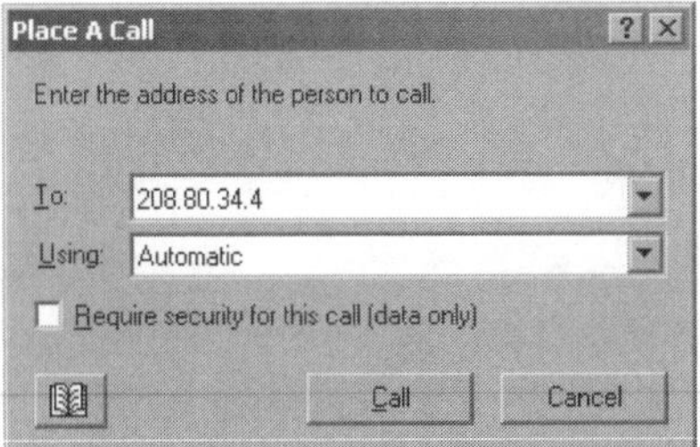

Figure 6.31
Placing a NetMeeting call.

Figure 6.32
Waiting for response message.

Figure 6.33
NetMeeting call.

Once a call is placed NetMeeting displays a waiting for response message. See Figure 6.32.

When the target PC host answers the call, the video from his or her Web camera is displayed in the NetMeeting control panel. Underneath the video display appears a listing of the PC hosts participating in this NetMeeting call. See Figure 6.33.

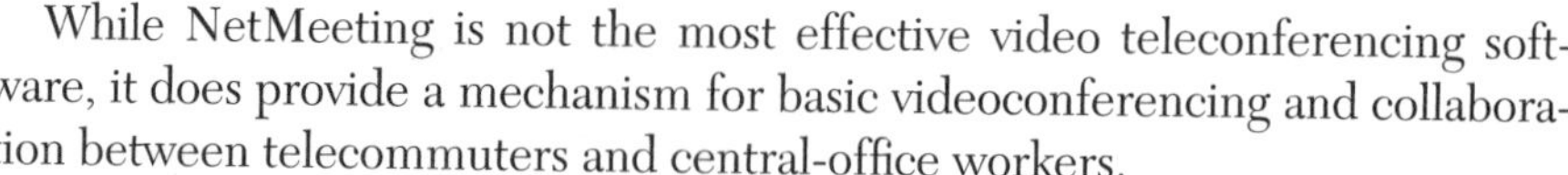
While NetMeeting is not the most effective video teleconferencing software, it does provide a mechanism for basic videoconferencing and collaboration between telecommuters and central-office workers.

Brain Teaser: NetMeeting

Check to see if Microsoft's NetMeeting client software is installed on your computer. If it is not installed try installing it and following the setup wizard. Otherwise, run the NetMeeting software and examine the configuration menu selections.

Was NetMeeting set up to access a central directory server? Did you try directly connecting across your LAN to another NetMeeting client PC host? What did you need to make the connection?

Telecommuting Administration

Through a series of checklists and thought-provoking questions, you can make an educated decision on whether telecommuting has the likelihood of being a successful way to run any given business. The remainder of this chapter presents telecommuting administration and the questions and checklists that help you determine whether telecommuting would be a benefit to your enterprise.

Telecommuting Enterprise Self Determination

Is your organization ready for telecommuting? The answers to some quick questions can determine if there are enough reasons to initiate a telecommuting program. The questions are as follows:

1. What percentage of your employees spend more than an hour a day commuting to work?
2. What size is your company?
3. Is your company located in places where state commuter trip reduction mandates are in effect?
4. To what extent does your organization use PCs?

5. What supporting infrastructure for remote communications exists within your organization? Can you identify and track your computer inventory and assets?
6. Is your business expanding? Contracting?
7. What organization climate is there? Is top management progressive? Conservative? Formal? Informal?
8. Who are the most successful managers—progressive or conservative? Employees?
9. Have storms been a problem?
10. Have storms destroyed employee residences?
11. Are employees likely to spend some of their own money to set up telecommuting?
12. Does your company already have experience with non-conventional work techniques such as flex time and video teleconferencing?
13. Does the work style of the company match a telecommuting profile? Or, do employees require direct face-to-face supervision, have high turnover, have constantly changing tasks, use special tools and machinery, or require special material/product distribution?
14. Are meetings regularly scheduled or are they mostly ad hoc meetings?

This self determination question list is likely to select out small companies in rural areas with low-paid workers who have short commutes to work.

Establishing a Telecommuting Program

The general steps to establishing a telecommuting program are as follows:

1. Define telecommuting for the organization and establish a common understanding of its objectives for the organization. Prepare a proposal outlining a plan, its benefits, the costs, the savings, and a request for action.
2. Select a telecommuting coordinator. Generally the one selling telecommuting gets to be the coordinator. Be careful because this may become a full-time, non-telecommuting job.
3. Form a telecommuting focus group/steering committee to develop telecommuting policies and procedures for your organization.
4. Write a telecommuting policy and telecommuter agreement answering:
   a. What are the criteria for becoming a telecommuter?
   b. What equipment does the organization provide the telecommuter?

   c. What equipment must the telecommuter provide?
   d. What types of telecommuting are supported? Satellite center or work at home?
   e. What is to be accomplished by the telecommuting program?
   f. How is telecommuting effectiveness going to be measured?
   g. What kind of statistics are going to be produced (trip reductions, absenteeism, etc.)?
   h. What is the basic agreement between the telecommuter and the organization?
   i. Must telecommuters have home inspections?
   j. Are telecommuters subject to audits?
   k. What are the security measures and procedures telecommuters must follow?
   l. What considerations and support are there for traditional commuters (non-telecommuters)?
5. Meet with employees and managers interested in telecommuting. This may be a series of short public meetings over a month's time. Be prepared to provide answers to the following:
   a. What is the organization's definition of telecommuting?
   b. What are the pros and cons for telecommuting for your organization?
   c. Why is your organization starting telecommuting?
   d. What are the specific telecommuting policies?
   e. Who can become telecommuters?
   f. How long is the telecommuting program to last? First-time programs are usually started with a pilot test, then expanded organization-wide if successful.
   g. What is in the telecommuting agreement?
   h. What are the responsibilities of the telecommuter? Of the organization?
   i. How can interested parties sign up for telecommuting?
6. Screen participants and select telecommuters and telecommuting workgroups.
7. Implement telecommuting—train your telecommuters technically!
8. Monitor and evaluate the telecommuting program results by surveying participants, managers, and co-workers before telecommuting and quarterly after telecommuting is in place.
9. Summarize and publish results semi-annually. Adjust policy accordingly.

Determining Enthusiasm

Enthusiasm for telecommuting from an organization's employees is readily gauged from their attendance at the public meetings held to explain telecommuting. The attendance and the questions are a sure gauge of employee interest.

If top management needs some measure of employee interest in telecommuting, a simple survey could be conducted. The survey form would need to describe what telecommuting is, its perceived benefits to the organization, and the potential benefits for the telecommuters. The results of this survey would determine the enthusiasm for telecommuting. Non-respondents to the survey are non-enthusiasts.

Setting Goals for Organizational Participation

Telecommuting program goals should be specific. Some specific goals are:

1. Does your organization expect to improve productivity?
2. Does your organization expect to reduce absenteeism?
3. Does your organization expect to reduce commuting trips?

The telecommuting goals explain what a telecommuting program is to accomplish and helps sell management on telecommuting. Selling a telecommuting program to employees and management can be easier when a mission statement and a logo for the program are developed.

Determining Whether Benefits to the Company are Measurable

Company benefits may be tangible (measurable) or intangible. For example, some productivity increases are easy to measure, such as more telephone contacts, increased sales, more invoices processed, more expense reports prepared, and other more or less mundane productivity measures. Other benefits are more difficult to assess, such as lower employee turnover and its long-term business impact or increased quality of work. How can one tell that telecommuting produced a better solution to a business problem than working in a normal commuting environment? Such questions are only answered from an overall historical business perspective.

Pitfalls to Watch Out For

Telecommuting is not for everyone. Further, the focus of the procedures described so far has been on the employees participating in telecommuting. Little has been heard from the technical people supporting the telecommuters. Rushing into telecommuting without having the requisite central site technical infrastructure in place is courting failure for telecommuting.

Because telecommuting is viewed from a telecommuter viewpoint or from a human resources viewpoint, we forget that the driving force behind telecommuting is technology. If the technologies were not available to support telecommuting, employee trip reduction programs would never consider telecommuting as an option.

Do **not** think the following:

1. The technical problems with telecommuting sort themselves out.
2. The organization adjusts to match the climate established by telecommuting.
3. It does not matter that non-telecommuters do not support telecommuting.
4. Once telecommuting is in operation its benefits become apparent to all.
5. All telecommuting participants are good workers.
6. Telecommuting produces immediate cost savings for the organization. Cost savings can only be determined by measuring all life-cycle costs.
7. Telecommuting benefits the telecommuter most.
8. There is no ongoing cost to the telecommuter. Telecommuters may not save money telecommuting—they may just spend their money differently.
9. Telecommuting turns employees into independent contractors.
10. Telecommuting employees can work 24 hours a day, 7 days a week.
11. Telecommuters have more personal time.
12. Telecommuting is the only way to meet state-mandated trip reductions.
13. Telecommuting reduces labor costs.
14. Telecommuting is only for big companies in big cities.
15. Telecommuters do not need any technical training.

Of these pitfalls, the most over looked is the cost of the infrastructure to support telecommuting. There is an immediate assumption that the savings in bricks and mortar pays for the organization's added costs associated with supporting telecommuting. This is clearly not so because office facilities are duplicated while the employee makes the transition from commuter to telecommuter. This transition may require a year or more.

Evaluating Effectiveness

Telecommuting program effectiveness has been evaluated by surveying the attitudes of telecommuters, co-workers, and supervisors. These surveys were conducted before and after telecommuting programs were started. The results, while helpful, are not necessarily a good measure of the impact of telecommuting on a specific organization. The surveys focused on behavioral perceptions and not statistical measures of job performance.

Other telecommuting cost saving claims have looked only at the savings that a single department realized and not at what overall savings, if any, were experienced by the organization or enterprise as a whole.

The effectiveness of a telecommuting program for a specific enterprise requires comparison of a telecommuting work group with a control group. By participation in the experiment both groups perform better, as was documented in the Hawthorne experiments of the late 1920s and early 1930s.

Measure before and after costs associated with telecommuting and non-telecommuting groups. True telecommuting costs would include the increased central site support costs attributed to the remote telecommuters as well as the cost of duplicate office space.

Measurements of productivity should be developed and tracked. The productivity measures should be similar for both telecommuters and non-telecommuters.

Behavioral attitude and perception surveys should be conducted on both groups.

Assessments of the intangible benefits should be made by neutral third parties. Intangible benefits may include measures of before and after product quality, contribution to the overall organization mission, employee enthusiasm for the job, and others.

The results of these evaluations should be combined into a telecommunications program assessment report. Such a report should be compiled annually or semi-annually and presented to management.

Telecommuting Policy

Telecommuting requires a corporate policy. It can be simple or complex. The following should be considered when writing a telecommuting policy:

1. What telecommuting means within your organization
2. A single-sentence policy statement defining the commitment made by your organization to telecommuting

3. The practices and standards for telecommuting, including statements of business needs, terms and conditions of employment, equipment requirements, work space designation, the telecommuting agreement, tax implications, dependent care, and scheduling
4. A statement establishing the voluntary nature of the program
5. A description of the selection criteria for telecommuting candidates including job characteristics, telecommuter characteristics, and supervisors' characteristics used in determining telecommuting employees
6. A general description of the organization equipment assigned to the telecommuter, including a definition of who is responsible for its care
7. A description of organization policies on proprietary information and security
8. An explanation of the process used to measure performance and evaluate the success of telecommuting
9. Guidelines for managing by objectives or results for potential telecommuters and their supervisors
10. A statement of telecommuting working hours and treatment of overtime
11. A description of a telecommuting safety policy that includes a statement on PC ergonomics

Policy statement examples can be found on the Internet from Pacific Bell and other sources. These policies can be readily adapted to other telecommuting organizations.

Sample Telecommuting Agreement

I have read and understand the attached Management Telecommuting Policy, and agree to the duties, obligations, responsibilities, and conditions for telecommuters described in that document.

I agree that, among other things, I am responsible for establishing specific telecommuting work hours; furnishing and maintaining my remote work space in a safe manner; employing appropriate telecommuting security measures; and protecting company assets, information, trade secrets, and systems in my possession. I also understand and have completed telecommuting site survey and personal survey forms.

I understand that telecommuting in my case is voluntary and I may stop telecommuting at any time. I also understand that the company may at any time change any or all of the conditions under which I am permitted to telecommute or withdraw permission to telecommute.

____________________________ __________________

Employee Signature Date

____________________________ __________________

Supervisor Signature Date

Setting up a Telecommuter

Generally, telecommuting is voluntary. Most employees being converted to telecommuting should not be required to telecommute. The most important factor in selecting the successful telecommuting employee is his or her motivation to telecommute. Employees that really desire to telecommute are the most successful telecommuters.

Employee Selection

Employee selection for telecommuting participation varies from organization to organization. It generally depends upon the employees' work, their access to technologies, their proficiency with technologies, and other factors. A typical employee selection survey should address the following:

1. The nature of the person's work—what percentage of time is spent working alone, in meetings, on the phone with co-workers, and on the phone with customers or vendors?
2. What are the potential benefits to the organization from their telecommuting?
3. What are the potential benefits to the employee from telecommuting?
4. What characteristics make them suitable telecommuters?
5. What is their supervisor's management style and attitude toward telecommuting?
6. How much time and money do they spend commuting?
7. Do they have room for separate office space at home?
8. What PC equipment do they have at home?

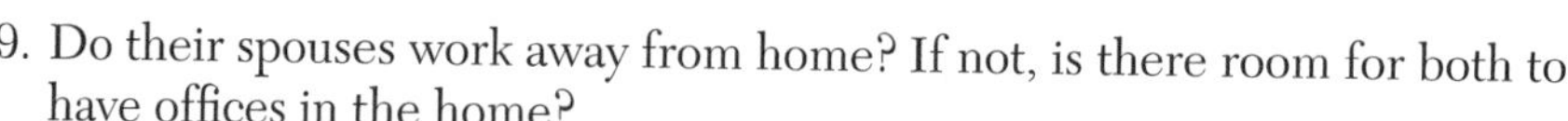

9. Do their spouses work away from home? If not, is there room for both to have offices in the home?
10. How long have they worked for the organization?
11. Are they full or part time?

Answering these questions carefully and accurately can give a good idea whether an employee is a candidate for telecommuting.

Set-up Costs

All telecommuters should be technically proficient with their telecommuting computer tools. When systems do not work as expected, it is no longer a simple case of having PC support come down the hall to fix the problem. Now they would be required to reverse commute to the remote site to correct any system problems. Every telecommuter should attend a PC troubleshooting seminar tailored to their specific PCs. This is an attempt to focus attention on one key factor in telecommuting success—technical competence of the telecommuting employees. This additional technical proficiency is needed to make effective use of the PC and communications tools. We have found that employees who cannot effectively use the technology at their disposal do not perform well on the job. Such training goes beyond simple PC troubleshooting into how to effectively integrate desktop publishing, fax, and Internet technologies into a home-based office. This is a cost of implementing telecommuting.

So, setup costs do not only include the cost of installing and configuring a remote PC system, but they also include the cost of the telecommuter is technically competent to handle installing and configuring Windows, troubleshooting basic printer/dialup communications/PC configuration problems, and operating his or her applications software. Employees desirous of becoming potential telecommuters who are not proficient with multimedia Windows PCs and the Internet should become proficient with these technologies.

Mail Distribution

Most mail for telecommuters is sent to the central site. This leaves three distribution methods:

1. Repackaging the mail and mailing it to the telecommuters' remote site
2. Having the telecommuters pick up the mail once or twice a week
3. Opening all mail and faxing key correspondence daily to the telecommuters

The trade-offs here are timeliness of response and privacy. Obviously, options one and two are more private but less timely than option three.

In the longer term, telecommuters are likely to have most correspondence in an electronic form. This means that they will e-mail or fax co-workers and customers rather than using snail mail.

Remote Office Visits

A tough area to cover is remote office visits by customers and vendors. Who is responsible for the liability insurance required to cover remote office visits by vendors and customers? Suppose a customer were to slip on ice and hurt his or her back during a visit to a telecommuter's office. Generally, businesses carry an umbrella liability insurance policy that protects them from such losses. Does this policy cover home-based telecommuting offices? If not, what is required to extend such liability insurance coverage to home-based offices? The answer here varies from insurance company to insurance company.

Based upon the difficulty we as a small business had in finding general business liability coverage, it may be very difficult for a home-based telecommuter to find adequate liability insurance coverage for visits from vendors and customers.

A solution is to prohibit customers to visit home-based workers. All such meetings must be luncheons at local restaurants. Further, office supplies would need to be picked up by the telecommuter from the office. They should not carry big boxes of paper home (for their laser printer) because this could cause lifting strain in their back. Just one to three reams of paper may be carried home at any one time.

These examples may be extreme, but they illustrate some of the legal issues surrounding telecommuter home-based offices.

Telecommuting Remote Sites

There are three basic types of telecommuting remote facilities. These are the home office, the mobile office (essentially, the car), and a satellite work site—either an enterprise established regional facility or an office suite rented daily like a hotel room. Let's look at these in more detail.

Home-based Offices. The easiest type of telecommuting to envision is the home office. In this case the telecommuter sets up a room at home containing a PC and ancillary hardware along with the requisite telephone connections. This room at home becomes his or her decentralized office. To be at work, he or she should be in the office.

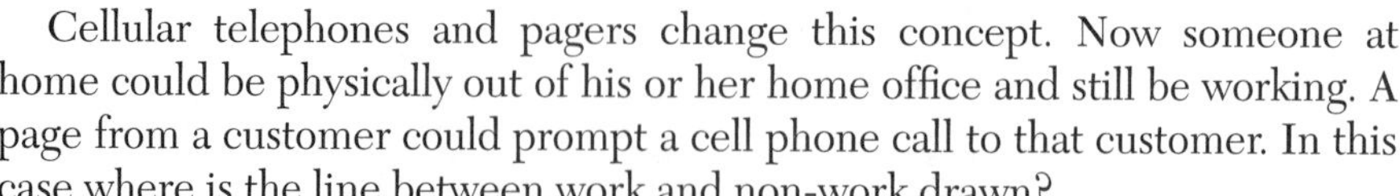

Cellular telephones and pagers change this concept. Now someone at home could be physically out of his or her home office and still be working. A page from a customer could prompt a cell phone call to that customer. In this case where is the line between work and non-work drawn?

Home-based offices may be relatively easy to establish with persons eager to telecommute. Most have a PC or are looking for a good reason to buy the very latest PC. They may be willing to purchase a computer and set up a room at their expense just to telecommute.

The main difficulty with a home-based office is that the equipment to operate it becomes technologically obsolete before the average three-year consumer loan is paid off. Further, as time goes on the telecommuter may become reluctant to re-invest in new technologies to maintain the work output and productivity of his or her home office. This means that it may be easy and somewhat inexpensive for an organization to start a bunch of telecommuters, but it quickly becomes much more expensive to maintain them. Without significant work output or productivity gains, such home-based office telecommuting withers and dies on the vine.

For small organizations this may be the only option because they are unable to construct facilities outside their central offices. With highly motivated telecommuters, the remote office equipment and facilities may be maintained at a technically current level at little cost to the organization.

Mobile Units. This type of telecommuting is performed by outside sales personnel and others who work from mobile offices. Industries with mobile offices include construction, transportation (truckers and pilots work from many remote locations), and various auditing and inspection services.

In this case, a laptop PC with a cellular phone with fax modem becomes the mobile office. Other ancillary support equipment is used depending upon the remote functions performed. New digital cameras might be one type of such support equipment. There an inspector or adjuster can take a picture, input it to the laptop PC, and transmit it as part of a report.

As these workers travel from site to site (hotel to hotel) they can, through their dialup modem connections, communicate with the central office. They send and receive reports, place customer orders, check order status, and so on using their laptop PC and dialup communications.

Generally, in this case the equipment is provided by the employer and not the telecommuter. Special high-performance modems and laptop PCs may be used in place of the standard-issue company PC. In this case the mobile telecommuter must become self-sufficient when it comes to technical support. He or she may also become responsible for upgrading his or her remote office equipment to avert technical obsolescence.

Regional Offices. A regional office is a facility set up specifically by an organization as a satellite to its central facilities. Telecommuters travel a short distance to the regional office, where they work each day instead of commuting to the central office facility. Employees may work at these regional centers more or less permanently.

Regional offices would need to be established at locations where a significant number of organization employees have a short commute. Their office would be permanently assigned to the satellite location. Commuting to a central office would be on an as-needed basis.

This sounds great until someone tries to decide where to locate satellite facilities. Further extensive communications infrastructure between the satellite facility and the central facility is needed to permit employees to more or less permanently work at the satellite facility. This is still an investment in bricks and mortar, but just cheaper bricks and mortar.

Daily Office Suites. This is similar to regional offices except that the organization just rents space from a regional telecommuting support facility owned by some organization specializing in providing telecommuting centers. Today few such centers exist, but the number is growing.

The telecommuter now drives to a nearby regional site. He or she goes to an assigned office cube—like a hotel room—and work for the day. The hoteled office cube has a PC and the necessary communications facilities to support the telecommuter's job functions. The company pays a daily rent on the office cube (hoteled office). This avoids investment in remote office equipment and bricks and mortar.

The bad news here is that the organization has little control over the quality and types of facilities that are available to the employee. Brand-new regional centers would have the latest equipment. In two years what will they be like? A rented regional telecommuter office must maintain its technology. What happens when telecommuters using a hoteled office site all use it on Tuesdays and Thursdays? How are the costs of maintaining the site passed on to the renters? This may result in higher telecommuting costs overall.

Business and Legal Considerations

Employers must consider factors that affect a final decision to telecommute or not from employee safety, worker's compensation, and other labor laws. Figure 6.34 illustrates the different business and legal considerations that must be addressed by an enterprise when setting up telecommuters. Some of these require a site inspection to document compliance.

A cursory examination of each of these areas is provided here to make you aware of what is involved with these business and legal considerations.

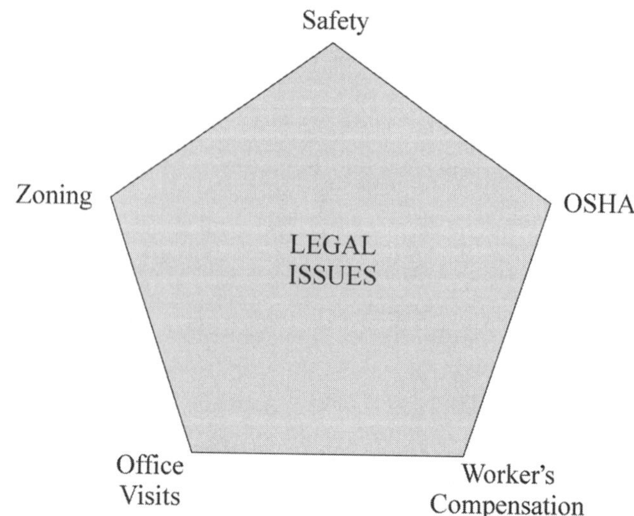

Figure 6.34
Telecommuter business and legal considerations.

Legal Issues. Laws for regional sites are equivalent to those for central sites. Generally the same laws that apply to a traditional office also apply to a home office. These laws are city, county, and state specific. Federal regulations generally do not cover home-office environments. A local business lawyer should be able to identify which laws in your area affect your business.

Safety Regulations. Localities have specific laws for health and safety. These laws may specify emergency egress, fire extinguishers, and other safety compliance conditions. A check with local fire and health and safety officials would clarify the requirements for a home office.

Zoning Regulations. Generally, zoning is approached with a do not ask, do not tell strategy. Many localities do not have zoning regulations that describe or permit telecommuting use of residential neighborhoods. As more localities enact telecommuting zoning regulations, telecommuting from residential locations will become more accepted and allowable.

Some cases may specifically be prohibited. Manufacturing or the use or production of certain products from home is prohibited in some areas. These prohibitions include catering and preparation of home-baked and edible food products, and businesses such as photography and photo development, printing, and painting, which use special chemicals.

Businesses may be required to register or obtain a permit or license to conduct business from a home-office location. A check with local zoning officials would clarify this requirement. A community may still enforce blue laws requiring all businesses to close on Sundays. Zealous officials can enforce such blue laws even against home offices.

OSHA Requirements. As of June 1996, OSHA had no specific requirements covering telecommuters. Since the Occupational Safety and Health Act of 1970 covers any work performed by any employee in any workplace within the United States, work at home is also covered. OSHA recognizes that an employee working at home controls his or her work environment.

OSHA Employer Requirements. OSHA mandates employers to furnish each employee a place of employment free from recognized hazards causing or likely to cause death or serious physical harm. All employers are responsible for complying with OSHA standards. According to law employers are responsible for protecting workers against hazards that they foresee and that they control. Practically, an employer's responsibility is limited to the employee's work area. An employer must ensure that a work area is suitable for the tasks performed and that the tools used are safe. Employees need suitable lighting, sufficient electrical outlets, and properly maintained equipment to work safely.

OSHA Compliance. Employers supporting telecommuting sometimes conduct an initial on-site evaluation of an employee's home work space. (We find this difficult to believe given the expense and privacy issues it raises.) Employees are then asked to certify annually or semi-annually that conditions remain the same as found during the inspection.

Other employers supporting telecommuting stipulate the use of only company-provided equipment at the home site to ensure that the equipment meets applicable requirements. (Again we find this difficult to believe because of the equipment capital expense incurred.)

Some OSHA home office/work areas to check are the following:

1. If an employee works at a computer, are ergonomic issues addressed?
2. Are aisles and passageways in the work area kept clear?
3. Is the work area adequately illuminated?
4. Is all electrical equipment effectively grounded or double insulated?
5. Do extension cords, if any, have a grounding conductor?
6. Are hand tools and equipment in good condition?
7. Are power tools and other machinery properly guarded?
8. Have appropriate provisions for any necessary material handling been made?
9. Is employee exposure to hazardous chemicals kept within acceptable levels?
10. When volatile chemicals are used, is ventilation adequate?

A very practical way to meet OSHA requirements is to develop a checklist of OSHA safety considerations. Using this list the telecommuter performs a

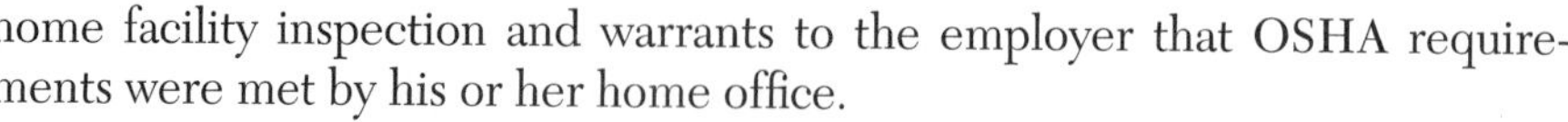

home facility inspection and warrants to the employer that OSHA requirements were met by his or her home office.

OSHA Checklist.

1. Do you have a dedicated home-office room?
2. Is there a fire extinguisher in the office? What type?
3. Is there a fire extinguisher in the home? What type?
4. Is there a fire detector in the office? In the home?
5. Is there more than one exit from the office? From the home?
6. Are passageways clear of furniture and other materials?
7. How many power outlets are in the office?
8. What is the rating of all office power outlets? 15 amp? 20 amp?
9. Does all equipment use three-prong, grounded power cords?
10. Are there desk lamps for each work area?
11. Is the viewing angle of the monitor below eye level?
12. Do computers have keyboards below the desktop?
13. Is the mouse or glide pad at the same level as the keyboard?
14. Do office chairs have ergonomic back support?

Worker's Compensation, Withholding, and Labor Laws. Labor laws apply to telecommuters just as they apply to all other employees. Just because a person telecommutes does not make him or her any less an employee than someone reporting to the office each day.

Worker's Compensation. A concern for employers is worker's compensation. Worker's compensation statutes are state laws with varying requirements. In most cases a worker injured at home while working for his or her employer is eligible to receive worker's compensation. More precise information on these issues is available from state worker's compensation authorities.

Organizations with employees working in home offices have to comply with workers' compensation laws. The state, local, and federal withholding regulations generally apply. Organizations must comply with them. Failure to comply with the withholding regulations means the officer charged with the responsibility for withholding and paying those taxes is personally liable.

In general there have been few legal tests of the applicability of worker's compensation claims to specific telecommuter claims. This is mainly because the employees telecommuting are the positive, proactive element in telecommuting. Employers typically establish limits to worker's compensation liability through clauses in their telecommuters' agreement. These clauses typically state the employee is protected when working within his or her workspace in the home office and not when he or she is someplace else. A telecommuter answering a business phone call from the hammock in the backyard and injuring his or her back falling out of the hammock is not covered.

Withholding Regulations. Businesses believe the problems with withholding and other employee-related obligations can be avoided by declaring an employee to be an independent contractor. The IRS has specific standards it applies to determine whether an individual is an independent contractor or an employee. There are tax penalties for employers who fail to withhold employer obligations for persons who are ultimately determined to be employees rather than independent contractors. Making an incorrect determination is very costly to the employer because he or she is responsible for all unpaid employer taxes if the person is determined to be an employee.

Outside payroll processing companies charge per month to process the payroll for all employees, including telecommuters. Pay checks are delivered to the central office. Telecommuters may desire to have their pay direct deposited to their bank accounts. Most payroll processing companies support direct pay check deposit. A payroll company should prepare all payroll tax returns and submissions as well as process pay checks.

Minimum Wage. The minimum wage law applies to telecommuters. Be sure you are paying at least minimum wage and otherwise complying with the wage and hours laws in your jurisdiction. Businesses operating in violation of them can be fined or shut down.

Americans with Disabilities Act (ADA). Telecommuting can help an organization's Americans with Disabilities Act (ADA) compliance. ADA is a law protecting otherwise qualified persons with disabilities from discrimination in employment, governmental programs, and places of public accommodation.

People are disabled under the Americans with Disabilities Act (ADA) if:

1. They have a physical or mental impairment that substantially limits one or more of life's major activities
2. They have a record of such impairment
3. They are perceived as having such impairment

Not everyone with a disability is protected by ADA. To have ADA protection a person has to meet eligibility requirements of the job. Next it must be determined if the person can do the essential functions of the job with or without reasonable accommodations. In the case of a program, it must be determined if reasonable modifications can be made in the program. Reasonable modifications or accommodations are general terms and do not equal inconvenience.

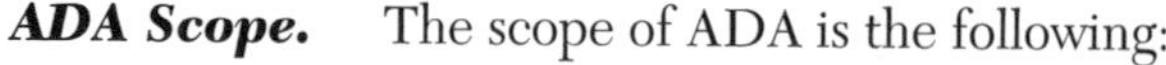

ADA Scope. The scope of ADA is the following:

1. All employers, besides the federal government, who have more than 15 employees are covered.
2. All government organizations regardless of the number of employees are covered.
3. All places of public accommodation are covered.

Preventing problems before they become big problems is an ideal strategy with the ADA. Title III of the ADA regulates removal of barriers and accommodation of the needs of disabled persons in all publicly accessed premises and work sites with disabled employees.

In reviewing premises for compliance, you should consider the following:

1. Inspecting hallways, tunnels, aisles, and other routes of access for protrusions and hazardous conditions that limit access. Hazardous conditions are fire extinguishers, bookcases, radiators, telephones, and other items that could be dislocated with the jarring of a wheelchair.
2. Inspecting ground, ramp elevations, and flooring surfaces. Carpet pile and levels, door jambs, and grading that limit access should be changed.
3. Inspecting elevators for markings or audio announcements for visually impaired persons, and wheelchair level access.
4. Determining if water fountains and water coolers are accessible to wheelchairs.
5. Determining if bathrooms are accessible and equipped with handicapped toilet stalls, urinals, lavatory fixtures, sinks, and mirrors.
6. Determining that signs and alarms are both visual and audible.
7. Determining that fixed or built-in fixtures, desks, seating, and tables, including reception areas, conference rooms, libraries, and cafeterias, are accessible.

Since telecommuters may work from their homes, and since handicapped telecommuters live in accessible homes, then presumably telecommuting handicapped workers would work in an ADA-compliant facility.

Of course if one handicapped worker worked at the central facility, it would then need to be ADA compliant. If handicapped workers were to attend meetings at the central facility, it would also need to be ADA compliant.

Company and Employee Responsibility. To resolve legal and other issues around telecommuting an agreement between the employee and employer should be established. The agreement must clearly spell out what responsibilities the employee has as well as those of the employer. Agreements generally cover the following:

1. Establishing specific telecommuting days and work hours
2. Furnishing and maintaining a remote work space
3. Responsibilities for maintaining remote office equipment and facilities
4. Safety during working hours and after working hours at the remote work space
5. Security measures for protecting company information and trade secrets
6. Security measures for protecting company equipment and systems
7. Employee Performance Assessment Techniques and time frames
8. Tax implications for having an office in the home
9. Obligations to participate in telecommuting program surveys and evaluations
10. Child and dependent care responsibilities
11. Applicability of organization policies and practices to working at the remote location

Enforcement measures usually mean the end to telecommuting and a return to the daily commute to the office.

To ensure that the telecommuter meets all the legal and enterprise requirements means that several questionnaires or compliance forms must be completed and the remote facility inspected. The inspection can be performed by the local Fire Department and followed up with an employee inspection documented by a photographic record of the parts of the facility used for telecommuting work.

After reviewing these administrative rules and checklists it may seem that telecommuting is not so desirable after all. Depending upon the size of your enterprise telecommuting administration can be very formal or informal. Larger enterprises will have a much more structured and formal policy and telecommuter administrative procedures. Smaller organizations can be less formal but nonetheless need to be cognizant of the administrative and legal ramifications of permitting telecommuting.

Because telecommuting is driven by technology it will be part of virtually every business enterprise in the long run. The degree to which it is incorporated into the culture and operation of the enterprise will depend on factors such as labor market competition, technology used in the workplace, and employee attitudes toward telecommuting.

Brain Teaser: Telecommuting Policies

Check to see if you can find your organization's telecommuting policies in its policies and procedures manuals.

Is there a telecommuter policy for your organization? Did you find that a telecommuter agreement was not in the policy and procedures manual? What kinds of inspections are required for the remote telecommuter office site?

Summary

This chapter looked at the technical and administrative issues involved in setting up telecommuting for SOHO LANs. Several central site and remote site network configurations were discussed. The functions of various central site components were presented. Different remote site configurations ranging from inexpensive to very expensive were explored. A major telecommuter application—video teleconferencing using Web cams and Microsoft's NetMeeting software—was presented. The chapter concluded with an examination of telecommuting administrative, business, and legal issues.

Key Technical Terms

ADA—The Americans with Disabilities Act sets out specifications for handicapped access to places where people with disabilities work.

NetMeeting—NetMeeting is Microsoft's video teleconferencing and collaborative groupware software included in Windows XP. Windows XP Home Edition and Professional both include the Windows NetMeeting client software. NetMeeting can establish connections point-to-point or through a common NetMeeting directory server.

OSHA—Occupational Safety and Health Administration, or Occupational Safety and Health Act, sets down rules for ensuring employee safety in the place where they work.

RADIUS—A Remote Authentication Dial-In User Service server acts as a central authentication authority for multiple RAS and VPN servers.

RADIUS servers collect information about remote connections for accounting and logging purposes.

RAS—Remote Access Service is Windows software that permits remote computers to use the PSTN to dial into a central facility network. RAS clients appear as though they are connected directly to the central site SOHO LAN.

Telecommuting—Telecommuting, sometimes referred to as telework, uses telecommunication facilities to support work outside traditional offices or workplaces. The telecommuter usually works at home in a small office/home office or in a mobile environment. Telecommuting is reported to be growing at 15 percent a year since 1990. Work at centralized company premises is not disappearing. However, video telephony and collaborative groupware are likely to make telecommuting more interactive with central site workers for telecommuters. Factors that continue to affect telecommuting include availability of high-speed Internet connections, business administrative procedures for balancing work control and work freedom, perceived values and economies in telecommuting, and opportunities and requirements for working collaboratively across the globe.

VPN—Virtual Private Network is point-to-point virtual connection across the Internet or a packet switched network implemented and controlled by software. The virtual connection remains private and secure because data is encrypted by the sending PC host and decrypted by the receiving PC host. Windows VPN software permits remote telecommuters to connect to a central site SOHO LAN using the Internet.

Review Questions

1. What two types of access are there for telecommuters to connect to a SOHO LAN?

   Answer: There is dialup access through a RAS server and Internet access through a VPN server.

2. A VPN server relies on what protocols to connect to remote telecommuting users?

   Answer: The VPN server uses TCP/IP to connect through the Internet to remote telecommuter PC hosts.

3. What legal and business issues must be addressed by an enterprise considering telecommuting?

   Answer: An enterprise considering telecommuting must address each of the same business and legal issues it faces at centralized facilities. In general the laws and regulations that apply to any centralized business facility also apply to the telecommuter's office. This means that OSHA, worker's compensation, zoning, and more must be addressed by the enterprise for each remote telecommuter site.

4. Why is telecommuting important at all?

   Answer: With advancing technology, changing social patterns, increased travel difficulty, and dispersed labor pools, some form of telecommuting is inevitable for most workers.

5. What application can improve the ability of the telecommuter to participate more effectively in project work at a central site?

   Answer: Video teleconferencing using Microsoft's NetMeeting software permits video teleconferencing and work collaboration over high-speed and dialup communications links.

6. What is a drawback of Microsoft's NetMeeting software?

   Answer: Video resources of a host PC are not effectively shared between NetMeeting and other video-intensive multimedia applications. For example, my TV viewing program does not effectively share the video output to the display screen with Microsoft's NetMeeting software. Consequently, I must run the TV viewing program or the NetMeeting software, but I cannot run both simultaneously without causing a conflict with the PC host's video resources.

Chapter 7

SOHO Network Security

Chapter Syllabus

- Network Security Threats
- Network Security Measures
- Summary
- Key Technical Terms
- Review Questions

Security is a constant concern for network attached PCs. E-mail-based exploits and other malevolent programs target servers and other network host PCs. Firewalls and Windows XP built-in security software were discussed in Chapter 5. This chapter takes a broader look at SOHO LAN security by first identifying and discussing different network security threats and then by addressing the steps and procedures that make a SOHO LAN secure from these threats.

Security experts can easily overstate the need for SOHO network security. This can be true from two perspectives. First, there are many SOHO LANs with Internet connections, including my own. A hacker/cracker would need to cast a wide net before he catches me. Do not get me wrong, my network can be caught, but it is likely many more networks would be caught before mine, creating an Internet-wide alarm and published software fixes that would mitigate the security threat. Secondly, one can spend so much time and money on security that the result renders one's network less than useful. Too much security is like the proverbial New York City apartment door with 23 deadbolt locks on the door: Before the renter can unlock them all and get safely in, he of she is mugged.

The SOHO LAN network security precautions discussed in this chapter provide a level of security adequate for most SOHO LANs. The chapter covers off-the-shelf products. I am sure there are additional products and Windows configurations that can make a SOHO LAN much more secure, but at what cost to a small business or home owner? These simple precautions are likely adequate for the foreseeable future.

There are many "small fish" in the sea of Internet-connected SOHO networks. These SOHO LANs are Internet connected with increasingly inexpensive and increasingly secure router/firewall products. Such products just get cheaper and better all the time. What was good last year is now supplanted by revised and newer products this year. Such inexpensive off-the-shelf security products are discussed in this chapter.

My small-office/home-office LAN has a definite security problem because of my surrogate autistic grandson, Padriac. He loves PCs and he avidly surfs the Internet. Consequently, when he passes by my office with the four PC monitors and the three computers, he goes immediately for every mouse and tries to surf the Web. He knows the exit command and control icon and how to run a Web browser. Once he runs amok on any PC, it is splattered with the Cartoon Network, Nickelodeon, and about three other cartoon or Muppet sites. The simple solution is to put a screen saver password on Windows XP and Windows 2000. But of course a security expert might recommend using biometrics to make my SOHO LAN more secure.

Network Security Threats

Security threats come in a variety of forms for a SOHO LAN. These threats vary from simple unauthorized access on the PC hosts; to virus and malevolent software attacks on PC hosts; to spyware observing, collecting, and reporting on user activity; and finally to direct attacks by hackers from the Internet.

The most common threat is from malevolent software sent as a package or attachment to e-mail; e-mail itself is basically text messages. Such malevolent software is commonly labeled virus software. By strict definition a virus is a program that hides itself as part of another program. In this book we use the term virus in both senses, as a general identifier of malevolent software and in its purer form as a program that hides in other programs. Text messages alone cannot pass malevolent software. No program code or scripts are contained in simple text messages. However, any file that can contain program instructions like keystroke macro commands (macros), executable programs, batch file commands, and other programmable code may be attached to a simple, seemingly harmless or innocuous e-mail message. If that file is opened by the e-mail recipient, then his or her system becomes infected with the malevolent code and disaster strikes. The malevolent software or program code often first finds other addresses to which to mail itself. In this manner it continues its propagation to other hapless Internet victims. Figure 7.1 illustrates this process.

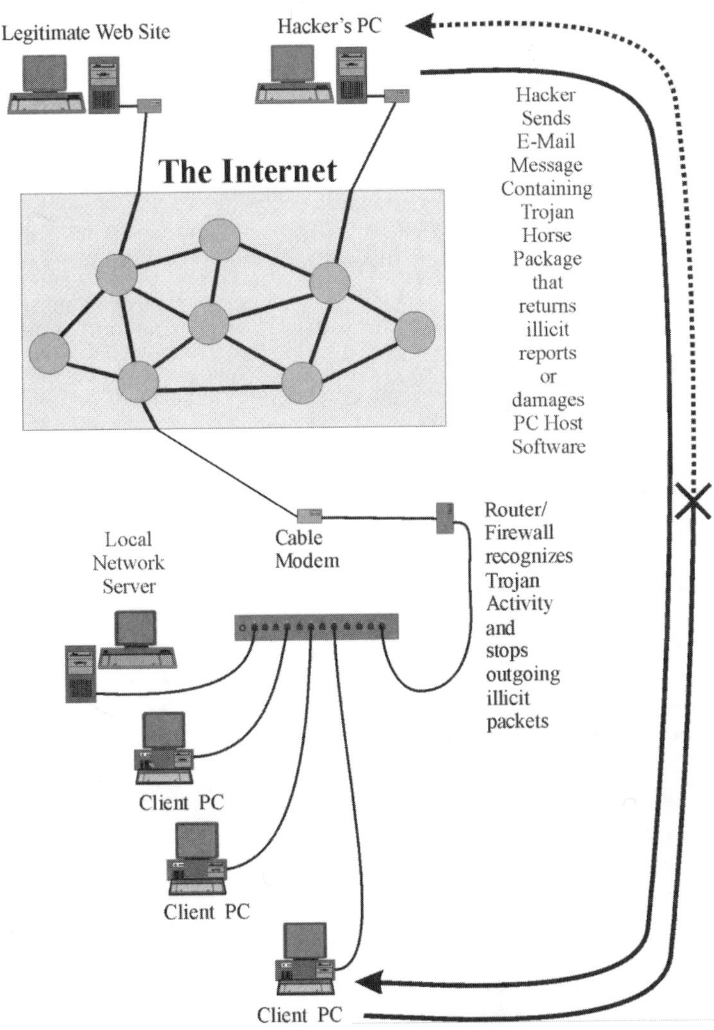

Figure 7.1 E-mail malevolent code attack.

When malevolent software is detected, the virus scanning programs try to remove the malevolent software in the attachment or more commonly they isolate or quarantine the attachment in a protected area where it cannot be accidentally executed. This is shown in Figure 7.2.

Firewalls do not stop malevolent software or program code attachments to e-mail. The best defense for such attacks is good virus scanning software. Such software scans all e-mail attachments and identifies those containing malevolent code of which it is aware. Permutations to malevolent code may also be spotted.

In some cases the malevolent software package is unknowingly installed by the recipient. Spyware is embedded in otherwise legitimate software, and it is used by companies to track Internet user activities for the purpose of marketing products and services to those recipients. It is nothing more than malevolent software in sheep's clothing. Spyware performs the same functions as other Trojan programs, but it is supposedly legitimate because the information is passed on to a marketing organization that uses it for commercial purposes.

Spyware is no different from a peeping Tom invading our privacy. Windows cookies that track our Web use at Web sites are a somewhat lesser compromise in privacy, but they compromise our privacy none the less. Such software should be legally banned because it is an invasion of privacy and can easily be used to gather intimate details on anyone using the Internet. No one should

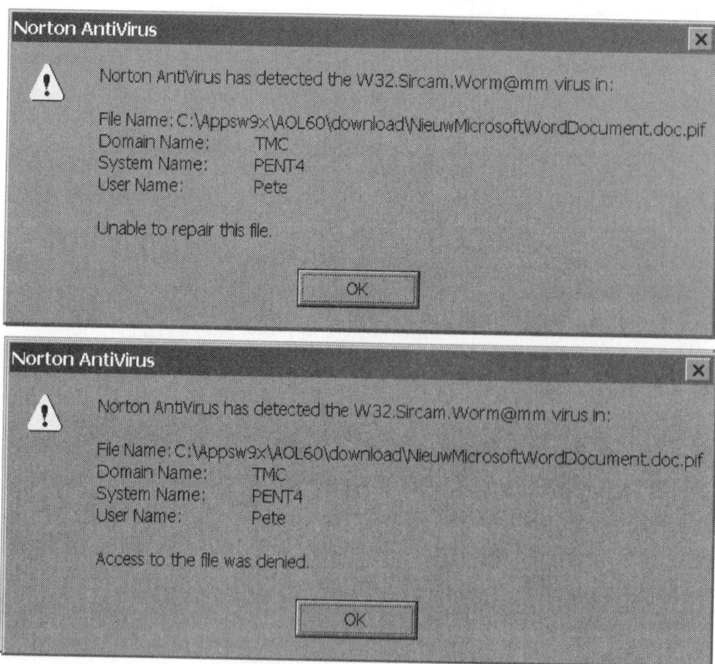

Figure 7.2 Sircam virus detection and isolation.

be able to install such software without a search warrant or other legal written permission because SOHO PC hosts reside in people's homes. Under United States law no one can search your house without a legal search warrant unless he or she has your permission. These same criteria should apply to spyware.

Brain Teaser: Spyware

Go to the Lavasoft Web site (*www.lavasoftusa.com*) and download their free Ad-aware scanning software. Install it and scan your PC host for spyware.

What spyware did you find? Was DoubleClick installed somewhere on your PC host?

From a SOHO LAN viewpoint, spyware steals PC host CPU cycles to perform its spying and makes PC hosts less reliable because they must perform added software tasks that may conflict with other legitimate software. Such software is just not needed. Further, I refuse to purchase any product that I see in a pop-up advertisement on my PC because I refuse to support their insidious marketing.

Other security attacks are made by hackers probing the SOHO LAN. They discover PC hosts to probe by sending out Packet Inter-Network Groper (PING) packets that use the Internet Control Message Protocol (ICMP) to determine whether an active PC at a specific Internet Protocol (IP) address responds. PING determines active IP addresses on a network and the Internet, resolves domain names to IP addresses using the Internet Domain Name Service (DNS), and measures the time required for the PING packet to make the round-trip journey from the PINGing PC host and the PINGed PC host. PING commands may also be used to update router tables. PING commands request an ICMP echo, which is fulfilled by an ICMP echo reply packet. Alternatives to PING are TRACERT (trace route) and Windows 2000/XP PATHPING utility programs.

When an active IP address is detected, more PING packets and other packets (e.g., HTTP packets, FTP packets, and more) are sent to probe the PC host's ports to see if data can be sent to the PC host. There are 65,000 ports to probe with 1,023 well-known ports frequently used by PC host applications and other software. Figure 7.3 identifies several of the most commonly used well-known ports. When data is accepted by a port, then many packets are sent that produce buffer overflows or other errors to expose vulnerabilities in Windows that permit malevolent code to be loaded into the PC host. The malevolent code is then executed to continue propagating the malevolent code attack on other SOHO

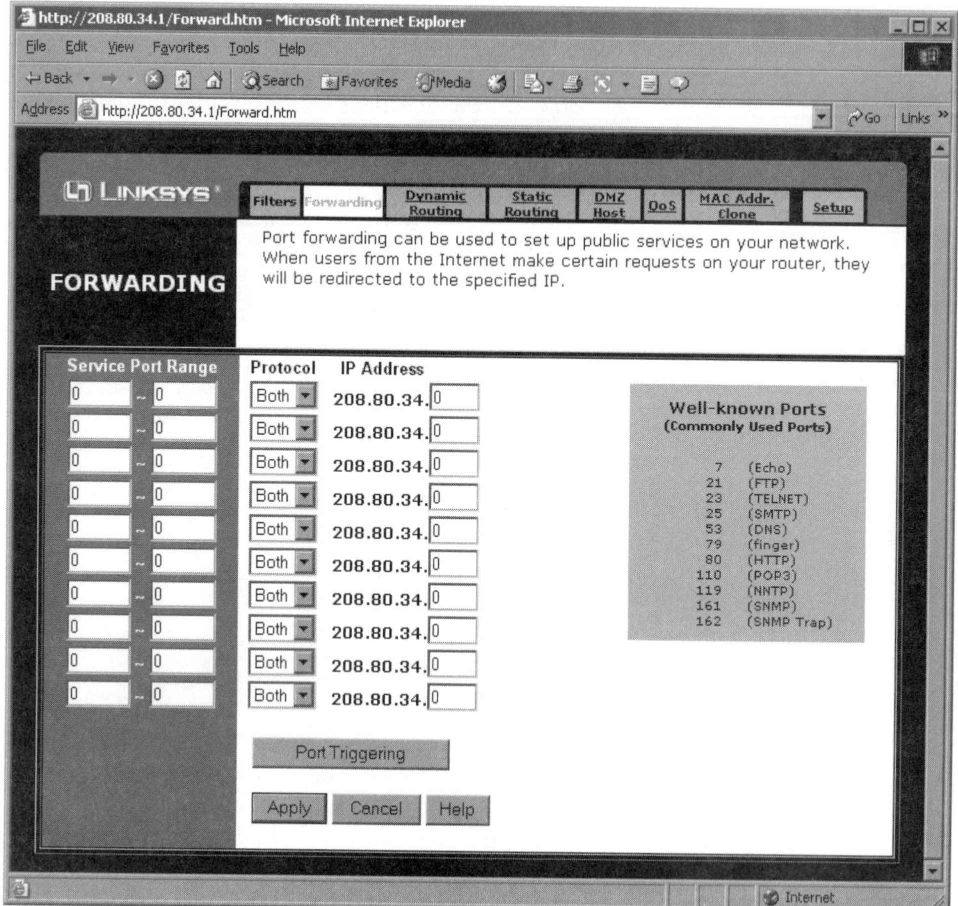

Figure 7.3 Some well-known ports.

LAN PC hosts. The Code Red worm used this approach to gain access to Windows PCs running the Internet Information Service (IIS) software.

A SOHO LAN attack originated by hackers to attack a SOHO LAN is illustrated in Figure 7.4. Firewalls protect from such attacks by blocking port probing.

FINGER displays names associated with e-mail addresses. FINGER may tell whether the e-mail named person is currently logged into their Internet host system and possibly other information, depending on the data maintained about users on the Internet host system. FINGER may also be used to attack PC hosts. Many Internet hosts have responses to FINGER requests turned off so that sensitive information cannot be obtained using FINGER. Figure 7.5 shows the Windows XP FINGER command options.

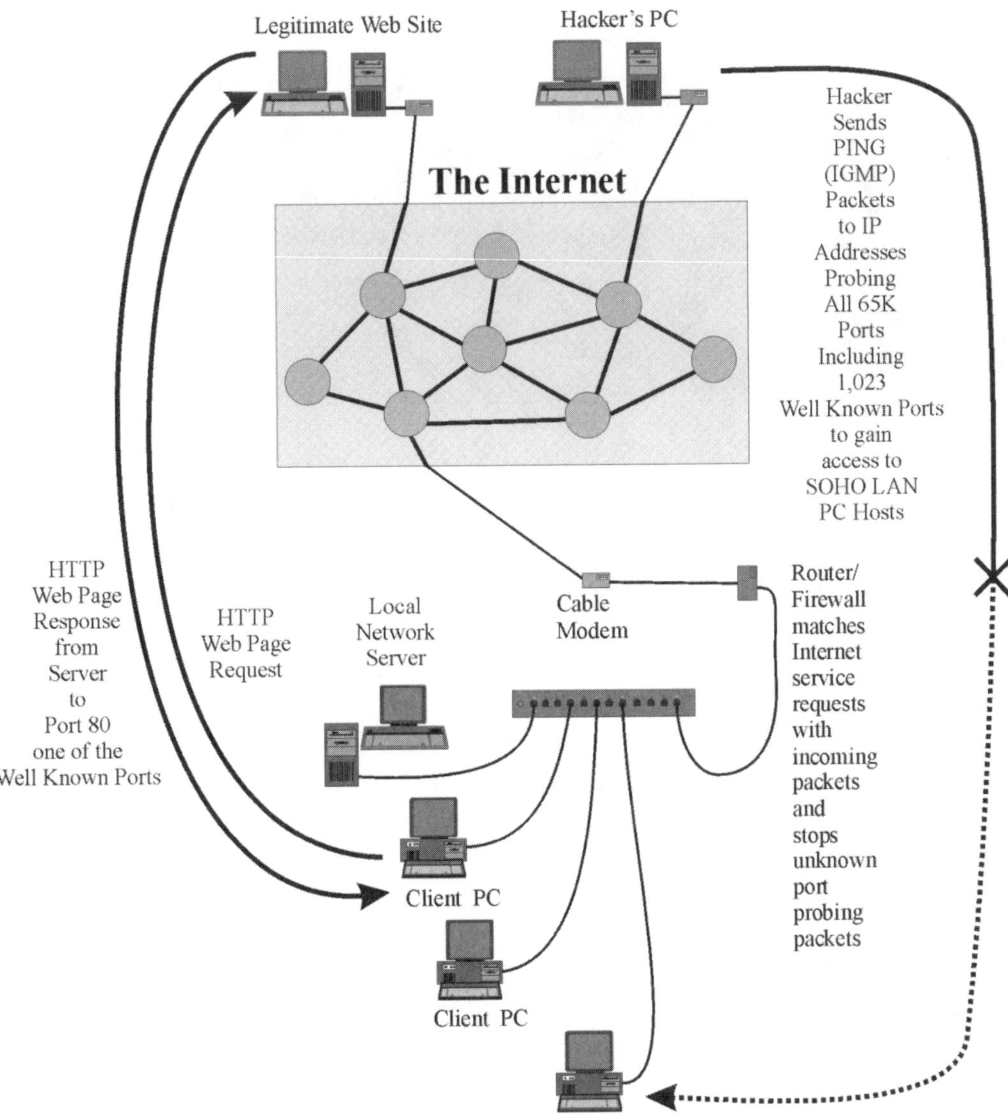

Figure 7.4 SOHO LAN external attacks.

To FINGER Internet users you enter the e-mail address. The server at the other end must be set up to respond to FINGER requests. If there is no server set up, the FINGER command times out.

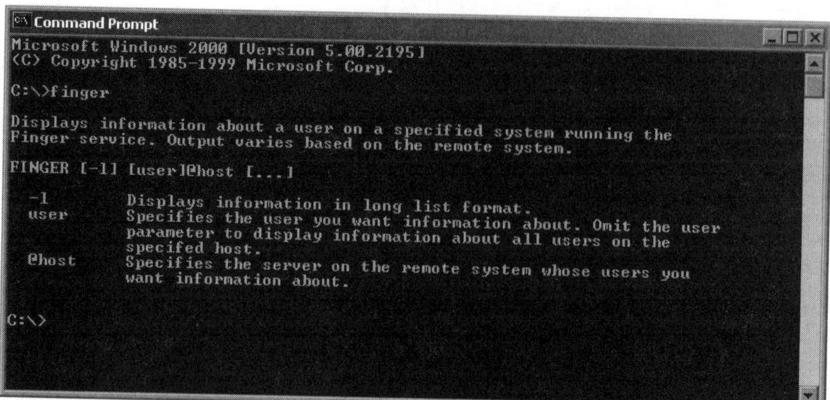

Figure 7.5 FINGER.

Virus Programs

A virus is a program that hides itself in other programs for the purpose of causing some unexpected and undesirable event. Virus programs are designed to automatically infect other PC hosts, spreading unknowingly to other users like a virus spreads by infecting animals.

Viruses were transmitted as code in diskette boot sectors and today are transmitted as attachments to e-mail or as program downloads from off-the-beaten-track Web sites. Such Web sites may be sites at which hackers and crackers post information. Such sites may be found by searching for warez.

Most times users passing the diskette, sending the e-mail, or posting the file for download are unaware of the virus. Viruses cause havoc when they are executed, while other viruses can lie dormant and quietly propagate themselves to other computers until specific events cause them to wreak their havoc. Viruses may be designed only to get your attention, while others can be much more irksome. They can erase data, corrupt Windows, or necessitate a complete Windows reinstall starting with repartitioning and then reformatting a PC's fixed disk.

The three common virus classes are as follows:

1. **File infecting viruses** imbed themselves into .COM and .EXE files. Some infect any executable code files including .DLL, .DRV, .MSI, .SYS, .OVL, .PRG, .MNU, and more. When Windows loads the infected program, the virus is loaded into memory and executed. Some file-infecting viruses arrive as programs or scripts sent as e-mail attachments. These file

infectors infect specific files and send off added e-mail messages with malevolent code attachments to infect other PC hosts.

2. **System or boot-sector infecting** viruses imbed themselves in executable code found in the system or boot records of a fixed disk. The boot-sector infecting viruses change the program loading code in a bootable floppy diskette disk boot sector or the primary fixed disk's master boot record. To become infected a PC host must attempt to boot from an infected floppy diskette. This booting process loads the virus, which then infects the PC's fixed disk and other diskettes. Reading and loading files on an infected diskette does not trigger the boot-sector infecting virus. Any attempt to boot from the diskette loads the virus. I had a diskette that was non-bootable placed into a system infected by a boot-sector infecting virus. The diskette became infected. Since I had not made it a bootable diskette, I was unaware of the infection. The diskette was accidentally left in drive A: of the computer. When the computer was powered on, it attempted to boot from drive A: and I got the message "operating system not found" which meant that I infected my computer with the boot-sector infecting virus. In this instance a DOS antivirus program identified the virus as a STONED virus variation and removed it.
3. **Macro code viruses** infect Microsoft applications that support script macros and Visual Basic programming. The macro scripts can be used to load .EXE, .DLL, or other virus payloads that in turn create more macro infected documents and e-mail to propagate themselves to other SOHO LAN PC hosts.

Worm Programs

A worm is a self-replicating program that does not embed itself in files. A worm uses seemingly unimportant or innocuous names to help it avoid detection. Worm programs reside in active memory and store themselves on a PC host's fixed disk so that they will be reloaded whenever the PC host is restarted. Worms duplicate themselves and pass themselves on to other PC hosts through e-mail or other Windows communication vulnerabilities. Worms use invisible or behind-the-scenes operating system components to perform replication and other nefarious tasks. Worm programs may only be noticed when their replication consumes system resources and slows or halts other programs.

Two types of worm programs are the following:

1. **Script worms**, which are programs using Visual Basic Script (VBS) language. The script language is a simplified programming language embedded in different documents. A script worm, when activated, propagates

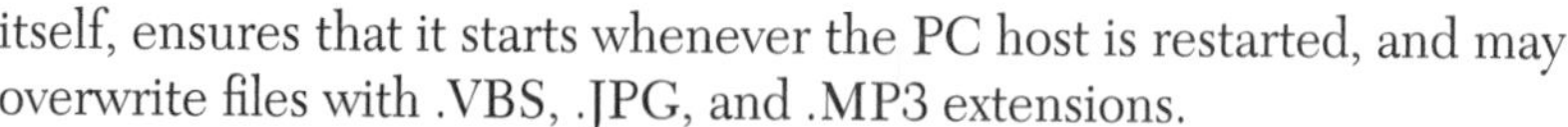

itself, ensures that it starts whenever the PC host is restarted, and may overwrite files with .VBS, .JPG, and .MP3 extensions.

2. **Internet worms** propagate like script worms but can also self-activate and spread using Windows and network security vulnerabilities.

A typical worm program is the MyLife or the Clinton worm program. The W32/MyLife-A worm when opened provides a screensaver of former President Bill Clinton playing the saxophone while in the background it copies itself to the Windows system directory, changes registry keys, and uses e-mail addresses from a PC host's Microsoft Outlook address book to send copies of itself to other PC hosts. MyLife variants infect a PC host by appearing as a screensaver attached to an e-mail. The e-mail message includes a line indicating it has been scanned by McAfee. This message contains spelling errors such as virus spelled "viruse."

Trojan Programs

Trojan horse programs hide malevolent code inside apparently harmless programs or data. When the apparently harmless program is run, the Trojan horse program is unleashed to capture and send sensitive information to outside Internet locations or to damage the PC host's software. See Figure 7.6.

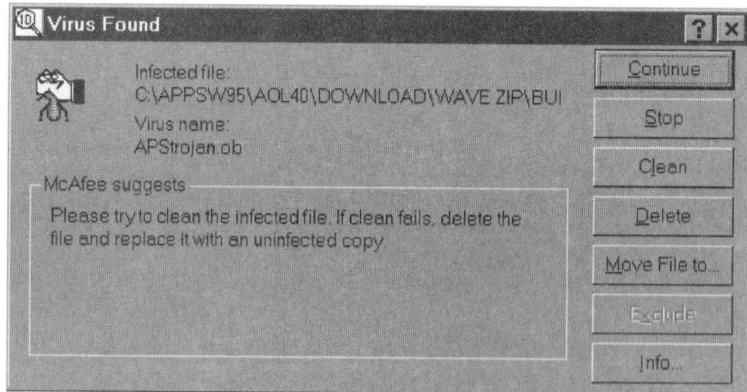

Figure 7.6 Trojan program detection.

Two types of Trojan programs are the following:

1. **Backdoor Trojan horse** programs, which modify the Internet or network connections. They add a hidden service to the PC host that permits a hacker (or cracker) to in some way upload other more malevolent programs to it. These programs can then damage the PC's software.

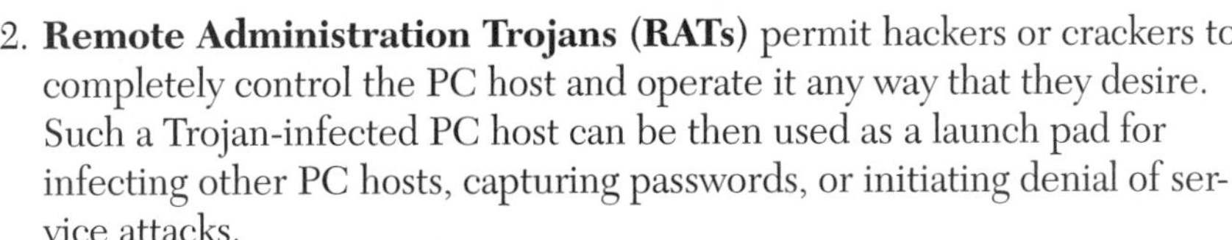

2. **Remote Administration Trojans (RATs)** permit hackers or crackers to completely control the PC host and operate it any way that they desire. Such a Trojan-infected PC host can be then used as a launch pad for infecting other PC hosts, capturing passwords, or initiating denial of service attacks.

Brain Teaser: Antivirus Software

Check to see if all PCs at work have antivirus software installed. An icon in the SYSTRAY should be displayed indicating that antivirus software is monitoring all files being opened on the PC. Antivirus software should appear as an option in the Start—Programs menus.

What is the last date that the antivirus software signature file was updated? Is there an automatic update or live update selection in the antivirus software menus? Run the automatic or live update to make the antivirus software signature file current.

Spyware

Spyware is technology that gathers and reports information without the PC host user's knowledge. Spyware is typically a program secretly installed in a PC host to clandestinely observe the PC host user's activities and relay such information to advertisers. Spyware is installed on a computer similar to other software viruses or when new software containing the spyware is installed. Data collecting programs installed with the PC host user's full knowledge would not be strictly defined as spyware. This would be especially true if the PC host user fully understood what data is collected and with whom the data is shared. Spyware programs are Gator, Ezula's TopText, and Surf+.

Cookies

Cookies are a well-known mechanism for storing information about an Internet user on his or her own computer. Cookies and their use are not concealed from users. Further, users can control how cookies are used. They may disallow access to cookie information on their PC host. Because Web sites store private Web site access information in a cookie that is not readily visible to the PC host user, cookies can be classified as a form of spyware. See Figure 7.7.

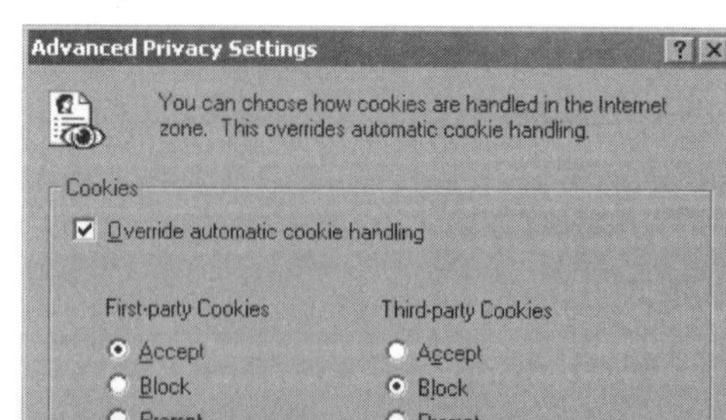

Figure 7.7
Windows IE cookie options.

DoubleClick is a leading banner ad serving company that uses cookies. It at one time planned to combine cookie information with database information from other sources for the purpose of targeting advertising campaigns directly at individuals without their permission. DoubleClick's current policy is not to collect private information about a user without the user's explicit opt-in permission. Sometimes the opt-in permission is not easily understandable by PC host users. Further, the DoubleClick opt-out procedure is involved and laborious, making it very difficult to opt out of DoubleClick monitoring.

Brain Teaser: Cookies

Find the cookies settings in the Internet Explorer by selecting Tools—Internet Options—Privacy. Select the Advanced privacy settings and set them to block third-party cookies and always allow session cookies.

Do these settings cause any cookie error messages to appear while you surf the Web? If these messages are annoying, reset the cookies settings.

Spyware and cookies are part of an overall public concern about privacy on the Internet.

Virus Costs and Prevention

Virus incidents cost companies in lost productivity. Large companies spend from $100,000 to $1 million annually to recover from virus attacks. New Tricks virus and worm writers are incorporating an e-mail SMTP engine into the virus or worm, avoiding securer versions of Microsoft Outlook, tricking unsuspecting users to clicking on infected Web site links, or sending viruses via instant messaging clients. Outlook 2002 no longer opens some attached files, such as files with macros, and it stops malevolent programs from stealing Outlook addresses to propagate by sending e-mail. One virus reads e-mail that is being sent and is no longer protected by Outlook. In this manner it circumvents Outlook's new virus protection features.

Heuristics are being used to more intelligently fight viruses. A heuristic is a procedure that detects malevolent program code and virus-like activity. Predictive antivirus software uses such heuristics to search for virus characteristics in software code. Normal virus scanning programs use virus signatures (a pattern of characters—bytes that are unique to that virus) to detect viruses. Signature protection relies on virus signatures gathered from known viruses.

Denial of Service (DoS)

An Internet DoS attack deprives a user or an organization of the Internet services they normally expect. A typical loss of service is a temporary loss of most all Internet connectivity. A severe DoS attack can force a Web site accessed by millions of PC hosts to temporarily cease operation. DoS attacks may also destroy programming and files. DoS attacks do not usually result in information thefts.

Common denial of service attacks are as follows:

1. **Buffer overflow attacks** are most common. They send more Internet packet traffic to an IP address than the PC host's packet buffers can hold. The result is a buffer overflow that may expose a PC host's software vulnerabilities or may temporarily overwhelm the PC host software. Some buffer overflow attacks have been sending e-mail messages with 256-character file name attachments to Netscape and Microsoft mail programs and sending oversized Internet Control Message Protocol (ICMP) packets (known as the PING of death).
2. **SYN attacks** use session-establishing packet's SYN fields. An attacker sends many connection requests rapidly and then fails to respond to the reply so the first packet remains in the buffer, blocking other legitimate connection requests. After a specific time period the blocking packet is dropped. However, many bogus connection requests make it difficult for legitimate requests to establish sessions.
3. **Teardrop attacks** exploit the Internet Protocol (IP) requirement to break up an IP packet that is too large for processing by the next router into smaller fragments. Fragmented packets contain an offset to the

beginning of the first packet that the receiving router uses to reassemble the entire packet. Teardrop attacks put a confusing offset value in the second or later IP packet fragments. When a receiving router does not handle such erroneous offset values, they can crash and route no more packets.

4. **Smurf attacks** send an IP PING or ECHO request to an IP address. The PING packet initiates a broadcast of the PING packet to other hosts within the local network and directs the PING or ECHO responses to another site that is the target site for the denial of service. Packets sent with a different return address are said to spoof the return address. The result is PING replies flooding back to a spoofed PC host. When the flood of PING packets is large, a spoofed host may not be able to receive or distinguish legitimate traffic.
5. **PING storm attacks** use the PING program to send a flood of packets to a server or router. This may be used to test a server, or router's ability to handle a high amount of traffic or may be maliciously used to overload the router or server, which would render it inoperable. The Windows PING command does not allow it to create a PING storm. However, in some UNIX-based systems the PING command can output PING packets as fast as they are returned from the target system or can increase the size of outgoing PING packets and thus increase the processing load of the receiving PC host.
6. **Viruses or worm attacks** can generate an enormous amount of e-mail messages in a network. These messages may incapacitate network routers and PC hosts.
7. **Physical infrastructure attacks** directly destroy the SOHO LAN components. Cutting a cable, kicking a server, or inflicting physical damage on some network component may result in denial of service because the network is down until the physical damage is repaired. Such physical infrastructure attacks are mitigated by rerouting network traffic.

Disgruntled Employees

Disgruntled and former employees pose a significant risk because they may know the details of your SOHO network and its security. Disgruntled employees may decide that whatever damage and hassle they can cause is justified because of their attitude toward the enterprise. Normal employees may not realize that they can also damage sensitive information through carelessness. And, since disgruntled employees know other employees, they may be able to get inside information at any time.

When any employee leaves an enterprise and the enterprise LAN is exposed to the Internet, it is imperative that the employee's password is changed and that his or her user ID is disabled or removed from the network immediately. For SOHO LAN security purposes the employee upon resigning must under supervision immediately clean out his or her desk and then be escorted from the facility. Often employees feel hurt by such abrupt departures, but to limit their access to sensitive SOHO LAN files employee resignations must be handled in such a fashion.

Network Security Measures

There are several SOHO LAN security measures that help ensure that SOHO LAN data is secure, its PC hosts are protected from viruses, and that the impact of DoS attacks are mitigated. To have a secure SOHO LAN all these measures must be implemented and monitored continually. If they are implemented and not monitored, then the SOHO LAN rapidly loses its protection from viruses and other external security threats.

Virus Scanning Programs

The most important SOHO LAN security measure is virus scanning programs. On several occasions virus attachments have been sent to me. Some have contained viruses themselves, while others no doubt directed my PC host to sites that contained virus-laden Web pages and software downloads. In these cases virus scanning software examined all files downloaded into my PC host, detected the virus, and quarantined the file so that it would not be inadvertently executed and infect my PC host with the virus.

Of the security measures identified and explored here, probably the most important for a SOHO LAN is implementing and maintaining virus scanning software. Figure 7.8 shows the Norton antivirus software included in Norton SystemWorks system status. The Live Update icon in the middle of the icons at the top of the figure links to the Norton Web site, where new virus signatures are downloaded into the PC host to update the antivirus software.

Norton antivirus software uses primarily virus signatures to detect potential PC host virus infections. Here a virus is used in its most general sense to represent all malevolent software. Norton antivirus also uses some heuristics to perform added virus detection for new "in the wild" viruses that have not yet been sampled and their signature extracted. Figure 7.9 shows the Norton Antivirus software heuristics configuration panel.

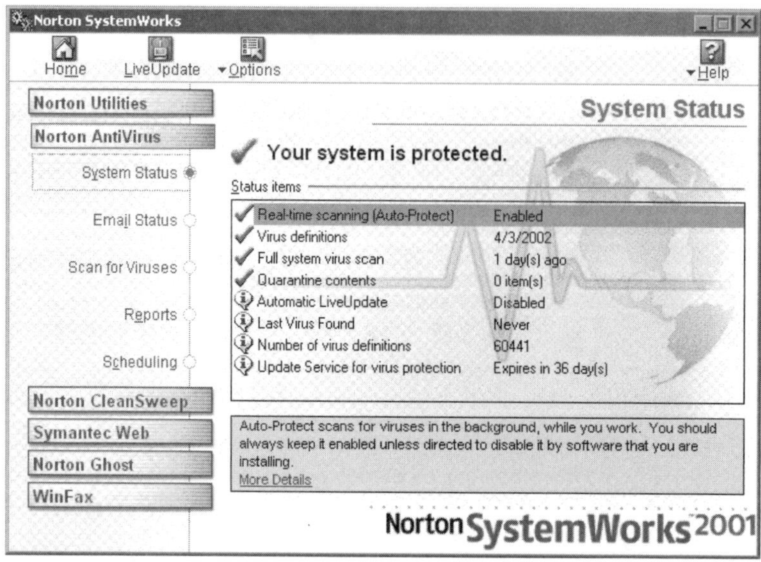

Figure 7.8 Virus scanning software maintenance.

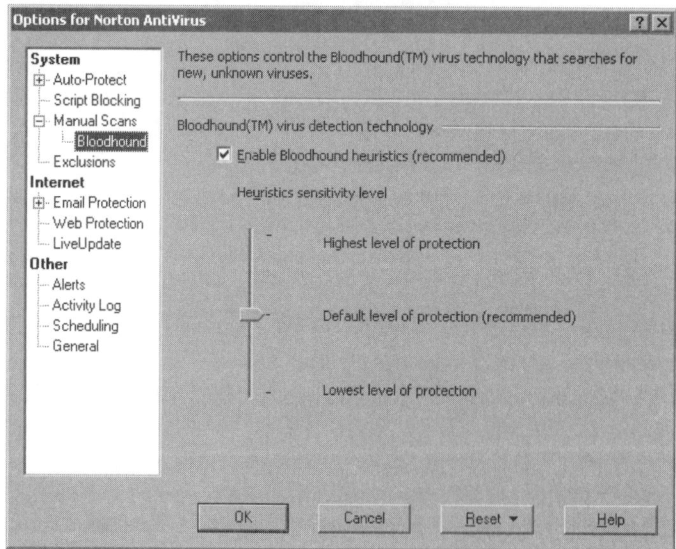

Figure 7.9 Antivirus heuristics.

The heuristics work to provide both automatic and manual protection.

The live signature file update feature can be performed automatically or by notifying the PC host user to permit him or her to manually perform the update. Virus signature file updates should be manually scheduled on a weekly basis to provide the most effective protection. Automatic updates help novice users maintain an effective level of virus protection without requiring their attention. Nonetheless an administrative procedure to check each PC host monthly to ensure that virus signature files are updated should be implemented. Even though such an administrative procedure is time consuming, it is much less time consuming than trying to recover a SOHO LAN from a virus infection. Figure 7.10 shows the Norton antivirus automatic update configuration panel.

The most popular antivirus software is equally effective when it comes to preventing a virus infection. Selecting one specific product over another is not as important as implementing virus protection with one antivirus software package and keeping it updated.

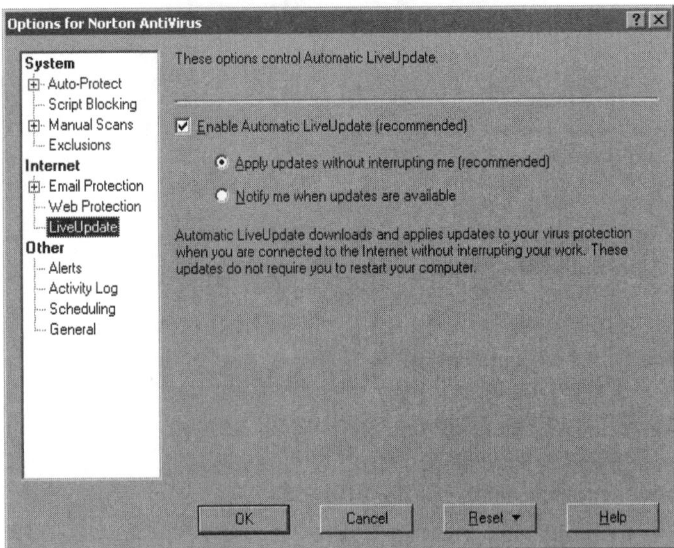

Figure 7.10 Automatic virus signature file live update.

Windows Update

The next most important security procedure is to run periodically the Windows software update. Figure 7.11 shows the link to the Microsoft Windows update site in the Windows XP Start menus.

When Windows Update does not appear in the Start menus, it can be accessed directly using the Windows update URL:

http://windowsupdate.microsoft.com

Windows critical updates deal primarily with resolving Windows security vulnerabilities that have been exploited by malevolent software. Effective security requires that these updates be implemented in both SOHO user PC hosts and in SOHO Windows servers. This is because Windows is the primary target of hackers and crackers. Other software is also a target, but the impact does not get the press coverage that Windows virus attacks get.

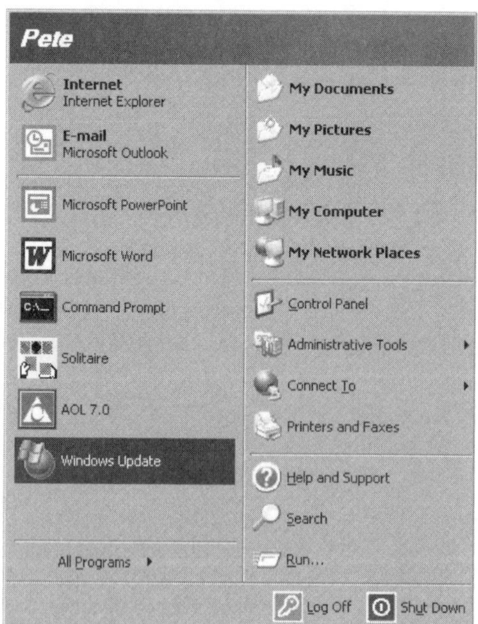

Figure 7.11
Windows XP update.

Brain Teaser: Windows Update

Run Windows Update on a PC host to see if any critical updates need to be installed. If there are missing critical updates, install them.

What other Windows updates did you find? If the DirectX 8.1 software needs to be installed, download the installation file from *www.microsoft.com/windows/directx/downloads/drx81.asp*.

Once the file is downloaded and saved on a server, it can be installed without running Windows Update.

Automatic download and notification of critical updates is provided in Windows XP and other Windows software and provides automatic notification when new critical updates are posted at the Windows Update Web site. Figure 7.12 shows the Windows XP automatic update configuration settings. Performing a Windows update once a week is probably best to provide the most effective SOHO LAN security.

Similar to antivirus protection, an administrative procedure to check all SOHO LAN user PC hosts and network servers to ensure that Windows critical updates have been installed should be implemented. Following such a procedure can avert the critical downtime that would occur if a SOHO LAN were infected with a virus.

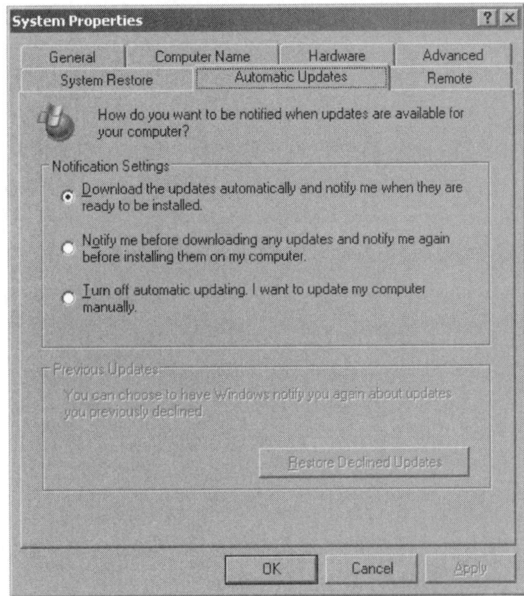

Figure 7.12
Windows XP automatic critical update notification.

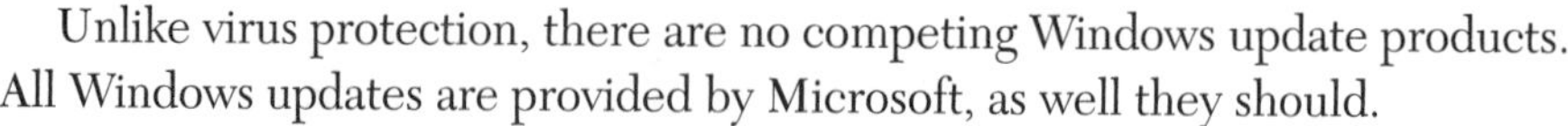

Unlike virus protection, there are no competing Windows update products. All Windows updates are provided by Microsoft, as well they should.

Firewalls

The third component in implementing effective SOHO LAN security is a firewall. Firewalls are either hardware components or software running in routers, PC hosts, or network servers. A firewall protects a network from external probing by matching packets sent from the Internet with legitimate requests for those packets generated by internal SOHO LAN PC hosts. Firewalls may also stop packets from Trojan horse and worm software from leaving the SOHO LAN. This is more difficult and technically sophisticated filtering. Finally, firewalls can detect unusual traffic activity from the Internet and from within the SOHO LAN and using traffic logs alert network administrators to potential security threats.

Router Firewall Devices

A basic SOHO LAN firewall is typically implemented in a cable modem/DSL router. This hardware device may incorporate router/gateway functions, quality of service functions, LAN switching, and firewall functions. They provide good security for small home-office and smaller-office LANs. Larger-office LANs may require a more sophisticated firewall device that requires constant monitoring and updating. Most such firewall products are better than no firewall products. However, more commonly implemented and less expensive devices are more likely to be compromised by hackers and crackers because of their availability for study and testing. The more popular a device and the more it is sold, the more attractive a target for hacking and cracking.

Linksys and D-Link make some popular hardware cable modem/DSL routers that incorporate firewall capabilities. When using one of these devices, the most important security consideration to implement is to immediately change the administrator ID and password from the default settings. Manuals for these devices are published on the Internet. These manuals contain the default settings for the administrative user ID and password. Consequently, any hacker or cracker encountering such a cable modem/DSL router will immediately try to access and determine the device configuration using these published administrator IDs and default passwords.

Software Firewalls

Software firewalls are some of the hottest-selling software today. This software implements firewall functions in SOHO LAN-attached PC hosts. This is personal firewall software. Several packages are popular sellers, including ZoneAlarm Pro, Norton Personal Firewall, McAfee Personal Firewall Plus, and BlackICE Defender.

All such personal firewalls have similar features that continually improve over time. Typical personal firewall protection features include the following:

1. E-mail attachment protection
2. Packet filtering to block external Internet intrusions
3. Logging to track hacker and cracker attacks
4. Blocking Internet performance and pop-up ads
5. Controlling cookies
6. Controlling internal PC host programs to prevent unauthorized Internet access

PC hosts connected 24/7 to the Internet are potential hacker and cracker targets. Crackers and hackers randomly send PING packets and attempt to scan a PC host's well known ports or any other of its 65,000 ports to find unprotected access to the PC host. When an open port is found, a hacker or cracker compromises the PC by sending a Trojan horse, spyware, or a malicious worm to the PC through the compromised port.

Personal firewall software protects PC hosts from intrusions and hostile attacks by rejecting packets received from the Internet that do not match legitimate requests coming from within the PC host. A personal firewall provides complete port blocking for all PC host ports. Personal firewalls protect against known and unknown Internet threats by monitoring all outbound traffic to the Internet. Only programs that have been specified as authorized for Internet access are permitted to send packets to the Internet. Malevolent programs attempting to transfer personal data, user IDs, passwords, e-mail addresses, and sensitive data to the Internet are thus detected and prevented from accomplishing the transfer. With a personal firewall the PC host user specifies which programs are trusted to access the Internet. See Figure 7.13.

Every personal firewall program provides the same basic features. As their development continues, the unique features of one product are incorporated into the competing products. So, using any personal firewall for a home-office LAN should provide effective security. Further, small-office LANs should con-

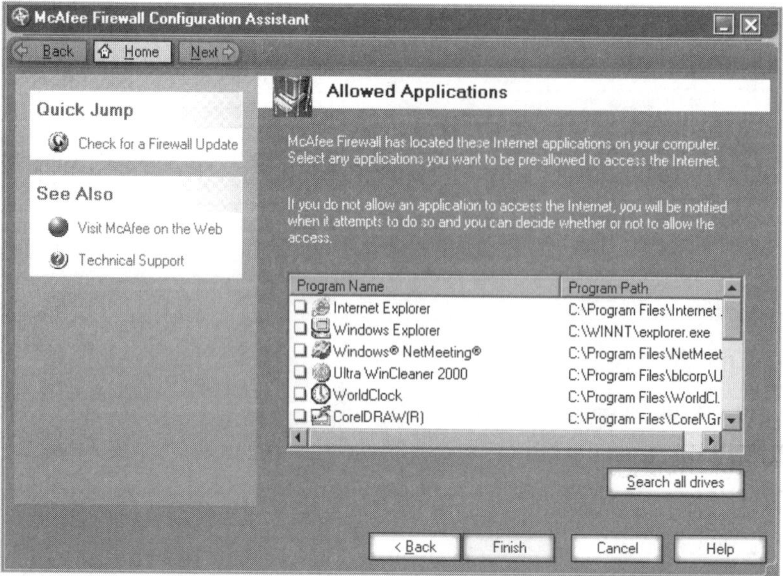

Figure 7.13 McAfee Firewall configuration.

sider personal firewall software for each PC client as a means of augmenting antivirus and other firewall security products.

Brain Teaser: Firewalls

Check to see if your SOHO LAN uses hardware or software firewalls or both.

What configuration options are there for hardware firewalls? Are there added configuration options for software firewalls? Generally software firewalls can be configured to limit PC programs from accessing the Internet while hardware firewalls do not generally support that feature.

SOHO Security Administration

Every SOHO LAN depends on a variety of detection mechanisms to protect PC hosts, servers, intranet Web sites, extranet Web sites, and Internet Web sites from malicious attacks and security breaches. One of the most important and more challenging tasks for an administrator is developing a tracking and detection system to alert him or her when a security breach or malicious attack is happening. Often, to determine when systems are compromised, log files must be sifted through to detect where and how the system was compromised and what damage was done.

This can be a very tedious process and may require a good knowledge of TCP/IP and the network monitoring tools employed. Consequently, preventing problems is the best defense. Some simple security measures for monitoring and securing Web traffic are the following:

1. **Ensure well known default Windows accounts are safe**—Windows comes with Administrator, Guest, and a variety of other built-in user accounts. Windows 2000 built-in accounts are shown in Figure 7.14. Ensure that these accounts have good passwords, their access to network resources is strictly limited, or they are disabled. Since everyone knows of these accounts and anyone can use these accounts to access a PC host, they should be checked to ensure effective SOHO LAN security.
2. **Use NTFS security and disk partitions**—NTFS provides added disk security that FAT partitions do not support. NTFS partition use can restrict access to files and directories to specific users and groups. With NTFS, access to a disk or folder can be revoked.

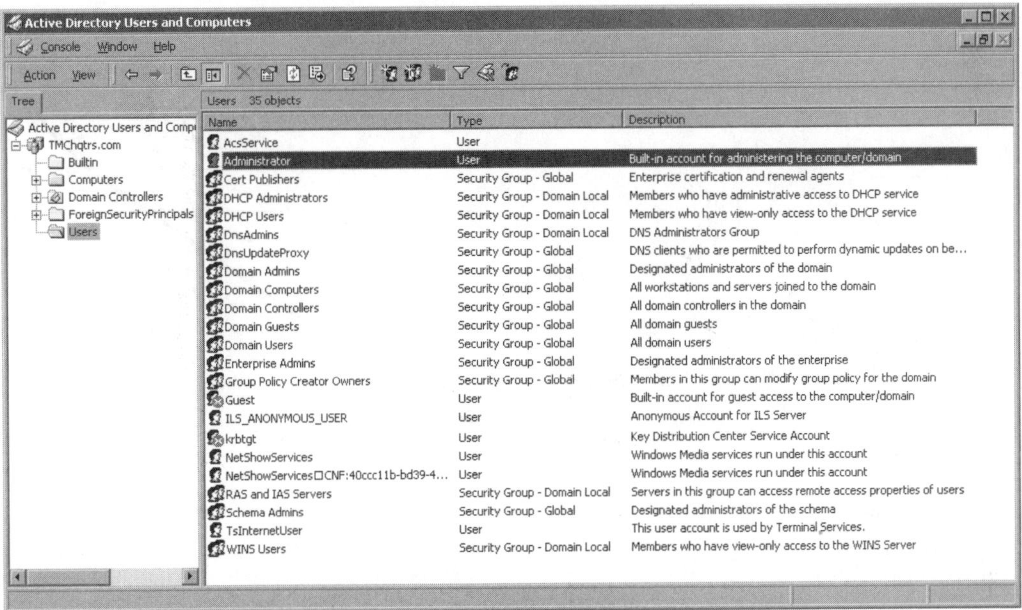

Figure 7.14 Windows 2000 built-in accounts.

3. **Control directory browsing**—When a Web browser follows a URL to a folder, a listing of files in the folder is displayed unless an INDEX.HTM is present in that folder. Web site security is increased when directory browsing is disabled in the IIS property sheet for a Windows IIS Web site or each folder has an INDEX.HTM file that controls access to that folder.
4. **Turn off all unnecessary server services**—Windows provides many services not required by a Web server. Remote Procedure Call (RPC) services are rarely used by a Web server. Turn off all Windows services unless they are proven to be absolutely needed.
5. **Turn on WWW and FTP logging**—Logging the activities at a Web site monitors a server's performance and tracks users' steps as they navigate through the Web site. By specifying when and what to log, you can reveal how well the Web site is performing and monitor malicious activity.
6. **Auditing**—Use Windows' resource auditing features to monitor critical server resources. Setting an audit policy is performed using the Microsoft Management Console (MMC). Running the MMC (Start button-Run-MMC) permits adding the Microsoft Group Policies Snap-in. Under this Snap-in audit policies can be set, as shown in Figure 7.15. Audit policy settings enable auditing and permit choosing which events to monitor. Be cautious because auditing too many things can overload the Windows event viewer making it difficult to focus on critical security events.

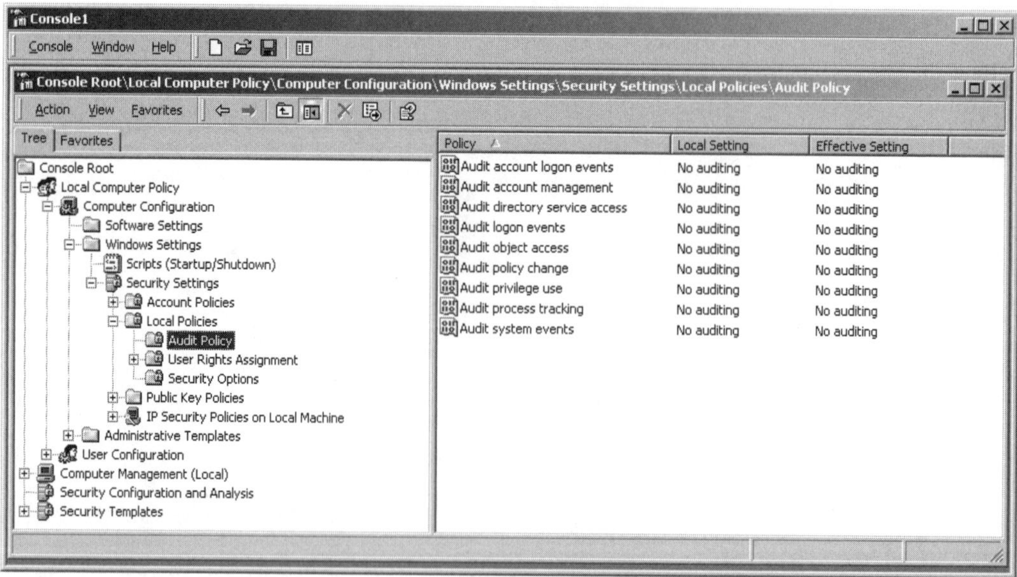

Figure 7.15 Setting auditing policies.

Once auditing is in place monitoring the event logs should identify an attack. An attack on a SOHO LAN is generally an attempt to violate or compromise system security on a server or other PC host connected to the Internet. As we have discussed, hackers or crackers have many different options for hacking into a SOHO LAN, so it's imperative to monitor system activity and logs regularly to maintain a secure environment. If a server is compromised, a hacker or cracker might control the machine enough to install software that makes the SOHO LAN server an acting participant in a denial-of-service attack.

When a SOHO LAN is secured, and logging and auditing are enabled and actively tracking any and all security violations, what happens when you detect suspicious activity on a SOHO LAN PC host or servers? Investigating security compromises can be frustrating. Knowing effective investigative steps saves considerable time. When hacking or cracking activity is suspected, first check the event viewer. Obvious traces of an attack are most likely discovered there. They may be a cluster of logon or other errors occurring in a short time interval.

After inspecting the event viewer, search the log files. The log files can be searched manually or by special software to find the IP address where the attack originated. Use the time clustering of the event log events to narrow the search. When you find a suspicious IP address, use *www.checkdomain.com* to find the name of the ISP from which the attack originated. Document every piece of information that you have found. Use listed e-mail addresses to report to the ISP the hacking abuse.

The `TRACERT` command can be used to trace the route that the hacking or cracking path followed. The log files provide details on the hacking or cracking attempt. Logging Internet activity is essential for securing a SOHO LAN. Logging does not keep attackers away—it only tells when they have attempted attacks.

Some added sources for SOHO LAN server security are the following:

www.microsoft.com/technet/treeview/default.asp?url=/technet/security/Default.asp

www.cert.org/tech_tips/intruder_detection_checklist.html

www.usdoj.gov/criminal/cybercrime/reporting.htm

www.securityfocus.com/

www.symantec.com

www.mcafee.com

www.zonealarm.com

www.antivirus.com/pc-cillin/

These Web site links may change. However, they provide additional security information, and some offer free one-time virus scanning and port scans.

Brain Teaser: Security Administration

Check the Windows Event Viewer. The Event Viewer is found by selecting the My Computer icon, clicking the right mouse button, and then selecting the Manage menu option. The event logs can also be reached using the Control Panel. Look at Security and System Events.

What warnings and errors were found? Do any events look like malicious activity? Can you disable Windows services not used to reduce warnings and errors in the event logs?

Summary

This chapter has discussed SOHO LAN security threats including the most common security threat, viruses and malevolent software; spyware observing, collecting, and reporting on user activity; and finally the less common direct attacks by hackers or crackers from the Internet. Countermeasures to mitigate the security threats were examined including virus scanning software, firewalls, and Microsoft Windows update services that fix Windows security vulnerabilities. A brief discussion of administrative procedures for monitoring network PC hosts and servers to detect and report security attacks concluded the chapter. The intent of this chapter is to provide an overview and introduction to inexpensive, common, and reasonably effective security products and procedures. Larger networks would need more sophisticated and more closely monitored security.

Key Technical Terms

Cookie—A cookie is a small file placed on a user's hard drive by a Web site. Cookies store user passwords to Web sites, and they are also used to record and report a PC host user's Web link selections and other information to marketing organizations. This information is used to advertise specific products to that Web site user. Some cookies cause targeted pop-up or banner advertisements to appear on the PC host user's monitor.

Cracker—A cracker is a 13- to 45-year-old male whose entire social life consists of cracking program code, creating virus programs that corrupt Windows, or breaking into other people's PCs. In this manner he gets his 15 minutes of fame, plus free food and an opportunity to twiddle his thumbs for from 5 to 20 years.

DoS—Denial of service is an attack on a SOHO LAN mounted from an external Internet source with the purpose of overloading the Internet connection or the LAN servers so that other requests are not processed and responded to normally.

Extranet—An extranet permits specific external users to access specific information stored on an enterprise's intranet.

FINGER—A program used to obtain information on e-mail accounts on remote PC servers that support the FINGER command.

Firewall—A firewall is a device or software that filters packets entering and leaving a SOHO LAN or a PC host attached to a SOHO LAN. The firewall matches packets received from the Internet, with requests sent by a PC host to the Internet, permitting these packets to be received by the PC host. Otherwise packets are discarded.

FTP—File Transfer Protocol is a protocol for transferring data or files between PC hosts on a TCP/IP network.

Hacker—A hacker is a 13- to 45-year-old male whose only social life is to break into someone else's PC to get attention. He cannot find a life anywhere else.

HTTP—Hypertext Transfer Protocol carries Web page information from an Internet server to a PC host running Web browsing software.

ICMP—Internet Control Message Protocol is an Internet or IP message control and error-reporting protocol. ICMP uses IP packets or datagrams to carry information between Internet hosts or other IP hosts. The ICMP messages are processed by the IP software and are not necessarily apparent to the PC host application. In the case of PING and TRACERT programs, the results of IP processing ICMP packets are displayed to the PC user.

ID—Identifier is the label placed upon a user account or other network resource.

IIS—Internet Information Service is Windows PC host software that implements hosting Web sites on that PC host. IIS software permits a SOHO LAN to host an intranet.

Intranet—An intranet is SOHO LAN supported Web servers and their associated Web pages within an enterprise's network. An intranet is generally not accessible from the Internet without special authorization.

ISP—Internet service provider is a commercial organization that provides access to the Internet for enterprises and other end users. An ISP may

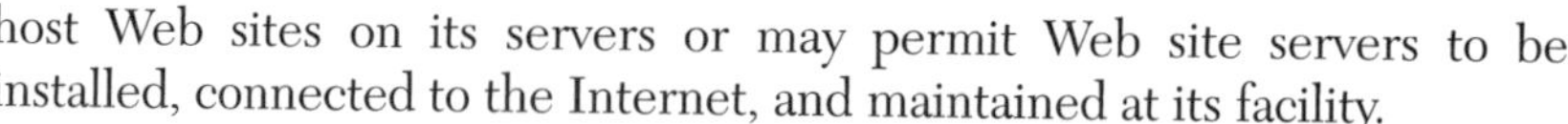

host Web sites on its servers or may permit Web site servers to be installed, connected to the Internet, and maintained at its facility.

Macro code—Macros are special combinations of key strokes that form a programming language of sorts. Macros automate processes in documents, spreadsheets, and database manipulation programs. Unfortunately, macros can be programmed to disseminate virus software via e-mail containing macros. A good security measure is to turn off Microsoft Word macro commands.

Malevolent software—Malevolent software is commonly called a virus but it can be a virus, a Trojan, or a worm program. Malevolent software in its least harmful form robs PC host CPU cycles and displays annoying messages to indicate its presence. Malevolent software in its most harmful form erases data and key files from PC host fixed disks, necessitating a complete rebuild of the PC host's Windows and application software.

MMC—Microsoft Management Console is Windows 2000/XP software that sets up auditing and other Windows management functions on Windows 2000/XP PC hosts or servers.

PATHPING—PATHPING is a Windows 2000/XP program for tracing the route packets follow from a source PC host to a target PC host. PATHPING times how long it takes for packets to traverse the route.

PING—Packet Inter-Network Groper is a Windows and UNIX program that uses the Internet Control Message Protocol (ICMP) to determine active IP addresses.

RPC—Remote Procedure Call is a Windows capability to run programs on other PC hosts across a SOHO LAN or the Internet.

Script—A script is a small application written in a simple programming language. Malevolent software can be distributed as scripts using Internet e-mail.

SMPT—Simple Mail Transfer Protocol is a protocol used to transfer e-mail messages between an Internet e-mail post office server system and a PC host sending and receiving e-mail messages. The PC host has mail box storage on the e-mail server.

Spyware—Spyware is software installed on a PC host without explicit user knowledge; it gathers and reports information on the PC host user generally for the purpose of selling him or her something.

TRACERT—Trace route is a Windows program using ICMP packets to trace the route between the requesting PC host and a target PC host on the Internet. It also performs some rudimentary timing of how long it takes packets to traverse the route from the requesting PC host to the target PC host.

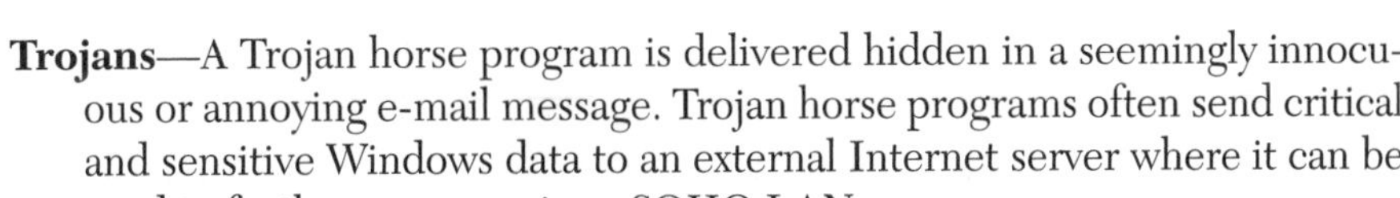

Trojans—A Trojan horse program is delivered hidden in a seemingly innocuous or annoying e-mail message. Trojan horse programs often send critical and sensitive Windows data to an external Internet server where it can be used to further compromise a SOHO LAN.

URL—A Uniform Resource Locator is the fully specified address of a Web page. For example, my DialANerd site's index page URL is http://www.dialanerd.com/index.htm.

VBS—Visual Basic Script is a basic programming language used to perform functions in many Windows applications.

Virus—A virus is malevolent software that hides itself as part of another program. Viruses replicate themselves through a SOHO LAN and may cause serious damage to Windows and critical PC data.

Worm—A worm is a self-contained program that has a seemingly legitimate Windows name. Worm programs like viruses replicate themselves through a SOHO LAN and may cause serious damage to Windows and critical PC data.

WWW—World Wide Web is servers supporting Web pages that are retrieved using HTTP and displayed using Web browsing software.

Review Questions

1. What is the most common SOHO LAN security threat?

   Answer: A virus, worm, or Trojan program sent to a PC host via e-mail.

2. What is a virus?

   Answer: A virus is a program that hides itself inside another legitimate Windows program. A virus makes the original program larger in size. In a general sense, "virus" is used to label any malevolent software.

3. What is Spyware?

   Answer: Spyware is software installed on a PC host without the user's knowledge or permission it gathers and reports information on the PC host user. The information reported is used to market products through targeted advertisements displayed on the PC host's monitor.

4. Why use Windows Update?

   Answer: Windows Update sends via the Internet software patches to Windows. These software patches often fix Windows security vulnerabilities.

5. What is a good administrative period for ensuring Windows PC hosts have current virus signatures and Windows updates? Daily—Weekly—Monthly—Annually?

   Answer: Weekly or monthly are both good update checking periods.

6. What do firewalls guard against?

   Answer: Firewalls protect SOHO LANs from penetration and attacks originating in the external Internet.

Chapter 8

VoIP Networking

Chapter Syllabus

- VoIP SOHO Network Application Configurations
- VoIP Network Components
- Summary
- Key Technical Terms
- Review Questions

A new SOHO application is VoIP telephony. For a small office this can save long-distance telephone charges and provide cost-effective PBX capabilities using the SOHO LAN. This chapter shows how to build a SOHO VoIP network.

The VoIP market is exploding with many new products. These products range from standalone devices that turn any phone into a VoIP network device that can call any other telephone, to sophisticated gateways aimed at providing VoIP telephony to large networks. Our focus is on products and services that can be effectively used in conjunction with a SOHO LAN. The main intent of these devices is to provide lower-cost voice communications.

VoIP products conform to a variety of standards. This chapter identifies and briefly describes the applicability of the standards most generally implemented in VoIP products. Many VoIP products interoperate. However, the safest strategy is to get VoIP products from a single vendor or VAR that guarantees they interoperate and perform as expected.

The goal of this chapter is to introduce you to some of the exciting VoIP products and services that can benefit your SOHO LAN. There are many VoIP products that are inexpensive enough for most home-office users. These products can help save long-distance costs, especially for international calls. By the time you finish this chapter you'll find out just what can be done to my SOHO LAN to use VoIP and how it can save communications costs.

VoIP SOHO Network Application Configurations

Both home-office and small-office LANs can benefit from VoIP products and services. Several of these configurations are examined to illustrate the products and benefits. These product configurations can vary from simple devices that connect analog PSTN telephones to the Internet to reduce long-distance charges, to more sophisticated small-office PBX systems that connect remote offices into the central-office PBX using VoIP and that can provide reduced long-distance costs by routing long distance and international calls over the Internet or private IP networks at reduced rates. The primary benefits of these VoIP products and services are reduced long-distance costs, centralized telephony operation and monitoring for remote workers, unified data and voice network wiring and operation, and cheaper telecommunications components such as PBX systems.

Home-Office Networks

Several products are targeted at small home-office LANs. A low-end product permits routing telephone calls across the Internet with the goal of saving costs. This French product requires that both the origination and termination calling points have a unit installed. The call is then initiated over the PSTN. When the terminating phone is answered, a button on the product is pushed and the product then reroutes the call over the Internet where the parties can talk toll free for an extended time period. Both originating and terminating stations must have their device set up to place and receive calls from a local ISP to enable the call to be rerouted across the Internet. The call must be initiated using the PSTN to ensure that the call terminating party is available to answer the phone. The device must also compress the voice into a small data stream because digital transmission is limited to 53 Kbps on a good day. However good voice quality today is realized with transmission speeds of a little as 9,600 bps. The coder/decoder (codec) used determines the compression and voice quality over the Internet.

More common devices are VoIP cable modem/DSL routers, or soft telephones (telephones implemented in software running in a PC host). These devices use a high-speed cable modem or DSL link to the Internet. An analog telephone is plugged into the port on the router or a PC host runs special soft phone software (in some cases a Java applet downloaded from a Web site). They then can place long-distance calls at very low rates. The router, or the soft phone program, converts the call into a VoIP call. It first authenticates the call and sets up billing for the connection, and it then uses an Internet telephony service provider (ITSP) to complete the call over the PSTN. Such ITSPs are Dialpad and Net2Phone. They can reduce long-distance charges to as low as three cents per minute for domestic calls. International calls enjoy considerably reduced rates as well. See Figure 8.1.

Because some TCP connections can be blocked, some soft phones require that ports on the router pass directly through the router to the soft phone PC host. The ports that should be opened include the following:

- TCP Port 5354
- TCP Port 7175
- TCP Ports 8680 through 8890
- TCP Port 9000
- TCP Ports 9450 through 9460
- UDP ports over 1024

The best strategy to follow when a soft phone does not work is to open these ports one at a time until the soft phone works. Once it works start closing down the ports just opened until the soft phone quits working. The reason for identifying only those ports that make the soft phone work is that for security purposes it is not necessarily a good idea to just open a lot of ports. Further, some routers have a limited ability to specify which ports are to be opened to which PC host and which are to be closed. Opening lots of ports may exceed the router's port controlling capacity.

Some routers expose a single PC host directly to the Internet. This bypasses the router's port filtering entirely. However, typically only a single PC host is exposed to the Internet, which may not help a SOHO LAN with five PC hosts using soft phones.

Dialpad soft phone long-distance service and rates are shown in Figure 8.2.

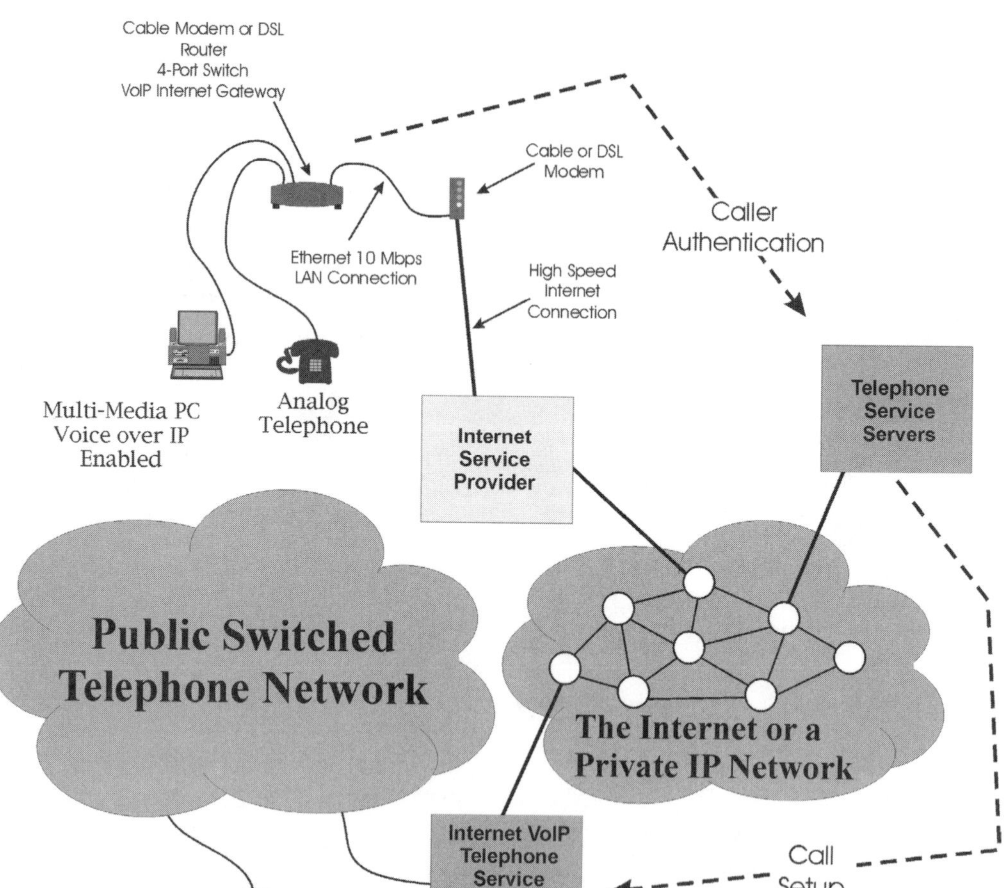

Call Connection Steps:

1. Top Phone Calls bottom PSTN phone
2. Cable Modem/DSL Router with VoIP Gateway
   connects to Telephone Service Servers
3. Telephone Service Servers authenticate caller
4. Telephone servers set up call with ITSP
5. Call is routed via High-speed Internet connection
   and the Internet
   to the Internet VoIP Telephone Service Provider (ITSP)
6. Internet VoIP Telephone Service Provider
   completes the call using the PSTN
7. Telephone Service charges from 2.9 to 7 cents a minute for the call.

Figure 8.1 Home-office VoIP configuration.

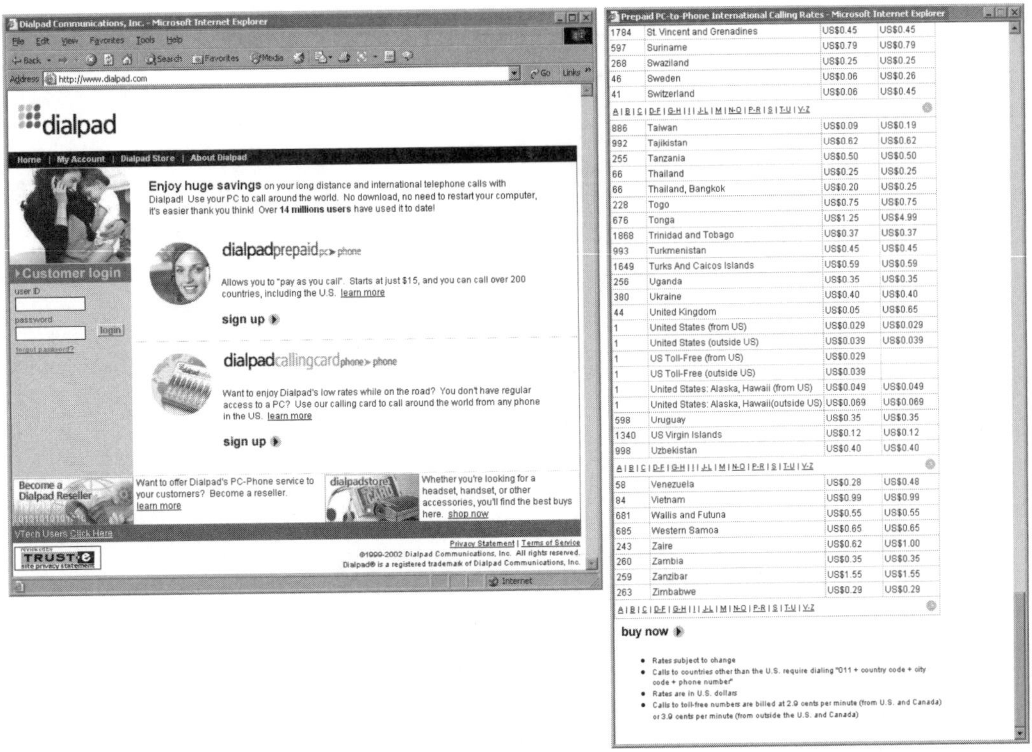

1784	St. Vincent and Grenadines	US$0.45	US$0.45
597	Suriname	US$0.79	US$0.79
268	Swaziland	US$0.25	US$0.25
46	Sweden	US$0.06	US$0.26
41	Switzerland	US$0.06	US$0.45
A | B | C | D-F | G-H | I | J-L | M | N-O | P-R | S | T-U | V-Z			
886	Taiwan	US$0.09	US$0.19
992	Tajikistan	US$0.62	US$0.62
255	Tanzania	US$0.50	US$0.50
66	Thailand	US$0.25	US$0.25
66	Thailand, Bangkok	US$0.20	US$0.25
228	Togo	US$0.75	US$0.75
676	Tonga	US$1.25	US$4.99
1868	Trinidad and Tobago	US$0.37	US$0.37
993	Turkmenistan	US$0.45	US$0.45
1649	Turks And Caicos Islands	US$0.59	US$0.59
256	Uganda	US$0.35	US$0.35
380	Ukraine	US$0.40	US$0.40
44	United Kingdom	US$0.05	US$0.65
1	United States (from US)	US$0.029	US$0.029
1	United States (outside US)	US$0.039	US$0.039
1	US Toll-Free (from US)	US$0.029	
1	US Toll-Free (outside US)	US$0.039	
1	United States: Alaska, Hawaii (from US)	US$0.049	US$0.049
1	United States: Alaska, Hawaii(outside US)	US$0.069	US$0.069
598	Uruguay	US$0.35	US$0.35
1340	US Virgin Islands	US$0.12	US$0.12
998	Uzbekistan	US$0.40	US$0.40
A | B | C | D-F | G-H | I | J-L | M | N-O | P-R | S | T-U | V-Z			
58	Venezuela	US$0.28	US$0.48
84	Vietnam	US$0.99	US$0.99
681	Wallis and Futuna	US$0.55	US$0.55
685	Western Samoa	US$0.65	US$0.65
243	Zaire	US$0.62	US$1.00
260	Zambia	US$0.35	US$0.35
259	Zanzibar	US$1.55	US$1.55
263	Zimbabwe	US$0.29	US$0.29
A | B | C | D-F | G-H | I | J-L | M | N-O | P-R | S | T-U | V-Z			

buy now

- Rates subject to change
- Calls to countries other than the U.S. require dialing "011 + country code + city code + phone number"
- Rates are in U.S. dollars
- Calls to toll-free numbers are billed at 2.9 cents per minute (from U.S. and Canada) or 3.9 cents per minute (from outside the U.S. and Canada)

Figure 8.2 Dialpad service. Courtesy of Dialpad Communications, Inc.

Typical rates for Dialpad service are 2.9 cents per minute for domestic U.S. calls. This rate is in the lower right of Figure 8.2.

Brain Teaser: VoIP Services

Use a Web browser and connect to the DialPad.com and net2phone.com Web sites. Check out their current long-distance rates for U.S. and some International calls.

Connect to the AT&T Web site and select calling plans to check out the AT&T rates for the same calls. How do these prices compare with the AT&T rates for domestic and international calls? Notice the unlimited plan disclaimers for universal connectivity charges and in-state connectivity fees.

A larger small-office LAN may use a VoIP PBX, as illustrated by Figure 8.3.

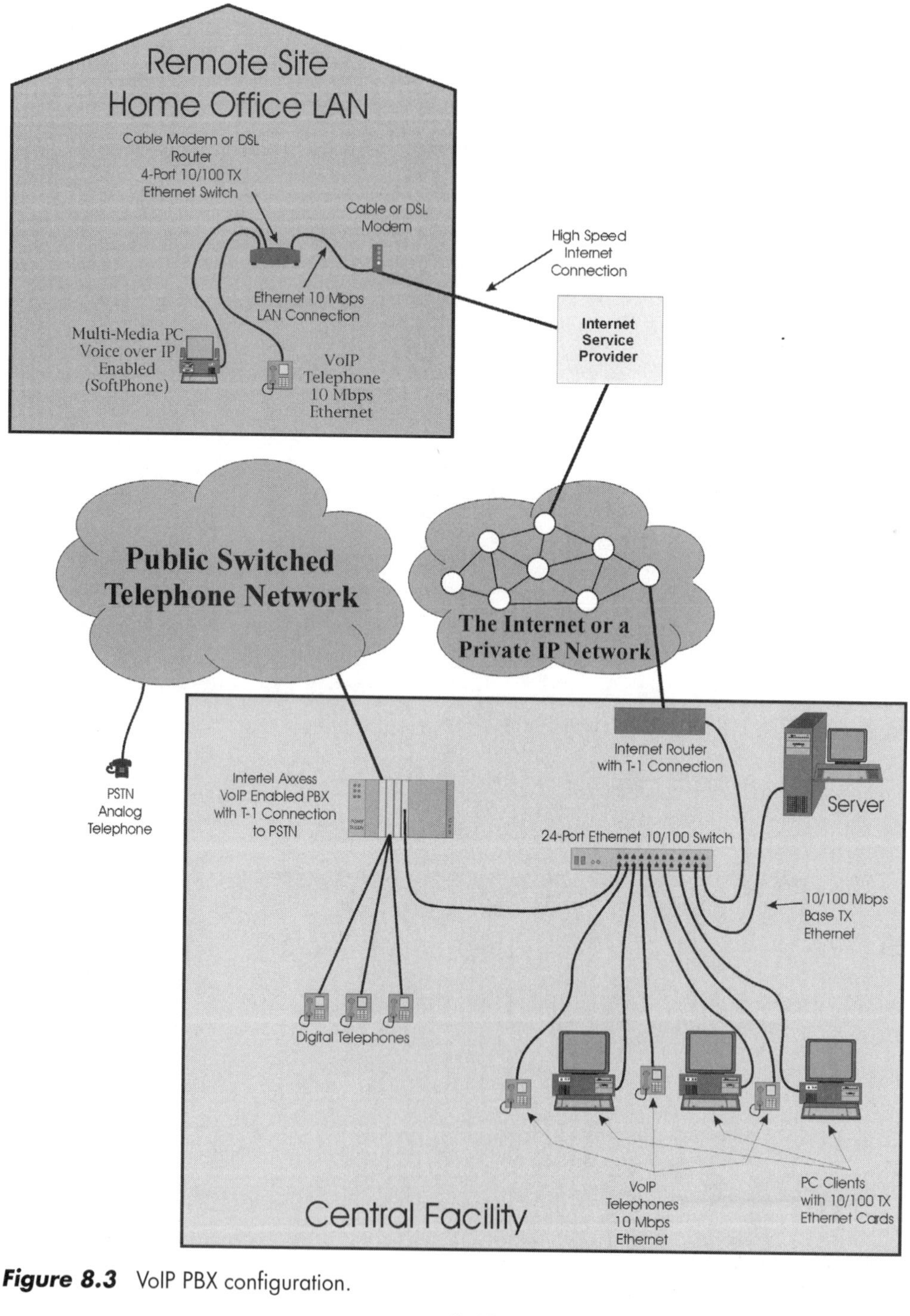

Remote Site
Home Office LAN
Cable Modem or DSL
Router
4-Port 10/100 TX
Ethernet Switch
Cable or DSL
Modem
High Speed
Internet
Connection
Ethernet 10 Mbps
LAN Connection
Internet
Service
Provider
Multi-Media PC
Voice over IP
Enabled
(SoftPhone)
VoIP
Telephone
10 Mbps
Ethernet
Public Switched
Telephone Network
The Internet or a
Private IP Network
Internet Router
with T-1 Connection
Intertel Axxess
VoIP Enabled PBX
with T-1 Connection
to PSTN
PSTN
Analog
Telephone
Server
24-Port Ethernet 10/100 Switch
10/100 Mbps
Base TX
Ethernet
Digital Telephones
VoIP
Telephones
10 Mbps
Ethernet
PC Clients
with 10/100 TX
Ethernet Cards
Central Facility

Figure 8.3 VoIP PBX configuration.

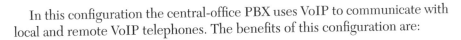

In this configuration the central-office PBX uses VoIP to communicate with local and remote VoIP telephones. The benefits of this configuration are:

1. Simplified central facility wiring because voice and LAN wiring are interchangeable Ethernet wiring
2. Seamless, step-by-step expandability of the central-office PBX—as one VoIP PBX reaches saturation in the telephones it can service (about 1,000), another VoIP PBX is added and combined with the first VoIP PBX to service the added telephones like a single large VoIP PBX
3. Centralized control and monitoring of remote telephones, which is especially useful for call center operation
4. Central facility long-distance telephone call origination, potentially reducing long-distance charges

The major drawbacks are that all remote telephones are dependent upon a high-speed Internet connection for the remote telephones to work and that each remote location requires an analog telephone to place local and 911 emergency calls. Each remote VoIP telephone acts like a local phone connected directly to the central-office PBX. This means that the remote VoIP phones can function as part of a centralized call center. They can perform extension dialing and operate with centralized voice mail regardless of their distance from the central facility. They are true extensions to the central facility VoIP PBX.

All calls placed by a remote VoIP telephone are completed through the central site PBX. Consequently, those calls are local to the central site PBX facility. When a remote VoIP telephone is located in another city or country, it is not making local calls in that city or country, but rather it makes local calls in the city or country where the central facility VoIP PBXs are located.

VoIP PBX/Router/Gatekeeper Configuration

The central component in a SOHO LAN VoIP network is the VoIP PBX. Such PBXs have evolved from traditional PBXs like my Inter-Tel Axxess PBX. Others have come from an Internet router heritage like the Cisco AccessPath-VS3. Finally, some were developed specifically to perform VoIP gatekeeper functions. Regardless of how these products came to be, they all perform similar functions. They act as the interface between both VoIP telephones and analog telephones to the VoIP packet network and to the Public Switched Telephone Network (PSTN). They provide traditional PBX functions for analog phones and provide a gateway for VoIP phones to use the analog telephone network. Typically, these PBXs can be combined together using VoIP connections to service a large population of telephones as though they were a single large PBX.

In acquiring and deploying these VoIP systems, the strategy is to use components from a single vendor. Trying to mix and match components at this time is more risky than selecting them from a single vendor. In the case of my Inter-Tel equipment, the VoIP telephones have equivalent features to my existing Inter-Tel digital telephones connected to my PBX. There is no need to make special software adjustments to the PBX to accommodate a display different from the six-line, 16-character one provided with both the digital and VoIP Inter-Tel telephones. A 3Com VoIP telephone has a two-line, 16-character display.

Integrating multiple switches into a single larger combined switch is supported by the products from a single vendor. Interoperability between components of different vendors in such a combined configuration is not assured. Even though VoIP equipment conforms to a variety of ITU telephony standards this is no assurance that products from different vendors interoperate as we would need them to. For example, suppose a hunt group (See Key Technical Terms) is split between two VoIP PBXs from different vendors. What determines that the hunt group telephones are selected in the desired order? What determines that all call group (See Key Technical Terms) telephones ring simultaneously when the call group telephones are split between multiple VoIP PBX systems? (Hunt groups are discussed later in this chapter.)

To save money on long-distance telephone calls, the VoIP PBX would need to connect to an ITSP such as Net2Phone or Dialpad. VoIP PBXs cannot as yet effectively interface directly with local telco Class 5 central-office switches because of interoperability issues. In the long run such interoperability issues will be resolved, but for the foreseeable future they are not. This means that a VoIP PBX vendor has its VoIP PBX work with a specific ITSP to provide low long-distance and international rates.

VoIP PBX interfaces are illustrated in Figure 8.4. These connections are briefly examined here.

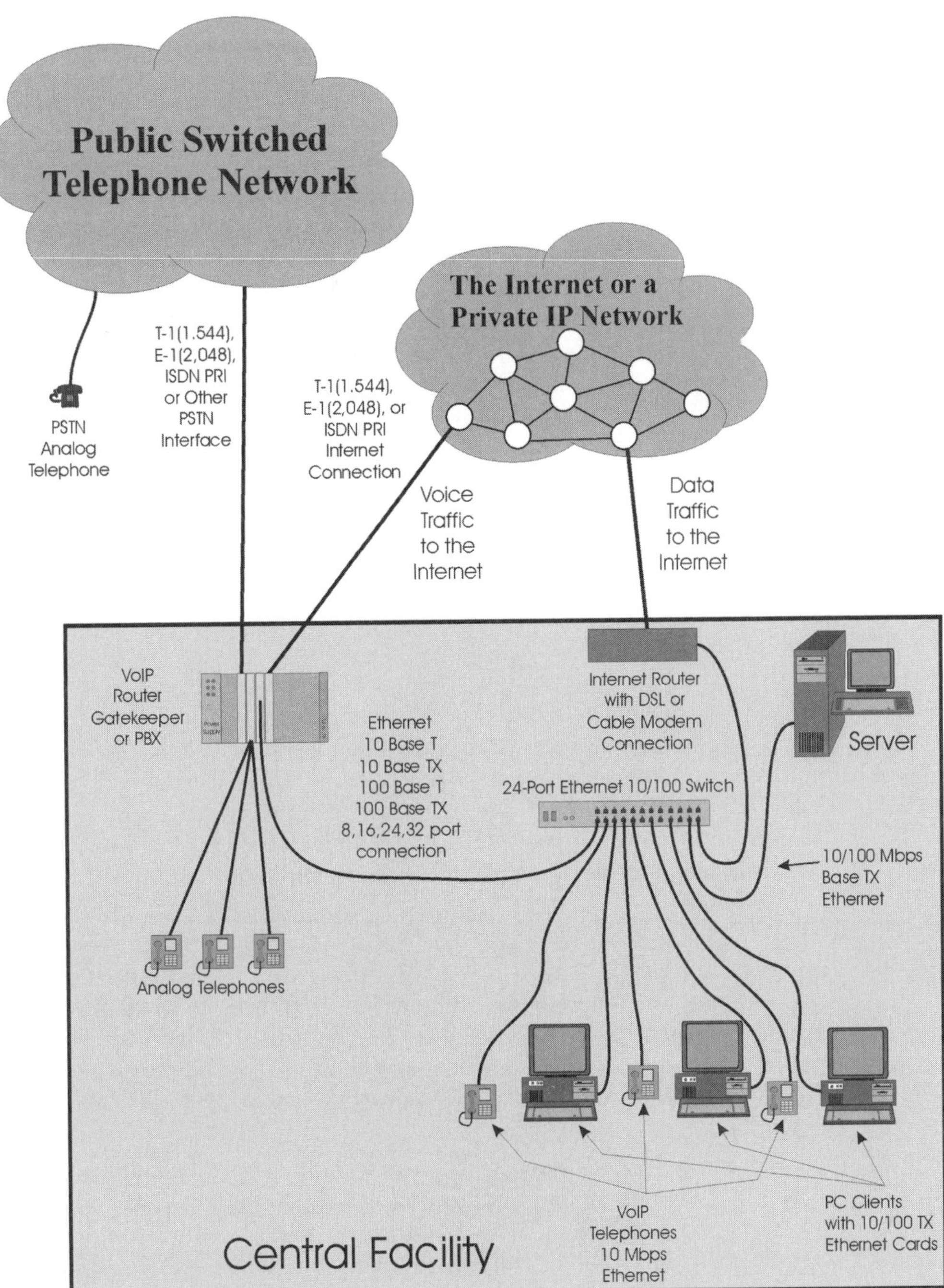

Figure 8.4 VoIP PBX, router, gatekeeper connections.

SOHO LAN Connections

The VoIP connection would connect through an eight-, 16-, 24-, or 32-port Ethernet PBX card. These VoIP PBX cards connect to VoIP telephones using specific IP addresses. The addresses are matched to ports on the VoIP PBX card. Local VoIP telephones get their IP address from the VoIP card installed in the VoIP PBX. Boot protocol (BootP) and DHCP (Dynamic Host Configuration Protocol) are used to connect the VoIP telephones to a specific port on the VoIP PBX by assigning their IP address. An eight-port VoIP PBX card services eight VoIP telephones and not 32 VoIP telephones. Each PBX VoIP card and each VoIP telephone must be assigned a compatible IP address. These addresses could be on a different subnet from the subnet used for SOHO LAN data. For example, a data subnet could be 208.80.34.x while the voice subnet would be 208.80.68.x.

Internet or IP Network Connections

VoIP Internet connections would typically use a high-speed T-1 link. In Figure 8.4, voice traffic would travel into the Internet over the direct high-speed link from the PBX to the Internet while data traffic would be routed through the Internet cable modem or DSL router.

For VoIP PBXs to connect to VoIP telephones across the Internet they must have IP addresses directly exposed to the Internet. A directly exposed Internet IP address is an IP address that is identified in an Internet Domain Name Service (DNS) server. SOHO LAN IP addresses in Windows 2000/XP are identified in the SOHO LAN DNS server but not necessarily in an Internet DNS server.

For example, to make a VPN connection into my SOHO LAN my VPN server must have an IP address directly exposed to the Internet. The VPN request does not effectively pass through my cable modem router-firewall. It may be possible to route VPN requests directly to the VPN server with a special firewall configuration. Such a configuration may not be possible with my firewall. Consequently, VPN connections into my SOHO LAN cannot be established.

Similarly, if my PBX were to be upgraded with a VoIP card and a remote VoIP telephone were to attempt to connect to it, the remote phone would be unable to find the PBX VoIP card's IP address. This is a simple router configuration issue that can be resolved by using IP addresses from my cable modem ISP that are directly exposed to the Internet or by a special router configuration.

Public Switched Telephone Network Connections

In Figure 8.4 the VoIP PBX, router, or gatekeeper connects to the PSTN via T-1, E-1 (international), ISDN PRI, E&M (ear and mouth) 4-wire tie line, analog loop start, or other common telephony circuit. Connections are made to normal analog telephones using DTMF signaling and two-wire loop start connections. PBX digital telephones would be similarly connected using an ISDN BRI or proprietary digital interface. Such interfaces are already installed and operational in VoIP PBXs. These interfaces use Signaling System 7 (SS7) and voice PSTN connections to complete calls in the PSTN.

Overall Configurations and Costs

Costs for VoIP components are not cheap. For my Inter-Tel Axxess PBX it would cost about $1,100 additional per VoIP phone. This cost is in addition to the basic PBX cost. The cost breaks down into about $1,600 per eight-port VoIP card and $900 per VoIP telephone, so that eight VoIP telephone connections would cost a total of $8,800 ($1,600 for the card plus $7,200 for the phones) or about $1,100 per connection. Other VoIP PBX systems would have similar costs. While these prices are not inexpensive, they should drop significantly over the next year. A typical VoIP eight-port card is shown in Figure 8.5.

The VoIP PBX configuration competes with Centrex service. Centrex permits remote locations to act as though they were part of a single centralized telephone switch, similar to the VoIP telephones being connected to the centralized switch through the Internet or a private IP network. The main difference is that the VoIP phones support a wider variety of call center reporting functions than is supported by Centrex. However, Centrex costs may be less than VoIP PBX costs, depending upon how long the VoIP PBX is used.

Brain Teaser: VoIP Products

Go to the Cisco Web site and try to find VoIP SOHO LAN products. Do the same for 3Com. Was it easy to find and understand how those products might apply to your network in 10 clicks or less? Which vendor's Web site provided information quicker? My vote is 3Com.

Can information be found quicker at the Inter-Tel Web site? Are the VoIP PBX features similar for all three vendors?

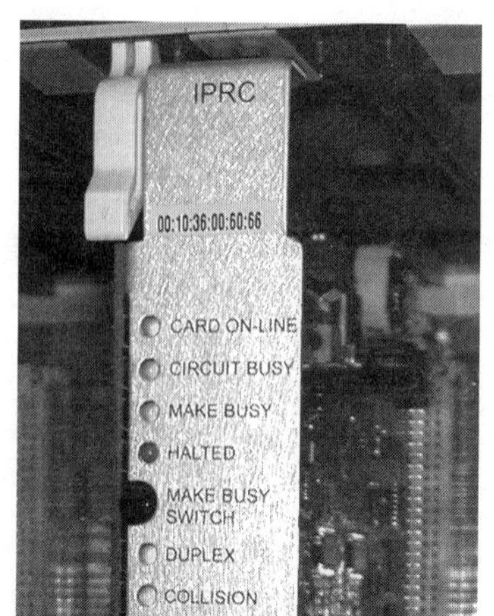

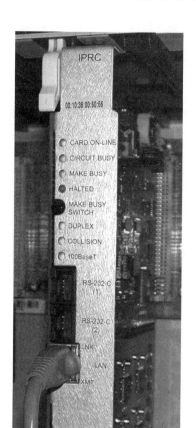

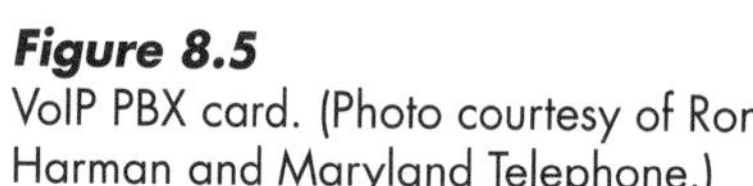
Figure 8.5
VoIP PBX card. (Photo courtesy of Ron Harman and Maryland Telephone.)

VoIP Network Components

VoIP network components are discussed here in more detail. Special focus is on the standards that VoIP components use to provide specific features and functions. These standards are often listed in the product sheets for these VoIP components.

VoIP Gatekeeper/Router/PBX

The central VoIP network component is the VoIP PBX. It may be called a gatekeeper, a router, or a PBX. We refer to it here as a VoIP PBX. Whatever the name, it performs the core inter-networking functions. These inter-networking functions are implemented in hardware and software that combines voice and data transmission over an IP network. The VoIP PBX supports analog telephones, emulates a telephony PBX by implementing signaling software functions, and connects the VoIP networking functions to the PSTN.

The VoIP PBX replaces other PBXs, uses the Internet or a private IP network to replace TIE trunks between facilities, and sometimes interfaces to cellular networks.

A VoIP PBX is typically administered using a Web browser like Internet Explorer or Netscape Navigator. This means that it must support the Hypertext Transfer Protocol (HTTP) to communicate with the Web browser software.

A VoIP PBX would implement hunt and call groups. A hunt group is a group or set of telephones that ring when a specific number is dialed. They ring in a designated sequence from the first phone in the hunt group to the last phone in the hunt group. Hunt groups are used to implement call centers.

In contrast, call groups are a set of telephones that all ring simultaneously when a specific number is dialed. The first phone answering the call services the call. Our phones use a call group so that anyone calling causes several phones to ring simultaneously. Anyone answering the phone first then answers the call. An alternative to call groups is automated attendant answering, a process in which the robot voice gives a menu listing and then finally asks for the extension number of the person whom you are calling.

Call detail reporting is used by call centers to track work and telephone activity. It is also used to allocate telephone costs to the different enterprise activities using the telephone system.

Unified voice mail/e-mail messaging is implemented using Internet Message Access Protocol version 4 (IMAP4). IMAP4 is a client/server protocol that works with e-mail received and held on an Internet or VoIP server. An e-mail client views just the heading and the sender information for the combined voice/e-mail message. The user then decides whether to download and listen to the voice mail or just read the e-mail message. Folders or mailboxes can be created and manipulated, voice mail and e-mail messages can be deleted, and specific information can be searched for in messages on the VoIP PBX server using IMAP4. IMAP4 requires constant access to the VoIP PBX server while the unified messaging is being worked upon.

Unified messaging also uses Microsoft's Telephony Application Program Interface (TAPI). TAPI is a standard program interface for PCs sending voice or video to other PCs or phone-connected resources. PCs equipped with TAPI can perform unified messaging tasks such as the following:

1. Initiating a call by clicking on an icon or other image
2. Setting up and attending conference calls

3. Viewing other callers individually or in a conference call
4. Adding a voice message to e-mail or listening to a voice message attached to e-mail received
5. Automatically receiving phone calls from specified numbers
6. Sending and receiving facsimile messages

TAPI permits PCs and other VoIP components to work with different telephone systems, including the PSTN, the Integrated Services Digital Network (ISDN), and PBXs, without having to understand their details because phone system hardware makers provide specific software drivers that interface directly with their hardware. TAPI/WAV (TAPI/Wave Form) is an audio file used to store and exchange voice information with VoIP components. TAPI/WAV files carry good quality audio that is not compressed. TAPI 2.1 adds client/server functionality to Windows TAPI. With TAPI 2.1 telephony hardware can be installed on a telephony server and then be accessed from any computer on a SOHO network. TAPI 2.1 includes administration software that controls access to remote resources.

VoIP PBXs use Internet Group Management Protocol (IGMP) to multicast phone number dialing information to other VoIP PBXs. In this manner they coordinate signaling information between VoIP PBXs.

VoIP PBX systems must resolve several differences between traditional circuit-switched telephony and VoIP telephony. These differences include latency, or delay, in the voice stream, jitter in the packet arrivals, lost packets, and echo compensation.

Latency is most noticeable in speaking to listening transitions. The latency, or delay, is the time it takes the voice signal to travel through the VoIP network connection. Such latency includes an accumulation delay from the voice codec, a processing delay in packaging digital speech into IP packets, and a network delay. Round-trip delays may be as high as several hundred milliseconds.

Latency makes satellite IP network services much less usable for implementing VoIP. When there is no other choice, satellite networks do work. But acceptable voice call latency (network delays) is a maximum of 250 ms one way. The recommended one way delay is 150 ms. These meet ITU (International Telecommunications Union) recommendations.

Typically a round trip delay over any satellite link like the Starband satellite links runs around 600 ms for geosynchronous or geostationary orbit satellites and much, much less for low earth orbit (LEO) satellites. The latency, or delay, is simply computed. The distance from an earth-bound antenna to the satellite is 22,300 miles. A single round-trip transmission must travel up and down from the satellite twice for a total of 89,200 miles. It takes light and radio waves traveling at 186,000 miles per second 480 ms (89,200/186,000) to make a round trip. Add a 100 ms electronic processing delay and the total is 580 ms or 600 ms (close enough for engineering work) round trip.

At a quarter of a second (250 ms) callers start to become uncomfortable with telephone voice communication because they can both speak simultaneously but not have a means to gracefully recover because they have been speaking too long. When the one-way delay is longer than 250 ms, callers must make a very conscious effort not to step on one another's speech. They almost must say "Over to you" when they complete speaking.

A second significant area of concern in VoIP telephony is jitter management. One approach to jitter management is using adaptive jitter management that measures jitter over time and adjusts a buffer size to match the jitter. This approach works well when jitter is consistent like jitter from Asynchronous Transfer Mode (ATM) or cell relay networks. An alternative approach uses an allowable late packet ratio to determine the jitter buffer size. This approach counts late packets and determines the ratio to good packets, and it then sets a buffer to match a specified allowable late packet to good packet ratio. This approach works well with highly variable times between packet arrivals such as is commonly found in IP networks. Some devices use a combined or hybrid approach.

The third significant area of concern for VoIP telephony is lost packets. Lost packets translate into dropped speech. Two approaches are used to compensate for lost packets' interpolation and redundancy. Interpolation guesses the lost packet speech using the information in received packets. This works well when there are infrequently lost frames. It is not very effective when large numbers of packets or bursts of packets are lost. Redundancy sends added data from which the lost packet speech can be reconstructed. The drawback here is that this uses extra transmission capacity or bandwidth. Some VoIP PBXs use a combination of approaches.

The final significant area is voice echoes interfering with speech. Voice echoes are caused by long round-trip delays for VoIP speech. In telephony, echoes are masked by side tones. With round-trip delays in excess of 50 milliseconds the side tones are prevented from masking the echoes. Echo compensation is described by G.165 Echo Cancellers (normal) and G.168 Digital Network Echo Cancellers (more stringent) ITU specifications.

VoIP PBXs connect to loop-start analog, digital, and VoIP telephones. The VoIP telephones conform to the H.323 ITU specification. The H.323 specification describes multimedia communications among terminals, network equipment, and services. H.323 belongs to the H.3x group of ITU recommendations for multimedia interoperability. H.323 originally provided consistency in audio, video, and data packet transmissions for IP networks, but it did not guarantee quality of service (QoS). H.323 is now the standard for interoperability in audio, video, and data transmission as well as Internet phone and

VoIP because H.323 specifies call control and management for point-to-point connections and multipoint conference connections. H.323 also specifies gateway administration for traffic, bandwidth, and user participation. The most recent version is ITU-T H.323-V3.

Calls are set up using the Media Gateway Control Protocol (MGCP). This is also called H.248 and Megaco. The MGCP-H.248-Megaco standard is a protocol for signaling and session management needed for multimedia conferencing. The MGCP-H.248-Megaco defines communication between a media gateway that converts data from a circuit-switched network format to packet-switched network and media gateway controller formats. MGCP-H.248-Megaco is used to establish, maintain, and terminate calls among multiple endpoints. Megaco and H.248 refer to enhanced versions of MGCP. MGCP-H.248-Megaco provides a single standard for controlling multimedia IP transmission gateway devices and connecting calls from a VoIP LAN to the PSTN.

The Session Initiation Protocol (SIP) initiates an interactive connection or session for video, voice, chat, gaming, and virtual reality communication. SIP establishes multimedia sessions or VoIP calls and terminates them. Both H.323 and SIP use Real-Time Protocol (RTP) for VoIP communications.

Real-Time Protocol or Real-time Transport Protocol (RTP) manages real-time transmission of multimedia communications. RTP was designed to support video conferences. RTP is now commonly used in VoIP applications. RTP does not guarantee real-time delivery of multimedia communications. Instead it provides the ability to manage multimedia transmission as it arrives at its destination to provide the best transmission quality over an IP network. RTP combines data transport with a Real-Time Control Protocol (RTCP), making possible data delivery monitoring. Such monitoring permits a receiver to detect packet losses and to compensate for latency and jitter. RTP headers tell receivers how to reconstruct the multimedia transmission and describe how codec-produced bit streams are placed into IP packets.

Trivial File Transfer Protocol (TFTP) provides a simple file transfer mechanism. VoIP components use TFTP to upgrade firmware and transfer other files containing control information.

VoIP PBXs work with different codecs used to compress VoIP communications for low bit rate (LBR) transmission. The codecs employ G.711 Pulse Code Modulation (PCM), producing a 64 Kbps digital data stream for a single voice call; G.726 Adaptive Pulse Code Modulation (ADPCM), producing 16, 24, 32, or 40 Kbps digital streams; G.728 Low Delay-Code Excited Linear Prediction (LD-CELP), producing 16 Kbps; and G.729 Conjugate-Structure Algebraic Code Excited Linear Prediction (CS-ACELP), producing an eight-Kbps digital data stream for a single voice call. The bottom line here is the resulting transmission speed required to carry a single voice call. The lower the speed the more calls that can be carried on a VoIP communications link. The trade-off is that greater compression may impact voice quality.

When an analog signal is converted to a digital signal by a codec, the signal is divided into a discrete number of smaller parts. This is called quantization. Quantization produces the output signal, which is an approximation of the input signal. Quantization distortion is perceived as noise. The magnitude of the quantization noise problem depends on the number of quantization steps used in encoding. The effect of quantization noise is more severe with small amplitude signals with a small signal-to-noise ratio. This problem is significantly reduced when logarithmic quantizing is used. This is called companding, for compressing and expanding. Companding is a means to represent a large dynamic range of speech sound using fewer bits. Two main quantization laws are used in telephony:

1. A-Law (CCITT), 13 segments
2. Mu-Law (U.S.), 15 segments

Both approaches to companding map a signal onto a logarithmic curve approximated by straight-line segments. Mu-Law (μ-Law) encoding is the ITU G.711 standard. In Europe, some systems still use A-Law. VoIP PBXs should work with both types of companding to provide effective international telephony.

Telephones connecting into VoIP PBXs use different signaling techniques to dial telephone calls. These techniques include Dual Tone Multi Frequency (DTMF) and Multi Frequency (MF, MF R1/R2) analog signaling, other Channel Associated Signaling (CAS), ISDN's Common Channel Signaling (CCS), and Network Call Signaling (NCS) used in cable modem networks. Signaling conforms to the E.164 ITU international public telecommunication numbering plan.

VoIP calls need a QoS guarantee when they are transported by an IP network with best effort delivery. Such guarantees are provided by IP-ToS, IP-DiffServ, and 802.1p/Q transport mechanisms. IP-ToS, IP-DiffServ, and 802.1p/Q are all approaches that assign greater priority to VoIP packets. Greater priority means that VoIPs are processed more quickly in IP network routers and other IP network components. In this manner a transmission speed or quality of service level is guaranteed for VoIP communications through an IP network.

VoIP components can use Digital Speech Interpolation (DSI) to increase the transmission efficiency by insertion of additional signals from other sources in the transmission stream during periods of silence or inactivity. DSI fills in gaps during speech pauses to increase transmission efficiency because silence comprises about 60 percent of voice communications. DSI transmits packets from one source only during voice bursts. Another active source uses the bandwidth during silent periods. Voice Activation Detection (VAD) prevents sending packets when no voice activity is present. Comfort Noise Generation (CNG) removes discomforting periods of dead air at the receiver caused by VAD. Comfort Noise Generation matches the natural background noise and uses it to fill in discomforting dead air periods.

VoIP PBXs work with Routing Information Protocol to perform routing in a SOHO LAN. RIP is based on a set of algorithms that use distance vectors to mathematically compare routes. The route with the lowest distance vector becomes the best path to a specific destination address.

Simple Network Management Protocol (SNMP) is used by VoIP components to perform component configuration and network management functions. SNMP works with specially designed management software.

Remote Authentication Dial-In Service (RADIUS) is a client/server protocol and software that remote access servers use to communicate with a central server, to authenticate dial-in users, and to authorize access to a requested system or service. RADIUS supports maintaining user profiles in a central database that all remote servers share. In this manner RADIUS provides better security by supporting the setup of a security policy applied at a single administered network database. A central RADIUS service makes it easier to track usage for cost allocation and to keep network operational statistics.

Data sheets for VoIP PBXs, gatekeepers, and routers may contain references to the features and specifications identified here. In some cases standards compliance may not be listed. VoIP components that comply or use Internet and other telephony standards tend to work better than components not conforming to those standards. This, however, does not guarantee interoperability with VoIP network components made by other vendors. To get the most out of VoIP components the best strategy is to use all components from a single vendor.

Figure 8.6 shows an Inter-Tel Axxess PBX with a VoIP card installed. The PBX uses two interconnected chassis, with the lower chassis being opened to expose the VoIP Ethernet card. This card connects to the SOHO LAN and to VoIP telephones. The Inter-Tel Axxess PBX also connects to other digital and analog phones as well as a local PSTN trunk line into a Class 5 central office. Other VoIP cards are installed in the top chassis as well.

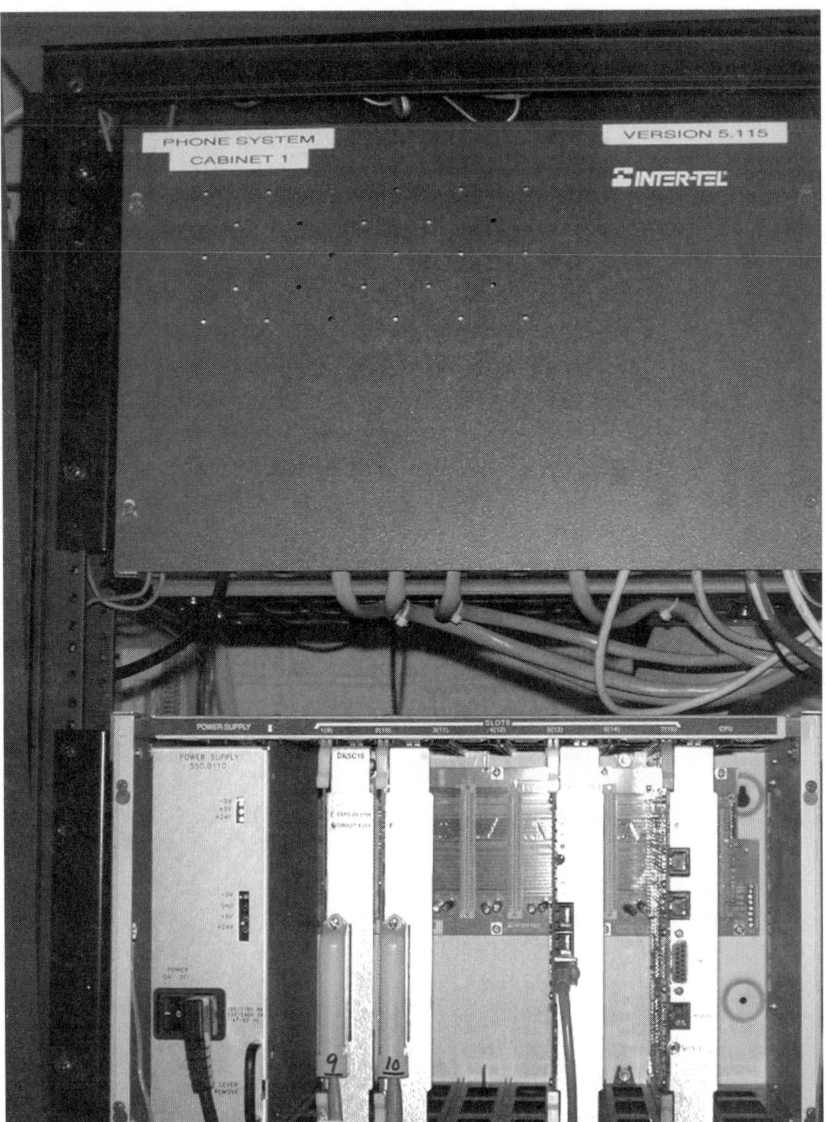

Figure 8.6 VoIP PBX. (Photo courtesy of Ron Harman and Maryland Telephone.)

PSTN-WAN Connections

The VoIP PBX uses standard interfaces to connect to the PSTN. These interfaces include high-speed T-1 (United States), E-1 (international), and ISDN-PRI interfaces. Such interfaces are common to all PBXs. The T-1 interface connects using a V.35 connector, fiber connectors, or an RJ-48C connector. RJ-48C means the T-1 or E-1 digital telephony wires and pin-outs physically terminate in an eight-pin modular plug (MOD-8 or RJ-45 connector). The ISDN Basic Rate Interface S/T is ISDN electrical signaling terminated in an RJ-45 connector.

Lower-speed interfaces include TR08, TR303, Loop Start Analog, and E&M. TR303 or TR08 interfaces are for Digital Loop Carrier (DLC) connections to the PSTN for voice traffic. A Loop Start Analog connection is the same as a single two-wire analog telephone line. Similarly, E&M and tie-line connections are analog connections between switching equipment. The term E&M denotes the telephony tip and ring wires. E&M is sometimes referred to as ear and mouth, indicating the receive function and the transmit function of the leads. E&M may have originated from rEceive and transMit. E&M and tie-line interfaces are four-wire interfaces as opposed to the loop start two-wire analog interface.

To complete PSTN calls a VoIP PBX must interface with SS7. Signaling System 7 performs out-of-band (common channel signaling) signaling to support the call-establishment, billing, routing, and information-exchange functions of the PSTN. It identifies functions to be performed by a signaling-system network and a protocol to perform them.

VoIP PBXs use QSIG (ISDN-PRI-QSIG) to provide signaling for Private Integrated Services Network Exchange (PINX) devices; for example, one corporate VoIP SOHO networked facility to another corporate VoIP SOHO networked facility. QSIG is a global signaling system that links corporate telecommunications networks. QSIG is based on the ISDN Q.931 standard. Using QSIG PRI signaling, a VoIP PBX can route incoming voice calls from a PINX across a WAN to a peer VoIP PBX. This VoIP PBX then transports the signaling and voice packets to its PINX.

A VoIP PBX may also support high-speed interfaces into the Internet, other private IP networks, or directly to other VoIP PBX systems. These connections can run over Frame Relay or ATM networks. Voice running over a Frame Relay network connection uses Q.922 data link protocols and Q.933 Voice over Frame Relay Signaling specifications. The Logical Management Interface (LMI) manages frame relay permanent virtual circuits. Voice IP packet encapsulation into Frame Relay frames is specified by RFC 1490 (RFC 2427) encapsulation. ATM networks use ATM Adaptation Layer 2 (AAL2) or ATM IP encapsulation to support VoIP communications.

LAN Connections

VoIP PBX SOHO LAN connections include 10 Base T connections, 10 Base T-MDI (Medium Dependent Interface) ports for direct connection to 10 Base T hubs, 100 Base T connections, and 100 Base TX connections. Some VoIP PBXs support only 10-Mbps Ethernet, while others support both 10-Mbps and 100-Mbps variations.

Some VoIP components interface to cable modems. They use the Data Over Cable Service Interface Specification (DOCSIS). The newest variation is DOCSIS 1.1, which adds QoS and security features for constant bit rate VoIP telephony. DOCSIS 1.2 is on the horizon. It is aimed at providing higher-speed service for future applications. The DOCSIS specifications are also known as ITU J.112 Data-over-Cable Service Interface Specifications.

Other components are needed to implement a VoIP SOHO LAN, as discussed below.

Multimedia PCs

Multimedia PCs become a VoIP network component with the addition of a soft phone application program. The soft phone program uses a microphone and speakers attached to the PC to turn it into a VoIP telephone. When installed on a laptop PC the soft phone application creates a mobile VoIP telephone that uses a dialup or a high-speed Internet connection to become a remote extension of the central facility VoIP system. Soft phone application software is unique for each VoIP PBX vendor, so that the soft phone-enabled computer fully integrates with its vendor's VoIP PBX features.

VoIP Telephones

VoIP telephones look and operate like a normal digital PBX telephone. This means that, similar to VoIP soft phones, they are designed to integrate fully with the specific features and functions of the VoIP PBX. Inter-Tel Axxess digital Executive phones have the same (or equivalent) control buttons that a regular digital Inter-Tel Axxess VoIP Executive phone has. Consequently, the VoIP telephones integrate with the features and functions provided by the VoIP PBX.

VoIP telephones are commonly configured using a Web browser. The configuration would set up how the IP address was assigned, the codec used (translating into the required VoIP bandwidth), and other similar functions. A typical VoIP telephone is shown in Figure 8.7.

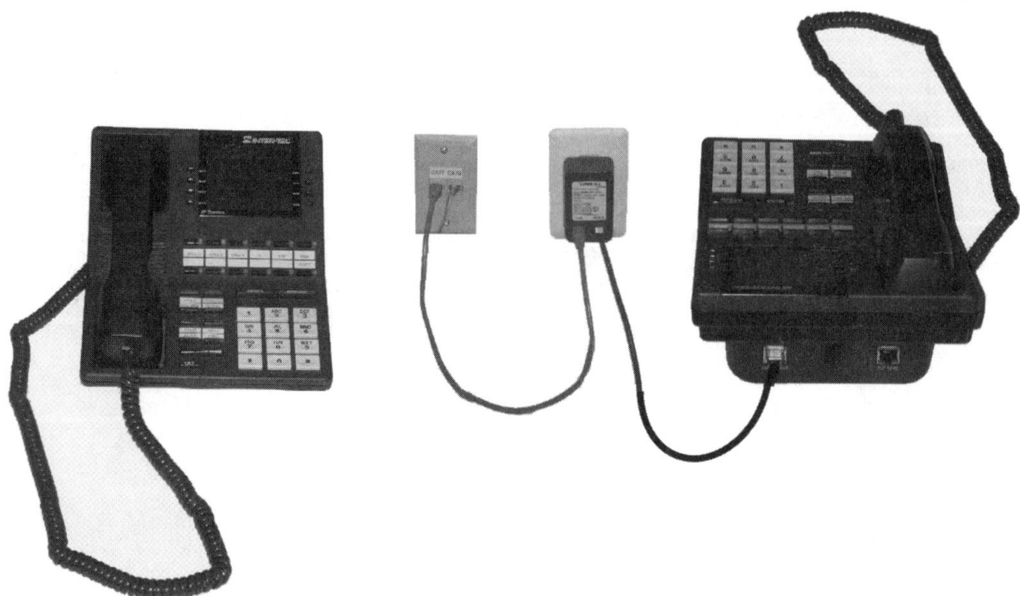

Figure 8.7 Inter-Tel Executive VoIP telephone. (Photo courtesy of Ron Harman and Maryland Telephone.)

The VoIP telephone requires a separate power source that runs through the CAT-5 UTP Ethernet cable into the phone. Ethernet uses two of the four pairs of wires in the CAT-5 Ethernet cable. One pair is the transmit pair and the other is the receive pair. This leaves two unused pairs, one of which Inter-Tel uses to power the phone from a wall socket transformer, as shown in Figure 8.7. The phones can be powered by the PBX when attached to a single head-end run back to the PBX, as long as the cable does not run through any intermediate switches or hubs.

Figure 8.8 shows a close-up of the LAN/power connection and a second hub connection on the VoIP telephone.

This phone permits one CAT-5 cable to be run from a hub to the phone and then extended to a PC host nearby. The only drawback here is that this VoIP phone only supports 10 Base T Ethernet and not 100 Base TX Ethernet. Consequently, connecting a PC host to the SOHO LAN would reduce its speed to 10 MBps.

Figure 8.8 VoIP telephone LAN connections. (Photo courtesy of Ron Harman and Maryland Telephone.)

Brain Teaser: VoIP PBX

Go to the Inter-Tel Web site and download PDF data sheets for its Axxess PBX, SoftPhone, and IP networking module.

What specifications referenced here appear in these data sheets?

Summary

This chapter has discussed VoIP network application configurations and VoIP network components. We examined simple home-office configurations aimed at reducing long-distance telephone costs. These can be quite cost effective when many long-distance and international calls are placed. Otherwise the capital recovery may occur over an extended time period. We also looked at small-office VoIP configurations. They provide a centralized telephone system for an enterprise with many remotely located personnel. With VoIP telephony all VoIP phones attach to a central VoIP PBX as though they were located in a single facility. This has special appeal for call center operations. It may also compete with CENTREX services from a functional and, perhaps in the longer term, a cost standpoint.

The second part of the chapter examined the functions and standards that are found in VoIP PBXs and other VoIP network components. The purpose of each specification in the VoIP component was briefly identified. The goal is to give a sense of what is being indicated in VoIP product literature by these standards. Because VoIP products conform to standards does not mean that they effectively interoperate. At this time the best strategy is to use the VoIP components from a single vendor to implement VoIP telephony in a SOHO LAN.

This chapter discussed several products that are inexpensive enough for most home-office users, especially if they plan to make international calls to children overseas. Further, a small office as large as 150 to 200 PC hosts often employs a PBX (I have 20 PCs and a PBX that is VoIP capable, if I spend another $2,600 for a board and a phone) and may have T-1 PSTN connectivity. VoIP is in some ways very usable for such a facility—or will certainly be so in the next few years. VoIP component prices are most assuredly dropping, making VoIP a component of many small-office LANs.

Key Technical Terms

802.1 p/Q—802.1p assigns priority levels to frames at the Media Access Control (MAC) layer (Layer 2) of the OSI model. The 802.1p standard also filters multicast traffic to ensure it does not proliferate over switched networks. The 802.1p standard works in tandem with 802.1Q VLAN tagging. 802.1Q defines a 32-bit tag header inserted after a frame's normal destination and source address header. Switches, routers, servers, and desktop systems can set 802.1 p/Q priority bits. In VoIP networking the 802.1 p/Q priority mechanism is a means for fulfilling VoIP QoS.

AAL2—ATM Adaptation Layer 2 encapsulates VoIP communications.

ATM—Asynchronous Transfer Mode is a high-speed cell relay networking technology.

Automated attendant answering—Telephones are answered by the robot voice announcing a menu of selections and then finally may ask for an extension number of the person whom you are calling.

Call groups—Telephones specially assigned to a group that all ring simultaneously when a specific number is dialed. The first phone answering the call services the call. My telephones use a call group so that anyone calling causes several phones to ring simultaneously. The person answering the phone first then answers the call.

CAS—Channel Associated Signaling embeds the signaling information in the same channel that carries the voice call. In this sense, DTMF is a form of CAS.

CCS—Common Channel Signaling sends the signaling information over a separate signaling channel. This technique is used in ISDN networks where the signaling information is sent as packets over the D-channel (data channel) separate from the B-channels (bearer channels carrying voice, video, and data).

CNG—Comfort Noise Generation removes dead air at the receiver caused by VAD by inserting simulated background noise during dead air periods.

Codec—Coder/decoder translates an analog voice signal into a digital data stream. The original telephony codec uses pulse code modulation to produce a 64 Kbps representation of a voice-grade (300 Hz to 3,400 Hz) telephone signal.

DOCSIS—The Data Over Cable Service Interface Specification defines requirements for cable modems that are used to distribute high-speed data over cable television networks.

DSI—Digital Speech Interpolation increases transmission efficiency by inserting additional signals from other sources in the transmission stream during silent or inactive periods.

DTMF—Dual Tone Multi-Frequency is the signaling or number dialing technology used by touch tone telephones.

E-1—The high-speed, 30-channel 2,048 Mbps trunk interface to the PSTN used internationally.

E.164—The international public telecommunication numbering plan that provides the number structure and functionality for telephone numbers used for international public telecommunication.

E&M—A four-wire analog connection between telephone switching equipment. E&M may also stand for Earth and magneto as opposed to ear and mouth.

G.165—Echo cancellation specification for normal voice networks.

G.168—Echo cancellation over digital networks for more stringent echo cancellation required in VoIP networks.

G.711—A Pulse Code Modulation (PCM) codec specification producing 64 Kbps digital data stream for a single voice grade channel.

G.726—An Adaptive Pulse Code Modulation (ADPCM) codec producing 16, 24, 32, or 40 Kbps digital streams for a single voice grade channel.

G.728—A Low Delay-Code Excited Linear Prediction (LD-CELP) codec producing 16 Kbps representation of a single voice-grade channel.

G.729—A Conjugate-Structure Algebraic Code Excited Linear Prediction (CS-ACELP) codec producing an eight-Kbps digital data stream for a single voice-grade channel.

H.248—An enhanced ITU specification for MGCP.

H.343—H.323 is the standard for interoperability in audio, video, and data transmission as well as Internet phone and VoIP. A current version is ITU-T H.323-V3.

Hunt groups—Telephones specially assigned to a group that ring when a specific number is dialed. They ring in a predetermined sequence from the first phone in the hunt group to the last phone in the hunt group. Hunt groups are used to implement call centers.

IGMP—Internet Group Management Protocol is used to multicast phone number dialing information to VoIP network components.

IMAP4—Internet Message Access Protocol version 4 is a client/server protocol that works with e-mail received and held on an Internet or VoIP server.

IP-DiffServ—IP Differentiated Services is an approach to differentiate between types of IP packets to provide QoS to VoIP transmission.

IP-ToS—IP Type of Service is a mechanism for providing higher transmission priority to VoIP packets and thus guarantee a higher quality of service.

ISDN-PRI—A high-speed, 23-bearer channel, 1.544-Mbps interface to the PSTN.

J.112—The ITU Data Over Cable Service Interface Specification.

LBR—Low bit rate or low-speed transmission of voice. This is voice transmission at any speed less than 64 Kbps.

LMI—Logical Management Interface in Frame Relay networks manages permanent virtual circuits.

Loop Start Analog Connection—A single two-wire analog telephone line.

Megaco—An enhanced variation of MGCP.

MF—Multi-frequency is an analog tone signaling technique used in telephony networks. MF R1/R2 are variations of multi-frequency signaling.

MGCP—Media Gateway Control Protocol defines communication between a media gateway that converts data from a circuit-switched network format to packet-switched network. MGCP establishes, maintains, and terminates VoIP calls among multiple endpoints.

NCS—Network Call Signaling sets up calls in cable modem networks.

PINX—Private Integrated Services Network Exchange is a private internal enterprise telephone system.

QoS—Quality of service describes the mechanisms that help deliver or guarantee a basic bandwidth or transmission speed to VoIP communications across an IP network. Since IP packets are delivered at best effort, there is no delivery guarantee for bandwidth or priority for VoIP traffic. QoS functions assign higher priority to VoIP traffic and thus provide some bandwidth or transmission speed guarantee.

QSIG (ISDN-PRI-QSIG)—A global signaling system that links corporate telecommunications networks.

RADIUS—Remote Authentication Dial-In Service is a client/server protocol and software used to communicate with a central server, to authenticate dial-in users, and to authorize access to a system.

RIP—Routing Information Protocol routes IP packets in a small network by using distance measurements or hop counts to compare routes. The route with the lowest hop count becomes the best path to a specific destination address.

RJ-48C—Terminates T1 or E1 digital telephony wires and pin-outs in an eight-pin MOD-8 or an RJ-45 Connector.

RTCP—Real-Time Control Protocol monitors data delivery, thus permitting a receiver to detect packet losses and to compensate for latency and jitter. RTCP works with RTP supporting VoIP communications.

RTP—Real-Time Protocol or Real-time Transport Protocol manages real-time multimedia transmission to provide the best transmission quality over an IP network.

SIP—Session Initiation Protocol initiates multimedia sessions or VoIP calls and terminates them.

SNMP—Simple Network Management Protocol is used to configure, monitor, and manage network devices.

Soft Switch—A software-based entity that provides call control functionality. Soft Switch software provides the same service you're used to getting today from a telco switch or an enterprise's PBX. But the important difference between this software and its telco and PBX counterparts is that it's been decomposed into functional elements, like the media gateway (MG), signaling gateway (SG), media gateway controller (MGC), and more. These components are connected by the Media Gateway Control Protocol (MGCP), Megaco (H.248), the Session Initiation Protocol (SIP), and H.323.

SS7—Signaling System 7 provides common channel signaling for call setup, billing, routing, and other information-exchange functions in the public switched telephone network (PSTN).

T-1—The high-speed, 24-channel, 1.544 Mbps trunk interface to the PSTN used in North America.

TAPI—Telephony Application Program Interface is a Windows standard program interface for PCs sending voice or video to other PCs or phone-con-

nected resources. The current client/server implementation of TAPI is TAPI 2.1.

TAPI/WAV—TAPI/Wave Form is an audio file format used to store and exchange voice information with VoIP components.

TFTP—Trivial File Transfer Protocol is used to update VoIP components' non-volatile RAM (NV-RAM).

Tie line—A four-wire dedicated permanent analog connection between telephone switching equipment. Tie lines are not dialed lines but rather full-period, non-switched connections.

TR08 (TR008)—A Digital Loop Carrier (DLC) connection to the PSTN for voice traffic.

TR303—A Digital Loop Carrier (DLC) interface for connecting to the PSTN.

V.35—The connector used to connect copper wire T-1 channels to telephony equipment.

VAD—Voice Activation Detection stops sending IP packets when no speech is present.

Review Questions

1. What is the goal of the simplest VoIP home-office LAN components?

   Answer: To enable reduction of long-distance and international telephone charges.

2. What do A-Law and Mu-Law describe?

   Answer: How the dynamic range of a voice signal is compressed and expanded while minimizing noise. Mu-Law is more universal than A-Law.

3. What is a codec?

   Answer: A codec is a coder/decoder that translates analog voice signals into a digital stream of data. Codecs can compress the signal to a very low bps digital stream.

4. Why use a VoIP PBX?

   Answer: A VoIP PBX can bring together VoIP phones and PBXs in local and remote offices so that they function as one single, large PBX. This is especially good for call centers using telecommuters.

5. What SOHO LAN is supported by VoIP components?

   Answer: Ethernet is the SOHO LAN used by VoIP components. Virtually all VoIP components work with 10 Base T Ethernet and some work with 100 Base TX Ethernet.

6. What are some functions of a VoIP PBX?

   Answer: Some functions of a VoIP PBX are translating voice in IP packets to 64 Kbps PSTN voice, interfacing with PSTN signaling, interconnecting with other VoIP systems servicing other Private Integrated Services Network Exchanges (PINX), and supporting a variety of telephone and network interfaces.

Chapter 9

WRAP-UP

Chapter Syllabus

- SOHO LANs Review
- The Future
- Key Technical Terms
- Put This Book to Use

This chapter reviews the SOHO networks and their use. It summarizes the configurations and costs for these network applications. A look to the future of SOHO networks is presented.

SOHO LANs Review

SOHO networks fulfill a multiplicity of applications, from simple peer-to-peer resource sharing to sophisticated client server configurations supporting mission-critical applications. The simplest of SOHO LANs is a home-office or home-entertainment resource-sharing network permitting PC hosts to share disk drive storage, printers, and high-speed Internet access. Such a network costs around $250 for Network Interface Cards (NICs), an Ethernet cable modem/DSL router/switch, and CAT-5 unshielded twisted pair wiring. A single Wireless Access Point, four-port switch and DSL/cable modem router combination runs $200 and wireless LAN cards run $80 each. Most homes with high-speed Internet access could easily benefit from this simple SOHO LAN configuration.

A more sophisticated small-office configuration would incorporate wireless LAN connections and a VoIP router/switch. The increased cost to add wireless and VoIP technologies can range from several hundred dollars to over tens of thousands of dollars depending upon the capabilities installed. Such a small-office VoIP LAN could realize savings by avoiding substantial LAN wiring coats and by reducing the cost of long-distance and international telephone calls. The VoIP savings should pay for the extra SOHO LAN component costs when the user makes many long-distance and international telephone calls.

Other benefits of a more sophisticated small-office LAN would be better integration of enterprise activities by providing an internal Web site, hosting an Internet Web site for the enterprise, supporting communication with customers and vendors, and integrating order entry and other enterprise business functions into a Web-centric environment. More sophisticated small-office LANs increase the SOHO LAN component investment, but these components in turn increase SOHO LAN functionality, making it more of an integral part of the enterprise's operation. For example, a client/server SOHO LAN configuration with an e-mail post office server, an SQL server, and an IIS server would be used to support internal and external e-mail, mission-critical database applications such as inventory control and client billing, and intranet and extranet Web servers. Integration of these functions in a Web-centric enterprise operation is the key to future enterprise success. While this does not necessarily come cheap, the benefits and productivity increases typically more than outweight the costs, particularly when a network upgrade is already required.

There is no escaping SOHO LANs and the changing technologies surrounding them. For many years in my seminars I predicted that most homes would have their own LAN. Today that is fast becoming true because networking is convenient, cheap, and easy to install and operate.

The Future

We have seen how easy it is to install and operate a SOHO LAN. What will the future bring? Sharing computer resources and Internet access in today's home is as important as everyone in today's home having his or her own PC or PCs. With PCs that can surf the Web dropping in price to around $500, who wants to share his or her PC with anyone? Kids need them for school. We can now use voice-to-text software to control our PCs. In the next several years this will become a standard PC feature. Since such voice recognition works best for individuals, and training of the PC is necessary to have voice recognition work most effectively, everyone will want his or her own non-shared PC. Then sharing information and Internet access via a SOHO LAN becomes necessary for all homes with PCs. Wireless Web cameras can be used to monitor the baby, the bird feeder, the garage, the front door, and more from any household PC.

Along with predicting that every home would have a LAN, I have said as I did in the Introduction to this book that I would have one of the first homes with a LAN connected to the refrigerator. This was a somewhat facetious statement because at the time I felt it would be done, but I was not exactly sure how I would use it. OK, so you do not believe me quite yet. Well, the networked refrigerator exists. There is more than one manufacturer! How do you like them apples? My only wish now is that this book sells enough copies so that I can afford the networked refrigerator. There is no turning back. Anything that you do with a SOHO LAN is critical for your personal and business life. Anything that you learn about PCs, LANs, VoIP, and the Internet is useful to your life today and in the future.

Please also try to keep your common sense when it comes to these new technologies. Do not necessarily—unless you are like me—purchase the leading (or bleeding) edge components because technologies and products change so rapidly. The most effective purchase time for any component is about one to one and one-half years after it is introduced. When new technologies are implemented we tend to make mistakes because we do not understand how to configure them. For example, I just implemented a new combined Internet cable modem router, wireless access point, and four-port switch in my home-office network. When I was configuring the firewall filtering in the switch, there was an SPI option. I had not enabled it. More importantly, I had forgotten that in Chapter 5, Stateful Packet Inspection (SPI) was described. This just illustrates that with technology and products changing all the time, it is very easy to forget or not know how to optimally configure them. "Defaults generally work best" has become my strategy to follow when installing new SOHO network components. As much as I am tempted to try what seems like a better configuration option, following the defaults results in a network that works, while my choice typically has not resulted in a network that works (but I learn something every time—"defaults always work best!").

I have said enough, so just jump into SOHO networking. Have fun and good luck!

Brain Teaser: Networked Refrigerator

Go to your favorite Internet search engine and search for networked refrigerator. Google reveals several news releases and articles including "The Coolest Internet Appliance," which identifies an Electrolux fridge and several press releases for the Whirlpool, Sun Microsystems, and Cisco networked refrigerator project. One of these will be mine....

Key Technical Terms

SPI—Stateful Packet Inspection is a form of packet filtering that examines both packet headers and packet contents. SPI determines more about the packet than just its source and destination. SPI examines packet contents to ascertain that the stated destination computer has previously requested the current communication. This is to ensure that all communications are initiated by a recipient computer and are from Web sources known and trusted from previous interactions. Stateful packet inspection firewalls close off ports until connection to a specific port is requested by a PC host application. This provides protection from port scanning threats.

Put This Book to Use

Having spent money on this book, why not put that money to use? Please write down 10 things that you will personally do as a consequence of reading this book. They can be as simple as shopping for a wireless access point, reconfiguring your router/firewall, or buying a second PC and networking your PCs. You have come this far, so why not? Review and revise this list in six months. If you do, this activity benefits you. Thanks.

Appendix

MULTIMEDIA PC ENTERTAINMENT SYSTEM NETWORKING

Chapter Syllabus

- Multimedia PC Entertainment System Components
- Multimedia PC Entertainment System Functions
- Networking a Multimedia PC Entertainment System
- Summary
- Key Technical Terms
- Review Questions

An emerging PC application is multimedia PC entertainment. Such systems use a large flat-panel monitor, a multimedia PC with 5.1 surround sound, DVD drive, and a TV tuner graphics card to perform multimedia entertainment center functions. What is an executive office without a TV and music? So, as a bonus, we need to look at multimedia PC entertainment systems.

Multimedia PC entertainment systems display TV programs and DVD movies, surf the Web, encode and play MP3 music, and much more. Once you have a television controlled by a PC there is no going back to regular TV. It is convenient to be able to surf the Web and check the weather radar, or go to the NBC Web site for details on a TV story while at the same time watching TV. A 42-inch plasma monitor helps as well by providing sufficient space to view TV and Web sites simultaneously. The PC permits taking pictures from the TV, recording programs on disk for instant playback, writing e-mail while viewing, and other functions. This is a way too cool application of PC and SOHO LAN technologies.

Among the entertainment functions such a system performs are that it:

1. Plays television programs from a TV antenna or cable TV source
2. Records TV programs for later playback
3. Captures images from TV programs
4. Plays DVDs
5. Plays MP3 files
6. Plays CD audio discs
7. Rips CD audio discs into MP3 files
8. Surfs the Web
9. Acts as an e-mail system
10. Gets digital images from new digital cameras (requires digital camera)
11. Acts as a security monitoring system using new Web cameras (requires Web cameras and software)
12. Prints images in color (requires color printer)
13. Runs essential applications like Microsoft Streets 2002, Quicken, and more

These functions and the components that support them are examined in detail in this chapter. This chapter shows how to build and use such a multimedia entertainment PC. Connecting a multimedia entertainment center PC to the Internet using a SOHO network is discussed.

Multimedia PC Entertainment System Components

The basic components for a multimedia PC entertainment system driven by a PC include a basic PC that runs at 1 GHz or better with an AMD Athlon, Pentium 4, or Pentium III CPU. Other CPUs would work, but remember that the system is going to be performing intensive multimedia processing functions.

The system should have 256, or better yet, 512 MB RAM. It is best to run Windows XP or Windows 2000. While other Windows operating systems will work, Windows XP and Windows 2000 are more reliable and targeted at multimedia entertainment.

To this basic PC system are added some special components. The components added do not have to be as specialized as the components suggested here, but to get maximum bragging rights you need to go whole hog and get top-of-the-line components. The specialized components include:

1. A specialized graphics card that acts as a TV tuner
2. A flat-panel monitor or big-screen monitor
3. A 5.1 surround sound card
4. A DVD drive
5. A CD/RW drive
6. A cordless keyboard and mouse
7. A LAN connection
8. Web cams
9. Software

Most PC graphics and audio cards have more than enough features to construct a sophisticated multimedia PC entertainment system. Let's look at each of these components individually so we can see just what features are essential and important for building a multimedia entertainment PC system.

Brain Teaser: Home Entertainment PC Systems

Use the Google search Web site (*www.google.com*) to search for home entertainment PC systems.

What did you find? I found a Speedy 3D article (*www.speedy3d.com/articles/builda_het/01.shtml*) that extols the cost and space-saving virtues of creating your own multimedia entertainment PC system.

Graphics Card

The first and central component to our multimedia PC entertainment system is the graphics card. This card drives our display. Most fast graphics cards work here, but special features are needed for a multimedia PC entertainment system. Basically we want to do the following:

1. View television
2. Record from television
3. Interface with a 5.1 speaker system

4. Input video from a camcorder or VHS deck
5. Run DVDs

In some cases all features are available on a single card and in others the TV features are separated from the graphics card driving the PC's monitor. Three companies that produce such TV tuning cards are Creative Labs, Matrox, and ATI.

The Creative Labs Digital Blaster VCR card is a TV tuning card by itself that works in conjunction with another graphics card. The benefit here is that the Creative Labs card is inexpensive and you can use any existing graphics card. It has inputs for composite and S-video, stereo audio, and CATV antennae. The software displays the images on the PC monitor and permits capturing video as MPEG-2 files on the PC's disk drive for later viewing, capturing stills, and other functions.

The Matrox Marvel G450 eTV card can use dual monitors. One monitor is a standard TV and the other is a PC display. TV can be viewed on a television while working as a PC on the other PC monitor. Similar to the Creative Labs card, the Matrox card can connect to standard AV composite, S-video, and stereo audio inputs from camcorders and VCRs. It can also send composite, S-video, and mini-jack audio outputs to a TV or VCR. At the same time it is connected to a normal PC monitor. In addition to capturing TV to disk it can operate both the TV and PC display in several modes. Both displays can be used as dual PC monitors (although TV resolution, being lower than PC resolution, can make the TV display appear extra large compared with the TV display), one display can blow up the image on the other display, the TV display can show TV while the PC display surfs the Web, or both displays can display the same image, with the TV display providing a very large image.

The ATI card drives a single digital or analog monitor and provides a variety of signal inputs and outputs. Figure A.1 shows the ATI All-In-Wonder Radeon graphics card with (from left to right) the video and audio input connector, the CATV coaxial connector, the video and audio output connector, and the DVI-I (Digital Visual Interface-Integrated) digital video output connector. The ATI digital video to analog RGB adapter is on the right, next to the All-In-Wonder Radeon board.

This board uses ATI's Radeon graphics processing unit, cooled by the heat sink and fan. The rear connectors attach to two special cables that provide more standard audio/video (AV) interfaces for camcorders, VCR decks, television monitors, and AV receivers. The input cable is shown at the top of Figure A.2 and the AV output cable is connected near the middle of the ATI graphics card.

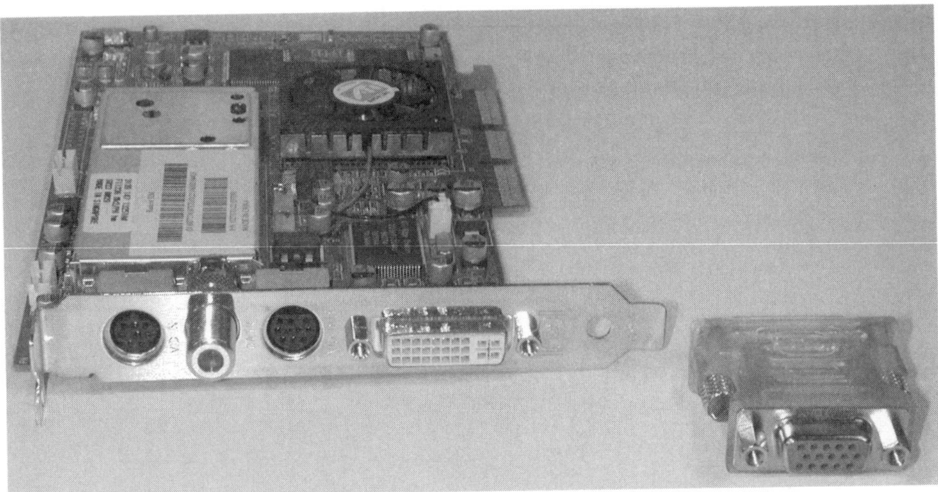

Figure A.1 ATI graphics board connectors.

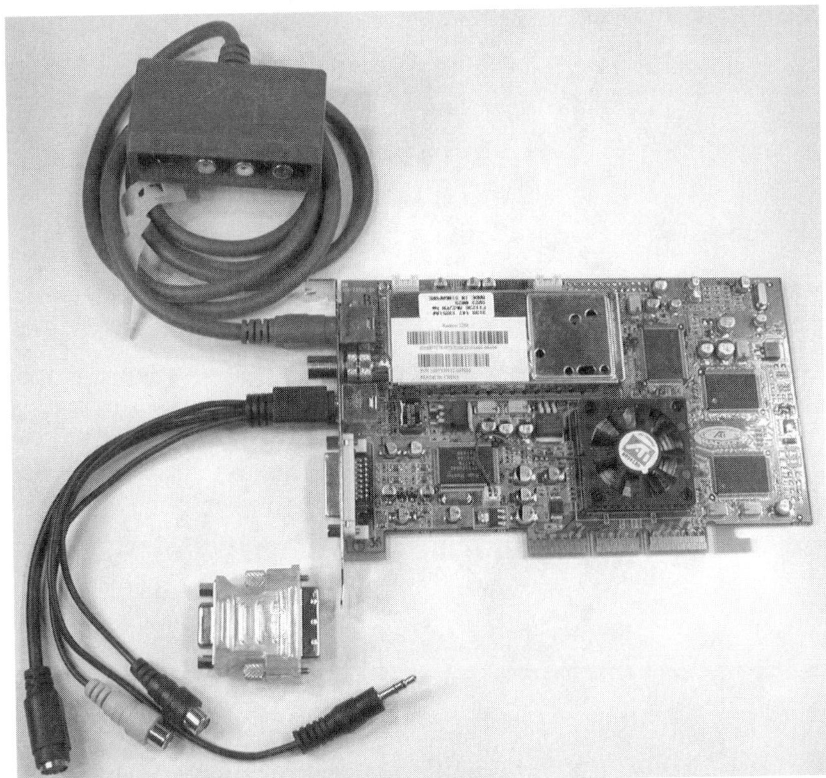

Figure A.2 ATI graphics board cabling and connectors.

These special cables provide composite video and S-video input and output connections. The input connections are shown close up in Figure A.3.

The four-pin S-video input connector is on the left in the figure for camcorders, VCR decks, and other video devices providing S-video output. Otherwise a yellow composite video jack is provided. The white left and red right stereo audio inputs are on the right side in the figure. Output connector details are shown in Figure A.4.

Similar to the input connectors, the output connectors include on the left a four-pin S-video connector, a composite video connector, and two audio output connectors. One connector is a coaxial cable output connector and the other is a stereo mini-jack connector. Table A.1 lists the types of video connectors and how they are used.

Figure A.3
ATI graphics board video and audio input connectors.

Figure A.4
ATI graphics board video and audio output connectors.

Table A.1 Video Connectors.

Connector Type	Shape	Use
Composite video	Round RC jack	TV monitor Low-quality video
S-video	Mini DIN 4-pin connector	TV monitor Medium-quality video
Analog RGB	D-shaped 15-pin connector	PC monitor High-quality resolution
DVI-I Digital Visual Interface—Integrated	D-shaped 28-pin connector or D-shaped 15-pin adapter	Flat-panel monitor High-quality resolution
DVI-D Digital Visual Interface—Digital	D-shaped 24-pin connector	Flat-panel monitor High-quality resolution
Component video connectors	BNC Three round push-and-turn connectors	AV system or monitor High-quality resolution

The newest ATI Radeon card is the All-In-Wonder Radeon 8500 DV. It supports DVD, viewing TV from 125 stereo TV channels, recording TV from any channel, and capturing and editing other video inputs. Similar to the All-In-Wonder Radeon card the All-In-Wonder Radeon 8500 DV card supports a variety of AV inputs and outputs. It adds IEEE 1394 (FireWire) iLink support for direct connection to and control of digital video camcorders.

These connections support a wide variety of AV configurations. Figure A.5 explores a possible configuration with the PC set up as a TV and DVD player. In this case a large plasma screen is used that has a VGA input connecting directly to an analog VGA output from the graphics card. The graphics card also connects into the CATV system and acts as the TV tuner using special TV tuning software. An AV receiver connects to a VCR and to a 5.1 speaker system. Outputs from both the graphics card and the sound card drive 5.1 speakers through the AV receiver. Some programs send sound output through the sound card while others send it out through the graphics card, so both connections to the AV receiver that drive the speakers are needed.

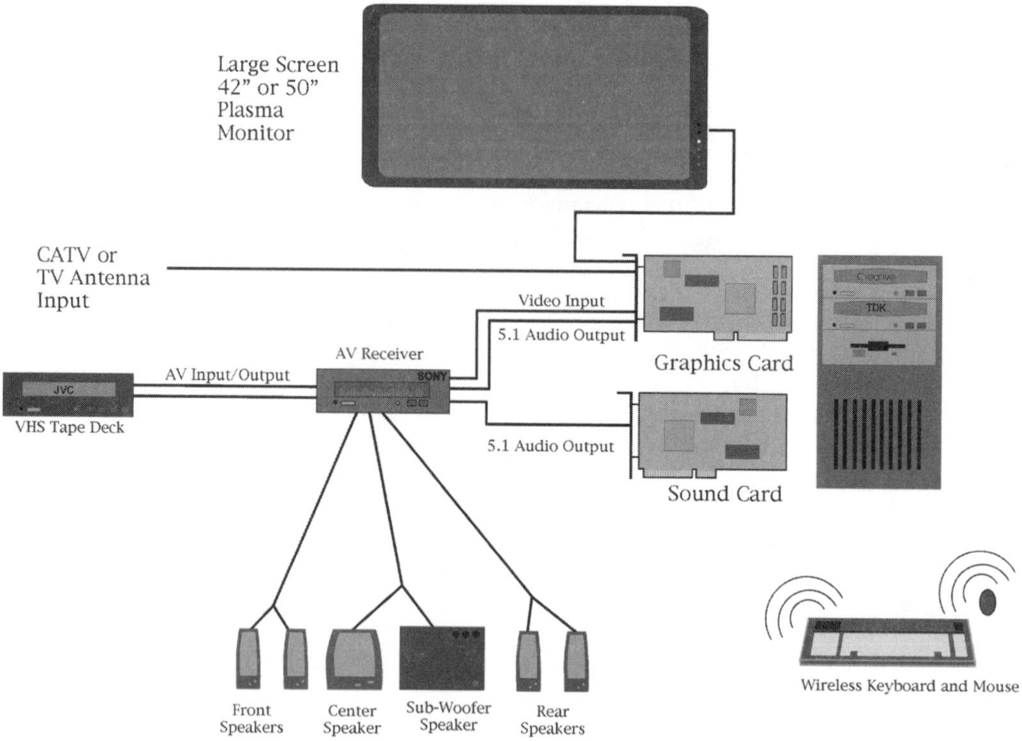

Figure A.5 Graphics card AV configuration.

In the example the AV receiver is needed because it supplies the power to drive the speakers. With the PC audio card, the outputs can produce sound on speakers, but powered speakers or speakers driven by external power are needed to realize theater-quality sound. In every case the subwoofer speaker needs to be powered because the bass sound it produces requires lots of power. The other speakers can be driven enough by the power from the sound card to produce the good quality higher frequency sounds.

The AV receiver can interconnect other AV components like VCR decks and DVD players to the PC. The main advantage here is that video can be stored on the PC's hard drive as an MPEG-2 file. This permits editing and publishing to the Web when encoded for Real Audio replay.

The dual audio connections in this configuration point out the complexity of configuring a multimedia entertainment PC system. There are just so many options it is difficult to determine exactly what hardware connections to make and what supporting software to run in the PC. There are enough jacks and connectors to confuse even Plug-Head (a character in a C sci-fi movie).

The AV connections in the configuration would use either S-video or composite video and then right and left audio connections. The 5.1 speaker connections would be made using a TosLink fiber cable or a digital coaxial cable connection. These connections would produce full 5.1 speaker sound for DVDs and enhanced surround sound for TV playback. TV is broadcast mainly in stereo sound. HDTV is broadcast in 5.1 speaker sound. Few HDTV broadcasts are available unless they come from specific direct broadcast satellites.

When configuring a TV graphics card you will not use all the AV connections. However, the large variety of connections and capabilities permit flexible configuration. The more options the graphics card provides, the more it can be tailored to your specific needs. More options permit you to start with some basic capabilities like receiving TV from antenna or cable and having the PC act as a VCR, and then later expand capabilities to permit the PC to become a video editing station for the camcorder tapes you have accumulated. This may be necessary as technology progresses from VHS tape to DVD or other media.

Brain Teaser: TV Graphics Cards

Search the Web for graphics cards that provide TV monitor functionality. Use the Google search site to search for graphics cards with TV antenna input.

What did you find? There was listed a CNET hardware review Web page (*computers.cnet.com/hardware/1,10121,0-1110-402-0,00.html*) that listed some 59 different products. Many of the products are video capture devices for connecting to digital camcorders, but quite a few are TV tuners. The Hauppauge TV tuner card mentioned in the Speedy 3D article is listed and reviewed. Its cost is around $50. Some USB TV tuner cards are also listed. These plug into a USB port on the PC and act as a TV tuner.

Check out the Tom's Hardware Guide article on TV tuner cards (*www4.tomshardware.com/video/00q2/000418/index.html*). It lists some analog and digital TV tuner cards that are needed for digital cable TV.

Monitor

The monitor used can be a TV monitor or a PC monitor. TV monitors are usually larger in size than PC monitors. This can make them more appealing than PC monitors, but size does not always matter. PC monitors typically have higher resolution than TV monitors. Further, they are becoming quite large in size. Let's examine some basic monitor characteristics, as shown in Table A.2.

Table A.2 Monitor Size, Resolution, and Price.

Monitor Type	Size	Resolution	Cost
Small PC CRT	15 inch	1,024 by 768	$200
Small PC flat panel	15 inch	1,024 by 768	$400
Medium PC CRT	21 inch	1,600 by 1,200	$400
Medium PC flat panel	18 inch	1,280 by 1,024	$1,000
Large PC CRT	24 inch	1,600 by 1,200	$1,700
Large PC flat panel	20 inch	1,600 by 1,200	$1,500
Small TV	26 inch	525 by 300	$400
Large TV	34 inch	800 by 600	$1,800
Plasma display	42 inch	1,024 by 768	$4,000
Plasma display	50 inch	1,280 by 768	$6,500

The premier monitor for a multimedia PC entertainment system would be a plasma monitor. The prices are dropping, so a 42-inch plasma display runs under $5,000. This is significantly less than the $6,500 I paid for my Sony 42-inch plasma display some time ago.

Any monitor works as a TV monitor. Further, since most graphics boards support both a PC monitor and a TV monitor, you can run both at the same time. The only drawback to dual monitors is that you soon run out of mounting space for both monitors. Further, the PC monitor tends to be smaller than the TV monitor so you must be close to it to read it.

The key for picking a monitor is the different connections it supports. The greater the number of connections and the greater the variety of connections, the easier it is to integrate the monitor into your multimedia PC entertainment system. As a minimum, a monitor should support an S-video connection as well as a PC VGA connection. Some typical plasma panel connections are shown in Figure A.6.

The Sony plasma monitor permits switching between the inputs using an infrared remote control. The audio inputs are also switched by the monitor so that if it were to receive video input from several sources, the infrared control could be used to switch both the audio and video from those sources. The video would be displayed on the monitor, and the audio would be output on

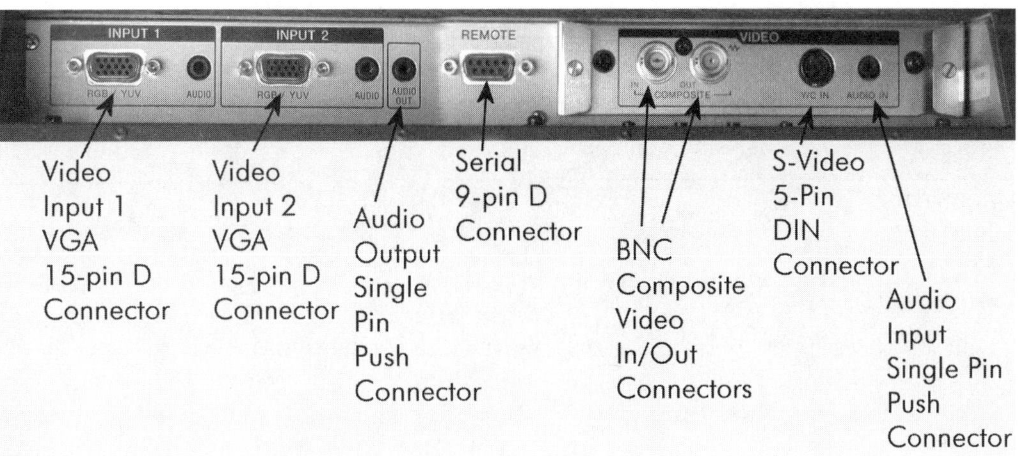

Figure A.6 Typical plasma monitor video and audio connectors.

the single audio output that presumably would be connected to a speaker system. This illustrates that when used with a multimedia PC entertainment system, many TV and monitor features are not connected.

The main function of the plasma display is to display video output. TV tuning, VCR functions, and DVD functions are performed by the PC, and 5.1 speaker output is generated by the PC when 5.1 sound information is encoded on a DVD or in a TV broadcast. So the TV tuner functions and audio switching functions are not performed by the TV display. In some cases the front speakers of a 5.1 speaker system may be the TV monitor speakers. In that case audio information would need to be supplied to the TV speakers.

Rows of horizontal and vertical pixels create pictures on a monitor. The native resolution is the physical resolution of a display and not the resolution of a delivered signal. When the delivered signal resolution differs from a flat panel's native resolution, the delivered signal is translated to the flat panel's native resolution by an internal converter.

The closer the incoming picture resolution is to the native resolution of the monitor, the better the picture. On my Sony plasma panel, this resolution is 1,024 by 768. On other panels it varies upwards to 1,280 by 768. Since my PC's graphics card output can be set to the monitor's native resolution, I get a very good picture. If the Sony panel had a lower 800 by 600 native resolution, the displayed image would not be as good when the PC's graphics card was set to 1,024 by 768 resolution.

There are other considerations dealing with the quality of the internal converter. Picture quality also depends upon whether the monitor is progressively scanned or interlaced. Forty-two inch plasma displays are HDTV ready, but few match exactly with true HDTV signals of 1080i (1,080 lines interlaced).

All monitors benefit from better signal and display better images as a result. Native plasma panel resolutions include 1,024 by 1,024; 1,024 by 768; 1,280 by 768; 1,365 by 768; 640 by 480; 825 by 480; and 853 by 480.

Plasma panels and TV displays can perform different aspect ratio shifts and zoom functions independent of the PC display card's output. The standard TV aspect ratio is 4:3 (normalized to 1.33:1), which produces a nearly square picture. High-definition TV uses an aspect ratio of 16:9 (normalized to 1.77:1). DVD movies use different aspect ratios including 2.35:1, 1.85:1, and 1.66:1. The DVD aspect ratios are in most cases higher than both the standard TV and HDTV aspect ratios. This means that even on HDTV screens, DVD movies appear in letterbox format unless the video is zoomed into full screen.

Zooming in on a picture causes distortion. It makes the picture wider and people appear wider (fatter) than they actually are. The zooming effect in plasma panels tries to keep the center part of the panel correctly proportioned while stretching the left and right sides of the picture horizontally. Since people focus on the center of the image, this gives them a sense of a wider image, but one that is not exactly crystal clear on the edges. This type of zooming produces acceptable images.

After monitors, the next key component of our multimedia PC entertainment system is the sound card.

Brain Teaser: Plasma Monitors

Check the Electrified Discounters site (Electrified.com then plasma displays or *www.electrifieddiscounters.com/plasma.html*) for current prices on plasma monitors.

What price did you find for the Sony PFM 42-B1? I paid $6,500 delivered in 2000. What could I get today for the same price? How about the nice Pioneer PDP-502MX plasma display panel? What is its native resolution? Although Electrified advertises UXGA as an accepted resolution, the native resolution is 1,280 by 768.

5.1 Sound Board

Sound cards convert digitally formatted sound into analog wave forms that produce sound on speakers. In some cases sound cards output digital sound directly to AV receivers that in turn convert the digital sound into analog speaker outputs. Sound boards decode AC-3 formats to drive 5.1 speaker systems. Sound boards provide both analog and digital speaker outputs. Some digital outputs use TosLink fiber cable connections. The digital outputs run into an AV receiver with an AC-3 decoder that decodes the digital signal (converting it to analog signals to the speakers), and also provides the power needed to drive the speakers.

To connect to a variety of speaker systems, some sound boards come with a second or child connector/driver board. This is illustrated in Figure A.7.

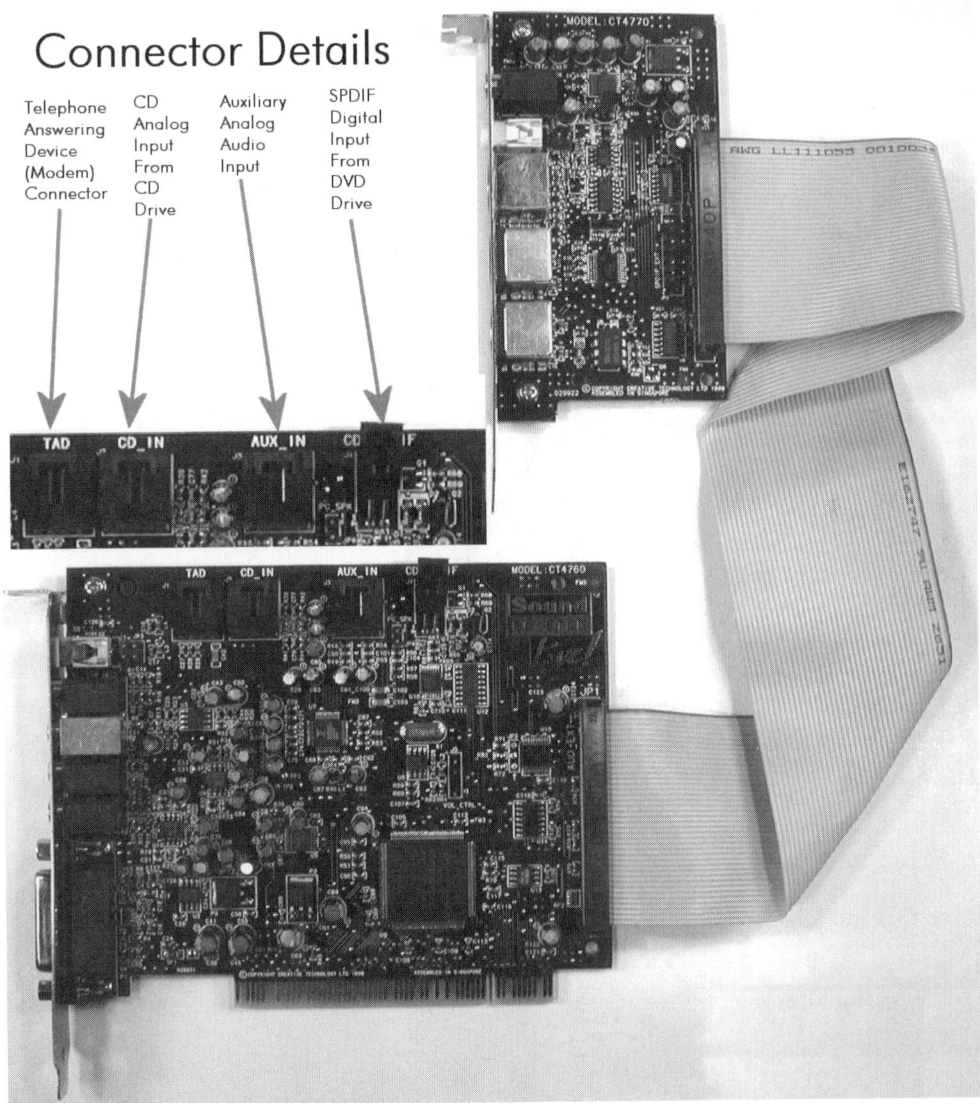

Figure A.7 5.1 surround sound board.

The connector details in the figure illustrate the internal connections to the sound board. The most typical connection is the CD stereo input from a CD-ROM drive. There is also an auxiliary analog input for a second CD or DVD drive's analog stereo output. The SPDIF connector goes to a DVD drive's SPDIF digital output so that 5.1 encoded digital sound on DVDs can be played through the sound board. The last internal connector is for a telephone answering device. This permits specially equipped modems to act as voice answering machines. The connection would go to one of these specially equipped modems.

The audio connectors provided by both the audio board and the child connector/driver board are shown in Figure A.8.

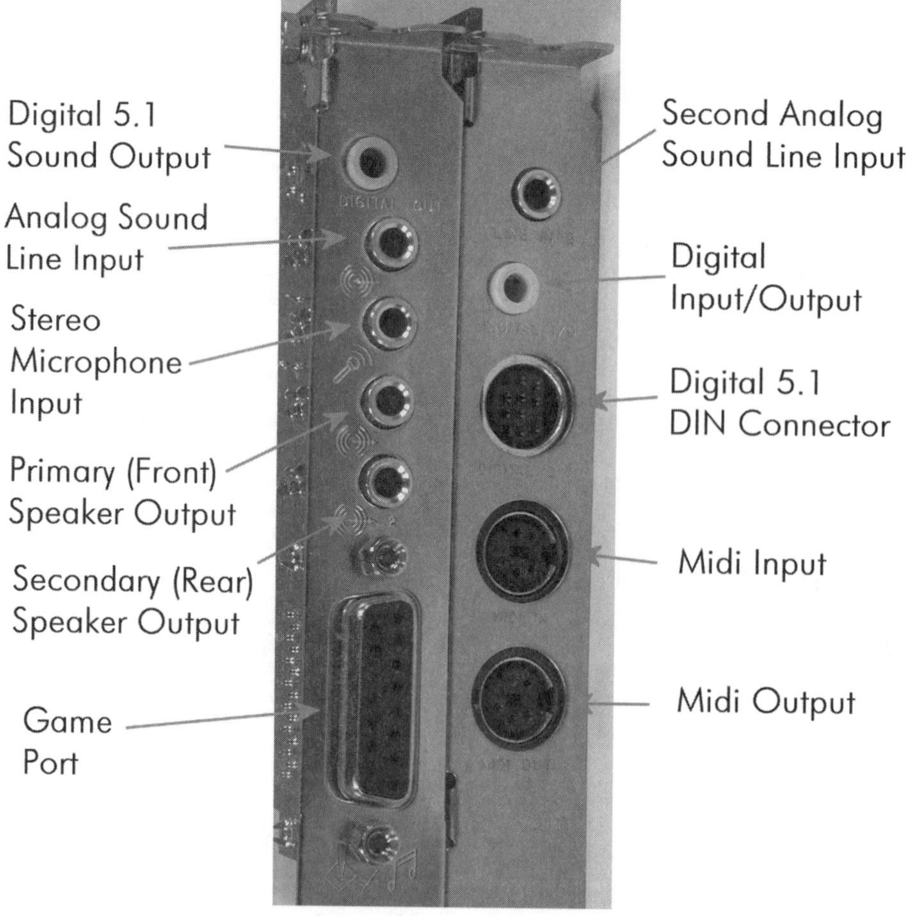

Figure A.8 Sound board connectors.

The left side connectors are those on the sound board and the right connectors are those on the child connector/driver board. The top-left connector provides the digital 5.1 speaker system output. It connects to a 5.1 speaker system using a mini-jack-to-DIN cable or a special digital output cable that provides optical TosLink. Figure A.9 shows a cable that converts the digital output from the mini-DIN jack on the sound card to TosLink or SPDIF coaxial cable connections for delivery to an AV receiver.

The other connectors on the sound card are stereo analog line inputs to permit other AV components to feed sound to the sound board, stereo microphone input (providing equivalent functionality to the line in jack), front and rear speaker analog outputs that would drive amplified speakers, and a game port to connect joystick and other game controller devices. The child driver/connector card adds a second analog line input, a second digital input/output connector, a mini-DIN 5.1 SPDIF output connector, and MIDI input and output connectors.

A benefit from using the TosLink fiber cables to connect speakers is that they provide no electrical connections between AV components.

Typical 4.1 and 5.1 speaker configurations with a sound board are diagrammed in Figure A.10. The top configuration uses the analog speaker outputs from the sound board to drive powered speakers. These speakers are a 4.1 speaker system. In reality the subwoofer is not a separate channel as it is on the 5.1 digital system but rather analog filters route the low-frequency sound to the subwoofer speaker and the high frequency sounds to the front speakers. The rear speaker sound is fed directly to powered rear speakers to produce the surround sounds.

In the second digital configuration the 5.1 speaker digital output is sent directly to an AV receiver. The AV receiver decodes the digital signal into the

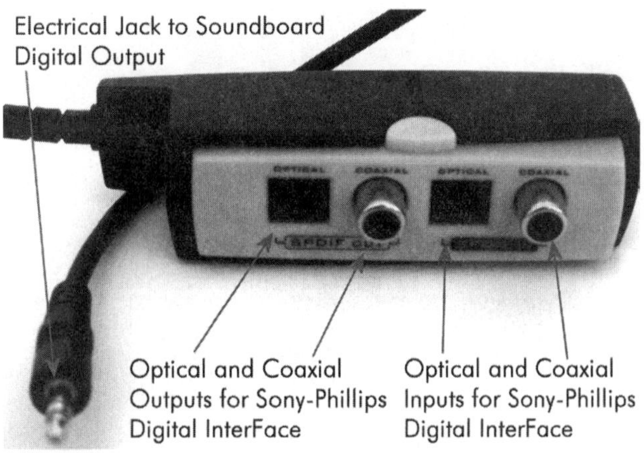

Figure A.9
Sound to digital optical conversion.

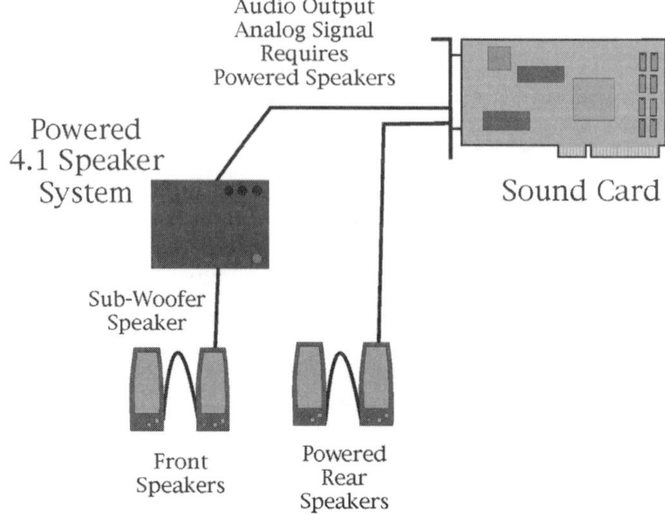

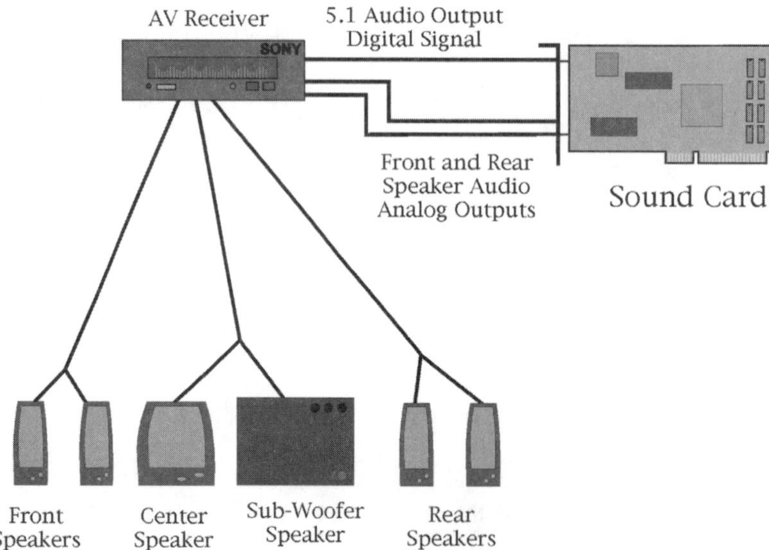

Figure A.10 Sound card/speaker configurations.

five discrete channels and the Low-Frequency Effects (LFE) channel (6 channels total) converts them to analog wave forms and then routes them to the appropriate speakers.

Digital 5.1 sounds are only produced for DVDs and not for regular TV broadcasts because normal TV is only broadcast in stereo sound. This also means that to hear both DVD 5.1 sound and TV sound, both the digital and the analog speaker outputs from the sound board need to be sent to an AV receiver. The AV receiver in turn routes both digital and analog sound outputs from the PC's sound card to the speakers.

Good sound depends upon good speakers. The next key component in our PC multimedia entertainment system is the speakers.

Speakers

Speaker systems have several configurations. They can be described as:

- 2.0 configuration—This would be a simple two-speaker stereo configuration. The speakers would be powered and accept analog input signals from the PC sound board's front speaker outputs.
- 2.1 configuration—This configuration would be a stereo speaker arrangement with a single subwoofer speaker. The speakers would be attached to the sound board's front speaker outputs. The subwoofer would be driven by a crossover matrix or filter, which routes low-frequency signals to the subwoofer and higher-frequency signals to the stereo speakers.
- 4.1 configuration—This configuration is identical to the 2.1 configuration, with the addition of two rear stereo speakers. The system produces four-channel sound from the sound board, with the subwoofer deriving its signals from the low-frequency analog signals sent to the front speakers.
- 5.1 configuration—This configuration uses the AC-3 digital output from the sound board. The AC-3 output has five discrete channels of sound and a LFE channel. This must be sent to a decoder that splits out the individual channels and sends them as amplified analog outputs to the appropriate speakers. Some 5.1 speaker systems perform the decoding themselves, particularly if they are designed to be connected to a PC sound board. The Creative Labs Inspire speaker systems perform such decoding as well as simultaneously accepting analog sound outputs from a sound card. They have a digital DIN input connector, a SPDIF coaxial input connector, a SPDIF TosLink optical input connector, a front analog line input connector, a rear analog line input connector, and a center/subwoofer analog line-in connector. In other words they cover all bases.
- 6.1 configuration—This is a 5.1 configuration with an extra speaker. To drive the speakers and derive the maximum surround sound effects, additional decoding of the digital signal is required. The extra speaker sounds are digitally derived from the AC-3 digital signal.
- 7.1 configuration—Similar to the 6.1 speaker configuration, the 7.1 speaker configuration is a 5.1 configuration with two extra speakers. The

added speaker outputs must be digitally derived from the AC-3 digital output of the PC sound board.

Good sound production depends upon good speakers. Real audiophiles go for only the very best speakers, or at least the speaker systems that sound best to them. With that said I can say for myself that adding a subwoofer to any speaker system makes it sound hugely better regardless of the speaker quality. A subwoofer is what makes the starship Enterprise throb when playing a *Star Trek* DVD. The subwoofer adds a dimension missing from normal speaker systems. Obviously, I am no audiophile and do not pretend to be one, either.

At any rate, any speaker system with a subwoofer is good from my viewpoint. It could be a 2.1, 4.1, or 5.1 speaker system for me. The extra speakers increase the spatial aspects of the sound, but good old stereo with a subwoofer can sound just fine.

Some speaker systems send sounds to the speakers using wireless communication or power line communication (sending signals through household power outlets). These speakers solve the problems of special wiring, which is the key to their salability.

Brain Teaser

Check the sound board in your PC. What outputs does it have?

Did you find four-channel analog speaker outputs? Did the sound card have a digital output? The digital output works only with DVDs and other video sources containing AC-3 encoded sound. Normal analog TV sends sounds out on the four-channel speaker outputs.

DVD Drive/CD-RW Drive

A DVD drive is essential for a multimedia entertainment PC system. It plays DVDs. This can provide a better DVD picture than some DVD players because the PC's monitor output is an analog RGB output, which is better than an S-video feed to the monitor.

The DVD player should have a SPDIF interface to feed digital sound to the PC's sound card. This is necessary to get the full surround sound with subwoofer (making the starship Enterprise rumble) effect. The faster a DVD drive the better. Speed is measured in X increments. Typical DVD drives run at 16X or 16 times faster than the original CD-ROM speed. They also act as a CD-ROM drive running at 40X. Some DVD drives also operate as DVD, CD-

ROM, and CD-RW combined drives. Their speed is slower than a DVD/CD-ROM drive combination. Toshiba offers one of them that has an 8X CD-R, an 8X CD-RW, an 8X DVD, and a 32X CD-ROM.

Most DVD drives come with DVD playing software that is independent of the graphics board used. One such player is the CyberLink PowerDVD player. It comes with many DVD drives and plays most DVDs. Some DVDs come with a software DVD player installed on them. If no other DVD player attempts to play the DVD, then this player self-installs and plays the DVD. See Figure A.11.

The PowerDVD software complies with Microsoft's DirectX technology. PowerDVD software uses DirectDraw to access hardware directly and increase graphics speed. With the matching hardware PowerDVD software can use the advanced video acceleration functions of display chips. When these video acceleration functions are activated, DVD playback is accelerated by transferring approximately 70 percent of the DVD decoding process onto the video card.

Figure A.11 PowerDVD software player.

The key to finding good DVD software is to test the software in the specific multimedia entertainment PC system.

A multimedia entertainment PC system can also use a fast CD-RW drive to burn MP3 files into CDs or save MPEG clips for future playback. A fast CD-RW drive is the TDK 32X/10X/40X drive. This CD-RW drive can burn CDs at 32X, write CD-RWs at 10X, and read CDs at 40X.

Cordless Keyboard and Mouse

To control a multimedia entertainment PC system from across a room, a cordless mouse and keyboard are needed. The important consideration here is how far from the RF transceiver unit the cordless mouse and keyboard can be and still operate properly. Generally, these units operate at a distance of 6 feet, which is not very far. Keep in mind that the typical family room is 12 feet by 16 feet. Some cordless units advertise an 8-foot range. All I can say here is that more is better and by all means use good batteries. Bad batteries cause cordless keyboards and mice to fail, particularly when they are at the edge of their operating range.

Some display cards come with an infrared or an RF remote control that controls the TV features from across a room just like it would control a TV/VCR system. This would work when operating the TV functions on a multimedia entertainment PC system.

Web Cameras

Every multimedia entertainment system needs a Web camera for capturing video and still images, permitting them to be sent in e-mail. Some key Web camera parameters are the capture resolution and rate. The resolution is the number of dots in the display being captured and the rate of capture is the frames per second captured at that resolution. An excellent camera operates at 640 by 480 resolution, capturing those images at a 30 frames per second rate.

Most Web cameras use a USB connection. The caution here is that they should not share that USB link with other devices. A USB link runs at the speed of the slowest device attached to the USB link. Mice and keyboards cause the USB link to run at 1.5 Mbps. Top USB link speed is 12 Mbps and moving to 480 Mbps with USB 2. A Web camera needs to operate at the highest USB speed of 12 Mbps to provide the highest resolution at 30 frames per second. A 640 by 480 image at 30 frames per second can easily generate about a 10 Mbps stream of data.

Once installed, Web cameras work with Microsoft's NetMeeting software. NetMeeting supports interactive video and other types of information exchange across a network.

LAN Connection

What makes a multimedia entertainment PC system very cool is that it can be networked to surf the Web at the same time it is playing a DVD or displaying a TV program. A wireless network connection provides sufficient speed to perform most Web browsing and other data transfers. The wireless LAN connection is needed to download TV schedules from the Web, send and receive e-mail, maintain the software on the PC, download or exchange MP3 files, and more. MP3 files are the only data-intensive transfer function in this group. Video captures from the Web camera and the TV can also generate large files that may demand significant capacity wireless LAN transmission to transfer.

During the Winter Olympics, while viewing the delayed broadcast events, I could display the daily results of the events by surfing the NBC Olympic Web site. Similarly, a football game could be watched while at the same time having the NFL.com Web site game summary displayed side by side on the screen. Or, alternatively you could be viewing cable headline news and reading detailed stories posted at news Web sites.

Brain Teaser: Cordless Mice and Keyboards

Check out cordless keyboards and mice at a local computer grocery store (Best Buy, Staples, or CompUSA).

Were there cordless keyboard/mouse combination products that provide optical mice? If you were to get a Logitech keyboard/mouse combination and then get a standalone optical mouse, the optical mouse could be substituted for the cordless combination mouse since they both use the same RF frequencies and transmission protocols. At what distance does the cordless keyboard/mouse operate from the transceiver connecting it to the PC? 6 feet? 8 feet? 10 feet?

Software

Windows XP is aimed at home entertainment and multimedia PC features. As an operating environment Windows XP seems like the first choice and Windows 2000 would be the second choice. However, because Microsoft's draconian copy-protection scheme implemented in Windows XP can make Windows XP PCs difficult to upgrade and maintain, Windows 2000 is the better OS choice.

Application software coming with the graphics card and with the DVD player provides the TV and DVD playing functions in the PC multimedia entertainment system. Further, Microsoft's media player that plays MP3s and other music is the same for Windows XP and Windows 2000. The sound board applications are provided by the sound board manufacturer and not by Microsoft. Consequently, whether you use Windows XP or Windows 2000 has virtually no impact on the performance of a multimedia entertainment PC system.

Multimedia PC Entertainment System Functions

The functions of a multimedia entertainment system are quite varied. Here we examine only the most basic of functions centered on the TV, video, and audio capabilities of the system. Multimedia entertainment systems can be used as a complete photographic studio when combined with a good digital camera, or they may act as a video editing studio when used with a digital camcorder. These functions are not examined here because they are a definite sidetrack to our SOHO LAN core theme.

Viewing TV

The primary functions of a multimedia entertainment PC system center on television viewing. Next to the refrigerator being the most used household appliance (it is on 24/7, cooling the beer) and the home heating and cooling system, the television is used more than almost anything else. It should be no surprise that the television functions of our multimedia entertainment PC system are used more than any other functions. Our multimedia entertainment PC system has several thousand hours of TV viewing versus a few hundred hours performing other tasks. Viewing a TV program in a small screen is shown in Figure A.12.

In the figure the television viewing program is shown on the desktop. The TV controls appear below the TV display window. The TV display can be maximized to full-screen view, making it appear to be no different from a normal TV.

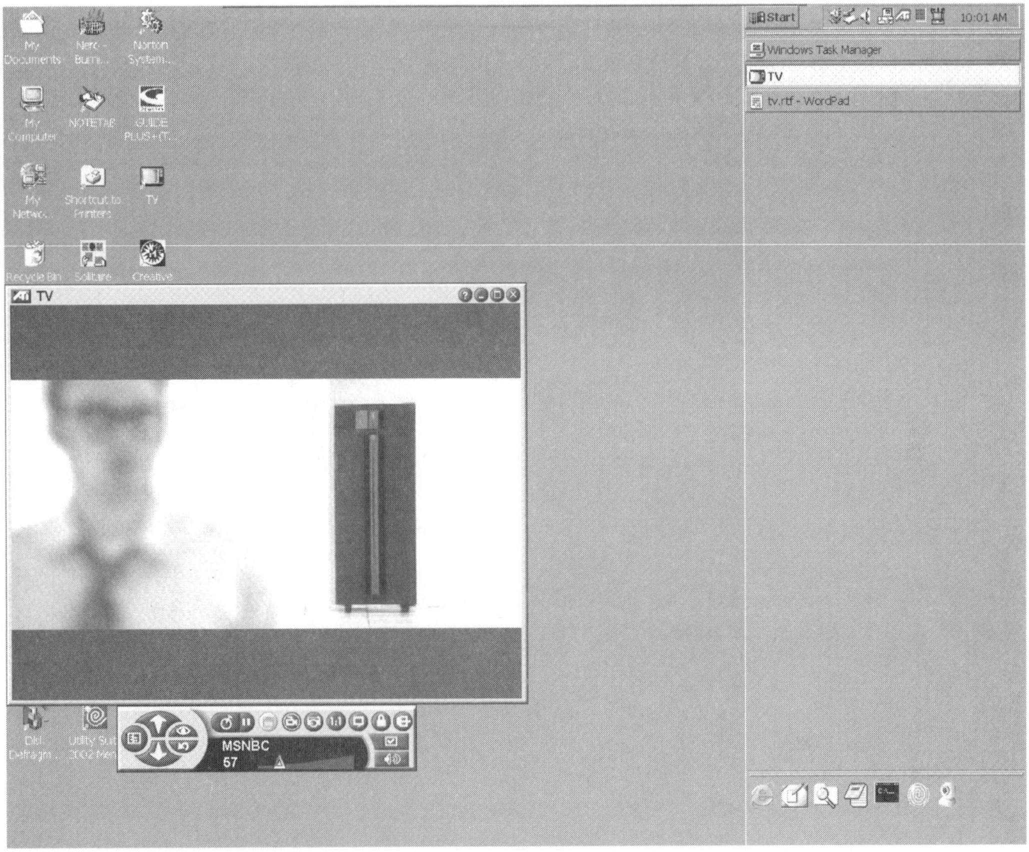

Figure A.12 Multimedia entertainment PC system television viewing.

TV viewing is mostly that—TV viewing. However, other functions like recording programs and capturing stills from programs may be used frequently.

Recording Programs

Television programs can be easily recorded or time shifted by clicking on the Record control. The TV video is saved to disk as shown in Figure A.13.

In the figure, over two hours of TV programming can be saved to the fixed disk. Each minute of recorded video requires about 60 MB of fixed disk space. Two hours of recording would thus require over 7 GB of disk storage space. If more disk space were allocated to the TV recording function, then more hours of TV programming could be saved to the PC's disk drive for later replay.

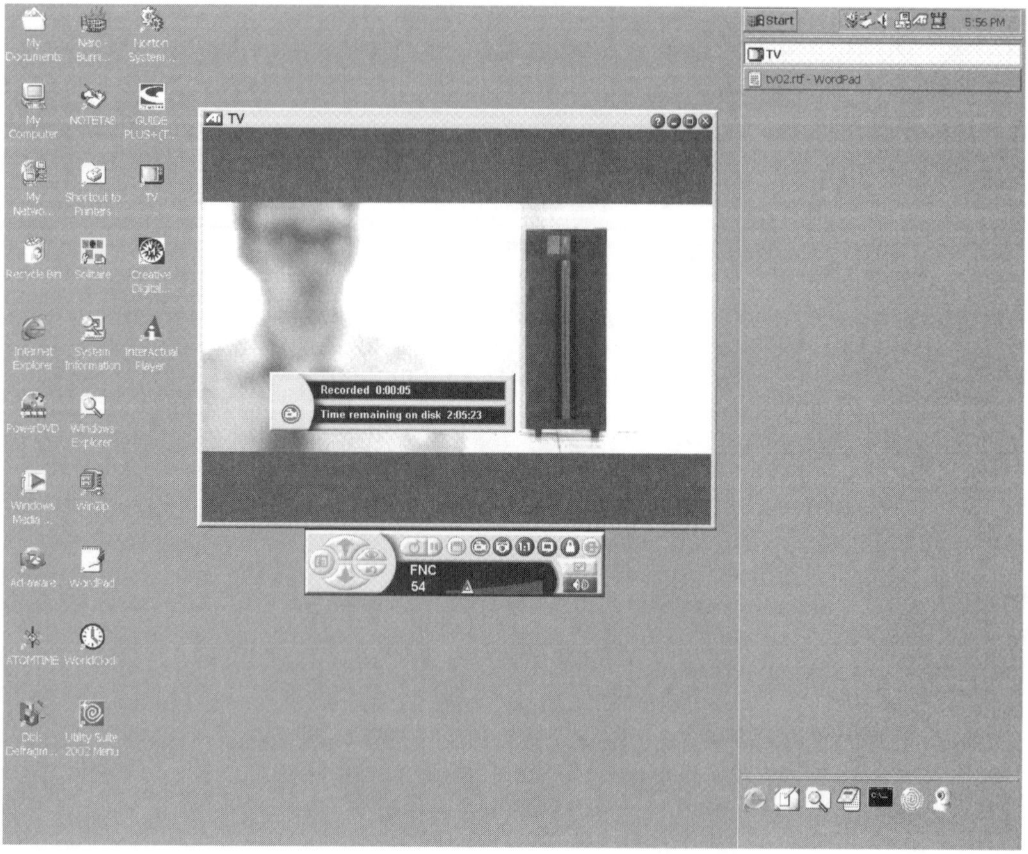

Figure A.13 Recording TV.

Once the TV image is captured, it is saved as an MPEG file on the PC's fixed disk drive. Figure A.14 shows the file being saved in the MP2 format. The file was renamed with an MPG extension to play it with the Windows XP Media player.

Video capture could be set up to create AVI files. These files play with almost any player. The only drawback is that they are very large in size.

The saved file could be written on a CD-R disc to conserve disk space on the PC. Saving MPEG-compressed video on a CD-R drive is not the same as a DVD video. DVD drives have much greater capacity than the 650 MB that can be stored on a CD-R drive. So the amount of MPEG-compressed video stored on a single CD-R drive is measured in minutes, not hours. At 60 MB per minute, a 650-MB CD-R disc could hold about 10 minutes of video.

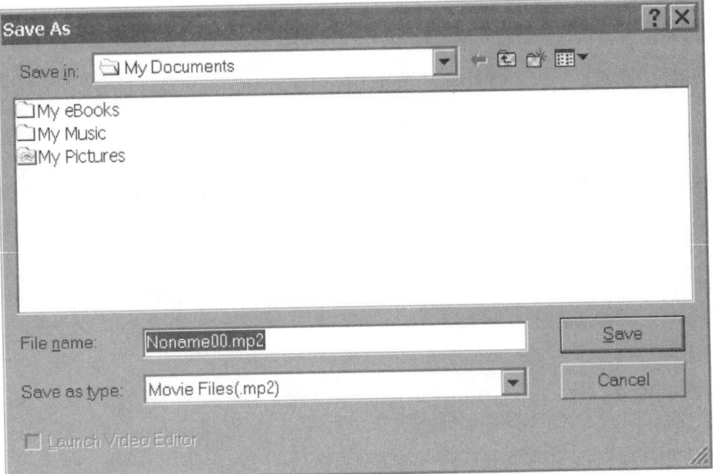

Figure A.14 Saving captured TV as an MPEG file.

Snapshot Pictures from TV

Capturing snapshots from broadcast television is very simple. The TV display program has an image capture icon. Clicking on the image capture icon captures the current TV image as a bit mapped picture (BMP) image. This image can be subsequently saved to disk as a BMP file, as shown in Figure A.15.

In the figure the image on the TV is captured as a still image and is being saved to disk as a BMP file. The captured image can be sent as an e-mail attachment, printed, included as a figure in a book, or used for many other purposes. The TV image cannot be captured by the traditional Windows Alt + Print Screen key combination. The Windows Alt + Print Screen key combination captures the TV program menus and display area, but the TV image itself appears as a black area in the TV display. Only the TV program snapshot function captures the live TV image.

Viewing TV and Web Sites

When viewing TV the Web can be surfed simultaneously. In Figure A.16 the TV program is running and displaying a live TV show in the top-most window in the lower left of the figure while at the same time Internet Explorer displays my intranet site in the rear-most window and the current weather radar image for Baltimore is shown in the middle window.

Figure A.15 TV image capture.

This is a function of the TV application combined with Windows 2000. Across the top of the display is the sound card control software menu. This permits modifying sound card effects while viewing the TV or any other video. The sound card effects add significant spatial dimension to the sounds from MP3 files and other digital sound sources.

TV Schedules

The Guide Plus+ TV schedule program uses the LAN connection to download weekly TV schedules to the multimedia entertainment PC. These schedules are localized using ZIP codes. The Guide Plus+ application displays the currently selected TV program in the upper left of the display screen and the schedule on the right side of the display, as shown in Figure A.17.

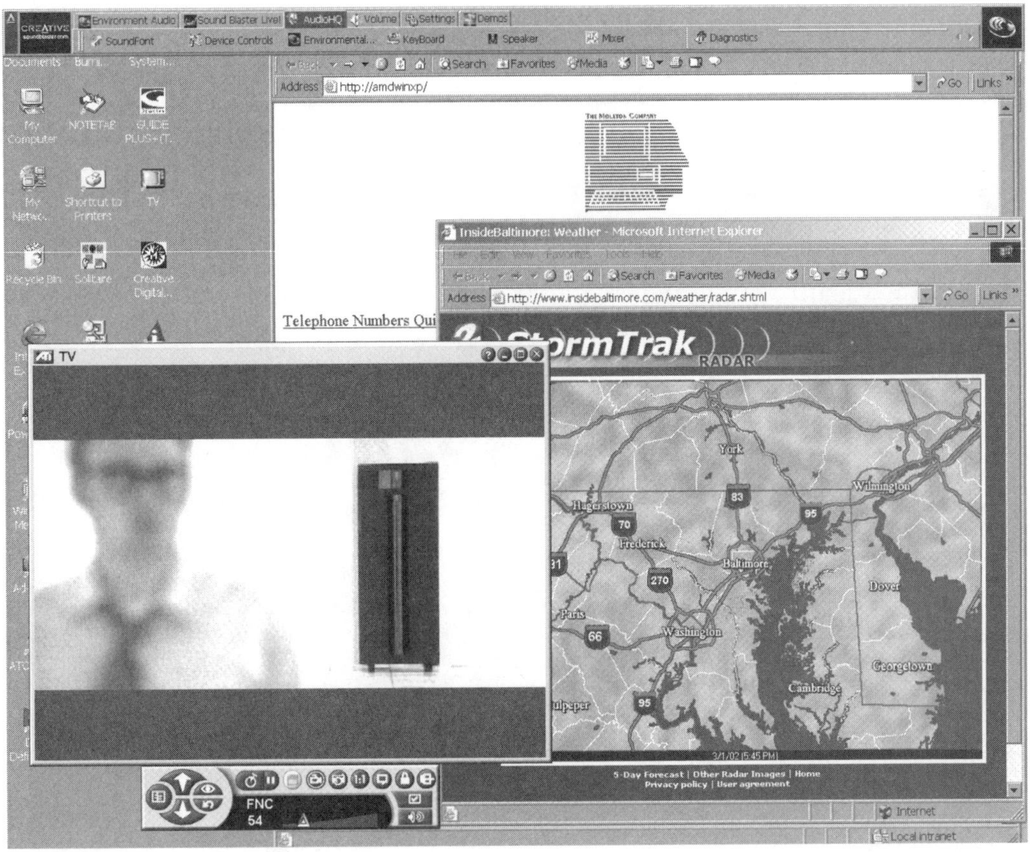

Figure A.16 TV viewing and Web surfing.

Below the current TV program display are two panel advertisements. Looks like you cannot get TV without some advertising. The Guide Plus+ display covers a day at a time and must be updated weekly to stay current.

Brain Teaser: TV Tuner Card Comparisons

A large part of the functionality of TV tuner cards is implemented by the software that comes with them. Check out and compare the ATI software with the Matrox software. Which software provides more features?

As I recall, the ATI board has more features, but they were not necessarily implemented better than the Matrox card's features. Further, some newer

ATI drivers actually mess up the TV tuner software so that not all channels are visible. Display and PC operation are highly dependent upon good display drivers. This is something that specifications alone cannot tell you.

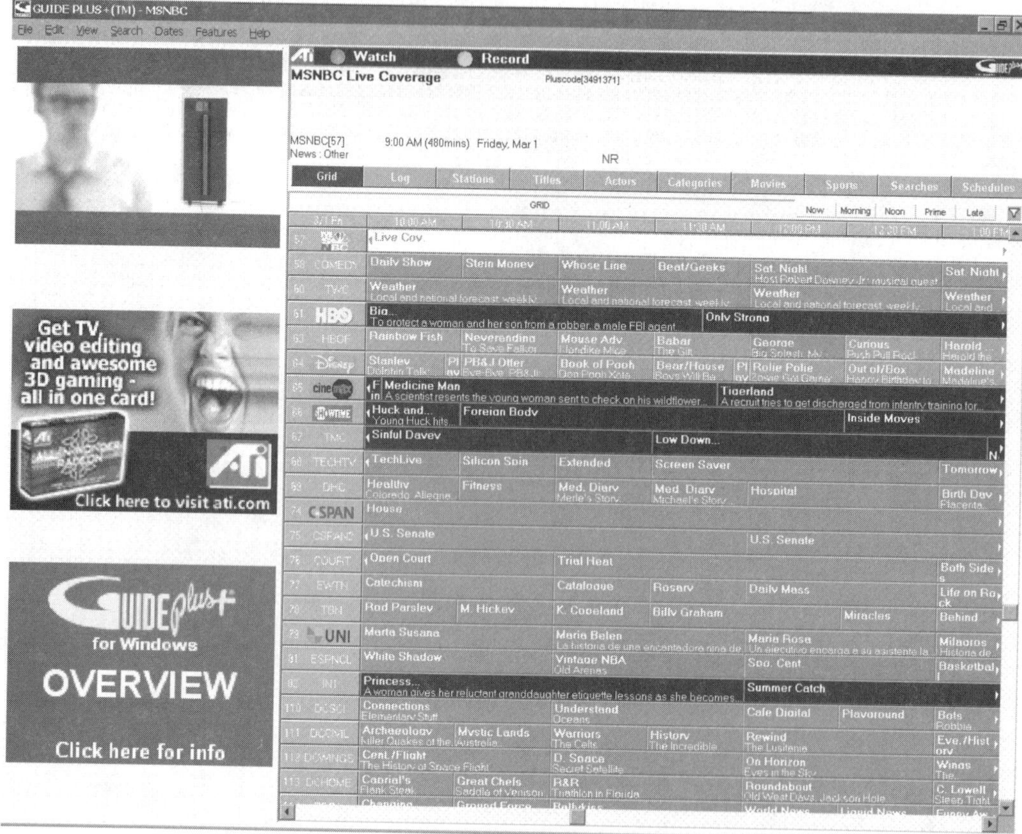

Figure A.17 Guide Plus+ local TV schedule display.

Viewing DVDs

Windows XP Media Player plays DVDs as well as various audio and video formats. In most cases when the DVD is inserted into the DVD drive, the DVD player's software automatically launches and begins playing the DVD. Depending upon the sound card support, the Windows XP media player makes it possible to play DVDs with the 5.1 Dolby digital sound. See Figure A.18. The DVD can be played full screen with the controls hidden.

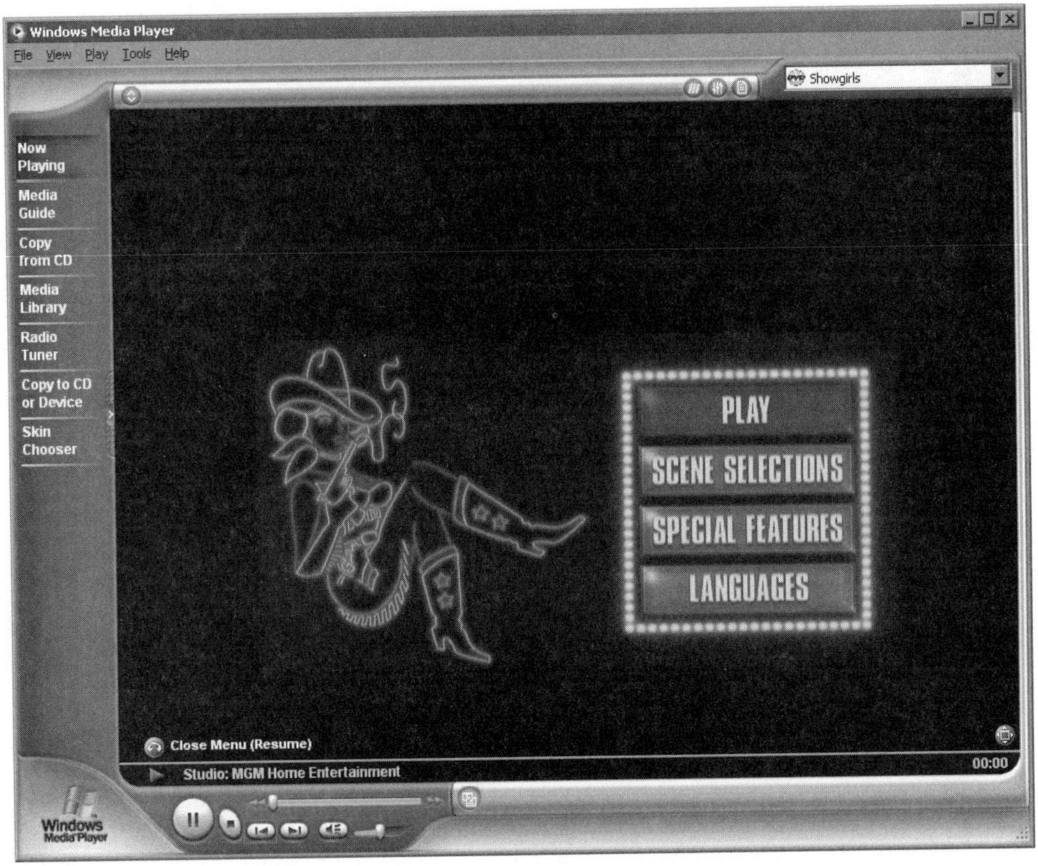

Figure A.18 Windows XP Media Player playing a DVD.

Clicking the right mouse button brings up the DVD player control menu. This permits setting the size of the playback image and some limited DVD menu selection and setup options. Other software DVD players have more configuration and control options for the DVD player that permit closed captions to be viewed, fast forward and reverse, zooming, bookmarking, screen snapshots, and more.

The main benefit of the Windows XP Media Player playing DVDs is that all multimedia PC entertainment functions are now found in that single program. While other programs provide more functionality, they do not necessarily provide all the functions in a single program. Further, since the media is bundled with Windows XP, the price is right if you are already purchasing Windows XP. The Windows 7.1 Media Player does not play DVD movies. It is only an audio player.

Playing Music

Digital music files are changing the way we get and play music. There are several different formats for digital music files. These formats include:

- MP3—MP3 was introduced in 1992 as part of the MPEG-1 standard. A German company, Fraunhofer Gesellschaft, developed MP3 audio compression and still holds key MP3 patents. Fraunhofer was granted a U.S. patent in 1996. With MP3 compression, an ordinary music CD can be compressed into one tenth of its original size. MP3 compression can store up to 12 hours of music on a single recordable CD. Napster made MP3 popular by enabling online peer-to-peer MP3 file sharing. Napster users exchanged millions of songs daily.
- WMA—Windows Media Audio format is used in Windows Multimedia software. The Windows Media Audio 8 format (WMA-8) was first released in products in December 2000. Other WMA formats preceded WMA-8. WMA formats are integrated in Microsoft's Windows Media Player 7.1 and above. WMA formats promise to deliver almost CD-quality audio with files a third of the original audio's file size. WMA formats also provide copyright protection to songs so that they cannot be republished. This is called Digital Rights Management. Windows multimedia formats Windows Media Audio (WMA) and WMV (Windows Media Video) support data streaming, important for Internet content delivery.
- WAV—WAV files were an early audio standard for digitally encoding sound. WAV files are digitally encoded at the same quality (data file size) as data on audio CDs. WAV files provide audio quality equivalent to CD quality sound. However, WAV files are uncompressed and very large (about 10 MB per minute of audio content). The large size makes WAV files unsuitable for exchange across the Internet.
- MIDI—MIDI files are sound files that are designed for music recording and playback on digital synthesizers. These files do not record the sound itself, but rather record how the how music is produced. The commands used by a digital synthesizer to create the music are stored in MIDI format files. These commands are then used by a PC card with a table of stored sounds to produce music.
- Others—There are several audio file formats with varying audio compression and quality that are used in PCs, including MP3pro, OGG, and VQF. However, the use of these formats is not widespread as yet.

MP3 files are the most popular format. MP3 files conform to the MPEG-1 Audio Layer 3 format. They compress sound at different bits per second rates.

A 64-Kbps compressed audio file is like FM radio quality sound, 128 Kbps is similar to CD quality sound, and 160 Kbps and up compression provides over-sampled higher quality audio files. This means that MP3 files vary in size depending upon how they were converted into digital information. The Windows Media Player also supports WMA format audio, MIDI, WAV, and other formats as well. Other players like Music Match Juke Box also play MP3 and other audio formats.

The Windows XP Media Player plays WMA and MP3 files and audio CDs in CDA format while displaying different visualizations that change as the music changes. Figure A.19 shows the Microsoft Windows XP Media Player playing music with the firestorm visualization. This is the standard skin or outside format for the media player. With all audio and video software the control layout and feel can be changed, similar to the plastic covers that change the colors of cellular phones.

For audio playback, the Windows XP Media Player plays most formats that a general multimedia entertainment system user needs. In particular, MP3 formats permit storing entire CD collections on disk and playing them in any sequence desired to suit a mood. With about 80 GB of MP3-formatted audio files, my multimedia entertainment system can play for a week without ever repeating an audio track.

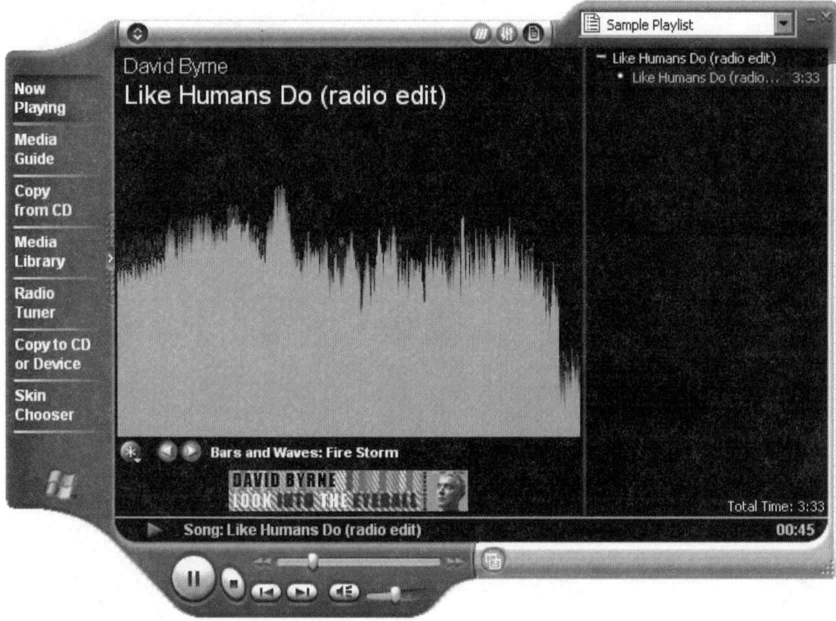

Figure A.19 XP Media Player.

Encoding WMA and MP3 Music from CDA Discs

The Windows Media Player can encode audio tracks from CDA formatted CDs. Selecting Copy from CD menu option while an audio CD is inserted in the CD-ROM drive enables the copying process. The Windows XP Media Player creates WMA digital files on the PC's fixed disk. With an extra cost add-in the Windows Media Player can encode MP3 files as well. There are programs that also convert the WMA format files to MP3 so that the extra add-in conversion program is not needed. The conversion process from CDA format to WMA format is being performed in Figure A.20.

During the conversion process the Windows Media Player presents the option to protect the audio file from unauthorized use. When this option is turned off the file can be moved from PC to PC for replay.

Figure A.20 Windows XP Media Player WMA format conversion.

Brain Teaser: WMA Files

Get a WMA file that is not copy protected. Test the audio player on your PC to see if it plays Microsoft's new audio format.

Most new digital music players play the new WMA format unless the file has copy protection on it. Does your music player play the WMA format? Windows PCs can update to Microsoft's Media Player 7.1, which plays the WMA format. The Microsoft 7.1 Media Player upgrade is at

www.microsoft.com/windows/windowsmedia/download/default.asp

Web Surfing

As on any other PC, Internet Explorer or Netscape can be used to surf the Web. There is nothing special about Web surfing on a multimedia entertainment PC system, except that if you want news or weather information and the TV is not playing news, then you can get it from the Web.

For example, newscasts only give a minute or two to the current Doppler radar image of the weather in the area. If you miss them showing the radar image, well then just too bad. You must wait until they review the weather at 11:00 PM. With a multimedia entertainment PC, you can get the current radar display in a Web browser window and then click to it any time you need an instant Doppler radar update.

Viewing and Writing E-Mail

Do you need to talk with your friends about what is happening in the afternoon soaps? Just e-mail them from the multimedia entertainment PC system. You can set up a free Hotmail or AOL account that permits you to paste images captured from the TV program to emphasize your point. Do the stars look especially tired? Who was in that episode? These questions are easily answered by sending video snapshots to your soap opera viewing buddies.

A Web camera makes it possible to send talking video or snapshots via e-mail to family and friends.

Captures and Displays Web Camera Images

Adding a Web camera to a multimedia PC entertainment system permits easy capture of snapshot images and short videos for e-mailing to family and friends. The Web camera also permits interactive video telephone calls when used with Microsoft's NetMeeting software. A Logitech Web camera with its QuickCam application is shown in Figure A.21. In the left panel is the active picture, and just above it are the Take a Picture and Record a Video buttons. In the right panel is the gallery of snapshots and videos that have been saved on this multimedia PC entertainment system. Other functions are listed in the menu running across the top.

This Web camera software makes it easy to capture pictures and video to e-mail. The images, once captured, are files that can be attached to e-mail messages. The hardest part of taking a picture for e-mail is to remember to look at the camera and not the PC monitor. When you look at the monitor it seems that you are not really talking to the e-mail recipients.

Figure A.21 Web camera snapshot and video capture.

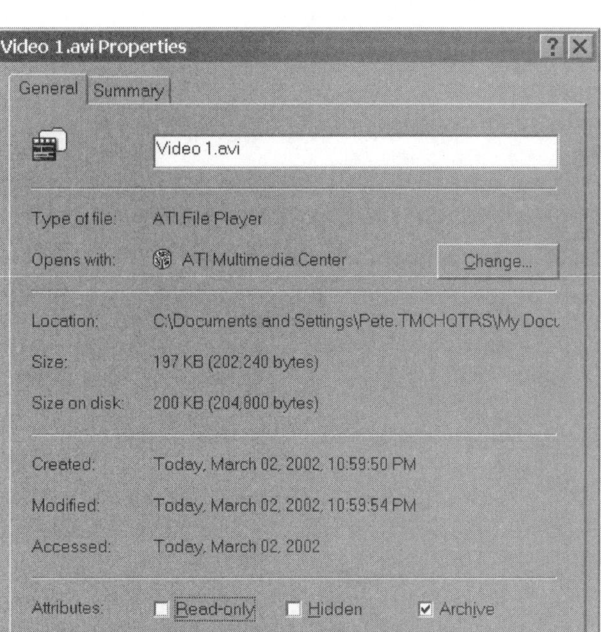

Figure A.22
Web cam video file properties.

When the Web camera captures a video clip, it saves the video clip as an Audio Video Interleaved (AVI) file. The low-resolution Web camera video file stored in an AVI format requires 200 MB of disk storage space for much less than a minute of video, as shown by Figure A.22. The primary difficulty with AVI files is that they are very large. I captured about 20 seconds of video and saved it as an AVI file. The 20-second file was about 388 MB. In contrast, about one minute of video captured and saved as an MPG file requires about 64 MB of disk space.

There are programs that convert file formats. They convert from AVI to MPG, saving huge amounts of disk space.

Prints Images in Color

The multimedia entertainment system can be a digital photographic studio with the addition of a color printer. Color inkjet printers are reasonably priced.

Digital cameras or digital film attach to the PC through a USB port. In this manner the camera takes the pictures, they are fed into the PC for editing (I am always correcting the color balance and brightness) and cropping, and finally printed on the color printer. Depending upon the paper used and the resolution, the printed color images can look like 8 × 10 glossy photographs.

The drawback here is that it is generally desirable to locate the printer somewhere other than where the multimedia entertainment PC is located. It just gets cumbersome to cram a printer into the same room as the television. Since many printers are directly network connected, it is not much of a problem to install them in the central hub room for the network and away from the multimedia PC entertainment system. Linksys makes a wireless print server and a WAP that includes a four-port switch and print server. The WAP with the print server would locate the printer in the central hub room. The wireless print server would permit the printer to be placed on a moving cart and moved throughout the house as needed. Moving the printer works for a lightweight inkjet printer but does not work for a much heavier color laser printer.

Acts as a Security Monitoring System

The coolest application is to turn your multimedia PC entertainment system into a facility security system. D-Link makes a wireless LAN Web camera that needs no PC to drive it. The wireless Web cameras connect directly to a wireless LAN and are accessed using any Web browser. They require only electrical power to function.

Here is how they work. Wireless Web cameras with internal Web servers are purchased for around $300 each. They are installed to view the front door, driveway, and rear of the house. They need some enclosure to ensure that they are not damaged by weather. The enclosure must ensure that the wireless Web camera stays dry and remains cool during summer. Excess heat could easily cause it to fail. The Web camera's built-in Web server permits the images it captures to be viewed using any Web browser. The wireless Web camera takes snapshots at regularly timed intervals. It can be configured to send an e-mail message whenever a picture is taken. This is especially useful when the camera is triggered by infrared, magnetic, or motion-detection sensors.

OK, so there you are watching TV on your multimedia PC entertainment system and the door bell rings. You click up the video of the front door in a Web browser to see who is there without leaving your chair. If the door bell is attached to the telephone system in your facility as is mine, then you can talk with the guest at the front door or choose to ignore him or her if he or she is soliciting door to door. Way cool!

Check on the kids in the basement when you are in the kitchen. Wireless LAN connections to the camera and a laptop PC are all that are needed. Just roam the house and watch the Web browser images from the wireless Web camera. Or watch TV and check using the multimedia PC entertainment system the Web browser images from the wireless LAN Web camera.

Ancillary Applications

Several applications not aimed specifically at home entertainment can be run on the multimedia PC entertainment system. Two of my favorites are Quicken and Microsoft Streets 2002. Quicken is a checkbook and bill-paying program. It makes it easy to write checks and pay bills by memorizing bills that are frequently paid. Balancing a checkbook is an easy chore because Quicken does most of the work for you. Quicken is similar to several other billpaying programs on the market.

Microsoft Streets 2002 and the DeLorme Street Map travel mapping programs both provide comprehensive street maps and other maps of the United States and parts of Canada. Whenever I need to go to an address that I am unfamiliar with, the address is easily looked up in the mapping programs and a route from my facility to the address is plotted and printed in both map form and list form (there are two types of people, list people and map or picture people—give me a list and I am lost, but a map lets me get there). This is an indispensable travel aid for any driving travel, be it local travel around town or vacation travel.

Networking a Multimedia PC Entertainment System

There are many other applications in different areas like cooking, home planning, and so on that are not listed here. Depending upon specific hobbies and interests, these applications are all potential candidates for a multimedia PC entertainment system that displays maps, recipes, and checkbook information on a large screen monitor for several family members to view together.

Multimedia PC entertainment systems can function as standalone devices, but they really become much more useful when networked. A wireless LAN is the best solution because the data volumes are typically not large and the flexibility of wireless installation permits locating the multimedia PC entertainment system anywhere in a room. Further, the Web camera security monitors are wireless. Consequently, a wireless home-office network is an ideal solution for connecting the multimedia PC entertainment system to the Internet, to the Web camera security monitors, and to printers located in other areas of the home. Wireless LANs were covered in detail in Chapter 4.

Brain Teaser: Web Cameras

Search for wireless Web cameras using the Google search site.

What did you find? There was one listed for around $2,000 that broadcast over a cellular link. Could you get to the X10 site? The link was found through an article on wireless Web cams. The site's Web camera data is at

www.x10.com/xrv/xraylanding1.htm

How does this wireless Web cam solution compare with the D-Link wireless Web cam? It appears to be less expensive for a couple of fixed cameras but a lot more work. Also, the camera images could be lower quality than the D-Link camera images. There are other components that can turn the X10 camera system into a formidable security observation system, but they drive up the price substantially. What are these components? (Hint: think Ninja.)

Summary

This chapter covered multimedia PC entertainment system components, including graphics cards, monitors, and sound cards; configuring a multimedia PC entertainment system; and using a multimedia PC entertainment system, including TV viewing, DVD playing, audio entertainment management, and other functions. While such systems are not very common today, their use is increasing.

A multimedia PC entertainment system provides the foundation for future home computing applications including Web surfing, e-mail, VCR functions, DVD viewing, Web camera snapshot/video captures, home security monitoring, and digital photography support. Depending upon personal interests, the list may go on and on.

Key Technical Terms

1080i—Interlaced scanning at 1,080 lines every 1/30 of a second or 540 lines every 1/60 second. This provides a better image than 480p (see 480p, below).

2.1 speaker system—This system contains two speakers plus a subwoofer. The two speakers are right front and left front.

4.1 speaker system—This system contains four speakers plus a subwoofer. The four speakers are right front, left front, right rear, and left rear.

480p—Progressive scanning at 480 lines every 1/60 of a second.

5.1 speaker system—This system contains five speakers plus a subwoofer. The five speakers are right front, left front, right rear, left rear, and center. 5.1 means that the soundtracks are recorded with five main channels: left, center, right, left rear, and right rear, plus a Low-Frequency Effects (LFE) bass channel. The LFE channel is designated a .1 channel because it carries a small portion of the frequency range of the main channels.

720p—Progressive scanning at 720 lines every 1/60 of a second. This would provide the best video image.

AC-3—Audio Coding-3 is a digital audio encoding/decoding algorithm that reduces the data needed to produce high-quality sound based upon the perceptions in human hearing. Perceptual digital audio coding is based on human hearing, screening out sound perceived as noise. By reducing, eliminating, or masking human-perceived noise the data needed to produce high-quality sound is reduced. Building upon Dolby's AC-1 and AC-2 coding algorithms, AC-3 is a coding system designed specifically for multi-channel digital audio. AC-3 is used in digital television, in DVDs, in HDTV, in cable, and in digital satellite transmission. AC-3 provides support for 5.1 speaker systems. This means that it provides five full-bandwidth channels: front left, front right, center, rear surround left, and rear surround right. AC-3 includes a LFE channel. AC-3 ensures compatibility with devices that do not support the 5.1 speaker system format with a down-mixing feature.

AVI—Audio Video Interleaved files are audio and motion video files. AVI files are formatted according to Windows's Resource Interchange File Format (RIFF) specification. AVI files are played by many different video players. Their major disadvantage is that they are very large in size.

CDA—CD Audio is the format of most music CDs. A single CD holds about one hour's music.

Dolby Digital 5.1—Music encoded in Dolby Digital 5.1 AC3 format, providing true 5.1 discrete multi-channel output for 5.1 speaker systems.

DVI-D—Digital Visual Interface–Digital supports only digital flat-panel monitors.

DVI-I—Digital Visual Interface–Integrated supports both analog (with a special DVI-I to VGA adapter) and digital flat-panel monitors.

Interlaced—A scanning method that alternately scans every other line of a display to produce images. A full image thus requires two scans. Since human vision sees full-motion images at 30 pictures per second, an interlaced image at 60 pictures per second (frames per second) produces a full image that refreshes at 30 frames per second.

LFE—Low Frequency Effect is a channel included in AC-3 digital encoding for special effects and action sequence sounds in movies. The LFE channel is one-tenth of the bandwidth of other AC-3 channels. The LFE channel is sometimes referred to as a subwoofer channel but that is not strictly its function.

MIDI—Musical Instrument Digital Interface is a data exchange protocol for digital synthesizers. It is designed for recording and playing back music. MIDI transmits information about how music is created on a keyboard device including note on/off, key velocity, pitch bend, and other keyboard/synthesizer controls. Sounds produced are already stored in a wave table (table of standard sounds) in the sound card. Because a MIDI file contains only player information, it requires less data than sound output, and therefore produces very small file sizes. MIDI uses asynchronous eight-bit serial transmission at 31.25 Kbps. The MIDI connection is a five-pin DIN plug.

MP3—MP3 file suffixes designate MPEG-1 audio layer-3 files. This is not the same as MPEG-3 files.

MPEG—Stands both for the Motion Picture Experts Group itself and for digital video and audio compression formats created by that group. MPEG is a working group of ISO (International Standards Organization). MPEG standards are evolving with each standard designed for a different purpose. To reduce the quantity of data in digital movies, MPEG compression algorithms describe each image using a base frame and the changes to that base frame. A talking-head video would have only the facial expression changing, so it could be compressed by keeping the background the same and only changing the facial expressions in the video image. Other mathematical techniques are used in MPEG compression to further reduce the amount of data required. To encode/decode MPEG video files requires a PC with a high-speed CPU, 256+ MB RAM, and hundreds of GB of fixed disk space. MPEG files or MPG files can be very large.

MPEG viewer software is needed to play MPG files. Shareware or commercial MPEG players can be downloaded from a number of Web sites.

MPEG-1—A standard for storage and retrieval of motion pictures and audio. Movies with 525 or 625 lines of resolution are compressed at 1.5 Mbps of video. MPEG-1 video quality is equivalent to VHS tapes. MPEG-1 is used to create video CDs, CD-ROMs, and videos distributed on the Web. MPEG-1 is the basis for MP3 files, which combine MPEG-1 and Audio Layer 3.

MPEG-2—A standard for digital television. It is used to create DVDs. MPEG-2 provides resolutions of 720 by 480 and 1,280 by 720 at up to 60 frames per second.

MPEG-4—Based on Apple's QuickTime standard. Previous MPEG formats focused mostly on compression. The MPEG-4 format adds bit rate scalability, animated sprites, interactivity, and copyright protection features.

NTSC—The National Television Standards Committee's standard protocol for broadcast television in North America. This standard has TV images composed of 525 horizontal lines per screen. These horizontal lines are scanned from left to right and from top to bottom. During scanning every other line is skipped. As a result, two scans are needed to produce a screen image. The first scan refreshes odd-numbered horizontal lines and the second scan refreshes even-numbered lines to produce the complete image. Each odd/even scan is about 1/60 of a second, resulting in images being refreshed every 1/30 second. Alternate-line scanning is called interlacing. The 30-frame-per-second image refresh rate is good for full motion video because the human eye refreshes at 30 frames per second.

PAL—Phase Alternate Line is an analog broadcast TV standard protocol used in Europe and internationally. PAL produces TV images by scanning horizontally 625 times to form a video image.

Progressive—Progressive scanning scans every line to produce an image. There is no interlacing of the line scanning.

SCART—Syndicat des Constructeurs d'Appareils Radio Récepteurs et Téléviseurs is a physical and electrical interconnection between audiovisual equipment. It is also known as a Euro-connector. Each device has a female 21-pin connector interface that carries stereo audio, composite video, and control signals. RGB video signals are input only. New television sets and VCRs in the European market using the PAL video standard come equipped with a SCART connector.

SECAM—Sequential Couleur avec Mémoire is a broadcast TV standard protocol used in France and parts of the former Soviet Union. Similar to

PAL, SECAM produces TV images by scanning horizontally 625 times to form a video image.

S/PDIF—Sony/Philips Digital Interface is a standard audio transfer file format. It is usually found on digital audio equipment such as DAT machines or audio processing devices. It allows the transfer of audio from one file to another without the conversion to and from an analog format, which could degrade the signal quality. The most common connector used with an S/PDIF interface is the RCA connector, the same one used for consumer audio products. An optical connector is also sometimes used.

SRS—Sound Retrieval System is the first generation of 3-D sound. SRS improves the quality of standard stereo. SRS is designed to retrieve the natural spatial cues and ambient information present in audio but masked by traditional recording and playback technologies.

THX—Identifies compliance with Lucasfilm THX parameters for cinema sound systems and acoustics. THX standards focus on the playback environment and parameters. A THX logo specifies home theater components such as sound processors and speaker systems complying with Lucasfilm THX performance parameters.

Time shifting—Time shifting is capturing video images or more specifically TV broadcast video to disk for viewing at another time.

TosLink—A popular optical digital audio interconnect standard often used by consumer and semi-pro equipment. TosLink is basically S/PDIF formatted data over an optical cable. Toshiba first developed the particular implementation in use, hence the name TosLink, which is short for Toshiba Link. TosLink optical digital audio output employs a fiber optic digital audio connection to connect a digital source component to a receiver or pre-amplifier. The data passed is the raw digital audio signal using laser (light) pulses. This means of interconnect minimizes signal interference and degradation.

TruBass—An audio enhancement technology that provides deep, rich bass on any speaker system without the need for a subwoofer. On systems with subwoofers TruBass enhances the bass performance.

WAV—Wave files are audio files identified by the extension .WAV. Microsoft created the WAV file format to store audio information for PC system sound themes. WAV has become a standard PC audio file format for many system and game sounds. The famous AOL "You've got mail" audio message is a 10-KB WAV file. My Windows XP laptop PC has over 350 WAV files stored on it. WAV files store uncompressed raw audio data, mono or stereo tracks, sampling rates, and bit depth.

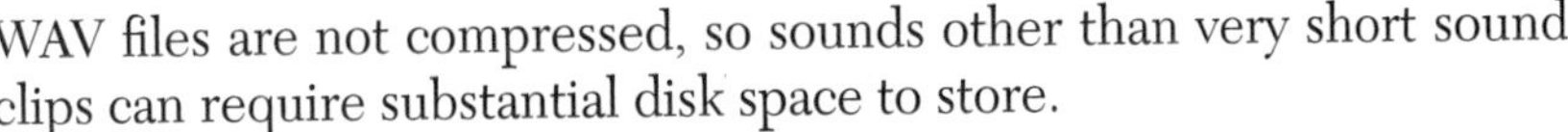

WAV files are not compressed, so sounds other than very short sound clips can require substantial disk space to store.

WMA—Windows Media Audio is an audio compression format developed by Microsoft. Windows Media Audio 8 format first emerged late in 2000. The Windows Media Audio format is integrated into Microsoft's Windows Media Player.

WOW—A combination of SRS audio technology and TruBass technology. WOW uses SRS 3-D technology to restore spatial cues and ambient information lost during standard stereo playback.

Review Questions

1. What are two popular compressed digital storage formats for audio signals?

   Answer: MP3 and WMA are digital storage formats for audio files that significantly reduce the information required to store the audio information. Windows XP Media Player can convert CDs with CDA uncompressed audio tracks into WMA and (with an extra cost add-in software) into MP3 files for subsequent playback.

2. What are the three components that differentiate a multimedia entertainment PC from any other home PC?

   Answer: The graphics card that makes TV viewing possible, the large-screen monitor that makes TV viewing pleasurable, and the sound card that delivers 5.1 sound for DVD playback.

3. What type of networking makes the most sense for a home PC?

   Answer: A wireless LAN gives the greatest flexibility in locating the PC components without the hassles of wiring. Further, wireless LANs support wireless print servers that locate printers anywhere in a facility and wireless Web cameras that can implement cool security monitoring applications.

4. What is AC-3?

   Answer: AC-3 is a Dolby audio encoding/decoding technology used in digital television, in DVDs, in HDTV, in digital cable, and in digital satellite transmission to provide support for 5.1 speaker systems.

5. Can stereo speaker systems produce surround sound?

   Answer: With special digital signal processing and enhancement, stereo speakers can produce fuller-sounding audio that simulates surround sound. This is not true surround sound produced by independent speaker channels such as those decoded by AC-3 systems.

6. What Windows operating system is the most closely aimed at multimedia applications?

   Answer: Windows XP is most closely aimed at multimedia and home entertainment applications. For example, the Windows XP Media Player plays DVDs, while the previous Media Player versions running on Windows 9x and Windows 2000 do not play DVDs.

INDEX

A

B

C

D

E

F

G

H

I

J

K

L

N

O

P

Q

R

S

T

U

V

W

Z

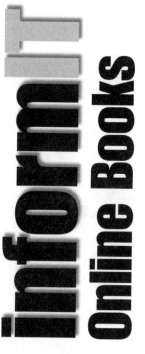